W9-BDD-548

FINANCIAL STATEMENT ANALYSIS
THEORY, APPLICATION, AND INTERPRETATION

The Willard J. Graham Series in Accounting
Consulting Editor   **Robert N. Anthony**   Harvard University

FINANCIAL STATEMENT ANALYSIS

THEORY, APPLICATION, AND INTERPRETATION

Leopold A. Bernstein, Ph.D., C.P.A.
Professor of Accounting
Bernard M. Baruch College
The City University of New York

1978
Revised Edition

RICHARD D. IRWIN, INC.   Homewood, Illinois   60430
Irwin-Dorsey Limited   Georgetown, Ontario   L7G 4B3

© RICHARD D. IRWIN, INC., 1974 and 1978

All rights reserved. No part of this publication may be
reproduced, stored in a retrieval system, or transmitted,
in any form or by any means, electronic, mechanical,
photocopying, recording, or otherwise, without the prior
written permission of the publisher.

ISBN 0-256-02004-3
Library of Congress Catalog Card No. 77-089791
Printed in the United States of America

2 3 4 5 6 7 8 9 0 MP 5 4 3 2 1 0 9 8

To
University Distinguished Professor

EMANUEL SAXE

Teacher, Colleague, and Friend

PREFACE

The major objective of this revised edition, as was that of the original work, is to present a comprehensive and up-to-date treatment of the analysis of financial statements as an aid to decision making. While financial statement analysis serves many and varied purposes, its major usefulness is in making investing and lending decisions. Such decisions, and the actions to which they lead, are, of course, at the heart of the free market system.

Investing and lending decisions require the application of thorough analysis to carefully evaluated data. They require, moreover, the ability to forecast—to foresee. Sound information is obtained by an *understanding* of the data from which it is derived as well as by the application of tools of analysis which aid in its extraction and evaluation. Foresight which is essential to the assessment of opportunity and risk is also rooted in understanding: understanding of the elements comprising the data and of the factors that can change them. The common denominator is *understanding*. Alfred North Whitehead assured us that foresight can be taught when he wrote: "Foresight depends upon understanding. In practical affairs it is a habit. But the habit of foreseeing is elicited by the habit of understanding. To a large extent, understanding can now be acquired by a conscious effort and it can be taught. Thus the training of foresight is by the medium of understanding."

Organization of this work

The keynote of this work, thus, is *understanding*. It focuses on understanding the data which are analyzed as well as the methods by which they are analyzed and interpreted.

Part I is concerned with the relationship between the discipline of accounting and that of financial analysis. It explores the objectives of accounting and the conventions which accountants have adopted for their achievement. It then proceeds to examine the objectives of the users of financial statements, and concludes with an overview of the analytical tools and techniques they employ.

Part II is devoted to an in-depth analysis of financial statements, and of the bases which underly their preparation. A thorough *understanding* of the processes of income determination and of asset and liability measurement, as well as the distortions to which these may be subject, are an essential prerequisite to the intelligent analysis of financial data. These, as well as other topics such as the effects of price-level changes and the significance of the audit function, are examined here from the point of view of their implications to the user of financial statements.

Part III examines the processes and the methodology of financial statement analysis. The focus here is on the major objectives of users of financial statements and on the analytical tools and techniques applied by them in reaching significant conclusions and decisions. The analysis and evaluation of financial data are time-consuming and demanding tasks. Considering the importance of the decisions based thereon, however, and the magnitude of the resources which may be committed as a result, a painstaking job of analysis and evaluation is essential. Thorough analysis not only removes, to some degree, the great uncertainties inherent in investing and lending decisions, but also imparts to the decision maker a degree of confidence which is an essential precondition to timely and decisive action.

Since the ultimate decisions here must be quantified, that is, expressed in terms of the price of a stock or the amount of a loan, Part III emphasizes the need to link qualitative judgments to as many factors that lend themselves to quantification as is possible.

Major users of this work

This book should prove of value to all those who need a thorough understanding of the uses to which financial statements are put as well as to those who must know how to use them intelligently and effectively. This encompasses *accountants, security analysts, lending officers, credit analysts, managers,* and all others who must make decisions on the basis of financial data. Teachers in this area will likewise profit greatly from its use.

Accountants should benefit from this book in two major ways:

1.   By obtaining a full appreciation of the uses to which the end-product of their work is put, they will be in a better position to improve upon it and to make it more responsive to the needs of users of financial statements.

2.   Primarily because the analysis of financial statements demands a thorough understanding of how and on what bases financial statements are constructed, accountants have often been called upon to aid in their analysis and interpretation. The study of the tools and techniques of financial statement analysis will open to the accountant important opportunities for the creative extension of his basic services into areas which are often as intellectually satisfying as they are financially rewarding.

Security analysts, lending officers, credit analysts, and investors, as well as others with financial responsibilities, will find in this work a discussion of accounting concepts and measurements undertaken from their point of view as users of such data. Following this they will, in Part III, learn how such knowledge of the accounting framework is integrated with the best tools and techniques that are available for the analysis and interpretation of financial statements.

Teachers of financial statement analysis will find that the organization and coverage of this work treats the subject matter of this field comprehensively and in depth and goes far beyond the superficial treatment often accorded to it. It offers the instructor in this subject enough challenging material of substance to form the basis for courses in this area on both the undergraduate and the graduate levels of study. The instructor's manual provided with this book contains further specific suggestions on the organization of different course levels by chapter and subject matter.

The revised edition

The major objective of this revision is to preserve and enhance those features of this work which have proved to be most valuable to its users and to update and improve that which experience indicated needed to be improved. The valuable feedback provided by students, colleagues, and other users of the original work have greatly aided me in this task. Also of considerable help was my continuing experience in the use of these materials in teaching graduate and undergraduate accounting students, professional security analysts preparing for the three levels of the Chartered Financial Analysts examinations, aspiring bank loan officers, and bond rating agency analysts as well as others. Valuable feedback of other users ranged from those using this work in finance and investment courses or for purposes of CPA Examination review, to those using it in the training of Chartered Life Underwriters and the teaching of Ph.D. candidates who were not accounting majors.

This revision reflects a comprehensive updating of all authoritative pronouncements on accounting and auditing standards and practices as well as the valuable suggestions of practicing financial analysts, credit analysts, and other users of financial data.

Numerous useful comments and suggestions by fellow educators have resulted in many modifications which are motivated by pedagogical considerations. The chapters on objectives of users of financial statements, accounting for price changes, the analysis of capital structure and long-term solvency, and the analysis of results of operations have undergone considerable expansion. Many modifications and new illustrations have been provided throughout. Appendixes have been added to chapters covering external sources of data and alternative methods of dealing with price level problems as well as the rating of debt securities. Many new problems have been added and existing problem material has been revised, enhanced, and expanded. A novel feature is the use of one comprehensive annual report as the basis of questions and problems for most chapters. Odd numbered problems appear at the end of the book and *additional*, even numbered, problems will be found in the instructor's manual.

Included are a significant number of problems taken from past examinations given by the Institute of Chartered Financial Analysts and by the American Institute of Certified Public Accountants whose permission to use these materials is hereby gratefully acknowledged.

ACKNOWLEDGMENTS

In performing the research for and the writing of this and the prior edition I was fortunate to benefit from the encouragement, help, and suggestions of many colleagues, professional associates, and students. University Distinguished Professor Emanuel Saxe, a teacher, an esteemed colleague, and friend, to whom this book is affectionately dedicated, has read the entire original manuscript as well as many revisions of it and has made numerous valuable suggestions. To me the thoroughness of his review served as a shining example of the kind of dedicated effort which a professional approach to financial statement analysis demands.

My colleagues at the City University of New York Abraham J. Briloff, Martin Mellman, Calvin Engler, Peter M. Gutman, Peter Lloyd Davis, Stanley C. W. Salvary, and Reed Storey have read portions of this work and have contributed valuable comments and suggestions, while Martin Benis, John Liapakis, Steven Lillien, and Harold Witner have contributed valuable comments as a result of class use of the book.

Other colleagues in Academe who provided valuable comments and suggestions include Robert N. Anthony, Harvard University; Fred Bien and Vince Brenner, Louisiana State University; Garry Bulmash, American University; Philip Chuey, Youngstown State University; John Gentis, Ball State University; Edwin Grossnickle, Western Michigan University; J. Larry Hagler, Mississippi State University; Henry Jaenicke, Franklin and Marshall College; Homer Kripke, New York University; Russ Langer, San Francisco State University; Burton T. Lefkowitz, C. W. Post College; Jerrold Weiss, Lehman College; Philip Wolitzer, Long Island University; and Stephen Zeff, Tulane University. Jon A. Stroble, a skillful teacher of bank officers, has also offered valuable suggestions as well as help with problem development.

In the field of professional accountancy I owe an intellectual debt to the firm of Coopers & Lybrand with whom I have now been associated for over 20 years, first as employee and mostly as consultant. Individual partners and members of the staff who have enhanced my understanding of accounting issues are too many to mention and, moreover, neither the firm nor its members are necessarily to be identified with views expressed in this volume. I do, however, want to express special appreciation to Coopers & Lybrand partner Fred Spindel, CPA, for many valuable review comments on Chapter 18. Robert Mednick, CPA, of Arthur Andersen; Paul Rosenfield, CPA, of the American Institute of Certified Public Accountants; and Samuel P. Gunther, CPA, of Richard Eisner & Co. have also contributed many valuable comments and suggestions. Professional debt or equity security analysts who have read portions of this work and made valuable suggestions include Kenneth Alterman, Hyman C. Grossman, Richard Huff, and Robert J. Mebus of Standard & Poor's Corporation; Clyde Bartter, Portfolio Advisory Company; Michael S. Hyland, First Boston Corporation; David Norr, First Manhattan Corporation; Thornton L. O'Glove, the *Quality of Earnings Report;* Frances Stone, Merrill Lynch, Pierce Fenner & Smith Inc.; and Jack L. Treynor, the *Financial Analysts Journal.*

I would like to single out for special mention the very dedicated and able service provided by my graduate assistants Tae-Whan Cho, CPA, and Mostapha El Makhsy. They rendered very effective research assistance, skillfully and creatively helped with problem development, and provided valuable comments on large portions of the manuscript.

Finally, I wish to express appreciation to my wife Cynthia for valuable editorial help, to my daughter Debbie and to my son Jeffrey for assistance with indexing, and to my mother Jeanette, as well as to

Cynthia, for their patience and understanding over the many years during which this work was being written and revised and for having provided me with the inspiration that helped bring it to a successful completion.

I earnestly solicit comments, suggestions, and constructive criticism from interested educators, professional financial and credit analysts, accountants, and other users in the hope that I shall be able to continue the unending task of improving this work.

December 1977   LEOPOLD A. BERNSTEIN

CONTENTS

*pricing model. The efficient market hypothesis. Implications for finan-
cial statement analysis. Objectives of management. Objectives of acquisition and merger analysts. Objectives of auditors. Objectives of other
interested groups.*

PART II
FINANCIAL STATEMENTS—THE RAW MATERIAL OF ANALYSIS

under leases: *Accounting by lessees. Accounting by lessors. Sales-type leases. Direct-financing leases. Operating leases. Principal disclosures. Leases involving real estate. Sale—leaseback. Leveraged leases. Effective date and transition. Capital versus operating lease—the effect on income. Implications for analysis.* Liabilities under pension plans: *Implications for analysis.* Liabilities at the "edge" of equity. Deferred credits (income): *Deferred taxes. Deferred investment tax credit. Implications for analysis.* Reserves and provisions. Accounting for contingencies: *Implications for analysis.* Commitments. Contingent liabilities.

search, exploration, and development outlays: *Types of research and development. The accounting problem. FASB statement 2. Exploration and development in extractive industries. Implications for analysis.* Goodwill: *Implications for analysis.* Interest costs: *Interest capitalization. Implications for analysis.* Income taxes: *Treatment of tax loss carry-backs and carry-forwards.* Tax allocation. *Accounting for income taxes by oil and gas producers. SEC disclosure requirements. Investment tax credit. Implications for analysis.* Analytical significance of the SEC disclosure requirements. Extraordinary gains and losses: *Cross currents of theory—the case of debt retirements. Discontinued operations. Implications for analysis.* The income statement—implications for analysis, an overview. Accounting changes: *Change in accounting principle. Change in accounting estimate. Change in reporting entity. Correction of an error. Materiality. Historical summaries of financial information. Implications for analysis.*

Major provisions of *APB Opinion No. 15: Simple capital structure. Computation of weighted average of common shares outstanding.* Complex capital structure: *Primary EPS. Fully diluted EPS. Requirements for additional disclosures in conjunction with the presentation of EPS data. Elections at the time EPS opinion became effective.* Comprehensive illustration of computation of EPS: *Facts and data.* Implications for analysis: *Statement accounting for changes in earnings per share.*

Significance and purpose. Two major concepts of liquidity. Statement of changes in financial position—a broader concept: *Basis of preparation. Arriving at "sources of funds from operations." The statement of changes in financial position. Illustration of "T-account" technique. Fixed assets. Accumulated depreciation. Goodwill. Bonds payable. Deferred income taxes. Capital stock and paid-in capital. Retained earnings. Analysis of changes in each element of working capital. Abbreviated method.* Statement of changes in financial position—cash focus: *Conversion of working capital provided by operations to cash flow provided by operations. Additional provisions of* APB Opinion No. 19. *Implications for analysis.* Cash flow. Depreciation—a source of funds?

Research and professional pronouncements. Intervention by governmental bodies. Accounting and reporting alternatives. Replacement cost accounting (RCA): *Estimating replacement costs.* Which framework will do the job? Implications for analysis: *General price level changes. Specific price changes.* Appendix 14A: General price level restated financial statements.

What the analyst needs to know: *Knowing the auditor. What the auditor's opinion means.* The auditor's report: *The scope of the audit. The opinion section. "Fair presentation." Modification of the opinion.* Circumstances giving rise to qualifications, disclaimers, or adverse opinions. Qualifications—"except-for" and "subject to." Disclaimer of opinion. Adverse opinions: *Adverse opinions versus disclaimers of opinion.* The form of the report. Limitations in the scope of the audit. Failure of financial statements to conform to generally accepted accounting principles. Financial statements subject to unresolved known uncertainties. Exceptions as to consistency. Special reports. Unaudited reports. The SEC's important role. Implications for analysis: *Implications inherent in the audit process. Implications stemming from the standards which govern the auditor's opinion. Qualification, disclaimers, and adverse opinions. Audit risk and its implications.*

PART III
FINANCIAL STATEMENT ANALYSIS—THE MAIN AREAS OF EMPHASIS

Significance of short-term liquidity. Working capital: *Current assets. Current liabilities. Other problem areas in definition of current assets and liabilities. Working capital as a measure of liquidity.* Current ratio: *Limitations of the current ratio. Implications of the limitations to which the current ratio is subject. The current ratio as a valid tool of analysis. Measures which supplement the current ratio. Measures of accounts receivable liquidity.* Average accounts receivable turnover ratio: *Collection period for accounts receivable. Evaluation.* Measures of inventory turnover: *Inventory turnover ratio. Days to sell inventory. The effect of alternative methods of inventory management.* Current liabilities: *Differences in the "nature" of current liabilities. Days purchases in accounts payable ratio. The capacity to borrow.* Interpretation of the current ratio: *Examination of trend. Interpretation of changes over time. Possibilities of manipulation. The use of "rules of thumb" standards. The net trade cycle. Valid working capital standards. The importance of sales. Common-size analysis of current assets composition. The liquidity index.* Acid-test ratio. Other measures of short-term liquidity: *Funds flow ratios. Cash flow related measures. Projecting changes in conditions or policies.*

Overview of cash flow and funds flow patterns. Short-term cash forecasts: *Importance of sales estimates. Pro forma financial statements as an aid to forecasting. Techniques of short-term cash forecasting. Differences between short-term and long-term forecasts.* Analysis of statements of changes in financial position: *First illustration of statement of changes in financial position analysis. Second illustration statement of changes in financial position analysis.* Evaluation of the statement of changes in financial position. Projection of statements of changes in financial position: *The impact of adversity. The funds flow adequacy ratio. Funds reinvestment ratio.*

Key elements in the evaluation of long-term solvency. Importance of capital structure. Accounting principles: *Deferred credits. Long-term leases. Liabilities for pensions. Unconsolidated subsidiaries. Provisions, reserves, and contingent liabilities. Minority interests. Convertible debt. Preferred stock. Effect of intangible assets. The significance of capital structure.* Reasons for employment of debt: *The concept of financial leverage. The effect of tax deductibility of interest. Other advantages of leverage. Measuring the effect financial leverage. Financial leverage index. Measuring the effect of capital structure on long-term solvency. Long-term projections—usefulness and limitations.* Capital structure analysis—common-size statements. Capital structure ratios: *Equity capital/total liabilities. Equity capital/long-term debt. Short-term debt. Equity capital at market value. Interpretation of capital structure measures.* Measures of assets distribution. Measures of earnings coverage. Earnings available to meet fixed charges. Fixed charges to be included: *1. Interest on long-term debt. 2. Interest implicit in lease obligations. 3. Capitalized interest. 4. Other elements to be included in fixed charges. 5. Principal repayment requirements. 6. Other fixed charges. 7. Guarantees to pay fixed charges.* Illustration of earnings-coverage ratio calculations. Times-interest-earned ratio: *Ratio of earnings to fixed charges. Coverage ratios of senior bonds. Fixed-charges-coverage ratio—the SEC standard. Fixed-charges-coverage ratios—expanded concept of fixed charges. Noninterest portion of capitalized rents ($110,000). Recognition of benefits stemming from fixed charges. Computation of coverage ratio—expanded concept of fixed charges. Pro forma computations of coverage ratios. Funds flow coverage of fixed charges. Other useful tests of funds flow relationships. Stability of "flow of funds from operations."* Earnings coverage of preferred dividends. Evaluation of earnings-coverage ratios: *Importance of earnings variability. Importance of method of computation and of underlying assumptions. Example of minimum standard of coverage.* Appendix 18A: The rating of debt obligations. Appendix 18B: Ratios as predictors of business failure.

Diverse views of performance. Criteria of performance evaluation. Importance of return on investment (ROI). Major objectives in the use of ROI: *An indicator of managerial effectiveness. A method of projecting earnings. Internal decision and control tool.* Basic elements of ROI: *Defining the investment base.* Book versus market values in the investment base: *Difference between investor's cost and enterprise investment base. Averaging the investment base. Relating income to the investment base. Illustration of ROI computations. Analysis and interpretation of ROI.* Analysis of asset utilization: *Evaluation of individual turnover ratios. Use of averages. Other factors to be considered in return on asset evaluation. Equity growth rate. Return on shareholders' equity. Equity turnover. Measuring the financial leverage index. Analysis of financial leverage effects.*

The significance of income statement analysis. The major objectives of income analysis: *What is the relevant net income of the enterprise?* Analysis of components of the income statement: *Accounting principles used and their implication. Tools of income statement analysis.* The analysis of sales and revenues: *Major sources of revenue.* Financial reporting by diversified enterprises: *Reasons for the need for data by significant enterprise segments. Disclosure of "line of business" data. Income statement data. Balance sheet data. Research studies. Statement of Financial Accounting Standards 14. SEC reporting requirements. Implications for analysis. Stability and trend of revenues.* Management's discussion and analysis of the summary of earnings: *Implications for analysis. Methods of revenue recognition and measurement.*

Analysis of cost of sales. Gross profit: *Factors in the analysis of gross profit.* Analysis of changes in gross margin. Example of analysis of change in gross margin: *Interpretation of changes in gross margin.* Break-even analysis: *Concepts underlying break-even analysis. Equation approach. Graphic presentation. Contribution margin approach. Pocket calculator problem—additional considerations. Break-even technique—problem areas and limitations. Break-even analysis—uses and their implications. Analytical implications of break-even analysis. The significance of the variable cost percentage. The significance of the fixed-cost level. The importance of the contribution margin.* Additional considerations in the analysis of cost of sales. Depreciation. Amortization of special tools and similar costs. Maintenance and repairs costs. Other costs and expenses—general: *Selling expenses. Future directed marketing costs.* General, administration, financial, and other expenses: *Financial costs. "Other" expenses.* Other income. Income taxes. The operating ratio. Net income ratio: *Statement accounting for variation in net income.*

Objectives of earnings evaluation. Evaluation of earnings level and its quality. The concept of earnings quality: *Evaluation of discretionary and future-directed costs. Maintenance and repairs. Advertising. Research and development costs. Other future-directed costs.* Balance sheet analysis as a check on the validity and quality of reported earnings: *Importance of carrying amounts of assets. Importance of provisions and liabilities. Balance sheet analysis and the quality of earnings. Effect of valuation of specific assets on the validity and quality of reported income. The effect of external factors on the quality of earnings.* Evaluation of earnings stability and trend: *Determining the trend of income over the years.* Extraordinary gains and losses: *Significance of accounting treatment and presentation. Analysis and evaluation.* Earnings forecasting: *SEC disclosure requirements—aid to forecasting. Elements in earnings forecasts. Publication of financial forecasts. Estimating earning power. Monitoring performance and results.* Interim financial statements: *Year-end adjustments. Seasonality.* APB Opinion No. 28. *SEC interim reporting requirements. Implications for analysis.*

PART I

FINANCIAL STATEMENT
ANALYSIS AND THE
ACCOUNTING FRAMEWORK

1

FINANCIAL STATEMENT ANALYSIS AND ACCOUNTING

THE FUNCTION OF FINANCIAL STATEMENT ANALYSIS

Financial statement analysis is the judgmental process which aims to evaluate the current and past financial positions and the results of operations of an enterprise, with the primary objective of determining the best possible estimates and predictions about future conditions and performance.

Financial statement analysis may be undertaken for many purposes. The security analyst is interested in future earnings estimates and in financial strength as an important element in the determination of security values. The credit analyst wants to determine future funds flows and the resulting financial condition as a means of assessing the risks inherent in a particular credit extension. Present owners of securities analyze current financial statements to decide on whether to hold, enlarge, or sell their positions. Merger and acquisition analysts study and analyze financial statements as an essential part of their decision processes leading to recommendations regarding the merger and acquisition of business enterprises. These are examples of situations involving outsiders—external analysts—trying to reach conclusions principally on the basis of published financial data.

Internal financial analysts, on the other hand, utilize an even larger and more detailed pool of financial data to assess, for internal management and control purposes, the current financial condition and results of operations of an enterprise.

3

THE RAW MATERIAL OF ANALYSIS

The analytical processes which underlie the conclusions of security analysts, credit analysts, and other external analysts, as well as internal analysts, make use of a vast array of facts, information, and data—economic, social, political, and other. However, the most important quantitative data utilized by these analysts are the financial data which are the output of an enterprise's accounting system. Presented for external use, principally in the form of formal financial statements, these data are among the most important quantified elements in the entire mix of inputs utilized by the decision maker. Since financial accounting data are the product of a whole range of conventions, measurements, and judgments, their apparent precision and exactness can be misleading. Such data cannot be intelligently used in financial analysis without a thorough understanding of the accounting framework of which they are the end product, as well as of the conventions which govern the measurement of resources, liabilities, equities, and operating results of an enterprise. This text examines the accounting framework which underlies financial accounting data as well as the tools of analysis which have been found useful in the analysis and interpretation of such data.

IMPORTANCE OF ACCOUNTING DATA

Decision processes, such as those relating to the choice of equity investments or the extension of credit, require a great variety of data possessing a wide range of reliability and relevance to the decision at hand. The information used includes data on general economic conditions and on industry trends, as well as data on intangibles such as the character and the motivation of the management group. Financial statements and other data emanating from the accounting process represent measurable indicia of performance already achieved and of financial conditions presently prevailing.

In any given decision situation, the relative importance of unquantifiable intangibles, as against quantified actual experience reflected in financial statements, will, of course, vary. Nevertheless, in most cases no intelligent, well-grounded decision can be made without an analysis of the quantifiable data found in financial accounting reports.

In the realm of data available for meaningful analysis, financial statements are important because they are objective in that they portray actual events which already happened; they are concrete in that they can be quantified; and being quantifiable they can, perhaps most importantly, be measured. This attribute of measurability endows financial statement data with another important characteristic: since they are expressed in the common denominator of money, this enables us to add and combine the data, to relate them to other data, and to otherwise manipulate them arithmetically. The above attributes contribute to the great importance of financial accounting data, both historical or projected, to the decision-making process.

LIMITATIONS OF ACCOUNTING DATA

Recognition of the importance of financial accounting data should be tempered by a realization of the limitations to which they are subject. The following sections discuss some of the more important limitations.

Monetary expression

The first and most obvious limitation is that financial statements can only present information that lends itself to quantification in terms of the monetary unit; some significant facts about the enterprise do not lend themselves to such measurement. For example, the financial statements, as such, contain very little direct information about the character, motivation, experience, or age of the human resources. They do not contain, except in terms of aggregate final results, information about the quality of the research and development effort or the breadth of the marketing organization. Nor can we expect to find in the financial statements any detailed information on product lines, machinery efficiency, or advance planning. Equally absent will be information on organization structure and on such behavioral problems as the fact that the marketing manager is not on speaking terms with the controller, or that the entire success of the enterprise hinges on the talents of a single person. Nevertheless, without a uniform unit of measurement, financial statements, as we know them, would not be possible.

Simplifications and rigidities inherent in the accounting framework

The portrayal by means of accounting statements of highly complex and diverse economic activities involves the need for simplification, summarization, and the use of judgments and estimates.

The simplification process is necessary in order to classify the great variety of economic events into a manageable number of categories. Inevitably, this simplification can be achieved only at the expense of clarity and detail which, in some instances, may be useful to the user of financial data.

The need to keep the size of and detail in the financial statements within reasonable bounds requires a high degree of summarization of economic events both in the initial recording of these events in the accounting records and subsequently in the preparation of the financial statements. Inevitably, in the process of such summarization, financial statements lose, perhaps more often than they should, comprehensiveness of description and clarity.

The simplifications and the rigidities inherent in the accounting framework as well as the high degree of summarization present in the financial statements make it imperative that the analyst be able to analyze and to reconstruct the events and the business transactions which they reflect. Indeed, it is an essential skill of the analyst to be able to recover from the financial presentations the realities imbedded in them and to recognize that which cannot be recovered and thus have a basis for asking meaningful questions of those able to provide additional information.

Use of estimation and judgment

The use of estimation and judgment in financial statements is inevitable. The limitation to be recognized here is the resulting variety in the quality and reliability of financial statement presentations. Financial statements may not be of uniform quality and reliability because of differences in the character and the quality of judgments exercised by accountants in their preparation.

Present-day financial statements are historical in nature, and their use for predictive purposes calls for the application of informed judgment by the user. Moreover, financial statements are general-purpose presentations; the extent of detail reflected therein is determined by the accounting profession's current view of the "average reader's" requirements and expectations. Such envisioned requirements do not necessarily coincide with those of a user with a specific purpose in mind.

Interim nature

A further limitation of financial statements stems from the need to report for relatively short periods of the total life-span of an enterprise. To be useful, accounting information must be timely; and therefore determinations of financial condition and results of operations must be made frequently. But such frequency of reporting, particularly on the results of operations, requires a great deal of calculation based on judgments; and the greater the degree of such estimation required, the greater the amount of uncertainty that is inevitably introduced into the financial statements.

It is important to clarify the connection between the length of a period reported on and the degree of accounting uncertainty introduced. Many business transactions and operations require a long period of time for final completion and determination of results. For example, fixed assets are acquired for a long period of usefulness. The longer such period of use, the more tentative must be the estimates of their ultimate useful life-span. Similarly, the value, if any, of investments in research and development may not become apparent until many accounting periods after the one in which they are incurred. Long-term contracts are another example in which the greater the length of time involved, the more tentative the estimation process must be.

Cost balances

As will be seen in Chapter 2, it still is a basic convention of accounting in the United States that accounting determinations be subject to objective ascertainment.[1] Since the cost of an asset arrived at by arm's-length bargaining may generally be objectively determined by inspection, it is claimed that the cost figure enjoys an objectivity surpassing any subsequent unrealized appraisal of value. Primarily for this reason accounting adheres, with few exceptions, to the cost concept. The price we pay for this objectivity in accounting adds up to yet another important limitation upon the usefulness of accounting statements. Cost balances do not, in most cases, represent current market values. Yet the users of financial statements usually look for an assessment of value and, to them, historical cost balances are of very limited usefulness. Moreover, the analyst must be aware of valuation bases other than cost which are used in financial statements.

Unstable monetary unit

The first accounting limitation which we discussed above identified accounting expressions as being limited to those which could be expressed in monetary terms. The advantage of the monetary expression is, of course, that it provides a common denominator and enables us to add up the cost aggregates of such diverse assets as, say, shares of stock, tons of lead, and store furniture.

Over the years, however, the value of money in terms of general purchasing power has undergone significant fluctuations and generally has had a pronounced downward trend. The monetary unit has not

---

[1] There is slow movement in this country and more determined movement abroad towards some forms of current value accounting. These moves are prompted particularly by a desire to give recognition to the effects of inflation on accounting determinations (see also Chapter 14).

retained its quality as a "standard of value" and, consequently, adding up the money cost of goods purchased in year 19X1 with those bought in 19X8 may result in serious distortions.

While the accounting profession has recognized that "the assumption that fluctuations in the value of money can be ignored is unrealistic," not much has been done so far in practice to issue supplementary statements which would shed light on the effect of price level changes on the conventional financial statements. Thus, the financial presentations found today remain subject to this serious limitation. The effect of price level changes on accounting determinations is examined in Chapter 14.

Having explored the relationship of financial statement analysis to the decision-making process and to the accounting framework on which it relies, we turn next to a more comprehensive consideration of the accounting process.

THE FUNCTION OF ACCOUNTING

Accounting is concerned with the quantitative expression of economic phenomena. As a discipline, it evolved from a need for a framework for recording, classifying, and communicating economic data. In the basic form existing today, it reflects the constant change and modification which it has undergone since its inception, in response to changing social and economic needs.

One of the best and most succinct definitions of the functions of accounting is found in *Accounting Research Study No. 1*, entitled "The Basic Postulate of Accounting," which had as its aim the identification of the postulates or conventions of the discipline. According to this study, the function of accounting is:

1. To measure the resources held by specific entities.
2. To reflect the claims against and the interests in those entities.
3. To measure the changes in those resources, claims and interests.
4. To assign the changes to specifiable period of time.
5. To express the foregoing in terms of money as a common denominator.[2]

The function and purposes of accounting are accomplished at two levels. One is the recording function which is that part of the discipline which governs the mechanics of recording and summarizing the multitude of transactions and economic events which occur in an enterprise and which can be quantified in terms of money. The other level, a more complex one and more subject to individual judgment and opinion, governs the methods, procedures, and principles by

---

[2] Maurice Moonitz, "The Basic Postulate of Accounting," *Accounting Research Study No. 1*. (New York: American Institute of Certified Public Accountants, 1961).

which accounting data are measured and presented. This chapter will concern itself with an examination of the recording level of the accounting discipline, while subsequent chapters will take up the conventions and principles which govern accounting measurements and their presentation.

The recording function

The recording function in accounting is governed by the principle of double-entry bookkeeping, an ingenious system of accounting which has stood the test of time since its description by an Italian mathematician in 1494.

The study of the theory of double-entry bookkeeping is an integral part of the study of accountancy. Users of accounting statements will find that a general understanding of the double-entry system will aid them significantly in the analysis of financial statements as well as in the reconstruction of business transactions.

The basic concept of the double-entry system is based on the duality of every business transaction. For example, if a business borrows $1,000, it acquires an asset (cash), and counterbalancing this is a claim against the enterprise (a liability) in an equal amount. Regardless of how many transactions an enterprise engages in, this duality and balance prevails at all times and provides the advantages of order, consistency, and control enjoyed under the system.

Continuing with a more generalized example, when an entity acquires an asset the counterbalancing effect results in one or a number of the following:

1. The incurrence of a liability.
2. The enlargement of the ownership's claim (capital funds).
3. The disposal of another asset.

Similarly, a liability is extinguished by:

1. The disposal of an asset, or
2. The enlargement of the ownership claim, or
3. Incurrence of another liability.

At all times the assets of an enterprise equal the outsider's claims against these assets (i.e., liabilities) and the equity of the ownership (i.e., capital). Thus, the basic equation prevailing under the double-entry system is:

$$Assets = Liabilities + Capital$$

An expense or a cost incurred in the operations of the enterprise is accompanied by one, or a combination of, the following:

1. Reduction of assets.
2. Increase in liabilities.
3. Increase in the ownership's claim.

Conversely, revenue received by the enterprise—

1. Increases assets, or
2. Decreases liabilities, or
3. Decreases the ownership's claim or affects a combination of the above.

Under the double-entry system, all transactions are recorded and classified and then summarized under appropriate account designations. Financial statements are formal, condensed presentations of the data derived from these accounts.

One of the best ways of visualizing the basic system of record-keeping and the principal interrelationships within it is by means of a diagram which portrays the major classes of accounts as well as the typical relationships among them.

Exhibit 1–1 is a graphic portrayal of the accounting cycle. A careful study of the illustration and the main movements reflected therein will

EXHIBIT 1–1

The accounting cycle

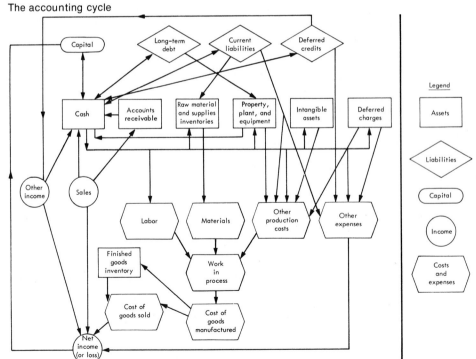

enable the reader to follow the principal basic financial relationships and flows within a manufacturing enterprise. For the sake of clarity, infrequent or unusual flows and relationships have not been included.

The arrows connecting the principal asset, liability, capital, income, cost, and expense accounts indicate the direction of the usual flows. They do not, of course, indicate the relative size of the flows, which vary considerably from business to business and from one set of circumstances to another. The reader will notice that no account is dead-ended, that is, there are flows in and out of all accounts. This simply emphasizes the dynamic aspects of business and the accounting system which portrays its financial flows. As management invests, buys, makes, incurs costs, and sells, the quantity of money represented in each account is changing while the system as a whole remains in balance, its debit accounts (generally assets, costs, and expenses) always equaling its credit accounts (generally capital, liabilities, and income).

The flows into and out of each account shown in Exhibit 1–1 can be clearly traced in the diagram, and the chapters which follow—on the measurement of assets, liabilities, capital, and income—should increase and sharpen the reader's understanding of these flows as well as the principles governing their measurement.

The flows shown in the diagram of Exhibit 1–1, while always expressed in dollars, can be in many forms, such as cash, costs, and so forth. Thus, for example, if we trace the inflows and outflows affecting the Property, Plant, and Equipment account in Exhibit 1–1, we can learn a great deal about the interrelationships among the various accounts. The reader can, of course, focus in similar fashion on any account or constellation of accounts. Exhibit 1–2 presents those accounts appearing in the accounting cycle diagram (Exhibit 1–1), which relate to the Property, Plant, and Equipment account and the flows into and out of it.

Three distinct phases can be discerned here:

1. The accounting for the acquisition and disposition of property, plant, and equipment (PPE).
2. The accounting for the use of PPE (depreciation).
3. Accounting for the recovery, out of revenue, of amounts invested in PPE.

Acquisition and disposition of PPE. The acquisition of PPE can be made by payment of cash or the incurrence of debt or both. Hence, the arrows in Exhibit 1–2 point to a flow from cash and/or long-term debt. Ultimately the debt is paid back by cash, and this accounts for the flow from cash toward long-term debt. The flow from PPE to cash represents instances where PPE is sold for cash at any stage of its use. In all

EXHIBIT 1–2
Typical flows to and from the Property, Plant, and Equipment account

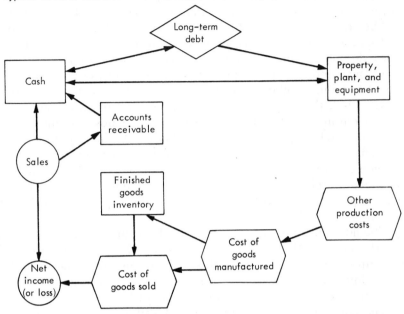

cases the flows are equal, for example, an increase in PPE will result in an equal decrease in cash or a commensurate increase in long-term debt.

Use of PPE.   PPE is acquired mostly for productive use. Consequently, its cost is allocated by means of the depreciation process (see Chapter 9) to "cost of goods manufactured." The flows shown in Exhibit 1–2 are from PPE to the "Other Production Costs" account from where they are charged to the "Costs of Goods Manufactured" account. The cost of goods manufactured which are sold is charged to the "Cost of Goods Sold" account which, in turn, flows into the Net Income (or Profit and Loss) account, where all cost and revenues of the period are accumulated. The unsold goods manufactured remain in the Finished Goods Inventory, which is an asset account to be carried over to the next period. Ultimately, when the finished goods are sold they find their way into the "Costs of Goods Sold" account.

Recovery of cost of PPE.   To complete the cycle, we observe in Exhibit 1–2 that the sales of finished goods, which normally are made at amounts designed to recover all costs and earn a profit, generate sales which are either for cash or result in claims, such as accounts receivable which are subsequently collected in cash. It is through these sales that the outlay for PPE is ultimately recovered by the enterprise.

This completes our tracing of the Exhibit 1–2 subcycle of the accounting system where cash was used to buy PPE and was finally collected from the sale of the products in whose production the PPE was used. Examination of Exhibit 1–1 will reveal the existence of numerous other subcycles which make up the integrated whole.

Financial statements

The accounting system which we examined above continually collects, summarizes, and updates data on assets, liabilities, capital, revenues, costs, and expenses. Periodically it is necessary to take stock in order to ascertain the financial condition and the results of operations of the enterprise. This is done by presenting in summary form the details contained in the accounts. Based on the accounts included in the diagram of the accounting cycle (Exhibit 1–1) we can illustrate the composition of two major financial statements as follows:

Balance sheet (statement of financial condition). Exhibit 1–3 shows all assets, liabilities, and capital accounts extracted from Exhibit 1–1 and presented in conventional balance sheet format. This presentation reveals a number of basic relationships worth noting. On the left side are all the assets and unexpired costs in which the resources of the enterprise are invested at a specific point in time. On the right side of the statement are the sources from which these invested funds were financed, that is, the liabilities and the equity (capital) accounts. Since the *current liabilities* represent a short-term claim against the enterprise, the balance sheet shows the *current assets* generally available to meet these claims, principally cash, accounts receivable, and inventories. The difference between current assets and current liabilities is the working capital.

Income statement (results of operations). The second major financial statement differs in some important respects from the balance sheet. The income statement format shown in Exhibit 1–4 does not show the account balances as of a certain date, as is the case with the balance sheet, but rather shows the cumulative activity in the revenue, cost, and expense accounts for the period reported upon. This is a report on the dynamic aspects of the enterprise—its results of operations. The final net income (or loss) is added to or deducted from capital through the Retained Earnings account. Thus, the capital accounts link the net results of operations with the statement of financial condition.

Other financial statements explain other aspects of change. Thus, changes in the Retained Earnings account are detailed in financial

EXHIBIT 1–3
Statement of financial condition (balance sheet)

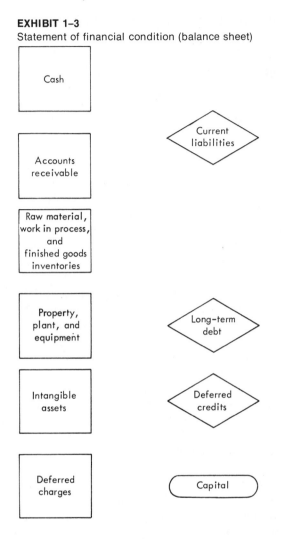

statements. The statement of changes in financial position, which is the third major financial statement, explains over a period of time changes in the funds available to the enterprise. It is examined more fully in Chapter 13.

Ingenious as the recording framework of accounting is, it represents only the mechanical aspects of the discipline. Controlling the method of recording of assets, liabilities, and capital, as well as the size and the timing of cost and revenue flows, is an elaborate and pervasive set of standards. These standards in turn reflect the application of the basic

EXHIBIT 1–4
Income statement

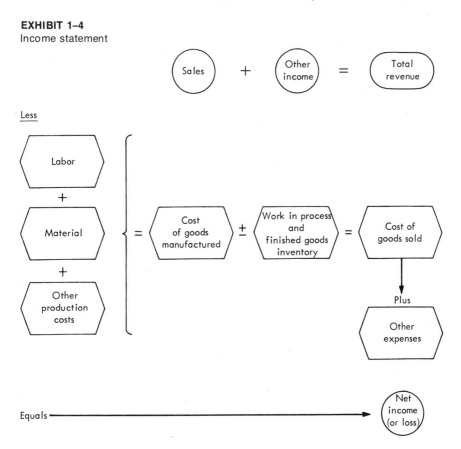

objectives and conventions of accountancy. Since this body of conventions and standards determines the methodology involved in the basic measurements in financial statements, as well as their form and the degree of disclosure therein, the intelligent analysis of these statements requires a thorough familiarity with, and an understanding of, these conventions and standards.

QUESTIONS

1. What is financial statement analysis?
2. Why are financial statements important to the decision process in financial analysis?
3. List some of the more important limitations to which accounting data are subject.

4. What are some of the simplifications and the rigidities inherent in the accounting framework?
5. Define briefly the function of accounting.
6. The functions and purposes of accounting are accomplished at two levels; describe them.
7. What is the basic equation prevailing under the double-entry system of bookkeeping?

2

ACCOUNTING OBJECTIVES, CONVENTIONS, AND STANDARDS

THE OBJECTIVES OF ACCOUNTING

While accountants have enjoyed some degree of success in agreeing upon the proper accounting in specific areas of practice, they have, so far, not been able to agree on the basic bedrock objectives of accounting. Not that there is a lack of broad generalizations on the subject—one firm suggested "fairness" as such basic underlying tenant—but there is no broad consensus on objectives in a way that would help accountants settle their differences of opinion by referring to them. Accounting is, after all, not an exact science. It is rather a social science—its concepts, rooted in the value system of the society in which it operates, are socially determined and socially expressed. Consequently, broad agreement on *useful* generalizations regarding its basic objectives may be as hard to achieve in the future as it was in the past. The fact that the setting of accounting standards is basically a political process involving many parties at interest, makes such agreement all the more difficult to attain.

In 1973, The Objectives of Financial Statements Study Group (Trueblood Committee) created by the American Institute of Certified Public Accountants and consisting of nine highly qualified individuals from varied backgrounds, reported its conclusions on the "Objectives of Financial Statements". After agreeing with the generally held conclusion[1] that "The basic objective of financial statements is to provide

---

[1] The FASB reports that only 37 *percent* of respondents to its First Discussion Memorandum on the Conceptual Framework of Accounting could agree even with this basic conclusion. This provides an insight into the magnitude of the problem of reaching agreement on even the most basic accounting objectives.

information useful for making economic decisions" the Study Group listed, among others, the following two significant objectives:

An objective of financial statements is to provide information useful to investors and creditors for predicting, comparing, and evaluating potential cash flows to them in terms of amount, timing, and related uncertainty.

An objective of financial statements is to provide users with information for predicting, comparing, and evaluating enterprise earning power.

These objectives established a definite link between accounting and the basic decision functions which it serves, i.e., the investing and lending processes. The Study Group recognized however that the objectives it enunciated can be attained only in stages and over time.

In late 1976, the Financial Accounting Standards Board (FASB) issued two documents in connection with its project on the conceptual framework for financial accounting and reporting. One document contains the "Tentative Conclusions on Objectives of Financial Statements of Business Enterprises" of the FASB. These tentative conclusions are based primarily on the first group of objectives set forth in the report of the above mentioned Study Group. The FASB had previously held a public hearing in connection with this document, and its tentative conclusions are based in part on the responses to an earlier discussion memorandum and on the results of the public hearing. The board is asking respondents to submit comments on these tentative conclusions.

The board's tentative conclusions on objectives begin with a broad concern with information that is useful to present and potential investors and creditors who have a reasonable understanding of business and are willing to study financial statements in making rational investment credit decisions. They then narrow that concern by reference to investors' and creditors' primary interest in the prospects of receiving cash from their investments in, or loans to business enterprises; and finally focus on the financial statements that provide information useful to assessing the prospects for cash flows to the business enterprise on which cash flows to investors and creditors depend and in an evaluating enterprise and management performance.

In addition to its tentative conclusions on the objectives of financial statements of business enterprises, the FASB has also issued a lengthy *Discussion Memorandum* on an analysis of issues related to "Conceptual Framework for Financial Accounting and Reporting: Elements of Financial Statements and Their Measurement." This *Discussion Memorandum* does not contain any conclusions of the board, and in this respect is different from the companion booklet on tentative conclusions and objectives.

The *Discussion Memorandum* is principally an analysis of issues related to defining and measuring the elements of financial statements. The first of its three parts is concerned with definitions of the elements of financial statements. These elements include assets, liabilities, earnings, revenues, expenses, gains, and losses. The second part of the memorandum discusses the qualitative characteristics of financial information, such as relevance, measurability, reliability, objectivity, and comparability. The final section deals with measurement of the elements of financial statements, including consideration of the attribute of those elements that is to be measured and of the unit of measure to be used.

Five measures (or attributes) discussed are historical cost/historical proceeds, current cost/current proceeds, current exit value in orderly liquidation, expected exit value in due course of business, and present value of expected cash flows. The discussion memorandum points out, that each of the five measures is equally susceptible to measurement either in terms of units of money or in terms of units of general purchasing power (see also Chapter 14).

The two documents are expected to lead ultimately to FASB pronouncements on issues that have been debated for decades.

The board has tentatively concluded that, for transitional purposes, the issuance in this area of pronouncements forming a class separate from the "statements" it now issues will be appropriate. The reason is that to insure orderly transition these pronouncements on concepts should not be subject to Rule 203 of the Rules of Conduct of the AICPA which requires adherence by members to statements of the FASB. We can thus foresee the elapse of a long period of time before the results of these deliberations become part of rules which are binding on members of the organized accounting profession.

USEFUL QUALITATIVE CHARACTERISTICS OF ACCOUNTING

The usefulness of accounting data is dependent on the achievement of certain normative objectives which are derived from the need experienced by users of financial information over time. Some of the most basic of these objectives can be described in terms of qualitative characteristics such as the following:

Relevance

Accounting information and presentations must be responsive to the informational needs of users of financial statements: It must bear on the problems for which it is intended. One of the most basic objectives of accounting is that financial statements be relevant, that is, that they serve the informational needs of users directly, comprehensively, and well. The achievement of this objective presupposes knowledge by the accountant of the needs of users of financial statements for information as well as an understanding of the tools and techniques used by them in analyzing such information.

Thus, we know, for example, that users of financial statements are interested in the elements of financial strengths and weaknesses of an enterprise and in data bearing on its vulnerability to adversity as well as its ability to weather it with the financial resources at its command. Moreover, users of financial statements are interested in all significant factors contributing to the results of a company's operations and in factors, such as nonrecurring and nonoperating elements included in such operations, which affect the validity of future projections. The last part of this text examines the various types of information needed by users of financial statements in order to make such statements relevant to their purposes.

Objectivity

Decisions made on the basis of financial statements inevitably affect the rights, resources, and the economic risks and rewards of parties at interest. Thus, for example, financial statements are used in the evaluation of management performance, and management as well as owners have an important stake in that evaluation. Similarly, the way accounting data are recorded and presented invariably affects anyone relying on them. This requires that financial statement determinations be objective—they must be free from bias, partisanship, and the effects of ulterior motive.

Two qualities attach to such objectively arrived at information. One is a high degree of verifiability. Objectively determined information can usually be traced and indentified as to origin or method, or both. The other quality is that of reliability, which derives from the conscientious effort to arrive at the most valid and supportable conclusions. Reliability allows users to depend on information with confidence.

Objectivity in accounting is a relative concept. A thermometer is an absolutely objective instrument. It records temperature as it senses it, and its conclusions are not affected by any extraneous factors. Such objectivity in accounting is well nigh impossible simply because its measurements are carried out by humans in the face of uncertainty. And humans have feelings, hunches, preconceptions, fears, and biases even if those are honest and not subject to ulterior motive. Yet, what is expected of accounting is that it be as objective as possible, that is, that it be neutral in its effects on the various parties at interest.

Comparability

One of the most basic tools of analysis for decision making is comparison. Almost all evaluations and alternative-choice judgments involve comparisons of one sort or another. Thus, the ability to compare sets of accounting data of the same enterprise over time, or those of one enterprise with that of another, is very important to the decision-making process. As a consequence, the usefulness of accounting presentations depends importantly on their comparability. This makes comparability an important objective in accounting.

In its ultimate form, comparability requires that like events be accounted for in like manner, so that differences arise from different circumstances rather than from the choice of different accounting methods or their application.

Clarity

The complexity of accounting information that results from the high degree of summarization of a multitude of economic events and transactions is one reason for the need for clarity and lack of equivocation in accounting presentations. The other obvious reason for the need for clarity is that users of accounting data vary greatly in their background, education, and in the competence to assimilate such information. While a minimum understanding of accounting processes and conventions is essential for the intelligent use of accounting data, clarity will contribute greatly to its maximum usefulness. This objective becomes even more obvious when we recognize that accounting is essentially a communications discipline and that clarity, for example, the absence of redundancy and ambiguity, can greatly facilitate the communication process.

Timeliness

Information always has a time value. In the case of economic and financial data, on the basis of which decisions have to be made, time is almost always of the essence. The older the information is, that is, the further in time it is removed from the events and circumstances which gave rise to it, the less useful and relevant it is likely to be for effective decision-making purposes. Thus, it is an important objective of accounting that financial statements be made available to users as soon as possible after the events reported upon have taken place.

Substance versus form

The ever present adverse and special interests which affect financial reporting often result in a tendency to emphasize form, in most cases legal form, over substance. Thus, for example, long term obligations under leases may be recorded in a way which ignores recurring future obligations (liabilities) and the related claims to benefits (assets). Moreover, transactions among related parties are often effected in ways that stress legal form over economic substance. Such a bias is contrary to good accounting, leads to distorted reporting and consequently should be avoided.

Generality of purpose

Accounting data are generally presented in the form of financial statements. These financial statements are used by many different parties having differing interests and points of view. Thus, we find accounting data used by present and potential owners of an enterprise and by creditors, suppliers, customers, employees, and governmental agencies. Representing some of these interests are specialized advisers and experts such as security and financial analysts, loan officers, lawyers, and officials of government regulatory agencies. Because the variety of interests and points of view of these users must be accommodated by the same set of financial statements, it is a basic objective of accounting to make these statements as complete, comprehensive, and "general purpose" as possible. This means that the statements should include as much information that is significant and of general interest as is possible without rendering the statements unduly elaborate, wordy, lengthy, and confusing. It also means that the statements should not be oriented towards the objectives of a special or specialized interest to the exclusion of other general interests.

Obstacles in the attainment of these objectives

The objectives enumerated above, while representing standards to strive for, are rarely if ever fully achieved in the presentation of accounting data. Limitations in the capabilities of the preparers of financial statements, imperfections in processes such as the interpretation of events and the estimation of future probabilities, as well as limitations inherent in human nature, are some obvious reasons for this.

Moreover, some of the objectives enumerated above are in conflict with each other. Thus, for example, the objective of relevance may be in conflict with that of generality of purpose because certain decision makers have specific information requirements which cannot be met in general-purpose statements.

The user of financial statements can resolve this conflict by obtaining the additionally needed information directly from the reporting enterprise, provided he has the influence necessary to persuade it to furnish such special-purpose information to him.

Another example of conflicting objectives is that of timeliness and relevance. In many instances the need to speed the issuance of data is made at the expense of its relevance and completeness. Similarly, relevance and objectivity represent to some degree conflicting objectives because the goal of objectivity prevents the inclusion of unverifiable data which, nevertheless, may be very relevant to the decision maker.

ACCOUNTING CONVENTIONS

Over the years, accounting objectives, such as those examined above, as well as other environmental factors influencing the discipline, have given rise to a series of conventions in accounting. Both the conventions of accounting as well as the objectives on which they are, in part, based represent a distillation of cumulative experience and, as such, are always subject to change and modification.

It is important to recognize that despite its many quantitative aspects, accounting is basically a social science. As such, its basic tenets are socially expressed and socially determined. Since accounting is man-conceived, its conventions and rules reflect the mores, concerns, and priorities of the society in which it is practiced.

To illustrate, accounting practices vary considerably from country to country. Many of these differences are due to differences in viewpoint. In some countries the creditors' point of view is accorded greater importance than that of the ownership. In this country, it is basically the ownership's viewpoint which is behind the move to prepare statements adjusted for general price level changes. Such statements would show the effect of price level changes on the owners' capital investment.

The purposes which accounting must serve as well as the priorities it must observe have made necessary agreement upon certain generally accepted conventions underlying the accounting principles which are the discipline's operative guides. Whether we refer to them as assumptions, postulates, standards, imperatives, or conventions (as this author prefers), they are the underlying tenets of accounting.

We consider here the following accounting conventions:

1. Entity.
2. Accounting period.
3. Continuity.
4. Conservatism.
5. Full disclosure.
6. Consistency.
7. Materiality.

Entity

To be meaningful, accounting is performed for business entities which comprise defined areas of interest. This convention is derived from the environment in which accounting functions and has developed in response to a need for accurate definition of what is being accounted for. Thus, we account for corporations as legal entities, for partnerships as units defined by agreement, and for proprietorships as circumscribed areas of business interest. Where presentations of the financial statements of a group of companies under common ownership is deemed more meaningful, the consolidated group is the entity accounted for.

Accounting period

While enterprise operations are conducted on a continuous basis, decision makers require, at frequent intervals, up-to-date information on its progress. This requirement, coupled with the objective of time liness, resulted in the convention of reporting by accounting period. The reporting for segmented periods, which requires cutoffs of various accounting measurements and determinations, is commonly done comprehensively at annual intervals and also at more frequent (e.g., quarterly) intervals for interim reporting purposes. The objective of comparability requires that the periodic reports cover time periods of equal length and that periods reported upon remain the same, unless a change is "flagged."

Continuity

Most modern enterprises have, or at least are intended to have, a life of indefinite duration. This is in contrast to the earlier prevailing single or joint ventures where on consummation of a specific undertaking, such as a voyage, the business entity would be terminated. The assumption of continuity of operations, or the going-concern convention, is a reasonable one under modern conditions and is presumed to prevail in all cases in which there is no evidence that a contrary assumption is warranted. However, where evidence of limited life does exist, accounting determinations must be oriented toward the probability of liquidation.

In practice, the continuity convention is based on the assumption that the enterprise will continue sufficiently far into the future so that its long-lived assets will be used for the purposes for which they were acquired. This convention is cited as one of the arguments for the *cost concept* in accounting. Thus, fixed assets in active use are carried at cost and allocated to future operations without regard to current market or liquidation values.

Conservatism

The convention of conservatism is one of long standing and is rooted in the experience of businessmen. It cautions not "to count one's chickens until they are hatched" and, in general, is on the side of caution and skepticism regarding future favorable outcomes or events. In order that this convention be not in conflict with the conventions of consistency and full disclosure, it is necessary that conservatism be not carried to the point of deliberate understatement of assets or overstatement of liabilities. Undue conservatism can be just as damaging to parties interested in financial statements as excessive optimism.

In its more modern version, conservatism can be best understood in terms of uncertainty and risk. The all-pervading uncertainty of business life makes it more prudent to err on the side of caution. The realization principle and the valuation principle involved in "the lower-of-cost-or-market" rule are based on the convention of conservatism. Realization requires an arm's-length sales transaction before gains are recognized. On the other hand, losses are recognized in the accounts as soon as they can be determined or reasonably foreseen and measured. The lower-of-cost-or-market rule is an extension of this principle. While the carrying value of, say, inventories should not exceed cost, a reduction in current market value must be recognized.

On the face of it, the "lower-of-cost-or-market" rule clashes with the convention of consistency in that the treatment of anticipated losses differs from that accorded anticipated gains. The explanation for this, as in so many other areas of accounting, is that under certain circumstances certain conventions do take precedence over others. Thus, in this particular case, the convention of conservatism supersedes that of consistency.

In terms of accounting objectives, the convention of conservatism satisfies the objective of objectivity in that the reliance on favorable future expectations is significantly reduced through the application of the conservatism convention.

Full disclosure

The convention of full disclosure satisfies many basic accounting objectives, the most prominent among which are relevance, objectivity, comparability, clarity, and the stressing of substance over form.

While the convention or standard of full disclosure is an eminently justified and logical one, it is, nevertheless, of relatively recent origin.

It was given full expression in the Securities Acts of the 1930s, wherein the prevailing theme is full disclosure of all facts needed by an investor to reach informed conclusions. The measure of full disclosure is sufficient information presented in such a way as to make the financial statements not misleading.

Full disclosure does not mean an abundance of facts and figures indiscriminately heaped upon the reader. It means, rather, the stress of substance over form and the arrangement and presentation of facts and figures in such a way as to allow the deducing of significant conclusions. As we shall see in the discussion of the convention of materiality, an overabundance of insignificant facts and trifles can be just as misleading to the reader as a lack of significant information.

Consistency

The convention of consistency is derived directly from the objective of comparability in accounting. The ability to compare, for example, the results of operations of one year with those of another year is basic to the decision-making process based on financial data. Yet such a comparison would, at best, be useless and, at worst, misleading if the principles underlying the preparation of the data being compared differed from year to year. This convention calls for adequate disclosure of any material change in the accounting principles employed in the accounting process as well as the disclosure of the effect of any such change. For positive assurance in this regard in audited financial statements the reader looks to the auditor's report wherein the statement is said to be "prepared on a basis consistent with that of the preceding year" or any departure from consistency is described.

Contrary to the impression of some, the convention of consistency does not preclude change from one principle of accounting to another, nor does it discourage such change as such. However, there is a general presumption in accounting that a change from one principle to another should be in the direction of better accounting, fuller disclosure, and a fairer presentation. Change is not warranted if its main purpose is the serving of a more narrow interest. This presumption has now been more forcefully stated in *Accounting Principles Board (APB) Opinion No. 20* which is discussed in more detail in Chapter 11.

Materiality

The convention of materiality is both basic and simple. Its basic meaning is that there is no reason to be concerned with what is not important and with that which is trivial. In accounting, this concept assumes special significance because by its nature accounting information is not comprehended easily by the reader. The introduction therein of redundancy can make the task of its absorption and analysis even more difficult. Hence, to keep the information from being misleading, trivia should be kept out of it. The concept of materiality contributes thus directly to the objectives of clarity and relevance.

If the issue were simply one of omitting trivia, where there is general agreement on what trivia are, materiality would not be the problem area it is. At its root, the problem of materiality rests on the claim by users that some preparers of financial statements and their auditors use the concept to avoid disclosing that which they do not wish disclosed. It is this aspect that makes this concept significant to users of accounting data who must realize that accountants do omit, reclassify, or ignore data and information on the basis of their materiality, but that there are, as of now, no set criteria which guide either the accountant or the user of information to distinguish between what is material and what is not.

This state of affairs has resulted in action on a number of fronts. Some professional pronouncements (such as those on earnings per share and intercorporate investments) contain quantitative materiality benchmarks, while recent Securities and Exchange Commission pronouncements (such as those requiring comments on operating results) also specify materiality boundaries. Moreover, the Financial Accounting Standards Board (FASB) has issued a voluminous *Discussion Memorandum* as the subject on which it accepted comments through early in 1976.

Effect of accounting conventions

The above-enumerated accounting conventions exercise an influence on practice in a number of ways. Some conventions (e.g., consistency or full disclosure) have direct influence in that they affect general standards of presentation and disclosure of financial statements. The influence of other conventions may be traced through the accounting principles which they underlie. Irrespective of the way these conventions exercise their influence on the ultimate accounting determinations, valid analysis requires that their impact be appreciated, understood, and assessed.

ACCOUNTING PRINCIPLES OR STANDARDS

Accounting principles are the rules and operative guides of accounting. These rules, which are now more accurately viewed as standards, determine such matters as how assets are measured, when liabilities are incurred, when income is recognized as earned, and when expenses and losses accrue. Thus, to the user of accounting data and statements, an understanding of these rules is essential. No intelligent and valid analysis of financial statements can be undertaken without ascertaining as fully as possible which accounting principles were used in the preparation of such statements and how they were applied.

How accounting standards are established

Accounting principles have been long in developing and are subject to continuous innovation, modification, and change. Thus, the principle of depreciation accounting, under which the cost of a productive fixed asset is allocated to revenue over the useful life of such asset, is well established today, but it was not fully accepted as recently as the turn of the century. The tremendous growth of leasing after World War II has moved the accounting profession to reconsider the accounting for leases and change it significantly. Over the years accounting principles have thus changed in response to developments in, and the needs of, the business community and its requirements and expectations.

It is now generally accepted that the primary responsibility for the fair presentation of financial statements rests with the reporting management of an enterprise. However, the responsibility for the development of accounting principles, which govern this reporting, has been borne primarily by the organized accounting profession and by the Securities and Exchange Commission and, to a lesser extent, by the American Accounting Association and the New York Stock Exchange.

The role of the accounting profession. The reasons for the accounting profession's assumption of early leadership in the development of accounting principles are not hard to find. One of the profession's major and unique functions is that of attesting to the fairness of presentation of financial statements. Yet, the term "fairness of presentation" requires a frame of reference by which it may be judged. Generally accepted accounting principles are intended to provide such a frame of reference, and the accounting profession is presumed to have both the independence and the technical capability required for their development. In pursuing the development of generally accepted accounting principles, the profession was not only performing a vital public service but was also catering to its own vital interests.

The earliest effort of the profession was a "Memorandum on Balance Sheet Audits" prepared by the American Institute of Certified Public Accountants (AICPA) at the request of the Federal Trade Commission. It was published in 1917 in the *Federal Reserve Bulletin* under the title "Uniform Accounts." A revision of this compendium of approved methods of preparing financial statements was prepared by the AICPA and published in 1929 by the Federal Reserve Board under the title "Verification of Financial Statements."

The winds of social and economic change which blew fast and furious starting with the 1929 financial collapse have exerted a strong and decisive influence on the pace of accounting change. While no knowledgeable source would place the major blame for the economic debacle at the door of poor accounting and inadequate reporting, there was, nevertheless, a general recognition of the fact that improvements in accounting principles and in disclosure were long overdue. The profession found a willing partner favoring change in the New York Stock Exchange whose reputation was, to say the least, tarnished by the debacle which began in 1929. Propelled by strong and renewed incentives to lift the financial accountability of companies listed with it to higher standards, the New York Stock Exchange cooperated with a Committee of the AICPA to spell them out. The result of a two-year correspondence between the AICPA Committee and the Committee on Stock List of the New York Stock Exchange was published in 1934. It embodied a number of basic principles of accounting to be followed by listed companies—clarification on the limitations of financial statements and agreement with regard to the wording of the auditor's opinion. This was the first recorded instance where the phrase "accepted accounting principles" (later changed to "generally accepted accounting principles") was used.

With the establishment of a research department, the AICPA undertook in 1938 to put the effort of developing accounting principles on a permanent basis. To this end, a Committee on Accounting Procedure was established whose purpose was to reduce the areas of difference in accounting and to narrow the choices available in the area of alternative accounting principles.

The Committee on Accounting Procedure at first endeavored to prepare a comprehensive statement on accounting principles but abandoned this goal for the more attainable one of dealing with individual areas of controversy and difficulty. During its tenure, the Committee considered a great many accounting problems and issued pronouncements in the form of 51 *Accounting Research Bulletins*. Issued with the approval of at least two thirds of committee members, the authority of the *Accounting Research Bulletins*, except in cases in which formal adoption by the Institute membership has been asked and secured, rested upon the general acceptability of opinions so reached.

By 1959, criticism from outside as well as from within the accounting profession led to the replacement of the Committee on Accounting

Procedure by the Accounting Principles Board. This larger body, vested with greater authority and supported by an enlarged research staff, was charged with the task of narrowing the areas of differences in accounting principles and in promoting the written expression of what generally accepted accounting principles are. The Accounting Principles Board (APB), which was replaced by the Financial Accounting Standards Board in 1973, issued 31 Opinions, some of which have improved the theory and the practice in significant areas (such as the area of pension accounting), some of which may have improved the theory but had an inadequate impact on practice (such as in the area of leasing), and some of which confused the areas of theory and practice requiring numerous amendments and clarifications (such as the areas of investment credit).

It is clear that in many cases the APB has attempted to change a principle adopted by its predecessor committee, not because the theory behind it was inherently deficient, but rather because it had been ignored or abused in practice. The adoption of a new theory does not, however, remedy the original deficiency, which was a lack of voluntary observance of the old one by members of the profession. It does not, moreover, assure observance of the new theory introduced in place of the old one. The crux of the matter, especially as concerns the user of financial data, is, in short, that he must not only understand the theory behind the accounting principles promulgated by the accounting profession but he must also know:

1. To what extent the spirit as well as the letter of these principles is observed in practice, and
2. What degree of latitude of implementation these principles, by their very nature, permit.

Generally, in determining the accounting standards applicable to a given situation, the auditor will first turn to official pronouncements of the FASB, which also incorporate pronouncements of its predecessors which are still in force, specialized sources such as AICPA Industry Guides and, as applicable, to official pronouncements of the Securities and Exchange Commission, such as their regulations pertaining to disclosure in financial statements, the Accounting Series Releases, or administrative rulings.

In the absence of any authoritative pronouncement in the first category, the auditor will turn to books and articles written by eminent and well-known authors. He may also review published financial statements with a view to finding authority and precedent for various principles.

It appears that under the AICPA's directives which required disclosure of departures from the pronouncements of the FASB and predecessors the auditor will, for all practical purposes, have to follow the accounting principles laid down or adopted by the FASB. Use of alternative principles also enjoying authoritative support will shift the burden of their defense on to the auditor.

A departure from promulgated principles is, however, far from easy to identify. The criteria of many pronouncements and opinions are often so vague and broad and so much subject to a wide range of interpretation that at present definite departures from such pro nouncements would be difficult to identify unequivocally. Consequently, the practical effect of the requirement to disclose departures from professional Opinions is more apparent than real.

Disclosure of accounting policies. In recognition of the fact that information about the accounting policies adopted and followed by both profit oriented and not-for-profit entities is essential to users of financial statements, the APB issued *Opinion No. 22,* "Disclosure of Accounting Policies."

The *Opinion* requires disclosure of accounting policies either in a summary or a footnote which is an integral part of the financial statements. The disclosure would identify and describe accounting principles followed and the methods of applying those principles that materially affect the determination of financial position, changes in financial position, or results of operations. Emphasis should be placed on describing principles and methods where a selection had been made from existing acceptable alternatives and where unusual, innovative or industry oriented principles and methods had been followed. In addition, the Opinion provides examples, not necessarily all inclusive, of the other types of disclosures which would be common.

The Financial Accounting Standards Board (FASB), composed of seven full-time paid members, began to function as the accounting standards-setting body of the accounting profession in mid-1973. Board members are appointed by a group of trustees which in addition to AICPA members include representatives from private industry, security analysts, and others.

In spite of expected criticism from many quarters the FASB represents a very significant improvement over its predecessors. Before issuing a Financial Accounting Standard on a subject the board issues, in most cases, a Discussion Memorandum which is exposed for public comment. Written comments can be filed with the board and oral comments can be voiced at public hearings which generally precede the issuance of an exposure draft of a Statement of Financial Accounting Standards (SFAS). After further exposure and comment a final SFAS is usually issued. Interpretations of previously issued pronouncements are also issued from time to time.

Another significant improvement in procedure is the inclusion in most SFAS of careful and elaborate explanations of the rationale of the board for the statements it issues, explanations of how comments to the board were dealt with, as well as examples of actual applications.

In 1977 the Financial Accounting Foundation (the FASB's parent body) adopted a number of structural changes in the FASB's operations, including greater participation by financial statement users in the rule-making process.

The influence of the Securities and Exchange Commission. The Securities and Exchange Commission, hereafter referred to as the SEC, which is an independent quasi-judicial agency of the U.S. government, administers, *inter alia,* the Securities Act of 1933 and the Securities Exchange Act of 1934.

The primary purpose of the 1933 Act is to insure that there be given to a potential investor in a security being offered for public sale all the material facts relating to the security that are needed in order to decide whether to buy it. Such facts are disclosed in a registration statement, which must be filed with the SEC and which must contain specified information.

The function of the SEC as regards a registration statement filed with it under the 1933 Act is to examine it to see that a full and accurate disclosure is made of all pertinent information relating to the company's business, its securities, its financial position and earnings, and the underwriting arrangements relating to the particular security that is being marketed. The SEC can require such changes to be made in the original registration statements as are necessary to achieve this objective. Until the SEC approves the statement, amended as necessary, it can prevent the registration statement from becoming effective and the securities from being sold. The SEC is not, however, concerned with the merits of any security registered with it.

Since its inception, the SEC has encouraged the development and improvement of accounting and auditing practice. That encouragement has, in practice, taken on a number of forms. The commission has issued specific rules and regulations concerning the preparation of financial statements which have to be filed with it and the degree of detail which they should contain. The commission's prosecution of numerous accounting and auditing infractions of its rules has resulted in a form of "case law" which provides important clues and precedents in the area of accounting principles and auditing procedure. Some of the most important decisions on accounting and auditing, as well as other important pronouncements on these subjects, are incorporated in Accounting Series Releases which now number well over one hundred. Less formal Staff Accounting Bulletins are also issued.

While many of the aforementioned sources on the SEC's position on accounting and auditing matters deal with specific instances and applications, the commission has recognized the impossibility of issuing rules to cover all possible situations. Thus, an important part of the SEC's influence on matters of accounting takes the form of conferences between companies and their accountants and the SEC staff and the numerous unpublished rulings and guidelines which are a result thereof.

The importance of the SEC position can be understood best in the light of the statutory authority vested in it. It has the ability to enforce the adherence to its rules over an ever-increasing number of companies that have come under its jurisdiction.

In the more than 40 years of its existence, the SEC has grown in competence and experience. It has wide regulatory authority over accounting and has the ability to enforce it. Moreover, it has assembled a fine and most experienced pool of accounting talent. It seems to have understood better than most the great difficulties and complexities involved in finding universally valid and acceptable accounting principles. As a result it has recognized the superiority of a system of widely diffused research efforts to mere promulgation by central edict. The SEC has recognized that the requirement for certification of financial statements to be filed with the commission have placed a heavy responsibility upon the accounting profession and have encouraged it to exercise leadership in accounting and auditing matters. "At the same time the commission has not hesitated to criticize and prod, to take exception to accounting presentations, and to discipline members of the profession when circumstances warranted."[2] In short, the Commission has so far exemplified, not a rigid and arbitrary exercise of governmental authority, but the sparing use of this authority in a helpful way.

The SEC approach toward accounting practice is, in large measure, determined by current public attitudes toward, and confidence in, financial reporting and to some extent by the personality and the temperament of its chief accountant. Both seemed to have changed in recent years and so we are witnessing a degree of impatience with the accounting professions rule-making process and novel approaches to the enforcement of auditing standards. Thus, in recent years audit firms were forced to consent to quality reviews of their practice by committees of peers and the FASB was confronted with a flood of new SEC requirements in areas it considered as being under its jurisdiction.

The SEC claims that it is responsible for matters of *disclosure* while the FASB's responsibility is in the area of accounting *measurement*. To

---

[2] Excerpts from testimony before the Subcommittee on Commerce and Finance of the Committee on Interstate and Foreign Commerce, House of Representatives, February 19, 1964, as reported in the *Journal of Accountancy*, June 1964, p. 58.

many this seems like a distinction without a difference. In any event the SEC has become increasingly aggressive in modifying FASB standards as, for example, by its modification of the effective date of SFAS 13 on leases.

In 1973 the SEC reiterated in *Accounting Series Release 150* its policy of "looking to the private sector for leadership in establishing and improving accounting principles and standards."[3]

In its desire to submit its major policies to periodic reevaluation the SEC appointed in early 1976 an Advisory Committee on Corporate Disclosure whose task it will be to examine the entire corporate disclosure system. So far the committee has recommended a number of changes including improvements in interim and segmental reporting, and its final conclusions do not appear to be far reaching.

The constructive influence which the SEC has been exercising over the development of accounting principles should, however, not mislead the financial analyst into believing that the financial statements included in documents filed with the Commission are more reliable than others from the point of view of the accounting used in their preparation. They are unfortunately not much more reliable because they rarely reflect a higher-than-average level of the "state of the art" and also because the staff of the SEC is far too limited in number and in capabilities to enable it to review thoroughly all the documents submitted to it.

The influence of other organizations.   Two other bodies whose influence on the formation of accounting principles must be considered are the American Accounting Association (AAA) and the Stock Exchanges, particularly the New York Stock Exchange.

The AAA has a membership composed primarily of accounting educators. Being one step removed from the practice of the profession, they have a more detached point of view and, by the very nature of their calling, a more scholarly and theoretical one. The AAA has long considered the inconsistencies in accounting theory as calling for a broad effort to establish an integrated framework of accounting theory. To this they have contributed significantly with a series of monographs (starting in 1937) and with statements on accounting principles and theory, the first one published in 1936 and the most recent in 1966. While the AAA statements on accounting theory have been influential in shaping accounting thought, they have no official standing in the accounting profession on which they are in no way binding.

---

[3] This delegation of authority has been challenged in court by one large accounting firm. Even more importantly, in late 1976 and in 1977 Congressional Committees have taken a critical interest in the workings and the regulation of the accounting profession and have called for its stricter regulation and supervision. They also called for an even more active role by the SEC in the setting of accounting standards.

The role of the New York Stock Exchange (NYSE) in the formulation of accounting theory has never been an active one. As already shown, the Exchange has in the early 1930s taken on active interest in financial reporting and in correspondence with the AICPA has promoted the setting down of accounting and auditing standards.

Like the SEC, the NYSE has the ability to enforce adherence to standards. The basic instrument by which the Exchange secures compliance to its standards is the listing agreement. This agreement defines, among other things, the minimum accounting disclosure required in the financial statements of the listed company.

One important way in which the New York and American Stock Exchanges have lent support to the efforts of the AICPA in the area of accounting improvements is by urging listed companies to comply with specific professional pronouncements.

Improvements in accounting principles—implications for financial analysts

In recent years substantial progress has been made by professional bodies and by the SEC in their endeavor to narrow the range of acceptable alternatives in accounting principles, to increase the amount of meaningful disclosure, and to improve the overall level of financial accounting. This progress notwithstanding, the serious user of published financial reports knows that the room for further necessary improvements is great indeed and that much remains to be done in these areas.

It would be naive and unrealistic to hope that the time is anywhere near when the financial analyst will no longer need to concern himself with the accounting principles which underlie the financial statements which he uses and "go forward from the figures" with his analysis rather than spending time and energy to first "go behind those figures." The critical examination, analysis, and evaluation of the accounting behind the financial statements will, for the foreseeable future, remain an important part of the totality of the analyst's task. Among the more important reasons for this conclusion are the following:

1. The vital interest of management in the results of operations and the financial position which it reports has in the past, and will continue in the future, to exert a strong influence on the manner in which it accounts for and presents these results. While the attesting auditor may, over the years, have increased his ability and his resolve to withstand management pressure, at the present time both his ability and his willingness to do so are limited. In addition to problems related to professional and financial independence, there are problems inherent in the accounting conventions and principles themselves:

a.   There is the difference between theory and practice. Rarely are accounting theory pronouncements so well and so comprehensively spelled out as to prevent practice from deviating from their spirit and intent.[4] Moreover, most accounting principles apply only to factors which are considered "material," and yet, so far the profession has failed to provide guidelines and a working definition of what is to be considered "material." (See also discussion earlier in this chapter.)

b.   A number of important areas of accounting theory, such as, for example, business combinations and product cost accounting and allocations, are not adequately covered by professional pronouncements. This contributes to even greater leeway and variety of practice.

c.   New industries, changing business practices, and the ingenuity of "financial architects" result in an inevitable lag of accounting theory behind accounting practice. In general, accounting theory is developed to cope with existing problems rather than to anticipate new and emerging ones such as those recently found in the real estate development and real estate investment trust industries.

2.   Progress toward the development of uniform and fair accounting principles has been and continues to be hampered by powerful interest groups. These exert pressure to have their interests represented in the formulation of accounting requirements which affect reporting practices in their particular industries. Recent examples of such lobbying are the efforts of bankers, of the insurance industry, the extractive industries, and the real estate industry to have their reporting interests reflected in the formulation of accounting principles.

A particularly ominous development in 1971 was the intervention of congressional legislation in the establishment of accounting principles.[5] In its apparent desire to allow reflection of the maximum improvement in corporate reported earnings from the investment tax credit, Congress has stated that no taxpayer shall be required to use any particular method of accounting for the investment credit in reports subject to the jurisdiction of any federal agency. This legislation thwarted the second attempt by the APB to develop a single uniform method of accounting for the investment credit.

---

[4] For an informative analysis of abuses in financial reporting, see A. J. Briloff *Unaccountable Accounting* (New York: Harper & Row, 1972) and by the same author, *More Debits than Credits* (New York: Harper & Row, 1976).

[5] Recent legislation obligates the SEC to prescribe accounting practices for the oil and gas industry in the United States. This specialized accounting topic is on the FASB's 1977 agenda.

3. Even if progress towards the establishment of sound and uniform principles of accounting were to proceed at a much more rapid pace than can now be envisaged, the analyst cannot safely abdicate the job of scrutinizing and evaluating the accounting assumptions and principles which underlie the financial statements which he analyses. As a prerequisite to a thorough and intelligent analysis, he needs a firm understanding of the data being analyzed. Experience has shown that improvements in accounting principles are accompanied by a significant increase in the complexity of accounting data and determinations. Financial analysis bears on decisions of such importance that under no circumstance can the analyst place undue reliance on the data with which he works without examining it and adjusting it to conform it to his own objectives.

4. Regardless of how well covered by sound and accepted theory accounting procedures may be, the analyst must realize that much of the data presented in financial statements is of the "soft" variety. This is true in spite of the appearance of precision conveyed by neatly balanced presentations. "Soft" information is information based on subjective evaluation, on heavy reliance on forecasts of future conditions, and on assumptions regarding the integrity, competence, intent or motives of managements which are generally expressed by means of unquantifiable adjectives. Such information must always be evaluated as part of a complete analysis.

5. Finally, a firm overall understanding of the accounting model is of fundamental importance to the analyst. Thus, at present the basic orientation of financial statements is towards the income statement with balance sheet amounts representing mostly residuals rather than amounts derived from a valuation process. Income statements are, for example, not based on current cash flows but are designed instead to measure long run average net cash inflows at a *current or assumed level of activity*. These orientations have significant implications for those who make decisions on the basis of financial communications.

The concept of accounting risk

The reader and user of accounting determinations must recognize a variety of risks. There is first the all-pervading risk associated with profit-seeking business enterprises: the risk of losses, of adversities, contingencies, and so forth. There is also the risk associated with reliance on audited financial statements on which we will elaborate in Chapter 15.

The user of financial statements prepared "in accordance with generally accepted accounting principles" must recognize yet another type of risk, best termed accounting risk.[6] This risk results from the imprecision inherent in the basic accounting process and is also due to the existence of alternative accounting principles, the loose criteria which define them, and the consequent loose standards of practice. This lack of assurance about the standards used or the method and rigor of their application may lead to a wide variety of results and hence to a great degree of uncertainty. In this concept of accounting risk we may also include the degree of conservatism of accounting principles in use or the lack of it. As we shall see in the following chapters, assumptions play an important role in accounting determinations; and such assumptions may be conservative or cautious, or they may be optimistic, daring, or too anticipative of favorable outcomes of things subject to normal doubt. Thus, the degree of conservatism found in the accounting principles in use will determine the magnitude of the setback that may result from assumptions which time shows to be overly optimistic. This aspect of analysis will be explored further in Chapter 22.

QUESTIONS

1. What is the basic purpose of financial accounting?
2. What are the objectives of financial statements as presented in the FASB's document "Tentative Conclusions on Objectives of Financial Statements of Business Enterprises"?
3. The usefulness of accounting data is determined by the achievement of certain objectives. List some of the most basic of these objectives.
4. Which are some of the more important obstacles in the achievement of the objectives of financial accounting?
5. What are accounting conventions? How did they develop? Name and elaborate on the meaning of the most important conventions of financial accounting.
6. Under certain circumstances certain conventions of accounting take precedence over other conventions. Give an illustration of such an instance.
7. How do accounting conventions exercise an influence on the practice of accountancy? Why is an understanding of accounting objectives and conventions essential to an intelligent analysis of financial statements?
8. What are accounting standards?
9. How are accounting standards established?
10. Does the FASB represent a significant improvement over its predecessors? Why?

---

[6] This risk is greatest in companies with a strong stock market orientation, whose managements need to produce earnings growth; companies in dire need for borrowed funds where accounting methods are regarded by managements as means of achieving reported results.

11. Trace briefly the accounting profession's endeavors to promulgate accounting principles.

12. Can the user of financial statements rely on the use of "generally accepted accounting principles" to produce reliable financial presentations? Of what implication to financial analysis is the rate of progress of improvement in accounting principles and practice?

3

OBJECTIVES OF FINANCIAL STATEMENT ANALYSIS

THE NATURE OF FINANCIAL ANALYSIS

The process of financial statement analysis consists of the application of analytical tools and techniques to financial statements and data in order to derive from them measurements and relationships which are significant and useful for decision making. Thus, financial statement analysis, first and foremost, serves the essential function of converting data, of which, in this age of the computer, there are a bewildering quantity and variety, into useful information, which is always in scarce supply.

The processes of financial analysis can be described in various ways, depending on the objectives to be attained. Thus, financial analysis can be used as a preliminary *screening* tool in the selection of investments or merger candidates. It can be used as a *forecasting* tool of future financial conditions and results. It may be used as a process of *diagnosis* of managerial, operating, or other problem areas. It can serve as a tool in the *evaluation* of management. Above all, financial analysis reduces reliance on pure hunches, guesses, and intuition, and this reduces and narrows the inevitable areas of uncertainty which attend all decision-making processes. Financial analysis does not lessen the need for judgment but rather establishes a sound and systematic basis for its rational application.

APPROACHES TO THE SUBJECT

There are a number of possible approaches to a discussion of the tools and techniques of financial analysis. One way, popularly employed in most works on the subject, is to describe the analysis of specific financial statements, such as balance sheets, without a concurrent emphasis of objectives to be attained. The approach employed here will be to examine the processes of financial statement analysis with emphasis on the major objectives (see "Building Blocks of Financial Statement Analysis"—Chapter 4) which they are designed to achieve. In order to do this we turn, first, to an examination of the information needs and the specific analytical objectives of the most important categories of users of financial data, namely:

Credit grantors.
Equity investors.
Management.
Acquisition and merger analysts.
Auditors.
Other interested groups.

Objectives of credit grantors

Credit grantors are lenders of funds to an enterprise. Funds are lent in many forms and for a variety of purposes.

Trade creditors usually extend very short-term credit. They ship goods or provide services and expect payment within the customary period which forms the terms of trade in their industry. Most trade credit ranges from 30 to 60 days, with cash discounts occasionally allowed for specified earlier payment. The trade creditor does not usually receive interest for an extension of credit. The trade creditor's reward takes the form of the business acquired and the possible profit which flows from it.

An enterprise receives other short-term and longer term credit or loans from a variety of sources. Short-term credit is often provided by various sources but mainly by banks. Longer term credit is provided by banks in the form of term loans and by financial institutions, such as insurance companies, through their purchase of bonds or notes or through private placements. Companies also obtain longer term funds through the public sale of notes or bonds in the securities markets. Leasing and conditional sales are other forms of long-term financing. The sale of convertible, and generally subordinated, bonds combines the borrowing of money with the added feature of an option to the lender to exchange his claim for an equity interest should he find it profitable to do so. Similarly, the issuance of preferred stock, which is senior to the common equity but junior to debt, combines the fixed reward features of a loan with the absence of definite principal repayment requirements which characterize equity securities.

One outstanding characteristic of all pure credit extension relationships is the fixed nature of the rewards accruing to the credit grantor. Thus, should the enterprise prosper, the credit grantor will still be limited to his contractually fixed rate of interest, or to the profit on the goods supplied. However, should the enterprise incur losses or meet other adversities, the credit grantor's principal may be placed in jeopardy. This uneven nature of the lender's risk-reward ratio has a major effect on his point of view and on the manner in which he analyzes the possibilities of credit extension.

The difference in the point of view of the lenders as compared to that of the equity investor results in differences in the way they analyze future prospects and in the objectives they seek. The equity investor looks for his reward primarily to future prospects of earnings and to changes in those earnings. The credit grantor, on the other hand, is concerned primarily with specific security provisions of his loan, such as the fair market value of assets pledged; and for repayment of principal and interest he looks to the existence of resources and the projections of future flows of funds and the reliability and stability of such flows. Lenders differ in their abilities to obtain supplementary financial information from borrowers. The equity investor, as a result of the theoretically unlimited nature of his rewards, may be receptive to highly abstract descriptions of "concepts," potentials, and future probabilities. The lender, on the other hand, requires a more definite link between the projections of the future and the resources already at hand as well as the demonstrated ability to achieve operating results. Thus, credit grantors generally are more conservative in their outlook and approach and rely on financial statement analysis to an even greater extent than do equity investors, for it serves to reassure them regarding the borrower's demonstrated ability to control the flow of funds and to maintain a sound financial condition under a variety of economic and operating circumstances. The more speculative the loan the more similar are the lender's analytical approaches to those of the equity investor.

The techniques of financial statement analysis used by lenders as well as the criteria of evaluation used by them vary with the term, the security, and the purpose of the loan.

In the case of short-term credit extension, the credit grantor is concerned primarily with current financial condition, with the liquidity of the current assets and the rate of their turnover.

The evaluation of longer term loans, which includes the valuation of bonds, requires a far more detailed and forward-looking inquiry and analysis. Such an analysis includes projections of cash flows, fund flows, and the construction of pro forma financial statements on the basis of a variety of assumptions regarding future conditions and requirements, and an assessment of the enterprise's ability to maintain its solvency under adverse economic conditions.

Since the profitability of an enterprise is a major element in the lender's security, the analysis of profitability is an important criterion to the credit grantor. Profit is viewed as the primary source for interest payments and as a desirable source of principal repayment.

Credit analysis, whether long term or short term, is concerned with capital structure because it has a bearing on risk and on the creditor's margin of safety. The relationship of equity capital to debt is an indicator of the adequacy of equity capital and of the cushion against loss which it provides. This relationship also reflects on the attitude of management toward risk and influences the income coverage of fixed charges.

Lenders, and bankers among them, generally look at asset values in the context of the going-concern assumption. Clearly, the assumption of liquidation would often lead to realizable values of assets that would generally be lower than those stated in accordance with generally accepted accounting principles. For this reason bankers tend to attach very conservative values to fixed and other assets, and to make allowance for all possible future contingencies.

Objectives of equity investors

The equity interest in an enterprise is the supplier of its basic risk capital. The capital is exposed to all the risks of ownership and provides a cushion or shield for the preferred or loan capital which is senior to it. This is why the equity interest is referred to as the *residual* interest. In the course of normal operations as a going concern, this residual interest may receive distributions (dividends) only after the prior claims of senior security holders for bond interest and/or preferred dividends have been satisfied. In liquidation, it has a claim only to what remains *after* the prior claims of creditors and preferred stockholders have been met. Thus, when an enterprise prospers the equity owners stand to reap all the gains above the fixed amount of senior capital contributors' claims and, conversely, the equity owners will be the first ones to absorb losses should the enterprise flounder.

From the above it is clear that the information needs of equity investors are among the most demanding and comprehensive of all users of financial data. Their interests in an enterprise, of which they own a share, are the broadest because their interest is affected by all aspects and phases of operations, profitability, financial condition, and captial structure.

Common stock valuation. The valuation of common stock is a complex procedure involving, in addition to financial statement analysis, an assessment of such factors as the general state of the economy, industry position, competitive stance, and the quality of management. Since the most thorough and sophisticated analysis and evaluation of equity securities, for the purpose of deciding whether to buy, sell, or hold, is performed by professional security analysts, their point of view will be examined here.

A common stockholder, having no legal claim to a definite dividend or to a capital distribution, looks for three principal rewards from his holdings: current dividends, special distributions such as rights, and a market value of the security at a given time in the future which will, hopefully, result in a capital gain. The most important determinant of both dividends and market values is earnings. Current earnings, which are the basic source of dividends and the accumulation of undistributed earnings, as well as the earnings record, current and prospective, form the basis for the market price of the common stock.

Approaches to common stock valuation.   The basis of most modern stock valuation techniques and models is present-value theory. This approach, first set forth in detail by John B. Williams,[1] maintains that the present value of a share of stock is equal to the sum of all dividends expected to be received from it, discounted to the present at an appropriate rate of interest. The difficulty here, of course, as in all other approaches based on this theory, is the estimation of such future distributions.[2] What is clear, however, is the fact that all expected distributions, be they of a current dividend or of a liquidation residual nature, are based largely on earnings and the earning power of assets.

Security valuation models used by security analysts bear out the proposition that earnings, and particularly estimated future earnings, are the most important determinant of the value of common shares.

Graham, Dodd, and Cottle emphasized the importance of earnings as follows:

The standard method of valuation of individual enterprises consists of capitalizing the expected future earnings and/or dividends at an appropriate rate of return. The average earnings will be estimated for a period running ordinarily between five and ten years.[3]

---

[1] *The Theory of Investment Value* (Cambridge, Mass: Harvard University Press, 1938).

[2] The importance of expected distributions is largely responsible for the focus on cash (or funds) flow. However, so far, most valuation models have not concerned themselves with the purchasing power equivalent of such cash flows, a consideration which looms large in times of price level changes. Thus, a security represents a contingent claim not only because of the uncertain outcome of future events but also (including here a "riskless" bond) because of an uncertain command over future goods and services. For a further discussion of these issues see Chapter 14.

[3] *Security Analysis* (New York: McGraw-Hill Book Co., 1962), p. 435.

Most common stock valuation models incorporate earnings growth and earnings payout ratios as factors of prime importance.

The normal procedure in dynamic models is to state the price of a stock as the present value of a growing stream of dividends with each component of this stream discounted at the rate k. One of the best known dynamic stock valuation models presented in recent years is that by Gordon and Shapiro. Assume that $E(t)$ are the earnings of an enterprise at time t; b is the dividend payout ratio; k is the market discount rate (the cost of capital); and g is the projected annual growth rate in earnings. The valuation formula for the company's justified market price V (intrinsic value) is:

$$V = \frac{bE(t)}{k - g}$$

The above formula reduces long and awkward statements to more manageable but nevertheless mathematically equivalent terms. It states in effect that the market value V is equal to the current dividend discounted at a rate $k - g$, i.e.,

$$V = \frac{\text{Current Dividend Rate}}{\text{Discount Rate} - \text{Growth Rate}}$$

The elegance and the simplicity of the above formula should not obscure the fact that the most critical element in this or similar approaches to equity valuation is the valid quantification of the variables or inputs themselves. The more conventional approach by practitioners in the field of security analysis is to value a security by multiplying its earnings, which are really a surrogate for present and future dividends, by a *price earnings ratio*[4] which is usually an imprecise expression of their assessment of external economic factors as well as of the growth prospects, financial strengths, capital structure, and other risk factors associated with the enterprise.

The similarity of the present-value models of common stock valuation to the conventional method of bond valuation is quite obvious. In the case of bonds the value, or proper purchase price, is calculated by discounting each coupon and the ultimate principal repayment to present value at a discount rate equal to the desired yield. In the case of growth stock valuations the expected dividend corresponds to the bond coupon and the assumed market price of the stock at the model

---

[4] Expressed in terms of the foregoing Gordon-Shapiro formula the price earnings ratio (P/E) can be stated as follows:

$$P/E = \frac{b}{k - g}$$

Thus, for example, if the dividend payout ratio (b) changes so would the P/E ratio.

target date corresponds to the repayment of bond principal at maturity date.

The similarity of the bond and stock valuation models under these theories has led Molodovsky and others to construct stock valuation tables which can be used in a fashion similar to the use of bond tables.[5] The formula used by them for the value (V) of a stock is:

$$V = D_0 + \frac{D_1}{1 + k} + \frac{D_2}{(1 + k)^2} + \cdots + \frac{D_n}{(1 + k)^n} + \cdots$$

where:

D_0 is the dividend initially.

D_n is the dividend in the nth year.

k is the discount rate, or the desired rate of return.

The model does not include a residual market value of the stock (similar to bond principal to be repaid) because it assumes dividend projections taken out to infinity. With regard to the latter the authors assure us that because the discount factor becomes so large in the distant future, these increments to value become negligible. It is easy to bring the model closer in form to a bond model by assuming a specified sales price (realization of principal) at a specified date, but that price will itself depend on the application of the foregoing formula.

While we can readily understand why the stock valuation model builders have been attracted by the logic as well as the mathematical elegance of the bond valuation model, we must recognize the important differences that exist between the inputs required by the bond model as opposed to those required by the stock model. The focus on these differences is all the more important since the basic purpose of our discussion in this chapter is to relate the scope and the techniques of financial statement analysis to the purposes which they are designed to serve—in this instance the valuation of equity securities.

In the case of bond valuation the bond coupon is known and so is the amount of principal to be repaid at the maturity of the bond. Thus, as we saw in the section dealing with the objectives of credit grantors, the major questions to be considered are the *availability* of funds for the payment of interest and the repayment of principal. While the assessment of the probabilities of such availability of funds does involve the totality of enterprise prospects, the process of estimation is nevertheless less complex than the one involved in arriving at the proper parameters for the stock valuation model.

It should also be noted that there is a basic and important difference

---

[5] N. Molodovsky, C. May, and S. Chottiner, "Common Stock Valuation—Principles, Tables, and Application," *Financial Analysts Journal*, March–April 1965.

in the certainty of results that can be expected from an analysis of debt instruments (such as bonds) and those that can be expected from the analysis of equity securities. In the case of debt instruments the results of the analysis depend almost entirely on a valid assessment of the borrower's ability to make timely payments of interest and principal. The relationship between analysis and the results achieved are far more complex in the case of equity securities. Thus, no matter how "right" the analyst is in assumptions and forecasts, a major part of the reward of that analysis, i.e., future capital values, depends on the perceptions of others. That is, on buyers agreeing with the analyst's conclusions and seeing things his or her way. No such dependence on validation by the market place exists in the case of results to be achieved from the analysis of debt instruments.

This difference, as well as the enormous complexities to which the analysis and evaluation of equity securities are subject, is in large part behind the skepticism with which many practicing security analysts treat those who attempt to compress the market reality into neat, streamlined, and elegant mathematical formulations.

Data required for stock valuation.   Let us now consider the data which are required in order to quantify the factors present in most of the stock valuation models discussed above.

The expected dividend stream in the future is dependent on earnings and dividend payout policy. The latter depends on the company's financial condition, capital structure, and its need for funds both in the present and in the future.

The projection of future earnings is always a complex process subject to varying degrees of uncertainty. The reported earnings must be evaluated and adjusted and, in turn, form the basis for projection. Unlike the bond coupon which remains constant, the further into the future that earnings are projected, the more conjectural the estimates become.

The size of the discount factor which may properly be used in computing the present value of a future stream of dividends and residual interests depends to a significant extent on the risk involved. The risk reflects such factors as the stability of the industry, the past variability in earnings, and the leverage inherent in its capital structure.

No stock valuation formula has yet been devised and published which has proved to be an accurate forecaster of security market values under all conditions. Perhaps the factors which bear on the determination of security values are too numerous and too complex for inclusion in a workable formula, and possibly not all such factors can be adequately measured, particularly because of the simplifying assumptions which are introduced in many such models.

Whatever method of stock valuation is used by the security analyst, be it either a simple short-term projection of earnings to be capitalized at a predetermined rate or a complex and sophisticated formula involving elegant mathematical techniques, the results can never reach a higher level of accuracy or be more reliable than the inputs used in such calculations. The reliability and the validity of these inputs, be they earnings projections, expected payout ratios, or various risk factors such as those inherent in capital structure, depend on the quality of the financial statement analysis performed.

The above view was best expressed by Douglas A. Hayes:

> Although the concept that investment results are likely to be heavily related to corporate performance in a long-term sense is generally accepted, some recent contributions to the field have alleged that the implementation methodology should be completely revolutionized. For example, Lerner and Carleton (A *Theory of Financial Analysis*, Harcourt, Brace, and World, Inc. New York: 1966, pp. 3–4) allege that a critical investigation of the past financial statements to reveal potential problems of consistency and comparability of reported income and balance sheet data can be largely discarded because accounting and disclosure standards have improved to the point where the underlying data require no critical review. Moreover, they allege that financial risk factors no longer require appraisal because of the greatly improved stability features of the economy; in lieu thereof, they suggest elegant mathematical techniques to develop the theoretical effects of assumed patterns of various management decisions and economic data on security values.
>
> However, the empirical evidence would suggest that these allegations are seriously in error. . . ."[6]

In short, while the goal of the analyst may be to go forward *from* the figures, a thorough job of the financial analysis requires that he also go *behind* the figures. No present or prospective developments in the field of accountancy justify the assumption that this can be significantly changed in the near future (see also discussion at end of Chapter 2).

RECENT DEVELOPMENTS IN INVESTMENT THEORY

In recent years the methods and approaches of practicing security analysts have come under repeated challenge by their academic counterparts who have developed a number of theories designed to provide insight into the overall investment process.

---

[6] "The Dimensions of Analysis: A Critical Review," *Financial Analysts Journal*, September–October 1966.

Portfolio theory

A pioneering contribution was that of Markowitz who addressed the problem of portfolio construction given analysts' estimates of possible future returns from securities.[7] He demonstrated that both risk and return must be considered, provided a formal framework for quantifying both and showed how the relationship among security risks and returns could be taken into account in portfolio construction.

He begins with the observation that the future return on a security can be estimated and he equates risk with the variance of the distribution of returns. Markowitz demonstrated that under certain assumptions there is a linear relationship between risk and return. Using these variables he provided a framework for deciding how much of each security to hold in constructing a portfolio. The two-dimensional risk-return approach offers the investor an ability to choose in the trade-off between risk and return.

Evaluation of risk and return

The relationship between the risk which must be accepted and the return which may be expected is central to all modern investing and lending decisions. It may seem obvious that the greater the perceived degree of risk of an investment or of a loan the greater is the required rate of return to compensate for such risk.

Categories of risk

Risk is commonly associated with the uncertainty surrounding the outcome of future events. While many investors and lenders make subjective evaluations of risk, academicians have developed statistical measures of risk which belong to the overall concept known as beta coefficient theory.

Under this theory the total risk associated with an investment is composed of two elements:

1. *Systematic risk* which is that portion of total risk attributable to the movement of the market as a whole.
2. *Unsystematic risk* which is the residual risk that is unique to a specific security.

In the application of the theory a quantitative expression of systematic risk (known as Beta) of one is attributed to the volatility of the market as a whole as measured by some broad based market index

---

[7] H. Markowitz, "Portfolio Selection" *Journal of Finance*, March 1952, pp. 77–91.

such as the Standard & Poor's 500. The higher a security's beta, the greater will be its expected return. Treasury bills have a beta of zero because they are essentially riskless, i.e., they do not fluctuate with the market. A stock having a beta of 1.20 could rise or fall 20 percent faster than the market while one having a beta of .90 would on average register market value changes 10 percent less in amplitude than those of the market as a whole. Thus high beta stocks can expect high returns in a "bull market" and also larger than average declines during a "bear market."

Since by definition unsystematic risk is the *residual risk* which is unexplained by market movements, no unsystematic risk exists for the market as a whole and almost none exists in a highly diversified portfolio of stocks. Consequently as portfolios become larger and more diversified their unsystematic risk will approach zero.

Adherents to this theory hold that the market will not reward those exposing themselves to nonsystematic risk which can be removed by proper diversification. They believe that the implication of the theory for common stock investors is to diversify, and if they expect the market to rise, to increase the beta of their portfolios and vice versa. Some experimental studies have indicated that between 30 and 50 percent of an individual stock's price is due to market (systematic) risk and that such influence reaches 85 to 90 percent in a well diversified portfolio of 30 or more stocks.[8]

It follows that the portfolio manager who does not wish to rely only on market action for his returns or who cannot forecast overall market action should seek nondiversification, i.e., exposure to the amount of unsystematic risk required for achieving the desired rate of return. Such a strategy would emphasize the analysis of individual securities, as discussed in this work, as opposed to overall portfolio risk balancing. Thus, reaping the rewards of exposure to nonsystematic risk is dependent on an ability to identify undervalued securities and on the proper assessment of their risk. (See discussion of efficient market hypothesis later in this chapter.)

Components of unsystematic risk

Those who want to obtain their rewards from exposure to unsystematic or nonmarket risk through the rigorous analysis of individual securities, must focus on the various components of such risk. While those components are undoubtedly interrelated and subject to the influence of such elements of systematic risk as overall political, eco-

[8] J. B. Cohen, E. D. Zinbarg, and A. Zeikel, *Investment Analysis and Portfolio Management*, 3d ed. (Homewood, Ill.: Richard D. Irwin, Inc., 1977), pp. 769–71.

nomic, and social factors they can nevertheless be usefully classified as follows:

Economic risk reflects risks of the overall economic environment in which the enterprise operates including general economic risk (fluctuations in business activity), capital market risk (including changes in interest rates) and purchasing power risk—some aspects of which are discussed in Chapter 14.

Business Risk is concerned with the ever present uncertainty regarding a business enterprise's ability to earn a satisfactory return on its investments as well as with the multitude of cost and revenue factors which enter into the determination of such a return. It includes the factors of competition, product mix, and management ability. (See chapters 19–22).

Financial Risk is basically concerned with capital structure and with the ability of an enterprise to meet fixed and senior charges and claims. These factors of short term liquidity and long term solvency are discussed in detail in Chapters 16 and 18.

For a discussion of the concept of *Accounting Risk* see Chapter 2.

Those who assume, as do beta theorists, that all investors are averse to risk and that they seek to diversify away the specific or unsystematic risks of a security thus exposing themselves only to market risk, must also realize that the historical betas for individual securities have proven quite unstable over time and that consequently such betas seem to be poor predictors of future betas for the same security.[9] Thus while overall concepts and theories are easier to apply to stock aggregates than to the evaluation of individual stocks they are at the same time far less reliable and accurate instruments for the achievement of investment results.

Another, and perhaps even more troublesome question is the assumption of beta theorists that past volatility alone is an acceptable measure of risk without reference to the current price of a security. Is a security which sells significantly *above* its value, as determined by some method of fundamental analysis, no more risky than a security of equal volatility (beta) which sells significantly *below* such fundamentally determined value? We know that paying an excessive price for a stable quality security can amount to as rank a speculation as investing in the most unseasoned of speculative securities.

While market theorists have not yet addressed the above trouble-

---

[9] W. H. Beaver, P. Kettler, and M. Scholes have found that a high degree of association exists between accounting risk measures (such as average payout, asset growth, coverage, etc.) and beta. Thus, these accounting measures of risk may be used in a way that can lead to better forecasts of market determined risk measures (betas) than would be possible using past observed betas. (*The Accounting Review*, October 1970, pp. 654–82.)

some question, they have addressed the problem of how securities are valued by the market.

The capital asset pricing model

Sharpe[10] and Lintner[11] have extended portfolio theory to a capital asset pricing model (CAPM) which is intended to explain how prices of assets are determined in such a way as to provide greater return for greater risk. This model is based on the assumption that investors desire to hold securities in portfolios which are efficient in the sense that they provide a maximum return for *a given level* of risk. Moreover the model was derived under the following simplifying assumptions:

1. That there exists a riskless security.
2. That investors are able to borrow or lend unlimited amounts at the riskless rate.
3. That all investors have identical investment horizons and act on the basis of identical expectations and predictions.

Based on these assumptions it can be shown that when capital markets are in a state of equilibrium the expected return on an individual security $E(\tilde{R}_i)$, is related to its systematic risk β_i in the following linear form:

$$E(\tilde{R}_i) = E(\tilde{R}_0) + [E(\tilde{R}_M) - E(\tilde{R}_0)]\beta_i,$$

The above formulation states in essence, that under conditions of equilibrium, a security's expected return equals the expected return of a riskless security, $E(\tilde{R}_0)$, plus a premium for risk taking. This risk premium consists of a constant, $[E(\tilde{R}_M - E(\tilde{R}_0)]$, which is the difference between the return expected by the market and the return on a riskless security (such as a short-term government bond) multiplied by the systematic risk of the security β_i (its beta) as discussed earlier.

The CAPM thus indicates that the expected return on any particular capital asset consists of two components: (1) the return on a riskless security and (2) a premium for the riskiness of the particular asset computed as outlined above. Thus under the CAPM each security has an expected return which is related to its risk. This risk is measured by the security's systematic movements with the overall market and it cannot be eliminated by portfolio diversification.

It remains for us to consider yet another theory which attempts to

---

[10] W. F. Sharpe, "Capital Asset Prices: A Theory of Market Equilibrium under Conditions of Risk" *Journal of Finance*, September 1964, pp. 425–42.

[11] J. Lintner, "The Valuation of Risky Assets and the Selection of Risky Investments in Stock Portfolios and Capital Budgets," *Review of Economics and Statistics*, February 1965, pp. 13–37.

describe a different property of security prices, i.e., the efficient market hypothesis.

The efficient market hypothesis

Efficient market hypothesis (EMH) deals with the reaction of market prices to financial and other data. The EMH has its origins in the random walk hypothesis which basically states that at any given point in time the size and direction of the next price change is random relative to what is known about an investment at that given time. A derivative of this hypothesis is what is known as the *weak form* of the EMH which states that current prices reflect fully the information implied by historical price time series. In its *semistrong form* the EMH holds that prices fully reflect all publicly available information.[12] Moreover, in its *strong form* the theory asserts that prices reflect *all* information including that which is considered "inside information."

The EMH, in all its terms, has undergone extensive empirical testing with much of the evidence apparently supportive of the weak and semistrong forms of the theory. Lorie and Hamilton[13] for example, present three studies in support of the semistrong form of the hypothesis indicating that:

1. Stock splits do not assure unusual profit for investors.
2. Secondary offerings depress the market price of a stock because such offerings imply that knowledgeable people are selling.
3. Unusual earnings increases are anticipated in the price of the stock before the company's earnings for the year are reported.[14]

None of these findings would, incidentally, clash with the intuition of experienced analysts or seasoned market participants.

Research supportive of the EMH by accounting scholars on the effect of accounting changes on security prices has found that changes from accelerated to straight-line depreciation had no significant long-term effect on stock prices.[15] Another study found that the stock market ignored the effects on income of changes in accounting procedures

---

[12] For one good discussion of this theory see E. F. Fama, "Efficient Capital Markets: A Review of Theory and Empirical Work," *Journal of Finance*, May 1970, pp. 383–417.

[13] J. H. Lorie and M. T. Hamilton, *The Stock Market: Theories and Evidence* (Homewood, Ill.: Richard D. Irwin, Inc., 1973).

[14] See for example R. Ball and P. Brown, "An Empirical Evaluation of Accounting Numbers," *Journal of Accounting Research* (Autumn 1968), pp. 159–78 and W. Beaver, "The Informational Content of Annual Earnings Announcements," *Empirical Research in Accounting Selected Studies*, 1968, University of Chicago, Graduate School of Business 1969, pp. 48–53.

such as those relating to inventories, depreciation, revenue recognition, and so forth.[16]

Implications for financial statement analysis

The EMH is almost completely dependent on the assumption that competent and well informed analysts, using tools of analysis such as those described in this work, will constantly strive to evaluate and act upon the ever changing stream of new information entering the market place. And yet the theory's proponents claim that since all that is known is already instantly reflected in market prices, any attempt to gain an advantage by rigorous financial statement analysis is an exercise in futility. As H. Lorie and M. T. Hamilton put it, "the most general implication of the efficient market hypothesis is that most security analysis is logically incomplete and valueless."[17]

This position presents an unexplained and unresolved paradox. The thousands of intelligent analysts are assumed to be capable enough to keep our security market efficient through their efforts but they are not intelligent enough to realize that their efforts can yield no individual advantage. Moreover, should they suddenly realize that their efforts are unrewarded the market would cease to be efficient.

There are a number of factors which may explain this paradox. Foremost among them is the fact that the entire EMH is built on evidence based on an evaluation of *aggregate* rather than individual investor behavior. The focusing on macro or aggregate behavior results not only in the highlighting of average performance and results but also ignores and masks the results achieved by individual ability, hard work, and ingenuity, as well as by superior timing in acting on information as it becomes available. Moreover, the reasoning behind the EMH's alleged implication for the usefulness of security analysis fails to recognize the essential difference between information and its proper interpretation. Even if all the information available on a security at a given point in time is impounded in its price, that price may not reflect *value*. It may be under- or overvalued depending on the degree to which an incorrect interpretation or evaluation of the available information has been made by those whose actions determine the market price at a given time.

Finally, the function and purpose of the analysis of equity securities

---

[15] R. Kaplan and R. Roll, "Accounting Changes and Stock Prices" *The Financial Analysts Journal* (January–February 1973), pp. 48–53.

[16] R. Ball, "Changes in Accounting Techniques and Stock Prices," *Empirical Research in Accounting: Selected Studies,* 1972 (Chicago: Institute of Professional Accounting, Graduate School of Business, University of Chicago, 1974) pp. 1–38.

[17] Lorie and Hamilton, *The Stock Market,* p. 100.

is construed much too narrowly by those who judge its usefulness in an efficient market.[18] While the search for overvalued and undervalued securities is an important function of security analysis, the importance of risk assessment and loss avoidance, in the total framework of investment decision making, cannot be overemphasized. Thus, the prevention of serious investment errors is at least as important as the discovery of undervalued securities. Yet, our review of the CAPM and of beta theory earlier in this discussion tends to explain why this important function of analysis is neglected by adherents to these macro models of the security markets. For to some it is a basic premise of these theories that the analysis of unsystematic risk is not worthwhile because that kind of risk taking is not rewarded by the market. They maintain that such risks should be diversified away and that the portfolio manager should look only to systematic or market risk for his rewards.[19]

Our basic premise here is that investment results are achieved through the careful study and analysis of *individual* enterprises rather than by an exclusive focus on market aggregates. Our approach in this area is to emphasize the value of fundamental investment analysis not only as a means of keeping our securities markets efficient and our capital markets rational and strong but also as the means by which those investors who, having obtained information, are willing and able to apply knowledge, effort, and ingenuity to its analysis.[20] For those investors, the fruits of fundamental analysis and research, long before being converted to a "public good," will provide adequate rewards. These rewards will not be discernable, however, in the performance of investors aggregated to comprise major market segments, such as mutual funds. Instead they will remain as individual as the efforts needed to bring them about.

The role of financial statement analysis in the professional decision process leading to the buying, selling, or holding of equity securities has always been the subject of controversy and debate. In times of high speculative market activity, fundamental factors inevitably give way in relative importance to the psychological or technical ones in

----

[18] For a more comprehensive discussion of these issues see the author's article "In Defense of Fundamental Investment Analysis," *Financial Analysts Journal*, January–February 1975, pp. 57–61.

[19] A current investment vogue, based on the efficient market adherents' disenchantment with investment results, is the index fund. An index portfolio is merely designed to copy the composition of a market index to such an extent that it will replicate its market performance. Like other schemes which represent mechanical substitutes for analysis and judgment this too is not likely to satisfy its adherents for too long.

[20] The value of such analysis for other purposes, such as credit evaluation, is not even at issue here.

the overall security appraisal and "valuation" process. The fact that these fundamental factors, based as they are on a concrete analysis of measurable elements, can lead to more sound decisions and to the avoidance of serious judgmental errors will not always prevent their abandonment in favor of the snap decisions which occur in times of speculative frenzy. Nevertheless, the ultimate return of more sober times after periods of speculation and the inevitable corrections of speculative excesses recurringly bring along with them a rediscovery of the virtues of thorough financial analysis as a sound and necessary procedure. In the aftermath of the 1969–70 bear market, David L. Babson urged such a return by stating:

> What we all should do now is to roll up our sleeves and go back to doing what we are paid for—to follow company and industry trends closely, to really dissect balance sheets and to dig into accounting practices—and maybe some future Jim Lings, Delbert Colemans and Cortes Randells won't make monkeys out of many of the prestigious firms in our industry again.[21]

The collapse in security values in the early 1970s was, of course, not the first such occurrence which was preceded by a widespread and reckless disregard for fundamentals. It is noteworthy that each generation of analysts has to relearn the lessons so heavily paid for by its predecessors. A. P. Richardson, in an editorial on "The 1929 Stock Market Collapse" published in the *Journal of Accountancy* of December 1929, emphasized this recurring phenomenon of the flight from facts and reason into the world of fancy and wishful thinking:

> The astounding feature of the decline and fall of the stock market in late October and early November was not the fact of descent itself, but the altogether unreasoning consternation which the public in and out of Wall Street displayed. There was nothing at all in the course of events which distinguished the break from its many predecessors. Month after month, even year after year, market prices of securities had climbed to even dizzier heights. Now and then a Jeremiah uttered warning and lament, but the people gave no heed. They thought and consequently dealt in far futures. What a company might earn when the next generation would come to maturity was made the measure of the current value of its stock. In many cases companies whose operations had never yet produced a penny of profit were selected, fortuitously or under artificial stimulation, as a sort of Golconda of the next voyage; and otherwise sane men and women eagerly bought rights of ownership in adventures whose safe return was on the knees of the sea gods. It was not considered enough to look ahead to what was visible. The unseen was the chief commodity. Good stocks, bad stocks and stocks neither good nor bad but wholly of the future rose with almost equal facility, until at last they were sold at prices which seemed to be entirely uninfluenced by the rates of dividend or

---

[21] "The Stock Market's Collapse and Constructive Aftermath," *The Commercial and Financial Chronicle*, June 4, 1970.

even by the earnings of the issuing companies. Government bonds and other "gilt-edged" securities were sold at prices nearer the actual interest yield than were the prices of highly speculative stocks to the dividend return or even to the net earnings, past or soon expected, of the companies concerned. Anything was possible when vision was so blurred by success.

Financial statement analysis, while certainly not providing answers to all the problems of security analysis, at least keeps the decision maker in touch with the underlying realities of the enterprise which is investigated. It imposes the discipline of comparing the results already attained with the wide ranging promises made for the future. As a very minimum it represents a safeguard against the repetition of the grievous mistakes of judgment recurringly made by investors in time of speculative euphoria.

We have, in this section, examined the needs for information by equity investors. Not all such information can be obtained by means of financial statement analysis nor is the information so obtainable always the most critical in the determination of security values. However, it should by now be clear to the reader that any rational and systematic approach to the valuation of common stocks must involve the use of quantified data which are mostly the end product of financial statement analysis, evaluation, and interpretation.

Objectives of management

Management's interest in an enterprise's financial condition, profitability, and progress is pervasive and all-encompassing. Management has a number of methods, tools, and techniques available to it in monitoring and keeping up with the everchanging condition of the enterprise. Financial data analysis is one important type of such methods.

Financial data analysis can be undertaken by management on a continuous basis because it has unlimited access to internal accounting and other records. Such analysis encompasses changes in ratios, trends, and other significant relationships. Ratio, change, and trend analysis is based on an intelligent, alert, and systematic surveillance of significant relationships in a business situation and the timely detection and interpretation of problem areas by an analysis of changes taking place.

Management's primary objective in utilizing the tools of analysis described in this work is to exercise control over and to view the enterprise in the way important outsiders, such as creditors and investors, view it.

Ratio change, and trend analysis make use of the numerous and inevitable relationships and interrelationships among the variables occurring in any business situation. Constant surveillance over the size and amplitude of change in these interrelationships provides valuable clues to important changes in underlying financial and operating conditions. Recognition of such changes and timely action to check adverse trends is the essence of control.

Management derives a number of important advantages from a systematic monitoring of financial data and the basic relationships which they display:

1. There is recognition that no event in a business situation is isolated and that it represents a cause or the effect of a chain of which it is but a link. This approach aims at discovering whether a given event or relationship is the cause or the effect of an underlying situation.
2. There is a recognition that one should not act on an isolated event, but rather by an examination of related changes, one should determine the basic causes of the event. Thus, an event cannot be judged as positive or negative until it has been properly related to other factors which have a bearing on it.
3. Such monitoring prevents management from getting submerged in a maze of facts and figures which, in the typical business situation, consist of a great variety of factors of varying sizes, velocities of change, and degrees of impact. Instead, it organizes the data and relates them to a pattern of prior experience and external standards.
4. Such monitoring calls for prompt and effective action as the situation unfolds, rather than for *"post mortem"* analyses of causes and effects.

Objectives of acquisition and merger analysts

The valuation of an enterprise in its entirety, for the purpose of purchasing a going concern or for the purpose of assessing the merger of two or more enterprises, represents an attempt to determine economic values, the relative worth of the merging entities, and the relative bargaining strengths and weaknesses of the parties involved. Financial statement analysis is a valuable technique in the determination of economic value and in an assessment of the financial and operating compatibility of potential merger candidates.

The objectives of the acquisition and merger analyst are in many respects similar to those of the equity investor except that the analysis of the acquisition of an entire enterprise must go further and stress the valuation of assets, including intangible assets such as goodwill, and liabilities included in the acquisition or merger plan.

Objectives of auditors

The end product of the financial audit is an expression of opinion on the fairness of presentation of financial statements setting forth the financial conditions and the results of operations of an enterprise. One of the basic objectives of the audit process is to obtain the greatest possible degree of assurance about the absence of errors and irregularities, intentional or otherwise, which if undetected could materially affect the fairness of presentation of financial summarizations or their conformity with generally accepted accounting principles.

Financial statement analysis and ratio change and trend analysis represents an important group of audit tools which can significantly supplement other audit techniques such as procedural and validation tests. This is so because errors and irregularities, whatever their source, can, if significant, affect the various financial operating and structural relationships; and the detection and analysis of such changes can lead to the detection of errors and irregularities. Moreover, the process of financial analysis requires of the auditor, and imparts to him, the kind of understanding and grasp of the audited enterprise which indicates the most relevant type of supportive evidence required in his audit work.

The application of financial statement analysis as part of the audit program is best undertaken at the very beginning of the audit because such analysis will often reveal the areas of greatest change and vulnerability, areas to which the auditor will want to direct most of his attention. At the end of the audit these tools represent an overall check on the reasonableness of the financial statements taken as a whole.

Objectives of other interested groups

Financial statement analysis can serve the needs of many other user groups. Thus, the Internal Revenue Service can apply tools and techniques of financial statement analysis to the audit of tax returns and the checking of the reasonableness of reported amounts.[22] Various governmental regulatory agencies can use such techniques in the exercise of their supervisory and rate-determination functions.

Labor unions can use the techniques of financial statement analysis to evaluate the financial statements of enterprises with which they engage in collective bargaining. Lawyers can employ these techniques in the furtherance of their investigative and legal work while economic researchers will find them of great usefulness in their work.

---

[22] Among the areas which can be analyzed are questions such as (1) whether the income reported is enough to support exemptions or expenses claimed, (2) whether the profit margin reported is out of line with that normal for that type of business, and (3) whether the return reported is less than that which can be earned by banking the money.

Similarly customers can use such approaches to determine the profitability (staying power) of their suppliers, the returns they earn on capital, and other factors of consequence to them.

CONCLUSION

This chapter has examined the points of view and the objectives of a variety of important users of financial statements. These various objectives determine what aspects of financial statement analysis is relevant to the decision-making process of a particular user. In the following chapters we shall first examine the tools and techniques of financial statement analysis in general, and this will be followed in Part III by an examination of the major missions or objectives of financial analysis and the means by which they are accomplished.

QUESTIONS

1. Describe some of the analytical uses to which financial statement analysis can be put.
2. Why are the information needs of equity investors among the most demanding of all users of financial statements?
3. Why is the measurement and evaluation of earning power the key element in the valuation of equity securities?
4. What is the essential difference between a bond valuation model based on the present value of future inflows and a stock valuation model based on the same principles?
5. Differentiate between systematic risk and unsystematic risk and discuss the various components of the latter.
6. Discuss the Capital Asset Pricing Model and explain how it deals with the problem of securities valuation by the market.
7. Explain how the Efficient Market Theory deals with the reaction of market prices to financial and other data?
8. Explain the concept of the trade-off between risk and return as well as its significance to portfolio construction.
9. Discuss the implications that the Capital Asset Pricing Model and the Efficient Market Theory present for financial statement analysis.
10. Why is the reliability and the validity of any method of stock valuation, no matter how complete and sophisticated, dependent on the prior performance of a quality analysis of financial statements?
11. Identify clearly three separate factors which have a significant influence on a stock's price-earnings ratio. (CFA)
12. What are the differences in point of view between lenders and equity investors? How do these differences express themselves in the way these two groups analyze financial statements and in the objectives which they seek?

13. *a.* Outline the principal risks inherent in a preferred stock as an investment instrument, relative to a bond or other credit obligation of the same company.

    b. Discuss the various influences of U.S. (or Canadian) income taxation trends on the inherent risks and yields of preferred stocks.

    c. What terms can be included in a preferred stock issue to compensate for its subordination to debt and its relationship to common stock? (CFA)

14. What uses can the management of an enterprise make of financial statement analysis?

15. Of what use can financial statement analysis be to the audit of an enterprise?

4

TOOLS AND TECHNIQUES OF FINANCIAL STATEMENT ANALYSIS—AN OVERVIEW

Basic approaches to financial statement analysis

In the foregoing chapter we have examined the various objectives of financial statement analysis as viewed from the point of view of specific user groups. In the performance of an analysis such objectives can, in turn, be translated into a number of specific questions to which the decision maker needs an answer. Thus, for example, the equity investor may want to know:

1. What has the company's operating performance been over the longer term and over the recent past? What does this record hold for future earnings prospects?
2. Has the company's earnings record been one of growth, stability, or decline? Does it display significant variability?
3. What is the company's current financial condition? What factors are likely to affect it in the near future?
4. What is the company's capital structure? What risks and rewards does it hold for the investor?
5. How does this company compare on the above counts with other companies in its industry?

The banker who is approached with a short-term loan request may look to the financial statements for answers to questions such as the following:

1. What are the underlying reasons for the company's needs for funds? Are these needs truly short term, and if so, will they be self-liquidating?

2. From what sources is the company likely to get funds for the payment of interest and the repayment of principal?
3. How has management handled its needs for short-term and long-term funds in the past? What does this portend for the future?

An important first step in any decision-making process is to identify the most significant, pertinent, and critical questions which have a bearing on the decision. Financial statement analysis does not, of course, provide answers to all such questions. However, each of the questions exemplified above can, to a significant extent, be answered by such analysis. Financial statement analysis utilizes a variety of approaches and techniques among which are the following.

Reconstruction of business transactions. Basic to the analyst's work is an ability to reconstruct the business transactions which are summarized in the financial statements. That requires an understanding of the *reality* underlying such business transactions as well as a knowledge of the *accounting entries* used to record it properly within the accounting framework.

The analyst must also know what information is not generally available in financial statements so that he may attempt to secure it. In addition to information such as commitments, lines of credit, and order backlogs, the analyst will also generally not find the *details* of changes in many important accounts. Thus, for example, a short-term bank loan account or a loan to officers account may show little or no change in year-end balances but may, in fact, have had significant interim balances which were liquidated during the year.

A knowledge of what information can be found in financial statements, where it is to be found and how to reconstruct transactions, including the making of reasonable assumptions, are important skills in the analysis of financial statements.

ILLUSTRATION 1.   The analyst of the financial statements of Beta Company (see Appendix 4-B to this chapter) wants to determine the actual amount of long-term debt paid off in 19X6. This involves the reconstruction and analysis of two accounts. To get all the pertinent information the analyst must refer to the balances of the long-term debt (current and noncurrent) accounts in the balance sheet, to footnote 8 as well as to the statement of changes in financial position.

Long-Term Debt—(Noncurrent)

Transfer to the current L.T.D. account (derived balancing figure)	124.1	Beginning balance	1,137.2
Ending balance	1,054.3	Long term borrowing (per statement of changes in financial position)	41.2
	1,178.4		1,178.4

Long-Term Debt—(Current)

→ Long-term debt paid off		Beginning balance	119.2
(balancing amount)	121.1	Transfer from L.T.D.—	
Ending balance	122.2	Noncurrent	124.1
	243.3		243.3

Direct measurements.   Some factors and relationships can be measured directly. For example, the relationship between the debt and the equity of an entity is a direct measurement. Both the amount of debt and that of equity can be measured in absolute terms (i.e., in dollars) and their relationship computed therefrom.

Indirect evidence.   Financial statement analysis can provide indirect evidence bearing on important questions. Thus, the analysis of past statements of changes in financial position can offer evidence as to the financial habits of a management team. Moreover, the analysis of operating statements will yield evidence regarding management's ability to cope with fluctuations in the level of the firm's business activity. While such indirect evidence and evaluation are often not precise or quantifiable, the data derived therefore nevertheless possess importance because the effects of almost all managerial decisions, or the lack of them, are reflected in the entity's financial statements.

Predictive functions.   Almost all decision questions, including those in the examples above, are oriented towards the future. Thus, an important measure of the usefulness of financial statement analysis tools and techniques is their ability to assist in the prediction of expected future conditions and results.

Comparison.   This is a very important analytical process. It is based on the elementary proposition that in financial analysis no number standing by itself can be meaningful, and that it gains meaning only when related to some other comparable quantity. By means of comparison, financial analysis is useful in performing important evaluative, as well as attention-directing and control, functions. Thus, it focuses on exceptions and variations, and saves the analyst the need to evaluate the normal and the expected. Moreover, by means of comparison, selection among alternative choices is accomplished.

Comparison may be performed by using:

1. A company's own experience over the years (i.e., internally derived data);
2. External data, such as industry statistics; or
3. Compiled yardsticks, including standards, budgets, and forecasts.

Historical company data can usually be readily obtained and most readily adjusted for inconsistencies.

Uses of external data. Useful comparison may also be made with external data. The advantages of external data are: (1) they are normally objective and independent; (2) they are derived from similar operations, thus performing the function of a standard of comparison; and (3) if current, they reflect events occurring during an identical period having as a consequence similar business and economic conditions in common.

External information must, however, be used with great care and discrimination. Knowledge of the basis and method of compilation, the period covered, and the source of the information will facilitate a decision of whether the information is at all comparable. At times, sufficient detail may be available to adjust data so as to render them comparable. In any event, a decision on a proper standard of comparison must be made by choosing from those available. Differences between situations compared must be noted. Such differences may be in accounting practices or specific company policies. It must also be borne in mind that the past is seldom an unqualified guide to the future.

SOURCES OF INFORMATION

For basic data on an enterprise and for comparative data of comparable entities in its industry, published financial statements provide the best and most readily available source.

Appendix 4–A to this chapter presents a listing of Sources of Information on Financial and Operating Ratios of various industries as well as sample presentations from these sources. These data, while representing valuable sources for comparison, must be used with care and with as complete a knowledge of the basis of their compilation as is possible to obtain. A realistic and sometimes superior alternative for the analyst is to use as a basis of comparison the financial statements of one or more comparable companies in the same industry. In this way, one can usually have a better command over and comprehension of the data entering into the comparison base.

Annual reports to shareholders contain an ever-expanding amount of information required by either generally accepted accounting principles or by specific SEC requirements.[1]

In addition, company filings with the SEC, such as Registration

---

[1] For example, rule 14c-3 of the Securities Exchange Act of 1934 specifies that annual reports furnished to stockholders in connection with the annual meeting of stockholders include the following information: "certified" comparative financial statements, a 5-year summary of operations, a management's analysis of the summary of operations, a brief description of the company's business, a 5-year line of business breakdown, identification of the company's directors and executive officers and their principal occupation, and a statement of the market price range and dividends paid on voting securities for each quarterly period during the past 2 fiscal years.

Statements[2] pursuant to the Securities Act of 1933, supplemental and periodic reports which are required to be filed (such as Forms 8-K, 10-K[3], 10-Q, 14-K and 16-K), or proxy statements contain a wealth of information of interest to the analyst.

THE PRINCIPAL TOOLS OF ANALYSIS

In the analysis of financial statements, the analyst has available a variety of tools from which he can choose those best suited to his specific purpose. The following principal tools of analysis will be discussed in this chapter:

1. Comparative financial statements
    a. Year-to-year changes
2. Index-number trend series
3. Common-size financial statements
    a. Structural analysis
4. Ratio analysis
5. Specialized analyses
    a. Cash forecasts
    b. Analysis of changes in financial position
    c. Statement of variation in gross margin
    d. Break-even analysis

The application of these tools as well as other aspects of analysis will be illustrated by means of the financial statements of the Beta Company presented in Appendix 4–B. Further examples of tabulations of analytical measures can be found in Chapter 23.

Comparative financial statements

The comparison of financial statements is accomplished by setting up balance sheets, income statements, or statements of changes in financial position, side by side and reviewing the changes which have occurred in individual categories therein from year to year and over the years.

The most important factor revealed by comparative financial statements is *trend*. The comparison of financial statements over a number of years will also reveal the direction, velocity, and the amplitude of

---

[2] SEC Regulation S-X which specifies the form and content of financial statements filed with the Commission contains numerous requirements for specific disclosures.

[3] A survey conducted in 1976, using the National Automated Accounting Research System Data Base, which aimed to identify the additional significant information that can be found in SEC annual reports (forms 10-K) when compared to annual reports to stockholders, found these to represent disclosures of compensating balances, income taxes and stock option, pension and profit sharing plans.

trend. Further analysis can be undertaken to compare the trends in related items. For example, a year-to-year increase in sales of 10 percent accompanied by an increase in freight-out costs of 20 percent requires an investigation and explanation of the reasons for the difference. Similarly, an increase of accounts receivable of 15 percent during the same period would also warrant an investigation into the reasons for the difference in the rate of increase of sales as against that of receivables.

Year-to-year change. A comparison of financial statements over two to three years can be undertaken by computing the *year-to-year change* in absolute amounts and in terms of percentage changes. Longer term comparisons are best undertaken by means of *index-number trend series.*

Year-to-year comparisons of financial statements are illustrated in Appendix 4–B. When a two- or three-year comparison is attempted, such presentations are manageable and can be understood by the reader. They have the advantage of presenting changes in terms of absolute dollar amounts as well as in percentages. Both have to be considered because the dollar size of the different bases on which percentage changes are computed may yield large percentage changes which are out of proportion to their real significance. For example, in the same financial statements, a 50 percent change from a base figure of $1,000 is far less significant than the same percentage change from a base of $100,000. Thus, reference to the dollar amounts involved is always necessary in order to retain the proper perspective and to reach valid conclusions regarding the relative significance of the changes disclosed by this type of analysis.

The computation of year-to-year changes is a simple matter. However, a few clarifying rules should be borne in mind. When a negative amount appears in the base year and a positive amount in the following year, or vice versa, no percentage change can be meaningfully computed. When an item has a value in a base year and none in the following period, the decrease is 100 percent. Where there is no figure for the base year, no percentage change can be computed. The following summary will illustrate this:

Item	19X1 $	19X2 $	Change increase (decrease) Amount $	%
Net income (loss)	(4,500)	1,500	6,000	—
Tax expense	2,000	(1,000)	(3,000)	—
Notes payable	—	8,000	8,000	—
Notes receivable	10,000	—	(10,000)	(100)

Comparative financial statements can also be presented in such a way that the cumulative total for the period for each item under study and the average for that period are shown.

The value of comparing yearly amounts with an average covering a number of years is that unusual factors in any one year are highlighted. Averages smooth out erratic or unusual fluctuations in data.

Index-number trend series

When a comparison of financial statements covering more than three years is undertaken, the year-to-year method of comparison may become too cumbersome. The best way to effect such longer term trend comparisons is by means of index numbers. Such a comparative statement for the Beta Company is illustrated in Appendix 4–B.

The computation of a series of index numbers requires the choice of a base year which will, for all items, have an index amount of 100. Since such a base year represents a frame of reference for all comparisons, it is best to choose a year which, in a business conditions sense, is as typical or normal as possible. If the earliest year in the series compared cannot fulfill this function, another year is chosen. In our example of the Beta Company comparative statements, the year 19X3, rather than the first year in the series, was chosen.

As is the case with the computation of year-to-year percentage changes, certain changes, such as those from negative to positive amounts, cannot be expressed by means of index numbers. All index numbers are computed by reference to the base year.

ILLUSTRATION 2.   Assume that in the base year 19XA cash has a balance of $12,000. Based on an index number of 100 for 19XA, if the cash balance in the following year (19XB) is $18,000, then the index number will be

$$\frac{18,000}{12,000} \times 100 = 150$$

In 19XC if the cash balance is $9,000, the index will stand at 75 arrived at as follows:

$$\frac{9,000}{12,000} \times 100 \left(\frac{\text{Balance in Current Year}}{\text{Balance in Base Year}} \times 100 \right)$$

It should be noted that when using index numbers, percentage changes cannot be read off directly except by reference to the base year. Thus, the change of the cash balance between 19XA and 19XB is 50 percent (index 150 − index 100), and this can be read off directly from the index numbers. The change from 19XB to 19XC, however, is not 75 percent (150–75), as a direct comparison may suggest, but rather 50 percent (i.e., 9,000/18,000), which involves computing the 19XB to 19XC change by reference to the amount at 19XB. The percentage change can, however, be computed by use of the index numbers only, for example, 75/150 = .5 or a change of 50 percent.

In planning an index-number trend comparison, it is not necessary to include in it all the items in the financial statements. Only the most significant items need be included in such a comparison.

Care should be exercised in the use of index-number trend comparisons because such comparisons have weaknesses as well as strengths. Thus, in trying to assess changes in the current financial condition, the analyst may use to advantage comparative statements of changes in financial position. On the other hand, the index-number trend comparison is very well suited to a comparison of the changes in the *composition* of working capital items over the years.

The interpretation of percentage changes as well as those of index-number trend series must be made with a full awareness of the effect which the inconsistent application of accounting principles over the years can have on such comparisons. Thus, where possible, such inconsistencies must be adjusted. In addition, the longer the period covered by the comparison, the more distortive are the effects of price level changes on such comparisons likely to be, and the analyst must be aware of such effects (see Chapter 14).

One important value of trend analysis is that it can convey to the analyst a better understanding of management's philosophies, policies, and motivations, conscious or otherwise, which have brought about the changes revealed over the years. The more diverse the economic environments covering the periods compared are, the better a picture can be obtained by the analyst of the ways in which the enterprise has weathered its adversities and taken advantage of its opportunities.

Common-size financial statements

In the analysis of financial statements it is often instructive to find out the proportion of a total group or subgroup which a single item within them represents. In a balance sheet, the assets as well as the liabilities and capital are each expressed as 100 percent and each item in these categories is expressed as a percentage of the respective totals. Similarly, in the income statement net sales are set at 100 percent, and every other item in the statement is expressed as a percent of net sales. Since the totals always add up to 100 percent, this community of size has resulted in these statements being referred to as "common size." Similarly, following the eye as it reviews the common-size statement, this analysis is referred to as "vertical" for the same reason that the trend analysis is often referred to as "horizontal" analysis.

Selected common size of Beta Company are presented in Appendix 4–B.

Structural analysis. The analysis of common-size financial statements may best be described as an analysis of the internal structure of the financial statements. In the analysis of a balance sheet this structural analysis focuses on two major aspects:

1. What are the sources of capital of the enterprise, that is, what is the distribution of equities as between current liabilities, long-term liabilities, and equity capital?
2. Given the amount of capital from all sources, what is the distribution of assets (current, fixed, and other) in which it is invested? Stated differently, what is the mix of assets with which the enterprise has chosen to conduct its operations.

The common-size balance sheet analysis can, of course, be carried further and extended to an examination of what proportion of a subgroup, rather than the total, an item is. Thus, in assessing the liquidity of current assets, it may be of interest to know not only what proportion of total assets is invested in inventories but also what proportion of current assets is represented by this asset.

In the case of the income statement, common-size statement analysis is a very useful tool transcending perhaps in importance the analysis of the balance sheet by such means. This is so because the income statement lends itself very well to an analysis whereby each item in it is related to a central quantum, that is, sales. With some exceptions the level of each expense item is affected to some extent by the level of sales, and thus it is instructive to know what proportion of the sales dollar is absorbed by the various costs and expenses incurred by the enterprise.

Comparisons of common-size statements of a single enterprise over the years are valuable in that they show the changing proportions of components within groups of assets, liabilities, costs, and other financial statement categories. However, care must be exercised in interpreting such changes and the trend which they disclose. For example, the table below shows the amount of patents and total assets of an enterprise over three years:

	19X3	*19X2*	*19X1*
Patents	50,000	50,000	50,000
Total assets	1,000,000	750,000	500,000
Patents as a percentage of total assets	5%	6.67%	10%

While the amount of patents remained unchanged, the increase in total assets made this item a progressively smaller proportion of total assets. Since this proportion can change with either a change in the absolute amount of the item or a change in the total of the group of which it is a part, the interpretation of a common-size statement comparison requires an examination of the actual figures and the basis on which they are computed.

Common-size statements are very well suited to intercompany comparison because the financial statements of a variety of companies can be recast into the uniform common-size format regardless of the size of individual accounts. While common-size statements do not reflect the relative sizes of the individual companies which are compared, the problem of actual comparability between them is a matter to be resolved by the analyst's judgment.

Comparison of the common-size statements of companies within an industry or with common-size composite statistics of that industry can alert the analyst's attention to variations in account structure or distribution, the reasons for which should be explored and understood. A comparison of selected common-size statement items of the Marine Supply Corporation with similar industry statistics is presented in Exhibit 23–8 (page 659.)

Ratio analysis

Ratios are among the best known and most widely used tools of financial analysis. At the same time their function is often misunderstood, and consequently their significance may easily be overrated.

A ratio expresses the mathematical relationship between one quantity and another. The ratio of 200 to 100 is expressed as 2 : 1 or as 2. While the computation of a ratio involves a simple arithmetical operation, its interpretation is a far more complex matter.

To begin with, to be significant the ratio must express a relationship that has significance. Thus, there is a clear, direct, and understandable relationship between the sales price of an item on one hand and its cost on the other. As a result, the ratio of cost of goods sold to sales is a significant one. On the other hand, there is no a priori or understandable relationship between freight costs incurred and the marketable securities held by an enterprise; and hence, a ratio of one to the other must be deemed to be of no significance.

Ratios are tools of analysis which, in most cases, provide the analyst with clues and symptoms of underlying conditions. Ratios, properly interpreted, can also point the way to areas requiring further investigation and inquiry. The analysis of a ratio can disclose relationships as well as bases of comparison which reveal conditions and trends that cannot be detected by an inspection of the individual components of the ratio.

Since ratios, like other tools of analysis, are future oriented, the analyst must be able to adjust the factors present in a relationship to their probable shape and size in the future. He must also understand the factors which will influence such ratios in the future. Thus, in the final analysis, the usefulness of ratios is wholly dependent on their intelligent and skillful interpretation. This is, by far, the most difficult aspect of ratio analysis. Let us, by way of example, consider the interpretation of a ratio derived from an area outside that of the business world: In comparing the ratio of gas consumption to mileage driven, A claims to have a superior performance, that is, 28 mpg compared to B's 20 mpg. Assuming that they drove identical cars, the following are factors which affect gas consumption and which will have to be considered before one can properly interpret the ratios and judge whose performance is better:

1. Weight of load driven.
2. Type of terrain (flat versus hilly).
3. City or country driving.
4. Kind of gasoline used.
5. Speed at which cars were driven.

Numerous as the factors which influence gas consumption are, the evaluation of the gas consumption ratio is, nevertheless, a simpler process than the evaluation of most ratios derived from business variables. The reason for this is that the interrelationships of business variables and the factors which affect them are multifaceted and very complex. In addition to the internal operating conditions which affect the ratios of an enterprise, the analyst must be aware of the factors, such as general business conditions, industry position, management policies, as well as accounting principles, which can affect them. As far as the latter are concerned, the discussion of accounting principles in Part II of this text points up their influence on the measurements on which ratios are based.

Ratios should always be interpreted with great care since factors affecting the numerator may correlate with those affecting the denominator. Thus, for example, it is possible to improve the ratio of operating expenses to sales by reducing costs which act to stimulate sales. If the cost reduction consequently results in a loss of sales or share of market such a seeming improvement in profitability may, in fact, have an overall detrimental effect on the future prospects of the enterprise and must be interpreted accordingly.

It should also be recognized that many ratios have important variables in common with other ratios thus tending to make them vary and be influenced by the same factors. Consequently, there is no need to use all available ratios in order to diagnose a given condition.

Ratios, like most other relationships in financial analysis, are not significant in themselves and can be interpreted only by comparison with (1) past ratios of the same enterprise, or (2) some predetermined standard, or (3) ratios of other companies in the industry. The range of a ratio over time is also significant as is the trend of a given ratio over time.

A great many ratios can be developed from the multitude of items included in an enterprises' financial statements. Some ratios have general application in financial analysis, while others have specific uses in certain circumstances or in specific industries. Listed below are some of the most significant ratios which have general applicability to most business situations. They are grouped by major objectives of financial analysis:

Major categories of ratios	*Method of computation*	*Beta Corporation ratio for 19X6 (see Appendix 4-B)*
Short-term liquidity ratios:		
Current ratio	$\dfrac{\text{Current assets}}{\text{Current liabilities}} = \dfrac{1,019.4}{513.7}$	1.98:1
Acid test	$\dfrac{\text{Cash + Cash equivalents + Receivables}}{\text{Current liabilities}}$ $= \dfrac{41.5 + 284.8 + 307.7 + 37.8}{513.7} =$	1.31:1
Days sales in receivables (collection period)	$\dfrac{\text{Accounts receivables}}{\text{Credit sales} \div 360} = \dfrac{307.7}{3,540.6 \div 360} =$	31 days
Inventory turnover	$\dfrac{\text{Cost of goods sold}}{\text{Average inventory during period}}$ $= \dfrac{2,513.8}{(343.7 + 347.6)/2} =$	7.27
Capital structure and long-term solvency ratios:		
Net worth to total debt	$\dfrac{\text{Net worth}}{\text{Total debt}} = \dfrac{1,826.5}{3,639.6 - 1,826.5} =$	1:1
Net worth to long-term debt	$\dfrac{\text{Net worth}}{\text{Long-term debt}} = \dfrac{1,826.5}{1,054.3 + 212 + 33.1}$	1.41:1
Net worth to fixed assets	$\dfrac{\text{Net worth}}{\text{Fixed assets}} = \dfrac{1,826.5}{2,382.3} =$	.77:1
Times interest earned	$\dfrac{\text{Income before interest and taxes}}{\text{Interest expenses}}$ $= \dfrac{379.5 + 92.4}{92.4} =$	5.11 times
Return on investment ratios:		
Return on total assets	$\dfrac{\text{Net income + Interest expense}(1 - \text{Tax Rate})}{\text{Average total assets}}$ $= \dfrac{253.6 + 92.4(1 - 0.332)}{(3,341 + 3,639.6)/2} =$	9%
Return on equity capital	$\dfrac{\text{Net income}}{\text{Average equity capital}} = \dfrac{253.6}{(1,501.6 + 1,826.5)/2} =$	15%

Major categories of ratios	Method of computation	Beta Corporation ratio for 19X6 (see Appendix 4-B)
Operating performance ratios:		
Gross margin ratio	$\dfrac{\text{Gross profit (margin)}}{\text{Sales}} = \dfrac{3,540.6 - 2,513.8}{3,540.6} =$	29%
Operating profits to sales	$\dfrac{\text{Operating profit}}{\text{Sales}} = \dfrac{379.5 + 92.40}{3,540.6} =$	13.3%
Pretax income to sales	$\dfrac{\text{Pretax income}}{\text{Sales}} = \dfrac{379.5}{3,540.6} =$	10.7%
Net income to sales	$\dfrac{\text{Net income}}{\text{Sales}} = \dfrac{253.6}{3,540.6} =$	7.2%
Asset-utilization ratios:		
Sales to cash	$\dfrac{\text{Sales}}{\text{Cash}} = \dfrac{3,540.6}{41.5} =$	85.3:1
Sales to accounts receivables	$\dfrac{\text{Sales}}{\text{Accounts receivable}} = \dfrac{3,540.6}{307.7} =$	11.5:1
Sales to inventories	$\dfrac{\text{Sales}}{\text{Inventories}} = \dfrac{3,540.6}{347.6} =$	10.2:1
Sales to working capital	$\dfrac{\text{Sales}}{\text{Working capital}} = \dfrac{3,540.6}{1,019.4 - 513.7} =$	7:1
Sales to fixed assets	$\dfrac{\text{Sales}}{\text{Fixed assets}} = \dfrac{3,540.6}{2,382.3} =$	1.5:1
Sales to other assets	$\dfrac{\text{Sales}}{\text{Other assets}} = \dfrac{3,540.6}{237.9} =$	14.9:1
Sales to total assets	$\dfrac{\text{Sales}}{\text{Total assets}} = \dfrac{3,540.6}{3,639.6} =$	.97:1
Market measures:		
Price/Earnings ratio	$\dfrac{\text{Market price}}{\text{Earnings per share}} = \dfrac{67^*}{5.60} =$	11.98
Dividend yield	$\dfrac{\text{Dividends per share}}{\text{Market price per share}} = \dfrac{2}{67^*} =$	2.98%
Dividend payout ratio	$\dfrac{\text{Dividends declared}}{\text{Net income}} = \dfrac{91.4}{253.6} =$	36.04%

* Average for last quarter of 19X6.

Each of the above five major objectives of financial statement analysis will be examined in subsequent chapters; and therein the computation, use, and interpretation of the ratios listed under each category as well as other ratios will be examined in detail and thoroughly discussed. The listing includes the respective ratios for 19X6 of the Beta Company (see Appendix 4–B).

TESTING THE UNDERSTANDING OF RELATIONSHIPS

The following is an example of an exercise designed to test the reader's understanding of various intra- and interstatement ratios and relationships.

ILLUSTRATION 3.   Given the following information we are to complete the balance sheet below:

$$
\begin{array}{ll}
\text{Cash} & \\
\text{Accounts Receivable} & \\
\text{Inventory} \dots\dots\dots\dots\dots\dots\dots & \$50 \\
\text{Building} & \\
\text{Land} & \\
\text{Current Liabilities} & \\
\text{Common Stock} & \\
\text{Retained Earnings} \dots\dots\dots\dots\dots & \$100
\end{array}
$$

Assets − Liabilities = $600.
Stockholders Equity = 3 times debt.
The carrying amount of Land is ⅔ of that of the building.
Acid test ratio = 1.25.
Inventory turnover based on Cost of Goods Sold is 15.
Gross Profit is 44% of the Cost of Goods Sold.
There are 20 days sales in Accounts Receivable.
The determination of the balance sheet which follows is based on the steps described below:

Cash	$190	Current Liabilities	200
Accounts Receivable	60	Common Stock	500
Inventory	50	Retained Earnings	100
Buildings	300		800
Land	200		
	800		

STEP 1
Assets − Liabilities = 600
Stockholders equity = 600
Retained Earnings = 100 (as given)
Common Stock   = 500

STEP 2
Equity = 3 × debt
         3 × current liabilities (which are the total debt) = $600
         Add current liabilities   200
         So total assets equal $800

STEP 3
Acid test = 1.25
$$\frac{\text{Cash + Accounts Receivable}}{200} = 1.25$$
hence
   Cash + Accounts Receivable = $250

STEP 4
Inventory + Buildings + Land   = $550 [i.e., Total Assets − (Cash + A/R)]
            Buildings and Land = 500

Land = ⅔ of building; thus, if x = carrying amount of building
  $x + ⅔x = 500$ $x = 300$ (building)

  Land = \$500 − \$300 = \$200

STEP 5

$$\frac{\text{Cost of Goods Sold (CGS)}}{\text{Inventory}} = \text{Inventory Turnover;} \quad \frac{\text{CGS}}{50} = 15$$

Cost of Goods Sold = \$750   Gross Profit 44% of 750 = \$330

STEP 6

Cost of Good Sold + Gross Profit (\$750 + \$330) = Sales = \$1080

Amount of Sales per day $\dfrac{\$1080}{360} = \$3$

Accounts Receivable = 20 days sales = 20 × \$3 = 60
Cash = \$250 − Accounts Receivable (\$60) = \$190

Specialized tools of analysis

In addition to the multipurpose tools of financial statement analysis which we discussed above, such as trend indices, common-size statements, and ratios, the analyst has at his disposal a variety of special-purpose tools. These tools focus on specific financial statements or segments of such statements or they can address themselves specifically to the operating conditions of a particular industry, for example, occupancy-capacity analysis in the hotel, hospital, or airline industries. These special purpose tools of analysis include cash forecasts, analyses of changes in financial position, statements of variation in gross margin, and break-even analyses.

BUILDING BLOCKS OF FINANCIAL STATEMENT ANALYSIS

Whatever approach to financial statement analysis the analyst takes and whatever methods he uses he will always have to examine one or more of the important aspects of an enterprise's financial condition and results of its operations. All such aspects, with perhaps the exception of the most specialized ones, can be found in one of the following six categories:

1. Short-term liquidity.
2. Funds flow.
3. Capital structure and long-term solvency.
4. Return on investment.
5. Operating performance.
6. Assets utilization.

Each of the above categories and the tools used in measuring them will be discussed in greater depth in Part III of this book. In this way the financial analysis required by any conceivable set of objectives may be structured by examining any or all of the above areas in any sequence and with any degree of relative emphasis called for by circumstances. Thus these six areas of inquiry and investigation can be considered as building blocks of financial statement analysis.

COMPUTER ASSISTED FINANCIAL ANALYSIS

The major emphasis throughout this work is on the application of thoughtful and logical analysis upon carefully evaluated and verified data. Financial statement analysis does, however, involve a significant amount of work of a computational nature as well as numerous logical steps which can be preplanned and programmed. It is in these areas that the financial analyst can utilize computers to great advantage.

The modern electronic computer has a remarkable facility for performing complex computations with great speed. Moreover, it can perform these computations, comparisons, and other logical steps for long periods of time without exhaustion and, once properly programmed, will do them without error. In today's environment, when business complexity has outstripped our ability to grasp it and when our ability to generate information has outrun our ability to utilize it, the computer can render vital assistance.

The intelligent use of the computer's formidable capabilities in financial analysis depends, however, on thorough understanding of the limitations to which this powerful tool is subject. Thus, the computer lacks the ability to make intuitive judgments or to gain insights, capabilities which are essential to a competent and imaginative financial analysis.

There is nothing that the computer can do which a competent analyst armed with a calculator cannot do. On the other hand, the speed and the capabilities of modern computers are such that to accomplish what they can do would require so many hours of work as to render most such efforts uneconomical or unfeasible. Computers have thus automated some of the statistical and analytical steps which were previously done manually.

The stored data bases on which computer assisted security analysis often relies do not include all the information which, as discussed in Part II of this text, is needed to adjust accounting data in order to render it comparable or in order to make it conform to the analyst's specific needs. This is particularly true for the following reasons:

1. The data banks generally lack information on accounting policies and principles employed by a given enterprise. This information is essential to an interpretation of the data and to its comparison to other data.

2. Footnotes and other explanatory or restrictive information usually found in individual enterprise reports containing the financial statements are also generally not available in any meaningfull detail.
3. Lack of retroactive adjustments, because the necessary data are often not available.
4. Errors and omissions may occur when large masses of financial data are processed on a uniform basis for purposes of inclusion in the data base.
5. The aggregation of dissimilar or noncomparable data results in a loss of vital distinctions and thus reduces its meaning and its value for analysis.

Given an understanding of the capabilities as well as the limitations to which the computer is subject, the following are the more significant uses which can be made of this important tool in the broad area of financial analysis:

1. Data storage, retrieval, and computational ability

A machine-accessible comprehensive data base is essential to the use of the computer in most phases of security and credit analysis. The ability of the computer to store vast amounts of data and to afford access to them is one of its important capabilities. Another is the ability to sift these data, to manipulate them mathematically and to select from among them in accordance with set criteria, as well as to constantly update and modify them. Moreover, the ability of computers to perform computations (of ratios etc.) is almost unlimited.

A large commercially available data base comprising financial information on many hundreds of corporations covering twenty or more years is available from COMPUSTAT, a service of Standard & Poor's Corporation. Many other specialized data bases and time-sharing services are available from various sources and those include the AICPA time-sharing program library.

2. Screening large masses of data

The computer can be used to screen for specified criteria as a means of selecting investment opportunities and for other purposes. A variation of these techniques consists of "filtering" data in accordance with a set of preselected criteria (e.g., certain sales levels, returns, growth rates, financial characteristics, etc.)

3. A research tool

It can be used as a research tool for uncovering characteristics of and relationships between data on companies, industries, the market behavior and the economy.

4. Specialized financial analyses

The computer can be an input tool for financial analysis in credit extension and security analysis.

A. *Financial analysis in credit extension*

(1) Storage of facts for comparison and decision making.

(2) Projection of enterprise cash requirements under a variety of assumptions.

(3) Projection of financial statements under a variety of assumptions showing the impact of changes on key variables. Known as *sensitivity analysis,* this technique allows the user to explore the effect of systematically changing a given variable repeatedly by a predetermined amount.

(4) The introduction of probabilistic inputs. The data can be inserted as probability distributions, either normally shaped or skewed, or random probability distributions otherwise known as "Monte Carlo trials."

B. *Security analysis*

(1) Calculations based on past data.

(2) Trend computations.
—Simple
—Regression analysis

(3) Predictive models.

(4) Projections and forecasts.

(5) Sensitivity analysis.

(6) Complex probabilistic analysis.

Given an understanding of the capabilities of the modern electronic computer, as well as the limitations to which it is subject, the financial analyst will find in it an important tool which promises to grow in importance as new applications to which it can be put are perfected in the future.

ANALYTICAL REVIEW OF ACCOUNTING PRINCIPLES—PURPOSES AND FOCUS

In the chapters which follow we shall present a review of accounting standards used in the preparation of financial statements. The purpose of this review is to examine the variety of standards which can be applied to similar transactions and circumstances, as well as the latitude which is possible in the interpretation and application of these standards in practice. Thus, the focus is on an understanding of accounting standards as well as on an appreciation of the impact which the application of these standards may have on the reported financial condition and results of operations of an enterprise. Such possible impact must be appreciated and understood before any intelligent analysis can be undertaken or any useful and meaningful comparison is made.

Example of importance of accounting assumptions, standards, and determinations: Illustration of a simple investment decision

The importance of standards and assumptions in accounting determinations can perhaps be best illustrated and understood within the framework of an exceedingly simple example of a business situation. Let us assume that the owner of an apartment building has found an interested buyer. How should the price be set? How should the buyer gain confidence in the soundness and profitability of such investment at a given price?

The first question is the method to be followed in arriving at a fair value of the building. While many approaches are possible, such as comparable current values, reproduction costs; and so forth, let us settle here on the most widely accepted method for the valuation of income-producing properties as well as other investments: the capitalization of earnings. If earning power is the major consideration, then the focus must be on the income statement. The prospective buyer is given the following income statement:

184 EAGLE STREET APARTMENT HOUSE
Income Statement
For the Year Ending December 31, 19X9

Rental revenue		$46,000
Garage rentals		2,440
Other income from washer and dryer concession		300
Total revenue		$48,740
Expenses:		
Real estate taxes	$4,900	
Mortgage interest	2,100	
Electricity and gas	840	
Water	720	
Superintendent's salary	1,600	
Insurance	680	
Repairs and maintenance	2,400	13,240
Income before depreciation		$35,500
Depreciation		9,000
Net income		$26,500

The first questions the prospective buyer will want to ask himself about the foregoing income statement are these:

1. Can I rely on the fairness of presentation of the income statement?
2. What adjustments have to be made so as to obtain a net income figure which can be used with confidence in arriving at a proper purchase price?

In our society the most common way of gaining assurance about the fairness of presentation of financial statements is to rely on the opinion of an independent certified public accountant. This professional is assumed to perform a skilful audit and to satisfy himself that the financial statements do accurately portray the results of operations and the financial position, in accordance with principles which are generally accepted as proper and useful in the particular context in which they are applied. Such an auditor is also presumed to understand that someone like our prospective buyer will rely on his opinion in reaching a decision on whether to buy and at what price. In Chapter 15 we will explore in more detail the function of the auditor and what his opinion means to the user of financial statements.

Our prospective buyer's second question is far more complex. The auditor's opinion relates to the income statement as representing fairly the net income for the year ended December 31, 19X9. That in no way means that this is *the* relevant figure to use in arriving at a valuation of the apartment building. Nor would an auditor ever claim that his opinion is directed at the relevance of financial statement figures to any particular decision. Let us then examine what information our buyer will need and what assumptions he will have to make in order that he may arrive at a figure of net income which can be used in setting the value of the apartment building.

Rental income.   Does the $46,000 figure represent 100 percent occupancy during the year? If so, should an allowance be made for possible vacancies? What are rental trends in the area? What would rents be in five years? In 10 years? Are demand factors for apartments in the area going to stay stable, improve, or deteriorate? The aim, of course, is to come nearest to that figure of yearly rental income which approximates a level which, on the average, can be expected to prevail over the forseeable future. Prior years' data will be useful in judging this.

Real estate taxes.   Here the trend of taxes over the years is an important factor. That in turn depends on the character of the taxing community and revenue and expense trends within it.

Mortgage interest.   This expense is relevant to the buyer only if he assumes the existing mortgage. Otherwise the interest cost which will be incurred as a result of new financing will have to be substituted.

Utilities. These expenses must be scrutinized with a view to ascertaining whether they are at a representative level of what can be expected to prevail.

Superintendent's salary. Is the pay adequate to secure acceptable services? Can the services of superintendent be retained?

Insurance. Are all forseeable risks insured for? Is the coverage adequate?

Repairs and maintenance. These expenses must be examined over a number of years in order to determine an average or representative level. Is the level of expenses such that it affords proper maintenance of the property or is the expense account "starved" so as to show a higher net income?

Depreciation. This figure is not likely to be relevant to the buyer's decision unless his cost approximates that of the seller. If the cost to the buyer differs, then depreciation will have to be computed on that cost using a proper method of depreciation over the useful life of the building, so as to recover the buyer's original cost.

The buyer must also ascertain whether any expenses which he will be properly expected to incur are omitted from the above income statement. Additional considerations concern the method of financing this acquisition and other costs related thereto.

It should be understood that most of the above questions will have to be asked and properly answered even if the auditor issues an unqualified opinion on the financial statements. Thus, for example, while "generally accepted accounting principles" require that insurance expense include accruals for the full year, they are not concerned with the adequacy of insurance coverage or of the maintenance policy, or the superintendent's pay, or with expected, as opposed to actual, revenues or expense levels.

If one views the many complex questions and problems that arise in the attempt to analyze this very simple income statement for decision-making purposes, one can begin to grasp the complexities involved in the analysis of the financial statements of a sizable, modern business enterprise.

It is clear that essential to an intelligent analysis of such statements is an appreciation of what financial statements do portray as well as what they do not or cannot portray. As we have seen, there are items which properly belong in such statements and there are items which, because of an inability to quantify them or to determine them objectively, cannot be included.

Those items which properly belong in the financial statements should be presented therein in accordance with principles of accounting which enjoy general acceptance. The wide variety of standards which are "acceptable" as well as the even greater variety in the ways in which they can be applied in practice make it imperative that the user of financial statements be fully aware of these possibilities and their implications. The following chapters will explore this important area.

The example of the apartment house buyer illustrates the obvious fact that despite their limitations, financial statements and presentations are indispensible to the decision-making process. While the potential buyer could not use the income statement without obtaining more information and making further assumptions and adjustments, he would not have had any basis for his decision without it. Had he not received one, he would have had to make one up without utilization of the objectivity and the benefit of the experience of actual transactions over a period of time. Thus, in most cases, the interpretation of historical financial statements represents the essential first step in the decision-making process.

APPENDIX 4A

SOURCES OF INFORMATION ON FINANCIAL AND OPERATING RATIOS

A good way to achieve familiarity with the wide variety of published financial and operating ratios available is to classify them by the type of source that collects or compiles them. The specific sources given under each category are intended to exemplify the type of material available. These are by no means complete lists:

Professional and commercial organizations

Dun and Bradstreet, Inc., Business Economics Division, 99 Church Street, New York, N.Y. 10007

Key Business Ratios. Important Operating and Financial Ratios in 71 Manufacturing Lines, 32 Wholesale Lines and 22 Retail Lines and published in *Dun's Review* of Modern Industry. Five year summaries are also published. The data is presented in three ranges: lower quartile, median, and upper quartile.

Cost-of-Doing Business Series. Typical operating ratios for 185 lines of business, showing national averages. They represent a percentage of business receipts reported by a representative sample of the total of all Federal tax returns.

Moody's Investor Service, New York, N.Y.

Moody's Manuals contain financial and operating ratios on individual companies covered.

National Cash Register Company. *Expenses in Retail Businesses.* Biennial.
   Operating ratios for 36 lines of retail business, as taken from trade associ-
   ations and other sources including many from *Barometer of Small
   Business*
Robert Morris Associates. *Annual Statement Studies.*
   Financial and operating ratios for about 300 lines of business—
   manufacturers, wholesalers, retailers, services and contractors—based on
   information obtained from member banks of RMA. Data is broken down
   by company size. Part 4 gives "Additional Profit and Loss Data."
Standard & Poor Corporation
   Industry Surveys in two parts: (1) Basic Analysis and (2) Current Analysis
   contains many industry and individual company ratios.
Almanac of Business and Industrial Financial Ratios, by Leo Troy. Prentice-
Hall, Inc., Englewood Cliffs, N.J.
   A compilation of corporate performance ratios (operating and financial). The
   significance of these ratios is explained. All industries are covered in the
   study, each industry is subdivided by asset size.

The federal government

Small Business Administration
Publications containing industry statistics:
   Small Marketers Aids.
   Small Business Management Series.
   Business Service Bulletins.

U.S. Department of Commerce
   Census of Business—Wholesale Trade—Summary Statistics. Monthly
   Wholesale Trade Report. Ratio of operating expenses to sales.
Department of the Treasury
   Statistics of Income, Corporation Income Tax Returns. Operating Statistics
   based on income tax returns.
Federal Trade Commission—Securities and Exchange Commission.
   Quarterly Financial Report for Manufacturing, Mining and Trade Corpo-
   rations. Contains operating ratios and balance sheet ratios as well as the
   balance sheet in ratio format.

Sources of specific industry ratios

Bank Operating Statistics. Federal Deposit Insurance Corporation. Annual.
Institute of Real Estate Management. Experience Exchange Committee. *A
   Statistical Compilation and Analysis of Actual (year) Income and Expenses
   Experienced in Apartment, Condominium and Cooperative Building Oper-
   ation.* Annual.
Discount Merchandiser. *The True Look of the Discount Industry.* June issue
   each year. Includes operating ratios.

The Lilly Digest. Eli Lilly and Company. Annual.

National Electrical Contractors Association. *Operation Overhead.* Annual.

National Farm & Power Equipment Dealers Association. *Cost of Doing Business Study.* Annual.

Journal of Commercial Bank Lending. "Analysis of Year End Composite Ratios of Instalment Sales Finance and Small Loan Companies."

Harris, Kerr, Forster & Company. *Trends in the Hotel-Motel Business.* Annual.

Ohio Lumber and Building Product Dealers Association. *Survey of Operating Profits.* Compiled by Battelle and Battelle. Annual.

American Meat Institute. *Financial Facts about the Meat Packing Industry.* Includes operating ratios.

Chase Manhattan Bank. *Financial Analysis of a Group of Petroleum Companies.* Annual.

National Office Products Association. *Survey of Operating Results of NOPA Dealers.* Annual.

American Paint and Wallcoverings Dealer. *Report on Annual Survey.*

Printing Industries of America. *Ratios for Use of Printing Management.* Annual.

Restaurants, Country Clubs, City Clubs: Reports on Operations. Laventhol Krekstein Horwath & Horwath. Annual.

National Association of Textile and Apparel Wholesalers. *Performance Analysis of NATAW Members.* Annual.

Bibliographies

Robert Morris Associates. *Sources of Composite Financial Data—A Bibliography.* 3d ed. N.Y., 1971. 28 pp.

An annotated list of sources, with an index by specific industry at front.

Sanzo, Richard. *Ratio Analysis for Small Business.* 3d ed. Washington, D.C., 1970. 65 p. (U.S. Small Business Administration, Small Business Management Series, No. 20).

"Sources of Ratio Studies": p. 22–35, lists the industries covered by basic sources such as D & B, Robert Morris Associates; also the names of trade associations which have published ratio studies. Published financial and operating ratios are also occasionally listed in the monthly *Marketing Information Guide.*

EXAMPLE A-1

Robert Morris Associates statement studies

	Not elsewhere classified—Construction sand & gravel*					Not elsewhere classified—Crude petroleum & natural gas mining†				
	Under $250M	$250M & less than $1MM	$1MM & less than $10MM	$10MM & less than $50MM	All sizes	Under $250M	$250M & less than $1MM	$1MM & less than $10MM	$10MM & less than $50MM	All size
Asset size										
Number of statements		24	15		46		16	42	35	97
Assets										
Cash		5.5%	3.4%		3.0%		7.3%	4.9%	5.3%	5.3%
Marketable securities		1.6	.7		2.3		7.7	1.2	2.5	2.3
Receivables net		16.9	17.2		16.0		15.9	14.9	12.9	13.3
Inventory net		4.8	6.5		4.4		7.5	8.0	6.8	7.0
All other current		2.0	1.6		1.0		4.9	3.7	3.4	3.5
Total current		30.7	29.3		26.7		43.3	32.7	30.9	31.3
Fixed assets net		59.5	50.9		61.9		45.5	54.9	62.2	60.8
All other noncurrent		9.8	19.8		11.4		11.2	12.4	6.9	7.9
Total		100.0%	100.0%		100.0%		100.0%	100.0%	100.0%	100.0%
Liabilities										
Due to banks—short term		6.6%	7.7%		4.3%		5.6%	8.5%	3.2%	4.1%
Due to trade		8.2	10.0		8.5		10.9	14.5	15.3	15.1
Income taxes		1.7	1.9		1.2		2.5	2.0	1.8	1.8
Current maturities LT debt		6.2	5.1		3.1		2.8	6.2	5.1	5.3
All other current		7.8	5.9		5.8		5.8	5.7	2.9	3.4
Total current debt		30.6	30.5		23.0		27.7	36.9	28.3	29.8
Noncurrent debt, unsub.		17.0	19.6		12.2		20.5	22.9	20.3	20.7

Total unsubordinated debt	50.5	48.6	59.8	48.2	35.2	50.1	47.6
Subordinated debt	1.4	1.4	1.3	1.7	.7	1.1	1.4
Tangible net worth	48.1	50.0	38.8	50.1	64.1	48.8	51.1
Total	100.0%	100.0%	100.0%	100.0%	100.0%	100.0%	100.0%
Income data							
Net sales	100.0%	100.0%	100.0%	100.0%	100.0%	100.0%	100.0%
Cost of sales	56.3	51.4	52.4	30.6	75.2	77.9	63.0
Gross profit	43.7	48.6	47.6	69.4	24.8	22.1	37.0
All other expense net	26.8	28.9	31.1	49.5	19.3	19.7	30.7
Profit before taxes	16.9	19.7	16.5	20.0	5.5	2.4	6.3
Ratios							
Quick	1.1%	1.2%	.8%	2.1%	1.2%	1.2%	1.2%
	.7	.7	.6	.8	.8	.8	.8
	.4	.5	.3	.5	.4	.3	.4
Current	1.5	1.5	1.1	2.3	1.5	1.5	1.4
	1.0	1.1	.9	1.2	1.1	1.2	1.1
	.8	.8	.6	.9	.6	.6	.5
Fixed/Worth	.8	1.0	.7	.5	.8	.6	.9
	1.2	1.3	1.3	1.1	1.2	1.0	1.2
	2.1	1.6	2.4	2.2	1.9	1.8	2.2
Debt/Worth	.5	.4	.5	.6	.5	.4	.6
	1.3	1.0	1.9	1.7	1.1	1.0	1.4
	2.5	1.9	4.0	2.4	2.1	2.3	2.3
Unsub. debt/Capital funds	.4	.4	.5	.3	.4	.4	.5
	1.2	.9	1.4	1.7	.9	.8	1.2
	2.5	1.9	4.0	2.4	2.0	2.3	2.1

* 14 statements ended on or about June 30, 1974. 32 statements ended on or about December 31, 1974.
† 51 statements ended on or about June 30, 1974. 46 statements ended on or about December 31, 1974.

EXAMPLE A–2

Dun & Bradstreet—Key Business Ratios (cost of doing business ratios—corporations)

Industry	Total number of returns filed	Cost of goods sold %	Gross margin %	Compensation of officers %	Rent paid on business property %	Repairs %	Bad debts %	Interest paid %	Taxes paid %	Amortization depreciation depletion %	Advertising %	Pension other employee benefit plans %
										Selected operating expenses		
All industrial groups	1,658,820	70.77	29.23	1.94	1.38	.85	.38	3.31	2.98	3.55	1.13	1.12
Contract construction	127,670	82.97	17.03	3.33	.53	.57	.19	.72	1.92	1.90	.20	.71
Building construction	42,597	89.34	10.66	2.38	.35	.20	.10	.76	1.20	.95	.20	.39
General contractors, except building construction	12,627	80.74	19.26	2.25	.62	1.36	.20	.96	2.10	3.94	.12	.77
Special trade contractors	72,446	76.95	23.05	5.14	.68	.49	.29	.52	2.65	1.69	.26	1.05
Retailers & wholesalers	524,586	77.44	22.56	1.86	1.42	.31	.22	.75	1.40	.92	1.02	.35
Retailers	351,819	72.55	27.45	1.88	2.08	.38	.24	.81	1.60	1.09	1.51	.37
Building materials, hardware & farm equipment	31,715	75.65	24.35	3.23	.99	.34	.48	.79	1.64	1.04	.79	.37

Note: The above operating ratios for 185 lines of business have been derived to provide a guide as to the average amount spent by corporations for these items. They represent a percentage of business receipts as reported by a representative sample of the total of all federal income tax returns filed for 1969–70.

EXHIBIT 4B–2

BETA COMPANY
Consolidated Statement of Changes in Financial Position
For the Five Years Ended December 31, 19X6
(in millions)

	19X6	19X5	19X4	19X3	19X2
Source of funds:					
Net earnings	$253.6	$218.0	$262.6	$159.8	$102.7
Expenses not requiring outlays of working capital:					
Depreciation	129.0	118.6	108.5	104.2	98.2
Depletion of oil and gas properties......................	50.5	45.1	—	—	—
Cost of timber harvested	33.3	28.8	26.6	17.7	14.3
Deferred income taxes—noncurrent	43.0	49.1	17.5	28.8	18.5
Funds provided from operations	509.4	459.6	415.2	310.5	233.7
Issuance of common stock	159.5	2.1	.1	—	.1
Issuance of long-term debt	41.2	191.2	170.7	40.7	38.9
Reduction of long-term investments	.4	47.9	24.6	(73.8)	6.1
Sales of properties.....................	5.3	2.8	4.1	38.6	3.5
Other sources—net	(5.6)	12.4	(3.9)	1.4	12.6
	710.2	716.0	610.8	317.4	294.9
Application of funds:					
Acquisition of General Crude Oil Company:					
Properties acquired...................	—	482.6	—	—	—
Long-term portion of debt issued and assumed	—	(288.1)	—	—	—
Other, net	—	5.0	—	—	—
Working capital required by the acquisition	—	199.5	—	—	—
Cash dividends paid	91.4	88.6	77.4	77.9	67.3
Invested in plants and properties	398.4	365.2	196.4	106.0	109.5
Invested in timberlands	37.5	95.7	216.3	35.6	13.6
Reduction of long-term debt	124.1	69.4	26.0	36.3	24.8
Purchase of treasury stock	.2	.4	.5	20.8	—
Environmental construction funds held by trustees	(8.9)	(.1)	13.8	3.1	(.1)
	642.7	818.7	530.4	279.7	215.1
Increase (decrease) in working capital	$ 67.5	($102.7)	$ 80.4	$ 37.7	$ 79.8
Changes in working capital:					
Increases (decreases) in current assets:					
Cash	($ 5.7)	$ 13.2	$ 19.0	$ 1.0	($ 11.6)
Temporary investments	92.2	(104.3)	90.2	60.5	145.3
Accounts and notes receivable	(14.4)	(11.7)	58.7	7.7	10.8
Inventories	3.9	19.3	96.5	(2.7)	(47.7)
Deferred income taxes	7.1	2.7	14.7	(2.8)	8.5
	83.1	(80.8)	279.1	63.7	105.3
(Increases) decreases in current liabilities:					
Notes payable and current maturities of long-term debt	(5.2)	(47.1)	(45.7)	(9.9)	18.3
Accounts payable and accrued liabilities	(12.4)	(86.8)	(43.2)	(12.9)	(34.6)
Accrued income taxes	2.0	112.0	(109.8)	(3.2)	(9.2)
	(15.6)	(21.9)	(198.7)	(26.0)	(25.5)
Increase (decrease) in working capital	$ 67.5	($102.7)	$ 80.4	$ 37.7	$ 79.8

EXHIBIT 4B-1

BETA COMPANY*
Consolidated Balance Sheet
(in millions of dollars)

Assets	December 31 19X6	December 31 19X5
Current Assets:		
Cash (Note 1)	$ 41.5	$ 47.2
Temporary investments	284.8	192.6
Accounts and notes receivable	307.7	322.1
Inventories (Note 2)	347.6	343.7
Deferred income taxes (Note 3)	37.8	30.7
Total Current Assets	$1,019.4	$ 936.3
Property:		
Plants and Properties (Note 4)		
Pulp and paper	$2,463.4	$2,187.3
Oil and gas	562.0	496.0
Other	547.1	531.7
	3,572.5	3,215.0

Liabilities and Share Owners' Equity	December 31 19X6	December 31 19X5
Current Liabilities:		
Notes payable and current maturities of long-term debt	$ 138.2	$ 133.0
Accounts payable	200.9	189.2
Accrued liabilities	146.1	145.4
Accrued income taxes	28.5	30.5
Total Current Liabilities	$ 513.7	$ 498.1
Long-term debt (Note 8)	$1,054.3	$1,137.2
Deferred income taxes (Note 3)	212.0	161.8
Reserves and deferred liabilities	33.1	42.3
Commitments and contingent liabilities (Notes 16 & 17)		
Share owners' equity (Note 9)		
Serial preferred stock, $1 par value	—	—

Less: Accumulated depreciation and depletion	1,624.6	1,471.7
Total Plants and Properties	1,947.9	1,743.3
Timberlands—net (Note 5)		
Owner in fee	398.8	388.8
Capitalized timber harvesting rights	35.6	48.6
Total timberlands	434.4	437.4
Total Property	$2,382.3	$2,180.7
Other Assets:		
Investments—at cost (Note 6)	$ 45.0	$ 45.4
Investments in affiliates—at equity	59.2	43.2
Notes and land contracts receivable (Note 7)	20.9	28.0
Cost in excess of assigned value of businesses acquired—net	52.6	49.1
Environmental construction funds held by trustees	18.7	27.6
Deferred charges and other assets	41.5	30.7
Total Other Assets	237.9	224.0
Total Assets	$3,639.6	$3,341.0

Cumulative $4 preferred stock, no par value	5.0	5.4
Common stock, $2.50 par value	118.5	112.5
Capital from conversion of 5% preferred stock	40.4	40.4
Capital surplus	582.7	427.4
Retained earnings	1,104.4	942.2
	1,851.0	1,527.9
Less: Common shares held in treasury, at cost	24.5	26.3
Total Share Owners' Equity	1,826.5	1,501.6
Total Liabilities and Share Owners' Equity	$3,639.6	$3,341.0

* A land resources management enterprise engaged in the production of paper, pulp, packaging and wood products as well as in the exploration for oil and other natural resources.

EXHIBIT 4B-3

BETA COMPANY
Consolidated Statement of Earnings and Retained Earnings
(in millions of dollars except per-share amounts)

	Years ended December 31		Increase (decrease)	
	19X6	*19X5*	*Amount*	*%*
Income:				
Net sales	$3,540.6	$3,080.8	459.8	14.9
Other income, net (Note 11)	40.9	29.2	11.7	40.1
Total Income	3,581.5	3,110.0	471.5	15.2
Costs and expenses:				
Cost of products sold	2,513.8	2,134.0	379.8	17.8
Distribution expenses	191.6	172.2	19.4	11.3
Selling and administrative expenses	191.4	156.6	34.8	22.2
Depreciation	129.0	118.6	10.4	8.8
Depletion of oil and gas properties	50.5	45.1	5.4	12.0
Cost of timber harvested	33.3	28.8	4.5	15.6
Interest	92.4	83.4	9.0	10.8
Total Costs and Expenses	3,202.0	2,738.7	463.3	16.9
Earnings before income taxes	379.5	371.3	8.2	2.2
Provision for income taxes (Note 3)	125.9	153.3	(27.4)	(17.9)
Net Earnings	253.6	218.0	35.6	16.3
Retained earnings—beginning of year	942.2	812.8	129.4	15.9
	1,195.8	1,030.8	165.0	16.0

Cash dividends	*19X6*	*19X5*				
	(per share)					
$4.00 preferred stock	$4.00	$4.00	.2	.2	0	0
Common Stock	$2.00	$2.00	91.2	88.4	2.8	3.2
Retained Earnings—end of year			$1,104.4	$ 942.2	162.2	17.2
Earnings Per Common Share			$ 5.60	$ 4.93	.67	13.6

Statement of significant accounting policies

Consolidation—The consolidated financial statements include the accounts of the company and its subsidiaries, except for a wholly-owned financial services subsidiary and, in 19X6, a real estate subsidiary in process of liquidation which are accounted for by the equity method. All significant intercompany items and transactions have been eliminated. Investments in affiliated companies, owned 20 percent or more, are accounted for by the equity method, and accordingly, the company's share of affiliates' net income has been included in the consolidated results of operations. Cost in excess of assigned value of businesses acquired is being amortized over a period of forty years.

Foreign currency translation—Cash and amounts receivable or payable that are denominated in local currency are translated at the rates of exchange in effect at the end of the respective periods (current rate). All other balance sheet accounts are translated using the rates of exchange in effect at the time of the transactions (historic rate). Depreciation expense is translated at the rates of exchange in effect when the related assets were acquired, and substantially all other income and expense accounts are translated at the rates in effect during each month. The net effects of gains or losses on foreign exchange are included in other income.

Inventories are stated at the lower of cost or market. Inventory costs include raw material, labor, and manufacturing overhead except for certain costs, principally depreciation. Cost of raw materials, paper and pulp products, lumber, and certain operating supplies is generally determined on the last-in, first-out basis. During periods of rising prices, this method results in charging increased inventory production costs to operations on a current basis and tends to eliminate inflationary gains on inventory balances from current operating results. If the first-in, first-out method had been utilized, it would have had the effect of increasing inventory balances by approximately $108 million and $94 million at December 31, 19X6 and 19X5, respectively. Other inventories are stated on the first-in, first-out or average cost basis.

Plants and properties are stated at cost. With regard to the company's oil and gas properties, the company follows the "full-cost" method of accounting under which all direct costs incurred in the acquisition, exploration, and development of oil and gas properties are capitalized and amortized on a company-wide composite method over the productive life of the producing properties.

Depreciation is computed principally on a straight-line method for financial reporting purposes and on accelerated methods for tax purposes, based upon estimated useful lives. Depreciation rates, for financial reporting purposes, are as follows: building 2.5 percent; machinery and equipment 5 percent to 25 percent; woods equipment 10 percent to 16 percent.

Depletion of oil and gas properties is determined on the basis of the percentage of the oil and gas revenues during the period to the total estimated future gross revenues from proven reserves.

Timberlands, including capitalized timber harvesting rights, are stated at cost, less cost of timber harvested. The portion of the cost of timberlands attributed to standing timber is charged against income as timber is cut, at rates determined annually, based on the relationship of unamortized timber costs to the estimated volume of recoverable timber. The costs of roads, park developments, and other land improvements are capitalized and amortized over their economic life.

The company capitalizes those timber cutting contracts where the gross price to be paid is fixed.

Income taxes—Deferred income taxes are provided for timing differences between financial and tax reporting. The investment tax credit is recognized currently in earnings.

The company provides deferred taxes on the income of its Domestic International Sales Corporation (DISC).

The company does not provide taxes on undistributed earnings that are considered permanently reinvested in the business outside the United States.

Research and development costs—The Company is committed to an ongoing research program which is primarily conducted at its four research centers in the United States and Canada. Such costs amounted to $20.1 million and $16.5 million in the years 19X6 and 19X5, respectively, and have been charged to operations as incurred.

Earnings per common share have been computed on the basis of the average number of shares outstanding—19X6-45.2 million; 19X5-44.2 million.

Notes to consolidated financial statements

Note 1.   Lines of credit—The Company maintains bank lines of credit ($232 million at December 31, 19X6) with certain U.S. and foreign banks. There have been no borrowings under these lines during 19X5 or 19X6 and, while the Company maintains deposits with some of these banks equal to approximately 10 percent of such lines, it is free to withdraw these deposits at any time.

Note 2.   Inventories by major category include:

(in millions)	19X6	19X5
Raw materials	$120.0	$118.1
Finished paper and pulp products	95.5	92.8
Finished lumber and plywood products	25.4	26.3
Operating supplies	96.4	95.1
Other	10.3	11.4
Total	$347.6	$343.7

Note 3.   Income taxes—The components of the provision for income taxes are:

(In millions)	19X6	19X5
Current:		
United States		
Federal	$ 45.5	$ 57.5
State	12.5	8.4
Outside U.S.	32.0	41.0
	90.0	106.9
Deferred:		
U.S. Federal	37.7	40.9
Outside U.S.	(1.8)	5.5
	35.9	46.4
Total	$125.9	$153.3

The principal items giving rise to deferred income taxes are:

(In millions)	19X6	19X5
Drilling and exploration		
costs, expensed for tax purposes	$17.9	$13.6
Depreciation	16.6	11.9
Discontinued operations	4.4	.1
DISC	2.5	8.8
Foreign exchange losses	(1.3)	(.1)
Other, net	(4.2)	12.1
	$35.9	$46.4

The principal components of the company's income tax rate are as follows:

	19X6	19X5
Ordinary U.S. income tax rate	48.0%	48.0%
Reduction resulting from:		
Income taxed at capital gains rate ...	5.5	3.7
Investment tax credit[1]	8.4	3.7
Other, net	.9	(.7)
Effective income tax rate	33.2%	41.3%

[1] Includes, in 19X6, an additional 1% investment tax credit (ITC) related to an Employee Stock Ownership Plan adopted by the Company in 19X6. This additional ITC ($2.9 million) has also been reflected in the accompanying income statement as compensation expense. Total ITC was: 19X6—$31.9 million; 19X5—$13.6 million.

Note 4.   Plants and properties by major classification, and related accumulated depreciation and depletion reserves, at December 31, 19X6 were as follows:

(In millions)	Cost	Accumulated depreciation depletion	Net
Pulp and paper facilities:			
Mills	$2,089.3	$1,125.7	$ 963.6
Packaging plants	374.1	171.2	202.9
	2,463.4	1,296.9	1,166.5
Oil and gas properties	562.0	94.5	467.5
Other properties:			
Wood products facilities	136.5	72.0	64.5
Woods equipment	206.0	103.6	102.4
Other	204.6	57.6	147.0
	547.1	233.2	313.9
Total	$3,572.5	$1,624.6	$1,947.9

Note 5.   Timberlands—At December 31, 19X6, timberlands owned in fee consisted of 7.2 million acres in the United States with a book value of $391.6 million and 1.3 million acres in Canada with a book value of $7.2 million.

Capitalized timber harvesting rights consist principally of those timber cutting contracts in the United States where the gross price to be paid has been fixed.

The company has timber harvesting licensing arrangements on a total of 12.4 million acres in the Canadian provinces of Quebec and New Brunswick plus additional harvesting rights measured in wood volume in the province of Quebec.

Legislation was enacted in Quebec in 19X4 directed towards the eventual replacement of existing licensing arrangements by guarantees of timber supplies from public lands. These guarantees are in the form of grants of rights to cut standing timber sufficient to supply wood processing plants for as long as such plants carry on normal operations. Such grants are expected to be economically equivalent to the rights presently held.

Note 6.   Investments at cost, include, at December 31, 19X6 and 19X5, $33.7 million representing the cost of 1,404,000 restricted shares of capital stock of C. R. Bard, Inc. Long-term debt of $53.3 million (4¼ percent Subordinated Debentures due 19X6) is exchangeable for the C. R. Bard, Inc. shares at a rate equivalent to $38 a share. The market price of C. R. Bard, Inc. shares was $14.63 per share on December 31, 19X6.

Note 7.   Notes and land contracts receivable include $6.9 million and $9.2 million at December 31, 19X6 and 19X5, respectively, representing the long-term portion of a secured interest-bearing note of Donald L. Bren Company. The note is payable in substantially equal annual installments through 19Y0, and is secured by 132,828 shares of the common stock of the Beta Company. The company has a warrant to purchase 49 percent of the oustanding stock of the Bren Company at any time through June 30, 19Y0 at its then book value.

Note 8.   Long-term debt—A summary of long-term debt follows:

(In millions)	*19X6*	*19X5*
5⅛% Notes—due 19X7-19Y6	$ 100.0	$ 110.0
5⅞% Notes—due 19X7-19Y6	20.0	22.0
6⅜% Notes—due 19X7-19Y8	120.0	130.0
8½% Notes—due 19X7-19Y2	275.6	323.3
9¼% Notes—due 19X7-19X8	69.1	103.9
8.85% Sinking fund debentures—due 19Y1-19Z5	150.0	150.0
8.85% Sinking fund debentures—due 19Y6-19Z9	150.0	150.0
4¼% Subordinated debentures—due 19Z6	53.3	53.3
Environmental bond issues	139.3[1]	112.1
Other	99.2	101.8
	$1,176.5	$1,256.4
Less—Current maturities	122.2	119.2
Total	$1,054.3[2]	$1,137.2

[1] Average interest rate of 6.5%.

[2] Total maturities over the next five years are as follows: 19X7—$122.2 million; 19X8—$113.5 million; 19X9—$77.8 million; 19Y0—$76.1 million; 19Y1—$78.4 million. Long-term debt at December 31, 19X6 includes local borrowings of Canadian and other subsidiaries outside the U.S. amounting to $73.1 million.

Note 9.   Capital stock—A summary of capital stock at December 31, 19X6 follows:

	Shares[1]	
	$4 preferred stock	Common 'stock[2]
Authorized	400,000	72,000,000
Issued	230,579	47,381,674
In Treasury........	180,686	684,716
Outstanding	49,893	46,696,958

[1] In April 19X6, the share owners approved the creation of a new class of serial preferred stock ($1.00 par value 15,000,000 shares) and the elimination of preemptive rights of common stock.

[2] Shares issued and outstanding increased by 2,447,414 shares during 19X6, principally due to the sale of 2.25 million shares in August for approximately $150 million. As a result of such sale, $143.9 million has been credited to capital surplus.

Note 10.   Operations outside the United States—A summary of operations outside the U.S. (principally Canada) follows:

(In millions)	19X6
Sales[1]	$826.4
Working capital	249.8
Assets	721.6
Undistributed earnings[2]	425.7

[1] Comparable sales for the year ended December 31, 19X5 were $780.6.

[2] Substantially all of these earnings have been permanently reinvested outside the U.S.

Note 11.   Other income, net—The major components of other income were as follows:

(In millions)	19X6	19X5
Interest income	$18.8	$17.6
Equity in earnings of affiliates	9.3	3.8
Sale of capital assets	5.5	1.7
Foreign exchange	(1.1)	(.6)
Miscellaneous	8.4	6.7
	$40.9	$29.2

Note 12.   Incentive plans—The company has a Profit Improvement Plan under which a maximum of 750,000 shares of treasury stock may be awarded. Under the plan, which terminates in 19Y0, contingent awards of shares of common stock, covering a three-year period, are granted by a committee composed of members of the Board of Directors who are not eligible for awards. Awards are earned in any year in which earnings per share, as defined, exceed the predetermined profit base. Through December 31, 19X6, 212,741 shares have been earned under the Plan, including 51,601 shares earned in 19X6 and

40,113 shares earned in 19X5. At December 31, 19X6, 52,276 shares have been contingently awarded for the year ending December 31, 19X7.

The company also has an Incentive Compensation Plan. Participants include those employees who are in a position to make substantial contributions to the management of the Company. Awards may be made in any year in which net earnings, as defined, exceed six percent of share owners' equity, but are limited to the lesser amount of eight percent of such excess or ten percent of the cash dividends declared on the outstanding common stock of the Company during the year. The awards may be in cash, payable immediately, or in treasury common shares, payable in the future.

Provision for the cost of the Company's two incentive plans amounted to $12.2 million and $8.5 million for the respective years of 19X6 and 19X5.

Note 13. Retirement plans—The company and its consolidated subsidiaries have several pension plans which provide retirement benefits to substantially all employees.

The company has amended its pension plans to conform to the provisions of the Employees Retirement Income Security Act which became effective on January 1, 19X6. The effect of such amendments on annual pension costs and the funding of such costs was not significant.

Annual pension costs, which reflect amortization of prior service costs over periods of up to 30 years, are funded currently by payments to the trustees of the various plans. Pension costs were $57 million in 19X6 and $45 million in 19X5. At December 31, 19X6, unfunded prior service costs amounted to $189 million, and it is estimated that the actuarially computed value of vested benefits exceeded the value of fund assets by approximately $76 million.

Note 14. Interim financial results (unaudited)

19X6	Sales	Net earnings	Earnings per common share
	($ in millions except per-share amounts)		
First	$ 866.8	$ 63.6	$1.43
Second	906.1	83.5	1.88
Third	884.0	58.8	1.29
Fourth	883.7	47.7	1.02
Year	$3,540.6	$253.6	$5.60[1]

[1] Total 19X6 per-share amount does not equal the sum of the individual quarters because of the effect on average shares outstanding of the sale of 2.25 million shares in August 19X6.

Note 15. Effects of inflation—(unaudited) During recent years, the overall rate of cost inflation has accelerated faster than the rate of productivity improvement in the company's operations. As a result, price increases have been necessary to achieve and maintain profit margins at acceptable levels. The company believes that over the next several years additional price increases, together with aggressive cost reduction and technological improvements, will be required to provide the profit margins necessary to justify new investment in the Company's principal businesses. In addition, future investment decisions will depend upon sound federal income tax policies and realistic environmental regulations.

The Company's Form 10-K, filed with the Securities and Exchange Commission, includes certain quantitative information with respect to the estimated replacement cost of inventories and plant and equipment at December 31, 19X6, and the related estimated effect of such costs on the cost of products sold, depreciation expense, and cost of timber harvested for the year then ended. A copy of Beta's Form 10-K is available upon request.

Note 16.   Commitments—Rent expense, principally relating to vessels and data processing equipment, was $33 million in 19X6 and $31 million in 19X5. At December 31, 19X6, rental commitments under existing leases were $22 million, $21 million, $20 million, $15 million, and $9 million for the five years ending 19X1, $27 million for the 19X2–19X6 period, and $10 million thereafter.

The Company has many purchase commitments involving such matters as timber supply contracts, material supply contracts, and construction contracts.

EXHIBIT 4B–4
Report of independent public accountants

To the Share Owners of Beta Company:

We have examined the consolidated balance sheet of Beta Company and consolidated subsidiaries as of December 31, 19X6 and 19X5, and the related consolidated statements of earnings and retained earnings and changes in financial position for the years then ended. Our examination was made in accordance with generally accepted auditing standards, and accordingly included such tests of the accounting records and such other auditing procedures as we considered necessary in the circumstances. The financial statements of Canadian Beta Company included in the consolidated financial statements (constituting approximately 15% of total consolidated assets and 20% of total consolidated sales for both 19X6 and 19X5) were examined by other independent public accountants whose report thereon has been furnished to us and our opinion expressed herein, insofar as it relates to the amounts included for Canadian Beta Company, is based solely upon such report.

In our opinion, based upon our examination and the report of other independent public accountants, the accompanying consolidated financial statements present fairly the consolidated financial position of Beta Company and consolidated subsidiaries as of December 31, 19X6 and 19X5, and the results of their operations and the changes in their financial position for the years then ended, in conformity with generally accepted accounting principles consistently applied during the periods.

New York, N.Y.,
February 8, 19X7

Good, Better & Co.

EXHIBIT 4B–5

BETA COMPANY
Ten Year Financial Summary
(in millions of dollars except per-share amounts)

	19X6	19X5	19X4	19X3	19X2	19X1	19X0	19W9	19W8	19W7
Ten year summary of earnings										
Income:										
Net sales	$3,541	$3,081	$3,042	$2,314	$2,093	$1,970	$1,841	$1,777	$1,574	$1,421
Other income, net	41	29	53	41	21	17	17	22	19	13
Total Income	3,582	3,110	3,095	2,355	2,114	1,987	1,858	1,799	1,593	1,434
Costs and expenses:										
Cost of products sold	2,514	2,134	2,128	1,661	1,514	1,432	1,323	1,246	1,115	1,028
Distribution expenses	192	172	186	156	157	148	139	132	120	106
Selling and administrative expenses	191	157	143	129	133	149	139	120	96	86
Depreciation	129	119	108	104	98	97	89	79	78	74
Depletion of oil and gas properties	51	45	—	—	—	—	—	—	—	—
Cost of timber harvested	33	29	27	18	14	14	10	9	7	3
Interest	92	83	45	41	38	41	39	26	17	9
Total Costs and Expenses	3,202	2,739	2,637	2,109	1,954	1,881	1,739	1,612	1,433	1,306
Earnings before income taxes	380	371	458	246	160	106	119	187	160	128
Provision for income taxes	126	153	195	86	57	37	37	73	62	44
Earnings before extraordinary items	254	218	263	160	103	69	82	114	98	84
Extraordinary items, net	—	—	—	—	—	(15)	(39)	—	—	—
Net Earnings	$ 254	$ 218	$ 263	$ 160	$ 103	$ 54	$ 43	$ 114	$ 98	$ 84

	$ 91	$ 89	$ 77	$ 78	$ 67	$ 67	$ 67	$ 66	$ 61	$ 59
Cash Dividends										
Financial position										
Current assets	$1,019	$ 936	$1,017	$ 738	$ 674	$ 569	$ 607	$ 572	$ 538	$ 453
Current liabilities	514	498	476	278	251	226	277	313	225	214
Working capital	505	438	541	460	423	343	330	259	313	239
Plants and properties—net	1,948	1,743	1,063	989	1,030	1,060	1,060	978	869	798
Timberlands—net	434	437	372	183	165	166	171	154	153	156
Long-term debt	1,054	1,137	727	583	578	564	534	373	359	181
Reserves and deferred liabilities ..	245	204	159	157	129	160	138	79	58	42
Common share owners' equity	1,822	1,496	1,361	1,173	1,106	1,069	1,081	1,105	1,068	1,036
Per share of common stock										
Earnings before extraordinary items	$ 5.60	$ 4.93	$ 5.95	$ 3.60	$ 2.30	$ 1.53	$ 1.84	$ 2.54	$ 2.18	$ 1.90
Extraordinary items, net	—	—	—	—	—	(.33)	(.89)	—	—	—
Net earnings	5.60	4.93	5.95	3.60	2.30	1.20	.95	2.54	2.18	1.90
Cash dividends	2.00	2.00	1.75	1.75	1.50	1.50	1.50	1.50	1.38¾	1.35
Common share owners' equity	39.01	33.81	30.84	26.62	24.83	24.03	24.38	24.93	23.95	23.11
Market price range per share* ... HIGH	80	62	56	57	42	46	40	46	40	32
LOW	58	35	32	33	33	28	28	35	26	25

Stock price by quarter*

19X6	Fourth	Third	Second	First
High	71	75	78	80
Low	63	64	69	58

19X5	Fourth	Third	Second	First
High	60	62	55	44
Low	50	49	41	35

* High and low market price on Composite Tape to nearest dollar.

EXHIBIT 4B-6

BETA COMPANY

	Trend analysis (index numbers)					Common size analysis				
Summary of Earnings	19X6	19X5	19X4	19X3†	19X2	19X6	19X5	19X4	19X3	19X2
Income:										
Net sales	153.0	133.1	131.5	100	90.5	100	100	100	100	100
Other income, net	100.0	70.7	129.3	100	51.2	1.2	.9	1.7	1.8	1.0
Total Income	152.1	132.1	131.4	100	89.8	101.2	100.9	101.7	101.8	101.0
Costs and expenses:										
Cost of products sold	151.4	128.5	128.1	100	91.1	71.0	69.3	70.0	71.8	72.3
Distribution expenses	123.1	110.3	119.2	100	100.6	5.4	5.6	6.1	6.7	7.5
Selling and administrative expenses	148.1	121.7	110.9	100	103.1	5.4	5.1	4.7	5.6	6.4
Depreciation	124.0	114.4	103.8	100	94.2	3.6	3.9	3.6	4.5	4.7
Depletion of oil and gas properties	113.3	100†	—	—	—	1.4	1.5	—	—	—
Cost of timber harvested	183.3	161.1	150.0	100	77.8	.9	.9	.9	.8	.7
Interest	224.4	202.4	109.8	100	92.7	2.6	2.7	1.5	1.8	1.8
Total Costs and Expenses	151.8	129.9	125.0	100	92.7	90.4	88.9	86.7	91.1	93.4
Earnings before income taxes	154.5	150.8	186.2	100	65.0	10.8	12.0	15.0	10.7	7.6
Provision for income taxes	146.5	177.9	226.7	100	66.3	3.6	5.0	6.4	3.7	2.7
Earnings before extraordinary items	158.8	136.3	164.4	100	64.4	7.2	7.0	8.6	7.0	4.9
Extraordinary items, net	—	—	—	100	—	—	—	—	—	—
Net Earnings	158.8	136.3	164.4	100	64.4	7.2	7.0	8.6	7.0	4.9
Cash Dividends	116.7	114.1	98.7	100	85.9	2.6	2.9	2.5	3.4	3.2
Financial Position*										
Current assets	138.1	126.8	137.8	100	91.3	28.0	28.0	37.3	33.6	32.5
Plants and properties—net	197.0	176.2	107.5	100	104.1	53.5	52.2	39.0	45.0	49.6
Timberlands—net	237.2	238.8	203.3	100	90.2	11.9	13.1	13.6	8.3	7.9
Other assets	83.0	78.1	96.2	100	71.9	6.6	6.7	10.1	13.1	10.0
Total Assets	165.6	152.0	124.2	100	94.4	100.0	100.0	100.0	100.0	100.0
Current liabilities	184.9	179.1	171.2	100	90.3	14.1	14.9	17.4	12.6	12.1
Long-term debt	180.8	195.0	124.7	100	99.1	29.0	34.0	26.6	26.5	27.8
Reserves and deferred liabilities	156.1	129.9	101.3	100	82.2	6.7	6.1	5.8	7.1	6.2
Total share owners' equity	154.8	127.3	115.8	100	94.7	50.2	45.0	50.2	53.8	53.9
Total liabilities and equity	165.6	152.0	124.2	100	94.4	100.0	100.0	100.0	100.0	100.0

* Reclassified from Form 10-K data.
† Base year.

In the opinion of management, no losses are anticipated in the liquidation of these commitments.

Note 17. Litigation—During 19X6, the company was fined $50,000 pursuant to a plea of *nolo contendere* to a charge of violation of federal antitrust laws in the sale of folding cartons. The company is one of the defendants in a number of purported class actions which were filed during 19X6 and which seek treble damages for alleged antitrust violations in the sale of folding cartons and the sale of box board used in the manufacture of folding cartons. All of these cases are in preliminary stages and the court has not yet determined which, if any, of the cases may be maintained as class actions.

In this increasingly litigious society, the company is also a defendant in other cases involving, among other matters, land sales, environmental protection, alleged discrimination in employment practices, securities matters, and private antitrust damage claims involving the sale of plywood. If the plaintiffs should prevail in various of the foregoing cases as class actions, damages against the company could be substantial. The company is also involved in several grand jury investigations concerning compliance with the antitrust laws. While any litigation or investigation has an element of uncertainty, the company believes that the outcome of any lawsuit or claim which is pending or threatened, or all of them combined, will not have a materially adverse effect on its financial condition or results of operations.

QUESTIONS

1. As a potential investor in a common stock, what information would you seek? How do you get such information?
2. The president of your client company approached you, the financial officer of a local bank, for a substantial loan. What could you do?
3. What, in broad categories, are some of the approaches utilized by the financial analyst in diagnosing the financial health of a business?
4. How useful is a comparative financial analysis? How do you make useful comparison?
5. What are some of the precautions required of a financial analyst in his comparative analytical work?
6. Give four broad categories of analysis tools.
7. Is the trend of the past a good predictor of the future? Give reasons for your argument.
8. Which is the better indicator of significant change—the absolute amount of change or the change in percentage? Why?
9. What conditions would prevent the computation of a valid percentage change? Give an example.
10. What are some of the criteria to be used in picking out a base year in an index number comparative analysis?
11. What information can be obtained from trend analysis?
12. What is a common-size financial statement? How do you prepare one?

13. What does a common-size financial statement tell about an enterprise?
14. Do all ratios have significance? Explain.
15. What are some of the limitations of ratio analysis?
16. Give five ratios that can be prepared by use of balance sheet figures only.
17. Give five ratios that can be prepared by use of income statement data only.
18. Give seven ratios that require data from both the balance sheet and the income statement.
19. Give four examples of special-purpose analytical tools commonly utilized by the financial analyst.
20. What are the steps generally taken by the financial analyst in his work? What do these steps achieve?
21. Identify and explain two significant limitations associated with ratio analysis of financial statements. (C.F.A.)
22. What are some of the principal uses of computers in investment analysis? (C.F.A.)
23. What are the most important limitations or disadvantages to the application of computers to security analysis? (C.F.A.)

PART II

FINANCIAL STATEMENTS—THE
RAW MATERIAL OF ANALYSIS

5

ANALYSIS OF CURRENT ASSETS

In considering the variety of standards which govern accounting transactions, determinations, and financial presentations, we shall be primarily concerned here with an examination of their significance to the intelligent user and analyst of financial statements. In this chapter we shall deal with the principles which underly the measurement and presentation of current assets.

CASH

Cash is considered the most liquid of assets. In fact, it represents the starting point, as well as the finish line, of what is known as the "accounting cycle." This cycle encompasses the purchase and manufacture of goods and services as well as their sale and the collection of the proceeds. The realization of a transaction is measured by sale and later by the ultimate conversion of the consideration received into cash. Excepting fixed commitments to the satisfaction of which cash must be applied, cash represents that point in the accounting cycle at which management has the maximum discretion with regard to the deployment and use of the resources.

By the very nature of its inherent liquidity, cash does not present serious valuation problems even though this characteristic requires special precautions against theft and defalcation. Care should be taken in the classification of cash items when restrictions have been placed on its disposition. For example, in the case of a segregation for plant expansion or for some other type of specific restriction, the cash balance involved should be separately shown. It may not, of course, be properly includible among current assets, which heading denotes liquidity and availability for the payment of current obligations. Cash set aside for "debt service" or "maintenance" under bond indenture is usually segregated on the balance sheet.

Accountants do not regard compensating balances maintained under a loan agreement as a restriction on cash because banks would generally honor checks drawn against such a balance. However, in accordance with guidelines promulgated by SEC *Accounting Series Release No. 148*, compensating balances must be segregated on the balance sheet if they are legally restricted. Otherwise such balances must be disclosed in notes to the financial statements.

Compensating balances constitute that part of a demand deposit which is maintained to support existing borrowing arrangements and to assure future credit availability. Even though informal, such arrangements have considerable practical significance. Thus, in assessing the current ratio the analyst must consider the repercussions which may follow from the breaking of a tacit agreement with the bank. This may involve the loss of a credit source, and thus have an effect on a company's liquidity and its future access to funds. Vulnerability in this area can be measured by computing the ratio of restricted cash to total cash.

MARKETABLE SECURITIES

Marketable securities represent in most instances temporary repositories of excess cash. Alternatively they may represent funds awaiting investment in plant and equipment, etc. They are usually shown among current assets. However, marketable securities which are temporary investments of cash designated for special purposes such as plant expansion or the meeting of requirements under sinking fund provisions should be shown among long-term investments.

Certain marketable equity securities carried as current assets must now be accounted for in accordance with SFAS 12 entitled "Accounting for Certain Marketable Securities." The following are some of the salient provisions of this statement, some of which apply also to marketable securities carried as noncurrent assets or carried in unclassified balance sheets and which are discussed under the appropriate heading in Chapter 6:

An equity security encompasses any instrument representing ownership shares or the right to acquire or dispose of ownership shares in an enterprise. This definition specifically excludes convertible bonds, treasury stock, and redeemable preferred stock.

The statement basically requires that marketable equity securities held by enterprises in industries that do not have specialized accounting practices (e.g., investment companies, security brokers and dealers, stock life insurance companies, and fire and casualty insurance companies) shall be stated at the lower of cost or market.

For those securities classified as current assets by the enterprise, market value changes recognized in applying the lower-of-cost-or-market rule are to be included in the determination of net income. This will be accomplished by use of a "valuation allowance" which will generally represent the net unrealized loss in the portfolio. Marketable securities classified as current are treated as one portfolio and those shown as noncurrent are considered a separate portfolio.

The lower-of-cost-or-market approach is based on the aggregate value of the portfolio of marketable equity securities rather than on the values of individual securities. A parent must group its securities with those of its consolidated subsidiaries (other than those in industries with specialized accounting practices) for the current and noncurrent classification.

Companies in certain industries where specialized acccounting practices are applied for marketable securities generally are not required to change their reporting practices for gains or losses on marketable securities. However, those that carry their marketable equity securities on the basis of cost would be required to change to the lower of cost or market for those securities, except that they could adopt the market basis of accounting where that basis is an accepted alternative.

When a subsidiary follows accepted accounting practices that differ from those of the parent company, those practices must be retained in the consolidated financial statements in which the subsidiaries are included. However, when the parent company does include realized gains and losses in net income, the accounting by the subsidiary must be adjusted in consolidation to conform to that of the parent company.

If there is a change in classification of a marketable security between current or noncurrent or vice versa, the security must be transferred at the lower-of-cost-or-market at the date of transfer. If the market value is less than cost it becomes the new cost basis and the write-down must be charged to income as if it were a realized loss.

The following disclosures are required:

1. Aggregate cost and market value of the separate portfolios as of the balance sheet date, with identification as to which is the carrying amount.
2. Gross unrealized gains or losses related to market value over cost or cost over market value for all marketable equity securities in the portfolio.
3. Net realized gain or loss included in income determination, the basis on which cost was determined and the change in the valuation allowance that has been included in the equity section of the balance sheet during the period and, when a classified balance sheet is presented, the amount of such change included in the determination of net income.

Post balance sheet changes in market prices or realized gains and losses shall not be cause for adjusting the financial statements although the effect of significant post balance sheet realized and unrealized gains and losses should be disclosed.

An exception to the general practice of valuing marketable securities at cost can be found in the stock brokerage industry where traditional thinking of necessity gave way to operating realities and needs. In this industry it was agreed that it was appropriate to carry marketable securities, including those held as investments, at market quotations and that it was also appropriate in this industry to carry securities which are not readily marketable at fair values.

The 1975 Annual Report of Reynolds Securities states:

Securities owned and securities sold—not yet purchased are carried at market value and the unrealized gains and losses on these securities are reflected in revenues.

"Specialized" industries, such as insurance, which have evolved their own methods of dealing with marketable securities are similarly unaffected by SFAS 12.

Implications for analysis

While SFAS 12 has, in general, improved the accounting for "certain" marketable securities there remain many gaps and inconsistencies in that accounting of which the analyst must be aware.

The definition of equity securities in the statement is somewhat arbitrary and inconsistent. Often convertible bonds derive all or most of their value from their conversion feature (as has, indeed, been recognized by *APB Opinion 15* on "Earnings per Share") and are much more akin to equity securities than to debt instruments. Thus, the exclusion of these securities from the equity classification is not logical. Nor, for that matter, is there a sound reason for excluding from the valuation process debt securities and marketable mortgages which can fluctuate in value significantly either due to interest rate changes or to changes in credit standing. The continued carrying at cost and above market of debt obligations of issuers in default is particularly unwarranted.

SFAS 12 does not define when marketable securities should be carried as current and when as noncurrent thus introducing a degree of arbitrariness in the decisions of how change in the market value of such securities should be accounted for. It is by no means self-evident that the manner of classifying securities in the balance sheet should determine whether changes in their value are reflected in income or not. While the statement requires the transfer of a marketable security from one category to the next at the lower of cost or market, category switching could still allow a company some leeway in the determination of future results. In recent years, (1969–71), for example, Signal Companies switched the classification of marketable securities four times. In 1975 Home Oil Co. reduced its holdings in Atlantic Richfield Co. substantially and the reclassification of its remaining holdings to marketable securities from long-term investment resulted in a write-down of $1.7 million.

While the statement does not address the question of how "cost" is determined the analyst must be aware that a number of methods of determining the "cost" of marketable securities exists (e.g., specific identification, average, first-in-first out) and that they can affect reported results.

It should be noted that under this statement the valuation concept accorded to marketable securities is analogous to that of accounts receivable valuation, and inconsistent with the concept of valuation applied to inventories—where once they are written down subsequent write-ups are not allowed. The statement also introduces an inconsistent treatment of anticipating gains, whereby it is acceptable to anticipate gains except when that would result in a valuation higher than original cost.

The aggregation of unrealized gains and losses can have an inconsistent effect on income recognition as is demonstrated by the following examples:

	End of Year 1	
	Cost	Market
Security A	$10	$15
Security B	20	30
Security C	10	5
Security D	40	10
	$80	$60

Example 1.   According to the statement, a valuation allowance of $20 would be provided in Year 1. If Security D were sold in Year 2 (assuming no change in market prices), an additional loss of $10 would be recorded (actual loss of $30 less elimination of $20 allowance). Thus, the $30 loss will have been recognized over two years rather than one.

Example 2.   If Security C is sold for a realized loss of $5, in Year 2 (assuming no change in other market prices) the loss would be completely offset by a decrease in the allowance for unrealized losses and there would be no impact on net income.

Example 3.   Assume that at the end of Year 2 the portfolio of marketable securities is as follows:

	Cost	*Market*
Security A	10	20
Security B	20	30
Security C	10	25
	40	75

Any security or combination of securities can now drop a total of 35 in value before any loss will be recognized. Thus, Security B could drop to 5 and Security A to 10 (with C remaining unchanged) without any need for recognition of the loss. This is so because as long as the aggregate market value of the portfolio remains above cost no individual gains or losses are recorded.

Additional considerations and analytical implications that relate to the accounting for marketable securities not carried as current assets will be considered in Chapter 6.

The current market value of investments is always relevant to an assessment of management performance. The argument that unrealized gains are only "paper profits" which could melt away before the investments are actually sold or otherwise disposed of does not recognize the fact that management makes the decision to hold or sell. Thus, a reduction in unrealized appreciation of an investment is as much a loss as would be a similar size loss on inventories or on equipment which became prematurely obsolete.

The analyst should treat with suspicion the amortization of bond discount (i.e., write-up of bond by crediting income) of an issue which from all available evidence sells at a discount because of doubt as to the ultimate collectibility of the principal amount.

The analyst, aware of accounting principles governing the presentation of investments, must pay particular attention to their valuation. On the one hand they can be grossly undervalued on the balance sheet because of the convention prohibiting their write-up to market value no matter how obvious and soundly based such value may be.

On the other hand the analyst must be alert to impairment of market value which because of loose standards in practice may not be fully reflected on the financial statements. If separately disclosed, the income generated by the investment may, at times, provide a clue to its fair value.

While the recognition of profits in nonequity securities must, according to present theory, await realization (i.e., in most cases sale), losses must be taken when they are deemed to be permanent in nature. However, the criteria for determining when a loss is "permanent" in nature are indefinite and allow for much leeway. With hope springing eternal, such write-downs occur in practice only when the evidence of loss in value is overwhelming. Since proper disclosure requires that the market value of securities be indicated, the alert analyst will be on the lookout for this information so that he can exercise his own judgment regarding the proper value to assign to these securities for the purpose of his analysis.

RECEIVABLES

Receivables are amounts due arising generally from the sale of goods or services. They may also represent accrued amounts due, such as rents, interest, and so forth. Notes receivable represent a more formal evidence of indebtedness due, but this characteristic does not make them more readily collectible than accounts receivable. Generally speaking, notes receivable are more easily negotiable and pledged for loans than are accounts receivable and, consequently, are considered the more liquid of the two. As a practical matter this is, however, a superficial distinction.

Receivables classified as current assets should be reasonably expected to be realized or collected within a year or within the normal operating cycle of a business. *The normal operating cycle* is a concept which is important in the classification of items as current or noncurrent. The operating cycle generally encompasses the full circle of time from the commitment of cash for purchases until the collection of receivables resulting from the sale of goods or services. Exhibit 5–1 illustrates the concept.

If the normal collection interval of receivables is longer than a year (e.g., longer term installment receivables), then their inclusion as current assets is proper provided the collection interval is normal and expected for the type of business the enterprise is engaged in. Because of their nature, certain types of receivables require separate disclosure. Examples are: receivables from affiliated companies, officers, or employees.

Certain types of receivables are established without formal billing

EXHIBIT 5–1
Operating cycle

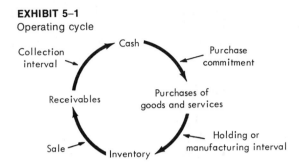

of the debtor. Thus, costs accumulated under a cost-plus-fixed-fee contract or some other types of government contracts are recorded as receivables as they accumulate.[1] Similarly, claims for tax refunds from the government are usually classified as receivables if no substantial question of technical compliance is involved.

To the financial analyst the valuation of receivables is important from two main points of view:

1. The realization value of the assets.
2. The impact on income.

These two aspects are, of course, interrelated. It is a fact supported by experience that not all receivables will be collected nor will they all necessarily be collected in their entirety.

While a judgment about the collectibility of any one account can be made at any appropriate time, the collectibility of receivables as a group is best estimated on the basis of past experience with due allowance for current conditions. The "accounting risk" here is that the past experience may not be an adequate measure of future loss or that current developments may not have been fully taken into account. The resulting loss can be substantial and will affect both the current asset position as well as the net income for the period under review.

ILLUSTRATION 1. Brunswick Corporation, in 1963, made a "special provision for possible losses on receivables" of $15,000,000 *after* taxes. The assumption is that factors which became clear in 1963 were not "visible" or obvious to the auditor at the end of 1962 when a substantial amount of the receivables provided for was outstanding. Management explained the write-off as follows:

"Delinquencies in bowling installment payments, primarily related to

---

[1] SEC *ASR 164* requires disclosure of amounts relating to long-term contracts included in receivables applicable to items billed but not paid under retainage provisions, items not yet billed or billable, and items representing claims subject to uncertainty as to their ultimate realization. Amounts expected to be collected after one year must also be disclosed.

some of the large chain accounts, *continued* at an unsatisfactory level. Nonchain accounts, which comprise about 80 percent of installment receivables, are generally better paying accounts.

"In the last quarter of 1963, average bowling lineage per establishment fell short of the relatively low lineage of the comparable period of 1962, resulting in an aggravation of collection problems on certain accounts. The bowling business may have felt the competition of outdoor activities associated with the unseasonably warm weather during the latter part of 1963. Some improvement in bowling lineage was noted in the early months of 1964 which tends to confirm this view. However, the fact that collections were lower in late 1963 contributed to management's decision to increase reserves. After the additional provision of $15,000,000, total reserves for possible future losses on all receivables amounted to $66,197,000, including $30,000,000 *transferred from defferred income taxes.* [Author's emphasis.]

While it may be impossible to define the precise moment when the collection of a receivable is doubtful enough to require provision, the question may be properly asked whether the analyst could not, in 1962, have made an independent judgment on the adequacy of the bad debt provision in the light of developments in the bowling industry with which he should have been thoroughly familiar. It should be noted that Brunswick's earnings peaked out in early 1962.

Another aspect of receivable valuation relates to long-term receivables which are noninterest bearing or which bear unrealistically low rates of interest.

APB Opinion No. 21—"Interest on receivables and payables"

Objective. The primary objective of this *Opinion* is to refine the manner of applying existing accounting principles when the face amount of a note (as defined below) does not reasonably represent the present value of the consideration given or received in an exchange.

The *Opinion* covers receivables and payables which represent contractual rights to receive or pay money on fixed or determinable dates. These are collectively referred to as "notes."

The *Opinion* does not apply to trade receivables and payables due within one year, progress payments, deposits, retainages, customary activities of lending institutions, notes which bear interest at rates prescribed by governmental agencies, or intercompany transactions.

Significant provisions. A note may be issued for cash or for property, goods, or services.

When issued for cash, a note is presumed to have a present value at issuance measured by the cash proceeds exchanged, unless other rights or privileges (stated or unstated) are included (such as the issuance of a noninterest bearing loan to a supplier who, in turn, charges less than the prevailing market price for products purchased by the lender under a contractual agreement).

When issued in a noncash transaction, the stated face amount of the note is generally presumed to represent the fair value of the consideration exchanged unless:

1. Interest is not stated,
2. The stated interest rate is unreasonable, or
3. The stated face amount of the note is materially different from the current sales price for the same or similar items or from the market value of the note at the date of the transaction.

When the stated face amount of the note does not represent the fair value of the consideration exchanged, the present value of the note must be established, taking into consideration:

1. The fair value of the consideration exchanged,
2. The market value of the note, or
3. The present value of all future payments.

The imputed rate of interest used for valuation purposes will normally be at least equal to the rate at which the debtor can obtain financing of a similar nature from other sources at the date of the transaction and may be influenced by:

1. An approximation of the prevailing market rates for the sources of credit that would provide a market for sale or assignment of the note;
2. The prime or higher rate for notes which are discounted with banks, giving due weight to the credit standing of the maker;
3. Published market rates for similar quality bonds;
4. Current rates for debentures with substantially identical terms and risks that are traded in open markets; or
5. The current rate charged by investors for first or second mortgage loans on similar property.

The difference between the present value and the face amount of the note should be treated as discount or premium and amortized as interest expense or income over the life of the note in such a way as to result in a constant rate of interest when applied to the amount outstanding at the beginning of any period (interest method).

The discount or premium should be reported in the balance sheet as a direct deduction from or addition to the face amount of the note.

Example of application of imputation of interest. The XYZ Corporation issued a noninterest bearing note (face amount $5,180) to Toro Machinery Company for purchase of machinery on August 17, 19X1. The face amount of the note is to be paid on July 31, 19X8. It is felt that for a similar type note an interest rate of 8 percent is applicable.

Toro Machinery Company will record as sales and as the receivable from XYZ, $3,032, representing the present value of $5,180 to be received on July 31, 19X8. Over the intervening periods, Toro Machinery will pick up as interest income the increases in the present value of the receivable from XYZ. If we assume that Toro's fiscal year-end is September 30, the pattern of interest income pickup on a yearly basis, and the carrying amounts of the receivable will be as follows:

Year	Month end	Face amount	Imputed interest income	Unamortized discount	Discounted value of receivable (rounded)
19X1	8	$5,180.00	—	$2,147.54	$3,032.00
19X1	9	5,180.00	$ 29.65	2,117.89	3,062.00
19X2	9	5,180.00	245.69	1,872.20	3,307.00
19X3	9	5,180.00	264.62	1,607.58	3,572.00
19X4	9	5,180.00	285.79	1,321.79	3,858.00
19X5	9	5,180.00	308.66	1,013.13	4,166.00
19X6	9	5,180.00	333.35	679.78	4,500.00
19X7	9	5,180.00	360.02	319.76	4,860.00
19X8	7	—	319.76	—	—
Total			$2,147.54		

Implications for financial analysis

The two most important questions facing the financial analyst with respect to receivables are:

1. Is the receivable genuine, due, and enforceable?
2. Has the probability of collection been properly assessed?

While the unqualified opinion of an independent auditor should lend assurance with regard to an affirmative answer to these questions, the financial analyst must recognize the possibility of an error of judgment as well as the lack of it.

1. The description of the receivables or the notes to the financial statement will usually not contain sufficient clues to permit an informed judgment as to whether a receivable is genuine, due, and enforceable. Consequently, a knowledge of industry practices and supplementary sources of information must be used for additional assurance.

In some industries, such as the phonograph record, toy, or bakery business, customers enjoy a substantial right of merchandise return, and allowance must be made for this.

ILLUSTRATION 2. The case of Topper Corporation, a manufacturer and marketer of toys, is quite instructive and should serve as a significant lesson and warning to financial analysts about the dangers inherent in the evaluation of accounts receivable.

In mid-1970 Topper issued a prospectus for the public sale of common stock. The 1970 calendar year financial statements indicated sales of $64 million and a terse footnote related to the accounts receivable of $31 million at 12/31/70 stated that "Approximately $14 million of sales made in December 1970 carried extended credit terms of five to eight months. The comparable amount for the prior year was $2 million."

While the credit terms granted under the December sales program were by no means unusual or excessively extended this "casual" footnote proved in retrospect to be an extraordinarily important piece of information for the analysts. For not only did the company, in its desire to report higher sales and earnings as a means to obtaining loans, grant its customers extended credit terms, free storage and substantial discounts, it also granted them substantial rights of merchandise return and exchange to the point where the risk of ownership did in effect not pass from Topper to its customers.

The auditors, who gave Topper a clean opinion for 1970, claimed that they first learned about letters giving Topper's customers the right of merchandise return only in early 1972 and a full year later withdrew their opinion on the 1970 financial statements.

In May 1972 Topper incurred huge write-downs of receivables and inventory and a year later was adjudged bankrupt. Losses to shareholders and to some large pension funds which extended credit on the basis of information contained in the 1971 prospectus were very substantial.

The analyst must be ever alert to the possibility that either "loose" agreements with customers by suppliers anxious to sell or swiftly changing demand conditions can seriously impair the collectibility of accounts receivable.

The following note to the financial statements appearing in the 1964 annual report of the O. M. Scott & Sons Company exemplifies the type of disclosure which does shed additional light on the contingencies to which receivables are subject:

Accounts receivable: Accounts receivable are stated net after allowances for returns, allowances, and doubtful accounts of $472,000 at September 30, 1964 ($640,000 at September 30, 1963).

Accounts receivable at September 30, 1964 include approximately $4,785,000 ($7,090,000 at September 30, 1963) for shipments made under a deferred payment plan whereby title to the merchandise is transferred to the dealer when shipped; however, the Company retains a security interest in such merchandise until sold by the dealer. Payment to the Company is due from the dealer as the merchandise is sold at retail. The amount of receivables of this type shall at no time exceed $11,000,000 under terms of the loan and security agreement. . . .

In some instances a receivable may not represent a true sale but rather a merchandise or service advance; they cannot be considered in the same light as regular receivables.

A sale of receivables with recourse does not effectively transfer the risk of ownership of the receivables. The analyst must be alert to accounting treatments which consider the risk as having passed to the buyer and which mention such sales as creating merely contingent liabilities for the seller.

2. Most provisions for uncollectible accounts are based on past experience, although they should also make allowance for current and emerging industry conditions. In actual practice the accountant is likely to attach more importance to the former than to the latter. The analyst must bear in mind that while a formula approach to the calculation of the provision for bad debts is convenient and practical for the accountant it represents a type of mechanical judgment which can easily overlook changing or emerging conditions. The analyst must use his own judgment and knowledge of industry conditions to assess the adequacy of the provision for uncollectible accounts (see example of the Brunswick Corporation earlier in this chapter).

Unfortunately, information that would be helpful in assessing the general level of collection risks in the receivables is not usually found in published financial statements. Such information can, of course, be sought from other sources or from the company directly. Examples of such information are:

1. What is the customer concentration? What percentage of total receivables is due from one or a few major customers? Would failure of any one customer have a material impact on the company's financial condition?
2. What is the age pattern of the receivables?
3. What proportion of notes receivable represent renewals of old notes?
4. Have allowances been made for trade discounts, returns, or other credits to which customers are entitled?

The financial analyst, in assessing the current financial position and a company's ability to meet its obligations currently, as expressed by such measures as the current ratio (discussed in Chapter 16), must recognize the full import of those accounting conventions which relate to the classification of receivables as "current." Thus, the operating cycle theory allows the inclusion of installment receivables which may not be fully collectible for years. In balancing these against current obligations, allowance for these differences in timing should be made.

INVENTORIES

With the possible exception of some service organizations, in most businesses inventories represent assets of great importance. From the point of view of the analyst of financial statements, inventories are significant for two main reasons:

1. They represent a significant, major component of the assets devoted to the conduct of the business.
2. They enter importantly in the determination of net income.

Asset valuation

Inventories are goods which are acquired for resale or which enter into goods produced for resale. In nonmanufacturing enterprises, such as retail establishments, purchased merchandise requires little or no additional work before resale. In manufacturing organizations we classify three main types of inventories:

1. Raw materials
2. Goods in process
3. Finished goods

depending on their stage of completion in the production process.

The importance attached to methods of inventory valuation and the controversies surrounding them is due primarily to the fact that they enter into the determination of the cost of goods sold and thus into the determination of net income. It is easy to understand why this is so. All material or goods purchased by an enterprise for resale are either sold or carried in inventory for use and sale at some future time. Thus, excluding material written off as worthless or missing, whatever is not on hand in the ending inventory must have been disposed of and, therefore, be part of the cost of goods sold and vice versa.

A most important factor to be recognized about accounting principles which govern the valuation of inventories is that they are primarily aimed at obtaining the best matching of cost and revenues. As a result of this orientation towards the income statement, the resulting, or residual, balance sheet inventory figure may be rendered inaccurate or even meaningless. This, as we shall see, can often be the case.

The basic principle of inventory valuation is that it be valued at "the lower-of-cost-or-market." This simple phrase belies the complexities and the variety of alternatives to which it is subject. This variety can, in turn, lead to significantly different figures of periodic income all "in accordance with generally accepted accounting principles."

What is cost?   The complexities of cost determination are caused by a diversity of assumptions and of practice in two main areas:

1. What is includable cost?
2. What assumptions do we make about the flow of inventory costs through an enterprise?

What is includable cost?   Let us start with a simple example. An office supply store buys a desk for resale. The invoice cost of the desk is obviously the basic cost. To that may properly be added the cost of freight-in as well as the costs of assembling the desk if that is the form in which it is kept in inventory. If the desk was imported, duty and other direct costs of clearing the desk through customs may properly be added. Suppose the president and others expend a great deal of time and effort in purchasing the desks. Should any part of the cost of their time be allocated to it, that is, inventoried if the desk is unsold at year-end? Here the answer is not so clear. Accounting principles would sanction allocation of such costs to inventories, but they would also sanction the current expensing of such costs. This will, of course, make a difference in the reported results for the year. Should expenses incurred in selling desks be added to their cost? Here there is more unanimity of view that such costs do not belong in inventory.

In spite of its importance, the matter of what costs are included in inventory or, conversely, excluded therefrom, is only rarely discussed or disclosed in published financial statements. The following example of disclosure, appearing in the 1967 annual report of the Eckmar Corporation, is an exception:

> *Note–inventories.* The carrying amounts of inventories as of December 31, 1967, include estimated amounts of costs, aggregating approximately $270,000, incurred for purchasing, freight, receiving, material handling, and warehousing applicable to materials and merchandise and for certain administrative functions considered to relate to manufacturing operations. Such costs previously had been charged to income when incurred. Inventories at December 31, 1967, also include certain items of supplies, amounting to approximately $30,000, not previously inventoried. The inclusion of these amounts in inventories as of December 31, 1967, had the effect of reducing cost of products and merchandise sold by approximately $150,000 and selling, administrative, and general expenses by approximately $150,000, and the net loss of the Corporation and subsidiaries for the year by approximately $300,000.

The need for this disclosure becomes clearer when we find that the auditor's opinion includes the following statement: "As explained in Note B to the financial statements, the Corporation revised as of December 31, 1967, its inventory policies to include in inventory additional amounts of overhead and supplies; our approval of these changes is conditioned upon the ability of the Corporation to recover such amounts in subsequent operations. In our opinion, subject (1) realization of the carrying amounts of inventories. . . ."

Consider the following note on inventories appearing in the 1976 financial statements of PPG Industries, Inc.:

> *Inventories.*   Most domestic and certain foreign inventories are stated at cost, using the last-in, first-out (Lifo) method, which is not in excess of market.

Other inventories are stated at the lower of cost or market. Cost is determined using either average or standard factory costs, which approximate actual costs, excluding certain fixed expenses such as depreciation and property taxes.

The exclusion of depreciation from inventories did not result in any comment on the part of the independent auditors.

It is important to understand the difference between the current expensing of a cost and its inclusion in inventory. The current expensing of a cost converts it into what is known as a "period cost," that is, a cost deemed to expire during the fiscal period in which it is incurred, rather than its continuance by virtue of its conversion into an asset. Conversely, a cost which is inventoried does not become a charge against current income and remains, instead as an asset to be charged against future operations which are presumed to benefit from it. It can be readily seen that a decision to inventory a cost rather than expense it *shifts* a charge to income from the present to the future.

Cost accounting

The foregoing desk inventory example was relatively simple because the inventory problem was that of a retailer. If we consider the cost problem of the desk manufacturer, additional complexities are introduced.

In producing the desk from its basic components, the manufacturer will incur three main types of cost:

1. Raw materials going into the desk.
2. Labor to produce and assemble the desk.
3. Indirect expenses such as wear and tear of machinery, auxiliary supplies, heat, light and power, various factory occupancy costs, supervisory costs, etc.

While the first two categories of expense may present some problems of classification, it is in the third group that we will find the greatest variety of treatments and the most problems. This category is also known as indirect expenses or overhead costs.

Overhead costs.   While it may be reasonably feasible to maintain control over the direct material and direct labor costs that go into the making of a desk, it is not practicable, if not impossible, to trace the specific overhead costs to the desk. This requires *allocation* of an entire pool of costs to the many products (e.g., desks, chairs, shelves, bookcases, etc.) which the manufacturer produces. This allocation requires a number of assumptions and decisions such as:

1. What items should be includable in overhead costs?
2. Over how many units (e.g., desks) do we allocate the overhead costs?

Includable costs in overhead. When we examine the costs which the retailer could include in the "cost per desk," we see that certain costs were generally accepted as includable while others were not clearly includable. In the area of manufacturing overheads, differences between theory and practice are even more prevalent because of the far greater variety of expenses involved and because of the wide variety of acceptable methods or because of practice which is not subject to meaningful restraints. In the matter of includable expenses, consider, for example, the following questions:

a. Should costs of testing new designs and materials of a desk be charged to inventories? If so, on what basis and over how many units?

b. Should general and administrative costs be included in inventory?

As of now there may be general acceptance of a number of ways in which to answer these questions. But there is by no means a single answer that is accepted more than all others.

Assumptions of activity. The allocation of overhead costs to all the desks, chairs, and other items produced must, of course, be done on a rational basis designed to get the best approximation of actual cost. However, this is far from an easy matter. The greatest difficulty stems from the fact that a good part of overhead represents "fixed costs," that is, costs which do not vary with production but vary mostly with the passage of time. Examples are rent payments and the factory manager's salary. Thus, assuming for a moment that only desks are produced, if the fixed costs are $100,000 and 10,000 desks are produced, each desk will absorb $10 of fixed costs. However, if only 5,000 desks are produced, each desk will have to absorb $20 of fixed costs. Clearly then, the level of activity itself is an important determinant of unit cost. In other words, wide fluctuations in output can result in wide fluctuations in unit cost.

Since the allocation of overhead depends also on an accurate estimate of total overhead costs which will be incurred during the period, variations between estimated and actual costs can also result in overabsorbed or underabsorbed overhead.

In order to allocate fixed costs over output, an assumption must be made at the outset of the fiscal period as to how many units (desks) the company expects to produce and that in turn will determine over how many units the overhead costs will be allocated. This procedure entails estimates of sales and related production. To the extent that the actual production differs from estimated production, the overhead will be either overabsorbed or underabsorbed. That means that production and inventory are charged with more than total overhead costs or with an insufficient amount of overhead costs.

A cost system which charges cost of goods sold and inventories with predetermined estimated costs is called a *standard cost* system. Variations between the estimates or standards and actual costs are called cost accounting variances. Generally speaking when an inventory is described as being valued at standard cost, that should mean that variances are insignificant or have been allocated or otherwise adjusted; in other words, standard costs would approximate actual costs. It is not permissible to carry inventories at only direct costs with the current expensing of all fixed overheads.

The next area of inventory cost determination which we will examine relates to assumptions regarding the *flow* of goods and their costs. While the methods used in this connection (Lifo, Fifo, average cost) are the most controversial methods associated with inventory accounting, it should be clear from the foregoing discussion that the problems of cost accounting and overhead allocations may produce even more variation in reported results than can the assumptions about cost flows.

Inventory cost flows

In order to keep the discussion simple let us return to our example of the office furniture retailer and assume that in the fiscal year ended December 31, 19X2, the inventory record of desks showed the following details:

Inventory on January 1, 19X2	100 desks @ $40	$ 4,000
First purchase in 19X2	200 desks @ $50	10,000
Second purchase in 19X2	100 desks @ $50	5,000
Third purchase in 19X2	200 desks @ $60	12,000
Total available for sale	600 desks	$31,000

Assuming that 50 desks are in inventory as at December 31, 19X2, how should they be valued?

There are a number of methods, all enjoying the "generally accepted" label, of which the three most common are discussed in the sections that follow.

First-in, first-out (Fifo). This method assumes what is probably the most common and justified assumption about the flow of goods in a business, that is, that those units bought first are sold (or used) first. This comforms also to the best inventory management practice. Under this method the 50 desks will be valued at $60 each, the unit cost of the last purchase, or $3,000. The resulting cost of goods sold is $28,000 ($31,000 representing the cost of all goods available for sale less $3,000 the value assigned to the ending inventory).

Last-in, first-out (Lifo). The assumption that the earliest purchases are the ones in inventory has been likened to the pile "flow" of
inventory. If an inventory consists of a pile of salt, or crushed rock or
coal, then the last quantity bought is likely to be the first removed and
sold. But this concern with a parallel to physical movement of inventories misses the real intention in inventory valuation. That relates
primarily to an assumption about the flow of *costs* rather than of physical units, and the flow of costs is chosen not because it parallels the
physical goods movement but rather because it achieves certain objectives of inventory valuation. The major objective of the Lifo method is
to charge cost of goods sold with the most recent costs incurred. Quite
obviously where the price level remains stable the results under either
the Fifo or the Lifo method will be much the same; but under a changing price level, as the advancing one in our example, the results in the
use of these methods will differ significantly. The use of the Lifo
method has increased greatly due to its acceptance for tax purposes.
Our tax law stipulates that its use for tax purposes makes mandatory its
adoption for financial reporting. The aim is to obtain a better matching
of current revenues with current costs in times of inflation. As will be
seen in the discussion of the effects of price level changes, this objective is not always achieved.

In our example the inventory of 50 desks under the Lifo method
will be valued at $40 each or $2,000. The cost of goods sold is $29,000
($31,000 − $2,000). The inventory figure of $2,000 on the balance
sheet will be one third below current market (or at least one third
below the latest cost), but the income statement will be more realistically presented in terms of matching current costs with current
revenues.

Average cost. The average cost method smoothes out cost fluctuation by using a weighted-average cost in valuing inventories and in
pricing out the cost of goods sold. While the weighted-average cost of
goods sold will depend on the timing of sales, we can, in this example,
consider the average cost of all purchases during the year and the
opening inventory. On that basis the average price per desk is $51.67
($31,000 ÷ 600), and the 50 desks will be valued at $2,583.50. The cost
of goods sold would be $28,416.50 ($31,000 − $2,583.50).

To summarize, under the three methods the following results are
obtained:

	Fifo	*Lifo*	*Average*
Ending inventory	$ 3,000.00	$ 2,000.00	$ 2,583.50
Cost of goods sold	28,000.00	29,000.00	28,416.50

Assuming that the sales of desks for the period amounted to $35,000,
the gross profit under each method would be as follows:

	Fifo	*Lifo*	*Average*
Sales	$35,000.00	$35,000.00	$35,000.00
Cost of goods sold	28,000.00	29,000.00	28,416.50
Gross profit	$ 7,000.00	$ 6,000.00	$ 6,583.50

It is clear that the choice of method (i.e., the assumption about cost flows) can make a significant difference in the determination of cost of goods sold and the valuation of inventories. Generally, the Fifo method provides a "good" inventory figure because it reflects the latest costs. The Lifo method, on the other hand, produces a better matching of costs and revenues. In times of changing prices, both virtues cannot be achieved simultaneously under the cost method.

A method of inventory valuation in use especially for interim statement results is the gross profit method. This method derives the inventory figure by estimating the cost of goods sold on the basis of a normal gross profit ratio experienced in practice. This method is accurate only if the gross profit ratio has in fact not changed and if there are no unusual inventory shortages or spoilage.

The retail method of inventory estimation is an extension of the gross profit method. It uses sophisticated techniques which involve physical inventory taking, priced first at retail, and the reduction of this inventory to cost by means of gross profit ratios.

Lifo and changing price levels

The accelerated inflation rate which started in 1973 renewed the business community's interest in the Lifo method. The rationale advanced for the flight to Lifo was that this method adjusts the financial statements for inflation. In fact it merely postpones the recognition of the effects of inflation although such postponement can be long-term if prices continue to rise and the Lifo inventory base is not liquidated. The major reason for the method's popularity is, of course, the long-term postponement of taxes under such conditions, which is a very real and tangible benefit.

The SEC has recognized the limited usefulness of Lifo as an adjuster for inflation and has, in *Accounting Series Release 151*, urged (but not required) disclosure by companies of "inventory profits," i.e., those resulting in time of rising prices from holding inventories and which are measured by the difference between historical costs and replacement costs at the time of sale. It has also called for disclosure of replacement cost (see Chapter 14) of inventories by certain companies.

A good way to understand the concept of inventory profits as well as the effect of changing price levels is to trace the operating results recorded under different inventory methods. The following examples and analysis are designed to accomplish this.

ILLUSTRATION 3.   The effects of price level changes on reported earnings under different inventory costing methods.

Following are inventory purchase costs and selling prices for quarterly periods starting with the fourth quarter of 19X2. It is assumed that prices rise steadily in the first, second, and third quarter of 19X3, that they level off in the fourth quarter, and decline in the first quarter of 19X4. It is also assumed—for simplicity's sake—that the Company's markup on cost is given as a constant $200 and that the Company holds three units in inventory at all times and buys and sells one unit each quarter.

	4thQ 19X2	1stQ 19X3	2dQ 19X3	3dQ 19X3	4thQ 19X3	1stQ 19X4
Selling price	$1,300	$1,400	$1,500	$1,600	$1,600	$1,500
Inventory purchase cost	$1,100	1,200	1,300	1,400	1,400	1,300

The following tables show the results under the three inventory costing methods, Fifo, Lifo and weighted average. The tables show cost of inventory on hand at the start of each quarter and also the gross profit recorded under the three methods.

TABLE 1
Fifo inventories on hand

Start of	Purchased						Balance sheet amount of inventory
	4thQ 19X2	1stQ 19X3	2dQ 19X3	3dQ 19X3	4thQ 19X3	1stQ 19X4	
2dQ 19X3	$1,100	$1,200	$1,300				= $3,600
3dQ 19X3		1,200	1,300	$1,400			= 3,900
4thQ 19X3			1,300	1,400	$1,400		= 4,100
1stQ 19X4				1,400	1,400	$1,300	= 4,100

TABLE 2
Fifo gross profit recorded

	2dQ 19X3	3dQ 19X3	4thQ 19X3	1stQ 19X4
Sales	$1,500	$1,600	$1,600	$1,500
Cost	1,100	1,200	1,300	1,400
(Purchased)	(4thQ-X2)	(1stQ-X3)	(2dQ-X3)	(3dQ-X3)
Gross Profit	$ 400	$ 400	$ 300	$ 100

TABLE 3
Lifo inventories on hand

Start of	Purchased						Balance sheet amount of inventory
	4thQ 19X2	1stQ 19X3	2dQ 19X3	3rdQ 19X3	4thQ 19X3	1stQ 19X4	
2dQ 19X3	$1,100	$1,200	$1,300				= $3,600
3dQ 19X3	1,100	1,200		$1,400			= 3,700
4thQ 19X3	1,100	1,200			$1,400		= 3,700
1stQ 19X4	1,100	1,200				$1,300	= 3,600

TABLE 4
Lifo gross profit recorded

	2dQ 19X3	3dQ 19X3	4thQ 19X3	1stQ 19X4
Sales	$1,500	$1,600	$1,600	$1,500
Cost	1,300	1,400	1,400	1,300
(Purchased)	(2dQ-X3)	(3dQ-X3)	(4thQ-X3)	(1stQ-X4)
Gross Profit	$ 200	$ 200	$ 200	$ 200

TABLE 5
Average cost inventories on hand

	Opening average cost[1]	Purchased						Balance sheet amount of inventory
		4thQ 19X2	1stQ 19X3	2dQ 19X3	3dQ 19X3	4thQ 19X3	1stQ 19X4	
2d Q 19X3..	—	$1,100	$1,200	$1,300				= $3,600
3d Q 19X3..	$2,400[2]				$1,400			= 3,800
4thQ 19X3..	2,533.3[3]					$1,400		= 3,933.3
1stQ 19X4..	2,622.2[4]						$1,300	= 3,922.2

[1] Balance sheet value of Inventory − Average cost of goods sold (B/S value ÷ 3)
[2] $3,600 − (3,600 ÷ 3) = 3,600 − 1,200 = $2,400
[3] 3,800 − (3,800 ÷ 3) = 3,800 − 1,266.7 = 2,533.3
[4] 3,933.3 − (3,933.3 ÷ 3) = 3,933.3 − 1,311.1 = 2,622.2

Average cost gross profits recorded

	2dQ 19X3	3dQ 19X3	4thQ 19X3	1stQ 19X4
Sales	$1,500	$1,600	$1,600	$1,500
Cost (average)	1,200	1,266.7	1,311.1	1,307.4[5]
Gross Profit	$ 300	$ 333.3	$ 288.9	$ 192.6

[5] Balance sheet value of inventory ÷ 3 = $3,922.2 ÷ 3 = $1,307.4

Analysis. *Under Fifo,* we note that the oldest cost in inventory at the start of the second quarter of 19X3, $1,100 is the first to be sold in that quarter. Compared with a sale price of $1,500, this produces a gross profit of $400.

This $400 is really composed of two elements. There is the normal $200 mark up on cost and an additional $200 resulting from the matching of an older, lower inventory cost with a current selling price. This $200 is the "inflation profit" so often referred to recently.

As long as the inflation rate remains unchanged, reported profits will include both the normal mark up of $200 and the inflation profit of $200. In the third quarter of 19X3, as the inflation continues, the gross profit remains at $400.

However, in the fourth quarter of 19X3, the price level remains unchanged from the third quarter. Following the established pattern, a higher priced Fifo inventory cost layer flows into cost of goods sold, but with the steady price level, the sales price does not rise and this results in a drop of

25 percent in gross profit to $300. In the first quarter of 19X4, there is a drop in price level, and both cost of new purchases and the sales price move down $100. The Fifo inventory system, however, continues as usual, to place the oldest unit (the item purchased for $1,400 in the third quarter of 19X3) into cost of goods sold to be matched against the reduced sale price of $1,500 with the gross profit dropping to $100.

Here then, is the vulnerability of Fifo. Inventory costs flow into cost of goods sold after a delay equal to the inventory turnover period. In periods of continuing inflation, this matching produces a continuous inflation of profit. When the rate of inflation declines, revenues should immediately reflect the change; costs will not. For the length of one inventory turnover period, costs will continue to reflect the earlier rate of inflation and will constantly increase. *Thus, any reduction in the rate of inflation will affect the profits of Fifo companies adversely.*

Under Lifo, we note that the gross profits reported are the same for all quarters and they equal the normal markup of $200. This is so because under the Lifo system, the most recent purchase is the first deemed to be sold. Thus, Lifo cost is close to current cost and the effects of inflation—both as the prices rise and as they fall—are largely eliminated from the income statement. Note, however, that in the real world, the correspondence between current cost and Lifo cost may not be quite as exact as in this illustration. However, there will rarely be any significant difference, unless there is a reduction in inventory *quantities*.

Thus, the Lifo inventory method will provide at least a temporary correction for the distorting effects of changing inflation rates, if purchases and sales are both made frequently and continually. In most cases, the price level at the time of the "last-in" purchase should be about the same as the price level at time of sale.

However, when purchases and sales are not closely linked, such as is the case with companies making seasonal purchases, the Lifo correction will not work. In this case, a time lag exists between purchase and sale. Reported income will tend to behave as if the company is on Fifo, even though it uses Lifo.

Under the average cost, we note that gross profits do vary with the price level, but not with as wide swings as under Fifo. This results because the time length of the time lag—in matching older costs with current revenues—is shorter under average cost than under Fifo, but longer than under Lifo. Thus, the inflation accounting problems of companies using average cost will be similar to those using Fifo, but the effects will be more moderate.

Inventory valuation at "market"

The inventory at cost must be compared with inventory at market and the lower of the two used.[2]

---

[2] The use of the lower of cost on market for Lifo inventories, while not permitted for tax purposes, can be used in the financial statements and would not violate the Internal Revenue Code requirement that if the tax return is on Lifo, reports to outsiders must also be on this basis.

"Market value" is defined as current replacement cost except that market shall not be higher than net realizable value nor should it be less than net realizable value reduced by the normal profit margin.

The upper limit of market value in effect considers the costs associated with sale or other disposition costs. The lower limit means that if the inventory is written down from cost to market it be written down to a figure that will insure the realization of a "normal" gross profit on its sale in a subsequent period.

Inventories under long-term contracts

The accumulation of costs under long-term contracts, reduced by progress billings, are in the nature of inventories. Two methods of accounting are acceptable here, but it is intended that their use should be dictated by surrounding circumstances.

1. Where estimates of the final outcome or results of the contracts are difficult or impossible to make and are too speculative to be reliable, the *completed-contract* method should be used. Under this method all costs of the contract, including related general and administrative costs, are accumulated and carried as assets (inventories) until completion of the contract when final net profit or loss is determined.
2. Where estimates of cost and related incomes at each stage of completion of the contract can be made, the *percentage-of-completion* method of long-term contract accounting should be used. Under this method the estimated proportionate profit earned up to any particular point in time may be credited to income and correspondingly included in accumulated costs (inventories).

Under either method, losses that are ascertainable at any point in time should be recognized and accounted for when first determined.

SEC *ASR164* requires separate disclosure of inventoried costs related to long-term contracts, methods of determining cost, methods of determining market, and description of method by which amounts are removed from inventory.

Classification of inventories

Generally, inventories are classified as current assets. Indeed they represent in most cases a very important part of the current asset group, although, ordinarily, they are considered less liquid than cash or receivables.

Under the "normal operating cycle" concept, inventories which would be kept beyond a year because of the requirements typical of an industry would nevertheless be classified as current. Thus, inventories in the tobacco industry or the liquor industry, which go through prolonged aging cycles, are nevertheless classified as current.

Inventories in excess of current requirements should not be classified as current.

ILLUSTRATION 4.   General Hobbies Corp. had the following footnote: Future operations (not covered by auditors' report):

> Inventory quantities at July 31, 1975 are considerably in excess of the Company's estimated requirements for the next fiscal year. In its continuing effort to reduce inventories and the related carrying costs, the Company is continuing its inventory reduction programs at prices which may result in a gross profit lower than that realized in prior years. These efforts may have a materially adverse effect on the Company's operations in the July 31, 1976 fiscal year.

IMPLICATIONS FOR FINANCIAL ANALYSIS

It is obvious that to the extent to which alternative choices of accounting principles, and the methods of their application, proliferate, the wider is management's flexibility in reporting results and in presenting the enterprise's financial condition. In the area of inventory accounting, where the impact of differing methods on income can be substantial, this flexibility is all the more likely to be availed of by management.

The auditor's opinion should provide assurance that certain minimum standards were upheld in the exercise of discretion with which such principles are applied. However, in some areas of inventory accounting the permitted leeway is so considerable that management can exercise a great deal of discretion in its choices. Thus, as a minimum, the financial analyst must understand what these choices are, and he must judge them in the light of conditions which apply to each specific situation.

With regard to inventories, the financial analyst will expect information and assurance as to the following:

1. Is the inventory physically in existence and is it fairly valued?
2. Has the accounting for inventories been consistent?
3. Can the effect of the different accounting methods used be measured?

Audit procedures designed to give assurance about the physical existence of inventories have been improving over the years and have been especially tightened up since the 1938 SEC hearings in the matter of McKesson & Robbins, Inc. In this case, large-scale fraud which resulted in a substantial overstatement of inventories was not uncovered by the audit primarily because no attempt was made by the auditors to establish physical contact with the inventories. The SEC stated:

> In our opinion, the time has come when auditors must, as part of their examination whenever reasonable and practicable, make physical contact with the inventory and assume reasonable responsibility therefor as had already become the practice in many cases before the present hearings. By this we do not mean that auditors should be, or by making such tests become, the guarantors of inventories any more than of any of the other items in the financial statements but we do mean that they should make all reasonable tests and inquiries, and not merely those limited to the books, in order to state their professional opinion, as auditors, as to the truthfulness of that item in the same way as they do for the other items in the statements.

The accounting profession responded by adopting the requirement that auditors observe the taking of physical inventories whenever it was reasonable and practicable to do so. This requirement, as well as the refinement of audit techniques, has brought about great improvements in the reliability of inventory audits. Nevertheless, exceptional cases still arise.

Thus, in the early 1970s Patterson Parchment Co. incurred a large inventory write-down because accountants in a key division counted the same inventory twice; Whittaker Corp. was forced to buy back two subsidiaries it sold because of multimillion inventory shortages discovered after their sale; and Cenco, Inc. was almost driven to insolvency because of inventory irregularities in a major division.

The fair statement of inventories is, of course, dependent not merely on a proper accounting for physical quantities but also on their proper pricing and summarization.

The analyst must be alert to the types of cost which are included in inventory. For example, under Internal Revenue Regulations adopted in 1975 marketing, sales, advertising and distribution expenses, interest costs, past service pension costs, and general and administrative costs pertaining to overall, rather than only to manufacturing activities, must be excluded from the overhead included in inventory under a full-absorbtion cost system. A reading of footnotes can reveal the inclusion of unusual costs. Sperry Rand, for example, included "learning curve" costs in inventories under a concept which involves deferral of costs early in a production cycle in the expectation that, with experience, subsequent costs will be reduced. However, should such expectations not materialize, future write-offs will occur:

> At September 30 and March 31, 1975, gross inventories included approximately $136,900,000 and $127,500,000, respectively, of costs related to long-term contracts or programs. The aggregate of deferred or other costs under

long-term contracts which exceeded the estimated average costs of all the units expected to be produced (learning curve concept) and included in inventories at September 30, 1975, and March 31, 1975, was not material.

While under the going-concern convention accountants are not concerned with the sale of inventories other than in the normal course of business, the analyst, and especially the credit analyst concerned with current values, may be interested in the composition of inventories. Thus, raw material may be much more readily salable than work in process since once raw material is converted into parts of certain specifications, it rapidly loses its value in case it then has to be liquidated.

Accepted reporting standards (which are part of generally accepted auditing standards) require that changes in the application of accounting principles be noted and the impact of the change reported. Thus, in audited financial statements the analyst will expect to be alerted to changes in principles of inventory accounting, such as, for example, from Lifo to Fifo. However, the analyst must be aware of the fact that changes in accounting principles call for a consistency exception, whereas other changes affecting comparability do not necessarily call for disclosure in the auditor's report.

Of the various inventory methods in use Lifo is the most complex and in addition has not only bookkeeping implications for management but behavioral ones as well. Thus, for example, in the case of Lifo the year-end inventory level makes a definite difference in results and management must plan and act accordingly.

The analyst must realize that the Lifo method of inventory accounting is not unitary but has rather many variations which can produce different results. It can be applied to all inventory components or to only a few.[3] It can be applied to material costs while other inventory methods are used for labor and overhead costs. Footnotes which merely disclose the variety of methods in use without giving breakdowns of respective inventory amounts lack analytical value.

The Lifo method permits income manipulation and analysts must be ever alert to this possibility. For example, changing purchasing policy at the end of the year can affect reported results. This is not possible under Fifo.

ILLUSTRATION 5.   The following purchases occurred in 19X1:

January to June	7,000 widgets at $1 per unit
July to November	5,000 widgets at $1.20 per unit
December	2,000 widgets at $1.30 per unit

---

[3] Some meat packers, for example, have used Lifo for pork but not for beef and lamb.

The ending inventory consisted of 1,000 units. Under Lifo these would be reported at a cost of $1 per widget. Now, assume the enterprise had purchased 3,000 widgets in December—an additional 1,000. The additional purchase would have cost $1,300 but the additional ending inventory would have been only $1,000 thus decreasing profits by $300. Under different conditions the act of buying more widgets could have increased profits.

When a reduction in the Lifo inventory quantities (base) takes place, old Lifo costs are matched with current revenues thus resulting in increased profit margins.

ILLUSTRATION 6. Assume that the widget company shows the results below for 19X2

Sales (2,000 @ $1.375)		$2,750
Cost of Sales:		
Beginning Lifo inventory (1,000 @ $1.00)	$1,000	
Purchases (2,000 @ $1.10)	2,200	
Ending Lifo inventory (1,000 @ $1.00)	(1,000)	2,200
Gross profit		$ 550
Gross profit percentage		20%

Assume that in 19X3 the company continues the policy of marking up widgets by 25 percent and that purchase and selling prices increase by 10 percent. However, a strike during the year prevents replacement of widget inventory and this part of the Lifo base is liquidated. As can be seen below this will increase profit margins as follows:

Sales (2,000 @ $1.5125)		$3,025
Cost of sales:		
Beginning Lifo inventory (1,000 @ $1.00)	$1,000	
Purchases (1,500 @ $1.21)	1,815	
Ending Lifo inventory (500 @ $1.00)	(500)	2,315
Gross profit		$ 710
Gross profit percentage		23.5%

In the same fashion managements can by deliberate action manipulate profit levels by dipping into Lifo inventory pools. Analysts must watch for disclosure of such charges. An example is the following forthright disclosure by DuPont:

If inventory values were shown at current cost (determined by the average cost method) rather than at Lifo values, inventories would have been $410.6 million and $382.7 million higher than reported at December 31, 1975, and December 31, 1974, respectively. During 1975 inventory quantities were reduced from the abnormally high year-end 1974 level. This reduction resulted in a liquidation of Lifo inventory quantities carried at lower costs prevailing in prior years as compared with 1975 costs, the effect of which increased net income by approximately $38.9 million, or 81 cents per share.

While spotting an undisclosed Lifo inventory chargeout is not always easy a crude check which the analyst can apply is to see whether the dollar value of the Lifo inventory has declined on a year-to-year basis. Moreover, information about such changes can also be found in the "Management's Discussion and Analysis of Results of Operations" section of published financial reports. It is important for the analyst to determine whether a Lifo inventory liquidation was temporary or permanent.

The analyst must be particularly wary about the reliability of quarterly results published by companies using Lifo. By definition of the tax laws Lifo is an *annual* calculation. Thus, at interim periods the preparation of quarterly statements requires forecasts of costs of inventory items purchased or produced as well as projections of future changes in inventory quantities and mix within the entire year. These estimates are bound to be subjective and thus subject to managerial manipulation. Chapter 22 contains a more extensive discussion of problems associated with interim reports.

As is clear from the discussion above and the example which will follow, the Lifo inventory method understates inventories significantly in times of rising price levels thus understating a company's debt-paying ability (as measured, for example, by the current ratio). It overstates inventory turnover and in addition contains the means of income manipulation. One defense available to the analyst is to adjust Lifo statements to the approximate pro-forma situation which would exist had they been prepared on a Fifo basis. This is possible when the current cost of Lifo inventories is disclosed, a disclosure now becoming increasingly available.

ILLUSTRATION 7.   Assume the following disclosure:

	Lifo	Current cost
Beginning inventory	$120	$140
Ending inventory	$150	$190

To make the adjustments the following steps are necessary:

1. Increase the inventory by the excess of the current cost over the Lifo cost.
2. Increase the current liability for deferred income taxes by the excess as determined in (1) above times the tax rate (approximately 50 percent).[4]

---

[4] If no such liability category exists one should be inserted. The reason for the tax deferral is that the pro forma balance sheet reflects an accounting method that differs from that used on the tax return (see also chapter 11).

3. Increase retained earnings by the balance (approximately 50 percent) of the excess.

To summarize;

	Beginning of period	End of period
Inventory	+$20	+$40
Deferred income taxes	+$10	+$20
Retained earnings	+$10	+$20

The income statement adjustments are as follows:

4. Increase cost of goods sold by the amount of the increase in the beginning inventory ($20).
5. Decrease cost of goods sold by the amount of the increase in ending inventory ($40).
6. The income before taxes will reflect the net change in the cost of goods sold. Thus the net decrease ($20) in the cost of goods sold will increase net income before taxes.
7. Increase income taxes by the effect in (6) above times the appropriate tax rate (here assumed at 50%) − $10.
8. Increase net income by the balance remaining after deducting (7) from (6) above − $10.

To summarize:

Cost of goods sold	−$20
Income before income taxes	+$20
Income taxes	+$10
Net income	+$10

The shorter the inventory turnover period the more reliable the above pro forma computations will be.

Analysts, such as lending officers or investors with clout, who have access to managements can ask additional questions about Lifo inventories as follows:

1. How are Lifo inventories calculated: on an item by item basis or by use of dollar value pools (in which different items are grouped)?
2. Was income affected by changes in inventory pools and if so by how much? Was it affected by year-end purchasing decisions?
3. Did the company record extra expenses or losses in order to offset income arising from the involuntary liquidation of Lifo inventories?
4. What assumptions concerning Lifo inventories underlie the quarterly reported results?

The "lower-of-cost-or-market" principle of inventory accounting has additional implications for the analyst. In times of rising prices it tends to undervalue inventories regardless of the cost method used. This in turn will depress the current ratio below its real level since the other current assets (as well as the current liabilities) are not valued on a consistent basis with the methods used in valuing inventories.

It is a fact that most published reports contain insufficient information to allow the analyst to convert inventories accounted for under one method to a figure reflecting a different method of inventory accounting. Most analysts would want such information in order to be able to better compare the financial statements of companies which use different inventory accounting methods.

To illustrate the effect which the use of a variety of inventory methods can have on reported net income or financial ratios, let us examine the case of a retailer who deals in only one product. We assume here no opening inventory, operating expenses of $5 million, and 2 million shares outstanding. The following purchases are made during the year:

	Units	Per Unit	
January	100,000	$10	$ 1,000,000
March	300,000	11	3,300,000
June	600,000	12	7,200,000
October	300,000	14	4,200,000
December	500,000	15	7,500,000
Total	1,800,000		$23,200,000

Ending inventory at December 31 was 800,000 units. Assets, excluding inventories, amounted to $75 million, of which $50 million were current. Current liabilities amounted to $25 million, and long-term liabilities came to $10 million.

The tabulation which follows shows the net income arrived at by

Computation of net income

	Fifo method	Lifo method	Average costs
Sales:			
1 million units @ 25	$25,000,000	$25,000,000	$25,000,000
Cost of sales:			
Beginning inventory	—	—	—
Purchases	$23,200,000	$23,200,000	$23,200,000
Cost of goods available for sale	$23,200,000	$23,200,000	$23,200,000
Less: Ending inventory	11,700,000	9,100,000	10,312,000
Cost of sales	$11,500,000	$14,100,000	$12,888,000
Gross profit	$13,500,000	$10,900,000	$12,112,000
Operating expenses	5,000,000	5,000,000	5,000,000
Net income	$ 8,500,000	$ 5,900,000	$ 7,112,000
Net income per share	$4.25	$2.95	$3.56

applying the Fifo, Lifo, and average cost method respectively. Sales are at $25 per unit, and taxes are ignored.

The Fifo inventory computation was based upon 500,000 units at $15 and 300,000 at $14 which yields a total of $11,700,000. The Lifo inventory cost was obtained following the assumption that the units purchased last were the first sold. Therefore, the 800,000 units are priced as 100,000 units at $10, 300,000 units at $11, and 400,000 units at $12, totaling $9,100,000. The average cost was obtained by dividing $23,200,000 by 1,800,000 units purchased, yielding an average unit price of $12.89. The $12.89 unit price multiplied by 800,000 ending inventory units gives a total inventory cost of $10,312,000.

The table below shows the effect of the three inventory methods on a number of selected ratios:

	Fifo method	Lifo method	Average costs
Current ratio	2.47:1	2.36:1	2.41:1
Debt equity ratio	1:5.17	1:4.91	1:5.03
Inventory turnover	2:1	3:1	2.5:1
Return on total assets	9.8%	7.0%	8.3%
Gross margin	54%	44%	49%
Net profit as % of sales	34%	24%	29%

As the above discussion and examples clearly show, the analysis of financial statements where inventories are important requires that the analyst bring to bear a full understanding of inventory accounting methods and their impact on results.

QUESTIONS

1. Under presently accepted but changing practice, compensating balances under a bank loan agreement are considered as unrestricted cash and are classified as current assets.
   a. From the point of view of the analyst of financial statements, is this a useful classification?
   b. Give reasons for your conclusion and state how you would evaluate such balances.

2. a. What are some of salient provisions of SFAS 12?
   b. What are the disclosures required by SFAS 12?

3. What are some of the gaps and inconsistencies in SFAS 12 of which the analyst must be aware?

4. a. What is meant by the "operating cycle"?
   b. What is the significance of the operating cycle concept to the classification of current versus noncurrent items in the balance sheet?
   c. Is this concept useful to those concerned with measuring the current debt-paying ability of an enterprise and the liquidity of its working capital components?

    d. Give the effect of the operating cycle concept on the classification of selected current assets in the following industries:

      (1) Tobacco.

      (2) Liquor.

      (3) Retailing.

5. *a.* What are the financial analyst's primary concerns when it comes to the evaluation of accounts receivable?

    b. What information, not usually found in published financial statements, should the analyst obtain in order to assess the overall risk of noncollectibility of the receivables?

6. Why do financial analysts generally attach such great importance to inventories?

7. Comment on the effect which the variety of accounting methods for determining the cost of inventories have on the determination of an enterprise income. As to the inclusion of which costs in inventories, is there considerable variation in practice? Give examples of three types of such cost elements.

8. Of what significance is the *level* of activity on the unit cost of goods produced by a manufacturer? The allocation of overhead costs requires the making of certain assumptions. Explain and illustrate by means of an example.

9. What is the major objective of Lifo inventory accounting? What are the effects of this method on the measurement of income and of inventories particularly from the point of view of the user of the financial statements?

10. Comment on the disclosure with respect to inventory valuation methods which is practiced today. In what way is such disclosure useful to the analyst? What type of disclosure is relatively useful to the reader?

11. Accountants generally follow "the lower-of-cost-or-market" basis of inventory valuations.

    a. Define "cost" as applied to the valuation of inventories.

    b. Define "market" as applied to the valuation of inventories.

    c. Why are inventories valued at the lower of cost or market? Discuss.

    d. List the arguments against the use of the lower-of-cost-or-market method of valuing inventories. (AICPA)

12. Compare and contrast effects of the Lifo and Fifo inventory cost methods on earnings during a period of inflation. (C.F.A.)

13. Discuss the ways and conditions under which the Fifo and Lifo inventory costing methods produce different inventory valuations. Do not discuss procedures for computing inventory cost.

14. What are some of the important questions about Lifo inventories that lending officers and investors with clout can ask?

6

ANALYSIS OF NONCURRENT ASSETS

In this chapter we conclude our examination of the measurement of assets by a discussion of the analysis of noncurrent assets.

LONG-TERM INVESTMENTS

Long-term investments are usually investments in assets such as debt instruments, equity securities, real estate, mineral deposits, or joint ventures acquired with longer term objectives in mind. Such objectives may include the ultimate acquisition of control or affiliation with other companies, investment in suppliers, securing of assured sources of supply, and so forth.

Marketable securities

With the exception of the accounting for investments in common stock of certain sizes, which is discussed below, and of convertible bonds, preferred shares with a stated redemption value and nonequity securities, marketable equity securities classified as noncurrent assets or shown in balance sheets of enterprises which issue unclassified balance sheets (e.g., finance or real estate companies), are now accounted for in accordance with the provision of SFAS 12, the salient points of which are covered in the "Marketable Securities" section of Chapter 5.

The following provisions of SFAS 12 apply to the equity securities not classified as current:

Market value changes are to be reflected directly in the equity section of the balance sheet and are not to enter the determination of net income except where the change is other than temporary. Marketable equity securities held by enterprises that issue unclassified balance sheets are to be regarded as noncurrent.

For those marketable equity securities not classified as current assets (including marketable securities in unclassified balance sheets), a determination must be made as to whether a decline in market value as of the balance sheet date for each individual security is other than temporary. If the decline is other than temporary, the cost basis is to be written down, as a realized loss, to a new cost basis. The new cost basis is not to be changed for subsequent recoveries in market value.

Accumulated changes in the valuation allowance of noncurrent marketable securities shall be included in the equity section of the balance sheet and presented separately.

The valuation allowance which may be called "net unrealized loss on noncurrent marketable equity securities" can be reduced for subsequent recoveries in market value, but at no time should the aggregate of marketable securities be carried on the balance sheet at an amount in excess of original cost.

Investments in common stock

Investments in common stock representing less than 20 percent of the equity securities of the investee must be accounted for in accordance with SFAS 12 as detailed above and in the preceding chapter.

Companies 20 percent to 50 percent owned. APB Opinion No. 18 concluded that even a position of less than 50 percent of the voting stock may give the investor the ability to exercise significant influence over the operating and financial policies of the investee. When such an ability to exercise influence is evident, the investment should be accounted for under the "equity method." Basically this means at cost plus the equity in the earnings or losses of the investee since acquisition, with the addition of certain other adjustments. The mechanics of the equity method are discussed in Chapter 9.

Evidence of the investor's ability to exercise significant influence over operating and financial policies of the investee may be indicated in several ways, such as management representation and participation, but in the interest of uniformity of application the APB concluded that in the absence of evidence to the contrary, an investment (direct or indirect) of 20 percent or more in the voting stock of an investee should lead to the presumption of an ability to exercise significant influence over the investee. Conversely, an investment in less than 20 percent of the voting stock of the investee leads to the presumption of a lack of such influence unless the ability to influence can be demonstrated.

It should be noted that while the eligibility to use the equity method is based on the percentage of voting stock outstanding, which may include, for example, convertible preferred stock, the percentage of earnings which may be picked up under the equity method depends on ownership of *common stock* only.

ILLUSTRATION 1. Company A owns 15 percent of the common stock of Company B. By virtue of additional holdings of convertible preferred stock, the total percentage of voting power held is 20 percent. While the total holdings entitle Company A to account for its investment in Company B at equity, it can only pick up 15 percent of Company B residual income because that is the percentage of ownership of *common* stock that it holds.

The above principle of picking up income under the equity method is not consistent with the concept of "common stock equivalents" used in the computation of earnings per share (see Chapter 12). The effect of possible conversions, etc. must, however, be disclosed.

Corporate joint ventures.   Joint ventures represent investments by two or more entities in an enterprise with the objective of sharing sources of supply, the development of markets, or other types of risk. A common form of joint venture is a 50–50 percent sharing of ownership, although other divisions of interest are also found. An investment in a *corporate* joint venture should, according to *APB Opinion No. 18,* be accounted for by the equity method. An investment in a joint venture not evidenced by common stock ownership may presumably be accounted for at cost.

Overview of how investments in common stock are accounted for.   Exhibit 6–1 presents a summary indicating how investments in common stock of different sizes are accounted for under *APB Opinion No. 18* and other pronouncements governing the principles of consolidation accounting.

Dealing with special risks

In the case of holdings of certain securities additional disclosures may be required because of special circumstances. Thus, in view of the city of New York's financial problems, including the moratorium on repayment of certain of its short-term obligations, the creation of the Municipal Assistance Corporation of the City of New York and related action by the legislature and Congress, the SEC adopted (in *ASR 188*) disclosure requirements with respect to certain of the securities affected by the moratorium (which has, since, been upset by the courts.)

EXHIBIT 6-1
Summary of accounting treatments by investor for investments in common stocks
Size of investment
in a given investee

0% ─┐
                Investors should, with certain exceptions, account for investments
                in marketable equity securities at the lower of cost or market.

20% ─┤
                Ownership of 20 percent or more of voting stock leads to the
                presumption that investor has the ability to influence operating
                and financial policies of the investee. In such cases the equity
                method should be used *(APB Opinion No. 18)*. Otherwise the
                accounting for investment positions of less than 20 percent is
                indicated (see above).

                Corporate joint ventures should be accounted for under the equity
50% ─┤   method *(APB Opinion No. 18)*.

                Subsidiaries (i.e., companies over 50 percent owned) should be
                consolidated. In certain cases use of the "equity method" may
                be appropriate. In case of serious doubt regarding the ultimate
                transferability or realization of subsidiary earnings, the "cost
                method" may be used (see discussion in Chapter 9).

100% ─┘

Implications for analysis

The analyst, aware of accounting principles governing the presentation of investments, must pay particular attention to their valuation. On the one hand they can be grossly undervalued on the balance sheet because of the convention prohibiting their write-up to market value, (except in certain industries) no matter how obvious and soundly based such value may be.

On the other hand the analyst must be alert to impairment of market value which, because of loose standards in practice, may not be fully reflected on the financial statements. If separately disclosed, the income generated by the investment may, at times, provide a clue to its fair value.

In Chapter 5 we considered some of the overall flaws and inconsistencies in the accounting for marketable securities brought on by SFAS *12*. Considered hereunder are some further considerations pertaining to the accounting for marketable securities not carried as current assets which the analyst must be aware of.

Statement 12 does require the write-down of marketable securities classified as noncurrent to market with a charge to income in cases where the change in value is deemed to be other than temporary. However, there is no agreement as to what constitutes "temporary" in this context. While the accounting profession has issued some guidelines of how to audit the carrying amounts of marketable securities (*Journal of Accountancy*, April 1975, p. 69) they by no means insure logical and consistent procedures in this regard. Thus practice will in all probability reflect arbitrary determinations which will make the carrying of marketable securities by one company not comparable to that of another. The analyst must also bear in mind that equity securities of companies in which the enterprise has a 20 percent or larger interest, and in some instances an even smaller interest than 20 percent, need not be adjusted to market but must instead be carried at equity which may at times be significantly below, and at other times above market. Thus, with regard to such relatively substantial blocks of securities the values at which they are carried on the balance sheet may be substantially in excess of their realizable values.

The creation of a new category in the equity sector of the balance sheet where the "net unrealized loss on noncurrent marketable securities" is lodged must be regarded as a somewhat regressive step. One of the achievements of *APB Opinion 9* was the elimination, except in cases of prior year adjustments, of direct charges of losses to equity accounts. SFAS *12*, brings us back, even if under different circumstances, to an area we were glad to leave in 1966.

The accounting for investments in substantial blocks of *common stock* has undergone significant improvement. The carrying of investments representing control of 20 percent or over at equity is an improvement over the practice which prevailed prior to the issuance of *APB Opinion No. 18*—that of carrying such investments at cost. While the equity method is more realistic than cost, it must be borne in mind that it is not the equivalent of fair market value which, depending on circumstances, may be significantly larger or lower than the carrying amount at equity.

The analyst must remember that the assumption that an investment in 20 percent or more of the voting securities of an investee results in significant influence over that investee is an arbitrary one which had to be made in the interest of accounting uniformity. If such influence is indeed absent, then there may be some question regarding the investor's ability to realize the amount stated at equity. The marketplace does not necessarily pay close attention to book values. An improvement brought about by *APB Opinion No. 18* is the requirement that where available, the market value of investments in common stock (other than in subsidiaries) be disclosed.

APB Opinion No. 18 states that "a loss in value of an investment which is other than a temporary decline should be recognized the same as a loss in value of other long-term assets." This leaves a great deal to judgment and interpretation, and in the past this approach has resulted in companies being very slow to recognize losses in their investments. Since the *Opinion* does not consider a decline in market value to be conclusive evidence of such a loss, the analyst must be alert to detect situations where hope rather than reason supports the carrying amount of an investment. It must be recognized that the equity method reflects only current operating losses rather than the capital losses which occur when the earning power of an investment deteriorates or disappears.

Another area where assumptions and management discretion influence accounting is that regarding the provision for taxes to be paid at some future time when earnings recognized under the equity method are distributed in the form of dividends by the investee to the investor. *APB Opinion No. 23,* "Accounting for Income Taxes—Special Areas," held that the nature of an investor's influence over an investee is significantly different from the influence exercised by a parent over a subsidiary and, consequently, the investor should provide for taxes that will be payable when the earnings of the investee are received or otherwise realized by the investor. Thus, whether taxes at regular or capital-gains rates are provided for remains a matter of judgment by management and the independent auditors.

In the case of joint ventures, *APB Opinion No. 23,* held that unless there are indications of a limited life for the joint venture, the same tax treatment as is applicable to subsidiaries should apply, that is, provision or nonprovision of taxes on unremitted earnings depends basically on management's judgment of whether these earnings are, or are not, to be permanently invested in the subsidiary or joint venture. Since the *Opinion* calls for disclosure of the tax provision which would have been made had permanent investment of earnings not been assumed, the analyst is not only able to form his own opinion regarding such probabilities but is also in a position to adjust for such taxes should his views of future probabilities differ from those of the reporting entity.

The accounting for other long-term investments (such as regular or convertible bonds) is presently not helpful to the analyst since historical cost is in most cases not relevant to decisions affecting the evaluation of profitability or of managerial performance. Moreover, the analyst must be alert to the overvaluation of longer term investments under the still persisting theory of lack of "permanent" impairment in value. Managements, as is well known, often take a very optimistic view of the final workout of their investments which have temporarily fallen in market value.

ACCOUNTING BY DEBTORS AND CREDITORS FOR TROUBLED DEBT RESTRUCTURINGS

SFAS 15 which is effective after December 31, 1977, specifies the accounting in situations where a creditor for economic or legal reasons related to a debtor's financial difficulties grants a concession to the debtor.

The statement divides troubled debt restructurings into two broad categories: (1) those in which the debtor transfers receivables, real estate, or other assets to the creditor or issues its stock or otherwise grants an equity interest to the creditor to satisfy the creditor's claim and (2) those in which the debt is continued but the terms are modified to defer or reduce cash payments the debtor is required to make to the creditor.

In cases falling under the first category both debtor and creditor are required to account for the fair value of assets transferred and equity interests granted in a troubled debt restructuring. The statement requires the debtors must recognize a gain and creditors a loss for a difference between those fair values and the recorded amount of the debt satisfied. Debtors must also recognize a gain or loss on assets transferred if their fair values differ from their recorded amounts.

The statement specifies that both debtor and creditor must account prospectively for the effects of modifications of terms of continuing debt as reduced interest expense or interest income for periods between the restructuring and maturity and should record no gain or loss at the time of restructuring. The one exception occurs when the total future cash payments specified by the new terms of the debt are less than the recorded amount of the debt at the time of restructuring. In that case, the debtor records a gain and the creditor records a loss to the extent of the differences.

Troubled debt restructurings which involve partial settlement by transfer of assets or grant of equity interests as well as modification of terms of the debt remaining outstanding after the restructuring are accounted for by combining the accounting for the two broad categories.

Implications for analysis

SFAS 15 raises serious questions for financial analysts regarding the realism and the validity of the accounting recommended therein.

The existing accounting framework of accounting for most receivables and payables, governed by *APB Opinions 21* and *26*, is based on the present value, at inception, of the cash flows embodied in them. SFAS *15*, in stressing form over substance, considers a modification of terms of debt to result in loss to the creditor (and gain to the debtor) only when the total future cash payments specified by the new terms of the debt (without regard to present value considerations) are less than the recorded amount of the debt. Thus, as shown in the following example, under SFAS *15* a loan which has been carried at $10,000,000 before a modification of terms will be carried as an asset of an identical amount after modification, even though its present value is 43 percent less.

	Before modification	After modification
Loan maturity	3 Years	10 Years
Effective interest rate	10%	3%
Total interest over life of loan	$ 3,000,000	$ 3,000,000
Principal amount of loan	$10,000,000	$10,000,000
Total Cash Receipts	$13,000,000	$13,000,000
Present value of total cash flow at market rate of interest (10%)	$10,000,000	$ 5,703,000

It is hard to understand how such disregard of reality can result in financial presentations which are useful to the analyst. In evaluating the carrying amounts of restructured loans, analysts, and particularly bank analysts, must be careful to question closely the basis of the computation.

TANGIBLE FIXED ASSETS

Assets that have an expected useful life of over a year and are used in operations and not acquired for sale in the ordinary course of business comprise this category. Property, plant, and equipment is the most important asset group included in it. They consist of those tangible assets used by business enterprises for the purpose of producing and distributing its goods and services.

Asset valuation

Currently the only permissible basis of accounting for fixed assets in this country is historical cost. Historical cost means the amount of dollars paid for the asset at the date of acquisition plus any other costs properly includable, such as freight, installation, setup costs, and so forth.

The primary reasons advanced for retention of the historical cost basis are that it is conservative in that it does not anticipate replacement costs; it is the amount for which management is accountable; and, above all, it is the best objectively determinable cost available. Moreover, after many years of acceptance as the basis at which fixed assets are stated, historical costs are recognized as not representing value but rather original costs which have not yet been charged to operations. Some even question the usefulness of costs based on some concept of current value which would change from year to year.

To the analyst of financial statements the concept of fixed assets at (historical) cost is not a complicated one. The distinction between a current expenditure and an outlay which results in an asset which will be allocated to future operations is a well-established one which depends primarily on the purpose of the outlay, the expected life of the asset, and for internal accounting expediency, on the amount involved. Accounting principles in this area, if consistently applied, do not lend themselves to serious distortion. Such, of course, is not the case with the determination of depreciation which is another matter to be discussed later.

One type of expense, sometimes included in the cost of fixed assets and which is subject to some debate, is interest cost during construction. This represents the cost of funds tied up while the property is being constructed and before it becomes productively utilized. This cost of funds committed to construction becomes part of the cost of the plant and equipment and is allocated to future operations along with all other costs. The inclusion of this cost in the cost of fixed assets is customary, primarily in the case of public utilities, where they are thus also included in the utility's rate base.

The SEC has established a moratorium on the capitalization of interest by companies other than electric, gas, water and telephone utilities, except with respect to types of assets for which they had, as of June 21, 1974, publicly disclosed an accounting policy of capitalizing interest (ASR 163).

In addition, the commission requires that all companies that capitalize interest costs disclose on the face of the income statement the amount of interest capitalized in each period for which an income statement is presented. Furthermore, companies other than electric, gas, water and telephone utilities that follow a policy of capitalizing interest are required to state the reason for their policy and the way in which the amount to be capitalized is determined.

Another area of controversy relates to costs included in fixed assets constructed in a company's own facilities. While most direct costs are includable without question, one problem area is the allocation of variable overhead and particularly fixed overhead cost to such assets. Where idle capacity has been utilized to construct capital assets, the inclusion of fixed overhead may be debatable. However, if usable production was foregone to build such assets, there is full justification for the inclusion of all proportionate overhead in the cost of the fixed assets.

One serious problem which confronts the analyst of financial statements which include fixed assets stated at historical cost is that these long-lived assets are not expressed in terms of a stable measuring unit. The accumulation of costs of assets purchased in different years represents the aggregation of units of differing purchasing power. Since depreciation—that is, the currently expired portion of the cost of these assets—is based on this original cost, the distortion is carried into the income statement. Thus, repeatedly the case has been made for adjusting original cost for changes in the price level—not as an attempt to arrive at some kind of current market value but rather to adjust the original cost for changes in the size of the dollar. This, it is argued, will not only result in more valid income statements and in a proper distinction between income and "real" capital, but will also present a fairer measure of how responsibly management has dealt with invested capital in terms of the purchasing power which has been entrusted to it.

The above discussion has pointed out the possible distortions to which historical cost accounting for long-lived assets may be subject. The SEC now requires disclosure of replacement cost of productive capacity by certain companies. Further discussion of this broad subject will be found in Chapter 14 dealing with the problem of accounting under changing price levels.

The Property, Plant, and Equipment account is assumed to include assets in active or productive use. If such assets are temporarily idle, disclosure of this fact will usually be made in notes or comments in order to explain the resulting excess cost and lower profit margins.

Should a substantial segment of assets be idle for a longer period of time and without definite prospects of use, they should no longer be included in the property, plant, and equipment designation where their inclusion would distort such relationships as that of sales to plant or the return on fixed assets. Instead, they should be segregated from other assets pending their reactivation, sale, or other disposition. Such idle assets represent not only an investment on which no return is earned but they often involve expenses of upkeep and maintenance.

Zenith Radio Corp. has the following footnote in its 1974 report:

The company has approximately $40 million invested in plant and equipment representing facilities not now being utilized and that may not be utilized in 1975. Depreciation expense of $4 million on these assets will be charged to expense in 1975 whether or not these facilities are utilized.

While the write-up of assets to current market or appraised values is not an accepted accounting procedure in the United States, the convention of conservatism requires that a permanent impairment of value and/or loss of utility of fixed assets be reflected in the accounts by a write-down. This is needed not only to reflect a loss of value and utility but also in order to relieve future periods of charges which the usefulness and productivity of the assets can no longer support and justify. Thus, for example, Cudahy Packing Company, after many years of unsatisfactory operating results, decided in 1965 to write-down some of its facilities and had the following explanation in its annual report:

Operating income at the Company's four midwestern meat packing plants (Omaha, Wichita, Denver and Salt Lake City) has been generally unsatisfactory in recent years, and management studies give no assurance that significant long-term improvement can be expected. Earnings of these plants have not been sufficient to cover applicable depreciation, general office administrative and interest costs. In recognition of the loss in value of these plants as measured by their demonstrated lack of earning power, the Board of Directors determined that a special reserve should be provided equal to the net book value of the property and equipment at the four plants. No salvage values were reflected in view of the substantial contingent liabilities under the labor contract covering employees at these plants. . . . This action was taken upon the recommendation of Arthur Andersen & Co., the Company's auditors. The special property reserve ($13,789,617) and the elimination of related deferred charges ($1,087,694) have been reflected as a special charge in the accompanying statements of income and earned surplus.

Depreciation expense for these plants has been provided for 1965 and 1964, and has been shown separately on the statement of income. Such depreciation provisions will no longer be required; however, property renewals, replacements and additions at these plants (which amounted to $175,000 in 1965 and $160,000 in 1964) will be charged directly to expense in future years.

The accompanying statement of income has been prepared to show the operations of the midwestern meat packing plants separately from other operations of the Company and its subsidiaries.

The significance of Cudahy Packing Company's action should not be lost to the financial analyst. The cost of plant and equipment is an outlay of capital which must be recovered through revenues generated by operations before net income can be recognized. The process by means of which the cost of productive assets is allocated to operations is called depreciation. Depreciation covers not only deterioration due to physical wear and tear but also loss of value due to obsolescence which is caused by technical innovation and other economic factors. Prior to 1960 Cudahy reported net income, and in retrospect it appears that the depreciation provision was inadequate in that it did not allow for the obsolescence of the company's plant. Losses in the years 1960 to 1965 convinced the management of the need to relieve future operations of heavy depreciation charges, and the write-off has achieved just that.

It is interesting to note that in 1967, after what management described as further "study and analysis" of the situation, management reversed itself and reestablished part of the 1965 write-down of plant and equipment. Thus, depreciation on the book values was resumed and retroactively restated. Possibly some of the impetus for this action may have had its origin outside the company. Such vacillating accounting is, to say the least, confusing to the analyst and completely baffling to the average reader. It destroys continuity and introduces confusion into the reporting of operating results.

The following example of write-offs due to reduced economic value appears in the 1974 Airco annual report:

Capital expenditures during 1974 aggregated $45,900,000 up from $28,800,000 spent in 1973. Depreciation and amortization amounted to $45,386,000 in 1974 and $27,530,000 in 1973, of which $4,281,000 and $1,470,000, respectively, was for depreciation provided for idle plant facilities and equipment. Also included in 1974 was additional depreciation of $11,515,000 in recognition of the reduced economic value of certain production facilities and equipment of the Vacuum Metals and Electronics Division.

The subject of depreciation, an important cost factor in most companies, is complex and subject to controversy. Its importance to the analyst cannot be overrated. It will be considered in Chapter 10 dealing with income determination.

Wasting assets

A category of assets which requires separate treatment is natural resources. With the exception of resources such as timber, which can be replenished by planned cutting and reseeding, most of such assets once exhausted cannot be used and lose most of their value. Examples of such resources are oil, gas, coal, iron ore, and sulphur.

Generally accepted accounting principles require that such assets be stated at original cost plus costs of discovery, exploration, and development. That means that the very significant value increment which occurs following the discovery of natural resources is not given immediate accounting recognition but shows up through the income stream when and as the resource is exploited.

The total cost of a wasting asset is generally allocated over the total units of estimated reserves available. This allocation process is known as depletion. Some companies in the mining field do not charge depletion to the income statement primarily because they believe the related assets to be grossly understated in terms of current and potential value. The subject of depletion will be discussed in Chapter 10.

Method of acquisition

Generally speaking, the method of acquiring assets or the use of assets should have no bearing on the basis on which they are carried in the accounting records. One method of acquisition which deserves separate mention, however, is leasing. Where leasing is short term, where it covers a period shorter than the asset's useful life, and where no property rights are acquired, no asset accounting is called for. In recent years, the practice of acquiring assets by means of leases which are in essence a financing method of purchases has grown and proliferated. Such leases should be accounted for as purchases, thus calling for the setting up of an asset at an amount equal to the present value of future rental payments, and this is essentially required by SFAS 13. Since the outstanding characteristic of this transaction is the *method* of financing, this topic will be considered in the chapter devoted to the measurement of liabilities.

Implication for analysis

In measuring property, plant, and equipment and in presenting it in conventional financial statements, accountants are concerned with a number of the objectives and conventions discussed in Chapter 2. They are concerned with the objectivity of original cost and the conservatism implicit therein, and with an accounting for the number of dollars originally invested in such assets. Judging from the resulting figures, they are quite clearly not overly concerned with the objectives of those who analyze financial statements. They are content to proclaim that "a balance sheet does not purport to reflect and could not usefully reflect the value of the enterprise." Not that the accountant is necessarily unmindful of the interests of those who use his statements; it is rather that his overwhelming concern lies in the real or imagined problems of his own art.

While clearly in the minority, some managements are concerned about the disparity between the original cost figures presented in their reports and the market values of assets which are potentially much more useful to the reader. Thus, the management of Utilities and Industries Corporation inserted the following footnote in their 1967 annual report:

1. The Board of Directors of the Corporation believes that the Corporation's properties have a present value materially in excess of the "original cost" basis at which its properties are carried on its books by reason of the

requirements of the Uniform System of Accounts prescribed by the Public Service Commission; and also that the reserve for depreciation, accrued at straight-line rates approved by the Commission, is in excess of the depreciation as demonstrated by the actual condition of the property. Pertinent to the Board's conclusion is the Corporation's experience in property condemnations (or sales in lieu thereof) since 1951. In these property dispositions, the Corporation and subsidiaries received awards or equivalent aggregating $48,637,000 for properties with a rate base carrying value of $23,869,000 on the several corresponding dates, as recorded on the books in conformity with Commission requirements.

In addition, there is included in other assets a parcel consisting of 66 acres of land in the Massapequa section of Nassau County, which land is not used in the utility operations of the Corporation and is being held for development, possibly by The South Bay Corporation, a subsidiary of the Corporation, or by others. This land is recorded in the above accounts at "original cost" to predecessors, which, in the judgment of the Board of Directors, is materially less than the value of said property.

In the context of the company's annual report, this disclosure merely hints at present market value and does not give the analyst the figure he may want, that is, what, in management's and other experts' opinions, the properties may really be worth. However, it does show a recognition of the problem faced by those who want to derive meaningful conclusions from financial statements.

Only by sheer coincidence can historical costs be useful to analysts. They are not relevant to questions of current replacement or of future needs. They are not directly comparable to similar data in other companies' reports. They do not enable us to measure the opportunity cost of disposal and alternative use of funds, nor do they provide a valid yardstick against which to measure return. Moreover, in times of changing price levels they represent an odd conglomeration of a variety of purchasing power disbursements.

It may be claimed that the value of assets is derived from their ability to earn a return and that consequently the key to their value lies in the income statement. While this is true in a significant number of cases, it does not provide the only avenue to an evaluation of an asset's worth. Thus, the earning of a return on an investment is dependent on managerial skill, and assets have a value tied to their capacity to produce. But in recognizing the importance of net income in the assessment of an asset's worth, the analyst must be aware of the problem which the method of depreciation has on the determination of net income. This aspect of the valuation of fixed assets and its effect on income is discussed fully in Chapter 10 on the analysis of income.

The effect of price level changes on fixed asset valuation will be explored more fully in Chapter 14 dealing with this general topic.

In utilizing the published figures of an enterprise's *gross* cost of property, plant, and equipment, the analyst must be aware of the fact that they are *undepreciated* balances of original cost. Thus, the first determination which he must make is whether such figures can be used for the purpose which he has in mind and, if not, what adjustments are necessary to make them more relevant.

Analysts who suspect that a company capitalizes interest without disclosure should determine first the existence of self-constructed assets, real estate, motion pictures, or other assets to which interest is customarily charged. The estimated total interest expense for a period can be determined by multiplying the average level of debt during the period by the applicable average interest rates. If the actual interest expense on the income statement is significantly lower than the estimate the possibility that some interest is capitalized exists and the analyst should seek clarification.

INTANGIBLE ASSETS

Intangible assets represent rights to future benefits. One distinguishing characteristic of these assets, which is not, however, unique to them, is that they have no physical existence and depend on such expected future benefits for most of their value. In many cases, the value of these benefits is inextricably tied to the continuity of the enterprise.

Some important categories of intangibles are:

1. Goodwill.
2. Patents, copyrights, and trademarks.
3. Leases, leaseholds, and leasehold improvements.
4. Exploration rights and cost of development of natural resources.
5. Formulae, processes, and designs.
6. Licenses, franchises, and memberships.

The basic rule in accounting for purchased intangibles is that they be carried at cost. If property other than cash is given in exchange for the intangible, it must be recorded at the fair market value of the consideration given. If liabilities are assumed, the intangible is valued by taking into consideration the present value of the future obligations.

There are some paradoxes in the valuation of intangibles which should be understood by the analyst. If a company spends material and labor in the construction of a "tangible" asset, such as a machine, these costs are capitalized and recorded as an asset which is depreciated over its estimated useful life. On the other hand, a company which spends a great amount of resources advertising a product or training a sales force to sell and service it, which, as we shall see, is a process of creating internally developed "goodwill," cannot usually capitalize such costs even though they may be as, or more, beneficial to the company's future operations than is the "tangible" machine. The reason for this inconsistency in accounting for the two assets is steeped in such basic accounting conventions (discussed in Chapter 2) as conservatism, which casts greater doubt on the future realization of unidentifiable intangible costs (such as advertising or training which create "goodwill") than costs sunk into tangible "hard" and visible goods.

APB Opinion No. 17 distinguishes between identifiable and unidentifiable intangible assets.

Identifiable intangibles

Identifiable intangibles can be separately identified and given reasonably descriptive names such as patents, trademarks, franchises, and the like. Identifiable intangibles can be developed internally, acquired singly or as part of a group of assets. In either case, they should be recorded at cost and amortized over their useful lives. Write-down or complete write-off at date of acquisition is not permitted.

Unidentifiable intangibles

Unidentifiable intangibles can be developed internally or purchased from others. They cannot, however, be acquired singly but form part of a group of assets or part of an entire enterprise. The excess of cost of an acquired company over the sum total of identifiable net assets is the most common unidentifiable intangible asset. *APB Opinion No. 17* refers to this unidentifiable mass of assets as "goodwill," and this is actually a residual amount in an acquisition after the amount of tangible and identifiable intangibles have been determined. It represents an expansion of the goodwill concept from what has obtained before this *Opinion* was issued.

The costs of developing, maintaining, or restoring intangibles which are unidentifiable, have indeterminate lives, or are inherent in a continuing enterprise should be expensed as incurred. By contrast, such intangible assets which are purchased must be carried at cost and amortized over their useful lives and cannot be written down or written off at date of acquisition.

Amortization of intangibles

Both types of intangibles, those identifiable as well as those unidentifiable, are believed to have limited useful lives and must be amortized accordingly. Depending on the type of intangible asset, its useful life may be limited by such factors as legal, contractual, or regulatory provisions; demand and competition; life expectancies of employees; and economic factors.

The cost of each intangible should be amortized over its individual useful life taking into account all factors which determine its length. The period of amortization cannot, however, exceed 40 years.

Other considerations regarding the accounting for intangibles

Goodwill is often a sizable asset. Since it can only be recorded on acquisition from a third party, it can be recorded only upon the purchase of an on-going business enterprise. The description of what is being paid for varies greatly, and the variety of views add to the confusion surrounding this subject. Some refer to the ability to attract and keep satisfied customers, while others point to qualities inherent in an enterprise that is well organized and is efficient in production, service, and sales. This distinction can also be seen in the difference that obviously exists between a business that is just starting and one that is successful and well-established in its industry and which has spent a great deal on training and research to get there. Thus, what is obviously being paid for here is earning power, and since any given amount of invested capital should expect a minimum return depending on risk, most accountants agree that goodwill is associated with a level of earnings over and above that minimum. These are otherwise referred to as "super-earnings." Thus goodwill implies exceptional profitability, and that should normally be evident when goodwill is being purchased, except in those cases where there is obvious mismanagement and the potential is evident and awaits to be tapped by good management.

Ipco Hospital Supply Corp. described its goodwill accounts as follows:

Intangible assets. Cost in excess of net assets acquired, which arose in connection with acquisitions prior to November 1, 1970, is not being amortized unless there is an indication of diminution in value; such cost relating to acquisitions made subsequent to October 31, 1970 is being amortized by the straight-line method over a period of 40 years.

General Motors, on the other hand, reported as follows:

Goodwill. Goodwill represents the excess of the cost over the value ascribed to the net tangible assets of businesses acquired and is amortized over ten years with the amortization applied directly to the asset account. Amortization amounted to $6.8 million in 1976 and $6.4 million in 1975.

When a business is being acquired, the book values, that is, the amounts at which its net assets are carried in accordance with accounting principles discussed in this book, are quite obviously not relevant in arriving at a purchase price, if only because they represent unamortized cost balances rather than values. Thus, the first requirement in purchase accounting is that the amount paid for the entity as a whole be allocated to all identifiable assets in accordance with their fair market values. If an excess remains after such allocation is made, it may be ascribed to the intangible "goodwill." If the fair market value of assets acquired exceeds the purchase price, a "bargain purchase credit" results and it can, after adjustments, be amortized to income over a reasonable number of years. A detailed examination of the accounting for business combinations will be found in Chapter 9.

Most other intangible assets have a useful life which is limited by law, regulation, or agreement. Thus, *patents* are rights conveyed by government authority to the inventor giving him the exclusive right to his invention for a term of years. Registered copyrights and trademarks also convey exclusive rights for specified periods of time. The cost of these assets should be written off against the revenues they help create over the maximum period coinciding with their legal life or over the minimum period of their estimated economic life.

The cost of franchises, licenses, or other such beneifts must be written off over the period during which they are deemed to be economically productive. The cost of leaseholds and leasehold improvements are benefits of occupancy which are contractually limited. Thus, their cost must be amortized over the period of the lease contract.

As is true with all assets, accounting principles require that if it is evident that an intangible has lost all or most of its value or utility, it should be written down to its net realizable value measured by either future estimated utility or selling price, whichever is more appropriate in the circumstances.

Implication for analysis

Because of their very nature, intangibles have often been treated with suspicion by financial analysts. In fact many analysts associate "intangibility" with riskiness. Quite obviously caution and clear understanding of the nature of these assets is required in the evaluation of their worth to the enterprise. However, since these assets may, in many instances, be the most valuable asset an enterprise owns and since they can be undervalued as well as, as is often the case, carried at inflated amounts, it is inadvisable to remove them from all consideration in financial analysis.

Goodwill is a case in point. Having understood the accounting conventions governing the recording of goodwill, the analyst realizes that only purchased goodwill will be found among the recorded assets and that more "goodwill" may exist off the balance sheet than on it.

Another key point here is that if there is value in goodwill it must be reflected in earnings. True, if a mismanaged situation with great potential was purchased, the profits may not become visible immediately; but if there is value to goodwill, then such an asset should give rise to superior earnings within a reasonably short time after acquisition. If those earnings are not in evidence, it is a fair assumption that the investment in goodwill is of no value regardless of whether it is found on the balance sheet or not. Goodwill represents an advantage that must become evident or else it does not exist.

Another important factor of which the analyst must be aware is that in practice, the accounting for goodwill is far from faithful to the theory. Due to the beneficial effect that an absence of write-off of assets has on the results of operations, goodwill and other intangibles may not be written off as speedily as a realistic assessment of their useful life may require. While the overall limitation of 40 years on the assumed useful life of intangibles is arbitrary and may, in some instances, result in excessive amortization, it is safe to assume that in most cases the bias will be in the direction of too slow a rate of amortization. The analyst must be alert to this possibility.

Regardless of the amount of outlays incurred in the acquisition or in the internal development of an intangible, the rule applicable to the carrying amount of any asset is that it be carried at an amount not in excess of realizable value in terms of sales price or future utility. That, at least, is the intention and the theory. But, as in most other categories of accounting theory, actual implementation in practice is another matter, and the analyst must be prepared to form his own judgment on the amounts at which intangible assets are carried. The analyst must also bear in mind that goodwill recorded as a result of business combinations initiated before November 1, 1970 does not have to be amortized at all and that at the cutoff date there were billions of dollars of unamortized goodwill on corporate balance sheets in this country. Only in extreme situations will the auditors qualify their opinion with respect to the continuing value of unamortized goodwill as was the case in the 1974 report of United Brands Co.

The analyst must also be alert to the consideration with which the enterprise has parted in the acquisition of goodwill, for this may affect the amount of the intangible recorded. Payments in promoter stock should be thoroughly scrutinized. Also of concern to the analyst is the rate at which goodwill is amortized. The 40-year maximum, after all, is a long period exceeding a generation. The assumption of useful life should be realistic and should reflect the proper allocation of costs to revenues. A lump-sum write-off of an intangible may bring the asset down to its proper realizable value but by no means does it make up for the implicit overstatement of earnings of prior years.

PREPAID EXPENSES AND DEFERRED CHARGES

Prepaid expenses and deferred charges distinguished

Prepaid expenses represent advance payments for services yet to be received. Examples are advance payments for rent or prepaid insurance on a longer term policy. Small supplies of stationery or stamps are often included in prepaid expenses. Prepaid expenses are generally classified among current assets because the services-due which they represent would otherwise require the use of current resources during the following operating cycle. For reasons of expediency and lack of materiality, services due beyond one year are usually included among prepaid expenses classified as current.

Unlike prepaid expenses which represent advance payments for services yet to be received, *deferred charges* represent charges already incurred which are deferred to the future either because they are expected to benefit future revenues or because they represent a proper allocation of costs to future operations.

Over the years the complexities of business operations as well as custom have sanctioned an ever increasing number and types of deferred charges.

Why costs are deferred

The basic theory behind the deferral of expenses and costs is relatively simple. If a cost incurred in one period is going to benefit a future period or periods by a contribution to revenues or reduction in costs, then such a cost should be deferred to such future period. The basic accounting convention involved here is that of matching costs and revenues. Thus, if a 20-year bond of $1,000 face value is issued for $950, the $50 discount (plus expenses of issue) is properly allocated to the 20 years which benefit from the use of the borrowed money. Looked at another way, the discount reflects an interest cost effectively higher than the coupon rate of the bond and should be treated as such.

While the future benefit, in terms of use of money which the bond discount affords, is pretty clear and obvious, such is not the case with many other kinds of deferred charges.

Research and development costs

Under FASB *Statement 2* almost all research and development costs are required to be charged to expense when incurred. That requirement applies to a tangible or intangible asset that is purchased for use in a single R&D project, although a purchased asset that has alternative future uses should be capitalized and amortized as such.

Some public utility regulatory commissions require the deferral and amortization of significant R&D expenditures and where they affect the rate-making process they can be accounted for in this manner.

The costs of research and development activities conducted for others under a contractual arrangement, including indirect costs which are specifically reimbursable, can be treated as work in progress or receivables under contracts and are not covered by the expensing requirement. A further discussion of the implications of the accounting for R&D outlays will be found in Chapter 11.

Other types of deferred charges

Another category of deferred charges which borders on a deferral of costs of dubious future benefit is that of moving expenses and to a lesser degree, start-up costs. Thus, Willcox & Gibbs, Inc., had the following note in its annual report:

The Comapny has deferred approximately $782,000 related to moving expenses and start-up costs associated with new facilities placed into operation during 1968. It is the Company's intention to amortize these costs over a five year period beginning in 1969.

Neptune International describes the deferral of start-up costs as follows:

Other assets. The Corporation has incurred costs prior to attaining normal levels of production in connection with the start-up of two new manufacturing facilities during 1973 and 1972, and the start-up of a new foundry during 1974. These costs are being amortized over three-year periods.

As indicated before, the variety of deferred costs has been growing due to new complexities in both technology and in business practice. Since deferred charges represent future intangible benefits, they are sometimes very close in nature to intangible assets. Regardless of terminology, the following list should give the reader an indication of the variety of deferred charges now found in financial statements:

1. Business development, expansion, merger, and relocation costs.
    a. Preoperating expenses, initial start-up costs, and tooling costs.
    b. Initial operating losses or preoperating expenses of subsidiaries.
    c. Moving, plant rearrangement, and reinstallation costs.
    d. Merger or acquisition expenses.
    e. Purchased customer accounts.
    f. Noncompete agreements.
2. Deferred expenses.
    a. Advertising and promotional expenses.
    b. Imputed interest.

    c. Selling, general, and administrative expenses.
    d. Pension plan costs.
    e. Property and other taxes.
    f. Rental and leasing costs.
    g. Vacation pay.
    h. Seasonal growing and packing expenses.
3. Intangible costs.
    a. Intangible drilling and development costs.
    b. Contracts, films, copyright materials, art rights, etc.
4. Debt discount and expenses.
5. Future income tax benefits.
6. Organization costs.
7. Advance royalties.

While we are here focusing on the validity of the assets represented by deferred charges, we must always bear in mind that each of these assets has "another side of the coin," that is, the deferral of a cost which would otherwise have been charged to results from operations. The impact of this aspect will be more fully discussed in Chapter 11, which is devoted to principles of income measurement.

Implications for analysis

While prepaid expenses are usually neither of the size or the significance sufficient to be of real concern to the analyst, deferred charges can be both sizable and significant and, hence, can present real challenges of understanding and interpretation.

Certain types of deferred charges, such as bond discount, can be easily understood and defended on the basis of accounting theory. Moreover, the period of their amortization is clearly dictated by the circumstances which gave rise to them. Deferred charges, such as organization costs, on the other hand, while clearly designated to benefit an organization in the future, cannot be amortized on a logical or obvious basis. Thus, while an indefinite life may be inferred from the going-concern or continuity convention of accounting, organization costs are nevertheless usually amortized over an arbitrarily determined period of time.

However, the validity of deferring many other charges, such as moving and start-up costs, promotional costs, or initial operating losses of, say, loan offices, is subject to many imponderables and estimates. Similarly, the period over which they should properly be amortized is often subject to serious doubt. The analyst must be alert to the situation where the deferred charge is not really an asset representing a future benefit but is rather a deferred loss which is being carried forward for no better reason than the desire of management not to burden current operating results. While the auditor's opinion or mention of such assets can be helpful to the analyst, he must be prepared to evaluate on his own the evidence and information regarding such deferrals. In any event deferred charges represent mostly assets which are incapable of satisfying claims of creditors. The other and perhaps even more significant implication which deferred charges carry is their effect on proper income determination, and this aspect will be examined in Chapter 11, which is devoted to this subject.

The analyst must, in general, treat with suspicion the propensity of managements to defer into the future the costs and problems of today. For example, following severe price increases of fuel beginning late in 1973 some electric utilities refused to face reality and deferred the absorption of these costs to future periods in the hope that these will be recouped through subsequent rate increases. This practice is symptomatic of the illusory accounting of which some companies are capable.

UNRECORDED INTANGIBLE OR CONTINGENT ASSETS

A discussion of principles of asset measurement would not be complete without an examination of that category of assets which under generally accepted accounting principles would not be recorded in a statement of financial condition.

One category of assets which are not recordable has already been mentioned in the discussion of goodwill. In this case, if the intangible is internally developed rather than purchased from an outside party, it cannot normally be capitalized and results instead in a charge to current operations. Thus, to the extent that a valuable asset has been created, one that can be either sold or which possesses earning power, the income charged with the expense of its development has been understated. This the analyst must realize and, if significant, take into account.

Another type of unrecorded asset is a tax loss carry-forward benefit which has a high probability of being realized in future years. Present accounting theory sanctions the recording of such a benefit only in those rare cases where its realization is "assured beyond any reasonable doubt." Thus, the analyst must look for evidence of such assets in the footnotes to the financial statements and other material containing comments about the company's financial condition.

Marhoeter Packing Co. presents the following disclosure of net operating loss carry-overs as well as the dates of expiration of such benefits:

Federal income taxes. The Company's federal income tax returns have been examined through fiscal year ended October 30, 1971. The Company has available net operating loss carryovers of approximately $2,430,000 to offset otherwise taxable income in future years. These carryovers expire as follows:

1976	$ 3,000
1977	1,300,000
1978	397,000
1979	730,000

In addition, the company has approximately $285,000 of investment tax credits available to reduce federal income taxes. These credits expire in varying amounts during the next seven years.

A contingent asset in the form of possible additional payments is disclosed by Ampco-Pittsburgh Corp. as follows:

The Corporation may receive an additional payment not to exceed $321,574, contingent upon the sum of the net income of Modulus Corporation for the years 1975 and 1976. No recognition has been given to this contingent payment.

Future contingent benefits are disclosed by Masonite Corporation as follows:

Timber contract. The company has a 10-year contract to supply St. Regis Paper Company with timber cut from a substantial portion of the company's timberlands. Cutting under the contract commenced in 1968. Income under the contract of $5,464,000 in 1970 and $3,725,000 in 1969 has been reflected in the accompanying income statements. Also reflected as a cost in the income statements is the acquisition of a portion of this timber from St. Regis Paper Company by Hood Industries Division acquired in 1970 and accounted for as a pooling-of-interests.

QUESTIONS

1. What are the provisions of SFAS *12* which apply to the equity securities not classified as current assets?
2. What accounting principles govern the valuation and presentation of long-term investments? Distinguish between the accounting for investments in the common stock in an investee of *(a)* less than 20 percent of the shares outstanding, and *(b)* 20 percent or more of the shares outstanding.
3. *a.* Evaluate the accounting for investments in between 20 percent to 50 percent of the common stock of an investee from the point of view of an analyst of the financial statements.
    b. When are losses in long-term investments recognized? Evaluate the accounting which governs the recognition of such losses.
4. What are some of the flaws and inconsistences of SFAS *12*, with regard to accounting for marketable securities not carried as current assets, of which the analyst must be aware?

5. How should idle plant and equipment be presented in the balance sheet? Explain the reasons for the presentation you describe.

6. The income of an enterprise from the exploration of wasting assets often bears no logical relation to the amount at which such investment is shown on the balance sheet.

   a. Why is this so?

   b. Under what circumstances would a more logical relationship be more likely to exist?

7. From the point of view of the user of financial statements, what are the objections to the use of original cost as the basis of carrying fixed assets?

8. a. What are the basic principles governing the valuation of intangible assets?

   b. Distinguish between the accounting for internally developed versus purchased intangibles.

   c. Of what significance is the distinction between (1) identifiable intangibles and (2) unidentifiable intangibles?

   d. What principles and guidelines underlie the amortization of intangible assets?

9. What are the implications for analysis of the accounting for goodwill?

10. List five categories of deferred charges and describe the rationale which is usually given for this deferral.

11. a. Give examples of two or more types of assets which are not recorded on the balance sheet.

    b. How should such assets be evaluated by the analyst?

7

ANALYSIS OF LIABILITIES

Liabilities are obligations to pay money, render future services, or convey specified assets. They are claims against the company's present and future assets and resources. Such claims are usually senior to those of the ownership as evidenced by equity securities. This discussion will be broadly construed to include current liabilities, long-term liabilities, and deferred credits which, as shall be seen, can vary significantly from conventional liabilities.

CURRENT LIABILITIES

Current liabilities are usually obligations for goods and services acquired, taxes owed, and any other accruals of expenses. They include deposits received, advance payments, trade acceptances, notes payable, short-term bank loans, as well as the current portion of long-term debt.

To be properly classified as current, a liability should require the use of current resources (assets) or the incurrence of another current liability for its discharge. As in the case of current assets the period over which such liabilities are expected to be retired is one year or the current operating cycle, whichever is longer.

As a general principle, the offsetting of assets against liabilities is permissible only where such a right specifically exists. Thus the availability of cash for the payment of a liability does not justify the offset of one against the other. In practice the only instances where offset is permissible is where government securities specifically designated as acceptable for the payment of taxes are acquired for that purpose.

The SEC in *Accounting Series Release 148* (1973) has significantly expanded the disclosure requirements in SEC filings (not necessarily in annual reports) regarding the terms of short term debt:

1. Footnote disclosure of compensating balance arrangements including those not reduced to writing.
2. Balance sheet segregation of *(a)* legally restricted compensating balances and *(b)* unrestricted compensating balances relating to long-term borrowing arrangements if the compensating balance can be computed at a fixed amount at the balance sheet date.
3. Disclosure of short-term bank and commercial paper borrowings:
    a. Commercial paper borrowings separately stated in the balance sheet.
    b. Average interest rate and terms separately stated for short-term bank and commercial paper borrowings at the balance sheet date.
    c. Average interest rate, average outstanding borrowings, and maximum month-end outstanding borrowings for short-term bank debt and commercial paper combined for the period.
4. Disclosure of amounts and terms of unused lines of credit for short-term borrowing arrangements (with amounts supporting commercial paper separately stated) and of unused commitments for long-term financing arrangements.

SFAS 6 (1975) superseded some provisions of the above by establishing criteria for the balance sheet classification of short-term obligations that are expected to be refinanced.

Certain short-term obligations such as trade accounts payable and normal accrued liabilities always should be classified as current and included in a total of current liabilities in companies' balance sheets. Other short-term obligations also should be classified as current liabilities unless the company intends to refinance them on a long-term basis and can demonstrate its ability to do so. Short-term obligations are those scheduled to mature in less than a year.

Refinancing on a long-term basis is defined to mean either replacing the short-term obligation with a long-term obligation or with equity securities; or renewing, extending or replacing it with other short-term obligations for an uninterrupted period extending beyond one year from the balance sheet date.

Ability to refinance on a long-term basis should be demonstrated either (1) by actually having issued a long-term obligation or equity securities to replace the short-term obligation after the date of the company's balance sheet but before it is released, or (2) by having entered into an agreement with a bank or other source of capital that clearly permits the company to refinance the short-term obligation when it becomes due. Financing agreements which are cancellable for violation of a provision that can be evaluated differently by the parties to the agreement (such as "a material adverse change" or "failure to maintain satisfactory operations") do not meet this condition. Also, an "operative" violation of the agreement has not occurred.

LONG-TERM LIABILITIES

Long-term liabilities may either represent bank term loans or more formal issuances of bonds, debentures, or notes. They represent obligations payable beyond the period of one year or beyond that encompassed by the operating cycle. Debt obligations may assume many and varied forms, and their full assessment and measurement requires disclosure of all significant conditions and covenants attached to them. Such information should include the interest rate, maturities, conversion privileges, call features, subordination provisions, and restrictions under the indenture. In addition, disclosure of collateral pledged (with indication of book and possible market values), sinking fund provisions subordination, revolving credit provisions, and sinking fund commitements should be disclosed. Any defaults in adherence to loan provisions, including defaults of interest and principal repayments, must also be disclosed.

Since the exact interest rate which will prevail in the bond market at the time of issuance of bonds can never be predetermined, bonds are sold in excess of par, or at a premium, or below par, that is, at a discount. The premium or discount represents in effect an adjustment of the effective interest rate. The premium received is amortized over the life of the issue, thus reducing the coupon rate of interest to the effective interest rate incurred. Conversely, the discount allowed is similarly amortized, thus increasing the effective interest rate paid by the borrower.

A variety of incentives are offered in order to promote the sale of bonds and to reduce the interest rates which would otherwise be required. They may take the form of convertibility features, attachments of warrants to purchase the issuer's common stock, or even warrants to purchase the stock of another company. It requires no great persuasion to understand that to the extent that these incentives are valuable they carry a cost to the issuing company. Whether the cost represents dilution of the equity or a fixed price call on an investment, these costs should be recognized. Although slow in doing so, accountants have recognized such costs and given expression to them as follows:

1. In the case of convertible features—through their effect on the computation of earnings per share (see Chapter 12).
2. In the case of warrants—by assigning a discount factor at the time of debt issuance which charge is amortized to income. In addition, the dilutive effects of warrants are given recognition in earnings per share computations. (Further discussion can be found under the topics of "equities" and "earnings per share.")

Generally the prohibitions against offsetting of assets against liabilities apply to the offsetting of debt against related assets. However, if a real estate company buys property subject to a mortgage which it does not assume, it may properly deduct the amount of the mortgage from the asset, thus showing it net.

When debt is not interest bearing, it is appropriate to show it at the present value of the amount that will be payable in the future discounted at the rate at which the company would otherwise borrow money. This not only shows debt as a proper amount, comparable to other interest bearing debt obligations, but it also provides for the computation of the interest charge which reflects the use of these funds. Moreover, if the debt is the result of the acquisition of an asset, this treatment insures that its cost is not overstated through the overstatement of the amount of debt incurred.

Reference to the discussion on the imputation of interest in the "receivables" section of Chapter 5 will show that under the provisions of *APB Opinion No. 21*, noninterest bearing obligations, or those bearing unreasonable rates of interest, must, under certain conditions, be shown at an amount which reflects the imputation of a reasonable discount rate.

Valuable disclosure, from the analyst's point of view, is the yearly loan payment requirement for a significant number of future years.

Occidental Petroleum Corp. presents an example of disclosure of terms and conditions to which its debt obligations are subject, including details of future maturities:

Long-term debt

Long-term debt, net of current maturities of $87,468,000 at December 31, 1975, consists of the following:

	Interest Rate (percent)	1975 (amounts in thousands)
Senior funded debt—		
Secured:		
Notes secured by mortgages on property, equipment and other assets—original cost $163,000,000	7⅜ to 7½	$136,940
Notes due through 1986, secured by mortgages on property, plant and equipment—original cost $25,000,000	5⅞	16,975
Unsecured:		
Revolving credit notes due through 1980	7¾	1,519
Notes due 1979–1993	8¾	105,000
Eurocurrency issues due through 1989	6½ to 10	131,963
Notes due through 1978	3⅝ to 8	34,669
Notes due 1979–1983	3⅝ to 12¼	185,127
Notes due 1984–1992	4⅝ to 7	44,927
Sinking fund debentures due through 1991	4⅜ to 5¼	20,364
Others due through 1992	various	50,841
		$728,325
Subordinated debt—convertible debentures due 1982–1996 (Note 12)	7½	$124,998

Repayment of notes secured by mortgages on property, equipment and other assets, being developed in the United Kingdom (North Sea), is related to production levels. If certain specified production and reserve levels have not been established, repayment must be made in January 1978, and, in any event, the loan must be repaid by 1983.

In February 1976, Occidental's wholly-owned subsidiary, Occidental Overseas Finance N.V., issued $30,000,000 of 9¾ per cent Euronotes, due 1981 which are not included in the above table.

The interest rate on certain notes may fluctuate from time-to-time in accordance with money market conditions. Certain of the above indebtedness has been borrowed under agreements which contain covenants relating to maintenance of financial ratios, borrowings, declaration of cash dividends, etc. At December 31, 1975, under the most restrictive of these covenants, retained earnings of approximately $320,000,000 were available for the payment of cash dividends to preferred and common shareholders.

Minimum principal payments on senior funded debt, including sinking fund requirements, after December 31, 1976, are as follows (amounts in thousands):

1977	$177,375
1978	37,494
1979	75,602
1980	51,316
1981	73,302
Thereafter	313,236
	$728,325

Occidental had unused domestic and foreign lines of committed bank credit aggregating $395,000,000 and $120,000,000 at December 31, 1975 and 1974, respectively, with a commitment fee of up to ½-of-1 per cent per annum.

IMPLICATIONS FOR ANALYSIS

Liabilities are prior claims against a company's assets and resources; and the analyst needs assurance that they are fully stated with proper descriptions as to their amount, due dates, and the conditions, encumbrances, and limitations to which they subject the company.

The means by which auditors satisfy themselves that all liabilities have been properly recorded are such procedures as scrutiny of board of director meeting minutes, the reading of contracts and agreements, and inquiry of those who may have knowledge of company obligations and liabilities. Since the nature of double-entry bookkeeping requires that for every asset, resource, or cost, a counterbalancing obligation, or investment must be booked, the areas subject to considerable difficulty are those relating to commitments and contingent liabilities because they do not involve the commensurate recording of assets or costs. Here, the analyst must rely on the information which is provided in the notes to financial statements and in the general management commentary found in the text of the annual report and elsewhere.

The analyst must be aware of the possibility that understatement of liabilities can occur and, when it does, income will most likely be adversely affected. Thus, for example, Rocor International reported early in 1976 that the accounts payable balance on its books may be understated by as much as $1 million. In another example the SEC found in 1976 that, Ampex Corp. in its 1971 10-K and 1972 10-Qs did not disclose that it was obligated to pay royalty guarantees to record companies totalling in excess of $80 million, that it did not disclose that it was selling substantial amounts of prerecorded tapes which were improperly accounted for as "degaussed" or erased tapes to avoid payment of royalty fees, and that it understated by several millions of dollars the allowances for doubtful accounts receivable and provisions for losses arising from royalty contracts and overstated income due to inadequate credit allowances for returned tapes.

If short-term bank debt is included in the current liability section, it may mean that the company does not plan to refinance or the company cannot get a refinancing agreement with a lender that meets the requirements of SFAS 6. The analyst should attempt to determine the reason for the current liability classification of bank debt since an inability to secure a satisfactory refinancing agreement could indicate the company has problems beyond those revealed in its financial statements.

Assessing uncertainties

Due to the uncertainties involved, the descriptions of commitments and especially of contingent liabilities in footnotes are often vague and indeterminate. In effect, that means that the burden of assessing the possible impact of the contingencies as well as the probabilities of their occurrence is passed on to the reader. The analyst should always determine whether the auditors feel that a contingency is serious enough and material enough to call for a qualification in their report. This was the case in the financial statements of Berry Petroleum Company where the opinion was made subject to the effect on the financial statement of the determination of the company's ultimate liability in respect to alleged price discrimination as explained in Note 6. That note reads in part:

During the year ended October 31, 1967 the state of Arkansas filed suits against the Company for alleged price discrimination in sales of asphalt. At the present time, counsel for the Company have been unable to make an evaluation of the claim: however, management of the Company denies that it has discriminated against the state. While the possibility exists that the Company's financial condition could be materially and adversely affected by the outcome of this litigation, counsel for the Company are of the opinion that these actions are not likely to have that result.

A situation such as Berry Petroleum's poses difficult problems of analysis. However, the auditor has at least unequivocally declared that not only is he unable to assess the ultimate impact of the contingency upon the company's financial position, but that the impact could be material enough to require him to qualify his opinion on the financial statement as a whole.

While utilizing all the information available, the analyst must nevertheless bring his own critical evaluation to bear on the assessment of all the contingencies to which the company may be subject. This process must draw not only on available disclosures and information but also on an understanding of industry conditions and practices.

Evaluation of terms of indebtedness

The disclosure of the terms and conditions of regular recorded indebtedness and liabilities is another area deserving the analyst's careful attention. Here, the analyst must examine critically the description of debt, its terms, conditions, and encumbrances with a view to satisfying himself as to the term's feasibility and completeness. Important in the evaluation of a liability's total impact are such features as:

1. The terms of the debt.
2. Restrictions on deployment of resources and freedom of action.
3. Ability to engage in further financing.
4. Requirements such as relating to maintenance of ratios of working capital, debt to equity, and so forth.
5. Dilutive conversion features to which the debt is subject.

Minimum disclosure requirements as to debt provisions vary somewhat, but auditors are bound by reporting standards to disclose any breaches in loan provisions which may restrict a company's freedom of action or set it on the road to insolvency. Thus, the analyst should be alert to any explanations or qualifications in the notes or in the auditor's opinion such as the following which appeared in the annual report of Lionel Corporation:

Reference is made to Note G to the financial statements relating to a provision of the indenture covering the 5½% Convertible Subordinated Debentures due in 1980 and to information contained therein as to the failure of the Company to maintain the net working capital required thereunder and to the possible failure to observe other indenture covenants. The management has represented to us that it is actively negotiating certain arrangements and planning certain actions, which, it believes, will have the ultimate effect of remedying any breaches of covenants that may exist under the indentures as referred to in Note G.

In view of the possible material effect which the final resolution of the matters referred to above could have on the consolidated financial position of the companies, and in view of the lack of knowledge at this time of the ultimate effect which the aforementioned negotiations and plans may have in finally disposing of the matters, we are precluded from expressing an opinion as to the fair presentation of the consolidated balance sheet and related consolidated statement of earned surplus of the companies.

Naturally, an analyst would like to be able to foresee developments such as those described in the Lionel situation. One of the most effective ways of doing this is by means of financial analysis that compares the terms of debt with the margin of safety by which existing compliance exceeds the requirements under those terms.

OBLIGATIONS UNDER LEASES

Leasing, as a means of acquiring assets and the services and use of assets, has been known for a long time, but in recent decades its use has grown considerably. Our consideration of lease obligations at this point is due to their similarity to debt. Lease terms usually oblige entities to make a series of payments over a future period of time, and it is well known that in many cases such payments may contain, among others, elements of interest and principal amortization. The debate over which features of a lease agreement clinch it as a purchase (i.e., as a financing method) and which characteristics cause it to retain the nature of a rental contract has been going on for a long time.

When the accounting profession first recognized the problem of accounting for leases in 1949 it recommended in *ARB 38* that long-term leases be disclosed. It was reasoned that if a lease arrangement was in substance an installment purchase of property it should be reflected as an asset and as a liability of the lessee. The spirit and intent of this pronouncement were largely ignored in practice.

As the attraction of leasing as a means of "off balance sheet financing" grew so did the clamor for a more realistic accounting. While *Accounting Research Study No. 4*, published by the AICPA in 1962, concluded that leases which give rise to property rights be so reported in the financial statements the *APB Opinion* which followed (*No. 5* of 1964) focused principally on the creation of a material equity in the property as a determining criterion requiring capitalization. This concept as well as the "soft" criteria which accompanied this opinion were no match to the countervailing forces against capitalization which were motivated by considerations of the most favorable financial structure presentation and income pattern determination. Thus, only relatively few of the most obvious financing leases were capitalized in the financial statements in accordance with the provisions of *APB Opinion 5.*

In its last *Opinion (No. 31—*1973) the outgoing APB called merely for improved lease disclosure. In an apparent reaction to slow progress the SEC issued in the same year *ASR 147* which called for footnote *disclosure* which went beyond those specified in *APB Opinion 31.* These included disclosure of details on the present value of financing leases, as defined, and of the impact on net income of the capitalization of such leases.

It was, however, not until November 1976 that a real tightening up of the accounting for leases occurred with the issuance of the more rigorous SFAS *13* which superseded most prior pronouncements. The provisions of the *Statement* derive from the view that a lease that transfers substantially all of the benefits and risks incident to the ownership of property should be accounted for as the acquisition of an asset and the incurrence of an obligation by the lessee and as a sale or financing by the lessor. All other leases should be accounted for as operating leases. The statement does not apply to leases relating to rights to explore natural resources or to licensing agreements. In 1977 the SEC moved to conform its lease accounting requirements to those of SFAS *13* (see footnote 3 on page 182).

Accounting by lessees

In the case of the lessee, the *Statement* requires that a lease be classified and accounted for as a capital lease (shown as an asset and an obligation on the balance sheet) if at the inception of the lease it meets one of four criteria: (1) the lease transfers ownership of the property to the lessee by the end of the lease term; (2) the lease contains an option to purchase the property at a bargain price; (3) the lease term is equal to 75 percent or more the estimated economic life of the property; or (4) the present value[1] of the rentals and other minimum lease payments, at the beginning of the lease term equal 90 percent of the fair value of the leased property less any related investment tax credit retained by the lessor. If the lease does not meet any of those criteria, it is to be classified and accounted for as an operating lease.

---

[1] A lessor shall compute the present value of the minimum lease payments using the interest rate implicit in the lease. A lessee shall compute the present value of the minimum lease payments using its incremental borrowing rate unless *(a)* it knows the lessor's computation of the implicit rate and *(b)* the implicit rate computed by the lessor is less than the lessee's incremental borrowing rate. If both of those conditions are met, the lessee shall use the implicit rate. The incremental borrowing rate is defined as the rate that, at the inception of the lease, the lessee would have incurred to borrow the funds necessary to buy the leased asset on a secured loan basis with repayment terms similar to the payment schedule called for in the lease.

With regard to the last two of the above four criteria, if the beginning of the lease term falls within the last 25 percent of the total estimated economic life of the leased property, neither the 75 percent of economic life criterion nor the 90 percent recovery criterion is to be applied for purposes of classifying the lease. As a consequence, such leases will be classified as operating leases.

The lessee shall record a capital lease as an asset and an obligation at an amount equal to the present value of minimum lease payments[2] during the lease term, excluding executory costs (if determinable) such as insurance, maintenance, and taxes to be paid by the lessor together with any profit thereon. However, the amount so determined should not exceed the fair value of the leased property at the inception of the lease. If executory costs are not determinable from the provisions of the lease, an estimate of the amount shall be made.

Amortization, in a manner consistent with the lessee's normal depreciation policy, is called for over the term of the lease except where the lease transfers title or contains a bargain purchase option; in the latter cases amortization should follow the estimated economic life.

In accounting for an operating lease the lessee will charge rentals to expense as they become payable except when rentals do not become payable on a straight-line basis in which case they should be expensed on such a basis or on any other systematic or rational basis which reflects the time pattern of benefits derived from the leased property.

Accounting by lessors

In the case of the lessor, except for leveraged leases, if a lease meets any one of the preceding four criteria plus two additional criteria, it is to be classified and accounted for as a sales-type lease (if manufacturing or dealer profit is involved), or as a direct financing lease. The additional criteria are: (1) Collectibility of the minimum lease payments is reasonably predictable; and (2) No important uncertainties surround the amount of unreimbursable costs yet to be incurred by the lessor under the lease. A lease not meeting those tests is to be classified and accounted for as an operating lease.

Sales-type leases

1. The minimum lease payments plus the unguaranteed residual value accruing to the benefit of the lessor shall be recorded as the *gross investment* in the lease.

---

[2] These include the following: *(a)* minimum rental payments, *(b)* any guarantee by the lessee of the residual value at the expiration of the lease term, *(c)* any payment the lessee must make upon failure to renew or extend the lease at its expiration and *(d)* the payment called for by a bargain purchase price.

2. The difference between gross investment and the sum of the present values of its two components shall be recorded as unearned income. The net investment equals gross investment less unearned income. Unearned income shall be amortized to income over the lease term so as to produce a constant periodic rate of return on the net investment in the lease. Contingent rentals shall be credited to income when they become receivable.

3. At the termination of the existing lease term of a lease being renewed, the net investment in the lease shall be adjusted to the fair value of the leased property to the lessor at that date, and the difference, if any, recognized as gain or loss. (The same procedure applies to direct financing leases—see below.)

4. The present value of the minimum lease payments discounted at the interest rate implicit in the lease shall be recorded as the *sales price*. The cost, or carrying amount, if different, of the leased property, plus any initial direct costs (of negotiating and consummating the lease) less the present value of the unguaranteed residual value shall be charged against income in the same period.

5. The estimated residual value shall be periodically reviewed. If it is determined to be excessive, the accounting for the transaction shall be revised using the changed estimate. The resulting reduction in net investment shall be recognized as a loss in the period in which the estimate is changed. No upward adjustment of the estimated residual value shall be made. (A similar provision applies to direct financing leases.)

Direct-financing leases

1. The minimum lease payments (net of executory costs) plus the unguaranteed residual value plus the initial direct costs shall be recorded as the *gross investment*.

2. The difference between the gross investment and the cost, or carrying amount, if different, of the leased property, shall be recorded as *unearned income. Net investment* equals gross investment less unearned income. The unearned income shall be amortized to income over the lease term. The initial direct costs shall be amortized in the same portion as the unearned income. Contingent rentals shall be credited to income when they become receivable.

Operating leases

The lessor will include property accounted for as an operating lease in the balance sheet and will depreciate it in accordance with his normal depreciation policy. Rent should be taken into income over the lease term as it becomes receivable except that if it departs from a straight-line basis income should be recognized on such basis or on some other systematic or rational basis. Initial costs should be deferred and allocated over the lease term.

Principal disclosures

The principal items of information required to be disclosed by lessees are (1) future minimum lease payments, separately for capital leases and operating leases, in total and for each of the five succeeding years and (2) rental expense for each period for which an income statement is presented. Information required to be disclosed by lessors includes (1) future minimum lease payments to be received, separately for sales-type and direct financing leases and for operating leases, and (2) the other components of the investment in sales-type and direct financing leases: estimated residual values, and unearned income.

Leases involving real estate

These can involve (1) land only, (2) land and buildings, (3) equipment as well as real estate or (4) only part of a building or building complex.

Generally the above discussed accounting procedures will apply here, however, with the following exceptions.

a. Real estate is always capitalized only if the first two capitalization requirements are met (see page 173).
b. Land is not normally amortized.
c. If the fair value of land is 25 percent or more of the total fair value of the leased property, land should be separately capitalized and the value of each component should be determined in proportion to their fair values at the inception of the lease. If the fair value of land is less than 25 percent the leased property should be treated as a single unit.
d. Equipment should be considered separately and the minimum lease payments applicable to it should be estimated by whatever means are appropriate in the circumstances.
e. If the fair value of the leased property is objectively determinable, it will be treated as in (b) above. If not, the lessee should classify the lease according to criterion (c) above under capital leases using the estimated economic life of the building in which the leased premises are located. The lessee should account for the

lease accordingly. The lessor should account for the lease as an operating lease.

f. Leases of certain facilities such as airport, bus terminal, or port facilities from governmental units or authorities are to be classified as *operating leases*.

Sale—leaseback

When the lease meets the criteria for treatment as a capital lease, any gain on the sale should be deferred and amortized over the lease term in proportion to the amortization of the leased asset. When a capital lease is not present, any gain should be recognized at the time of the sale if the fair rental for the lease term is equal to or greater than the rental called for by the lease. If the lease rental exceeds the fair rental, any gain on the sale should be reduced by the amount of such excess.

When the leaseback is for only a portion of the property sold, an assessment should be made as to whether the leaseback of the portion of property sold at a profit represents a continued involvement in the property sufficient to require deferral of all or part of the profit on the sale.

Leveraged leases

Leveraged leasing, in which a lessor borrows heavily in order to finance a leasing transaction with a small, or even negative, equity in the leased property is a highly specialized topic.

Basically, the accounting method prescribed for use by lessors for leveraged leases, as they are defined in the statement, is called "the separate phases method." This method recognizes the separate investment phases of a leveraged lease in which the lessor's net investment declines during the early years of the lease and rises during the later years. In the case of lessees, leveraged leases are to be classified and accounted for in the same manner as nonleveraged leases.

Effective date and transition

The accounting of SFAS 13 is required for leases *entered* into, on or after January 1, 1977. Applying the new accounting rules to existing leases is optional—for three years—that is, companies may continue to apply the new *Standard* only to new leases through December 31, 1980. See, however, footnote 3 on page 180 for more stringent SEC requirements. Companies may voluntarily include all leases immediately or at any time until the 1980 deadline. The *Statement* requires, however, that until companies adopt full retroactive accounting in the financial statements, they must disclose, *in a footnote*, the amount of the capitalized asset and liability and the income statement impact of the capitalization, computed on a retroactive basis.

ILLUSTRATION 1.   Accounting for capital leases by lessees and lessors.

I.   Lease terms and assumptions
    A.   Lessor's cost of leased property (equipment) $10,000
    B.   Fair value of the leased property at inception of the lease 1/1/19X1 .... $10,000
    C.   Estimated economic life of the leased property .... 8 years
    D.   The lease has a fixed noncancelable term of 5 years with a rental of $2,400 payable at the end of each year. The lessee guarantees the residual value at the end of the 5-year lease term in the amount of $2,000. The lessee is to receive any excess of the sales price of property over the guaranteed amount at the end of the lease term. The lessee pays executory costs.
    E.   The rentals specified are determined to be fair, and the guarantees of residual value are expected to approximate realizable value. No investment tax credit is available.

II.   Additional information
    A.   The lessee depreciates its owned equipment on a straight-line basis.
    B.   The lessee's incremental borrowing rate is 10 percent per year.
    C.   At the end of the lease term the equipment is sold for $2,100.

1.   *Determination of minimum lease payments*
Minimum lease payments for both the lessee and the lessor are computed as follows:

Minimum rental payments over the lease term = ($2,400 × 5 years)	$12,000
Lessee guarantee of the residual value at the end of the lease term	2,000
Total minimum lease payments	$14,000

2.   *Determination of lessor's rate of interest implicit in the lease*
This is the rate which equates the recovery of the fair value of the property at the inception of the lease ($10,000) with the present value of both the minimum lease payments ($2,400 × 5) plus the lessee's guarantee of the residual value at the end of the lease ($2,000). This rate can be arrived at on a trial and error basis. At 10 percent the two discounted amounts add up to $10,340; at 11 percent to $10,057; while at 12 percent they equal $9,786. Through interpolation we arrive at an implicit interest rate of 11.21 percent.

3.   *Classification of the lease*
The *lessee* will classify this as a capital lease because the present value of the minimum lease payments at $10,340 (using its incremental borrowing

rate of 10 percent) exceeds 90 percent of the fair value of the property at the inception of the lease ($10,000). The lessee will use its incremental borrowing rate (10 percent) in discounting because it is less than the implicit interest rate in the lease. The *lessor* will classify the lease as a direct financing lease because the present value of the minimum lease payments using the implicit rate of 11.21 percent ($10,000) exceed 90 percent of the fair value of the property, cost and fair value of the amount are equal at inception of lease, and all other conditions of capitalization have been met.

4. *Accounting on the lessee's books*

1/1/19X1:

Leased property under capital leases	10,000	
Obligations under capital leases		10,000

To record the capital lease at the fair value of the property.

12/31/19X1:

Obligations under capital leases	1,279	
Interest Expense	1,121 (a)	
Cash		2,400

To record first year rental payments.

(a) Obligation balance outstanding × implicit interest rate = $10,000 × 11.21% = $1,121.

Depreciation Expense	1,600 (b)	
Accumulated depreciation of leased property under capital leases		1,600

To record first year depreciation.

(b) $\dfrac{\text{Cost-Residual Value}}{\text{Term of Lease}} = \dfrac{\$10,000 - \$2,000}{5} = \$1,600.$

12/31/19X5:

Cash	100	
Obligations under capital leases	2,000	
Accumulated Depreciation, leased property under capital leases	8,000	
Leased property under capital leases		10,000
Gain on Disposition of leased property		100

To record liquidation of obligations under capital leases and receipt of cash in excess of guaranteed residual value.

5. *Accounting on the lessor's books*

1/1/19X1:

Minimum Lease Payments Receivable	14,000	
Equipment		10,000
Unearned income		4,000

To record investment in direct financing lease.

12/21/19X1:

Cash	2,400	
Minimum Lease Payments Receivable		2,400
To record receipt of first year's rental.		

Unearned Income	1,121 (c)	
Earned Income		1,121

To recognize the portion of unearned income
that is earned during first year of investment.

(c) Net investment × implicit interest rate = 10,000 ×
    11.21%   = $1,121

12/31/19X5:

Cash	2,000	
Minimum Lease Payments Receivable		2,000
To record the receipt of the lessee's guarantee.		

Capital versus operating lease—the effect on income

As can be seen from the tabulation that follows, the interest expense
pattern of the capital lease follows that of a fixed payment mortgage
with interest expense decreasing over time as the principal balance
decreases. The attraction of operating lease accounting to the lessee is
also clear because under the capitalization procedure expenses incident to the lease, i.e., interest plus depreciation ($1,121 + $1,600),
exceed the rental expense by $321. In later years this excess reverses,
as over the lease period total expense under either method is equal,
but the pattern of expense recognition is an important consideration to
many enterprises, and the higher beginning charge under capitalization is viewed as a distinct disadvantage of that method.

The tabulation also indicates the pattern of finance income recognition by the lessor which is proportional to the investment at risk.

Year	Rental	Interest expense	Payment for obligations	Balance of obligations
19X0	—	—	—	$10,000
19X1	$ 2,400	$1,121	$1,279	8,721
19X2	2,400	977	1,423	7,298
19X3	2,400	818	1,582	5,716
19X4	2,400	641	1,759	3,957
19X5	2,400	443	1,957	2,000
Total	$12,000	$4,000	$8,000	$ 2,000

Capital versus operating lease—the effect on funds

It should be noted that, as far as the flow of funds is concerned, there is only one reality, i.e., the yearly outflow of the $2,400 rental.

Under capital lease accounting "funds from operations" are reduced yearly by declining interest charges (i.e., $1,121, $977 . . .), while the payment of lease obligations represents an "other" (non-operating) use of funds which increases yearly (i.e., $1,279, $1,423 . . .). The two always equal the rental payment of $2,400. The amortization (depreciation) of the property right of $1,600 annually has no effect on funds because it is a non-fund-using expense.

Implications for analysis

Leasing as a means of financing is an area deserving the analyst's particular scrutiny. The major objective here is to make sure that accounting form is not permitted to mask the economic substance of debt and its effect on capital sturcture, as well as exposure to fixed charges and the effects of leverage.

It is quite obvious that many long-term leases have all or most of the earmarks of debt. They create an obligation for payments under an agreement which is not cancellable. This represents a commitment to fixed payments which is what a debt obligation amounts to. The adverse effects of debt are also present in the case of a lease, that is, an inability to pay may result in insolvency. The fact that statutory limitations on lease obligations in case of bankruptcy limit the obligation to pay rent to one or a number of years is not a mitigating factor of substance because the process of financial analysis is usually designed to evaluate the probability of insolvency and the attendant adverse effects on asset values and credit standing, rather than an evaluation of the amount and standing of the obligations after insolvency proceedings have been started. The importance of the leased property to company operations is also a factor, since it may be so vital as to preclude the company's abandonment of the lease in reorganization proceedings.

It is very difficult, if not impossible, to compare the financial position of companies which use different methods of financing, including installment purchase in the form of a lease, for the financing of different assets. That is also true of comparisons of income, since when accounted as an operating lease, rentals are usually less than interest expense and depreciation expenses in the early stages of ownership in the form of a lease.

SFAS 13 represents a major step in the direction of providing the analyst with the information required for the proper reflection of leases in the financial statements and the evaluation of their impact on the financial position and results of operations of an enterprise. The criteria as well as the disclosure requirements embodied in this *Statement* are much more comprehensive and explicit than those contained in any former pronouncements and this should assure that the abuses and distortions of the past will not inhibit the process of analysis. Nevertheless, the analyst, mindful of the historical tendencies and developments in areas of accounting which are affected by strong special interests, should be ever alert to the possibility that managements, aided by the seemingly inexhaustible ingenuity of their accountants, lawyers, and other financial advisers will, in time, devise ways to circumvent this statement. Accounting standards may, in time, be changed to meet these challenges and so it is the interim period that presents the time of greatest risk exposure for the analyst.

Until the expiration of the transitional period in 1980 additional analytical steps may be required to make the financial statements of lessors and lessees fully comparable and the analyst will have to refer to the additional footnote information provided.[3] While, under the standards which preceded SFAS 13, only relatively few leases were capitalized, the new rules will require the capitalization of most leases where there is an effective transfer of substantially all of the benefits and risks of ownership from lessor to lessee.[4]

The effect of these changes will result in the increase of debt and of fixed assets; the impairment in debt/equity ratios; the reduction in current and acid test ratios (the current portion of long-term lease obligations will increase current liabilities); and in the increase of expenses in the early stages of a lease. Because of the requirement that enterprises use their "normal" depreciation policies in accounting for the depreciation of leased property the income of entities using accelerated depreciation methods for book purposes will be more substantially affected.

The provisions of SFAS 13 which entail assumptions of fair values, selling prices, salvage or residual values, implicit rates of interest, and incremental borrowing rates are not so tight as to preclude substantive changes in accounting through manipulations of these relatively "soft" factors. Thus, as in the past, the analyst will also in the future,

---

[3] Under rules proposed by the SEC, companies will be required to retroactively capitalize and restate existing leases by 12/25/77 unless they are unable to resolve problems in connection with restrictive clauses of loan indentures or other agreements and that fact is disclosed. Public utilities which are considered exempt from the lease capitalization provisions of SFAS 13 would be required to make substantial footnote disclosures.

[4] The exemption of facilities leased from governmental units is an expedient step not entirely supported in logic.

have to be alert and vigilant when analyzing the impact of leases on financial statements.

LIABILITIES UNDER PENSION PLANS

Like the accounting for most obligations, that for pensions also has a dual aspect. Their impact on results of operations will be considered in Chapter 11 while the liability aspect will be discussed here.

While the FASB has the topic of pension plans under consideration, as of now *APB Opinion 8* remains the authoritative pronouncement on the subject of pension accounting.

Two basic cost categories are associated with pensions. The *current cost* which is the actuarially determined obligation incurred for pension benefits bestowed upon employees during a given period of time, and *prior service* costs representing pension credit given to employees for work performed before the inception of the pension plan or incident to a retroactive revision of plan terms.[5]

It is important to understand the difference between the *accrual* of the proper pension cost which is a bookkeeping entry and the *funding* of that cost which involves the transfer of funds from the entity to the pension trustee.

Liabilities for current costs represent accruals which, for whatever reason, the company has not funded. However, pension legislation as well as tax considerations require that current service costs be funded promptly.

On the assumption that the payment of past period benefits obligations can be delayed and avoided indefinitely, *APB Opinion 8* states that "unfunded prior service cost is not a liability which should be shown in the balance sheet."

The *Opinion* does require disclosure of the excess of vested benefits over the total of the pension fund net assets adjusted for accruals and prepayments. It does not, however, require the disclosure of vesting terms nor the size of the pension fund.

Implications for analysis

The analyst must be aware that both the shortcomings of present accounting and disclosure rules for pension liabilities as well as new developments such as the Employee Retirement Income Security Act of 1974 (ERISA) can cause financial statements to understate significantly the actual and potential corporate liabilities for pensions.

---

[5] There is a technical distinction between "past" and "prior" service cost which need not concern us here.

While *APB Opinion 8* does not require the disclosure of unfunded past service benefits Rule 3-16(g) of Regulation S-X calls for disclosure of "the estimated amount that would be necessary to fund or otherwise provide for the past service cost of the plan." Thus, the analyst should, in most cases, be able to determine the size of the unfunded past service liability.

Moreover, whenever vested benefits (those belonging to an employee in any event) exceed the net pension fund assets the analyst is faced with a kind of "off balance sheet liability" which he must recognize and take into account. Knowing only the excess of the liability over the assets available to meet it, is incomplete information because the relationship of the deficiency to total fund assets holds important clues to how large a percentage recovery in the value of fund assets is needed to bridge the gap.

ERISA has added weight to the argument that unfunded past service costs represent real liabilities because of requirements of the law that they be funded (i.e., paid) generally over a 40 year period.

Comparisons between unfunded liabilities of companies are difficult because of variations due to:

1. Methods of evaluating assets and liabilities of the fund.
2. Methods of recognizing realized and unrealized gains and losses.
3. Discrepancies between actuarial assumptions and actual performance.
4. Different dates of actuarial valuations.

Thus, for example, carrying assets at "adjusted" cost at the bottom of a bear market can understate the unfunded vested benefits liability as was, for example, the case with General Electric in 1974.

The potential seriousness of the size of unfunded vested benefits liabilities can be appreciated from the results of a study which showed that the average company in a 1974 survey of 40 large corporations had a liability equal to five percent of net worth.[6] However, Uniroyal had a liability equal to 78 percent of net worth, Chrysler 45 percent, Bethlehem Steel 41 percent, Western Union 40 percent, and Republic Steel 34 percent. Lockheed's liability exceeded its net worth 16 times.

This survey also found that while the size of fund assets held by the 40 companies was $27 billion at the end of 1974 their unfunded vested benefits stood at $12 billion (44 percent of pension funds assets) and their unfunded past service costs were about $20 billion.

Finally, ERISA provides that on liquidation of an enterprise or the termination of a pension plan, up to 30 percent of the enterprise net

[6] Patrick J. Regan, "Potential Corporate Liabilities under ERISA", *Financial Analysts Journal*, March–April 1976, pp. 26–31.

worth (which may be greater or less than book value net worth) may be attached to make good pension fund deficiencies. This potential liability for "guaranteed unfunded benefits," which ranks in priority with a tax lien, is an additional element which may affect the debt-equity ratio of many enterprises.

So far the Financial Accounting Standards Board has stated that it does not believe that ERISA creates a legal obligation for unfunded pension costs that warrant recognition as a liability on the balance sheet except generally for that unpaid portion currently required to be funded and where a legal liability is created as a result of the termination of the pension plan. As we have seen the obligations may be very real and even the exception may become important. The analyst must be careful to assess pension liabilities fully and thoroughly.

LIABILITIES AT THE "EDGE" OF EQUITY

The analyst must be alert to the existence of equity securities (typically preferred stock) which because of mandatory redemption provisions are more akin to debt than they are to equity. Whatever their name, these securities impose upon the issuing companies obligations to lay out funds at specified dates which is precisely a burden which a true equity security is not supposed to impose. Such preferred issues exist, for example, at Lockheed Corporation (Preferred A), at Reliance Group (preferred Series B and C—a close to $116 million obligation) and are described by Getty Oil Co., as follows:

Note 6: Capital stock. Under the sinking fund provisions of the preferred stock, the company is required to redeem 40,917 shares of its $25 par value stock on each January 10 and July 10. The sinking fund provisions may be satisfied from treasury stock previously purchased on the open market, and accordingly, 81,834 treasury shares were retired during each of the years 1974 and 1973.

The preferred stock contains provisions which restrict the payment of cash dividends on common stock and the purchase or redemption of such stock. On December 31, 1974, approximately $185 million of consolidated retained earnings were restricted under these provisions.

DEFERRED CREDITS (INCOME)

An ever-increasing variety of items and descriptions is included in this group of accounts. In many cases these items are akin to liabilities; in others, they represent deferred income yet to be earned, while in a number of cases, they serve as income-smoothing devices. The confusion confronting the analyst is compounded by a lack of agreement among accountants as to the exact nature of these items or the proper manner of their presentation. Thus, regardless of category or presentation, the key to their analysis lies in an understanding of the circumstances and the financial transactions which brought them about.

At one end of this group's spectrum we find those items which have the characteristics of liabilities. Here we may find included such items as advances or billings on uncompleted contracts, unearned royalties and deposits, and customer service prepayments. Quite clearly, the outstanding characteristic of these items is their liability aspects, even though, as in the case of advances of royalties, they may, after certain conditions are fulfilled, find their way into the company's income stream. Advances on uncompleted contracts represent primarily methods of financing the work in process, while deposits of rent received represent, as do customer service prepayments, security for performance of an agreement. Even though found sometimes among "deferred credits," such items are more properly classified as liabilities, or current liabilities if due within the company's operating cycle.

Next, we consider deferred income items which represent income or revenue received in advance and which will be earned over future periods through the passage of time, the performance of services, or the delivery of goods. Examples of deferred income items are: magazine subscription income, representing the receipts by magazine publishers of advance payment for long-term subscriptions; and unearned rental income, which represents receipt of advance payment for rent. Other examples are unearned finance charges, deferred profit on installment sales, deferred gain on sales-and-leaseback arrangements, and unrealized profit on layaway sales.

It should be noted that this category includes a liability for future performance as well as a possible profit component in such income items received but not yet earned as, for example, subscription income, the future earning of which is dependent on the delivery of magazines. It also includes unearned finance charges which have already been deducted but which are allocated to the future on the assumption that they are earned with the mere passage of time. Still further along the "earned" scale are profits on installment sales which are deferred, not because they have not been earned but rather because the collection of the receivable resulting from such sales is going to occur over a period of time in the future. The preferred accounting treatment is not to defer such gains on installment sales but rather to give expression to any doubts about future collectibility of receivables by establishing a provision for doubtful accounts for that purpose.

Further on the other extreme of the deferred credit spectrum are so-called "bargain purchase credits" which arise in cases where the fair value of certain assets of an acquired company exceeds the consideration given. (Purchase accounting which is governed by *APB Opinion No. 16* is discussed in Chapter 9.) In such cases the resulting credit is amortized to income over what is usually an arbitrarily determined number of years. What we have here is a benefit derived from what is presumably an advantageous acquisition. The reason for the deferral of this benefit and its taking up in income over a number of years is not necessarily that this benefit has not been realized, but because of a desire to spread it out, or smooth its effect over a number of years.

One of the most complicated and controversial, as well as most substantial, of deferred credits are deferred income taxes.

Deferred taxes

Tax allocation which is the accounting process giving rise to deferred tax credits (or debits in reverse circumstances) is primarily a device for matching the applicable tax expense with corresponding pretax income. A more comprehensive analysis of this accounting technique and its implications will be undertaken in Chapter 11 on the measurement of income. Here we will examine primarily the nature of the deferred credit to which it gives rise.

For purposes of understanding how this deferred tax credit arises, let us consider the example of the depreciation deducted under circumstances where a company may elect an accelerated-depreciation method for tax purposes while using the straight-line method for book purposes. Since more depreciation is deducted for tax purposes in the early years, two things are evident: (1) there is a tax deferral in the early years and (2) that will have to be made up in the later years since in no event can depreciation for tax purposes exceed the total original cost. Thus, in theory, the tax savings are temporary; and under tax allocation these savings are not used to reduce the tax expense but are rather accumulated as a deferred tax credit.

In practice, as a study by the accounting firm of Price Waterhouse and Company shows, this "deferred tax liability" is rarely paid in full. The reason for this is that most companies keep expanding their plant so that every year there is new accelerated depreciation on new facilities to balance—and usually outweigh—the reduced depreciation on facilities that got the accelerated treatment earlier.[7]

The accounting profession which, in *APB Opinion No. 11*, adopted the concept of comprehensive tax allocation, states that it does not regard deferred taxes as a liability but considers them rather a deferred

---

[7] It is interesting to note that in Britain, chartered accountants have proposed in 1977 that most deferred tax accounting be abolished.

credit account which must be established for the proper matching of costs and revenues. Be that as it may, the analyst must understand what this account represents when he finds it included within the deferred credits category. While we used depreciation as an example here, deferred taxes may arise in any instance where expense or income items are treated one way for tax purposes and another for book purposes.

Deferred investment tax credit

Frequently included among deferred income taxes is the deferred investment credit. While also a tax benefit, the similarity between the deferred income taxes, discussed above, and the deferred investment credit is more apparent than real.

Under various revenue acts, as amended, up to 10 percent of the cost of certain depreciable assets purchased and put into service during the year has been allowed as a credit against federal income taxes. Unlike deferred income taxes, which represent a postponement of tax liability, the investment credit is an effective reduction of taxes in the years in which it is earned. Under one alternative treatment, it is taken into income by means of a reduction of tax expenses in the year in which it is taken on the tax return, while under another alternative, it is taken into income over the productive lives of the assets whose acquisition gave rise to it. It is in the latter case that the deferred investment credit account is found on the balance sheet; and what it represents is, in essence, a device for spreading a benefit already earned over a number of years, in order to achieve a more fair determination of income. The income aspect of the investment credit will be considered more fully in the chapter devoted to this subject.

Now that we have covered the entire spectrum of that family of accounts designated as deferred credits, we can clearly see that each must be examined and understood on its own merits if its significance to the analyst is to be properly assessed.

Found among liabilities, and sometimes in the equity section, but not really representing an immediate claim on company resources, are the minority interests in consolidated entities. These represent the proportionate interest of minority stockholders in a majority-owned subsidiary which is consolidated. Since all the net assets (i.e., assets less liabilities) of the subsidiary are included in the consolidated statements, the minority's portion is shown as a liability in the consolidated balance sheet.

Implications for analysis

The key to the proper analysis of deferred credits is a clear understanding of what has brought them about. In the discussion concerning the accounting principles involved, we have pointed out that they encompass a wide variety of dissimilar items.

Those items which represent prepayments on services yet to be performed or goods yet to be delivered must be regarded as temporary sources of funds. In fact, often advances on contracts yet to be executed serve exactly the purpose of affording temporary financing to the supplier.

Deferred reserves may be viewed by the analyst as items which are on their way to the income stream of a company. What should not be lost sight of is the fact that many such items do not represent pure income elements as may be the case with interest on deferred installment sale profit which are deemed to be earned by the mere passage of time without the incurrence of additional expense. Thus, deferred subscription income represents the amount received in advance for magazines yet to be delivered. In spite of the fact that the earning of such subscription revenue will require paper, printing, editorial, and postage expense, such costs are usually not provided for when the revenue is deferred. Thus, while such items do represent temporary sources of funds, they are not sources of net profit and may, in fact, ultimately result in a net loss.

Certain deferred income items are clearly created, not for the purposes of fair presentation of financial positions but rather for purposes of income smoothing or equalization. Thus the "bargain purchase credit" discussed earlier has as its main purpose and justification the smoothing of income over a period of years and must be regarded as such. Similarly the ratable taking up of installment sales profit is designed to provide for the contingency of possible noncollection of the sales price.

Perhaps the most confusing deferred credit to many analysts is the deferred tax credit. Because of its size, it is, by far, the most important item in this category. Its location in the twilight zone between liabilities and equity indicates that it is neither, but that in itself does not shed light on its true nature.

The reason that the deferred tax credit is not a liability is that it lacks some of the more important characteristics of debt. The government has no present claim for taxes nor is there a timetable for repayment. While the deferred tax account represents the loss of future deductibility of assets for tax purposes, the drawing down of this account to reduce tax expenses depends on future developments, such as asset acquisition and depreciation policies which are not predictable with certainty.

This kind of uncertainty attests to the fact that the deferred tax credit is also not in the nature of equity capital because it represents a tax benefit in the nature of a postponement of taxes rather than a savings of taxes.

The most meaningful thing that can be said about this account from the point of view of financial analysis is that it represents a temporary source of funds derived from the postponement of taxes and that the duration of the overall postponement depends on factors such as the future growth or stability of the company's depreciable assets pool. It is the assessment of such factors and their future likelihood that will be helpful to the analysis of the deferred tax account.

RESERVES AND PROVISIONS

Another group of accounts, found between long-term liabilities and the stockholders' equity section, is that of reserves and provisions. These accounts are often lumped together or even found among current liabilities or as deductions from related asset accounts; consequently it is most useful to classify them broadly so as to facilitate an understanding of their true nature.

The first category is most correctly described as comprising provisions for liabilities and obligations which have a higher probability of occurrence, but which are in dispute or are uncertain in amount. As is the case with many financial statement descriptions, neither the title nor the location in the financial statement can be relied upon as a rule of thumb guide to the nature of an account. Thus, the best key to analysis is a thorough understanding of the business and financial transactions which give rise to the account. The following are representative items in this group: provisions for product guarantees, service guarantees, and warranties, which are established in recognition of the fact that these undertakings involve future costs which are certain to arise though presently impossible to measure exactly. Consequently, the provision is established by a charge to income at the time products covered by guarantees are sold, in an amount estimated on the basis of experience or on the basis of any other reliable factor.

Another type of obligation which must be provided for on the best basis available is the liability for unredeemed trading stamps issued. To the company issuing the trading stamps, there is no doubt about the liability to redeem the stamps for merchandise. The only uncertainty concerns the number of stamps which will be presented for redemption.

Another important group of future costs which must be provided for is that of employee compensation. These, in turn, give rise to provisions for deferred compensation, incentive compensation, supplemental unemployment benefits, bonus plans, welfare plans, and severance pay.

Finally the category of estimated liabilities includes provisions for claims arising out of pending or existing litigation.

The second category comprises reserves for expenses and losses, which by experience or estimate are very likely to occur in the future and which should properly be provided for by current charges to operations.

One group within this category comprises reserves for operating costs such as maintenance, repairs, painting, or furnace relining. Thus, for example, since furnace relining jobs may be expected to be required at regularly recurring intervals, they are provided for rateably by charges to operations in order to avoid charging the entire cost to the year in which the actual relining takes place.

Another group comprises provisions for future losses stemming from decisions or actions already taken. Included in this group are reserves for relocation, replacement, modernization, and discontinued operations.

ACCOUNTING FOR CONTINGENCIES

SFAS 5 (1975) sets definitive criteria for the accrual and disclosure of loss contingencies.

A loss contingency is defined in the *Statement* as an existing condition, situation, or set of circumstances involving uncertainty as to possible loss that will be resolved when one or more future events occur or fail to occur. Examples provided of loss contingencies are: litigation, threat of expropriation, collectibility of receivables, claims arising from product warranties or product defects, self-insured risks, and possible catastrophe losses of property and casualty insurance companies.

The *Statement* specifies two conditions, both of which must be met before a provision for a loss contingency should be charged to income. First, it must be probable that an asset had been impaired or a liability incurred at the date of a company's financial statements. Implicit in that condition is that it must be probable that a future event or events will occur confirming the fact of the loss. The second condition is that the amount of loss can be reasonably estimated. The effect of applying these criteria is that a loss will be accrued only when it is reasonably estimable and relates to the current or a prior period.

In the board's opinion, losses from uncollectible receivables and obligations related to product warranties and product defects would normally meet the conditions for accrual at the time a sale is made. On the other hand, accrual for loss or damage of a company's property and loss from injury to others, damage to the property of others, and business interruption—sometimes referred to as self-insurance risks— would not be appropriate until the actual event of loss has taken place. Catastrophe losses of property and casualty insurance companies and reinsurance companies would not be accruable until the catastrophe has occurred. According to the *Statement,* catastrophe losses do not meet the conditions for accrual because predictions of losses over relatively short periods of time are subject to substantial deviations. Accruals for losses from such matters as expropriation, litigation, claims, and assessments would depend on the facts in each case.

The *Statement* permits appropriations of retained earnings for specified risks provided these are kept in the equity sector of the balance sheet and are not used to relieve the income statement of actual losses (see also Chapter 8).

The *Statement* requires that if no accrual is made for a loss contingency because one or both of the conditions for accrual are not met, disclosure of the contingency shall be made when there is at least a reasonable possibility that a loss may have been incurred. The disclosure shall indicate the nature of the contingency and shall give an estimate of the possible loss or range of loss, or state that such an estimate cannot be made.

Implications for analysis

Provisions, such as for service guarantees and warranties, represent, in effect, revenue received for services yet to be performed. Of importance to the analyst is the adequacy of the provision which is often established on the basis of prior experience or, absent that, on the basis of other estimates. Concern with adequacy of amount is a prime factor in the analysis of all other reserves, whatever their purpose. Reserves and provisions appearing above the equity section should almost invariably be created by means of charges to income. They are designed to relieve the income statement of charges which, while belonging to the present, will be incurred in the future.

Reserves for future losses represent a category of accounts which require particular scrutiny. While conservatism in accounting calls for recognition of losses as they can be determined or clearly foreseen, companies tend, particularly in loss years, to overprovide for losses yet to be incurred such as a disposal of assets, relocation, or plant closings. Overprovision does, of course, shift expected future losses to a present period which already shows adverse results. (A more extended discussion of such practices will be found in Chapter 11.) The problem with such reserves is that once established there is no further accounting for the expenses and losses which are charged against them. Only in certain financial statements required to be filed with the SEC (such as Form 10-K) are details of changes in reserves required, and even here there is no requirement for detailed disclosure of the nature of the changes. Normally no information is given, and the analyst must adopt a critical attitude towards the establishment of such reserves and the means of their disposition.

Reserves have traditionally been a popular management device for earnings manipulation and smoothing. Overprovision of loss reserves were recorded in years when results of operations were richer than management wanted to report, or when they were so poor that the creation of a cushion for the future did not matter to reported results.

SFAS 5 has gone a long way towards removing or at least reducing this management option. The much stricter criteria which must now be met means that greater earnings volatility will be experienced by companies subject to foreign risks, casualty insurers, self-insurers, and companies in certain industries such as oil (e.g., risks affecting offshore rigs and tankers.)

The *Statement* also recognized that "accounting reserves" do not protect against risk, have no "cash flow" significance and do not provide an alternative to insurance.

The analyst cannot, however, safely assume that overprovisions or, for that matter, underprovisions for losses are a thing of the past. Analysts should always attempt to obtain the full details of reserves by category and amount. Under the Internal Revenue Code the only anticipated losses that are specifically tax deductible are provisions for bad debts and inventory write-downs to the lower of cost or market (for companies not on Lifo). Thus, one method by which the analyst can detect undisclosed provisions for future expenses or losses is by an analysis of deferred taxes. The book expense not currently allowed for tax purposes should have its effect on the deferred (prepaid) tax account.

It is interesting to note that the disclosure requirements of SFAS 5 with respect to contingency losses charged to income appears weaker than those concerning unbooked amounts. The analyst needs as much disclosure as possible because it is important to assess the adequacy of provisions for future losses particularly in such areas as claims and litigation where existing guidelines and standards are far from clear or rigorous.

COMMITMENTS

Commitments are claims which may occur upon the future performance under a contract. They are not given expression in accounting records since the mere signing of an executory contract or the issuance of a purchase order does not result in a completed transaction.

Examples of commitments are long-term noncancellable contracts to purchase goods or services at specified prices or purchase contracts for fixed assets which call for payments during construction. In a sense, a lease agreement is also regarded by some as a form of commitment.

Commitments call for disclosure of all the factors surrounding the obligation, including amount, conditions, timing, and other facts of importance.

For example, Storer Broadcasting Company revealed the following commitment in its annual report:

The Company has entered into contracts, covering rentals of television films, under which it is obligated to make payments totaling approximately $7 million during the next six years. Payments under these contracts are recorded as deferred film rentals which are charged to expense as the films are used by the Company.

Cummins Engine Co. disclosed the following in its annual report:

The contract with a foreign engine parts supplier requires that the Company take minimum quantities at prices negotiated annually, or pay 45 percent of the difference between purchases and the minimum. Should the Company terminate the agreement, it will pay the supplier book value of plant and equipment acquired for the manufacture of these parts.

Commitments for additional plant, property and equipment for 1975 totaled approximately $33 million at December 31, 1974. In addition, there is a further commitment of $15 million to equip the new components plant by December 31, 1977.

CONTINGENT LIABILITIES

Business enterprise is subject to constant and all-pervading uncertainty. It is assumed that the informed reader of the financial statements is aware of this. However, certain events may point to specific probabilities and contingencies in the future and should be disclosed as such. *Accounting Research Bulletin No. 50* states that "in accounting, a contingency is an existing condition, situation, or set of circumstances, involving a considerable degree of uncertainty, which may, through a related future event, result in the acquisition or loss of an asset, or the incurrence or avoidance of a liability, usually with the concurrence of gain or loss."

The basic nature of a contingency is its dependence on a future development or intervening factor or decision by an outside factor. Usually the contingency is uncertain as to probability of occurrence, timing, and amount. The financial statements must disclose the degree of probability of occurrence and, if possible, the best estimate of financial impact (Refer also to the discussion of SFAS 5 under "Reserves").

Examples of contingent liabilities are those which could arise from litigation, from guarantees of performance, from agreements and contracts, such as purchase or repurchase agreements, and from tax assessments or renegotiation claims.

The AMAX INC., annual report includes the following:

Contingent Liabilities and Guarantees—At December 31, 1974, AMAX and its consolidated subsidiaries were contingent guarantors of notes and other liabilities aggregating $30,000, principally in connection with the 50 percent-owned aluminum smelter operated by an affiliate of Alumax Inc. In addition, AMAX has guaranteed liabilities of $17,000 applicable to Botswana RST Limited which could, in certain circumstances, be increased $11,000.

QUESTIONS

1. What are the major disclosure requirements in SEC *Accounting Series Release No. 148* regarding the terms of short-term debt?
2. What are the conditions required by SFAS 6 that will demonstrate the ability of a company to refinance its short-term debt on a long-term basis?
3. How do bond discounts and premiums usually arise? How are they accounted for?
4. Both the conversion feature of debt as well as warrants attached to debt instruments aim at increasing the attractiveness of debt securities and at lowering their interest cost. Describe how the costs of these two similar features are accounted for.
5. What should the analyst be aware of if a company includes short-term bank debt in its current liabilities?
6. How does the analyst of financial statements evaluate an enterprise's liabilities—both present and contingent?
7. *a.* What are the criteria, stipulated by SFAS 13, for classifying leases by the lessee?
   b. Provide a summary of accounting for leases by lessee according to SFAS 13.
8. *a.* What are the different classification of leases—according to SFAS 13—by lessors? What are the criteria for classifying each type?
   b. What are the accounting procedures for leases by lessors according to SFAS 13?
9. What are the principal disclosures required by lessees and lessors according to SFAS 13?
10. What are the implications of SFAS 13 for the financial analyst?
11. What liabilities or potential liabilities must the financial analyst recognize with regard to pension plans?
12. Comparisons between unfunded pension liabilities of different companies are difficult for various reasons. Discuss.
13. What types of equity securities are akin to debt? Discuss.
14. Distinguish between different kinds of "deferred credits" appearing on a balance sheet. How should those be analyzed?

15. Describe the nature of deferred tax credits. How should the analyst interpret this account?

16. Into what types should reserves and provisions be subdivided for purposes of financial statement analysis?

17. Why must the analyst be particularly alert to the accounting for reserves for future costs and losses?

18. *a.* What is a loss contingency? Give some examples.

    b. What two conditions (as specified by SFAS 5) must be met before a provision for a loss contingency can be charged to income?

8

ANALYSIS OF STOCKHOLDERS' EQUITY

The stockholders' equity section of the balance sheet represents the investment of the ownership in the assets of a business entity. While the claims of the ownership are junior to those in the current and long-term liability sections of the balance sheet, they represent, on the other hand, residual claims to all assets, once the claims of creditors have been satisfied. Thus, while being exposed to the maximum risk associated with the enterprise, the ownership is entitled to all the residual rewards that are associated with it.

The accounting for the equity section as well as the presentation, classification, and footnote disclosure associated therewith have certain basic objectives, the most important among which are:

1. To classify and distinguish the major sources of capital contributed to the entity.
2. To set forth the rights and priorities of the various classes of stockholders and the manner in which they rank in partial or final liquidation.
3. To set forth the legal restrictions to which the distribution of capital funds may be subject for whatever reason.
4. To disclose the contractual, legal, managerial, or financial restrictions to which the distribution of current or retained earnings may be subject.
5. To disclose the terms and provisions of convertible securities, of stock options, and of other arrangements involving the future issuance of stock, contingent and otherwise.

CLASSIFICATION OF CAPITAL STOCK

There are two basic kinds of capital stock—preferred and common. There are a number of different varieties within each category, and these, too, have basic differences worth noting.

The preferred stock is usually preferred in liquidation and preferred as to dividends. It may be entitled to par value in liquidation or it may be entitled to a premium. On the other hand its rights to dividends are generally fixed, although they may be cumulative, which means that preferred shareholders are entitled to arrearages of dividends before the common stockholders may receive any dividends. The preferred features, as well as the fixed nature of the dividend, give the preferred stock some of the earmarks of debt with the important difference that preferred stockholders are not generally entitled to demand redemption of their shares. Nevertheless, there are preferred stock issues which have set redemption dates and which may require sinking funds to be established for that purpose. These are more akin to debt than to equity and are discussed in Chapter 7.

Characteristics of preferred stock which may make them more akin to common stock are divided participation rights, voting rights, and rights of conversion into common stock.

Within the preferred stock classes we may find a variety of orders of priority and preference relating to dividends and liquidation rights.

The common stock is the basic ownership equity of a company having no preference but reaping all residual rewards as well as being subject to all losses. Occasionally there is more than one class of common stock. In such cases the distinctions between one class and the other express themselves in dividend, voting, or other rights.

The preferred stock generally has a par value which may or may not be the amount at which it was originally sold. Common stock may have a par value, and if not, it is usually assigned a stated value. The par value of the common stock has no substantive significance for analytical purposes.

Disclosure regarding capital stock

Proper disclosure requires that an analysis and explanation of changes in the number of shares of capital stock be given in the financial statements or in the notes related thereto. Such changes may be due to a variety of reasons including the following:

1. *Increases in capital stock outstanding:*
   a. Sale of stock.
   b. Conversion of debentures or preferred stock.

  c. Issuance pursuant to stock dividends or stock splits.
  d. Issuance of stock in acquisitions or mergers.
  e. Issuance of stock pursuant to stock options granted or warrants exercised.
2. *Decreases in capital stock outstanding:*
  a. Purchase and retirement of stock.
  b. Purchase of treasury stock.
  c. Reverse stock splits.

Another important aspect of disclosure with regard to the various classes of capital stock is the various options held by others which, when exercised, would cause the number of shares outstanding to be increased. Such options include:

1. Conversion rights of debenture or preferred stock into common.
2. Warrants outstanding for a specified period entitling the holder to exchange them for stock under specified conditions.
3. Stock options under supplementary compensation and bonus plans which call for the issuance of capital stock over a period of time at prices fixed in advance, such as qualified stock option plans and "employee stock purchase plans."
4. Commitments to issue capital stock, such as under merger agreements which call for additional consideration contingent on the happening of an event such as the reaching of certain earning levels by the acquired company, etc.

The importance of such disclosures lies in the need to alert all interested parties to the potential increase in the number of shares outstanding. The degree of the resultant dilution in earnings and book value per share depends, of course, on such factors as the amount to be paid in per share and other rights given up when conversions of securities are effected.

Up to the mid-1960s the accounting profession has almost completely ignored the effect that potential dilution has on such basic valuation yardsticks as earnings per share and, to a lesser extent, book value per share. More recently, alerted by the use of even more complex securities, the profession has finally recognized that dilution represents a very real cost to a company, a cost which had been given little if any formal recognition in financial statements. The impact of dilution on earnings per share will be examined in Chapter 12. Problems in the computation of book value are examined at the end of this chapter.

Disclosure must be made of a variety of terms to which preferred stock may be subject, including:

1. *Dividend rights,* including participating and cumulative features.
2. *Liquidation rights.* In *APB Opinion No. 10* the board stated:

> Companies at times issue preferred (or other senior) stock which has a preference in involuntary liquidation considerably in excess of the par or stated value of the shares. The relationship between this preference in liquidation and the par or stated value of the shares may be of major significance to the users of the financial statements of those companies and the Board believes it highly desirable that it be prominently disclosed. Accordingly, the Board recommends that in these cases, the liquidation preference of the stock be disclosed in the equity section of the balance sheet in the aggregate, either parenthetically or "in short" rather than on a per share basis or by disclosure in notes.

Such disclosure is particularly important since the discrepancy between the par and liquidation value of preferred stock can be very significant as is the case, for example, in General Aniline & Film Corporation where at one point in time the par value was $3.9 million as against a liquidation value of $85.7 million!

3. *Voting rights,* which may change with conditions such as arrearages in dividends.
4. *Conversion rights.*
5. *Sinking fund provisions,* which are not too common.
6. *Call provisions,* which usually protect the preferred stockholder against premature redemption. Call premiums often decrease over time.

In addition to a description of terms, disclosure must be made of any conditions affecting the relative standing of the various classes of stock such as, for example, dividend arrearages on preferred stock, which must generally be paid before the common stock can get any distribution at all.

An example of such disclosure is provided by Jim Walter Corporation:

> The $2 convertible series 1-third preferred stock (i) is convertible into three shares of common stock (141,927 shares of common stock are reserved for such conversion at August 31, 1975), (ii) is callable in whole or in part on any quarterly dividend date for $45 per share plus cumulative dividends, (iii) upon liquidation is entitled to $40 per share plus cumulative dividends, and (iv) holders are entitled to receive quarterly cumulative dividends at an annual rate of $2 per share. Sinking fund payments at $40 per share are required, subject to reductions for redemptions and conversions after July 31, 1977, equal to 5 percent annually of shares outstanding at that date. During 1975 and 1974, 1,555 and 53,973 shares of $2 convertible series 1-third preferred stock were converted into 4,665 and 161,919 shares of common stock, respectively.

Additional capital

Amounts paid in for capital stock are usually divided into two parts. One part is assigned to the par or stated value of capital shares, and the rest is shown in the capital surplus section. The term "surplus" is actually falling into disuse so that the additional capital section contains accounts having such descriptive titles as "capital in excess of par or stated value," "additional capital," "additional paid-in capital," and "paid-in capital." No matter what the title, these accounts signify the amounts paid in for capital stock in excess of par or stated value.

The additional accounts in the "capital" group do not result only from amounts paid in excess of par but include also charges or credits from a variety of other capital transactions, examples of which are:

1. Gains or losses from sale of treasury stock.
2. Capital changes arising from business combinations.
3. Capital donations, usually shown separately as donated capital.
4. Capital stock expenses, merger expenses, and other costs of a capital nature.
5. Capitalization of retained earnings by means of stock dividends.

Informative financial statements must contain a reconciliation of all capital surplus accounts so as to explain the changes which have occurred therein.

Treasury stock

Treasury stock is stock which has once been issued and was outstanding and which has been subsequently reacquired by the company. Treasury stock is generally carried at cost, and the most common method of presentation is to deduct such cost from the total equity section. Some companies which reserve their own treasury stock for such purposes as profit sharing, contingent compensation, deferred compensation, or other compensation plans, or for purposes of acquisitions of other companies do sometimes present such stock among assets which, while not a very logical procedure, is nevertheless acceptable.

RETAINED EARNINGS

While the capital stock and capital surplus accounts show primarily the capital contribution by various classes of stock, the Retained Earnings account represents generally the accumulation of undistributed earnings since inception. Conversely, a deficit account represents the accumulated net losses of the corporation.

Although some states permit distributions to shareholders from capital surplus accounts such distributions represent, in effect, capital distributions. Thus, the Retained Earnings account is the prime source of dividend distributions to shareholders, and amounts distributed by charge to other accounts do not, strictly speaking, deserve the label "dividend."

Dividends

The most common form of dividend is the cash dividend which, once declared, becomes a liability of the company. A second form of dividend is the dividend in kind, such as dividends in goods (e.g., cases of liquor) or dividends in the stock of another corporation. Such dividends should be valued at the fair market value of the assets distributed.

American Express provides an example of questionable accounting treatment for dividends in kind. In prior years the company acquired shares in a brokerage firm. At the time it distributed these shares to stockholders in 1975 as a dividend, it carried them at a cost of $26.8 million. However, the market value of the shares at the time of distribution was only $6.2 million and by calling it a $26.8 million dividend (the amount charged to retained earnings) the company avoided charging a $20 million dollar loss to income.

A third form of dividend is the stock dividend which, in effect, represents the permanent capitalization of company earnings. As evidence of such a shift from retained earnings to the permanent capital accounts, shareholders receive additional shares. Generally accepted accounting principles require that the stock dividends be valued at the fair market value of the shares to be issued as determined at the date of declaration. This principle is designed to put a realistic limit to the number of shares that can be issued as stock dividends. A stock distribution exceeding 20–25 percent is no longer to be accounted as a stock dividend and should instead be accounted for as a stock split. The latter represents, in essence, the subdivision of the net corporate pie into smaller shares.

Prior period adjustments

SFAS 16 requires that, except for corrections of errors in the financial statements of a prior period and adjustments that result from realization of income tax benefits of pre-acquisition operating loss carryforwards of purchased subsidiaries, all items of profit and loss recognized during a period, including accruals of estimated losses from loss contingencies, be included in the determination of net income for that period. The statement permits limited restatements in interim periods of an enterprise's current fiscal year.

In addition to dividends and prior year adjustments, changes in retained earnings may include adjustments due to business combinations and other capital adjustments such as premiums on redemption of preferred stock, losses on sales of treasury stock, and so forth.

Appropriations of retained earnings

By managerial action, or in compliance with legal requirements, retained earnings are often appropriated or reserved.

Appropriated retained earnings, also known as reserves, established by managerial action include reserves for general contingencies, plant expansion, self-insurance, and other business contingencies. The basic idea here is to preserve a specific amount of capital which is available for absorption of possible losses or is frozen to provide permanent funds, such as for expansion. Thus, such appropriations should never be used to relieve the income statement of charges which are properly chargeable against it. After having served their purpose, such appropriations should be restored to unappropriated retained earnings.

Appropriations of retained earnings in an amount equal to the cost of treasury stock purchased is an example of appropriations established under the legal requirements of certain states. Such appropriations are restored to retained earnings after the treasury stock is sold, retired, or otherwise disposed of.

Restrictions on retained earnings

An important aspect of disclosure relating to retained earnings involves restrictions imposed on its distribution as dividends. This is, obviously, information of importance to potential investors and others. Examples of such restrictions which stem from debt indentures are:

SEARS INDUSTRIES
Long-term debt. The terms of a loan agreement provide for the corporation to maintain a specified amount of working capital and linen in circulation and to restrict dividend payments (except stock dividends) and purchases of its capital stock to $1,250,000 plus 75 percent of consolidated net income (as defined) since December 29, 1973. At December 28, 1974, consolidated working capital (as defined) and linen in circulation exceeded the required amount by $4,406,138 and consolidated retained earnings available for dividends was $1,916,426.

GOLDBLATT BROS. INC.
Note: Under the most restrictive provisions of the long-term debt agreements, the company, among other things, may not pay dividends or reac-

quire its capital stock in excess of $2 million plus 75 percent of net income (as defined) subsequent to January 27, 1973; accordingly, at January 25, 1975, approximately $860,000 is available for the payment of dividends. In addition, working capital must always be at least equal to the greater of $20 million or 150 percent of long-term debt. At January 25, 1975, the company is restricted from entering into any new obligations for the payment of additional rentals.

BOOK VALUE PER SHARE

The term "book value" is conventional terminology referring to net asset value, that is, total assets reduced by the senior claims against them. Thus, the book value of the common stock equity is equal to the total assets less liabilities and claims of securities senior to the common stock, such as preferred stock, mostly at amounts at which they are carried on the financial statements but also unbooked claims of the senior securities. A simple way of computing book value is to add up the common stock equity accounts and reduce the total by any senior claims not reflected in the financial statements such as preferred stock dividend arrearages, liquidation premiums, or other asset preferences to which the preferred shares are entitled.

Book value is almost always presented on a per share basis (the significance of this figure will be considered later in the chapter). Once the underlying principles of computation are understood, the calculation of book value is relatively simple.

ILLUSTRATION 1*.   The following is the equity section of the Zero Corporation for years ended in 19X4 and 19X5:

	19X5	19X4
Preferred stock, 7% cumulative, par value $100 (authorized 4,000,000 shares; outstanding 3,602,811 shares)	$ 360,281,100	$ 360,281,100
Common stock (authorized 90,000,000 shares; outstanding 54,138,137 shares at December 31, 19X5 and 54,129,987 shares at December 31, 19X4)	3,264,581,527	3,122,464,738
Par value $16⅔ per share ..... $ 902,302,283		
Income reinvested in business 2,362,279,244		
Total	$3,624,862,627	$3,482,745,838

The preferred shares are nonparticipating but are callable at 105. Dividends for 19X5 are in arrears.

Required:

Calculate the book value per share of both the common and preferred stock as of December 31, 19X5.

Computations

	Preferred	+	Common	=	Total
Preferred stock* (@ $100)	$360,281,100				$ 360,281,100
Dividends in arrears (7%)	25,219,677				25,219,677
Common stock			$ 902,302,283		902,302,283
Retained earnings (net of amount attributed to dividend in arrears)			2,337,059,567		2,337,059,567
Total	$385,500,777		$3,239,361,850		$3,624,862,627
Divided by number of shares outstanding	3,602,811		54,138,137		
Book value per share	$107.00		$59.84		

* The call premium does not normally enter into the computation of book value per share because the call provision is at the option of company.

ILLUSTRATION 2.   The following is the stockholders' equity section of the balance sheet of the XYZ Company on June 30, 19X1:

Preferred stock—authorized 200,000 shares, issued and out-standing 100,000 shares, par value $100, 6% cumulative, nonparticipating	$10,000,000
Common stock—authorized 375,000 shares, issued and out-standing 200,000 shares, par value $100	20,000,000
Capital contributed in excess of par value	5,000,000
Retained earnings (deficit)	(7,000,000)
Total Stockholders' Equity	$28,000,000

The preferred shares have a liquidation value of $105 and are callable at $110. No dividends have been declared or paid by the company for either the preferred or common shares for two years. Assume that the preferred stock has a preference on assets in liquidation.

Required:

Compute the book value (equity) per share of all classes of stock as of June 30, 19X1.

Computations

	Preferred	Common
Par value	$10,500,000	$20,000,000
Dividends in arrears	1,200,000	
Net deficit (all applicable to common stock)		(3,700,000)
Total	$11,700,000	$16,300,000
Divided by number of shares outstanding	100,000	200,000
Book value (equity) per share	$117.00	$81.50

Explanations:
1. Liquidation value for preferred shares ($105) is used; call value does not enter into the computation of book value per share.
2. Preferred shares are entitled to two years' dividends (12% of $10,000,000 = $1,200,000).

3. Preference of assets for preferred shares means that the deficit is wholly applicable to the common.
4. Computation of net deficit:

Retained earnings (deficit)	$(7,000,000)
Paid-in capital	5,000,000
Dividends in arrears........................	(1,200,000)
Preferred liquidation premium	(500,000)
Net deficit	$(3,700,000)

As can be seen from the above illustrations, the major adjustments in book value per share computations arise from rights and priorities of securities which are senior to the common. In most cases these are premiums, and liquidation priority rights of a variety of classes of preferred stock.

Care must be taken to determine the liquidation value of preferred stock. Some companies have preferred stock issues outstanding which give the right to very substantial liquidation premiums which are far above the par value of such shares. The effect of such liquidation premiums on the book value of the common and other junior equities can be substantial.

ILLUSTRATION 3   In a listing application (A-25189) of Glen Alden Corporation appear the following details of book value computation:

Equity per Share:

Equity per share of Glen Alden, Warner and the Surviving Corporation, based on the initial redemption values of the preferred stocks and on the consolidated balance sheets of Glen Alden and Warner at December 31 and August 27, 1966, respectively, and the pro forma combined balance sheet follows:

Initial redemption per share values	Preferred stocks	Glen Alden December 31, 1966	Warner, August 27, 1966	Pro forma surviving corporation
$ 52.50	Senior stock	$52.50		$ 52.50
$107.00	Class B senior stock			$100.70
$110.00	Preferred stock	$88.89		None
$ 90.00	Class stock	$72.73		None
None	Common stock	None	$19.51	None

Based on the pro forma combined balance sheet there would be no book value attributable to the preferred stock, class C stock and common stock of the Surviving Corporation when the equity applicable to the senior stock and the class B senior stock is considered at aggregate initial redemption value. The aggregate initial redemption value of the senior stock and class B senior stock exceeds total pro forma stockholders' equity by approximately $141,816,000.

The pro forma initial redemption and liquidation prices of the preferred stocks in the aggregate ($343,821,848) exceed their stated values by $296,179,211, and such excess exceeds the aggregate amount of common stock and surplus by approximately $141,816,000. Upon liquidation the senior stock is first in order of preference, followed by the class B senior stock. The preferred stock and class C stock are junior to the class B senior stock, but rank on a parity with each other. There are no restrictions upon surplus arising out of such excess.

As the above example shows, the liquidation premium of the senior stocks is of such magnitude as to wipe out the entire residual book value of the junior preferred and common stock issues.

The accounting profession has, in *APB Opinion No. 10,* recognized the problem posed by preference rights in involuntary liquidation which are substantially in excess of stated par values. Thus, the *Opinion* recommends that the aggregate liquidation preference be prominently disclosed in the equity section of the balance sheet. The *Opinion* also calls for disclosure of call prices and dividend arrearages.

Judging by actual practice, the rules involving "common stock equivalents" which govern the computation of earnings per share (see Chapter 12) do not seem to apply to the computation of book value per share. Nevertheless, a case can be made for extending the earnings per share rules to book value computations. The recent merger movement has given rise to increasingly complex securities, and there is not much justification for ignoring these in book value computations.

ILLUSTRATION 4.   Company A has the following simplified balance sheet:

Assets less current liabilities	$1,000,000
Convertible debentures	100,000
Net assets	$ 900,000
Common shares	100,000

The debentures are convertible into 20,000 shares of common stock.

The company also has warrants outstanding entitling the holder to buy 10,000 shares at $6 per share. Stock options to buy 10,000 shares at an average price of $8 per share are also outstanding.

The conventional method of book value calculations would yield a book value per share of $9 (net assets/common shares = $900,000/100,000).

Giving effect to possible conversions, the book value computation will look as follows:

Net assets (as above)..	$ 900,000
Add convertible debentures	100,000
Proceeds from exercise of warrants (10,000 × $6)	60,000
Proceeds from exercise of stock options (10,000 × $8)	80,000
Adjusted net asset value	$1,140,000

Common shares outstanding	100,000
Add:	
Conversion of debentures	20,000
Exercise of warrants	10,000
Exercise of options	10,000
Adjusted number of common shares	140,000
Book value per share ($1,140,000/140,000)	$8.14

Clearly, the effect of conversions of debentures, options, and so forth, on book value depends on the conversion terms. If stock is converted at prices below conventional book value per share, the effect is, as in the above example, dilutive. Conversely, if the conversion is at prices above conventional book value, the effect will be antidilutive. Applying the conservative principles which have been devised by the accounting profession for the computation of earnings per share (see Chapter 12), antidilutive effects (i.e., those which enhance book value per share) would not be allowed to enter the computations.

Significance of book value

Once an important variable in investment decision making, book value has gradually dwindled in importance. The basic reason for this is that investment analysis generally emphasizes earning power and not asset size. Thus, the value of a company's securities is based primarily on the earning capacity of its asset base rather than on its size.

There are, of course, exceptions to this generalization, and they account for the continued use of the book value per share statistic:

1. Book value, properly adjusted, is often used in an assessment of merger terms.
2. Due to the fact that the rate base of public utilities often approximates its book value, this measure is important in this industry.
3. The analysis of companies which have mostly liquid assets such as those in the finance, investment, insurance, and banking fields, rightfully affords greater than usual importance to book values.
4. The analyst of high-grade bonds and preferred stock usually attaches considerable importance to asset coverage in addition to earning capacity.

There are, of course, other factors which make net assets a measure of some importance in financial analysis. A company's earnings growth is sooner or later dependent on growth in assets and, consequently, on a choice of how to finance them. A large asset base has, depending on its composition, a certain potential of profitable utilization.

The accounting considerations that enter into computation of book value should be thoroughly understood by any user of this statistic:

1. The carrying values of assets, particularly long-lived assets such as plant and equipment, long-term investments, and some inventories, is usually at cost and may differ significantly from current market values.[1] Moreover, such carrying values will, as was seen in the preceding chapters, vary according to the accounting principles selected. Thus, for instance, in times of rising prices the carrying value of inventories under the Lifo method of inventory accounting will be lower than under the Fifo method.
2. Intangible assets of great value may not be reflected in book value nor are contingent liabilities, which may have a high probability of occurrence, usually so reflected.

The decline in the use of book value may be due to a lack of usefulness of this measure. It is, undoubtedly also due to the very crude approaches taken in its reporting and application. Thus, for example, the blanket exclusion from book value of goodwill, patents, franchises, and other intangibles cannot make up for the lack of the analysis required to adopt this measure to the particular objective it is designed to meet. Either book value is computed on a "current value" basis or on a cost basis. In the latter case, the arbitrary exclusion of intangible assets makes no sense. If, for example, book value is to be used in comparing the relative value of two companies engaged in merger negotiations, adjustments, such as the following, may be required so that an intelligent comparison can be made:

1. The carrying value of assets should be adjusted to current market values.
2. Differences in the application of accounting principles should be adjusted for.
3. Unrecorded intangibles should be given recognition.
4. Contingent liabilities should be assessed and given appropriate recognition.
5. Accounting and other errors should be adjusted on the books of both companies.

Other adjustments may also be called for. Thus, if the preferred stock has the characteristics of debt, it may be appropriate to capitalize it at the prevailing interest rate, thus reflecting the benefit or disadvantage of it to the company.

---

[1] The new SEC disclosure requirements of the replacement value of certain assets of specified companies (see Chapter 14) may be helpful in arriving at more realistic book value figures.

The emphasis of earning power has, as was discussed above, resulted in a deemphasis of asset size. Sterile or unproductive assets are worse than worthless. They are often a drag on earnings because they require a minimum of upkeep and management expenses. Like any other analytical tools, book value is a measure which can be useful for certain purposes provided it is used with discrimination and understanding.

IMPLICATIONS FOR ANALYSIS

The accounting principles which apply to the equity section do not have a marked effect on income determination and, as a consequence, do not hold many pitfalls for the analyst. From the analysis point of view, the most significant information here relates to the composition of the capital accounts and to the restrictions to which they may be subject.

The composition of the equity capital is important because of provisions affecting the residual rights of the common equity. Such provisions include dividend participation rights, conversion rights, and the great variety of options and conditions which are characteristic of the complex securities frequently issued under merger agreements, most of which tend to dilute the common equity.

An analysis of restrictions imposed on the distribution of retained earnings by loan or other agreements will usually shed light on a company's freedom of action in such areas as dividend distributions, required levels of working capital. Such restrictions also shed light on the company's bargaining strength and standing in credit markets. Moreover, a careful reading of restrictive covenants will also enable the analyst to assess how far a company is from being in default of these provisions.

QUESTIONS

1. What are the objectives of the classifications and the footnote disclosure associated with the equity section of the corporate balance sheet? Of what significance are such disclosures to readers of financial statements?

2. What features of a preferred stock issue make it akin to debt? What features make it more like common stock?

3. Why is it important from the point of view of the analyst of financial statements that the liquidation value of preferred stock, if different from par or stated value, be clearly disclosed?

4. Presidential Realty Corporation reported as follows on distributions paid on common stock:

"The cash distributions on common stock were charged to paid-in surplus because the parent company has accumulated no earnings (other than its equity in undistributed earnings of certain subsidiaries) since its formation. . . ."

a. Are these cash distributions dividends?

b. Why do you suppose did this realty company make such distributions?

5. Why does the proper accounting for stock dividends require that the fair market value, rather than the par value, of the shares distributed be charged against retained earnings?

6. What conditions must a gain or loss conform to before it may be treated as a prior period adjustment?

7. Some companies present "minority interests in subsidiary companies" between the long-term debt and the equity sections of the consolidated balance sheet; others present them as part of equity capital.

a. What is a "minority interest"? (Refer to Chapter 9.)

b. Where on the consolidated balance sheet does it belong? What different points of view do these differing presentations represent?

8. What is book value per share? How is it computed? What is its significance? (C.F.A.)

9. Why has the use of the "book value per share" declined in relative importance over the past decades? What valid uses of book value are still made today?

10. What are some of the accounting considerations which enter into the computation of book value and about which the analyst should be aware?

11. What adjustments may be necessary to render the book value per share measure comparable as between two enterprises?

9

INTERCORPORATE INVESTMENTS, BUSINESS COMBINATIONS, AND FOREIGN OPERATIONS

In this chapter we shall examine the analytical implications of a number of specialized topics in accounting, most of which straddle the areas of asset, liability, and income measurements and are thus discussed best in their entirety and in a separate and distinct fashion.

INTERCORPORATE INVESTMENTS

When one corporation owns all or a majority of the voting equity securities of another corporation, a parent-subsidiary relationship is said to exist. The reasons why one company may form or buy control of another entity are many and include sources of supply, enlargement of market coverage, entrance into new lines of business, taxes, reduction of risk because of limited liability, and the requirements of government regulation.

There are three basic methods by which a parent company can account for its ownership in a subsidiary. These are:

1. Consolidated financial statements.
2. Equity method.
3. Cost method.

We shall examine these hereunder in this order, which is the order of their preference from an accounting theory standpoint. This order of preference coincides also with that from the point of view of the financial analyst since, as we will see from the discussion which follows, the methods differ significantly in the amount of information they provide the analyst about the financial condition and results of operations of the combined parent-subsidiary entity.

Consolidated financial statements

On the parent company's financial statements the ownership of stock in a subsidiary is evidenced by an investment account. From a legal point of view the parent company owns the stock of its subsidiary; it does not own the subsidiary's assets nor is it normally responsible for the subsidiary's debts, although it frequently guarantees them. Consolidated financial statements disregard the legality of this situation in favor of its business substance and reflect the economic reality of a business entity under centralized control. There is a presumption that in most cases, consolidated financial statements are more meaningful than separate financial statements and that they are required for fair presentation of financial conditions and results of operations.

Basic technique of consolidation. Consolidated financial statements combine the assets, liabilities, revenues, and expenses of subsidiaries with the corresponding items in the financial statements of the parent company. To the extent that the parent does not own 100 percent of a subsidiary's equity securities, the minority interest of outsiders is recognized in the consolidation. Intercompany items are eliminated in order to avoid double counting and the premature recognition of income.

ILLUSTRATION 1.   Exhibit 9–1 presents the simplified balance sheet of Company P (the parent) at the time of its acquisition of Company S (the subsidiary). The assets and liabilities included in the balance sheet of Company S are already stated in terms of their fair market values at the time of acquisition. Company P paid $78,000 for 90 percent of Company S's common stock. Accounts receivable of Company P include $4,000 owed it by Company S.

The adjustments in the work sheet which combine the two companies are as follows:

a.   The investment at acquisition is eliminated against 90 percent of the equity (capital stock plus retained earnings) of Company S. The remaining 10 percent of Company S's equity belongs to outside stockholders and is shown as "minority interest" in the consolidated balance sheet. The amount of $6,000 which Company P paid in excess of the fair value of 90 percent of the tangible net assets of Company S is carried as "goodwill" in the consolidated balance sheet. The method of determination of goodwill will be discussed later in this chapter under "purchase" accounting.

b.   The accounts receivable of Company P and the corresponding payable of Company S are eliminated in consolidation.

EXHIBIT 9–1

COMPANY P AND COMPANY S
Consolidated Balance Sheet Worksheet
Date of Acquisition

	Company P	Company S	Adjustments and eliminations	Minority interest	Consolidated
Assets					
Cash	16,000	11,000			27,000
Accounts receivable	32,000	19,000	(*b*) 4,000		47,000
Inventories	42,000	18,000			60,000
Fixed assets	64,000	42,000			106,000
Investment in Company S:					
Fair value at acquisition	72,000	—	(*a*) 72,000		—
Excess of cost over fair value (goodwill)	6,000	—			6,000
Total Assets ...	232,000	90,000			246,000
Liabilities and Equity					
Accounts payable	12,000	10,000	(*b*) 4,000		18,000
Capital stock:					
Company P	120,000				120,000
Company S		50,000	(*a*) 45,000	5,000	
Retained earnings:					
Company P	100,000				100,000
Company S		30,000	(*a*) 27,000	3,000	
Minority interest					8,000
Total Liabilities and Equity	232,000	90,000			246,000

Under the consolidation method the income statement of Company S will be combined with that of Company P, and the 10 percent share of the minority interest in the net income or loss of Company S for the period will be deducted from the consolidated income (or loss) in order to show the consolidated net results of operations of the group.

In consolidating the income statement of subsidiary Company S with parent Company P, intercompany profits on sales of inventories which remain within the consolidated group at year-end and intercompany profits on other assets, such as fixed assets, must be eliminated. This is so because the equity interest in the earnings of a consolidated entity relate to earnings with parties *outside* the group. Transactions among members within the group are viewed as incomplete, and the profit as unrealized.

Principles governing consolidation policy. There is a general presumption that consolidated statements are more meaningful than separate parent and subsidiary statements. Consequently, consolidation is the preferred method of presenting the financial statements of a parent and its subsidiaries. There are, however, a number of valid reasons why a subsidiary should not be consolidated. They are:

1. *Incomplete or temporary control.* In general, in order to consolidate a subsidiary, a parent should have ownership or effective management control over the subsidiary. Thus, ownership of over 50 percent of the voting stock is generally required for consolidation, and consolidation is inappropriate where the control is temporary or where it will be disposed of or otherwise lost in the near future.

2. *Lack of homogeneity.* The concept of what constitutes a homogenous unit has undergone considerable change over the years. More recently, corporate diversification has led to the creation of conglomerates which have interests in many different types of industries and activities. Generally speaking, a mere difference in the nature of business is not sufficient reason to bar consolidation. Nevertheless, certain businesses are so different in nature that consolidation is considered by some as misleading. Thus, credit or financial subsidiaries of industrial parents are mostly omitted from consolidation.

In recent amendments to its regulations the SEC increased the number of situations where separate financial statements must be submitted for consolidated subsidiaries engaged in financial activities (e.g., life, casualty and fire insurance, securities broker dealers, finance savings and loan, or banking).

3. *Uncertainty as to income.* Where there is reason for serious doubt whether an increase in equity in a subsidiary has really accrued to the parent, consolidation is not appropriate. Such doubt can occur particularly in the case of foreign subsidiaries when there are restrictions on the conversion of foreign currencies or on the remittance of foreign earnings.

The need to consolidate leasing subsidiaries. APB Opinion No. 18 and *SFAS 13* reaffirm the requirement that subsidiaries whose principal business activity consists of leasing property or facilities to their parents or other affiliates be consolidated with such parents. The reason for this requirement is the significance of the assets and liabilities of such subsidiaries to the consolidated financial position of the entire group.

The equity method

The equity method should be used in consolidated financial statements for investments in common stock of all unconsolidated subsidiaries (foreign or domestic) where for reasons, such as those discussed above, consolidation is not appropriate. Under *APB Opinion No. 18* the equity method is not a valid substitute for consolidation and should not be used to justify exclusion of a subsidiary when consolidation is otherwise appropriate.

The difference between consolidation and the equity method lies in the details reported in the financial statements. Under the equity method the parent's share of the subsidiary results are presented in its income statement as a line item, and this has resulted in the equity method being also referred to as "one line consolidation."

As we saw in the discussion of the accounting for intercorporate investments in Chapter 6, the equity method of accounting should, generally, be used for investments in common stock which represent interests 20 percent or over in the voting stock of a company's equity securities, and it may be appropriate in some cases even for investments representing an interest of less than 20 percent.

Recognizing the wide application of the equity method to investments in subsidiaries, to investments in corporate joint ventures, as well as to investments in less than majority owned investees, *APB Opinion No. 18* listed a number of procedures which should be followed in applying this method:

1. Intercompany profits and losses should be eliminated until realized by the investor or investee as if a subsidiary, corporate joint venture, or investee company were consolidated.
2. A difference between the cost of an investment and the amount of underlying equity in net assets of an investee should be accounted for as if the investee were a consolidated subsidiary. (*APB Opinion No. 17* requires amortization of goodwill over a term not exceeding 40 years.)
3. The investment(s) in common stock should be shown in the balance sheet of an investor as a single amount, and the investor's share of earnings or losses of an investee(s) should ordinarily be shown in the income statement as a single amount except for the extraordinary items and prior period adjustments which should be separately classified in the income statement of the investor.
4. A transaction of an investee of a capital nature that affects the investor's share of stockholders' equity of the investee should be accounted for as if the investee were a consolidated subsidiary.
5. Sales of stock of an investee by an investor should be accounted for as gains or losses equal to the difference at the time of sale between selling price and carrying amount of the stock sold.
6. If financial statements of an investee are not sufficiently timely for an investor to apply the equity method currently, the investor ordinarily should record its share of the earnings or losses of an investee from the most recent available financial statements. A lag in reporting should be consistent from period to period.

7. A loss in value of an investment which is other than a temporary decline should be recognized the same as a loss in value of other long-term assets. Evidence of a loss in value might include, inability to recover the carrying amount of investment, decline in market value, etc. All relevant factors must be evaluated.

8. The investor ordinarily should discontinue applying the equity method when the investment (and net advances) is reduced to zero and should not provide for additional losses unless the investor has guaranteed obligations of the investee or is otherwise committed to provide further financial support for the investee. If the investee subsequently reports net income, the investor should resume applying the equity method only after its share of that net income equals the share of net losses not recognized during the period the equity method was suspended.

9. When an investee has outstanding cumulative preferred stock, an investor should compute its share of earnings (losses) after deducting the investee's preferred dividends, whether or not such dividends are declared.

10. The carrying amount of an investment in common stock of an investee that qualifies for the equity method of accounting as described above may differ from the underlying equity in net assets of the investee. The difference should affect the determination of the amount of the investor's share of earnings or losses of an investee as if the investee were a consolidated subsidiary. However, if the investor is unable to relate the difference to specific accounts of the investee, the difference should be considered to be goodwill and amortized over a period not to exceed 40 years, in accordance with *APB Opinion No. 17*.

The cost method

The cost method is, under the prevailing system of accrual accounting, the method least preferred among the three alternative ways of presenting investments in subsidiaries. Under this method the investment in a subsidiary is recorded at cost and income is recognized only as it is received in the form of dividend distributions. A permanent impairment in the value of the investment, due to losses or other causes, should be recognized by a write-down of the investment.

The use of the cost method is now restricted to cases where there is considerable doubt that the equity in the earning of a subsidiary is effectively accruing to the benefit of the parent. Such cases include foreign subsidiaries which operate under conditions of exchange restrictions, controls, or other uncertainties of a type that casts doubt on the parent's ability to achieve an ultimate realization of these earnings.

Example of difference in income recognition—equity versus cost method

On January 1, 19X1 Company P acquired 80 percent of Company S for $900,000. The net assets of Company S at date of acquisition were $1,000,000.

During 19X1 Company S earned $100,000 and paid $40,000 in dividends, while in 19X2 it lost $20,000 and paid a dividend of $30,000. Exhibit 9–2 contrasts the accounting by Company P for the investment in Company S and the income derived from it under (1) the cost method and (2) the equity method:

EXHIBIT 9–2
Cost and equity methods of accounting for investment in subsidiary

	Cost method		Equity method	
	Invest-ment	Income (loss)	Invest-ment	Income (loss)
Cost at acquisition	$900,000		$900,000	
Earnings for 19X1			80,000	$ 80,000 (1)
Amortization of goodwill			(2,500)	(2,500) (2)
Dividends—19X1		$32,000 (3)	(32,000)	
Earnings pickup— 19X1		$32,000		$ 77,500
Loss for 19X2			(16,000)	$(16,000) (4)
Amortization of goodwill			(2,500)	(2,500) (2)
Dividends—19X2		$24,000 (5)	(24,000)	
Earnings (loss) pickup—19X2		$24,000		$(18,500)
Investment at 12/31/X2	$900,000		$903,000	

(1) 80% equity in earnings of $100,000.	
(2) Cost of 80% interest in Company S	$900,000
80% of net assets ($1,000,000—assumed to represent fair market value)	800,000
Excess of cost over net assets (goodwill)..................................	$100,000
Yearly amortization (40-year basis)	$ 2,500
(3) 80% of $40,000.	
(4) 80% of $20,000.	
(5) 80% of $30,000.	

The disparity in the amount of income reported by the parent under the two methods is readily apparent. Under the cost method the income pickup bears no relationship to actual results achieved during the period but is, instead, dependent on the amount of dividend distributions.

The amount at which the investment is carried on the books of the parent company also varies considerably among these two methods. Under the cost method the investment account remains unchanged (except in the case of losses which lead to a permanent impairment in value), while under the equity method the investment account reflects the parent company's equity in the underlying net assets of the subsidiary. Goodwill should, however, be amortized also under the cost method.[1]

Intercorporate investments—less than majority ownership

Investments by one company in less than the majority of the voting security of another enterprise and investments in joint ventures are discussed in Chapter 6.

Implications for analysis

From the analyst's point of view the financial reporting of intercorporate investments has undergone consistent improvement. This improvement is due in large measure to the sharp restrictions which are now placed on the use of the cost method of accounting.

Under the cost method, dividends remitted, rather than income earned, are the basis on which a parent company recognizes the earnings accruing from an investment in a subsidiary. The obvious disadvantage of the cost method is that the cost basis does not reflect the results of operations of the subsidiary and lends itself to income manipulation. Thus, dividends included in the parent company's income may be unrelated to the subsidiary's earnings, and losses of the subsidiary may go unreported for a number of periods. The trend in earnings can be completely distorted by use of the cost method.

Validity of taking up earnings. Consolidation and the equity method are based on the assumption that a dollar earned by a subsidiary is at least equal to a dollar's worth of parent company earnings. Even disregarding the possible tax liability which the parent company may incur on the remittance of earnings by the subsidiary, this dollar-for-dollar equivalence in earnings cannot be taken for granted. The following are some possible reasons for this:

1. The subsidiary may be under the supervision of a regulatory authority which can intervene in dividend policy.
2. The subsidiary may operate in a foreign country where there exist restrictions on the remittance of earnings abroad and/or where the

---

[1] The goodwill element can, of course, also be present in an investment account of an unconsolidated subsidiary.

value of the currency can deteriorate rapidly. Furthermore, changes in political climate may result in hampering the subsidiary's operations.

3. Dividend restrictions in loan agreements may become effective.
4. The presence of a stable or powerful minority interest may reduce the parent's discretion in setting dividend and other policy.

While considerations such as the above should govern the independent accountant's decision on whether or not to use the cost method, the analyst should, as a check on that judgment, form his own opinion in each given situation on whether a dollar earned by a subsidiary can indeed be considered the equivalent of a dollar earned by the parent company.

There are other problems in the analysis of consolidated financial statements or investments in subsidiaries carried at equity which the financial analyst must consider carefully.

Provision for taxes on undistributed earnings of subsidiaries. APB Opinion No. 23, "Accounting for Income Taxes—Special Areas," concluded that including undistributed earnings of a subsidiary in the pretax accounting income of a parent company, either through consolidation or accounting for the investment by the equity method, may or may not require a concurrent provision for taxes depending on the actions and intent of the parent company.

The Board believes that it should be presumed that all undistributed earnings will be transferred to the parent and that a provision for taxes should be made by assuming that the unremitted earnings were distributed to the parent in the current period and that the taxes provision is based on a computation benefiting from all the tax-planning alternatives to which the company may be entitled.

The foregoing presumption can be overcome if persuasive evidence exists that the subsidiary has or will invest the undistributed earnings permanently or that the earnings will be remitted in a tax-free liquidation.

The analyst should be aware that the decision of whether taxes on undistributed earnings should or should not be provided is, in effect, left largely to management. However, the amount of earnings on which no income taxes were provided by the parent must be disclosed.

In contrast, ownership in an investee (20 percent to 50 percent owned) calls for provision of taxes on equity in earnings because a presumption of an ability to reinvest earnings is assumed not to exist.

Debt shown in consolidated financial statements. Liabilities shown in the consolidated financial statements do not operate as a lien upon a common pool of assets. The creditors, be they secured or unsecured, have recourse in the event of default only to assets owned by the individual corporation which incurred this liability. If, on the other hand, a parent company guarantees a specific liability of a subsidiary, then the creditor would, of course, have the guarantee as additional security.

The consolidated balance sheet obscures rather than clarifies the margin of safety enjoyed by specific creditors. To gain full comprehension of the financial position of each part of the consolidated group, the analyst needs also examine the individual financial statements of each subsidiary. Legal constraints are not always effective limits to liability. Thus American Express made good on obligations of a warehousing subsidiary not because it was legally obliged to do so but because of concern for its own financial reputation.

Additional limitations of consolidated financial statements. Consolidated financial statements generally represent the most meaningful presentation of the financial condition and the results of operations of a group. However, they do have limitations in addition to those discussed above:

1. The financial statements of the individual companies in the group may not be prepared on a comparable basis. Accounting principles applied and valuation bases and amortization rates used may differ, thus destroying homogeneity and the validity of ratios, trends, and relationships. Year-end dates of individual members of a group can vary by as much as 90 days.
2. Companies in relatively poor financial condition may be combined with sound companies, thus obscuring information necessary for analysis.
3. The extent of intercompany transactions is unknown unless *consolidating* financial statements are presented. The latter generally reveal the adjustments involved in the consolidation process.
4. Unless specifically disclosed, it may be difficult to establish how much of the consolidated Retained Earnings account is actually available for payment of dividends.
5. The composition of the minority interest, for example, as between common and preferred, cannot be determined because the minority interest is generally shown as a combined amount in the consolidated balance sheet.

ACCOUNTING FOR BUSINESS COMBINATIONS

The combination of business entities by merger or acquisition is not a new phenomenon on the business scene. What is relatively new is the utilization of the merger technique as an instrument for the creation of "glamour" or of an image of growth, and as a means of increasing reported earnings.

Reasons for mergers

There are, of course, many legitimate reasons for *external* business expansion, that is, expansion by means of business combinations under which two or more entities are brought under common control. These reasons include: (1) acquisition of sources of new materials, productive facilities, production know-how, marketing organizations, and established shares of a market; (2) the acquisition of financial resources; (3) the acquisition of competent management; (4) savings of time in entering new markets; and (5) achieving economies of scale and acquiring tax advantages such as those relating to tax-loss carry-overs.

Distortions in accounting for mergers

In addition to the above legitimate reasons for entering into business combinations, financial "architects" and operators of the 1960s have utilized merger techniques and loose merger accounting to serve up to a stock market obsessed with "earnings growth" a picture of growth which was, in large part, illusory.

The means by which such illusions of earnings growth were achieved were many. Briefly, some were as follows:

1. A great variety of convertible securities were issued without any recognition being given to their future potential dilutive effects on the common stockholder's equity. This phenomenon reached such heights of abuse that it was finally remedied by the issuance of *APB Opinion No. 15.* Chapter 12 contains a more extended discussion of this subject.

2. The merger of growing companies which have earned a high price-earnings ratio in the marketplace with companies of lesser growth prospects was achieved by payment in high price-earnings ratio stock. This contributed to further earnings per share growth, thus reinforcing and even increasing the acquiring company's high price-earnings ratio. However, in many cases the market failed to take into account the lower quality of the *acquired* earnings. This is mostly a transitory problem inherent in the market evaluation mechanism and is not readily subject to remedy by external factors.

3. The utilization of loose accounting rules governing merger accounting in order to create the illusion of earnings growth where, in fact, there is none. This is to be distinguished from the genuine

economies and advantages which can accrue from business combinations. This problem area will be discussed below in our consideration of alternative accounting methods for business combinations.

Accounting for business combinations: Two methods

Prior to World War II the accounting for business combinations was governed by the legal form which it assumed and that resulted in a majority of acquisitions by one company of another being treated as purchases. To businessmen, the one immediate disadvantage of purchase accounting was the creation of "goodwill" as an asset representing usually the excess of cost of acquisition over the amounts at which the acquired company's net assets were recorded on the acquiring company's books. Not only was goodwill a nontax deductible item which, if amortized, would have resulted in a reduction of earnings, but it was also an asset which bankers and other lenders considered of dubious value.

Pooling of interests.   For this and other reasons, the search for an alternative method of accounting for business combinations led to the pooling of interests method. The rationale behind this method is that instead of an acquisition of one company by another, a pooling of interests reflects the merging of two stockholder groups which share in future risks and opportunities.

This accounting convention, which has gained wide acceptance in the post-1945 period, is based on the following assumptions about the two corporations combining—

1. That they would exchange voting securities; essentially, ownership would be continuing.
2. That the two corporations would be roughly comparable in size.
3. That management personnel would continue with the merged corporation.

The great attraction of the pooling method along with the vague criteria which were promulgated to govern its accounting led to a significant deterioration in actual practice. The criterion of relative size erroded, all manner of equity securities became acceptable, various means of circumventing the continuity of ownership provisions were devised, and where it was clearly impossible to justify the use of a full pooling, a part-pooling part-purchase method was devised. In short, we had here a classic illustration of the operation of Gresham's law in accounting.

With the growth in these abuses the chorus of criticism grew, and this resulted in a call by many for the abolition of pooling of interests accounting. Instead, members of the APB compromised and issued *Opinion No. 16* which, as we shall see, established stricter and more specific conditions for use of this method of accounting in the future.

Purchase accounting.   In the permissive atmosphere of the 1960s, accounting under the "purchase" convention also deteriorated in relation to its original intent. Abuses occurred in two major areas:

1. Assets and liabilities of purchased entities were not revalued at fair value before being included in the accounts of the acquiring company.
2. The resulting "goodwill" represented merely the excess of amounts paid over the carrying amounts of assets and liabilities assumed without even the pretense that such assets and liabilities were fairly valued. This resulting "goodwill" was very rarely amortized. It thus became a repository for all kinds of costs incurred in acquiring the company, costs which were thus kept out of present and future income statements. The curt note found in the Gould Inc. prospectus dated 2/17/70 was characteristic of this kind of treatment: "The cost of acquired businesses in excess of recorded net assets at dates of acquisition are considered to be attributable to intangible assets which will not be amortized."

While, in theory, a purchase is in substance, quite a different business combination from a pooling of interests, by the late 1960s the accounting for them became in *effect* quite similar. Under the pooling method the understatement of assets took the form of carrying forward the merged company's assets at book value, while under the "polluted purchase"[2] method the assets were similarly understated and the excess of cost over these understated assets was merely carried as a nondescript composite intangible which was rarely amortized. Thus, under either method substantial costs were kept out of the income statement.

REVISED OPINIONS ON ACCOUNTING FOR BUSINESS COMBINATIONS

In an attempt to improve the accounting for business combinations, the APB issued in 1970 *Opinions No. 16* and *No. 17*. However, in late 1976 the FASB issued a voluminous Discussion Memorandum on the subject which is designed to lead to public hearings in 1977 and to a reconsideration of the entire subject.

---

[2] This term was coined by Professor Abraham J. Briloff who has done more than anyone else to expose the abuses under both pooling and purchase accounting. Starting in 1967 his incisive and analytical articles, appearing mostly in the *Financial Analysts Journal* and *Barron's*, contributed greatly to a wider understanding of the distortions for which this type of accounting was responsible.

We shall first consider the accounting required under these two *Opinions*. Following this consideration we shall consider the implications which the present accounting holds for the analyst.

Pooling of interests and purchase accounting compared

Pooling of interests accounting is based on the assumption that the combination is a uniting of ownership interests achieved by means of an exchange of equity securities. Under this method the former ownership interests continue and the recorded assets and liabilities of the constituents are carried forward to the combined entity at their recorded amounts. Since this is a combining of interests, income of the combined corporation includes income of the constituents for the entire fiscal period in which the combination occurs. Prior periods are also restated to show the combined companies as merged since their respective inceptions.

The purchase method of accounting views the business combination as the acquisition of one entity by another. The acquiring entity records the acquired assets, including goodwill, and liabilities at its cost which is based on fair values at date of acquisition. The acquiring entity picks up the income of the acquired entity, based on its cost, only from date of acquisition.

APB Opinion No. 16 concluded that if a business combination meets the 12 specific criteria enumerated in it, it must be accounted for as a pooling of interests. Otherwise it must be accounted for as a purchase.

Conditions for the pooling of interests method. There are 12 conditions which must be met under the provision of *APB Opinion No. 16* before a business combination may be accounted for as a pooling of interests. These can be grouped under three main categories:

 I.   Attributes of the combining companies.
 II. Manner of combining interests.
III. Absence of planned transactions.

 I.   Attributes of the combining companies
       A.   Each of the combining companies should be autonomous and not have operated as a subsidiary or division of another company within two years before the plan of combination is initiated. An exception to this condition concerns the divestiture of assets which was ordered by a governmental or judicial body. A subsidiary which is divested under an order or a new company which acquires assets disposed of under such an order is considered autonomous for this condition.

B. Each of the combining companies must be independent of
    each other. That means that no combining company or
    group of combining companies can hold as an intercom-
    pany investment more than 10 percent of the outstanding
    voting common stock of any other combining company. To
    illustrate the 10 percent requirement, let's assume that
    Company A plans to issue its voting common stock to ac-
    quire the voting common stock of Companies B and C. If
    Companies A and B each own 7 percent of Company C's
    outstanding common stock, A can pool with B, but the com-
    bined entity cannot subsequently pool with C since more
    than 10 percent of Company C's outstanding stock would
    have been held by the other combining companies.

II. Manner of combining interests

C. The combination should be effected in a single transaction
    or should be completed in accordance with a specific plan
    within one year after the plan is initiated. The *Opinion*
    provides an exception to this one year rule when the delay
    is beyond the control of the combining companies because
    of proceedings of a governmental authority or pending
    litigation.

D. The combination should involve the issuance of voting
    common stock only in exchange for substantially all of the
    voting common stock interest of the company being com-
    bined. "Substantially all" in this context means at least 90
    percent of the voting common stock interest of the company
    being combined. Thus, the issuer may purchase for cash or
    other nonvoting common stock consideration up to 10 per-
    cent of the voting common shares of the company to be
    pooled. Such a cash outlay may be necessary to eliminate
    fractional shares or to pay dissenting stockholders. The ra-
    tionale of this criterion is that substantially all of the voting
    common stock interest in each party to a pooling should be
    carried forward as a voting common stock interest in the
    issuer in the pooling. The payment of cash, debt, or an
    equity instrument which does not satisfy this test destroys
    the most fundamental basis of a pooling. If the company
    being combined has securities other than voting stock, such
    securities may be exchanged for common stock of the issu-
    ing corporation or may be exchanged for substantially iden-
    tical securities of the issuing corporation.

E. None of the combining companies should change the
    equity interest of their voting common stock in contempla-
    tion of effecting the combination. This restriction applies

during the period from two years preceding the date the plan is initiated through the date the plan is consummated. Changes in the equity interest of the voting common stock which may violate this condition include distributions to shareholders, additional issuance or exchange of securities, and the retirement of securities. The purpose of this rule is to disallow changes in equity interests prior to a combination because such changes indicate a sale rather than a combining and sharing of risks.

F. Each combining company may reacquire shares of voting common stock only for purposes other than business combinations, and no company may reacquire more than a normal number of shares between the date the plan of combination is initiated and consummated.

G. The ratio of the interest of an individual common stockholder to those of other common shareholders in a combining company should remain the same as a result of the exchange of stock to effect the combination. This condition insures that no common stockholder is denied his potential share of a voting common stock interest in a combined corporation.

H. The stockholders of the resulting combined corporation cannot be deprived of, nor restricted in, their ability to exercise their voting rights on common stock of the combined corporation. For example, establishing a voting trust to hold some of the shares issued in the combination disqualifies the combination as a pooling of interests.

I. The combination must be resolved at the date the plan is consummated, and there must be no contingent arrangements for the issuance of additional securities or other consideration. All consideration to be given to effect the combination of the companies, must be determinable as of the date the plan of combination is consummated. The only exception to this would be a provision to adjust the exchange ratio as a result of a subsequent settlement of a contingency such as an existing lawsuit.

III. Absence of planned transactions

J. The combined corporation should not agree directly or indirectly to retire or reacquire any of the common stock issued to effect the combination.

K. The combined corporation cannot enter into other financial arrangements for the benefit of the former stockholders of a combining company, such as a guarantee of loans secured by stock issued in the combination. This financial arrangement may require the payment of cash in the future which would negate the exchange of equity securities, and thus the combination would not qualify for pooling of interests treatment.

L. The combined corporation may not intend to plan to dispose of a significant part of the assets of the combining companies within two years after the combination. Some disposal of assets may be effected within the two-year period provided the disposals would have been in the ordinary course of business of the formerly separate companies or if the disposals were to eliminate duplicate facilities or excess capacity.

If a combining company remains a subsidiary of the issuing corporation after the combination is consummated, the combination could still be accounted for as a pooling of interests, as long as all the conditions for a pooling are met. Any business combination which meets all of the above conditions *must* be accounted for under the pooling of interests method.

Application of the purchase method. As we have seen in the foregoing discussion, under purchase accounting the business combination is viewed as the acquisition of one entity by another.

Problem of valuation of the consideration. One of the major problems in accounting for a purchase is to determine the total cost of an acquired entity. The same accounting principles apply whether determining the cost of assets acquired individually, in a group, or in a business combination. It is the nature of the transaction which determines which accounting principles apply in arriving at the total cost of assets acquired.

There usually is no problem in determining the total cost of assets acquired for cash, since the amount of cash disbursed is the total cost of the acquired assets. The difficulty is, however, in the proper allocation of the total cost to the individual assets acquired.

If assets are acquired by incurring liabilities, total cost of the assets is the present value of the amounts to be paid in the future. The present value of a debt security is the fair value of the liability. If the debt security has been issued at an interest rate which is substantially above or below the present effective rate for a similar security, the appropriate amount of premium or discount should be recorded. In some cases the characteristics of a preferred stock may be so similar to a debt security that it should be valued in the same manner.

If assets are acquired in exchange for stock, the general rule for determining the total cost of the assets acquired would be that it is the fair value of the stock given or the fair value of the assets received, whichever is more clearly evident.

The fair value of securities traded in the market is normally more clearly evident than is the fair value of the acquired company. Quoted market price should serve as a guide in determining total cost of an acquired company after considering market fluctuations, the quantities traded, issue costs, and so forth.

If the quoted market price is not a reliable indicator of the value of stock issued, it is still necessary to determine the fair value of the assets received, including goodwill, even though this valuation is difficult.

In these cases the best means of estimation should be used, including a detailed review of the negotiations leading up to the purchase and the use of independent appraisals.

Contingent additional consideration. The amount of any additional contingent consideration payable in accordance with the purchase agreement is usually recorded when the contingency is resolved and the consideration is to be issued or becomes issuable. Two of the most common types of contingencies are based on either earnings or security prices.

The following guides to the accounting for such contingent additional consideration are contained in *APB Opinion No. 16:*

1. A contingent issuance of additional consideration should be disclosed but should not be recorded as a liability or shown as outstanding securities unless the outcome of the contingency is determinable beyond a reasonable doubt.
2. A contingent issuance of additional consideration based on future earnings should be recorded as an additional cost of the acquisition when the contingency is resolved. In this case the total amount of consideration representing cost was not determinable at the date of acquisition.
3. A contingent issuance of additional consideration which is based on future security prices should be considered as an adjustment of the amount originally recorded for the securities at the date of acquisition.

Allocation of total cost. Once the total cost of an acquired entity is determined, it is then necessary to allocate this total cost to the individual assets received. All identifiable assets acquired and liabilities assumed in a business combination should be assigned a portion of the total cost, normally equal to their fair value at date of acquisition. The excess of the total cost over the amounts assigned to identifiable assets acquired, less liabilities assumed, should be recorded as goodwill. Such goodwill must be amortized over a period not to exceed 40 years.

It may be possible in some cases that the market or appraisal values of identifiable assets acquired, less liabilities assumed, exceeds the cost of the acquired company. In those cases, the values otherwise assignable to noncurrent assets acquired (except long-term investments in marketable securities) should be reduced by a proportionate part of the excess. Negative goodwill should not be recorded unless the value assigned to such long-term assets is first reduced to zero. If such allocation results in an excess of net assets over cost, it should be classified as a deferred credit and should be amortized systematically to income over the period estimated to be benefited but not in excess of 40 years.

North American Philips Corp. provides the following example of a "bargain purchase" acquisition:

> Note 2: Acquisitions.   Effective October 1, 1974, a subsidiary of NAPC acquired approximately 84 percent of the common stock of The Magnavox Company (Magnavox) for an aggregate cash purchase cost of approximately $142 million. The transaction has been accounted for as a purchase and accordingly the operations of Magnavox are included in the consolidated statement of income from October 1, 1974. The equity in the net assets of Magnavox exceeded acquisition cost by $18,977,000. Of such amount, $12,552,000 was assigned to specific assets and liabilities and $6,425,000 was allocated to remaining noncurrent assets acquired on a pro rata basis in accordance with the provisions of Accounting Principles Board Opinion No. 16 . . .

Guidelines for valuation of assets and liabilities.   APB Opinion No. 16 established general guides for assigning amounts to individual assets and liabilities assumed, except goodwill, as follows:

1. Marketable securities should be recorded at current net realizable values.
2. Receivables should be recorded at the present values of amounts to be received, determined at appropriate current interest rates, less allowances for uncollectibility and collection costs, if necessary.
3. Inventories:
   a. Finished goods should be recorded at selling prices less cost of disposal and reasonable profit allowance.
   b. Work in process inventories should be stated at estimated selling prices of finished goods less the sum of the costs to complete, costs of disposal, and a reasonable profit allowance for the completing and selling effort of the acquired corporation.
   c. Raw materials should be recorded at current replacement costs.
4. Plant and equipment to be used in the business should be stated at current replacement costs for similar capacity unless the expected future use of the assets indicates a lower value to the acquirer. Replacement cost may be determined directly if a used asset market exists for the assets acquired. Otherwise, replacement cost should be approximated from replacement cost new, less estimated accumulated depreciation.
5. Indentifiable intangible assets should be valued at appraised values.
6. Other assets, such as land, natural resources, and nonmarketable securities, should be recorded at appraised values.
7. Accounts and notes payable, long-term debt, and other claims payable should be stated at present values of amounts to be paid, determined at appropriate current interest rates.

An acquiring corporation should not record as a separate asset goodwill previously recorded by an acquired company, and it should not record deferred income taxes previously recorded by an acquired company. Amounts assigned to identifiable assets and liabilities should recognize that their value may be less, if part or all of the assigned value is not deductible for income taxes. However, the acquiring corporation should not record deferred tax accounts for the tax effect of these differences at the date of acquisition.

Treatment of goodwill. APB Opinion No. 17 provides that for the intangible assets acquired in a business combination, the method of allocating the total cost of the acquired company depends on whether or not the asset is identifiable, such as a patent, or unidentifiable, such as goodwill. The cost of an identifiable intangible asset should be based on the fair value of the asset. The cost of an unidentifiable intangible asset is measured by the difference between total cost and the amount assigned to other assets acquired and liabilities assumed.

The cost of an intangible asset should not be written off in the period of acquisition but instead should be amortized based on the estimated life of that specific asset; the period of amortization, however, should not exceed 40 years. The straight-line method of amortization should be used unless the company can demonstrate that another systematic method is more appropriate. The method and period of amortization should be disclosed in the financial statements.

Pro forma supplementary disclosure. Under the purchase method, notes to the financial statements of the acquiring corporation for the period in which a business combination occurs should include as supplemental information the following results of operations on a pro forma basis:

1. Combined results of operations for the current period as though the companies has combined at the beginning of the period unless the acquisition was at or near the beginning of the period.
2. If comparative financial statements are presented, combined results of operations for the immediately preceding period should be reported as though the companies had combined at the beginning of that period.

This supplemental pro forma information should, as a minimum, show revenue, income before extraordinary items, net income, and earnings per share.

Illustration of accounting mechanics: Purchase versus pooling of interest accounting

Company Buy has agreed to acquire Company Sell in a transaction under which it will issue 1,200,000 of $1 par value common shares for all the common shares of Company Sell. The transaction qualifies as a pooling of interests, and consequently the fair market value of Sell's assets and liabilities at date of the merger do not enter into the accounting for it. Exhibit 9–3 presents in columnar fashion the balance sheets of Company Buy and Company Sell as well as the adjustments needed to effect the combination under pooling of interests accounting.

EXHIBIT 9–3

Merger of Company Sell into Company Buy

Summary of Pro Forma Condensed Combining Balance Sheet
(in thousands of dollars)

	Company Buy	Company Sell	Combining adjustments		Com- bined
			Debit	Credit	
Assets	157,934	28,013	—	—	185,947
Liabilities	42,591	11,218	—	—	53,809
Stockholders' equity:					
Company Buy:					
Preferred stock	810	—	—	—	810
Common stock	7,572	—	—	1,200	8,772
Company Sell:					
Common stock	—	1,285	1,285	—	—
Additional paid-in capital	31,146	137	—	85	31,368
Retained earnings	75,815	15,373	—	—	91,188
Total Stockholders' Equity	115,343	16,795	1,285	1,285	132,138
	157,934	28,013	1,285	1,285	185,947

Pooling accounting

Briefly, the pooling method requires taking up Sell's assets and liabilities at recorded amounts and carrying forward the equity account balances, subject to adjustments required by differences in the par values of the securities exchanged.

Since the amount of the par value of the common stock of Company Buy ($1,200,000) is smaller than the amount of the par value of the stock of Company Sell which is exchanged ($1,285,000), the difference is credited to "Additional Paid-In Capital." In a pooling where the reverse to the above situation prevails, additional par value is taken out first of the existing "paid-in capital" accounts of the constituents and, if sufficient, from retained earnings. The balance in the retained earnings accounts is carried forward.

The entry on Company Buy's books of the pooling with Company Sell will be as follows:

	Debit	Credit
	(in thousands of dollars)	
Assets	28,013	
Liabilities		11,218
Common stock		1,200
Additional paid-in capital		222
Retained earnings...................................		15,373

To record the issuance of 1,200,000 shares of $1 par value common stock for the merged net assets of Sell and to credit to Retained Earnings the balance of retained earnings of Sell at date of acquisition.

Exhibit 9–3 reflected the pooling as a "statutory merger," that is, the assets and liabilities of the two companies were combined and Company Sell ceased its separate existence. If we assume that Company Sell was to continue as a wholly owned subsidiary of Company Buy, the pooling would be recorded as shown in Exhibit 9–4.

EXHIBIT 9–4
Merger of Company Buy and Company Sell (Company Sell remains as a fully owned subsidiary of Company Buy)

Summary of Pro Forma Condensed Balance Sheet
(in thousands of dollars)

	Company Buy	Parent company only		
		Adjustments		
	Before pooling	Debit	Credit	After pooling
Assets	157,934	—	—	157,934
Investment in Sell		16,795	—	16,795
	157,934	16,795	—	174,729
Liabilities	42,591	—	—	42,591
Stockholders' equity:				
Company Buy:				
Preferred stock	810	—	—	810
Common stock	7,572	—	1,200	8,772
Company Sell: Common stock	—	—	—	—
Additional paid-in capital	31,146	—	222	31,368
Retained earnings	75,815	—	—	75,815
Retained earnings from pooled company	—	—	15,373	15,373
Total Stockholders' Equity	115,343	—	16,795	132,138
	157,934	—	16,795	174,729

The accounting entries made on the parent company's books are as follows:

	Debit	Credit
Investment in Company Sell	16,795	
Common stock		1,200
Additional paid-in capital		222
Retained earnings from pooled company		15,373

To record the issuance of 1,200,000 shares of $1 par value common stock for the common stock of Sell and to credit to Retained Earnings the balance of retained earnings of Sell at date of acquisition.

The investment in Company Sell will continue to be carried on an equity basis by Company Buy, the parent. In consolidation the investment account in Company Sell will be eliminated against subsidiary Company Sell's common stock, additional paid-in capital, and the parent company's retained earnings from the pooled company, all in accordance with normal consolidation procedure.

Purchase accounting

Let us now assume that instead of acquiring Company Sell in an exchange of common stock, Company Buy acquires Company Sell for $25,000,000 in cash. Since this acquisition must be accounted for as a purchase, it is necessary to determine the fair values of Company Sell's assets and liabilities. The following tabulation compares Company Sell's recorded asset and liability amounts with indicated fair values at date of acquisition:

	Amounts on Company Sell books	Fair values determined at date of acquisition
	(in thousands of dollars)	
Assets	28,013	34,000
Liabilities	11,218	13,000
Net assets	16,795	21,000
Cost to Company Buy	—	25,000
Amount assigned to goodwill	—	4,000

Assets and liabilities are valued in accordance with the valuation principles outlined in *APB Opinion No. 16*. The excess of purchase price over the fair value of net assets acquired assigned to goodwill must be amortized over its useful value not to exceed 40 years.

Exhibit 9–5 presents the consolidated balance sheet of Company Buy right after the purchase of Company Sell so as to enable a contrast with the balance sheet obtained right after the pooling accounting presented in Exhibit 9–3 on page 232.

A cash acquisition is, of course, not the only method requiring purchase accounting. As described earlier, under a great number of condi-

EXHIBIT 9–5
Purchase of Company Sell by Company Buy

Summary of Pro Forma Condensed Consolidated Balance Sheet
(in thousands of dollars)

	Company Buy	Company Sell (at fair values on date of acquisition)	Combining and consolidating adjustments		After purchase
			Debit	Credit	
Assets					
Assets (exclusive of goodwill)	157,934	34,000		25,000	166,934
Goodwill			4,000		4,000
Total Assets	157,934	34,000			170,934
Liabilities and Stockholder's Equity					
Liabilities	42,591	13,000			55,591
Stockholder's Equity:					
Company Buy:					
Preferred stock	810				810
Common stock	7,572				7,572
Additional paid-in capital	31,146				31,146
Retained earnings	75,815				75,815
Net assets at fair value of company sell..................		21,000	21,000		
Total Stockholder's Equity.....................	115,343	21,000			115,343
Total Liabilities and Stockholder's Equity.................	157,934	34,000	25,000	25,000	170,934

tions involving an acquisition for stock purchase accounting would be required.

The following difference between the pooling and the purchase accounting should be noted. In the purchase—

1. The assets and liabilities are recorded at fair value. Goodwill is recognized. These will result in higher charges to income reflecting the higher net asset values acquired.
2. The total stockholder equity remains unchanged. There has been an exchange of resources, that is, Company Sell's net assets of $25,000,000 for Company Buy's cash.

Implications for analysis

An examination of the revised guidelines and principles governing the accounting for mergers and acquisitions reveals a serious attempt by the accounting profession to improve the accounting in this area and to prevent some of the glaring distortions and abuses of the past, as they perceived them, from recurring.

The new rules which govern the accounting for pooling of interests and for purchases are the result of a lengthy process of compromise; another important objective was the elimination of *specific* abuses of practice. The analyst must recognize this as well as the fact that the rationale which accountants use in distinguishing pooling of interests from purchases combinations are not necessarily relevant to his attempt to measure and analyze the economic consequences of business combinations.

Thus, in determining the implications which the new accounting rules on business combinations hold for the analyst of financial statements, we must examine the impact which these rules have on the realistic portrayal of the results of mergers and acquisitions.

Pooling versus purchase accounting

Before we examine the effect of pooling accounting on the financial statements of a combined entity, let us summarize the main arguments which have been advanced in defense of this method:

1. If cash is given as consideration in a business acquisition, the acquirer parts with a resource. But if a company's own unissued stock is given in exchange, no resource is given; instead the equity is increased.
2. In exchange of common stock, the "seller" is getting back a part of itself as well as part of the buyer. Since he does not part with ownership in his own company, there is no valid basis for establishing new values.
3. In a combination of equals, which results from an exchange of stock, it is hard to determine who acquired whom.

It is not at all clear that cash is a resource while unissued stock is not. After all, if stock is an acceptable consideration to a seller, it should also command a price on the market. Some regard the ability to issue stock as equivalent to "a license to print money." The valuation of noncash consideration is a problem which accountants have to face frequently. Moreover, if a combination fails as a pooling on any one of the technical conditions enumerated in *APB Opinion No. 16*, a valuation of the stock issued will become necessary in order to account for the combination as a purchase.

There is some validity to the second argument above, but in most business combinations the relative size of the pooled-in company to the surviving entity is small indeed.

The third argument is rarely relevant today because the size-test of poolings has been abandoned and consequently a large company can acquire a very small enterprise and still account for the combination as a pooling.

Aside from the above considerations, from the point of view of the analyst it is the results of pooling accounting which really matter. These can be best illustrated by means of a simplified example.

Assume that Company B which wants to acquire Company S earns $1,000 of net income and has 500 shares outstanding. Company S's condensed balance sheet is as follows:

Fixed assets*	$ 400	Liabilities	$ 200
Other assets	600	Capital accounts	800
	$1,000		$1,000

* Current value $600

Company S has a net income of $200 after deduction of $20 for depreciation (10 percent of $400 in fixed assets less 50% tax effect).

Let us now consider the operating results of Company B one year after the acquisition of Company S for a price of $1,400 paid in (1) cash or (2) stock. Let us assume that the earnings of both companies remain unchanged and that the $1,400 purchase price (of Company S) is arrived at as follows:

Fixed assets (current value)	$ 600
Other assets	600
Goodwill	400
	$1,600
Less liabilities assumed	200
Purchase consideration	$1,400

Payment in cash.   If the purchase price was in cash, the combined company's income statement would be accounted for on a purchase basis as follows:

Income of B			$1,000
Income of S (before depreciation)		$220	
Depreciation (10% of $600)	$30*		
Goodwill amortization (2½% of 400†)	10	40	180
Net income of the combined enterprise			$1,180

* After tax effect.
† Assuming amortization over 40 years, no tax deduction.

Payment in stock.   If, however, the purchase price was in stock, under the pooling method of accounting the income statement of the enterprise would be as follows:

Income of B	$1,000
Income of S	200
Net income of the combined enterprise	$1,200

The difference in the net income is due to the inclusion, under the pooling method, of fixed assets at $400, the original cost on the books of Company S, and the complete omission of the goodwill which Company B paid in the acquisition of Company S.

Whether the reported income of the combined company is $1,200 or $1,180 depends in this case on how the purchase price was paid. Moreover, if the purchase price is paid in common stock and *any* of the other 11 conditions of a pooling are not met, the acquisition would have to be accounted for as a purchase and the reported income would be $1,180 instead of $1,200.

This, then, is the basic difference between pooling and purchase accounting. The nonrecording or suppression of asset values for which the acquiring company paid generally results in an understatement of assets and an overstatement of income. This is the primary reason why earnings which are the result of pooling combinations are viewed as being overstated in comparison with similar earnings resulting from purchase accounting.

As an astute financial analyst put it "Dow Chemical with a market value of near $6 billion, offered stock worth $419 million for General Crude. The basis of accounting in a pooling will remain book value of General Crude which is about $82 million. Suppose instead International Paper had been successful and offered $419 in cash in a purchase. Then the new basis of General Crude's assets could have been $419 million. It seems that form prevails over substance in permitting pooling."[3]

APB Opinion No. 16 has done nothing to remove this problem which is inherent in the pooling of interests method. It has removed some of the abuses of the original criteria of the pooling of interests concept such as part pooling-part purchase, issuance of complex securities other than common stock in a pooling, retroactive pooling, and contingent additional consideration. But these features, while enabling the application of pooling accounting to many mergers, are not in themselves responsible for the suppression of asset values. This suppression is *inherent* in the pooling of interests concept, and all that *APB Opinion No. 16* achieved in this regard is to limit significantly the application of the concept by making it more difficult for companies to meet the criteria of a pooling. But once having met these criteria, many of the old problems and distortions remain.

---

[3] D. Norr, *Accounting Theory Illustrated*, First Manhattan Co., 1974, p. 4.

Let us now summarize the most important features of pooling of interests accounting which, from the point of view of the analyst, differentiate it from purchase accounting:

1. Assets acquired are carried at "book value" rather than at the current fair values reflected in the consideration given. To the extent that "goodwill" is paid for, the amount is not shown on the acquiring company's balance sheet.
2. The understatement of assets leads to an understatement of capital employed by the enterprise.
3. The understatement of assets such as inventory, property, plant, and equipment, as well as goodwill and other intangibles, will lead to an understatement of expenses such as cost of goods sold, depreciation, and amortization of goodwill and intangibles. In turn, this will lead to an overstatement of income.
4. The understatement of assets can lead not only to an understatement of expenses but can also result in an overstatement of gains realized on their disposition. Thus, the acquiring corporation can claim as part of its results of operations gains on the sale of assets which at the time of their acquisition were carried forward at unrealistically low amounts, amounts which are actually far below the amount which, in the negotiations preceding the merger, was the agreed fair value of these assets. In these cases income is overstated and management performance is overrated. What we have here is clearly a recovery of cost rather than a profit.
5. Both the understatement of invested capital and the overstatement of income will lead to an overstatement of the return on investment.
6. The retained earnings of the acquired enterprise can be carried forward to the surviving company.
7. The income statements and the balance sheets of the combined enterprise are restated for all periods presented. Under purchase accounting they are combined only since the date of acquisition, although pro forma statements showing preacquisition combined results are also furnished.

A crude way of adjusting for omitted values in a pooling is to determine the difference between the fair or market value of assets acquired. This difference can then be amortized against reported income on some reasonable basis in order to arrive at results which would be comparable to those achieved under purchase accounting.

Purchase accounting

Since purchase accounting is designed to recognize the acquisition values on which the buyer and seller of a business entity bargained, it is a more meaningful method of accounting from the analyst's point of view. Purchase accounting is more relevant to the analyst's needs because he is interested in values which were exchanged in a business combination rather than in amounts which represent original costs to the seller.

As we have noted earlier in this chapter, the abuses in purchase accounting which preceded the issuance of *APB Opinions No. 16* and *No. 17* centered on attempts by acquiring companies to suppress the fair values of net assets acquired and paid for and to transplant the values paid for to a nondescript intangible asset account which was not amortized.

The Effect of APB Opinions No. 16 and No. 17.   *APB Opinions No. 16* and *No. 17* have directly and forthrightly addressed themselves to the problem and have as their primary objective the elimination of these abuses. However, the analyst must not confuse theory with practice: It must be realized that the objectives of many merger and acquisition-minded managements with respect to the accounting for these business combinations were in the past and are now likely to remain—

1. To reduce as much as possible the impact on present and future income of charges arising from assets acquired in the purchase.
2. To increase the post-acquisition income by understating assets acquired or by overproviding for future costs and contingencies.

Remaining room for distortions.   While *APB Opinion No. 16* contains specific provisions on the valuation of assets and liabilities, room for abuses and loose interpretations remains. In addition to the leeway which inevitably exists when broad rules of valuation and appraisal are applied, the analyst must be particularly alert to understatements of assets and overstatement of liabilities which result from provisions for future costs and losses. A profession which tolerates the provision of such indeterminate reserves in the normal process of income determination (see discussion in Chapter 10) cannot be expected to forbid their use in the general process of realignment of values which occurs in purchase accounting.[4] Two examples of such kind of provisions and adjustments will illustrate what we have in mind:

1. City Investing Company in its prospectus dated August 12, 1971 disclosed the following:

Certain Accounting Adjustments made in connection with the Acquisition of The Home Insurance Company. City accounted for its acquisition of The Home Insurance Company on August 31, 1968 as a "purchase of assets" rather than as a "pooling of interests." As a result, City was required, in accordance with generally accepted accounting principles, to establish a new cost basis of Home's net assets at the date of acquisition based upon the fair values of Home's assets and liabilities in the light of conditions then prevailing. In arriving at such fair values, it was determined that the reserves for underwriting losses and loss expenses on Home's books at the date of acquisition did not adequately reflect the amounts that could reasonably be expected to be paid in

---

[4] See however the discussion of the restricting provisions of SFAS 5 in Chapter 7.

respect of casualty losses which actually occurred prior to the acquisition. Accordingly, such reserves were increased by $43,181,000 through a charge to the income of Home for the eight-month period ended August 31, 1968, the period prior to the acquisition of Home by City. As a result of this adjustment, payments by Home in respect of casualty losses which occurred prior to the acquisition will not be deducted from City's income unless they exceed by $43,181,000 the reserves on Home's books for such losses prior to such adjustment. In addition, in determining the estimated realizable value of Home's investment portfolio as of the date of acquisition, it was considered appropriate, in the opinion of Lehman Brothers, to recognize a discount from quoted market of 15%, or $65,709,000, in the case of equity securities and 5%, or $14,074,000 in the case of debt instruments so as to reflect liquidation factors such as block transaction discounts, type of market, trading volume and similar factors. As a result of this adjustment, the aggregate amount of gains ultimately recognized in City's income from the sale of all portfolio securities held by Home at the date of acquisition (when and if all such securities are sold) will exceed by $79,783,000 the amount that would have been recognized if such adjustments had not been made. Net pre-tax gains on the sale of investments include approximately $13,000,000 and $25,000,000 during the years ended April 30, 1969 and 1970, respectively, and $1,356,000 and $15,661,000 during the eight months and year ended December 31, 1970, respectively, attributable to such portfolio adjustment.

Here are substantial provisions for costs and expenses which are not normally provided for and which, apparently, the auditors of the Home Insurance Company did not insist on in prior years.

2. General Leisure Products Corporation in its prospectus dated July 27, 1971 disclosed the following:

Effective January 31, 1971, the company was acquired by Arctic Enterprises, Inc. in a transaction which was accounted for as a purchase. As a result, management of Arctic Enterprises, Inc. decided not to proceed with previous management's policies with regard to inventories. . . . Based on the change in management policies and the physical inventory taken as of January 31, 1971, an inventory reserve of $1,139,000 was recorded and has been included in cost of sales in the unaudited statement of operations for the six months ended January 31, 1971. Based on decisions of new management, the inventory reserve was established to provide for quantities which are in excess of current sales requirements, parts related to discontinued models and defective and obsolete parts.

In addition, new management wrote-off the unamortized deferred product line development costs . . . to conform with the accounting practices followed by Arctic Enterprises, Inc. Accordingly, $78,363 of such unamortized deferred product line development costs have been expensed and included in cost of sales in the unaudited statement of operations for the six months ended January 31, 1971.

Here too we have substantial provisions for expected losses which are charged by the acquiring management to preacquisition results in order to achieve management decisions and conformance with stated accounting policies.

In assessing the effect of a business combination accounted for as a purchase, the analyst must evaluate in detail the disclosures which he finds regarding the process of valuation applied by the acquiring company. On the basis of such information he must reach his own conclusions on the fairness of presentation of the acquired companies assets and liabilities.

Acquisitions for equity securities. When an acquisition accounted for as a purchase is effected for stock or other equity securities, the analyst must be alert to the valuation of the net assets acquired in the combination. In periods of high market price levels, purchase accounting may tend to introduce inflated values when net assets, and particularly the intangibles assets, of acquired companies are valued on the basis of market prices of the stock issued. Such values, while determined on the basis of temporarily inflated stock prices, remain on a company's balance sheet and affect its operating results on a long-term basis.

The effect of goodwill amortization. APB Opinion No. 17 recognized that a payment made in anticipation of future earnings should be recovered from those earnings over the period of those excess earnings. The mandatory amortization of goodwill is, from the point of view of realistic income determination, a step in the right direction. The analyst must, however, remain alert to the possibility that many companies will use the maximum period of 40 years for amortization purposes rather than the "reasonable" estimate of useful life which *APB Opinion No. 17* calls for.

ACCOUNTING FOR FOREIGN OPERATIONS

When the user of financial statements attempts to analyze an entity which has investments and operations in a foreign country,[5] he or she must add to the problems which are discussed throughout this book those which are peculiar to foreign operations. These subdivide, broadly speaking, into two major categories:

1. Problems related to differences in accounting principles and practices which are peculiar to the foreign country in which the operations are conducted.
2. Problems which arise from the translation of foreign assets, liabilities, equities, and results of operations into the U.S. dollar.

---

[5] SFAS *14* now requires information about Foreign Operations and Export Sales (see also Chapter 20).

Foreign accounting practices and auditing standards

Accounting practices can vary significantly among countries. There are a variety of reasons for this including a lack of agreement on objectives of financial statements, the requirements of national "company laws, the influence of tax laws and differences in the strength" and the development patterns of local professional bodies.

In recent years serious attempts have begun to bring more conformity into international accounting practices. The most ambitious program for the establishment of international accounting standards was the establishment in 1973 of the International Accounting Standards Committee (IASC) by the professional institutes of nine countries. Its objective is to "formulate and publish in the public interest, basic standards to be observed in the presentation of audited accounts and financial statements and to promote their worldwide acceptance and observance." The IASC published a number of papers since its first standard entitled "Disclosure of Accounting Policies" was published in early 1975.

These are modest, if important, beginnings and much remains to be done if the significant differences between the accounting practices of various countries are to be narrowed.

Differences in auditing standards.   In the area of auditing, which is discussed in Chapter 15 and is concerned with the function of attesting to the reliability of financial statements, a wide variety of standards in international practice exist. In some countries, such as the United Kingdom and Canada for example, the auditing profession is strong and well regarded, while in others its standing may be weak and, consequently, the reliability of financial statements may be subject to considerable doubt. Nevertheless, an auditing firm of international repute can enhance the credibility of a company's financial statements regardless of the location of the company's home base. Thus, the analyst must assess the reliability of the financial statements which are used on the basis of the individual circumstances surrounding their preparation and attestation.

Peculiarities of foreign accounting practices.   One of the central theses of this text is that no intelligent analysis of financial statements is possible without a thorough understanding of the assumptions and principles on the basis of which such statements were prepared. It follows that in the case of foreign companies the analyst must at least obtain a working familiarity with such assumptions and principles.

While the differences in accounting practice between those obtaining in the United States and those in other countries vary significantly from country to country, they can be substantial. The following are merely indicative of the nature and extent of such differences. Thus, in some countries—

1. Inventory reserves and other secret reserves may be sanctioned.
2. Excessive depreciation may be recorded.
3. Because of substantial price level changes, restatements of property accounts may be effected based on coefficients established by, and frequently revised by, the local government.
4. "Legal reserves" amounting to a fixed percentage of net income may be established.
5. Tax allocation may not be practiced.
6. Stock dividends may be recorded only on the basis of the par value of the stock issued.
7. Pooling of interests accounting may not be sanctioned.
8. Consolidation of parent and subsidiary financial statements may not be required.
9. The recognition of pension liabilities can vary widely.

A recitation of the differences in accounting as practiced in the United States and in other countries is beyond the scope of this text. The analyst must consult up-to-date sources of information which are relevant to the proper understanding and analysis of financial statements.[6]

In consolidating their foreign subsidiaries, U.S.–based multinational companies will usually conform their subsidiaries' accounting to the principles generally accepted in this country.

Translation of foreign currencies

In the discussion of intercorporate investments earlier in this chapter, it was emphasized that the consolidation of majority-owned subsidiaries is now a generally accepted procedure and the reasons for nonconsolidation are few and well defined. With respect to subsidiaries of U.S.–based multinational companies, the most common reasons for nonconsolidation would be substantial uncertainty regarding the ultimate realization or transferability of foreign earnings.

In addition to the above provisions, *APB Opinion No. 18* requires a parent company to recognize in its financial statements the equity in earnings or losses of (1) unconsolidated foreign subsidiaries, (2) corporate joint ventures, and (3) other companies, less than 50 percent owned, over which the investor company exerts a significant influence.

---

[6] See for example, *Professional Accounting in 30 Countries* (New York: AICPA, 1975); and Gerhard G. Muller, *International Accounting* (New York: Macmillan Co., 1967).

The translation process. The consolidation of, as well as equity accounting for, foreign subsidiaries and affiliates requires that their financial statements be translated into U.S.–dollar equivalents. This is, of course, necessary before the accounts of such foreign subsidiaries or affiliates can be combined with those of the U.S.–based company.

The practical effect of the translation into dollars of an asset or a liability expressed in terms of a foreign currency can be best visualized by focusing on a few concrete examples:

1. If a foreign subsidiary holds an amount of foreign currency, then the value of that currency to the U.S. parent is the amount of U.S. dollars it will buy. That calls for translation at the current (balance sheet date) rate. If the value of the foreign currency falls in relation to the dollar, then the parent will experience a loss on conversion. Should the dollar decline in relation to that foreign currency, the parent company will sustain a gain on translation.

2. When the foreign subsidiary incurs a debt payable in the currency of the country in which it conducts its operations, then a decline of that currency in terms of dollars will result in a translation gain, that is, fewer dollars will be needed to obtain the amount of foreign currency in order to repay the loan. But suppose that the subsidiary took out a long-term loan and the value of the dollar declined in relation to the foreign currency. The dollar equivalent of the liability has now increased. While a translation loss must now be recognized, there are those who feel that because of the long-term nature of the obligation, only a contingent loss has been incurred or that an additional borrowing cost exists which should be charged off over the term of the loan.

3. When the foreign subsidiary acquires property, plant, and equipment with foreign currency, should it be translated at the current exchange rate, that is, should the translated dollar equivalent vary with fluctuations in the exchange rates? The general view is that it should not because such assets are "nonmonetary," that is, in this case the subsidiary is not holding assets expressed in fixed amounts of the foreign currency. Thus, translation into dollars continues at the rate at which these assets were acquired, that is, the "historical rate," on the assumption that foreign-currency selling prices will increase under inflationary condition and that this will prevent deterioration in the economic value of assets such as property, plant, and equipment.

SFAS 8 (1975) sets forth the Accounting for the Translation of Foreign Currency Transactions and Foreign Currency Financial Statements.

The basic objective of the translation process (known also as the "temporal method") is to preserve the accounting basis used in the original (foreign currency) statements. That is, if an item is carried in that statement at historical cost (such as fixed assets or inventories) to preserve the carrying basis by translating it at the historical rate. Conversely, items stated in terms of foreign money (such as cash receivables and payables) are converted at the current exchange rate. Under this method as the carrying basis of items changes so should the translation basis change, e.g., inventory carried at cost is translated at historical rates; if written down to market it should be translated at the current rate.

The following are the basic translation procedures:

Before translation occurs, the statements should be prepared in conformity with U.S. generally accepted accounting principles.

Cash, receivables and payables denominated in other than local currency should be adjusted to reflect the current rate between local and foreign currency. The adjusted balances and other balances representing cash and accounts receivable or payable that are denominated in the local currency should be translated into dollars at the current rate.

Other assets and liabilities should be translated in a manner that retains their measurement basis, thus, they are to be translated at the historical foreign exchange rate in effect when the assets were acquired or the liabilities were incurred. However, the current rate should be used to translate those other assets and liabilities that are accounted for on the basis of current prices, such as marketable securities or inventories carried at market price and estimated warranty obligations.

Revenue and expense transactions should be translated in a manner that produces approximately the same dollar amounts that would have resulted had the underlying transactions been translated on the dates they occurred. Use of weighted average rates for the period is permitted as a practical matter.

Summary of applicable translation rates

	Translation rate
Cash, current receivables, current payables	Current
Inventories, current prepaids, current unearned revenue ...	Historical
Noncurrent receivables, long-term liabilities	Current
Fixed assets, deferred charges, noncurrent unearned revenue	Historical
Income and expenses other than depreciation	Average (weighted)
Depreciation and amortization of long-lived assets	Historical

Interperiod tax allocation is appropriate if taxable exchange gains or tax-deductible exchange losses resulting from foreign currency transactions are included in financial statement income in a different period than for tax purposes.

Special procedures should be followed in applying the test of cost or market, whichever is lower, to inventory valuation and translating timing differences that affect deferred tax accounting.

Gain or loss pertaining to a forward exchange contract should be included in determining net income for the period in which the rate changes unless the contract represents a hedge (as described) of a foreign currency commitment.

Gain or loss pertaining to a forward exchange contract intended to be a hedge of an identifiable foreign currency commitment should be deferred and included in the dollar basis of the related foreign currency transaction.

Exchange gains and losses should be included in determining net income for the period in which the rate changes. The same accounting for exchange gains and losses is to be followed at interim and year end dates.

The dividend remittance rate to translate foreign statements should be used when multiple foreign exchange rates exist.

The current rate used to translate the financial statements of a foreign subsidiary should be the rate in effect at the subsidiary's year-end date.

If the exchange rate changes significantly after the balance-sheet date—this, and possible effect on financial position, should be disclosed—but not given effect to.

For foreign currency transactions—if multiple rates exist, the transaction should be recorded at the rate at which the transaction could be settled at that date. For subsequent balance sheet dates, the rate at which the related transaction can be settled at these dates should be used.

The use of averages or other methods of approximation is appropriate provided the results do not differ materially from the results prescribed by the standards.

Disclosure requirements

Aggregate exchange gain or loss included in determining net income for the period.

Effects of rate changes on reported results of operations, other than the effects included in the disclosure required above, if predictable, should be described and quantified. If quantified, the methods and the underlying assumptions used to determine the estimated effects should be explained.

Treatment of gains and losses from translations of foreign currencies

In accordance with *APB Opinion 30* (See Chapter 10) *all* gains or losses from translations of foreign currencies, including those relating to major devaluations and revaluations, are to be treated as ordinary rather than extraordinary items. Such treatment does not, however, imply that such gains and losses cannot be separately disclosed in the income statement as "one line" items above "income before extraordinary items."

Implications for analysis

The principles of accounting which govern the translation of foreign accounts were originally developed in times of deteriorating foreign currencies and a relatively stable U.S. dollar. More recently there has occurred a fundamental change in these relationships.

SFAS 8 has brought substantial change in the accounting for foreign currency transactions compared to the methods which were acceptable prior to its promulgation. Among the most substantial changes which affect many companies with multinational operations are the requirements that:

1. Companies which translated inventories at current rates must now change to historic rates.
2. Companies which translated long-term debt and receivables at historical rates will now have to convert these at current rates.
3. Reserves and deferrals created by exchange gains and losses must now be eliminated.
4. The use of exchange gain and loss deferrals and reserves to smooth out foreign earnings will no longer be available.

The above changes will, aside from their effect on income, also affect such important financial position relationships as the current ratio, the acid test ratio, debt-equity ratios as well as performance in areas such as the return on investment.

Balance sheet effects.   In assessing and in estimating the impact of the new translation rules on future financial position and results of operation of companies with foreign operations, the analyst will have to pay close attention to the capital structure as well as the composition of the assets and liabilities of affected companies.

Thus, when the dollar declines—foreign income and assets generated and located in strong currency countries translate into more dollars—thus enhancing translated foreign results provided foreign liabilities do not offset these effects. Balancing of foreign assets and liabilities insulates a parent somewhat from the effect of changing exchange rates on translated foreign results.

Exhibit 9–6 illustrates the effects of exchange rate changes on balance sheet translation gains and losses. Situation A represents the start-

EXHIBIT 9–6

Illustration of balance sheet translation

A. Initial exchange rate $1 = 10 pesos

Cash	Ps. 1,000 ÷ 10 =	$100	Payables	Ps. 1,000 ÷ 10 =	$100
Accounts			Capital	3,000 ÷ 10 =	300
Receivable	1,000 ÷ 10 =	100			
Inventory	1,000 ÷ 10 =	100			
Fixed Assets	1,000 ÷ 10 =	100			
Totals	Ps. 4,000	$400		Ps. 4,000	$400

B. Peso weakens—Exchange rate $1 = 12½ pesos

Cash	Ps. 1,000 ÷ 12½ =	$ 80	Payables	Ps. 1,000 ÷ 12½ =	$ 80
Accounts			Capital	3,000 ÷ 10 =	300
Receivable	1,000 ÷ 12½ =	80	Exchange		
Inventory	1,000 ÷ 10 =	100	Loss		(20)*
Fixed Assets	1,000 ÷ 10 =	100			
Totals	Ps. 4,000	$360		Ps. 4,000	$360

C. Peso gains—Exchange rate $1 = 8 pesos

Cash	Ps. 1,000 ÷ 8 =	$125	Payables	Ps. 1,000 ÷ 8 =	$125
Accounts			Capital	3,000 ÷ 10 =	300
Receivable	1,000 ÷ 8 =	125	Exchange		
Inventory	1,000 ÷ 10 =	100	Gain		25*
Fixed Assets	1,000 ÷ 10 =	100			
Totals	Ps. 4,000	$450		Ps. 4,000	$450

* Charged or credited directly to profit or loss of period.

ing point. In situation B the weakening peso results in a loss from the translation of items subject to exchange risks (i.e., translated at current rates) which are Cash (loss of $20), Accounts Receivable (loss of $20) and Payables (gain of $20) or a net exchange loss of $20. Conversely, in situation C a stronger peso results in a net translation gain. Thus, an important clue to the prediction of future translation gains or losses is the net exposed position by foreign country.[7]

---

[7] The conclusion in SFAS 14 that disclosure of working capital and property plant and equipment should not be required by geographic area represents a setback to analysts attempting to measure exposure to currency fluctuations.

Thus, under the new rules which require the translation of most monetary assets and liabilities at current rates, a highly leveraged foreign subsidiary will be less affected by changes in exchange rates than will an equity financed one. This is so primarily because debt must be repaid in the foreign currency subject to translation. For that reason also debt which is a U.S. dollar obligation (i.e., the parent's currency) can be considered for purposes of measuring exposure to currency fluctuation risks, as being more akin to equity than to debt.

Since inventories valued at the lower of cost or market (which is the usual case) are now to be translated at historical rates a company with large inventories, such as a tobacco company, and thus showing an excess of liabilities over cash plus receivables, will show a gain on foreign devaluation and a loss on foreign revaluation. Conversely, a company with small inventories, such as in the case of some service industries, is likely to show a gain on revaluation and a loss on devaluation.

Income statement effects.   While most revenue and expense items in the income statement are translated at weighted average rates for the year, depreciation and amortization are geared to the historical rates at which the related assets are stated. Consequently to the extent that depreciation and amortization is a factor in the total income statement the impact of the translation of income statement items is magnified. The more capital intensive the foreign operation the greater the impact of this magnification.

The following example will illustrate this point:

ILLUSTRATION 2.   Assume that a foreign subsidiary has unchanged operations in 19X2 compared to 19X1 but that the exchange rate of currency of the country in which it operates has increased on average against the dollar by 10 percent in 19X2.

	19X1	19X2	% Change
Sales	$1,000	$1,100	10%
Expenses (except depreciation)	600	660	10%
Depreciation-at historical rates	200	200	—
Total Costs......................	800	860	
Net Income	$ 200	$ 240	+20%

Thus, because of the importance of depreciation, a 10 percent exchange rate change resulted in a 20 percent change in net income because assets bought in prior years are depreciated at the lower historical rates.

Conversely, a decline of 10 percent in the rate of exchange of the foreign currency against the dollar could have produced the following results:

	19X1	19X2	% Change
Sales	$1,000	900	−10%
Expenses (except depreciation)	600	540	−10%
Depreciation (at historical rates)	200	200	
Total Costs...........................	$ 800	$ 740	
Net Income	$ 200	$ 160	−20%

The analytical conclusion that can be derived from the above is that the less profitable the foreign operation relative to sales, or the greater the relative importance of depreciation to sales, the greater will be the effect of changes in exchange rates on net income.

It should be noted that while the impact of a currency rate change on the balance sheet occurs at the time of that change the impact on income statement comparisons will persist for twelve months. This is so because in the translation of operating results we compare each period with the corresponding period of a year ago and thus the impact is stretched out.

As we saw in the preceding illustration the mix in the income statement of items translated at historical rates and those which must be translated at current rates contributes to the volatility of results. The effect of inventory acquired in prior quarters at one exchange rate level and charged against currently quarterly results which experience a different exchange rate can be traced in Exhibit 9–7. Such conditions can cause significant fluctuations in profit margins from quarter to quarter.

It should also be noted that the amount that appears in the income statement, or in notes to financial statements, as the gain or loss on currency translation relates ordinarily only to the results of *balance sheet* translation; the impact of translating the income statement is shown as part of overall results and is not separately identified.

One basic reason for this is that the translations of balance sheets are *comparative* translations, i.e., differing rates of exchange are applied at differing times to the same kinds of assets and liabilities and the exchange gain or loss arises therefrom. In contrast the income statement of each period is separate and unique to that period and is not carried forward except for its transfer to retained earnings.

That is not to say that changes in exchange rates do not affect the income statement because, as we saw in the above illustrations, they most certainly do. However, unlike our simplified illustrations which assured no changes in volume, prices, unit costs, and so forth, in reality these elements are much influenced by the same factors which influence exchange rate changes. Thus, as a practical matter the com-

EXHIBIT 9–7

Illustration of the lagging effect of currency rate changes on quarterly gross profit margins (SFAS 8 method)

Assumptions: Stable 800 pesos inventory level, Fifo inventory method and an inventory turnover of 4

	Pesos				Explanation
First quarter 19X1—$1 = 10 pesos					
Sales	1,000	÷	10	= 100	
Cost of sales	800	÷	10	= 80	Rate at Inventory Acquisition
Gross profit	200			= 20	"Normal" Profit Margins
Second quarter 19X1—Exchange rate changes to $1 = 12½ pesos (at 4/1)					
Sales	1,000	÷	12½	= 80	Translated at current rate
Cost of sales	800	÷	10	= 80	Inventory at 1st qtr. rate
Gross profit	200			0	
Third quarter 19X1 exchange rate stable throughout at $1 = 12½ pesos					
Sales	1,000	÷	12½	= 80	At current rate
Cost of sales	800	÷	12½	= 64	Inventory at 2d qtr. rate
Gross profit	200			16	
Fourth quarter 19X1—Exchange rate changes to $1 = 10 pesos (at 10/1)					
Sales	1,000	÷	10	= 100	At current rate
Cost of sales	800	÷	12½	= 64	Inventory at 3d qtr. rate
Gross profit	200			36	
First quarter 19X2—Exchange rate remains at $1 = 10 pesos					
Sales	1,000	÷	10	= 100	At current rate
Cost of sales	800	÷	10	= 80	Inventory at 4th qtr. rate
Gross profit	200			20	

putation of income statement effects is such a complex procedure that SFAS 8 requires that when it is presented, the methods and the *assumptions* used to arrive at it must be disclosed. The analyst must be alert to these disclosures as well as to the possibility that some companies will use guesswork or will merely translate the latest year's foreign income statements at the rates of the previous year and consider the difference as the translation income effect. This may be too simplistic an approach to be really informative and significant.

Continuing controversy. While the required accounting for foreign currency translation has now been settled, controversy regarding its provisions persists. Some observers take issue with the requirement that inventories and fixed assets be translated at historical rates while requiring the short- and long-term debt incurred to finance these to be converted at the current rate of exchange. This, they maintain, causes the translated results and relationships to differ significantly from those reflected in the foreign currency financial statements of the foreign subsidiary.

Furthermore, critics of these requirements maintain that the requirement that foreign *assets* be translated one way while foreign *debt* be translated in a different way may cause distortions and serious fluctuations in income which may be misinterpreted by investors.

Finally, it is claimed by some that the current recognition of *unrealized* foreign exchange gains is not in accord with principles of conservative accounting.

The analyst must also be aware of the fact that fluctuating currency rates are but one of the variables, albeit an important one, which determine the final effect of foreign operations on a company's financial statements. Among the other factors which the analyst must take into account are: The location of assets and liabilities, intercountry transactions, foreign taxation trends, differing fiscal years of foreign entities, restrictions on remittances of funds and the currencies in which sales are effected.

QUESTIONS

1. *a.* List and explain three main reasons why a parent company may not choose to include certain subsidiaries in its consolidated financial statements.
    b. What significant information may be disclosed by inspection of individual parent company and subsidiary statements in addition to the consolidated statements? (C.F.A.)
2. "A parent company is not responsible for the liabilities of its subsidiaries nor does it own the assets of the subsidiaries. Therefore, consolidated financial statements distort legal realities." Evaluate this statement from the financial analyst's viewpoint.
3. Which of the following cases would require consolidated financial statements?
    a. The parent company has a two-fifths ownership of the subsidiary.
    b. The parent company has temporary but absolute control over the subsidiary.
    c. The parent company has a controlling interest in the subsidiary but plans to dispose of it.
    d. Control of the subsidiary is to be relinquished in the near future as a result of a minority shareholder's derivative suit.
    e. A conglomerate parent company has a majority interest in diversified subsidiaries.
    f. The parent company has a 100 percent interest in a foreign subsidiary in a country where the conversion of currencies and the transfer of funds is severely restricted by the governmental authorities.
    g. The parent company has a 100 percent interest in a subsidiary whose

principal business is the leasing of properties to the parent company and its affiliates.

4. Why is the cost method of accounting for investments in subsidiaries regarded as the least desirable?

5. Give some examples of situations in which the use of the cost method, rather than the equity method, is more appropriate.

6. What are some of the important limitations to which consolidated financial statements are subject?

7. The following note appeared in the financial statements of the Best Company for the period ending December 31, 19X1:

"*Event subsequent to December 31, 19X1:* In January 19X2 the Company acquired Good Products, Inc. and its affiliates by the issuance of 48,063 shares of common stock. Net assets of the combined companies amounted to $1,016,198 and net income for 19X1 approximated $150,000. To the extent that the acquired companies earn in excess of $1,000,000 over the next five years, the Company will be required to issue additional shares not exceeding 151,500, limited, however, to a market value of $2,000,000."

   a. Is the disclosure necessary and adequate?
   b. If the Good Products, Inc. was acquired in December 19X1, at what price should the Best Company have recorded the acquisition, assuming the Best Company's shares are traded at $22 on that day?
   c. On what is the additional consideration contingent?
   d. If the contingency materializes to the maximum limit, how should Best Company record the investment?

8. How would you determine the valuation of assets acquired in a purchase in the following cases?
   a. Assets acquired by incurring liabilities.
   b. Assets acquired in exchange of common stock.

9. Assuming the total cost of a purchased entity is appropriately determined, how should the total cost be allocated to the following assets?
   a. Goodwill.
   b. Negative goodwill (bargain purchase).
   c. Marketable securities.
   d. Receivables.
   e. Finished goods.
   f. Work in process.
   g. Raw materials.
   h. Plant and equipment.
   i. Land and mineral reserves.
   j. Payables.
   k. Goodwill recorded in the book of the acquired company.

10. One of the arguments for pooling of interests is that in pooling no resource is given in exchange for the acquisition: since the acquiring company gives its unissued stock, the acquisition cannot be regarded as purchase. Do you agree?

11. Company A accounts as a pooling of interests the acquisition of Company B, the market value of whose net assets is much higher than their book value. What will be the effect of the pooling of interests method on Company A's income statement? On its balance sheet? What significance does *APB Opinion No. 16* have on such effects?

12. How is "goodwill" treated in an acquisition accounted for as a pooling of interests?

13. If assets are understated as a result of a pooling of interests, what effect(s) would the understatement have on the following:
    a. Capital account.
    b. Various expenses.
    c. Disposition of assets acquired.

14. Is there any way an analyst can adjust the income statement under the pooling of interests method so that it can be comparable to a purchase method income statement?

15. From the analyst's point of view, which method of accounting for a business combination is preferable and why?

16. When an acquisition accounted for as a purchase is effected for stock or other equity securities, what should the analyst be alerted to?

17. When the balance sheet shows a substantial amount of goodwill, to what should the analyst be alert?

18. A current accounting controversy concerns the widespread use of pooling in mergers. Opponents of the use of pooling believe that the surviving company often uses pooling (rather than purchase) to hide the "true" effects of the merger. What may be "hidden" and how is the analysis of a company's securities affected by pooling practices? (C.F.A.)

19. Company X has engaged in an aggressive program of acquiring other companies through exchange of common stock.
    a. Explain briefly how an acquisition program might contribute to the rate of growth in earnings per share of Company X.
    b. Explain briefly how the income statements of prior years might be adjusted to reflect the potential future earnings trend of the combined companies. (C.F.A.)

20. What are some factors which could change management's original estimates of the useful life of intangible assets?

21. What are some significant problem areas in accounting for foreign operations?

22. When a consolidated financial statement includes foreign operations, to what must the financial analyst be particularly alert?

23. Although cash generally is regarded as the simplest of all assets to account for, certain complexities can arise for both domestic and multinational companies.
    a. What are the normal components of cash?
    b. Under what circumstances, if any, do valuation problems arise in connection with cash?

    c. Unrealized and/or realized gains or losses can arise in connection with cash. Excluding consideration of price level changes, indicate the nature of such gains or losses and the context in which they can arise in relation to cash. (AICPA)

24. For the fiscal year ended December 31, 1970, International Business Machines Corporation reported record earnings per share of $8.92, up 9 percent from earnings per share of $8.21 in 1969. "For the first time, net earnings of IBM World Trade Corp., the foreign subsidiary, accounted for more than half of the huge computer maker's total annual—50.27%."

    In what ways does the growing importance of international operations such as World Trade make more difficult the analysis of the income statements of multinational corporations? (C.F.A.)

25. Discuss the major changes that were introduced by SFAS 8 on translation of foreign currency.

26. What are the major causes that contribute to the volatility of results of operations under foreign currency translation rules?

10

ANALYSIS OF THE INCOME STATEMENT—I

The income statement portrays the net results of operations of an enterprise. Since results are what enterprises are supposed to achieve and since their value is, in large measure, determined by the size and quality of these results, it follows quite logically that the analyst attaches great importance to the income statement.

This chapter and the one that follows will examine the principles which underlie the preparation and presentation of the income statement. The analysis and interpretation of this important financial statement is discussed in Chapters 20 and 21. Such analysis can be intelligently undertaken only after the principles outlined in this chapter are fully understood.

What is income? An examination of this subject will reveal that significant differences of opinion exist among thoughtful and competent accountants, economists, and financial analysts on what income is and on how the net income of an enterprise for a given period should be measured.

A simple illustration

Take, for example, the very simple case of a business unit which has only $1,000 in cash, with which it buys, at the beginning of the year, a bond priced at par, and carrying a 6 percent coupon. While we may readily agree that the gross income is $60 (the interest), the determination of net income depends, among other factors, on the value of the bond at year-end. Thus, if the market price at year-end is $950, the $50 loss would be recognized by the economist while the accountant may or may not recognize it, depending on a judgment of whether there has been a permanent impairment in the value of the bond and, also, on whether the loss must be recognized if it is the present intention of the enterprise to hold it to a not too distant maturity date. The economist would claim that it is not right to recognize the income of $60 without the offsetting shrinkage in capital in the amount of $50. The essence of this argument is that the enterprise was not as well off at the end of the period as it was at the beginning if the $60 is all recognized as income and so distributed.

If, instead, the bond had a market quotation at year-end of $1,100, then some economists would consider the $100 accretion as a gain to be added to the $60 in interest earned. This the accountant would not do, because the gain is not realized and the market value of the bond could fluctuate in either direction before it is finally sold. Other theoreticians would not rely on the current market price of the bond but, taking the going interest rate into account, would value the bond at the present value of future interest receipts ($60 a year) plus the present value of the bond principal at maturity discounted at the appropriate rate and would use such value in the determination of net income for the period. There again, accountants have, so far, shied away from such approaches mostly because the variables which make up the bond value can change very frequently before final realization through sale or redemption of the bond. They consider such realization as the necessary objective evidence needed to warrant recording of the gain.

Price level changes complicate matters even further and their effect as well as significant proposed accounting modifications are considered in Chapter 14.

If such a simple income-producing asset as a bond, which involves no complexities on the expense side, can give rise to so many possible interpretations of what the amount of the net income it produced is, it is obvious that the determination of the amount of net income of a full-fledged business enterprise is far more complex. It is in this light that one can, at least, understand, even if not fully agree with, the principles of income determination which accountants have established over the years.

A variety of concepts of income

Going from our simple specific example to generalizations, we see that the economist's concept of income is the amount that could be consumed or distributed by an entity during a period and still leave it as "well-off" at the end of the period as it was at the beginning.

It is in the area of measuring the degree of "well-offness" of an enterprise that the gap between the economist's view and that of the accountant is widest. The economist maintains that capital value can be measured by the present value of future net receipts. But such receipts are based on highly subjective and constantly shifting estimates of future probabilities applying to both the *size* of the net receipts and the discount factors to be applied to them. The degree of uncertainty present here dwarfs that involved in estimating, for example, the future useful life of plant and equipment or the probability of debt collection, which are estimates of a kind which accountants now make. Thus, while the economist, cognizant of the uncertainty pervading all of business life, is impatient with the accountant's great concern for objectivity, verifiability, and conservatism, the latter believes that the very utility of his professional service to the community is dependent upon his upholding these qualities and characteristics.

Because of the divergencies in viewpoint such as those discussed above, the differences in the concepts of income of economists and accountants have not been appreciably narrowed. This is, in large measure, also due to difficulties which a practicing profession found in implementing in practice the theoretical concepts of economic thought.

One way in which income can be measured is by comparing the capital balances at the beginning and end of a period. Since capital is the excess of assets over liabilities, the problem of income determination is thus inseparable from the problem of asset and liability measurement. While, as we have seen, the economist focuses on a comparison of capital balances at successive points in time, in modern accounting the income determination process centers around the matching of current costs and revenues within a specific span of time. To the analyst who is interested in using the income statement as a means of predicting future streams of income and expense, this is a much more useful approach, because he is very much interested in all the elements which make up the final net income figure.

The process of income determination thus involves two basic steps: (1) identification of the revenues properly attributable to the period reported upon and (2) the matching of the corresponding costs with the revenues of this period either through direct association with the cost of the products sold therein or by assignment as expenses properly applicable as period costs.

THE ACCRUAL OF REVENUE

For every profit-seeking enterprise the first step in the process of profit recognition is the accrual of revenue. Thus, the very important question arises when, that is, at what point in the entire sequence of revenue-earning activities in which an enterprise is engaged, is it proper to recognize revenue as earned? The improper accrual of revenue can have one of two undesirable effects:

1. Revenue may be recorded prematurely or belatedly, that is, it may be assigned to the wrong fiscal period.
2. Revenue may be recorded before there is a reasonable certainty that it will actually be realized. This in turn can lead to reporting of gain derived from such revenue in one period and the cancellation or reversal of such profit, with a resultant loss, in a subsequent period. The effect of this is to overstate net income in one period and to understate it in a subsequent period.

Conditions for revenue realization

These two effects are, of course, highly undesirable and misleading, and in order to minimize such possibilities accountants have adopted strict and conservative rules regarding the recognition or realization of revenues. The following criteria exemplify the rules which have been established to prevent the premature anticipation of revenues. Thus, realization is deemed to take place only after the following conditions have been met:

1. The earning activities undertaken to create revenue have been substantially completed, for example, no significant effort is necessary to complete the transaction.
2. In case of sale, the risk of ownership has been effectively passed on to the buyer.
3. The revenue, as well as the associated expenses, can be measured or estimated with substantial accuracy.
4. The revenue recognized should normally result in an increase in cash, receivables, or marketable securities, and under certain conditions in an increase in inventories or other assets.
5. The business transactions giving rise to the income should be at arm's length with independent parties (i.e., not with controlled parties).
6. The transactions should not be subject to revocation, for example, carrying the right of return of merchandise sold.

While the above criteria may appear to be pretty straightforward, they are, in fact, subject to a number of exceptions and have, in practice, been interpreted in a variety of ways. The best way to understand these variations is to examine the application of these concepts in a variety of circumstances.

Uncertainty as to collection of receivables

In normal circumstances, doubts about the collectibility of receivables resulting from a sale should be reflected in a provision for doubtful accounts. *APB Opinion No. 10* affirms this when it states that "profit is deemed to be realized when a sale in the ordinary course of business is effected, unless the circumstances are such that the collection of the sales price is not reasonably assured." At what point the collection of a receivable is no longer reasonably assured is, of course, a matter of judgment based on all the surrounding circumstances. Moreover, such judgment may be conservative or it may be based on liberal or optimistic assumptions.

Installment sales. Installment sales normally result in a receivable which is collectible over a period of many months or even many years. Time is an important dimension in the assessment of risk, for the more distant the time of the collection of the proceeds of the sale, the more uncertain the final collection of the receivable. Conceivably, then, the length of time of collection is an important factor in assessing the probability of ultimate collection. Except in situations where the doubt about the collection of installment receivables is such as to make a reasonable estimate impossible, profit on installment sales is properly recognized at the time of sales.

Real estate accounting. The sale of real estate is often characterized by payment terms stretching over long time periods. A long-delayed collection period increases uncertainty, and thus the recognition of profit on such sales is dependent on an ability to assess the probability of collection of the full sales price. For this reason, real estate companies have frequently taken up the profit on sale of real estate on an installment basis, that is, on a basis which takes up profit only in proportion to the actual cash collection of the sales price.

The SEC has expressed reservations about certain types of attending circumstances by issuing *Accounting Series Release No. 95* which stated that—

. . . circumstances such as the following tend to raise a question as to the propriety of current recognition of profit:

1. Evidence of financial weakness of the purchaser.
2. Substantial uncertainty as to amount of costs and expenses to be incurred.
3. Substantial uncertainty as to amount of proceeds to be realized because of form of consideration or method of settlement; e.g., nonrecourse notes, non-interest-bearing notes, purchaser's stock, and notes with optional settlement provisions, all of indeterminable value.
4. Retention of effective control of the property by the seller.
5. Limitations and restrictions on the purchaser's profits and on the development or disposition of the property.

6. Simultaneous sale and repurchase by the same or affiliated interests.
7. Concurrent loans to purchasers.
8. Small or no down payment.
9. Simultaneous sale and leaseback of property.

Any such circumstance, taken alone, might not preclude the recognition of profit in appropriate amount. However, the degree of uncertainty may be accentuated by the presence of a combination of the foregoing factors.

While this release is concerned with sales of real estate in particular, these principles may be applied, of course, to other sales as well, and that adds to their overall significance.

As to liability for future performance, General Development had this to say: "The AICPA Industry Accounting Guide (1973) on Recognition of Profit Sales of Real Estate concluded that recognizing the full profit at time of sale is inappropriate unless the buyer has paid a down payment equal to a major part of the difference between usual loan limits and the sales value of the property."

Significant problems have arisen in the accounting for revenues and profits of retail land sales companies. Often lots are sold with small down payments with the balance due over very long periods. These conditions resulted in abuses which the AICPA Industry Accounting Guide on Retail Land Sales was designed to correct. Accordingly, stringent criteria were set forth before any profit on sale could be recorded. Thus, before a "sale" can be recorded as such 10 percent of the sales price must be collected and if the profit is to be accounted for on other than an installment base, collection experience, as defined, must warrant it.

General Development had the following description of its accounting policy in the 1973 report:

Homesite sales—Installment method. The company sells land principally under installment contracts which require payments over an average period of ten years. Under the installment method, the company records homesite sales when aggregate payments (including interest) equivalent to 10 percent of the contract price have been received. Costs and direct selling expenses (including commissions) related to a homesite sale are recorded at the time the sale is recognized. Costs include the cost of unimproved land (including interest on purchase money mortgages), estimated real estate taxes, estimated closing costs and estimated cost of improvements, such as roads and drainage. Land cost for each project is allocated to homesites sold based on the total number of homesites which the project is expected to yield. All other costs, which are estimated in total, are allocated to homesites sold based upon the relationship of their sales price to the aggregate estimated sales price of all plotted homesites in the project.

The gross profit less direct selling expenses relating to recorded homesite sales is recognized in income on a pro rata basis as payments of principal under the installment contracts are received.

Guidelines for recognizing the liability for future performance by the seller were also included in both aforementioned guides. In the case of retail land sales profit at time of sale is to be based upon the stage of completion of the required future performance. Estimating the cost of future construction may be difficult due to escalating costs. If the seller's involvement with the property carries, in essence, the same kinds of risk as does ownership, the transaction should not be treated as a sale at all.

As to liability for future performance General Development had this to say:

Estimated homesite improvement cost. Sales of homesites are generally made in advance of the completion of land improvements and the cost of such improvements to be completed in the future is accrued as an estimated liability when the homesite sale is recorded. The estimated homesite improvement cost is reevaluated at least annually. The remaining deferred profit on sales previously recorded is adjusted for the retroactive effect of any changes in these estimates as of the date of such changes. Under the terms of the company's installment sales contracts the required improvements must be completed no later than the year of the customer's scheduled final installment payment.

Revenue recognition when right of return exists

A Statement of Position of the AICPA (1975) bearing the captioned title deals with the serious and important problem of right of return existing in many industries such as agricultural products, farm machinery, perishable foods, newspapers, books, records, and toys. A "sale" with right of return is not really a sale and the resulting receivable is not an asset (see also chapter 5).

The above mentioned statement maintains that a transaction should not be recognized as a sale unless all of the following are present:

Selling price is substantially fixed.

Buyer becomes indebted to the seller and payment is not contractually or implicitly excused until product is resold.

Buyer's obligation would not be changed by theft or physical destruction or damage of the property.

Buyer has economic substance apart from that provided by the seller.

Seller does not have significant obligations for future performance to bring about resale by the buyer.

Amount of future returns can be reasonably predicted.

The ability to estimate future returns is an important consideration. Items which would appear to impair the ability to reasonably predict returns include:

Susceptibility to significant external factors, such as technological obsolesence or swings in market demand.

Long return privilege periods.

Absence of appropriate historical return experience.

When sales are recorded, reported sales and cost of sales should exclude the portion for which returns are expected. Provision should also be made immediately for any costs or losses which may be expected in connection with returns.

Other problem areas

When receivables are sold with recourse, a professional Statement of Position held that the differential between the amount of the net receivable sold and the proceeds received should be treated as financing income and it should be amortized to income as the risks of the seller diminish.

The field of franchising provides another example of a problem area. The buyer of a franchise undertakes, among many other obligations, to pay a franchise fee. However, only a minor portion is usually paid in cash to the franchise issuer, the balance being evidenced by a note payable over a period of years. The problem involved in recognizing the entire franchise fee at the time the agreement is signed revolves around the value of the note received for a substantial portion of the fee and the issue of the franchisor's performance obligation.

An Industry Acccounting Guide on this subject insists that in the case of sales of franchises all profit be deferred as long as the franchisor bears an obligation for significant future performance, a test even more stern than in the case of future performance requirements under land sale contracts.

Timing of revenue recognition

A major problem area in revenue recognition is the matter of *timing*. It is a basic principle of accounting that gains accrue only at the time of sale and that gains may not be anticipated by reflecting assets at their current sales prices. There are some exceptions to the rule such as in the case of gold and silver production, where a government controlled fixed price market exists, or as in the case of some agricultural, mineral, or other fungible products which enjoy immediate marketability at quoted market prices. After completion, such products may be recorded at market price less costs of disposal. Another area of seeming exception is contract accounting where, in effect, the sale normally precedes production or construction and where profit may, under certain conditions, be taken up in proportion to activity.

Contract accounting

The basis of recording income on short-term construction or production contracts poses no special problems. Profit is ordinarily recognized when the end product is completed and has been accepted by the owner.

Long-term construction contracts, be they for buildings, battleships, or complex machinery, present a more difficult accounting problem. Here the construction cycle may extend over a number of accounting periods while substantial costs accumulate, financed in part by progress billings. Two generally accepted methods of accounting are in use:

1. The *percentage-of-completion* method is preferred when estimates of costs to complete and estimates of progress towards completion of the constract can be made with reasonable dependability. A common basis of profit estimation is to record that part of the estimated total profit which corresponds to the ratio that costs incurred to date bear to expected total costs.[1] Other methods of estimation of completion can be based on units completed on qualified engineering estimates, or on simple lapse of time.
2. The *completed-contract* method of accounting is preferable where the conditions inherent in the contracts present risks and uncertainties which result in an inability to make reasonable estimates of costs and completion time. Problems under this method concern the point at which completion of the contract is deemed to have occurred as well as the kind of expenses to be deferred. Thus, some companies defer all costs to the completion date, including general and administrative overhead, while others consider such costs as period costs to be expensed as they are incurred.

Under either of the two contract accounting methods, losses, present or anticipated, must be fully provided for in the period in which the loss first becomes apparent.

Finance company accounting

Generally the accrual of interest is a function of time. The income on a bond or a loan to others depends on principal outstanding, time elapsed, and rate.

---

[1] Under this method the current year contract revenue equals =

$$\left[\frac{\text{Total Costs Incurred to Date}}{\text{Estimated Total Costs}} \times \frac{\text{Contract}}{\text{Price}} \right] \text{less} \left[\begin{array}{c} \text{Contract Revenue Recognized} \\ \text{in Prior Years} \end{array} \right]$$

Finance companies, such as in the consumer or sales finance fields, make loans under which a finance charge is added on to the face amount of the rate, that is, discount and add-on loans.

A number of alternative methods of taking up this discount exist. Thus, if the face of the note is $2,400 and the cash advanced is $2,160, the $240 unearned finance charge can be taken up over, say, 12 months, in a number of ways:

1. Under the *straight-line method,* one twelfth or $20 would be taken up each month as an installment is collected.

2. Under the *sum-of-the-months'-digits* method, larger amounts of income are recognized in the early part of the loan contract than in its latter period. In the case of a 12-month loan, the sum of the digits is 78. In the first month of the contract, 12/78th of the finance charge ($36.92) is taken into income; and in the last month, 1/78th ($3.14) is taken up. Under this method the interest earned bears a closer relationship to funds out at risk than it does under the straight-line method. That is also true of other methods which take up income in proportion to the decreasing balance of the loan outstanding.

3. A variation of either of the above methods involves taking into income, immediately on granting of the loan, an amount, also called "acquisition factor," which is designed to offset the initial loan acquisition expenses incurred by the company. The balance of the unearned finance charge is then taken into income by means of one of alternative methods.

When should the recording of interest income be discontinued

An AICPA Statement of Position (1975) on "Accounting Practices of Real Estate Investment Trusts" states that the recognition of interest revenue should be discontinued when it is not reasonable to expect that it will be received. The following conditions should be regarded as establishing such a presumption:

1. Payments of principal or interest are past due.
2. The borrower is in default under the terms of the loan agreement.
3. Foreclosure proceedings have been or are expected to be initiated.
4. The credit-worthiness of the borrower is in doubt because of pending or actual bankruptcy proceedings, the filing of liens against his assets, etc.
5. Cost overruns and/or delays in construction cast doubt on the economic viability of the project.
6. The loan has been renegotiated.

Accounting for lease income

Another special branch of revenue accounting is found in the case of companies leasing property to others. Their methods of revenue recognition are discussed in Chapter 7.

"Sales" to leasing subsidiaries

Before revenue under a sale can be considered as realized there must be a genuine transfer of risk from seller to buyer. An interesting example of the importance of this principle is provided by the furor caused by the attempt by Memorex Corporation to treat as an immediate sale the transfer of equipment to the company's unconsolidated leasing subsidiary.

The basic flaw in the proposed accounting was (1) that the subsidiary had not been capitalized by the infusion of third-party capital and could, as a consequence, not pay Memorex for the equipment; and (2) that Memorex had agreed to protect the subsidiary against losses. In short, these conditions clearly demonstrated that there was no transfer of the risk of ownership from Memorex to third parties, and consequently there was no genuine sale. Thus, the company had to agree to treat the transfer of the leased equipment as a lease rather than as an outright sale.

Additional examples of income recognition problems

Additional examples of problems regarding the timing of revenue recognition can be found in a number of industries.

Thus, Time, Inc. reports as follows on the accounting for unearned subscription income:

Unearned portion of paid subscription. Sales of magazine subscriptions are credited to Unearned Portion of Paid Subscriptions at the gross subscription price at the time of sale. Accounts receivable resulting from charge sales have been deducted from Unearned Portion of Paid Subscriptions. As magazines are delivered to subscribers, proportionate shares of the gross subscription price are credited to revenues. All costs in connection with the procurement of subscriptions are expensed within the year incurred.

In the liquor industry, Schenley Industries, Inc., reported on a timing aspect of income recognition as follows:

The company sells certain whiskey in barrels in bond under agreements which provide for future bottling. In prior years, profits on such transactions were reflected as of the date of sale. The present company policy, effective as of September 1, 19X9, is to treat such profits as deferred income until the whiskey is bottled and shipped.

Income of subsidiaries and affiliates

When a company owns a part or the whole of another entity, the interest of the company in the subsidiary's income may be accounted for in a number of ways. (see also Chapter 9.)

1. Consolidated financial statements may be prepared, thus including the subsidiary's income in the consolidated income statement while excluding any minority interest in that income. It is generally recognized that they do in most cases represent the best and more meaningful presentation of the financial position and the results of operations.

2. If a subsidiary is not consolidated, two methods of reporting the parent company's investment in it are possible:

a. *The cost method* under which only dividends received are recorded as income by the parent. Because the latter has the power to control the amount and timing of dividend declarations by the subsidiary, the dividends may not reflect the actual earnings performance of the subsidiary and thus may lead to income distortion or manipulation.

Because of the above-mentioned possible distortions, *APB Opinion No. 18* now requires that if consolidation is not appropriate, for whatever reason, the investments in subsidiaries be carried "at equity."

b. *The equity method* takes up the parent company's proportionate part of a subsidiary's profits and losses, thus reflecting best the parent company's share of the subidiary's results. The equity method is, thus, appropriate in all cases except those where there are serious limitations or restrictions on remittance of dividends, or where control is likely to be temporary or where it is not adequate.

When the parent company and its subsidiary are consolidated or when the parent picks up the equity with earnings of the subsidiary, intercompany sales and profits must be eliminated.

Jointly owned companies. Frequently two corporations join in forming a new corporation which, in effect, represents a joint venture in which each owns a 50 percent interest and has a voice in management. *APB Opinion No. 18* concluded that the equity method reflects best the underlying nature of investments in such ventures and calls for accounting for the investment at equity, thus recording a proportionate share of the results as they are earned. This method may be used even when the ownership is less than 50 percent provided the corporate joint venture is operated by a small group of businesses for their mutual benefit and encompasses a pooling of resources and a sharing of risks and rewards as well as participation in the overall management of the investee.

Implications for analysis

The income statement, presenting as it does, the results achieved by an enterprise and the return achieved on invested capital is of great importance to the analyst in his evaluation of the worth of the enterprise. For exactly this reason and for such reasons as pride, bonuses based on income, and the value of stock options, management is greatly interested in the results it reports. Consequently, the analyst can expect managements to choose those accounting principles and procedures which come closest to achieving their purposes.

The objectives of income reporting which management is desirous of achieving do not always result in the fairest or most proper measurement of results, and consequently the analyst must be aware of management's propensities as well as the choices available to it.

Since the recording of revenue is the first step in the process of income recognition and on which the recognition of any and all profit depends, the analyst should be particularly inquisitive about the accounting methods chosen so as to ascertain whether they reflect economic reality. Thus, for example, if a manufacturer records profits on sale to the dealer, the analyst must inquire about dealer inventories because the real earning activity consists in selling to the ultimate consumer. Similarly, when a membership fee to a golf club is recorded at the time a contract is signed, the analyst must determine whether the crucial earning activity consists of selling memberships or in delivering the services of the golf club.

Problem of collectibility.   One element which casts doubt on the recording of revenue is *uncertainty about the collectibility* of the resulting receivable. We have examined the special problems relating to installment sales, real estate sales, and franchise sales. Problems of collection exist, however, in the case of all sales, and the analyst must be alert to them. Sales with right of return can often turn out not to be sales at all (see chapter 5) and the analyst should be alert to these.

Let us conclude the consideration of the collection problem by an example from the bowling equipment manufacturing industry. The early 1960s witnessed a bowling boom which was attended by the building of a large number of bowling alleys which competed for a limited amount of business in restricted territories. The two major manufacturers of bowling equipment sold it to inexperienced and poorly financed operators against notes and receivables, mostly secured by the equipment itself. The full profit on this equipment was immediately taken up while the provision for bad debts concurrently established underestimated by a wide mark the special risks involved. Brunswick Corporation wrote off very substantial amounts of accounts receivable in 1963, while American Machine & Foundry made similarly substantial write-offs of receivables only five years later. Long before the write-offs were announced, the alert analyst could have taken his cue from the deteriorating business conditions in the bowling industry. There was, however, little in the financial statements of the bowling manufacturers to forewarn him of the losses yet to come.

Timing of revenue.　The emphasis on transactions rather than performance has resulted often in the anticipation of earnings ahead of completion of the earnings process. The analyst must be alert to the problems related to the *timing of revenue recognition.* We have examined the accounting concept of realization and the reasons for the accountant's great preoccupation with objective and verifiable evidence in this area. While the justification for this position is the subject of much debate both within and outside of the accounting profession, it behooves the analyst to understand the implications of present accounting in this area on his work.

The present rules of realization generally do not allow for recognition of profit in advance of sale. Thus, increases in market value of property such as land, equipment, or securities, the accretion of values in growing timber, or the increase in the value of inventories are not recognized in the accounts (see, however, chapter 14). As a consequence, income will not be recorded before sale, and the timing of sales is in turn a matter which lies importantly within the discretion of management. That, in turn, gives management a certain degree of discretion in the timing of profit recognition.

Contract accounting.　In the area of contract accounting, the analyst should recognize that the use of the completed-contract method is justified only in cases where reasonable estimates of costs and the degree of completion are not possible. In fact, from the statement user's point of view it is a poor method because results can be unpredictable and very erratic.

The percentage-of-completion method of accounting is, however, not free of problems and pitfalls. This can be seen from the following examples:

ILLUSTRATION 1.　Stirling Homex, a company which built modular houses, had strong incentives to show earnings growth because it was a "glamour company" and needed financing as well. Invoking percentage-of-completion-contract accounting principles it recognized the earnings process as completed when housing modules were "manufactured and assigned to specific contracts." In fact, this method was nothing but an earning-by-producing process and the spurious "sales" were reversed in 1972—a process which triggered loan defaults and ultimately led to bankruptcy.

ILLUSTRATION 2.　The case of Four Seasons Nursing Centers, which collapsed around the turn of this decade, presents a particularly vivid example of the dangers and the pitfalls of percentage-of-completion contract accounting *in actual application.* When, during their 1969 audit, the auditors, for whatever reasons, found physical engineering estimates of job completion to be unacceptable the company was forced to base the degree of contract completion on the percentage that the costs incurred to date bore to total estimated costs. The company, which was at the time on the "glamour treadmill" of Wall Street with strong incentives to produce increasing earnings, proceeded to supply the auditors with cost invoices which later proved fictitious or inapplicable to the situation at hand. These formed the basis for a higher percentage of completion with the resultant increased profit pickup. That was the road to the company's ultimate collapse.

In addition to the basic choice of method, the matter of which costs are to be considered contract costs and which period costs remains, to a significant degree, an area of management discretion.

Other problem areas of revenue recognition.   In finance company accounting, the analyst must be aware of the variety of methods, as outlined earlier in this chapter, available in the recognition of income as well as the option of taking into income at the inception of loan agreements of amounts designed to offset loans acquisition costs.

Other alternative methods of taking up revenue, as in the case of lessors, must be fully understood by the analyst before he attempts an evaluation of a company's earnings or a comparison among companies in the same industry.

Concept of materiality in income determination.   The analyst must be aware of the fact that the concept of materiality remains undefined in accounting and is consequently subject to abuse and uncertainty. It is all too often employed by auditors in defense of the omission of disclosure when their clients are adamant in their resistance to certain disclosures. The analyst must also realize that the accountant's concept of materiality is presently a very narrow one indeed. It does not attempt to take into account the future implications of an emerging situation. All too often, what looks like a small problem area may be the beginning of a serious future problem. Recent examples of this were provided by Celanese Corporation; which lost heavily from what was initially a relatively small foreign venture, and American Express Company, which had to make good the losses of its relatively insignificant warehousing subsidiary when large-scale defalcations in the famous "salad oil swindle" were discovered. The FASB has the entire subject under study.

COST AND EXPENSE ACCRUAL

Costs and expenses are resources (assets) and service potentials consumed, spent, or lost in the pursuit or production of revenues. The major problems of accounting for costs concern the measurement (size) of costs and the timing of their allocation to production time periods.

A basic objective of income accounting is to match costs to the revenues recognized during a period. This is far from easy to do. There are many kinds of costs, and they behave in a variety of ways. Some costs can be specifically identified with a given item of revenue. At the other end of the spectrum are costs which bear no identifiable relationship to specific elements of revenue at all and can be identified only with the time period during which they are incurred. This variation in behavior of costs has given rise to certain useful classifications which are helpful in understanding the matching and allocation problems.

Variable costs are those which vary in direct proportion to activity, whether the latter is measured by means of sales, production, or other gauges of activity. Thus, for example, in the manufacture of electric cable, the consumption of copper wire may be said to vary in direct proportion to a given unit of wire length. The higher the cable sales figure the higher the copper wire cost. In practice many costs, while varying somewhat in proportion to activity, do not vary in exact proportion to it and are usually referred to as semivariable costs.

Fixed costs are those which remain relatively constant over a considerable range of activity. Rent, property taxes, and insurance are examples of fixed costs. No category of cost can remain fixed indefinitely. For example, after reaching a certain level of activity an enterprise will have to rent additional space thus bringing the rent expense to a new and higher level.

Costs can be classified in many additional ways depending on the purpose. Focusing on the problem of matching costs with revenues, we have *product costs* which attach to a specified good or service from which revenue is derived. Costs which cannot be identified with a product or service are called *period costs* because they can be identified only with the period in which they occur. We have already touched on this distinction of costs in our examination of inventory and related cost-of-goods-sold accounting in Chapter 5. The allocation of costs to products sold and particularly manufactured products gives rise to a distinction among three major classes of cost:

1. *Direct product costs* represent charges which can be identified specifically with a product. Thus, for example, in a retailing business it is the cost of the item sold as well as the direct freight and other acquisition cost incurred in obtaining it. In a manufacturing enterprise it represents the specific or direct cost of material and labor entering the production of the item. Direct product costs generally vary in amount in direct proportion to revenues, a characteristic which results in their being classified as variable costs. Direct product costs are among the easiest costs to match with specific revenue flows.

2. The cost of materials acquired for resale or manufacture should logically include in addition to invoice costs such additional costs as receiving, inspecting, purchasing, and storing. In reality most enterprises find it impractical to allocate such costs or costs such as indirect labor directly to specific products. Consequently such *indirect costs* are allocated to relate products on some reasonable bases. Most fixed costs, such as depreciation or supervision, are treated as indirect overhead costs and are allocated to products or services on bases which attempt to reflect consumption or benefits derived.

3. *Joint product costs* are costs which cannot be identified with any of a number of products which they jointly benefit as for example is the case in the meat-processing industry. Such costs are usually allocated on some reasonable basis which may include that based on the selling prices of end products.

Having outlined some basic aspects of cost behavior and the methods of cost allocation which have been devised in response to it, we shall now proceed to examine the accounting problems which are encountered in the measurement and allocation of major categories of costs and expenses. Generally, a cost is a measure of service potential or utility which may be utilized in one accounting period or another. Those costs which are to be matched with the revenue of future periods may be viewed as deferred costs and are shown as assets on the balance sheet. Major examples of such assets are inventories; property, plant, and equipment; intangibles; and deferred charges. The accounting problems of inventories are examined in Chapter 5. Property, plant, and equipment gives rise to allocations of costs in the form of depreciation and depletion, and they will be considered in this chapter. The allocation and amortization of intangibles and deferred charges have been examined in the chapter on asset measurement, and the income measurement aspects of these costs will be further considered in this chapter.

Generally, expenses are costs which are immediately chargeable to income. Most period costs become current expenses; and some categories of expense, such as selling and administrative, are not usually deferred to the future. The measurement of costs and expenses is complicated whenever a significant lapse of time occurs between the time of payment for or incurrence of the cost and the time of its utilization in the earning of revenues. The longer such lapse of time the more complicated and speculative such allocations and measurements become.

Let us now consider some important categories of costs and the principles governing their allocation to revenue.

Depreciation and depletion

The cost of assets which are in productive use, or otherwise income-producing, must be allocated or assigned to the time periods which comprise their useful life. It is a basic principle of income determination that income which benefits from the use of long-lived assets must bear a proportionate share of their cost. Thus, the cost of the long-lived assets should, at the end of their useful lives, have been charged to operations.

Depreciation is the process whereby the cost of property, plant, and equipment is allocated over its useful life. The purpose of depreciation is to recover from operations, by means of this allocation, the original cost of the asset. Consequently, if operations are not profitable, the depreciation becomes an unrecovered cost, that is, a loss. This is as true of depreciation as it is of any other cost which cannot be recovered because of inadequate revenues. The depreciation process in itself is not designed to provide funds for the replacement of an asset. That objective can only be achieved by means of a financial policy which accumulates funds for a specific purpose to be available at a given time.

The above principles of depreciation accounting are now so firmly established that there are no significant differences of opinion about them. Nevertheless, depreciation remains an expense item which is the subject of confusion and controversy among users of financial statements. The controversy and confusion stems from the methods and the assumptions on the basis of which the cost of assets is allocated to operations over their useful life.

Factors influencing the rate of depreciation

1. Useful life

Almost all assets are subject to physical deterioration. A major exception is land which is consequently not subject to depreciation. While the "indestructible powers of the earth" have an unlimited life-span, this quality does not insure a similar resistance to loss of economic value. Such loss is, however, not provided for by means of depreciation but is instead recognized as and when it occurs. The exhaustion of natural resources lodged in or above the earth is recognized by means of depletion accounting which will be discussed later.

Useful lives of assets can vary greatly. The *Depreciation Guidelines and Rules,* published by the Internal Revenue Service, list the useful life of warehouses as 60 years, while assets used in heavy construction are assumed to have a useful life of 5 years. The assumption as to the useful lives of assets should be based on economic and engineering studies, on experience, and on any other available information about an asset's physical and economic properties.

Physical deterioration is one important factor which limits the useful life of an asset. The frequency and quality of maintenance has a bearing on it. Maintenance can extend the useful life but cannot, of course, prolong it indefinitely.

Another limiting factor is obsolescence. Obsolescence is the impairment of the useful life of an asset due to progress or changes in technology, comsumption patterns, and similar economic forces. Ordinary obsolescence occurs when technological improvements make an asset inefficient or uneconomical before its physical life is fully exhausted. Extraordinary obsolescence occurs when inventions of a revolutionary nature or radical shifts in demand take place. Electronic data processing equipment and propeller driven aircraft were subject to rapid obsolescence. The development of Xerography brought about extraordinary obsolescence in equipment using alternative methods of reproduction.

The integrity of the depreciation charge, and with it that of income determination, is dependent on a reasonably accurate estimate of useful life. That estimate should be determined solely by projections relating to physical life and economic usefulness and should not be influenced by management's desires with regard to the timing of income reporting.

2. Methods of allocation

Once the useful life of an asset has been determined, the amount of the periodic depreciation cost depends on the method used to allocate the asset's cost over its useful life. As will be seen hereunder, that cost can vary significantly depending on which method is chosen from the array of acceptable alternatives available:

Straight-line method.   This method of depreciation assigns the cost of the asset over its useful life on the basis of equal periodic charges. Thus, in Table 10–1 we can see how an asset which cost

TABLE 10–1
Straight-line method of depreciation

Year	Depreciation	Accumulated depreciation	Undepreciated asset balance
			110,000
1	10,000	10,000	100,000
2	10,000	20,000	90,000
.			
.			
.			
9	10,000	90,000	20,000
10	10,000	100,000	10,000

$110,000, has an estimated useful life of 10 years, and an estimated salvage value of $10,000 at the end of that period is depreciated. Every one of the 10 years is charged with an allocation of one tenth of the asset's cost less the estimated salvage value.

The basic rationale of the straight-line depreciation method is that the process of physical deterioration occurs uniformly over time. This is a more valid assumption with regard to fixed structures than with regard to, say, machinery where utilization or running time is a more important factor. Moreover, the other element of depreciation, that is, obsolescence, does not necessarily occur at a uniform rate over time. However, in the absence of concrete information on the probable rate of actual depreciation in the future, the straight-line method has the advantage of simplicity. This faculty, perhaps more than any other, accounts for the method's popularity and widespread adoption in practice.

There are other theoretical flaws in the straight-line depreciation method. If the service value of an asset is to be charged evenly over its useful life, then the loss of productivity and the increased maintenance costs should not be ignored. Under the straight-line method, however, the depreciation charges in the first years is the same as in the last years when the asset can be expected to be less efficient and to require higher cost of repairs and maintenance.

Another objection to the straight-line method, one which is of particular interest to the financial analyst, is that it results in a distortion in the rate of return on capital by introducing a built-in increase in this return over the years. Assuming that the asset depreciated in Table 10–1 is a heavy crane which yields a uniform return of $20,000 per year *before* depreciation, we can see that the return on investment will be as follows:

Year	Book value	Income before depreciation	Depreciation	Net income	Return on book value
1	$110,000	$20,000	$10,000	$10,000	9.1%
2	100,000	20,000	10,000	10,000	10.0
3	90,000	20,000	10,000	10,000	11.1
10	10,000	20,000	10,000	10,000	100.0

Increasing maintenance costs may render the constant "income before depreciation" assumption a bit too high but will not negate the overall effect of a constantly increasing return on investment. Obviously, this increasing return on the investment in an aging asset is not an entirely realistic portrayal of the economic realities of investments.

Under accelerated methods of depreciation, this kind of distortion in the return on book value of the asset can be even more marked.

Decreasing charge method.   The decreasing charge method of depreciation, also known as declining balance or accelerated depreciation, is a method whereby charges for depreciation decrease over the useful life of an asset.

The strongest support for this method arose from its approval by the Internal Revenue Code in 1954. Its value for tax purposes is obvious and relatively simple to understand. The earlier an asset is written off for tax purposes the larger amount of tax deferred to the future and the more funds are available for current operations.

The theoretical justification of the decreasing charge method of depreciation for financial accounting is not clear-cut. Arguments in its favor are that over the years an asset declines in operating efficiency and service value and that lower depreciation charges would offset the higher repair and maintenance costs which come with the older age of assets. Moreover, it is claimed that to compensate for the increasing uncertainty regarding the incidence of obsolescence in the future, the earlier years should bear a larger depreciation charge.

There are two principal methods of computing the decreasing charge to depreciation. One, the declining balance method applies a constant percentage to the declining asset balance. Given the salvage value *(S)*, the original cost *(C)*, and the number of periods over which the asset is to be depreciated *(N)*, the rate (percentage) to be applied to the asset can be found by the following formula:

$$\text{Rate } (\%) = 1 - \sqrt[N]{\frac{S}{C}}.$$

In practice an approximation of the proper rate of declining charge depreciation is to take it at twice the straight-line rate. Thus an asset with an assumed 10-year useful life would be depreciated at a declining balance rate of 20 percent. This is referred to as the double-declining balance method.

The other method, involving simpler computations, is known as the sum-of-the-years'-digits method. Thus, the cost of an asset to be depreciated over a 5-year period is written off by applying a fraction whose denominator is the sum-of-the-years'-digits $(1 + 2 + 3 + 4 + 5)$, that is, 15 and whose numerator is the remaining life from the beginning of the period, that is, $5/15$ in the first year and $1/15$ in the last year of assumed useful life.

Table 10–2 illustrates the depreciation of an asset having a cost of $110,000, a salvage value of $10,000, and an assumed useful life of 10 years under the double-declining balance method and the sum-of-the-years'-digits method. Since under the first method an asset can never be depreciated to a zero balance, salvage value is not deducted before applying the yearly rate (20 percent) to the original cost.

TABLE 10–2
Accelerated depreciation methods

| | Depreciation | | Cumulative amount | |
Year	Double declining	Sum-of-the-years'-digits	Double declining	Sum-of-the-years'-digits
1	$22,000	$18,182	$22,000	$ 18,182
2	17,600	16,364	39,600	34,546
3	14,080	14,545	53,680	49,091
4	11,264	12,727	64,944	61,818
5	9,011	10,909	73,955	72,727
6	7,209	9,091	81,164	81,818
7	5,767	7,273	86,931	89,091
8	4,614	5,455	91,545	94,546
9	3,691	3,636	95,236	98,182
10	2,953	1,818	98,189	100,000

The main theoretical justifications for the decreasing charge method are that charges for depreciation should decrease over time so as to compensate for (1) increasing repair and maintenance charges; (2) decreasing revenues and operating efficiency; and, in addition, to give recognition to the uncertainty of revenues in the later years of assumed useful life.

Other methods of depreciation. A method of depreciation found in some industries, such as steel and heavy machinery, relates depreciation charges to activity or intensity of use. Thus, if a machine is assumed to have a useful life of 10,000 running hours, then the depreciation charge will vary with number of hours of running time rather than the lapse of time. In order to retain its validity it is particularly important that the initial assumption about useful life in terms of utilization be periodically reviewed in order to check its validity under changing conditions.

Another method of depreciation once advocated by some utilities but not now in general use is the compound interest method of depreciation. This method views an investment in property as the present value of anticipated earnings. Thus, the depreciation charge is the amount which, invested yearly at a capital cost rate, will equal the cost of the asset, less any salvage value, at the end of its useful life. The addition of this interest factor causes this method to result in systematically increasing depreciation over the years. One advantage claimed for it is that it will result in a more uniform rate of return on investment than is the case with the other methods.

Depletion. Depletion is the process by means of which the cost of natural resources is allocated on the basis of the rate of extraction and production. The essential difference between depreciation and depletion is that the former represents an allocation of the cost of a productive asset over time, and the latter represents the exploitation of valuable stocks such as coal deposits, oil pools, or stands of timber. Thus, in the case of depletion the proportionate allocation of cost is entirely dependent on production, that is, no production, no depletion.

The computation of depletion is easy to understand. If the cost of an ore body containing an estimated 10,000,000 recoverable tons is $5,000,000, then the depletion rate per ton of ore mined is $.50. A yearly production of 100,000 tons would result in a depletion charge of $50,000 and a cost balance in the asset account at the end of the year of $4,950,000. The analyst must be aware of the fact that here, as in the case of depreciation, a simple concept may nevertheless result in a multitude of complications. One is the reliability of the estimate of recoverable resources, and it should be periodically adjusted in accordance with experience and new information. Another is the definition of "cost," particularly in case of a property still in process of development. Also, in the case of oil fields, for example, the depletion expense will vary with the definition of what constitutes an "oil field," since the depletion computation is not based on individual wells but rather on entire fields. The depletion expense can vary with the definition of the boundaries of the field.

The argument, sometimes advanced, that the discovery value of a natural resource deposit is so great in relation to its cost that no depletion need be allowed for, is not a valid one nor is the argument that depletion should be ignored because of the very tenuous nature of the estimate of reserves.

Implication for analysis

Most companies utilize long-lived productive assets in their operations, and whenever this is the case, depreciation tends to become a significant cost of operations. If we add to this the fact, as we have seen in the foregoing discussion, that many subjective assumptions enter into the determination of the depreciable basis, and of useful lives of assets and that alternative methods of depreciation coexist and that these factors can result in widely differing depreciation charges, all "in accordance with generally accepted accounting principles," it is obvious that the financial analyst needs a thorough understanding of all the factors entering into the depreciation computation before he can assess a reported earnings figure or before he attempts to compare it with that reported by another company.[2]

---

[2] For a discussion of possible variations in practice see "Accounting for Depreciable Assets" Accounting Research Monograph No. 1, AICPA, 1975.

The information on depreciation methods presently available in corporate reports varies and, generally speaking, more is available in documents filed with the SEC than is available in annual reports. Thus, typically the more detailed information will contain the method or methods of depreciation in use as well as the range of useful lives assumptions which are applied to various categories of assets. Two things are obvious to the intelligent reader of this information. One is that it is practically useless for purposes of deriving any conclusion from it. After all, what can one conclude from a statement which talks about this or that method being used without a quantitative specification of the extent of its use and the assets to which it applies. The second is that this information is supplied because it is required and not because of the supplying company's conviction about its usefulness.

Giving the ranges of useful lives or depreciation rates looks more informative than it is. It actually contributes very little to the basic objectives of the analyst, that is, the ability to predict future depreciation charges or the ability to compare the depreciation charges of a number of companies in the same industry.

The typical information supplied appears something like this:

The annual rates of depreciation used were as follows:

Land improvements	2–12½%
Buildings	2½–10
Machinery and equipment:	
Acquisitions prior to 1954	2–5
Acquisitions subsequent to 1953	5–33⅓
Furniture and fixtures	6–25

There is usually no identification of the relationship between the depreciation rates disclosed and the size of the asset pool to which such rates apply. Moreover, there is normally no identification between the rate used and the depreciation method applied; that is, which rates are used in conjunction with straight-line methods of depreciation and which with accelerated methods.

There are, of course, additional complications. While the straight-line method of depreciation enables the analyst to approximate future depreciation charges with some degree of accuracy, accelerated methods of depreciation make this task much more difficult unless the analyst is able to obtain from the company additional data not now disclosed in public reports.

Another problem area in depreciation accounting arises from differences in the methods used for book purposes and those used for tax purposes. Three possibilities exist here:

1. The use of straight-line depreciation methods for both book and tax purposes.
2. The use of straight-line depreciation for book purposes and accelerated methods for tax purposes. The favorable tax effect which results from the higher depreciation for tax purposes compared to that for book purposes is offset by the use of tax allocation which will be discussed in the next chapter. The advantage to the reporting company is the postponement of tax payments, that is, the cost-free use of funds.
3. The use of accelerated methods for both book and tax purposes. This method gives a higher depreciation charge than does method 1 in early years, and for an expanding company, even in subsequent years.

Unfortunately, the amount of disclosure about the impact of these differing methods is not always adequate. The best type of disclosure is the one which gives the amount of depreciation which would have been charged under a number of alternatives, such as, for example, what the difference in depreciation would have been under an accelerated method as opposed to a straight-line method. If a company gives the amount of deferred taxes which arose from accelerated depreciation for tax purposes, the analyst can get the approximate amount of extra depreciation due to acceleration by dividing the deferred tax amount by the current tax rate. See the information yielded by expanded requirements of the composition of deferred taxes, discussed in the next chapter.

Analysts who have despaired of making meaning out of depreciation information have tended to ignore it altogether by looking at income before depreciation in comparing company results. As will be more thoroughly discussed in the chapter on fund flows, depreciation is an expense which derives from funds spent in the past and thus does not require the outlay of current funds. For this reason income before depreciation has also been called cash flow, an oversimplication for what is meant to be described as funds inflow from operations. This is, at best, a limited and superficial concept since it involves only selected inflows without considering a company's commitment to such outflows as plant replacement, investments, or dividends. Nor is this inflow strictly of a cash nature because funds provided by the recovery of depreciation charges from revenue are not necessarily kept as cash but may be invested in receivables, inventories, or other assets.

Another and even more dangerous misconception which derives from the cash flow concept, and against which the analyst must guard, is that depreciation is a kind of bookkeeping expense, somehow different from such expenses as labor or material and that it can be ignored or at least accorded less importance than is accorded to other expenses.

One reason for this thinking is the cash outlay aspect already mentioned above. This represents, of course, entirely fallacious thinking. The purchase of a machine with a useful life of, say, five years is, in effect, a prepayment for five years of services. Let us assume that the machine is a bottle-filling machine and that its task can be performed normally by a worker working eight hours a day. If, as is not common but quite feasible, we contract with the worker for his services for a five-year period and pay him for it in advance, we would obviously have to spread this payment over the five years of his work. Thus at the end of the first year, one fifth of the payment would be an expense and the remaining four-fifth prepayment would represent an asset in the form of a claim for future services. It requires little elaboration to see the essential similarity between the labor contract and the machine. In year 2 of the labor contract no cash is spent, but can there be any doubt about the validity of the bottle-filling labor cost? The depreciation of the machine is a cost of an essentially identical nature.

Another reason for doubts about the genuine nature of depreciation expense is related to doubts about the loss of value of the asset subject to depreciation. On further examination we can break these doubts into two major categories:

1.   Doubts about the rate of loss in utility of productive equipment.
2.   Doubts about loss in market value of assets such as real estate.

1.   When we see one airline depreciating a jet plane over eight years and another airline spreading the depreciation of an identical aircraft over, say, 12 years, we realize that depreciation rates are matters of opinion. What is not a matter of opinion is that the effect on income of such differing assumptions can be significant and can distort comparisons. Thus, the effect must be assessed by the analyst as best as he can in the light of industry practice as well as the apparent reasonableness of the useful life assumption. While there may be some guidelines about useful lives of assets for tax purposes, there are practically none for financial accounting purposes. Auditors are not specialists in the longevity or useful life of equipment, and they will challenge management's estimates only when they are way out of line with industry practice or recorded experience. Where recorded experience is nonexistent, as in the case of a new industry such as computer leasing, the auditor's willingness to question management's estimate is further reduced. All this leaves a great deal of room for interpretation and income manipulation. While it does nothing to render depreciation as less of a genuine expense than any other, it does raise questions about the proper allocation of a productive asset's cost over time. Moreover, as between two estimates of useful life on similar equip-

ment in an industry, there is obviously more risk to the longer life assumption than to the lower.

The rate of write-off is another aspect of depreciation the analyst must be alert to. When the tax laws first permitted a variety of accelerations in the computation of depreciation, many companies adopted the method for both book and tax purposes. Later, however, a number of companies, such as those in the steel and paper industries, wanted to soften the impact of depreciation on reported income and switched back to the straight-line method while retaining accelerated methods for tax purposes. Such switching back and forth can usually not be said to be made in the interest of better reporting. Thus, though mostly unjustified and contributing to a discontinuity in comparability, it is nevertheless accepted by the accounting profession whose limited self-imposed responsibility it is to highlight the change and report its effect in the year in which it occurs. This practice along with the leeway allowed in setting useful lives has contributed in good measure to the skepticism regarding the measurement of depreciation expenses. *APB Opinion No. 20,* "Accounting Changes," which is more fully considered below, is designed to remedy this obvious reporting deficiency by insisting that changes be made only in the direction of "preferable" accounting principles. Since the concept of "preferable" in relation to accounting principles remains undefined, the analyst must retain a vigilant and critical attitude towards this area of accounting practice.[3]

2.   In the case of assets such as real estate, the problem of depreciation is somewhat different. For one thing, constant maintenance can prolong its useful life considerably more than can maintenance of, say, machinery or automobiles. Moreover, those who look at loss of market value as a true index of depreciation, claim that in times of rising price levels buildings gain rather than lose in value.

These are, however, not arguments against depreciation as such but rather questions of useful economic life and the proper time period over which an asset's cost should be written off. There is not more justification to a depreciation rate which is excessive than there is to one that is insufficient. Possibly, those companies which depreciate buildings at a rate exceeding their physical and economic decline do so in order to justify the rates they use for tax purposes. This procedure does not, however, result in proper income determination and must be understood as such by the analyst.

Rising real estate values are, of course, no reason to discontinue providing for depreciation. The adequacy of depreciation is dependent on many factors both physical and economic. The process of

---

[3] See, however, chapter 15 for a discussion of new SEC requirements that the auditor take a position on the preferability of a switch in accounting methods.

depreciation can be retarded but never abolished or reversed. The following note to the financial statements of Louis Lesser Enterprises, Inc., covering a period of generally rising prices, makes this clear:

As a result of the general decline in certain aspects of the real estate industry, accentuated by conditions in the money market and continuing vacancy factors in certain of the Company's rental properties, management is of the opinion that the full cost of certain properties and investments in and advances to companies not majority owned will not be recovered in the normal course of operations or through sale. Accordingly, the carrying values of such properties and investments and advances have been reduced to the amount of expected recovery.

The losses above provided for exceeded $4 million in a year when the company's total revenues were only about $6 million. In retrospect it is clear that management and its auditors underestimated the process of depreciation and value erosion of the company's income-producing properties. The values of such properties depend more on their income-generating capacity under a variety of economic conditions than on physical characteristics and maintenance levels.

As the above case illustrates, it is not prudent to rely on temporary economic conditions or market quotations to redress overoptimism which results in the willful underestimation of depreciation. After all, the depreciation concept encompasses a number of factors such as physical life, economic usefulness, and technological and economic factors which affect obsolescence. The difficulties of such real estate operators as Zeckendorf, Kratter and Glickman attest to the fact that real estate values move in a two-way street.

Changing price levels also introduce many complexities to the depreciation problem. Particularly in industries which are based on holdings of real estate, the argument is often advanced that rising prices (due in great measure to the decline in the purchasing power of money) obviate or reduce the need for depreciation charges. These arguments confuse the problems resulting from price level changes, which affect all accounts rather than only the fixed assets, with the function of depreciation which is designed to allocate the cost of an asset over its useful life. Price level changes in themselves do not, of course, prolong the useful life of an asset. The problem of price level changes must be dealt with fully and apart from that of depreciation. Price level problems will be examined in Chapter 14.

The analyst should realize that the variety of depreciation methods in use will cause not only problems of comparisons with other companies but internal measurement problems as well. This is particularly true with regard to the rate of return earned on the carrying value (book value) of an asset subject to different methods of depreciation. As the following example shows, only the "annuity" method of depreciation provides a level return on investment over the useful life of an asset. This method is, however, rarely found in practice.

ILLUSTRATION 3. Assume that a machine costing $300,000 and having a useful life of five years with no salvage value generates a yearly income before taxes of $100,000. According to the annuity method of depreciation, the cost of depreciable assets is the present value of an anticipated stream of future services, determined at some rate of discount. In our illustration the assumed rate of discount is 19.86 percent. The following are the rates of return realized annually under *(a)* straight-line, *(b)* sum-of-the-years'-digits, and *(c)* annuity depreciation methods (which is identical to the sinking fund depreciation method):

Year	Income before depreciation	Depreciation	Income after depreciation	Asset book value at beginning of year	Rate of return
		a. Straight-line depreciation			
1	$100,000	$ 60,000	$ 40,000	$300,000	13.3%
2	100,000	60,000	40,000	240,000	16.7
3	100,000	60,000	40,000	180,000	22.2
4	100,000	60,000	40,000	120,000	33.3
5	100,000	60,000	40,000	60,000	66.7
	$500,000	$300,000	$200,000		
		b. Accelerated depreciation (sum-of-years'-digits)			
1	$100,000	$100,000	$ . . .	$300,000	0.0
2	100,000	80,000	20,000	200,000	10.0
3	100,000	60,000	40,000	120,000	33.3
4	100,000	40,000	60,000	60,000	100.0
5	100,000	20,000	80,000	20,000	400.0
	$500,000	$300,000	$200,000		
		c. Annuity depreciation			
1	$100,000	$ 40,421	$ 59,579	$300,000	19.86
2	100,000	48,450	51,550	259,579	19.86
3	100,000	58,076	41,924	211,129	19.86
4	100,000	69,612	30,388	153,053	19.86
5	100,000	83,441	16,559	83,441	19.86
	$500,000	$300,000	$200,000		

From the foregoing discussion it is clear that the accounting for depreciation, which is a very real and significant cost of operation, contains many pitfalls for the analyst. Moreover, the information frequently supplied in published reports is mostly useless from the point of view of meaningful analysis. Thus, the analyst has to approach the evaluation of this cost with an understanding of the factors discussed above and with an attitude of questioning independence. In assessing the depreciation provision, he may have to evaluate its adequacy by such measures as the ratio of depreciation expense to total asset cost as well as its relationship to other factors which affect its size.

QUESTIONS

1. Why does the financial analyst attach great importance to the analysis of the income statement?

2. What conditions should usually be met before revenue is considered realized?

3. What conditions should usually be present before a sale with "right of return" can be recognized as a sale and the resulting receivable can be recognized as an asset?

4. The ability to estimate future returns (when right of return exists) is an important consideration. What are some of the factors that might impair such ability to predict returns?

5. Distinguish between the two major methods used to account for revenue under long-term contracts.

6. According to the AICPA statement of position (1975) on "Accounting Practices of Real Estate Investment Trusts", the recognition of interest income should be discontinued when it is not reasonable to expect that it will be received. What are some of the conditions that would be regarded as establishing such a presumption?

7. How is income in a jointly owned company accounted for?

8. To what aspects of revenue recognition must the financial analyst be particularly alert?

9. Can the analyst place reliance on the auditor's judgment of what consti- tutes a "material" item in the income statement?

10. Distinguish between (a) variable, (b) semivariable, and (c) fixed costs.

11. Depreciation accounting leaves a lot to be desired; and no real progress, from the analyst's point of view, is imminent. Comment on the following observation:

    "The analyst of course cannot accept the depreciation figure unques- tioningly. He must try to find out something about the age and efficiency of the plant. He can obtain some help by comparing depreciation, current and accrued, with gross plant, and by comparisons among similar com- panies. Obviously, he still cannot adjust earnings with the precision that the accountant needs to balance his books, but the security analyst doesn't need that much precision."

12. What means of adjusting for inconsistencies in depreciation methods are sometimes employed by analysts? Comment on their validity.

13. Which method of depreciation would result in a level return on asset book values? Why?

11

ANALYSIS OF THE INCOME STATEMENT—II

This chapter continues and concludes the discussion of the analysis of the income statement which was begun in Chapter 10.

PENSION COSTS AND OTHER SUPPLEMENTARY EMPLOYEE BENEFITS

Pension costs

Pensions are a major employee-benefit cost designed to contribute to security after retirement. Pension commitments by companies are formalized in a variety of ways by means of pension plans. As pensions grew in importance and in size as a significant cost of operations, so did the accounting for such costs become a matter of great significance.

APB Opinion No. 8, issued after years of loose accounting practice in this area, represents a significant improvement in the prescribed accounting for pension costs. Basically, the *Opinion* views pension costs as long term in nature because they encompass the entire work-span of a group or groups of employees. Thus, such costs must be provided for on an accrual basis based on the actuarial assumptions which govern the pension plan. Limitations of legal liability to pay pensions should not normally affect accruals which are based on an assumption of indefinite continuance of benefits. Nor should the method used to fund the pension obligation affect the accrual of proper cost. Funding of pension obligations is essentially a matter of financial management, and it may or may not coincide with proper accrual for accounting purposes, which is a decision as to the appropriate charge of pension costs against the operations of a given period. Chapter 7 contains a discussion of liabilities under pension plans.

APB Opinion No. 8 establishes both a floor and a ceiling for the annual accrual of pension costs. Under *either* the minimum or the maximum pension cost provision, the *normal accrual cost* must be provided for. This must be arrived at by use of an actuarial cost method which is rational, systematic, and consistently applied and which relates to years after adoption of the pension plan.

The minimum and maximum cost provision is as follows:[1]

Minimum pension cost provision:

1. The normal cost.
2. A provision of interest on unfunded prior service cost.
3. A supplementary provision called for in cases where the value of vested benefits at the beginning of the year are not reduced by at least 5 percent in relation to the comparable amounts at the end of the year. Such comparison should be made exclusive of any net increase of vested benefits occurring during the year. If a supplementary provision for vested benefits is required, the total pension provision may be the lesser of the amount computed above or an amount sufficient to make the aggregate annual pension provision equal to:

    a. The normal cost.
    b. Amortization of prior service cost on 40-year basis (including interest).
    c. Interest equivalents on the difference between the provisions for pension costs accrued and the amount of such costs actually funded.

Maximum pension cost provision:

1. The normal cost.
2. Ten percent of past service cost at inception of plan and of increases and decreases in prior service cost arising from plan amendments. Since the 10 percent includes an interest factor, it will require, depending on interest rate assumed, more than 10 years for full amortization.
3. Interest equivalents on the difference between provision for pension costs and the amount of such costs actually funded.

---

[1] In the light of new pension legislation (ERISA) the AICPA Accounting Standards Executive Committee concluded that the minimum expensing level should be revised to require amortization of unfunded past and prior service costs in conformity with the minimum funding requirements of the law and that the maximum expensing level should be revised to permit amortization of such cost over ten years. The FASB has the entire topic under reconsideration.

In the above context "past service cost" refers to the portion of the total pension cost that under the actuarial cost method in use is identified with periods prior to the adoption of the pension plan. "Vested benefits" refers to benefits accrued which are not contingent on the employee's continuing in the service of the employer.

APB Opinion No. 8 generally aims at avoiding wide year-to-year fluctuations in pension costs. Consequently it prescribed the averaging of actuarial gains and losses as well as of unrealized appreciation or depreciation of fund investments.

To the extent that actual experience subsequent to an actuarial valuation differs from the actuarial assumptions (e.g., those relating to employee turnover, mortality or income yield of investments), actuarial gains or losses will arise. Under the *Opinion* such losses or gains should be spread or averaged over a period from 10 to 20 years.

The *Opinion* calls for recognition of unrealized appreciation or depreciation of fund assets in the determination of pension cost on a rational and systematic basis that avoids giving undue weight to short-term market fluctuations. Thus, the *Opinion* recommends the averaging of such appreciation or depreciation or its recognition on the basis of expected long-term performance.

The following is designed to illustrate the actual workings of the minimum-maximum pension cost provision approach. For purposes of this illustration, we assume the following:

Normal pension cost for the year (i.e., the cost arrived by an acceptable actuarial method) .... $	400,000
Prior service cost:	
Unfunded at beginning of year	3,000,000
Funded in prior years	2,000,000
Amortization of actuarial gains	7,000
Amortization of unrealized appreciation	3,000
Unfunded pension accruals	100,000
Actuarial value of vested benefits:	
Beginning of year	10,000,000
End of year	10,600,000
Fund assets:	
Beginning of year	4,000,000
End of year	4,800,000
Assumed rate of interest	4%

Under the above assumptions the computation of minimum and maximum allowable provisions for current pension costs would be as shown on page 290.

APB Opinion No. 8 also specified a greater degree of disclosure then hitherto required. The following are considered by the board to be appropriate disclosures on pension plans:

1. A statement that such plans exist, identifying or describing the employee groups covered.

2.   A statement of the company's accounting and funding policies.
3.   The provision for pension cost for the period.
4.   The excess, if any, of the actuarially computed value of vested benefits over the total of the pension fund and any balance sheet pension accruals, less any pension prepayments or deferred charges.
5.   Nature and effect of significant matters affecting comparability for all periods presented, such as changes in accounting methods (actuarial cost method, amortization of past and prior service cost, treatment of actuarial gains and losses, etc.), changes in circumstances (actuarial assumptions, etc.), or adoption of amendment of a plan.

		Minimum		
		A	*B*	*Maximum*
1.	Normal cost	$400,000	$400,000	$400,000
2.	Interest on unfunded prior service cost	120,000		
3.	Provision for vested benefits (Note 1)	95,000		
4.	Amortization of prior service cost:			
	I on a 40-year basis, interest included (Note 2)		252,500	
	II at 10% per year			500,000
5.	Interest on excess of prior years' accounting provisions over amounts actually funded		4,000	4,000
6.	Amortization of actuarial gains	(7,000)	(7,000)	(7,000)
7.	Amortization of unrealized asset appreciation......................	(3,000)	(3,000)	(3,000)
	Total	$605,000	$646,500	$894,000

The pension expense for the year may not exceed the maximum amount and may not be less than the lesser of columns A or B under the minimum provision caption.

Note 1:   The provision for vested benefits is arrived at as follows:

		This year's valuation	*Preceding valuation*
1.	Actuarial value of vested benefits	$10,600,000	$10,000,000
2.	Amount of pension fund	4,800,000	4,000,000
3.	Unfunded amount (1 − 2)	$ 5,800,000	$ 6,000,000
4.	Net amount of balance sheet pension accruals	100,000	100,000
5.	Actuarial value of unfunded (unprovided for) vested benefits (3 − 4)...	$ 5,700,000	$ 5,900,000
6.	5% of item 5 for prior year	295,000	
7.	Year-to-year change in item 5	200,000	
8.	Excess of item 6 over item 7 which represents provision for vested benefits.......................................	$ 95,000	

Note 2:   Level annual charge which will amortize total prior service cost of $5,000,000 (with interest) on a 40-year basis; amortization will cease when the unfunded component of $3,000,000 has been amortized.

The following is considered by the board to be an example of appropriate disclosure regarding pension plans:

The company and its subsidiaries have several pension plans covering substantially all of their employees, including certain employees in foreign countries. The total pension expense for the year was $ . . . . , which includes, as to certain of the plans, amortization of prior service cost over periods ranging from 25 to 40 years. The company's policy is to fund pension cost accrued. The actuarially computed value of vested benefits for all plans as of December 31, 19 . . . , exceeded the total of the pension fund and balance-sheet accruals less pension prepayments and deferred charges by approximately $ . . . . A change during the year in the actuarial cost method used in computing pension cost had the effect of reducing net income for the year by approximately $ . . . .

Other supplementary employee benefits

Social pressures, competition, and the scarcity of executive talent have led to the proliferation of employee benefits which are supplementary to wages and salaries. Some fringe benefits, such as vacation pay, bonuses, current profit sharing, and paid health or life insurance are clearly identifiable with the period in which they are earned or granted and thus do not pose problems of accounting recognition and accrual.

Other supplementary compensation plans, because of the tentative or contingent nature of their benefits, have not been accorded full or timely accounting recognition, but accounting pronouncements have recently resulted in improvements in this area.

Deferred compensation contracts are usually awarded to executives with whom the company wants to develop lasting ties and who are interested in deferring income to their post retirement and lower taxbracket years. Generally, provisions in such contracts which specify an employee's undertaking not to compete or which specify his availability for consulting services are not significant enough to justify deferring the current recognition of such costs. Thus, *APB Opinion No. 12* requires that at least the present value of deferred compensation to be paid in the future "be accrued in a systematic and rational manner over the period of active employment from the time the contract is entered into, unless it is evident that future services expected to be received by the employer are commensurate with the payments or a portion of the payments to be made." Similar accruals are called for in cases of contracts which guarantee minimum payments to the employee or his beneficiaries in case of death.

Stock options are incentive compensation devices under which an executive receives the right to buy a number of shares at a certain price over a number of years and subject to conditions designed to identify him with the employer's interests.

The usual rationale advanced in defense of stock options is that business will be run better by managers who are important share owners. Options allow executives to build an estate and offer significant tax advantages.

In theory the accounting for stock options defines the compensation to be recognized as the excess of the fair value of the optioned shares, at the dates the options are granted, over the option price. In practice, since the spread, if any, between the market price and the option price at the date of grant is negligible, the compensation inherent in stock options was generally not recorded on the basis of lack of materiality.

APB Opinion No. 25, issued in 1972, "Accounting for Stock Issued to Employees," specifies that when stock options are granted, the excess of the market price of the stock over the option/price should be accounted for as compensation over the periods benefited. In this computation the discounting of market value to allow for restrictions placed on the use or disposition of the stock by the employee is not permitted.

Implications for analysis

By providing for full and systematic accrual of all pension costs, *APB Opinion No. 8* has narrowed the areas of differences in pension accounting and improved the underlying theory. The financial analyst is, however, not yet entitled to assume that the intent of the APB Opinions will be adhered to in all cases. There remains a great deal of room for maneuvering in this area.

The question of materiality is one aspect of the problem. Thus, the 1968 annual report of the Youngstown Sheet and Tube Company contains the following note on pensions:

The company has contributory and noncontributory retirement plans covering hourly and salaried employees. It is the policy to accrue and fund pension costs each year in an amount approximating current service costs and interest on unfunded past service costs, adjusted for estimated long-term appreciation of trust fund assets. In determining 1968 pension costs actuarial assumptions as to the interest rate and the rate of appreciation of trust assets were increased to reflect investment experience, thus reducing pension costs by $3,300,000. Trust funds at December 31, 1968 were sufficient to cover the estimated liability for pensions already granted as well as pensions for those employees eligible for retirement.

We know that *APB Opinion No. 8* requires the spreading of actuarial gains and losses such as the $3.3 million reduction in pension costs of Youngstown. The apparent reason the benefit was all taken into 1968 rather than spread over 10 to 20 years is the lack of materiality of the $3.3 million as against an income before taxes of $61 million. However, if such changes are made frequently and are all deemed "immaterial" in relation to the particular year in which they were made, the cumulative effect on earnings may, nevertheless, be considerable thus defeating the intent of the pension cost Opinion.

Changes in actuarial methods and assumptions can have a significant effect on earnings as the following note in Westvaco Corporations report indicates:

> *Employee retirement plans.* The cost of employee retirement benefits for the year 1974 was $12,641,000 (1973-$7,610,000). The company, in keeping with its policy of utilizing conservative actuarial methods and assumptions to insure that retirement benefits are properly provided for, has changed certain assumptions and methods. Primarily as a result of these changes, net income after applicable income taxes for 1974 was reduced $1,954,000 ($.18 per-share).

The accounting problem regarding stock options is serious. Basically there is a failure to reflect in operating costs compensation granted to employees. No serious student of accounting and finance can deny the real cost to a company of selling its shares at prices below what it could get on the open market. The justification of the lack of accounting for the cost of stock option is a sort of "coin clipping" operation whereby the small annual dilution of stockholder equity is overlooked without an assessment of its more significant cumulative effect.

The plain fact is that the compensation inherent in stock options is unrecorded under present generally accepted accounting principles. The improvements brought about by *APB Opinion No. 25* are more apparent than real. This *Opinion* continues the accounting profession's long-standing reluctance to face up to the fact that an option to buy a share of stock for a number of months or years at the current market price is a valuable privilege. The prices at which call options as well as longer term warrants sell in the marketplace is adequate testimony to this.

In 1972 the United States Pay Board faced the problem of valuing stock options and decided that their value is equivalent to 25 percent of the fair market value of the stock at the date of grant plus the excess of fair market value of the shares over the option price at the time of grant (Regulation 201.76). This rule is somewhat arbitrary in that it may fail to take into account restrictions to which a stock option is subject or the length of its duration. Nevertheless, it proves that stock options can be valued, and this valuation is a far more realistic approach than that adopted by the accounting profession in this matter. Financial analysts may well use the Pay Board's valuation rule as a rough guide whenever they want to estimate the unbooked compensation inherent in stock option plans.

One saving feature in the stock option accounting problem is a development brought about through "the back door" by *APB Opinion No. 15* on "Earnings per Share." Under this *Opinion,* stock options which have a dilutive effect on earnings per share must enter into the computation of that figure, thus showing in this statistic some of the effect which is missing in the reported "net income" figure. The computation and evaluation of earnings per share is discussed in Chapter 12.

RESEARCH, EXPLORATION, AND DEVELOPMENT OUTLAYS

Research, exploration, and development efforts are undertaken by business enterprises for a variety of reasons, all aiming at either short-term improvements or longer term profit and improved market position. Some research efforts are directed towards maintaining existing product markets while others aim at the development of new products and processes.

Types of research and development

One type of research is *basic* or *pure research,* that is, directed towards the discovery of new facts, natural laws, or phenomena without regard to the immediate commercial application to which the results may be put. Benefits from such research programs are very uncertain, but if successful, they may be among the most rewarding of all.

Unlike pure research, *applied research* is directed towards more specific goals such as product improvement or the perfection and improvement of processes or techniques of production.

Exploration is the search for natural resources of all kinds. Exploration is always an "applied" kind of activity in that it has a definite and known objective.

Development begins where research and exploration end. It is the activity devoted to bringing the fruits of research or the resources discovered by exploration to a commercially useful and marketable stage. Thus development may involve efforts to exploit a new product invention or it may involve the exploitation of an oil well, a mineral deposit, or a tract of timber.

Research and development may be one part of many activities of an ongoing enterprise or it may be the almost sole activity of an enterprise in its formative stages.

The accounting problem

The problem of accounting for research and development costs is difficult and defies easy solutions. There are a number of reasons for this, among which the most important are:

1. The great uncertainty of ultimate results which pervades most research efforts. Generally, the outcome of a research project is more uncertain than that of an immediately productive operation.
2. In most cases there is a significant lapse of time between the initiation of a research project and the determination of its ultimate success or failure. This, in effect, is another dimension of uncertainty.
3. Often the results of research are intangible in form, a fact which contributes to the difficulty of evaluation.

It is this all-pervading uncertainty of ultimate results which causes the difficulty in accounting for research and development costs rather than the absence of logical reasoning or a lack of clear objectives of accounting. Such objectives are clear and well known:

1. Costs should be matched with the revenues to which they are related.
2. Costs should not be deferred unless there is a reasonably warranted expectation that they will be recovered out of future revenues or will benefit future operations.

FASB *Statement 2*

After a great deal of discussion and deliberation, the FASB has arrived in its *Statement 2* at a rather simple solution to the complex problem of accounting for research and development costs: They should be charged to expense when incurred.

FASB *Statement 2* has expanded considerably the definition of what is to be included in research and development costs. It maintains that only a very small percentage of research and development projects are successful (recognizing the difficulty in defining what constitutes a successful project) and that even if the rate of success could be predicted with reasonable accuracy it still would be difficult to forecast the period of future benefit.

The board concluded, therefore, that subject to exceptions indi-

cated below, all research and development costs should be charged to
expense as incurred.

Definition of research and development activities

Research activities are aimed at discovery of new knowledge for the
development of a new product or process or in bringing about a
significant improvement to an existing product or process.

Development activities translate the research findings into a plan or
design for a new product or process or a significant improvement
to an existing product or process.

R&D specifically excludes routine or periodic alterations to ongoing
operations and market research and testing activities.

Accounting for research and development costs

The majority of expenditures incurred in research and development
activities as defined above constitutes the costs of that activity
and should be charged to expense when incurred.

Costs of materials, equipment, and facilities that have alternative
future uses (in research and development projects or otherwise)
should be capitalized as tangible assets.

Intangibles purchased from others for R&D use that have alternative future uses should also be capitalized.

Elements of costs that should be identified with R&D activities are:
  a. Costs of materials, equipment, and facilities that are acquired
      or constructed for a particular research and development
      project and purchased intangibles, that have no alternative
      future uses (in research and development projects or
      otherwise).
  b. Costs of materials consumed in research and development
      activities, the depreciation of equipment or facilities, and the
      amortization of intangible assets used in research and
      development activities that have alternative future uses.
  c. Salaries and other related costs of personnel engaged in R&D
      activities.
  d. Costs of services performed by others.
  e. A reasonable allocation of indirect costs. General and admin-
      istrative costs that are not clearly related to R&D activities
      should be excluded.

Disclosure requirements

For each income statement presented, the total R&D costs charged
to expense shall be disclosed.

Government regulated companies that defer R&D costs in accordance with the addendum to APB 2 must make certain additional disclosures.

While it is difficult to estimate the future benefits from research and development outlays, it is even more difficult and speculative to estimate the future benefits to be derived from costs of training programs, product promotions, and advertising. Consequently deferral of such costs is very difficult to justify.

The FASB's simplistic solution to the accounting for research and development outlays has been described as "really a way of avoiding responsibility" and as arriving at "too easy a solution to an extremely difficult problem."[2] Professors Bierman and Dukes, in questioning the basic reasoning which led the FASB to arrive at the expensing solution, maintain that it is "incorrect to conclude that, because it has been difficult to observe a significant correlation between expenditures and subsequent benefits, future benefits are not generated by research and development expenditures." The professors conclude that "From the point of view of accounting theory, the expenditures for R&D, which are made in the expectation of benefiting future periods, should not be written off against the revenues of the present period. Justification for such practice must be found elsewhere, if it is to be found."

The analyst should realize that while SFAS 2 assures that there will be no overstated research and development deferrals on the balance sheet it does so at the expense of any reasonable attempt to match the expenditure of the resources against the revenues which it helps produce. Thus, this new accounting is safe rather than more useful; it overlooks the history of productivity of many ongoing research efforts as opposed to the uncertainty involved in one-shot research projects.

Exploration and development in extractive industries

The search for new deposits of natural resources is the function of a very important industry segment encompassing the oil, natural gas, metals, coal, and nonmetallic minerals industries. While the unique accounting problems of these industries deserve separate consideration, it should be borne in mind that no new accounting principles are involved here but rather the application of such principles and concepts to special circumstances. Thus, while the search for and development of natural resources is characterized by exposure to high degrees of risk, so is, as we have seen, the search for new knowledge, new processes, and new products. Risk involves uncertainty; and

---

[2] Harold Bierman Jr. and Ronald E. Dukes, "Accounting for Research and Development Costs" *The Journal of Accountancy*, April 1975.

within a framework of periodic income determinations, uncertainty always presents very serious problems of income and expense determination.

In extractive industries the major problems lie on the cost and expense side. Essentially, the problem is one of whether exploration and development costs which may reasonably be expected to be recoverable out of the future lifting of the natural resources should be charged in the period incurred or should be capitalized and amortized over future recovery and production.

While many companies charge off all exploration costs currently, some charge off only a portion and capitalize another portion. A few companies capitalize almost all development costs and amortize them over future periods.

The following note in Sun Oil Company's financial statements illustrates the variety of principles in use:

. . . Sunray has followed the generally accepted accounting principle prevalent throughout the industry of capitalizing intangible development costs and charging income for the amortization thereof over a period of years. Sun's method, which is also in accordance with generally accepted accounting principles, has been to charge these costs to expense as incurred. . . .

The accounting profession has recognized that the divergent practices create a need for reforms in this area. As a first step, *Accounting Research Study No. 11,* "Financial Reporting in the Extractive Industries," recommends, among others, that:

Expenditures for prospecting costs, indirect acquisition costs and most carrying costs should be charged to expense when incurred as part of the current cost of exploration.

Direct acquisition costs of unproved properties should be capitalized and the estimated loss portion should be amortized to expense on a systematic and rational basis as part of the current cost of exploration.

Unsuccessful exploration and development expenditures should be charged to operations even though incurred on property units where commercially recoverable reserves exist.

The adoption, in practice, of these as well as the other guidelines of the study, including rational bases of deferred cost amortization, will go a long way towards improving accounting in this important segment of industry.

In mid-1973 the Committee on Extractive Industries of the APB rendered its final report with the purpose of providing the FASB with a summary of the committee's research in accounting for the oil and gas industry. The committee stated:

Throughout the committee's deliberations it became increasingly clear that there exists in practice two basic concepts or philosophies regarding accounting in the oil and gas industry; namely, full-cost accounting and successful efforts accounting. The basic concept of the full-cost method is that all costs, productive and non-productive, incurred in the search for oil and gas reserves should be capitalized and amortized to income as the total oil and gas reserves are produced and sold. The basic concept of the successful efforts method is that all costs which of themselves do not result directly in the discovery of oil and gas reserves have no future benefit in terms of future revenues and should be expensed as incurred. It was equally clear that the application of the two concepts in practice varies to such an extent that there are in fact numerous different methods of accounting.

In mid-1977 the FASB issued an exposure draft of a SFAS "Financial Accounting and Reporting by Oil and Gas Producing Companies" which proposed that use of a form of the "successful efforts" method of accounting be required.

Implications for analysis

The evaluation of research and development outlays presents a serious problem in the analysis of financial statements. Often the size of these outlays is such that they must be taken into account in any analysis of current income and of future prospects.

It is possible that the FASB's pragmatic solution which requires the current expensing of practically all research and development outlays will help accountants achieve a uniformity of approach in this area and at the same time avoid the difficult choices and judgments which a policy of capitalization and deferral imposes. It is, however, doubtful that such a policy of, in fact, nonaccounting for research and developments costs along with the very limited disclosure requirements it requires will really serve the needs and interests of serious analysts of financial statements.

Granting the difficulty of measuring and estimating the future benefits to be derived from research and development outlays, it is nonetheless reasonable to assume that managements enter into such projects with firm expectations of returns on these investments. Moreover, in many cases they have specific expectations about such potential returns that the realization or nonrealization of which can be monitored and estimated as a research project progresses. In the past a policy of deferral of research and development costs afforded managements and their independent accountants, who normally judge uncertainties and estimate results in most of their work, an opportunity to carry to the reader their estimate of the future potential promise of such outlays at a given point in time. Under the new rules all research and development is treated as if it has no future value, and the analyst will no longer have the benefit of the estimates of those in the best position to offer them.

FASB *Statement No. 2* requires only disclosure of total research and development outlays charged to expense in a given period. In order to form an opinion on the quality and the future potential value of research outlays, the analyst needs to know, of course, a great deal more than the totals of periodic research and development outlays. Information is needed on the types of research performed, the outlays by category, as well as the technical feasibility, commercial viability, and future potential of each project assessed and reevaluated anew at the time of each periodic report. He or she also needs information on a company's success-failure experience in its several areas of research activity to date. Of course, present disclosure requirements will not give the analyst such information and it appears that, except in cases of voluntary disclosures, only an investor or lender with the necessary clout will be able to obtain such information.

In general one can assume that the outright expensing of all research and development outlays will result in more conservative balance sheets and fewer painful surprises stemming from the wholesale write-offs of previously capitalized research and development outlays. However, the analyst must realize that along with a lack of knowledge about future potential he or she will—unless the analyst probes widely and deeply—also be unaware of the potential disasters which can befall an enterprise tempted or forced to sink ever greater amounts of funds into research and development projects whose promise was great but whose failure is nevertheless inevitable.

With regard to exploration and development costs in the extractive industries, the analyst faces at present the problem of a variety of acceptable methods of treating such costs. This in turn hampers the comparison of results among companies in the same industry. With issuance of a proposed standard on accounting by oil and gas producing companies the FASB is moving towards the establishment of more uniform rules for the treatment of such costs. Even the establishment of such uniform rules will not solve all of the analyst's problems in this area. The considerations entering into the measurement and allocations of these costs are so complex and varied (e.g., what constitutes a unit of production?) as to allow for a great deal of diversity of treatment. Moreover, in the quest for uniformity, accounting rules must inevitably be somewhat arbitrary. This may lead to the current expensing of costs holding benefits for future operations. The analyst must be aware of these possibilities and adjust for them on the basis of available information.

GOODWILL

Finally in a consideration of intangible costs, we should add here to the discussion of goodwill which was begun in Chapter 6.

Goodwill is usually the measure of value assigned to a rate of earnings above the ordinary. It is, in some respects, similar to the premium paid for a bond because its coupon rate exceeds the going interest rate. That goodwill has value at the time it is purchased cannot be disputed. Otherwise corporations would be spending billions for assets devoid of value. The real problem with the accounting for purchased goodwill is that of measuring its expiration. There is no need to write off against earnings an asset whose value does not expire. Land is a prominent example of this. However, the superior earning power of an enterprise is not indestructible or everlasting. Goodwill can, at times, be the major part of the consideration paid for a going business. Thus, Standard & Poor's Corporation reported as follows:

. . . Standard & Poor's purchased all the stock of Trendline Corp. and O. T. C. Publications, Inc., for a price of approximately $2,425,000, which exceeded the net tangible assets of the acquired companies by $2,154,061. That amount was charged to goodwill.

As can be seen in the more comprehensive discussion of the subject in Chapters 6 and 8, *APB Opinion No. 17* requires that the excess paid over fair market value of net assets acquired in a purchase, that is, goodwill, be amortized to income over a period not to exceed 40 years.

Implications for analysis

One of the most common solutions applied by analysts to the complex problems of the analysis of goodwill is to simply ignore it. That is, they ignore the asset shown on the balance sheet. And yet by ignoring goodwill, analysts ignore investments of very substantial resources in what may often be a company's most important asset.

Ignoring the impact of goodwill on reported periodic income is, of course, also no solution to the analysis of this complex cost. Thus, even considering the limited amount of information available to the analyst, it is far better that he understand the effects of accounting practices in this area on reported income rather than dismiss them altogether.

Goodwill is measured by the excess of cost over the *fair market value* of tangible net assets acquired in a transaction accounted for as a purchase. It is the excess of the purchase price over the fair value of all the tangible assets acquired, arrived at by carefully ascertaining the value of such assets. That is the theory of it. At least up to 1970 when *APB Opinion No. 17* took effect, companies have failed to assign the full fair market value to tangible assets acquired and have, instead, preferred to relegate as much of the purchase price as possible to an account bearing the rather literally descriptive, but meaningless, title of "excess of cost over book value of assets acquired." The reasons for this tendency are simple to understand. Costs assigned to such assets as inventories, plant and equipment, patents, or future tax benefits must all ultimately be charged to income. Goodwill, prior to *APB Opinion No. 17,* had to be amortized only when its value was impaired or was expiring and such a judgment was difficult to prove let alone to audit or second-guess. Thus, many companies have included much of the cost of acquisition over the book value on the *seller's* books in the "excess of cost . . ." account and thereafter proceeded to claim that the amount is not amortized because its value to the enterprise is undiminished. We may add here that since the amortization of goodwill is not a tax-deductible expense, its deduction for financial reporting purposes has a magnified adverse impact which managements desire to avoid. The change in accounting requirements toward mandatory amortization will change the effects of the aforementioned practices over time. Financial analysts should, however, be aware of the large stagnant "pools" of goodwill which will remain on the books of many corporations. Eastern Company reports this as follows:

Goodwill attributable to businesses purchased prior to November 1, 1970 is considered to have continuing value over an indefinite period and is not being amortized. Goodwill purchased subsequent to October 31, 1970 is being amortized over a 20-year period.

The financial analyst must be alert to the makeup and the method of valuation of the Goodwill account as well as to the method of its ultimate disposition. One way of disposing of the Goodwill account, frequently chosen by management, is to write it off at a time when it would have the least serious impact on the market's judgment of the company's earnings, for example, a time of loss or reduced earnings. Goodwill should be written off when the superior earning power originally justifying its existence is no longer present. Lehigh Portland Cement Company described such a write-off as follows:

Write-off of excess of cost over net assets. The rug and carpet operations of the Home Furnishings Division continued to experience operating losses in 1974. The original cost of these operations exceeded the net assets acquired by approximately $2,800,000. A management study in 1974 of existing economic conditions in this industry indicated that the future value of this intangible is questionable. Accordingly, the company decided to write off the unamortized balance of the intangible ($2,034,000) as of December 31, 1974.

In the case of United Brands the auditors qualified their opinion concerning, among others, the uncertainty regarding "the continuing value of the excess of cost over the fair value of net assets acquired."

Under normal circumstances goodwill is not indestructible but is rather an asset with a limited useful life. Whatever the advantages of location, of market dominance and competitive stance, of sales skill or product acceptance, or other benefits are, they cannot be unaffected by the passing of time and by changes in the business environment. Thus, the amortization of goodwill gives recognition to the expiration of a resource in which capital has been invested, a process which is similar to the depreciation of fixed assets. The analyst must recognize that a 40-year amortization period, while adhering to the minimum accounting requirement, which represents a compromise position, may not be realistic in terms of the time expiration of economic values. Thus, he must assess the propriety of the amortization period by reference to such evidence of continuing value as the profitability of units for which the goodwill consideration was originally paid.

INTEREST COSTS

The interest cost to an entity is the nominal rate paid including, in the case of bonds, the amortization of bond discount or premium. A complication arises when companies issue convertible debt or debt with warrants, thus achieving a nominal debt coupon cost which is below the cost of similar debt not enjoying these added features.

After trial pronouncements on the subject and much controversy, *APB Opinion No. 14* has concluded that in the case of *convertible debt* the inseparability of the debt and equity features is such that no portion of the proceeds from the issuance should be accounted for as attributable to the conversion feature.

In the case of debt issued with stock warrants attached, the proceeds of the debt attributable to the value of the warrants should be accounted for as paid-in capital. The corresponding charge is to a debt discount account which must be amortized over the life of the debt issue, thus increasing the effective interest cost.

Interest capitalization

Interest, being an expense that accrues with the lapse of time, is generally regarded as a period cost. In certain instances, however, such as in real estate held for development and sale or as in the case of long-term capital projects which require financing during construction, interest may be deferred and included as part of the cost of the asset. This latter practice is particularly prevalent in public utility accounting where regulatory authorities attach great importance to the allocation of costs between present and future consumers of services and where the rate-making process practically assures the recovery of costs.

In recent years, the practice of interest capitalization has been spreading and has encompassed industrial companies. Thus, American Metal Climax reported that:

During 1972 the capitalization of interest applicable to major construction projects was extended to include interest on general corporate borrowings, as well as specific project borrowing (previous policy was to capitalize interest during construction only on those projects for which specific project borrowings had been made).

This increasing and spreading practice of interest capitalization has led the SEC to issue *ASR 163* (1974) which precludes companies other than public utilities, savings and loan associations and real estate, to adopt a policy of capitalizing interest if such policy was not already publicly disclosed at 6/21/1974. The Commission cited questions of theory and of difficulties with cost measurement as reasons for this moratorium and will reconsider its position only after the FASB acts on this subject. The commission also requires all companies to show the amount of capitalized interest within each income statement presented.

Implications for analysis

Financial analysts should realize that in spite of the position taken in *APB Opinion No. 14,* there are many who disagree with the *Opinion's* position on convertible debt. The dissenters, which included members of the APB, contend that by ignoring the value of the conversion privilege and instead using as a sole measure of interest cost the coupon rate of interest, the *Opinion* specifies an accounting treatment which ignores the true interest cost to the corporation.

It should be noted, however, that *APB Opinion No. 15* on "Earnings per Share" by requiring, in specified circumstances, the inclusion in the computation of earnings per share of the number of shares issuable in the event of conversion of convertible debt, in effect creates a cost additional to the coupon interest cost by thus diluting the reported earnings per share figure.

In spite of the present moratorium on new interest capitalization imposed by the SEC, many companies can continue an established capitalization practice and do so. Occidental Petroleum Corporation reports that:

The company follows the policy of capitalizing property additions, including interest costs during major plant construction and mine development, major renewals and betterments, and major improvements at cost. The policy of capitalizing interest provides a more realistic matching of expense with the revenue generated by the asset.

The new SEC capitalized interest disclosure requirements should provide the analyst information he often did not have before but if he suspects that some capitalized interest is still undisclosed he can determine the amount by estimating total interest costs on debt (i.e., debt times the reasonable average interest rate) and deduct therefrom the interest *expense* shown in the income statement. The balance, if any, should represent capitalized interest.

INCOME TAXES

Income taxes are a very substantial cost of doing business. In most cases they will amount to roughly half a corporation's pretax income. It follows that the accounting for income taxes is an important matter which should be clearly understood. This discussion is not concerned with matters of tax law but rather with the accounting principles which govern the proper computation of the periodic tax expense. *APB Opinion No. 11* is the accounting profession's authoritative pronouncement on this subject. The SEC has additional important requirements.

The current provision for taxes is governed by any number of tax regulations which may apply in a given situation. Regulations such as those concerning the depletion allowance or capital gains treatment can reduce the effective tax rate of a corporation below normal levels. Proper disclosure requires that information be given regarding the reasons for deviations from normal tax incidence.

Treatment of tax loss carry-backs and carry-forwards

A corporation incurring an operating loss may carry such loss *back;* and if it cannot be fully utilized in the preceding three years, it may be carried *forward* for five years. The status of a tax loss *carry-back* is usually simple to determine: either it is available or it is not. The value of a tax loss *carry-forward* depends on a company's ability to earn taxable income in the future, and that in most cases is not a certainty.

Thus, the tax effects of a tax loss carry-back should be recognized in the determination of the results of the loss period. The benefits of tax loss carry-forward should not normally be recognized until they are actually realized. The only exception to this rule occurs in unusual circumstances when realization of the tax loss carry-forward is assured "beyond any reasonable doubt."

The SEC has insisted on strict adherence to both requirements which must exist before tax loss carry-forward benefits can be booked as assets, to wit: *(a)* the loss results from an identifiable, isolated, and nonrecurring cause and the company either has been continuously profitable over a long period or has suffered occasional losses which were more than offset by taxable income in subsequent years, and (b) future taxable income is virtually certain to be large enough to offset the loss carry-forward and will occur soon enough to provide realization during the carry-forward period.

In its 1975 Annual Report Kaufman and Broad disclosed that on SEC insistence it reversed a $12 million future tax benefit booked in an earlier period.

Tax reductions resulting from tax loss carry-forwards are, if material, shown as extraordinary credits so as not to distort the normal relationship prevailing between a company's income and the tax to which it is subject. Analytically these tax loss carry-forward benefits are best related to the loss year(s) which gave rise to them.

Tax allocation

It is well known that financial accounting, which is governed by considerations of fair presentation of financial position and results of operations, does not share in all respects the principles which govern the computation of taxable income. Thus, there are a great many cases of difference between tax and "book" accounting. Some of the differences are permanent, that is, they are not equalized over time. For example, certain items of revenue, such as interest on municipal bonds, are excludable from taxable income, while certain expenses, such as premiums on officers' life insurance, are not deductible for tax purposes.

Another type of tax-book difference stems from the timing of the inclusion of such items for book purposes as opposed to tax purposes.

ILLUSTRATION 1. For financial accounting purposes a company depreciates a $1,000 asset over 10 years on a straight-line basis. To conserve its cash, the company elects for tax purposes to use the double declining-balance method of depreciation. In the first year the book depreciation is $100 while the tax depreciation is $200. In later years, the book depreciation will exceed the tax depreciation because under either method the total depreciation cannot exceed $1,000. Thus the difference is one of timing.

There are a variety of timing differences between tax and financial accounting. The following are some examples:

1. Revenue or income is deferred for tax reporting purposes but is recognized in the current period for financial reporting purposes.
   a. The installment method is used for tax purposes; the accrual method is used for financial reporting purposes.
   b. The completed-contract method is used for tax purposes; the percentage-of-completion method is used for financial reporting purposes.

2. Expenses deducted for tax purposes in the current period exceed
    expenses deducted for financial reporting purposes.
    a. Accelerated depreciation is taken for tax purposes; straight-
        line depreciation is used for financial reporting purposes.
    b. Pension costs are deducted earlier for tax purposes than for
        financial reporting purposes.
    c. Land reclamation and similar costs are deducted for tax pur-
        poses; capitalization and amortization are utilized for financial
        reporting purposes.
3. Revenue or income is recognized for tax purposes in the current
    period, but all or part of the amount is deferred for financial report-
    ing purposes.
    a. Rent income or other income received in advance is recog-
        nized for tax purposes.
    b. Unearned finance charges and other deferred credits are rec-
        ognized for tax purposes but are taken into income over a
        number of years for financial reporting purposes.
4. Expenses deducted for financial reporting purposes in the current
    period exceed expenses deducted for tax purposes.
    a. Estimated expenses (repair and maintenance, warranty servic-
        ing costs, and vacation wages) are accrued for financial report-
        ing purposes but not deducted for tax purposes.
    b. Estimated refunds due the government for price redetermina-
        tion and renegotiation are accrued for financial reporting
        purposes.

The basic problem with these timing differences, from the accounting point of view, is that there will be differences between the income
before tax shown in the income statement and the taxable income
shown in the tax return. Thus, if the actual tax paid is considered as the
period expense, it will not match the pretax income shown in the
income statement. This would violate the basic accounting principle
that there should be a matching of income and related costs and expenses. Interperiod tax allocation is designed to assure that in any one
period income shown in the financial statements is charged with the
tax applicable to it regardless of how such income is reported for tax
purposes.

The following example will illustrate the principle of tax allocation:

A retailer sells air conditioners on the installment basis. On January
1, 19X1, he sells a unit for $720 payable at the rate of $20 a month for
36 months. For purposes of this illustration, we ignore finance charges
and assume a gross profit to the retailer of 20 percent and a tax rate of
50 percent.

In accordance with proper accrual accounting, the retailer will recognize in the year of sale (19X1) a gross profit of $144 (20 percent of

$720). For tax purposes he can recognize profit based on actual cash collections as follows:

	Cash collection	Taxable gross profit (20%)	Actual tax payable
19X1	$240	$ 48	$24
19X2	240	48	24
19X3	240	48	24
Total	$720	$144	$72

In the absence of tax allocation the results shown by the retailer on this transaction would be as follows:

	Pretax profit	Tax payable	Profit (loss)
19X1	$144	$24	$120
19X2	—	24	(24)
19X3	—	24	(24)
Total	$144	$72	$ 72

The flaws in this presentation are readily apparent. The book profit of 19X1 does not bear its proper share of tax, thus resulting in a profit overstatement of $48, which distortion is carried over to 19X2 and 19X3, whose profits will be understated by $24 each because they will bear a tax without inclusion of the revenues which gave rise to it. Moreover, this kind of accounting would appear to suggest that in 19X1 our retailer is more profitable than his competitor who may have sold the air conditioner for cash ($720), realized a gross profit of $144, and paid a tax of $72, thus realizing an after-tax profit of $72 (versus $120 on the installment sale).

Tax allocation is designed to remedy the above distortions by means of a deferred tax account, which results in the matching of tax with the corresponding revenue as follows:

Year	Pretax profit	Taxes			After-tax profit	Deferred tax account
		Actually payable	Deferred	Total		
19X1	$144	$24	$ 48	$72	$72	$48
19X2	—	24	(24)	—	—	24
19X3	—	24	(24)	—	—	—

APB Opinion No. 11 has adopted the position that the deferred tax account (e.g., the $48 in 19X1) is not a liability but rather a deferred credit meaning an equalization account which is used to achieve a matching of income and expense. Such an equalization account would appear on the asset side as a deferred charge when, due to timing differences, the taxable income is higher than the book income. The present-day emphasis on the importance of the income statement has resulted in balance sheet items designed specifically to serve such expense and revenue allocation purpose. The deferred tax account may also be viewed as a source of funds, and this aspect will be discussed further in Chapter 13.

The above installment sale example is a simplification of a complex process. While the tax deferral pertaining to the *specific* air conditioner is, as shown in the example, completely extinguished at the end of the third year, the aggregate tax deferral account will usually not behave this way. Thus, if another air conditioner is sold in 19X2, the aggregate deferred tax account will stay the same; and if a growing number of air conditioners are sold, the deferred tax account will also grow. In the case of tax-book differences attributed to depreciation, where the assets are long lived, the deferred tax account may grow over the years or at least stabilize. A study by Price Waterhouse & Company of 100 major corporations concluded that the bulk of the deferred tax accounts were not likely to be "paid off" or drawn down. There are also those who claim that only taxes actually due should be accrued. While the matter of accepted accounting practice for taxes has been settled by *APB Opinion No. 11*, the controversy surrounding it has not ended.

Another form of tax allocation concerns the distribution of the tax effect within the various segments of the income statement and the retained earnings of a period. The basic principle here is that each major category should be shown net of its tax effect. Thus, for example, an extraordinary item should be shown net of its appropriate tax effect so that the tax related to operating results is properly stated. This is known as *intra*period allocation.

Accounting for income taxes by oil and gas producers

FASB *Statement No. 9* requires now the allocation of income taxes for timing differences arising from intangible drilling and development costs and other costs associated with the exploration for and development of oil and gas reserves that are charged to expense in income statements in one period, but deducted for income tax purposes in a different period.

Prior to 1975 most oil and gas producing companies did not provide income taxes on these timing differences because the percentage depletion allowances in the income tax law were expected to be larger than costs amortized from prior periods for accounting purposes. The "interaction" of percentage depletion with these costs was considered sufficient to warrant omission of tax allocation. Changes effected in the income tax law have reduced substantially, or have eliminated, the percentage depletion benefits for many oil and gas companies as of January 1, 1975. As a result, this interaction will generally not be effective in reducing future taxes for these companies.

Commencing January 1, 1975, oil and gas producing companies that have not allocated taxes with respect to these costs must begin doing so using the prospective net method of accounting. The prospective net method requires the allocation of income taxes on the net change in timing differences originating in the period and the reversal during the period of similar differences that arose in prior periods.

The *Statement* provides for an election that permits oil and gas producing companies to take interaction with percentage depletion into account when using the prospective net method.

Prior to 1975, certain oil and gas producing companies allocated income taxes in accordance with the provisions of *Accounting Principles Board Opinion No. 11* without recognizing interaction with percentage depletion. FASB *Statement No. 9* permits a company wishing to change to that accounting method to do so, but if it does, the company must apply the method retroactively by restating prior period financial statements.

When using the prospective net method or when recognizing interaction with percentage depletion, SFAS 9 requires disclosure of the amount of cumulative financial accounting/tax differences attributable to intangible drilling and development costs and other costs with respect to which income taxes have not been allocated. In addition, when it becomes probable that future reversals of those costs will exceed future originating differences of a similar nature, and that the excess income tax effect will be charged to income tax expense, the company must disclose that probability.

SEC disclosure requirements

To enable users of financial statements to understand better the tax accounting of an enterprise, its effective tax rate, and the current and prospective cost drains associated with tax payments, the SEC has called in *ASR 149* (1973) for disclosure in Form 10-K of:

A reconciliation between the effective income tax rate and the statutory Federal income tax rate.

Components of deferred tax expense.

"Substantial" future reductions in deferred income taxes in the balance sheet.

Investment tax credit

The investment tax credit has been used as an instrument of economic policy for the stimulation of capital investment when this is deemed a desirable objective. Thus, for example, a 7 percent investment credit was allowed in the year of an asset's acquisition. An industrial company acquiring an asset of $100,000 would have its tax bill for the year reduced by $7,000.

The APB has repeatedly tried to obtain acceptance of an accounting treatment whereby the investment credit benefit would be spread over the useful life of the asset acquired. The basic argument in favor of this method is that one does not enhance earnings by the act of buying assets but rather by using them. Under the deferral method, if the above-mentioned asset has a useful life of 10 years, the $7,000 investment credit would be taken into income (as a reduction of taxes) at the rate of $700 per year.

The APB has not been successful in obtaining acceptance of this view. The position of those who favor the immediate reflection of the investment credit in income (also known as the "flow-through" method) is that the investment credit is a selective reduction in taxes unrelated to the use of the asset. The "flow-through" method of taking the investment credit into income in the year of the asset purchase is in more widespread use than the deferral method. Both methods enjoy the label of "generally accepted accounting principles."

Implications for analysis

Taxes are almost always substantial expense items, and the analyst must be sure that he understands the relationship between pretax income and the income tax expense.

The analyst should note that the procedures applied to loss carry-forwards differ from those applied to carry-backs. While the tax loss carry-back represents a reduction of tax in the loss year and is recognized as such, a loss carry-forward which should have a similar impact is not so recognized because its realization is not usually "assured beyond any reasonable doubt." Thus, in this situation the "realization convention" in accounting takes precedence over the "matching concept." The subsequent actual realization of a tax loss carry-forward is designated as an extraordinary item so as to indicate that it has really nothing to do with the normal tax for the year.

In spite of all the heated arguments surrounding tax allocation, it is obvious that this accounting principle makes an important contribution to proper tax accrual and, hence, income reporting. It separates tax strategy from the reporting of results of operations, thus removing one possibility of management determining the size of results by means of bookkeeping techniques alone.

Another good argument for tax allocation, from an analytical point of view, is the fact that assets whose future tax deductibility is reduced cannot be worth as much as those which have a higher tax deductibility. Thus, for example, if two companies depreciate an identical asset costing $100,000 under different tax methods of depreciation which result in a first-year depreciation of $10,000 and $20,000 respectively, then it is obvious that at the end of that year, one company has an asset which it can still depreciate for tax purposes to the tune of $90,000 while the other can depreciate it only to the extent of $80,000. Obviously the two assets are not equally valuable, and the tax deferral adjustment recognizes this fact.

One of the flaws remaining in tax allocation procedures is that no recognition is given to the fact that the present value of a future obligation, or loss of benefits, should be discounted rather than shown at par as today's tax deferred accounts actually are. This was a question which was also debated within the APB, but the board decided to postpone a decision on this matter.

The failure of the accounting profession to face the issue of discounting squarely should cause the analyst to be even more aware of the serious objections many in industry continue to have to the tax deferral concept in general and to the relentless buildup of deferred tax credits which, while reducing income, do not represent a legal obligation to an outsider. When forced to adopt deferred tax accounting Exxon's management expressed its objection as follows:

It is the opinion of Management that the total of these deferred tax credits, which do not represent liabilities, will continue to grow rather than be restored to income. Management believes that its former method of accounting for income taxes was more realistic than the new method it was required to adopt in 1968.

So far its prediction has proved correct.

An error sometimes committed by analysts is to assume that deferred tax accounting acts as a complete offset to differences between tax and financial accounting methods. Actually, if we assume that the accelerated depreciation method used for tax purposes is more realistic than the straight-line method used in reporting income, then the effect of deferred taxes is to remove only approximately *half* of the overstatement of income which results from the use, for book purposes, of the slower depreciation method.

FASB *Statement 9* on tax allocation by petroleum companies represents more of a compromise with a divided industry than a creditable attempt to provide similar accounting for similar circumstances. Given the highly technical and complex provisions which provide for alternative ways of deferred tax computations the analyst must now be aware that the use of these different methods by the oil companies can affect comparability among their reported results.

Accounting for the investment credit is subject to two very different acceptable alternatives. In our example of the company which buys a 10-year life asset for $100,000, one allowable method is to take the $7,000 investment credit into income in the first year while under the alternative, and preferred method, only $700 is so taken into the first year income. It is obvious that the $6,300 tax difference on a $100,000 asset purchase may have a significant impact on results and on intercompany comparability. The fact is that the "flow-through" method enjoys substantial acceptance and the analyst must be aware of this in his evaluation of relative results.

ANALYTICAL SIGNIFICANCE OF THE SEC DISCLOSURE REQUIREMENTS

The SEC disclosure requirements *(ASR 149)* provide the analyst with significant income tax information beyond that required by *APB Opinion 11.*

The requirements for an explanation of why the effective tax expense percentage differs from the statutory rate of 48 percent, if it does, gives the analyst important means of judging whether the present tax benefits, which an enterprise enjoys, can be expected to continue in the future. Thus, such benefits as the Investment Tax Credit, DISCS, foreign tax shelters (e.g., Puerto Rico), depletion allowances, and capital gains treatment depend on legislative sanction and are always subject to change, repeal, or expiration. Other differences, such as those arising from foreign tax differentials, depend on conditions which must be carefully monitored. The continuation of accounting related differentials, such as those relating to the use of the equity method of income pickup or the amortization of goodwill, can be evaluated by the analysis of underlying transactions. New information can also be obtained by an analysis of the reconciliation. Thus, for example, if the analysis indicates that tax-free interest reduced taxes by $144,000 one can determine the amount of tax-free income by dividing $144,000 into $0.48 which equals $300,000.

A reconciliation of the tax rate of the Beta Company can be found on page 95.

The analysis of components of the deferred income tax expense can lead to significant analytical insights. The analyst may through this medium find out about the capitalization of costs, the early recognition of revenues, or about other book accounting methods of which he would otherwise not have known. Beta Company's analysis of the principal items giving rise to deferred income taxes is found on page 95.

Information about expected "substantial" future reductions in deferred income taxes, which do, of course, spell higher tax expense cash outlays is valuable for the liquidity implications that it carries. Whenever a deferred tax credit "reverses" it means that the book tax *expense* is reduced by the amount of the reversal but that the *actual* tax bill is higher than the net expense appearing in the income statement. The implication is a cash drain.

Puerto Rican Cement described such a projected situation as follows:

Based upon currently anticipated expenditures and operations, it is expected that the deferred income tax balance will be reduced in 1975, 1976, and 1977 and the cash outlay for taxes associated with those years will exceed tax expense by approximately $1,550,000, $1,640,000 and $1,640,000, respectively, primarily due to the reversal of flexible depreciation taken in prior years for tax purposes over depreciation for book purposes.

It should be noted again that a lack of agreement among accountants on what constitutes a "substantial" or material amount may result in a lack of disclosure of items which the analyst may consider material.

EXTRAORDINARY GAINS AND LOSSES

Most items of revenue and cost discussed so far in this chapter are of the ordinary operating and recurring variety. Thus, it can be assumed that their inclusion in the income statement results in a figure which is a fair reflection of the period's operating results. Such reported results are a very important element in the valuation of securities, in the evaluation of managements, and in many other respects; and they are used as indicators of a company's earning power (see Chapter 22). Consequently, ever since the income statement became the important financial statement it is today, the treatment of unusual and extraordinary gains and losses and prior period adjustments has been a major problem area of income measurement and reporting.

Extraordinary items are distinguished by their unusual nature *and* by the infrequency of their occurrence. Examples of extraordinary items include substantial uninsured losses from a major casualty (such as an earthquake) or a loss from an expropriation.

Items affecting results of prior years are now limited by SFAS *16* to correction of errors in prior period financial statements and to adjustments resulting from realization of income tax benefits of pre-acquisition operating loss carry-forwards of purchased subsidiaries.

There are two main schools of thought on how to handle extraordinary gains and losses. One is the "all-inclusive" concept, which gives recognition in determining net income to all items affecting the change in equity interests during the period except dividend payments and capital transactions. The other is the so-called "current-operating-performance" concept. This concept would exclude from net income any items which, if included, would impair the significance of the net income as a measure of current earning power. Under this latter concept, prior to 1966, actual income reporting practice had deteriorated to such an extent that a complete reversal in philosophy and approach became necessary.[3] The change came in stages, first with *APB Opinion 9* (1966) and in 1973 with *APB Opinion No. 30* which restricted still further the use of the extraordinary category by requiring that in order to qualify for this designation an item be *both* unusual in nature and infrequent of occurrence. It defined these terms thus:

a. *Unusual nature*—the underlying event or transaction should possess a high degree of abnormality and be of a type clearly unrelated to, or only incidentally related to, the ordinary and typical activities of the entity, taking into account the environment in which the entity operates.
b. *Infrequency of occurrence*—the underlying event or transaction should be of a type that would not reasonably be expected to recur in the foreseeable future, taking into account the environment in which the entity operates.

APB Opinion No. 30 held that certain gains and losses should not be reported as extraordinary items because they are usual in nature and may be expected to recur as a consequence of customary and continuing business activities. Examples include:

1. Write-down or write-off of receivables, inventories, equipment leased to others, deferred research and development costs, or other intangible assets.
2. Gains or losses from exchange or translation of foreign currencies, including those relating to major devaluations and revaluations.
3. Gains or losses on disposal of a segment of a business.
4. Other gains or losses from sale or abandonment of property, plant, or equipment used in the business.
5. Effects of a strike, including those against competitors and major suppliers.
6. Adjustment of accruals on long-term contracts.

---

[3] For a comprehensive discussion of all aspects of this issue see the author's book *Accounting for Extraordinary Gains and Losses* (New York: Ronald Press, 1967).

The *Opinion* also calls for the separate disclosure in income before extraordinary items of unusual *or* nonrecurring events or transactions that are material but which do not meet both conditions for classification as extraordinary.

Cross currents of theory—the case of debt retirements

When the APB considered in 1972 the question of gains and losses on debt retirement its desire to limit further the items qualifying for the "extraordinary" label led it to the conclusion that these should be shown as ordinary items of gain and loss. Gains and losses on debt retirement arise when, due to changes in interest rates and or credit standing, a debt can be satisfied by repurchase in the open market or otherwise at amount below (gain) or above (loss) par.

Thus, when in 1974 soaring interest rates reduced the price of older, low coupon bonds, companies rushed to exchange high coupon bonds of lower aggregate par values for outstanding low coupon bonds. The resulting "profits" were substantial, as was the case of General Host which included in ordinary income $16 million of such gains which in turn represented 9 percent of net income.

Cases such as that of General Host prompted the SEC to induce the FASB to issue SFAS 4 (1975) which requires material debt retirements of all kinds, except for sinking fund purchases, to be separately disclosed as extraordinary items. Material sinking fund gains and losses must, however, be aggregated and separately identified in the income statement.

These shifting theories reflect an ambivalence, i.e., a desire to do away with the label "extraordinary" on the one hand and on the other an attempt to counter the ever present propensity of some managements to augment income with a variety of "profits."

Discontinued operations

APB Opinion No. 30 also deals with the accounting for and the presentation of discontinued operations and the disposal of a segment of a business. These are not extraordinary items but should be presented separately as in the statement on page 317.

The analyst will recognize that in the estimation of *future* earning power results from discontinued operations can be omitted. The losses on disposal must be treated analytically in a way similar to that accorded to extraordinary items, i.e., while not entering the computation of the results of a single year, they must be included in the longer-term earnings record of the enterprise.

Income from continuing operations before income taxes............ $xxx
Provision for income taxes xxx

    Income from continuing operations xxx
Discontinued operations (described in a note)
  Income (loss) from discontinued operations (less applicable
    income taxes of $xxx)(A) .... $xxx
  Loss on disposal of discontinued operations including
    provision of $xxx for operating losses during phase-out
    period (less applicable income taxes of $xxx)(B) xxx   xxx

    Net income .... $xxx

(A) Includes operating losses to date of committment to formal disposition of a segment, i.e., a separately identifiable entity—physically, operationally, and financially.

(B) Includes estimated operating losses from date of decision to discontinue to expected disposal date. (Expected net gains on disposals can be recorded only *when realized*.)

Implications for analysis

To the intelligent analyst the single most desirable characteristic in the income statement is that of adequate disclosure. Most analyses of the income statement, except possibly for evaluation of the quality of management, are predictive in nature. Analysts rely on factors whose stability of relationship and recurrence facilitate the extrapolation and forecasting function. Similarly, adjustments must be made for the erratic, sporadic, and nonrecurring elements of reported income. For all this the analyst needs, above all, sufficient information about the nature of all the material elements entering the determination of the results of operations of a period. He needs such information presented in adequate detail so as to enable him to form an opinion as to its impact on his conclusions and projections, and he needs it presented without bias so that he can use it with confidence. This, then, is the reason for the need for the largest possible measure of fair and adequate disclosure.

While there is need for full details of all normal operating elements of revenue and expense, the need for information regarding the nature of extraordinary gains and losses is even more essential. This is true because of the material nature of such items as well as the need to form judgments and conclusions regarding how they should be treated in an assessment of the overall results of operations and what probability of recurrence should be assigned to them. It is this special nature of extraordinary items that has caused so much debate and controversy within the accounting profession as to their treatment.

The financial analyst should realize that one important aspect of that controversy is of no real concern to him. It focuses on the one figure of net income which many superficial users of financial data rely upon almost to the exclusion of all other factors. In such a context the matter of whether an extraordinary item is or is not included in the determination of net income is of great importance. To the analyst who most carefully analyzes all elements of the income statement, the exact positioning of the extraordinary item within the income statement is not of great import. He is much more concerned with the adequate description of the extraordinary item as well as the circumstances which gave rise to it, so that he can classify it properly in the context of long run as well as short-term analysis.

APB Opinion No. 9 represented the start of a reversal of attitude on the part of the accounting profession with regard to its responsibilities towards income reporting. Apparently discouraged by the abuses which resulted under the former approach, the profession has all but abandoned its professed intention to arrive at a meaningful or reliable measure of current operating performance. Instead, in order to insulate itself from the pressures of managements, the profession decided that with the exception of "rare" prior year adjustments, *all* items of income and expense shall be included in the determination of a "net income" figure which thus assumed a new and altogether different meaning.

While one may wonder whether those who rely on the sole "net income" statistic will be helped by this new approach, the analyst must clearly understand the implications which the reporting under *APB Opinion No. 30* and *SFAS 16* holds for him.

To begin with, the analyst should not assume that the accountant's designation of an item as "extraordinary" even under the stricter criteria set forth by *Opinion No. 30* renders it automatically excludable from the measure of periodic operating results. The best that can be expected here is that under the requirements of the *Opinion,* full disclosure will be made of all *material* credits and charges in the income statement regardless of their designation. However, despite the fact that "materiality" is an important criterion in determining whether an item is "extraordinary" or not, the profession has, so far, not developed a meaningful standard that would guide it in distinguishing between items which are material and those which are not. Consequently, practice enjoys an undue amount of flexibility in this area.

An extraordinary item is now defined as being nonrecurring and outside an enterprise's normal operations. It is, sometimes, the result of a freak or of an unexpected or unpredictable occurrence. However, this concept of normalcy is one which must not be taken too seriously. Business is always subject to contingencies and to the unexpected. This is the very essence of business risk.[4] Moreover, variability is a fact

---

[4] See Chapter 3 for a discussion of unsystematic risk.

of business life; and in spite of management's desire for stable growth trends, business results do not come in neat uniform installments. Thus, the "bunching up" of positive and negative factors which often causes items to become extraordinary should not lead to the conclusion that since they require adjustment of any one year's result they should be disregarded in an evaluation of an entity's long-term average performance.

Extraordinary items should never be completely disregarded. They often bear the mark of the particular type of risks to which an enterprise is subject. While they may not recur yearly, the fact of their occurrence attests to the possibility of their recurrence. In their final impact on a business entity, they are not different from operating items. After all, a loss from a flash flood affects the entity's wealth every bit as much as does an equal loss on the sale of merchandise below cost. Moreover, the cumulative importance of extraordinary items can be considerable.

The analyst should always be aware of management's reporting propensities and the fact that often it is in its power to decide both the size and the *timing* of gains and losses. Thus, management can decide when to sell an asset, when to discontinue a product line, or when, subject to the limiting provisions of SFAS 5 discussed in Chapter 7, to provide for a future loss; and often the timing of such decision is affected by its probable impact on reported results. Since materiality is a consideration in the determination of whether an item is "extraordinary" or not, losses which are small and considered "operating" can be permitted to accumulate to the point where they are large enough to be labeled "extraordinary." In assessing extraordinary items, the analyst should be aware of the possibility that both their size and their timing can be "managed."

Chapter 22 contains a more thorough discussion of the significance of extraordinary and other unusual items to the financial analyst. What must be emphasized here is that regardless of the good intentions of those who promulgate official accounting policies, the analyst can never assume that the intent and spirit of these pronouncements will be implemented in practice. Instead he must pay close attention to actual practice. For example, the author has documented the serious abuses of practice which have occurred after the promulgation of *APB Opinion No. 9*.[5] The following examples will illustrate that in spite of a

---

[5] See "Reserves for Future Costs and Losses—Threat to the Integrity of the Income Statement," *Financial Analysts Journal*, January–February 1970, pp. 45–48; and "Reporting the Results of Operations—A Reassessment of *APB Opinion No. 9*," *Journal of Accountancy*, July 1970, pp. 57–61.

considerable tightening up of the rules, opportunities for violating their spirit or their letter still exist:

ILLUSTRATION 2.   In a 1975 refinancing, Reliance Group sold to banks for $53.4 million lease receivables with a book value of $57 million. It labeled the resulting $3.6 million loss as "extraordinary" because it regarded it as resulting "from the early extinguishment of debt. . ." In fact the purchase agreements which led to the transfer of the leases to the banks indicate that this was a sale and not a debt swap.[6] We have here an example of management's use of accounting standards (i.e., SFAS 4) to further its particular interests which seem to be the exclusion of an ordinary loss from reported operating income.

ILLUSTRATION 3.   Norton Simon Inc. in its 1976 annual report had the following note:
In accordance with the provisions for the initial application of Statement 12 of The Financial Accounting Standards Board, the marketable equity securities transferred from short-term to long-term investments at December 31, 1975 were transferred at cost, and a valuation allowance was established by a charge to shareholders' equity. The short-term valuation allowance of approximately $10 million, established in prior years, was included in other income. Other income in 1976 was charged with provisions aggregating approximately $8 million against the realization of certain noncurrent receivables, investments other than marketable equity securities, and for certain other nonrecurring items. The net aftertax effect of the above items was to increase earnings by approximately $.01 a share.

In 1973 Western Union and United Brands, among others, used profits from debt retirements as the opportunity to absorb substantial unrelated write-offs. These are illustrations of the persisting technique of offset. The propensity of management to offset items of gains with provisions for present and future losses is not difficult to understand. It accomplishes two objectives: (1) it removes from the income stream an unusual profit boost which an earnings-trend conscious company may find difficult to match in the following year and (2) it provides a discretionary "cushion" against which future losses and expenses can be charged so as to improve the earnings trend, or it provides for losses which up to now it did not find expedient to provide for. Thus the timing of income and loss recognition can be "managed."[7]

In a partial response to these problems of income presentation Accounting Series Release No. 138 of the SEC contains requirements for rather detailed information relating to extraordinary items in Form 8-K. For example, there is a requirement for a statement setting forth the years in which costs being reflected in a charge were or are ex-

---

[6] For further details see A. J. Briloff, "Whose Deep Pocket," Barron's, July 19, 1976.

[7] Chapter 11 of the first edition of this work contains additional examples in this area.

pected to be incurred and the amount of cost for each year by main components, reasons for the charges or credits, and a description and detailed schedule (with follow-up reconciliations) of provisions for future losses. Also required is a description of accounting principles followed in connection with the charge or credit and the estimated net cash outlays associated with a charge.

The above discussion makes it obvious that the financial analyst must adopt an independent and critical attitude towards items in the income statement be they classified as unusual, extraordinary or in any other fashion. Only on the basis of a full understanding of the nature of such items can a conclusion be reached regarding their impact on the earnings performance of a business entity.

THE INCOME STATEMENT—IMPLICATIONS FOR ANALYSIS, AN OVERVIEW

The position of importance and predominance assumed by the income statement is due to a number of factors. For one, it is the financial statement which presents the dynamic aspects of an enterprise, the results of its operations, and the quality of its performance. Moreover, it is the basis on which extrapolations and projections of future performance are built. The income statement's importance is emphasized by the accounting process which favors it and focuses on it, often to the detriment of the balance sheet. The attempt to increase the significance of the income statement has often resulted in distortions in the balance sheet. Thus, for example, the use of the Lifo method of inventory accounting in times of rising price levels introduces current costs into the income statement but undermines the significance of the balance sheet where inventories are carried at unrealistically low amounts. The balance sheet is cast mostly in a supporting role, containing as it does residual balances of assets and deferred credits which will ultimately become costs and revenues, the investments and working funds necessary to conduct operations, and the various sources of funds such as the liability and capital accounts.

As we have seen throughout this and the preceding chapters, the accounting rules governing the determination and measurement of periodic income are far from uniform, and much leeway exists in their selection, interpretation, and application. It may be useful to conclude this discussion with an overview of the possibilities that exist in the distortion of reported income.

If we accept the proposition that there is such a thing as "true" or "real" income, that is, income that could be determined when all the facts are known and all the uncertainties are resolved, then it is obvious that most reported income must deviate somewhat from this ideal figure. We can never be sure about the useful life of an asset until it has actually come to an end; we cannot be certain about the ultimate profitability of a contract until it is fulfilled, nor can we be certain about the revenue received from a transaction until the sales price is actually collected. There is nothing one can do about these uncertainties except to estimate their ultimate disposition on the basis of the best information and judgment available. Periodic income reporting requires that we not wait for final disposition of uncertainties but that we estimate them as best we can. Such a system is subject to many errors: errors of estimation, errors of omission, and errors of commission. The better and the more conscientious a company's management and the better its internal controls the less likely it is that such errors will substantially distort reported results.

The more serious and frequent cases of income distortion arise when managements set out to "manage" reported results in such a way that instead of portraying economic results as they are, they are presented as nearly as possible as management wants them presented.

We have seen that such distortions can be accomplished by means of the timing of transactions, the choice from a variety of generally accepted principles, the introduction of conservative or, alternatively, very optimistic estimates, and the arbitrary choice of methods by which elements of income and expenses are presented or their nature is disclosed.

Generally, an enterprise wishing to benefit current income at the expense of the future will engage in one or a number of practices such as the following:

1. It will choose inventory methods which allow for maximum inventory carrying values and minimum current charges to cost of goods or services sold.
2. It will choose depreciation methods and useful lives of property which will result in minimum current charges as depreciation expense.
3. It will defer all manner of costs to the future such as, for example:
    a. Interest costs.
    b. Preoperating, moving, rearrangement, and start-up costs.
    c. Marketing costs.
    Such costs would be carried as deferred charges or included with the costs of other assets such as property, plant, and equipment.
4. It will amortize assets and defer costs over the longest possible period. Such assets include:
    a. Goodwill.
    b. Leasehold improvements.
    c. Patents and copyrights.

5. It will elect the method requiring the lowest possible pension and other employment compensation cost accruals.
6. It will inventory rather than expense administrative costs, taxes, etc.
7. It will choose the most accelerated methods of income recognition such as in the areas of leasing, franchising, real estate sales, and contracting.
8. It will take into income right away, rather than defer, such benefits as investment tax credits.

Enterprises which wish to "manage" the size of reported income can still resort to classification as "extraordinary" of items which arise from the normal and usual risks to which the business is subject or can regulate to some extent the flow of income and expense by means of reserves for future costs and losses.

Exhibit 11–1 illustrates the possible impact on reported income of some of the alternative accounting principles available to managements.

EXHIBIT 11–1
Example of the effect of the variety of accounting principles on reported income

RIVAL MANUFACTURING COMPANY
Consolidated Statement of Income
For Year Ended 19XX

	Method A	Method B
Net sales	$365,800,000	$365,800,000
Cost of goods sold (1) (2) (3) (4) (5)	(276,976,200)	(274,350,000)
	$ 88,823,800	$ 91,450,000
Selling, general, and administrative expenses (5) (6)	(51,926,000)	(42,700,000)
	$ 36,897,800	$ 48,750,000
Other income (expenses):		
Interest expenses	(3,085,000)	(3,095,000)
Net income—subsidiaries	1,538,000	1,460,000
Amortization of goodwill (7)	(390,000)	(170,000)
Miscellaneous expenses	(269,000)	(229,000)
Income before taxes	$ 34,691,800	$ 46,715,800
Taxes:		
Income taxes—deferred (8)	(756,000)	(850,000)
Income taxes—current	(16,716,900)	(22,397,900)
Reductions from investment tax credits (9)	10,400	758,400
Net income	$ 17,229,300	$ 24,226,300
Earnings per share	$5.74	$8.08

Explanations:
(1) Inventories:
    A uses last-in, first-out
    B uses first-in, first-out
       Difference—$1,780,000

(2) Administrative costs:
     A includes some administrative costs as period costs
     B includes some administrative costs as inventory costs
          Difference—$88,000
(3) Depreciation:
     A uses sum-of-the-years'-digits method
     B uses straight-line method
          Difference—$384,200
(4) Useful lives of assets:
     A uses conservative assumption—8 years (average)
     B uses liberal assumption—14 years (average)
          Difference—$346,000
(5) Pension costs:
     A uses "maximum provision" under APB *Opinion No. 8*
     B uses "minimum provision" under APB *Opinion No. 8*
          Difference—$78,000
(6) Executive compensations:
     A compensates executives with cash bonuses
     B compensates executives with stock options
          Difference—$840,000
(7) Goodwill from acquisition:
     A amortizes over 10 years
     B amortizes over 40 years
          Difference—$220,000
(8) Taxes on subsidiary profits:
     A makes provision as income earned
     B makes no provision until dividends received
          Difference—$67,000
(9) Investment tax credits:
     A amortizes over useful lives of equipment
     B credits against current taxes
          Difference—$748,000

ACCOUNTING CHANGES

In an attempt to reduce the unwarranted switching by management from one accepted method of accounting to another, *APB Opinion No. 20* states that:

. . . in the preparation of financial statements there *is a presumption that an accounting principle once adopted should not be changed in accounting for events and transactions of a similar type.* Consistent use of accounting principles from one accounting period to another enhances the utility of financial statements to users by facilitating analysis and understanding of comparative accounting data.

*   *   *   *   *

The presumption that an entity should not change an accounting principle *may be overcome* only if the enterprise justifies the use of an alternative acceptable accounting principle on the basis that *it is preferable.*[8] . . . (Emphasis supplied.)

---

[8] In *ASR 177* (1976) the SEC introduced the requirement that when an accounting change is made:

. . . a letter from the registrant's independent accountants shall be filed as an exhibit indicating whether or not the change is to an alternative principle which in his judgment is *preferable* under the circumstances . . . (emphasis added)

The Board distinguishes in this *Opinion* among three types of accounting changes, that is, a change in (1) an accounting principle, (2) an accounting estimate, and (3) the reporting entity.

Change in accounting principle

As a general rule (see exceptions below), the cumulative effect of the change (net of taxes) on the amount of retained earnings at the beginning of the period in which the change is made should be included in net income and shown in the statement of income between "extraordinary items" and "net income." This is the so-called "catch-up adjustment." Previously issued financial statements should *not* be adjusted.

A change in the method of allocating the cost of long-lived assets to various accounting periods, if adopted only for newly acquired assets, does not result in the "catch-up adjustment" described above.

Under this general rule the following disclosures are called for:

1. Nature of and justification for adopting the change.
2. Effect of the new principle on income before extraordinary items and net income for the period of change, including related earnings per share data.
3. Pro forma effects of retroactive application of the accounting change on income before extraordinary items and the net income (and related earnings per share data) should be shown on the face of the income statement for all periods presented.

When pro forma effects are not determinable, disclosure must be made as to why such effects are not shown.

There are three specific exceptions to the general rule that previously issued financial statements not be restated. In the case of the following accounting changes previously issued statements should be restated:

1. Change *from* Lifo to another inventory pricing method.
2. Change in accounting method for long-term construction type contracts.
3. Change *to* or *from* the "full cost" method used in extractive industries.

These exceptions were included presumably because these adjustments normally result in large credits to income. The FASB has extended the exceptions to include changes resulting from the adoption of accounting standards required in SFAS 2, 5, 8, and 9.

Change in accounting estimate

In accounting, periodic income determination requires the estimation of future events such as inventory obsolescence, useful lives of property, or uncollectible receivables. These are known as accounting estimates. The following provisions in *APB Opinion No. 20* apply to changes in accounting estimates:

1. Retroactive restatement is prohibited.
2. The change should be accounted for in the period of change and, if applicable, future periods.
3. A change in accounting estimate that is recognized by a change in accounting principle should be reported as a change in estimate.
4. Disclosure is required of the effect on income before extraordinary items and net income (including related earnings per share data) of the current period when a change in estimate affects future periods as well.

Change in reporting entity

A change in the reporting entity can occur in the following ways:

1. Initial presentation of consolidated financial statements.
2. Changing the consolidation policy with respect to specific subsidiaries.
3. A pooling of interests.

APB Opinion No. 20 calls for restatement of all periods presented in the financial statements and for disclosure of the nature of the change and the reasons therefor.

Correction of an error

APB Opinion No. 20 does not consider the correction of an error as being in the nature of an accounting change. Consequently, the correction of an error should be treated as a prior period adjustment and disclosure should include:

1. The nature of the error.
2. The effect on previously reported income before extraordinary items and net income (and related earnings per share data).

Materiality

The materiality of an accounting change for reporting and disclosure purposes should be considered in relation to current income on the following bases:

1. Each change separately.
2. The combined effect of all changes.
3. The effect of a change on the trend of earnings.
4. The effect of a change on future periods.

The APB, in what appears to be a reaction to the increasing dissatisfaction of financial statement users with the failure of the profession to promulgate criteria for judging materiality, has narrowed its interpretation of this concept as applied to *Opinion No. 20.* Particularly noteworthy is the recognition by the Board of the importance which the analyst and other users of financial statements accord to earnings *trends.*

Historical summaries of financial information

APB Opinion No. 20 also applies to historical summaries of financial information which customarily appear in published financial statements or elsewhere. However, since these summaries are not normally covered by the auditor's opinion and their presentation is not mandatory, companies can avoid the need for restatement by merely shortening the period which they cover or by omitting them altogether.

Implications for analysis

The requirement that changes in accounting principles be undertaken only when the change is in the direction of preferable accounting is a significant development. Much depends on the judgment which independent accountants will use in deciding when a change is in the direction of preferable accounting and when it is not. The potential for improvements in financial reporting which *APB Opinion No. 20* holds is undeniably great.

Similarly, the SEC's controversial rule on preferability is a favorable development from the analyst's point of view. To reduce an accountant's propensity for liberal interpretation of this rule the commission stated that it would expect accounting firms to be consistent between clients when making their preferability judgments.

The inclusion of the "catch-up" adjustment, which results from accounting changes, in the determination of the net income of the period in which the change takes place strengthens the need to deemphasize the net income of any one year and to focus instead on the average earnings achieved over a number of years.

The financial analyst, while welcoming improvements in the scope and quality of financial statements as well as in their integrity and reliability, must nevertheless be ever alert to the innumerable possibilities and avenues available for the distortion of reported results.

QUESTIONS

1. Name some key provisions of *APB Opinion No. 8* dealing with the accounting for pension costs.

2. Which are some of the important disclosure requirements of *APB Opinion No. 8?*

3. How is compensation granted by means of stock options measured? Does *APB Opinion No. 25* call for a realistic recognition of the compensation cost inherent in stock options granted?

4. *a.* Discuss the accounting standards that govern Research and Development costs as stipulated by SFAS 2.
   b. What are the disclosure requirements as stipulated by the same statement?

5. What information does the financial analyst need regarding R&D outlays, especially in light of the limited disclosure requirements stipulated by SFAS 2?

6. To what aspects of the valuation and the amortization of goodwill must the analyst be alert?

7. Contrast the computation of total interest costs of a bond issue with warrants attached with that of an issue of convertible debt.

8. How can the financial analyst estimate capitalized interest charges if he suspects that they are undisclosed?

9. What are the requirements that must be met before tax-loss carry-forward benefits can be booked as assets?

10. List four circumstances giving rise to book-tax timing differences.

11. Describe "income tax normalizing." (C.F.A.)

12. Discuss the accounting treatment of income taxes by oil and gas producers as stipulated by SFAS 9.

13. *a.* What are the major SEC disclosure requirements regarding income taxes?
    b. What is their significance to the financial analyst?

14. Name one flaw to which tax allocation procedures are still subject.

15. How has the accounting profession defined an extraordinary item? Give three examples of such items.

16. What conditions are necessary before an item qualifies as a prior period adjustment?

17. In the never-ending debate on the proper treatment of extraordinary items, what should be the financial analyst's main interest?

18. Describe some of the abuses in the area of extraordinary item reporting which are found in practice and which have not been dealt with by recent APB pronouncements on this subject.

19. Why do some companies try to offset items of gains with provisions for present and future losses?

20. Why is it impossible to arrive at an absolutely "precise" measure of periodic net income?

21. What are some of the types of methods by means of which income can be distorted?

22. For each of the items below (1–3), explain:
    a. Two acceptable accounting methods for corporate reporting purposes.
    b. How each of these two acceptable accounting methods will affect the earnings of the current period.
       (1) Depreciation.
       (2) Inventory.
       (3) Installment sales. (C.F.A.)

23. What are the objectives of *APB Opinion No. 20?* It distinguishes among four types of accounting changes. Which are they?

12

EARNINGS PER SHARE—
COMPUTATION AND EVALUATION

The determination of the earnings level of an enterprise which is relevant to the purposes of the analyst is a complex analytical process. This earnings figure can be converted into an earnings per share (EPS) amount which is useful in the evaluation of the price of the common stock, in the evaluation of dividend coverage and dividend paying ability, as well as for other purposes. The analyst must, consequently, have a thorough understanding of the principles which govern the computation of EPS.

The intelligent analyst will never overemphasize the importance of, or place exclusive reliance on, any one figure, be it the widely used and popular EPS figure or any other statistic. In using the EPS figure he should always be alert to the composition of the "net income" figure used in its computation.

In the mid-1960s, when a wave of mergers brought with it the widespread use of convertible securities as financing devices, the attention of analysts and of accountants turned also to the denominator of the EPS computation, that is, the number of shares of common stock by which the earnings should be divided. It became obvious that the prior practice of considering only the common shares actually outstanding without a consideration of the future potential dilution which is inherent in convertible securities, had often led to an overstatement of EPS.

The managements of merger-minded companies had discovered that it was possible to buy the earnings of a company by compensating its owners with low-yield convertible securities which in effect represented a deferred equity interest. Since the acquired earnings were immediately included in the combined income of the merged enterprise while the dilutive effect of the issuance of convertible securities was ignored, an illusory increase in EPS was thus achieved. Such growth in EPS increased the value of the securities, thus enabling the merger-minded company to carry this value enhancing process even further by using its attractive securities to effect business combination at increasingly advantageous terms for its existing stockholders.

ILLUSTRATION 1. Merging Company A, which pays no dividend and whose stock sells at $35, issued to merged Company B, which is earning $3 per share, $1 convertible preferred, on a share-for-share basis which allows for conversion into Company A's common at $40 per share. Because of the dividend advantage there is no prospect of an early conversion of the convertible preferred into common. Thus, prior to *APB Opinion No. 15*, Company A realized "instant earnings" by getting a $3 per share earnings boost in return for a $1 preferred dividend requirement. It is obvious that the $1 convertible preferred derives most of its value from the conversion feature rather than from its meager dividend provision.

MAJOR PROVISIONS OF *APB OPINION NO. 15*

APB Opinion No. 15, issued in 1969, put an end to this unrealistic disregard of the potential dilutive effect of securities convertible into common stock. The *Opinion* looks to the substance of a securities issue rather than merely to its legalistic form.

Simple capital structure

If a corporation has a simple capital structure which consists only of common stock and nonconvertible senior securities and does not include potentially dilutive securities, then most of the provisions of the *Opinion* do not apply. In that case a single presentation of EPS is called for and is computed as follows:

$$\frac{\text{Net Income less claims of senior securities}}{\begin{array}{c}\text{Weighted Average Number of Common Shares Outstanding during}\\\text{the period after adjustments for stock splits and dividends (including}\\\text{those effected after balance sheet date due before completion of}\\\text{financial statements)}\end{array}}$$

In the above computation dividends of cumulative senior securities, whether earned or not, should be deducted from net income or added to net loss.

Computation of weighted average of common shares outstanding

The theoretically correct weighted average number of shares is the sum of shares outstanding each day divided by the number of days in the period. Less precise averaging methods, such as on a monthly or quarterly basis, where there is little change in the number of shares outstanding, is also permissible.

In the computation

1. Reacquired shares should be excluded from date of acquisition.
2. Previously reported EPS data should be adjusted retroactively for changes in outstanding shares resulting from stock splits or stock dividends.

Example of computation or weighted average number of shares outstanding

19X1	Transactions in common stock	Number of shares
January 1	Outstanding	1,200
February 2	Stock options exercised	200
April 15	Issued as 5% stock dividend	70
August 16	Issued in pooling of interests	400
September 2	Sale for cash	300
October 18	Repurchase of treasury shares	(100)
		2,070

Computation of weighted average number of shares

	Shares outstanding		Product: Share—days
	Number	Days	
Date of change:			
January 1	1,200		
Retroactive adjustment:			
For stock dividend (5%)	60		
Issued in pooling	400		
January 1—adjusted	1,660	32	53,120
February 2—stock option 200			
+5% stock dividend 10	210		
	1,870	212	396,440
September 2—sale for cash	300		
	2,170	46	99,820
October 18—repurchase	(100)		
	2,070	75	155,250
		365	704,630

19X1 weighted average number of shares $\dfrac{704,630}{365} = 1,930$ shares

As can be seen in the illustrations above, shares issued in a pooling of interests are included in the computation of EPS as of the beginning of all periods presented. This is so because under the pooling of interests concept the merged companies are assumed to have been combined since their respective inceptions. In the case of purchases the EPS reflect new shares issued only from date of acquisition.

Example of computation

Pooling of interests

Assumptions: On July 1, 19X2 Company A and B merged to form Company C. The transaction was accounted for as a *pooling of interests.*

	Company A	Company B
Net income January 1 to June 30, 19X2	$100,000	$150,000
Outstanding shares of common stock at June 30, 19X2 ...	20,000	8,000
Shares sold to public April 1, 19X2	10,000	

	Company C
Net income July 1 to December 31, 19X2	$325,000
Common shares issued for acquisition of:	
Company A	200,000
Company B	400,000
Computation:	
Net income ($100,000 + $150,000 + $325,000)	575,000

Average shares outstanding during year, using
  equivalent shares for pooled companies:

Company A:		
100,000 × 3 months	300,000	
200,000 × 3 months	600,000	
Company B:		
400,000 × 6	2,400,000	
Company C:		
600,000 × 6	3,600,000	
	6,900,000	
Average	575,000	

Net income per weighted average number of shares of common stock outstanding during the year (equivalent shares used for pooled companies) $1.00

Purchase

Assumptions: Company X has outstanding at December 31, 19X2, 120,000 shares of common stock. During the year (October 1) Company X issued 30,000 shares of its own common stock for another company. This transaction was accounted for as purchase. Net income for 19X2 was $292,500.

Computation:

9 months × 90,000 shares outstanding	810,000
3 months × 120,000 shares outstanding	360,000
	1,170,000

$$\text{Average shares } \frac{1,170,000}{12} = 97,500$$

Net income per weighted average number of shares of common

$$\text{stock outstanding during the year} \frac{\$292,500}{97,500} = \$3.00$$

COMPLEX CAPITAL STRUCTURE

A company is deemed to have a complex capital structure if it has outstanding potentially dilutive securities such as convertible securities, options, warrants, or other stock issue agreements.

By dilution is meant a reduction in EPS (or increase in net loss per share) resulting from the assumption that convertible securities have been converted into common stock, or that options and warrants have been exercised, or that shares have been issued in compliance with certain contracts.

A company having a complex capital structure has to give a dual presentation of EPS if the aggregate dilutive effect of convertible and other securities is more than 3 percent. Such dual presentation is to be effected with equal prominence on the income statement and show: (1) primary EPS and (2) fully diluted EPS.

Primary EPS

Primary EPS is the amount of earnings attributable to each share of common stock outstanding plus dilutive common stock equivalents.

Definition of common stock equivalents (CSE). The concept of CSE is basic to the approach adopted in the *APB Opinion No. 15*. It denotes a security which derives the major portion of its value from its common stock characteristics or conversion privileges. Thus, a CSE is a security which, because of its terms or the circumstances under which it was issued, is in substance equivalent to common stock. The following are examples of CSE.

1. *Convertible debt and convertible preferred stocks* are CSE only if at the time of issuance they have a cash yield (based on market price) of less than 66⅔ percent of the then current bank prime interest rate. If a convertible security is issued which is a CSE and that same security was previously issued when it was not a CSE at time of issuance, the earlier issued shares or debt should be considered a CSE *from the date of issuance of the later shares or*

debt. Prior periods EPS should not be restated. Similarly, any subsequent issuance of shares or debt with the same terms as previously issued shares or debt classified as a CSE should be classified as a CSE at its time of issuance even though the later issue of shares or debt would not be a CSE under the yield test at the later date of issue. This requirement can be overcome by a change in a term having economic significance which is expected to affect prices in the securities market.

2. *Stock options and warrants (including stock purchase contracts)* are always to be considered as CSE.

3. *Participating securities and two-class common stocks* are CSE if their participation features enable their holders to share in the earnings potential of the issuing corporation, on substantially the same basis as common stock, even though the securities may not give the holder the right to exchange his shares for common stock.

4. *Contingent shares*—if shares are to be issued in the future upon the mere passage of time, they should be considered as outstanding for purposes of computing EPS. If additional shares of stock are issuable for little or no consideration upon the satisfaction of certain conditions, they should be considered as outstanding when the conditions are met.

5. *Securities of subsidiaries* may be considered common stock equivalents and conversion or exercise assumed for computing consolidated or parent company EPS when—

   a. *As to the subsidiary*

   (1) Certain of the subsidiaries' securities are CSE in relation to its own common stock.

   (2) Other of the subsidiary's convertible securities, although not CSE in relation to its own common stock, would enter into the computation of its fully diluted earnings per share.

   b. *As to the parent*

   (1) The subsidiary's securities are convertible into the parent company's common stock.

   (2) The subsidiary issues options and warrants to purchase the parent company's common stock.

Computation of primary EPS. If CSE with a dilutive effect are present, then primary EPS should be based on the weighted average number of shares of common stock and CSE. The computation is also based on the assumption that convertible securities which are CSE were converted at the beginning of the period (or at time of issuance, if later), and that requires adding back to net income any deductions for interest or dividends, net of tax effect, related to such securities.

Use of treasury stock method for options, warrants, and other securities requiring "boot" for conversion. The *treasury stock* method recognizes the use of proceeds that would be obtained upon exercise of options and warrants in computing EPS. It assumes that any proceeds would be used to purchase common stock at current market prices. For options and warrants the treasury stock method of computing the dilution to be reflected in EPS should be used (except for two exceptions to be explained). Under the treasury stock method:

1. EPS data are computed as if the options and warrants were exercised at the beginning of the period (or at time of issuance, if later) and as if the funds obtained thereby were used to purchase common stock at the average market price during the period.
2. But the assumption of exercise is not reflected in EPS data until the market price of the common stock obtainable has been in excess of the exercise price for substantially all of three consecutive months ending with the last month of the period to which EPS relate.[1]

Example of treasury stock method
Assumptions:
    1,000,000 common shares outstanding (no change during year)
        $80 average market price for the common stock for the year
        100,000 warrants outstanding exercisable at $48
Computation:
    Shares
    100,000 shares issuable on exercise of warrants (proceeds $4,800,000)
    (60,000) shares acquirable with $4,800,000 proceeds (at $80 per share)
    ―――――――
      40,000 CSE
  1,000,000 common shares
  1,040,000 shares used for computing primary EPS

First exception to treasury stock method. Warrants or debt indentures may permit or require certain uses of funds with exercise of warrants. Examples:

1. Debt is permitted or required to be tendered towards exercise price.
2. Proceeds of exercise are required to retire debt.
3. Convertible securities require cash payments upon conversion.

―――――――

[1] The following formula will yield the number of incremental shares which will result from applying the treasury stock method to options or warrants (Y);

$$Y = \frac{M - E}{M}(N)$$

where M is the market price per share, E is the exercise price of option or warrant per common share and N is the total number of shares obtainable on exercise.

In these cases, an "if converted" method, which assumes conversion on exercise at the beginning of the period should be applied as if retirement or conversion of the securities had occurred and as if the excess proceeds, if any, had been applied to the purchase of common stock under the treasury stock method.

Second exception to treasury stock method. If the number of shares of common stock obtainable upon exercise of outstanding options and warrants in the aggregate exceeds 20 percent of the number of common shares outstanding at the end of the period for which the computation is being made, the treasury stock method should be modified. In these circumstances all the options and warrants should be assumed to have been exercised and the aggregate proceeds therefrom to have been applied in two steps:

1. As if the funds obtained were first applied to the repurchase of outstanding common shares at the average market price during the period (treasury stock method) but not to exceed 20 percent of the outstanding shares; and then
2. As if the balance of the funds were applied first to reduce any short-term or long-term borrowings and any remaining funds were invested in U.S. government securities or commercial paper, with appropriate recognition of any income tax effect.
3. The results of steps 1 and 2 of the computation (whether dilutive or antidilutive) should be aggregated, and if the net effect is dilutive, it should enter into the EPS computation.

Example of second exception of treasury stock method

	Case 1	Case 2
Assumptions:		
Net income for year	$ 4,000,000	$ 3,000,000
Common shares outstanding (no change during		
year)	3,000,000	3,000,000
Options and warrants outstanding to purchase		
equivalent shares............................	1,000,000	1,000,000
20% limitation on assumed repurchase	600,000	600,000
Exercise price per share	$15	$15
Average market value per common share to		
be used.....................................	$20	$14*
Interest rate on borrowings	6%	6%
Computations:		
Application of assumed proceeds ($15 × 1,000,000		
shares) toward repurchase of outstanding common		
shares at applicable market value (600,000 × $20)		
and (600,000 × $14)	$12,000,000	$ 8,400,000
Reduction of debt	3,000,000	6,600,000
	$15,000,000	$15,000,000

Adjustment of net income:

Actual net income	$ 4,000,000	$ 3,000,000
Interest reduction on debt (6%) less 50%		
tax effect......................................	90,000	198,000
Adjusted net income (A)	$ 4,090,000	$ 3,198,000

Adjustment of shares outstanding:

Actual number outstanding	3,000,000	3,000,000
Net additional shares issuable		
(1,000,000–600,000)	400,000	400,000
Adjusted shares outstanding (B)	3,400,000	3,400,000

Primary EPS:

Before adjustment	$1.33	$1.00
After adjustment (A ÷ B)	$1.20	$0.94

* The three consecutive months test has previously been met.

Provisions concerning antidilution.   Antidilution is an increase in EPS resulting from the assumption that convertible securities have been converted or that options and warrants have been exercised or other shares have been issued upon the fulfillment of certain conditions. For example, although stock options and warrants (and their equivalents) and stock purchase contracts should always be considered CSE, they should not enter into EPS calculations until the average market price of the common stock exceeds the exercise price of the option or warrant for preferably three consecutive months before the reporting period.

Computations of primary EPS should not give effect to CSE or other contingent issuance for any period in which their inclusion would have the effect of increasing the EPS amount or decreasing the loss per share amount otherwise computed.

Fully diluted EPS

Definition of fully diluted EPS.   Fully diluted EPS is designed to show the maximum potential dilution of current EPS on a prospective basis. Fully diluted EPS is the amount of current EPS reflecting the maximum dilution that would have resulted from conversions, exercises, and other contingent issuances that individually would have decreased EPS and in the aggregate would have had a dilutive effect. All such issuances are assumed to have taken place at the beginning of the period (or at the time the event or contingency arose, if later).

When required.   Fully diluted EPS data are required for each period presented if shares of common stock (1) were issued during the period on conversions, exercise, etc., or (2) were contingently issuable at the close of any period presented and if primary EPS for such period would have been affected (dilutively or incrementally) had such actual issuances taken place at the beginning of the period or would have been reduced had such contingent issuances taken place at the beginning of the period.

Computation of fully diluted EPS. The computation should be based on the assumption that all such issued and issuable shares were outstanding from the beginning of the period (or from the time the contingency arose, if after the beginning of the period). Interest charges applicable to convertible securities and nondiscretionary adjustments that would have been made to items based on net income or income before taxes—such as profit-sharing expense, certain royalties, and investment credit—or preferred dividends applicable to the convertible securities should be taken into account in determining the balance of income applicable to common stock.

Use ending market price for treasury stock method. The treasury stock method (with the two exceptions) should be used to compute fully diluted EPS if dilution results from outstanding options and warrants; however, in order to reflect maximum potential dilution, the market price at the close of the period reported upon should be used to determine the number of shares which would be assumed to be repurchased (under the treasury stock method) if such market price is higher than the average price used in computing primary EPS.

Example of computation of fully diluted EPS. Assume that there are 1,000,000 shares of Class A preferred stock and 1,500,000 shares of Class B preferred stock outstanding, both issues convertible into common on a share-for-share basis. Two million shares of common are outstanding. Class A preferred is a CSE with a $1.80 dividend; Class B is a nonCSE preferred with a $1 dividend. Net income before either preferred dividend was $7,300,000.

Computation

	Shares	Net income	EPS
Net income		$7,300,000	
Shares outstanding	2,000,000		
$1.80 preferred dividend....................		(1,800,000)	
$1.00 preferred dividend....................		(1,500,000)	
($2 per share)	2,000,000	4,000,000	
Assume conversion of CSE Class A preferred ..	1,000,000	1,800,000	
	3,000,000	5,800,000	
Primary EPS			$1.93
Assume conversion of nonCSE Class B preferred	1,500,000	1,500,000	
	4,500,000	$7,300,000	
Fully diluted EPS (beginning with primary EPS			$1.62

Since the intention in presenting fully diluted EPS is to show the *maximum* dilution possible, an alternative computation is possible in this case which would yield a lower figure of fully diluted EPS. This computation has as a starting point the outstanding common shares and income after preferred dividends rather than the primary EPS.

Computation

	Shares	Net income	EPS
Shares outstanding and income after dividends	2,000,000	$4,000,000	
Assume conversion of nonCSE Class B preferred	1,500,000	1,500,000	
	3,500,000	$5,500,000	
Fully diluted EPS–beginning with outstanding shares and income after preferred dividends			$1.57

The reason why the alternative computation yields a lower fully diluted EPS is that while the $1.80 preferred issue is dilutive for purposes of computing primary EPS, it is antidilutive for purposes of computing the fully diluted EPS.

Provisions regarding antidilution. As with primary EPS, no antidilution should be recognized. Consequently, computations should exclude those securities whose conversion, exercise, or other contingent issuance would have the effect of increasing the EPS amount or decreasing the loss per share amount for each period.

Requirements for additional disclosures in conjunction with the presentation of EPS data

Complex capital structures require additional disclosures either on the balance sheet or in notes. Financial statements should include a description sufficient to explain the pertinent rights and privileges of the various securities outstanding.

With regard to EPS data, disclosure is required for—

1. The bases upon which both primary and fully diluted EPS are calculated, identifying the securities entering into computations.
2. All assumptions and any resulting adjustments used in computations.
3. The number of shares issued upon conversion, exercise, etc. during at least the most recent year.

Supplementary EPS data should be disclosed (preferably in a note) if

1. Conversions during the period would have affected primary EPS (either dilutive *or* incremental effect) if they had taken place at the beginning of the period, or
2. Similar conversions occur after the close of the period but before completion of the financial report.

This supplementary information should show what primary EPS would have been if such conversions had taken place at the *beginning* of the period or date of issuance of security if within the period.

It should be understood that the designation of securities as CSE is done solely for the purpose of determining primary EPS. No changes from present practices in the accounting for such securities or in their presentation within the financial statements are required.

Elections at the time EPS opinion became effective

APB Opinion No. 15 became effective for fiscal periods beginning after December 31, 1968, for *all* EPS data (primary, fully diluted, and supplementary) regardless of when the securities entering into computations of EPS were issued. In addition, an election was available as of May 31, 1969, for all securities whose time of issuance had been prior to June 1, 1969. This election is only for purposes of computing primary EPS. Under this election a computation is made by either:

1. Determining the classifications of all such securities under *APB Opinion No. 15* or,
2. Determining the classification under *APB Opinion No. 9* regardless of how they would be classified under *APB Opinion No. 15*. This election in effect "freezes" securities as previously classified.

This means that in determining EPS for reporting after May 31, 1969, certain securities can be classified as CSE under either the old rules or the new. Regardless of the election made, computations of EPS should be based on the guidelines set forth in *APB Opinion No. 15*.

COMPREHENSIVE ILLUSTRATION OF COMPUTATION OF EPS

The following illustration of the computation of EPS shows the application of many of the provisions included in the foregoing discussion of *APB Opinion No. 15*. To facilitate comprehension the illustration is organized as follows:

Schedules

	Facts and data
I	EPS: Computation
II	EPS: Summary of share computations
A	Weighted average common shares outstanding
B	Share computations—5% subordinated debentures
C	Share computations—5% convertible preferred stock
D	Share computations—warrants
E	Share computations—options
F	Share computations—contingently issuable—purchase

Facts and data

The Multiplex Corporation has the following capital structure, with special factors as noted:

5% subordinated debentures, convertible into common stock at $50 per share:

Issued 4/1/X1	$1,000,000	Not a CSE at
Issued 4/1/X2	1,000,000	time of issue
Issued 8/1/X2 (bank prime rate 8½%)	1,000,000	
Converted 12/1/X2 into 30,000 shares of common	(1,500,000)	
Outstanding 12/31/X2 convertible into 30,000 shares of common	1,500,000	

7% prior preference stock, authorized, issued, and outstanding:

December 31, 19X1 and 19X2	100,000
Annual dividends	$ 700,000

$5 convertible preferred stock, convertible into common stock at $50 (2 shares for 1), authorized 1,000,000 shares, issuable in series:

Series A—issued 2/1/X1 in a pooling of interests	100,000	A CSE since time of issue
Series B—issued 6/1/X2 in a purchase (bank prime rate, 7½%; market value at issuance was $100)	100,000	
Converted 11/1/X2 into 25,000 shares of common— Series A	(12,500)	
Outstanding, 12/31/X2:		
Series A	87,500	
Series B	100,000	
Total (convertible into 375,000 shares of common)	187,500	

Warrants to purchase common stock at $50 per share—issued with Series A preferred:

Total number	100,000
Exercised 12/1/X2	(20,000)
Outstanding 12/31/X2	80,000

Options granted under executives stock option plans at market value on date of grant:

Plan B—granted 3/1/X1 at $30 per share	8,000
Exercised 7/1/X2	(8,000)
Plan C—granted 12/1/X2 at $60 per share, none exercised	5,000

Shares contingently issuable in connection with 6/1/X2 purchase:

If acquired net earnings for the three years 19X2–19X4 are at least equal to certain amounts, a total number of additional shares will then be issued, as shown:

$1,500,000	10,000 shares
2,250,000	20,000
3,000,000	40,000

Net earnings of the purchased company for 19X2 were $520,000.

Other relevant hypothetical facts about the hypothetical corporation are as follows:

1. On April 1, 19X2 the corporation completed a public offering of 200,000 common shares.
2. On October 1, 19X2 the corporation purchased 60,000 common shares for its treasury.
3. Market prices of the company's common stock during 19X2 were:

	First	Average	Quarterly	19X2 average
January	40	34		
February	30	30	32	
March	30	32		
April	35	35		
May	40	43	42	
June	45	48		
July	50	47		
August	40	38	43	
September	35	44		
October	55	51		
November	50	54	55	
December	60	60		43

The closing market price on December 31 was 65.

4. For the year 19X2, the corporation's earnings, in condensed form, were:

Income before extraordinary items	$5,000,000
Extraordinary credits, net of taxes	1,000,000
Net income	$6,000,000

5. Included in the above is pretax interest on the subordinated debentures, as follows:

January 1–March 31	$12,500
April 1–July 31	33,333
August 1–December 1	50,000
December 1–December 31	6,250

6. Not included are total preferred dividends (paid quarterly, March 1, June 1, September 1, and December 1) as follows:

7% prior preference stock	$700,000
Series A	484,375
Series B	250,000

SCHEDULE I
EPS: Computations

	Income before extra-ordinary item	Extra-ordinary item	Net income
Amounts before adjustment	$5,000,000	$1,000,000	$6,000,000
Less: Dividend on 7% prior preference stock	(700,000)		(700,000)
Amounts after preferred dividends	$4,300,000	$1,000,000	$5,300,000
Adjustments for computing primary EPS:			
Interest on 5% convertible subordinated debentures, net of tax effect (assumed 50% rate)	28,125		28,125
Income for primary EPS	$4,328,125	$1,000,000	$5,328,125
Adjustments for computing fully diluted EPS:			
Interest on 5% convertible subordinated debentures, net of tax effect (assumed 50% rate)	$ 22,916		$ 22,916
Income for fully diluted EPS	$4,351,041	$1,000,000	$5,351,041
Adjustments for computing supplementary EPS:			
Income for primary EPS, as above	$4,328,125	$1,000,000	$5,328,125
Add: Additional interest on 5% convertible subordinated debentures (net of assumed 50% tax effect)	18,750		18,750
Income for supplementary EPS	$4,346,875	$1,000,000	$5,346,875

Note: Interest is eliminated (*a*) for primary EPS, for period after 8/1/X2 (date on which entire issue became a CSE), and (*b*) for fully diluted EPS, for all earlier months. For supplementary EPS, interest eliminated for primary EPS is increased to reflect the assumption that the actual conversion of debentures took place as of the beginning of the year (or date of issuance).

Weighted average common and common equivalent shares (from Schedule II)	1,490,900	1,490,900	1,490,900
Related income, as above	$4,328,125	$1,000,000	$5,328,125
Earnings per common share and common equivalent share	$2.90	$.67	$3.57
Weighted average shares adjusted for full dilution (from Schedule II)	1,529,649	1,529,649	1,529,649
Related income, as above	$4,351,041	$1,000,000	$5,351,041
Earnings per common share, assuming full dilution	$2.84	$.66	$3.50

Note: Dilution is less than 3%, and could therefore be considered immaterial.

Supplementary data:

Weighted average common and common equivalent shares adjusted to give pro forma effect to actual conversions as though made at the beginning of the year (from Schedule II)	1,505,900	1,505,900	1,505,900
Related income, as above	$4,346,875	$1,000,000	$5,346,875
Supplementary earnings per common and common equivalent share, giving pro forma effect to conversions	$2.89	$.66	$3.55

Note: Effect on primary EPS is clearly immaterial, and disclosure would probably be confined to noting that that is the case.

SCHEDULE II
EPS: Summary of share computations

	Shares
Weighted average common shares outstanding (Schedule A)..	1,147,333
Weighted average CSE:	
5% subordinated debentures (Schedule B)	22,500
$5 convertible preferred (Schedule C)	312,500
Warrants (Schedule D)	1,977
Options (Schedule E)	757
Contingently issuable—purchase (Schedule F)	5,833
Weighted average common and common equivalent shares	1,490,900 *(To Sch. I)*
(Used to compute primary EPS)	
Adjustments for full dilution:	
5% subordinated debentures (Schedule B)	18,333
$5 convertible preferred (Schedule C)	—
Warrants (Schedule D)	19,541
Options (Schedule E)	875
Contingently issuable—purchase (Schedule F)	—
	38,749
Weighted average shares adjusted for full dilution	1,529,649 *(To Sch. I)*
(Used to compute fully diluted EPS)	
Weighted average common and common equivalent shares, as above..	1,490,900
Adjustment for supplementary purposes:	
5% subordinated debentures (Schedule B)	15,000
Weighted average shares giving pro forma effect to conversions of debentures as though made at begining of year (or date of issue)	1,505,900 *(To Sch. I)*
(Used to compute supplementary EPS)	

SCHEDULE A
Weighted average common shares outstanding

Number of shares

Date	Source	Increase (decrease)	Total	Months	Weighted product
Jan. 1	Balance		1,000,000	3	3,000,000
Apr. 1	Public offering	200,000	1,200,000	3	3,600,000
July 1	Stock options exercised	8,000	1,208,000	3	3,624,000
Oct. 1	Treasury stock	(60,000)	1,148,000	1	1,148,000
Nov. 1	Conversion—Series A preferred	25,000	1,173,000	1	1,173,000
Dec. 1	Conversion—debentures	30,000 ⎫	1,223,000	1	1,223,000
	Exercise of warrants	20,000 ⎭			
				12	13,768,000
Weighted average common shares outstanding					1,147,333

SCHEDULE B
5% subordinated debentures

	Total shares	Weight	Weighted average shares
CSE for primary EPS:			
Equivalent shares—issue of 4/1/X1	20,000	5/12	
Equivalent shares—issue of 4/1/X2	20,000	5/12	25,000
Equivalent shares—issue of 8/1/X2	20,000	5/12	
Less: Shares issued on conversion 12/1/X2 and included in shares outstanding	(30,000)	1/12	(2,500)
Weighted CSE—debentures— primary EPS			22,500

Note: Issue of 8/1/X2 was a CSE at time of issuance because cash yield was less than two thirds of the bank prime rate. Accordingly, earlier issues of this security with same terms acquired CSE status at that time.

	Total shares	Weight	Weighted average shares
Fully diluted EPS:			
Equivalent shares—issue of 4/1/X1	20,000	12/12	20,000
Equivalent shares—issue of 4/1/X2	20,000	9/12	15,000
Equivalent shares—issue of 8/1/X2	20,000	5/12	8,333
			43,333
Less: Shares issued on conversion 12/1/X2 and included in shares outstanding (as above)			(2,500)
Share equivalents included in CSE above			(22,500)
Net additional shares—debentures— fully diluted EPS			18,333

Note: For fully diluted EPS, convertibility before acquiring CSE status relates to entire period during which issues were outstanding.

	Total shares	Weight	Weighted average shares
Supplementary EPS:			
Equivalent shares—actual conversions as though made at beginning of year (or date of later issuance):			
Issue of 4/1/X1 (entire)	20,000	12/12	20,000
Issue of 4/1/X2 (part)	10,000	9/12	7,500
Equivalent shares—not converted:			
Issue of 4/1/X2 (remainder)	10,000	5/12	4,167
Issue of 8/1/X2	20,000	5/12	8,333
			40,000
Less: Shares and CSE reflected in primary EPS (as above)			(25,000)
Net additional shares—debentures— supplementary EPS			15,000

SCHEDULE C
$5 convertible preferred stock

	Total shares	Weight	Weighted average shares
CSE for primary EPS:			
Series A—equivalent shares	200,000	12/12	200,000
Less: Shares issued on conversion 11/1/X2 and included in shares outstanding	(25,000)	2/12	(4,167)
			195,833
Series B—equivalent shares—issue of 6/1/X2	200,000	7/12	116,667
Weighted CSE—preferred—primary EPS			312,500

Note: The cash yield of Series B at time of issuance was *not* less than two thirds the prime rate. This security, which thus would not have been a CSE, assumes that status because Series A—an outstanding security with the same terms—was a CSE. (Because the issuance involved a *purchase*, Series B is a CSE only from 6/1/X2.)

Fully diluted EPS:
   No additional effect: convertible preferred was a CSE during entire period outstanding.

Supplementary EPS:
   Had the conversion of Series A taken place at the beginning of the year, primary EPS would not have been affected, because the issue was a CSE during the entire period. Accordingly, this conversion does not call for supplementary EPS disclosure.

SCHEDULE D
Warrants

	Total shares	Weight	Weighted average shares
CSE for primary EPS:			
As to warrants exercised Dec. 1:			
Number of shares.................	20,000		
Exercise price—proceeds $1,000,000			
Average market price, 4th quarter, prior to exercise $52.50			
Treasury stock shares	(19,048)		
Net shares added in respect of period before exercise	952	2/12*	159
As to warrants outstanding Dec. 31:			
Number of shares.................	80,000		
Exercise price—proceeds $4,000,000			
Average market price, 4th quarter........................ $55			
Treasury stock shares	(72,727)		
Net shares added in respect of outstanding	7,273	3/12	1,818
Weighted CSE—warrants— primary EPS			1,977

*Note:*Average quarterly market prices were *anti*dilutive during the 1st, 2d, and 3d quarters, and *dilutive* during the 4th quarter. Accordingly the first three quarters are ignored in the computation, which is based on the average market price during the 4th quarter. For warrants exercised, the average price used is that for the portion of the 4th quarter prior to exercise.

	Total shares	Weight	Weighted average shares
Fully diluted EPS:			
As to warrants exercised Dec. 1:			
Number of shares.................	20,000		
Exercise price—proceeds $1,000,000			
Market price at date of exercise $60			
Treasury stock shares	(16,667)		
Shares added in respect of period before exercise	3,333	11/12*	3,056
As to warrants outstanding Dec. 31:			
Number of shares.................	80,000		
Exercise price—proceeds $4,000,000			
Market price at December 31 ..... $65			
Treasury stock shares	(61,538)		
Shares added in respect of outstanding	18,462	12/12	18,462
Total shares added			21,518
Less: CSE added (as above)			(1,977)
Weighted average additional shares—warrants, for fully diluted EPS			19,541

Note: For fully diluted EPS, market prices at *date of exercise* and *year-end* as appropriate, are used rather than *averages.*

* The exercised warrants enter the computation of primary EPS only for the two months preceding their exercise because only during this period was the average market price of the common stock above the exercise price. For fully diluted EPS the end of period coincides with date of exercise on which date the market price was $60 per common share.

SCHEDULE E
Options

	Total shares	Weight	Weighted average shares
CSE for primary EPS:			
Plan B: Shares optioned at beginning of year	8,000		
Exercise price—proceeds $240,000			
Average market price during the 6-month period before exercise $37			
Treasury stock shares	(6,486)		
Shares added (to date of exercise)	1,514	6/12	757
Plan C: Shares optioned December 1	5,000		
Exercise price $60			
Average market price, December $60			
No effect			
Weighted CSE—options— primary EPS			757
Fully diluted EPS:			
Plan B: Prior to exercise	8,000		
Exercise price—proceeds $240,000			
Market price at date of exercise $50			
Treasury stock shares	(4,800)		
Shares added to date of exercise	3,200	6/12	1,600
Less: CSE added (as above)			(757)
Net shares added—Plan B			843
Plan C:	5,000		
Exercise price—proceeds $300,000			
Market price at December 31 ...... $65			
Treasury stock shares	(4,615)		
Shares added—Plan C	385	1/12	32
Weighted average shares— options—fully diluted EPS			875

Note: For fully diluted EPS, market prices at *date of exercise* and *year-end*, as appropriate, are used rather than *averages*.

SCHEDULE F
Contingently issuable—purchase

	Total shares	Weight	Weighted average shares
CSE for primary EPS:			

CSE for primary EPS:
   If total earnings for 19X2–X4 of the acquired company are $1,500,000, an additional 10,000 shares will be issued. This is equivalent to annual earnings of $500,000 for each of these three years; since this level has been attained, the entire 10,000 shares are regarded *as though issued*, for primary EPS:

	Total shares	Weight	Weighted average shares
Shares (weighted from date of purchase	10,000	$^{7}/_{12}$	5,833

Fully diluted EPS:
   Both of the other earnings levels (i.e., $750,000 and $1,000,000 average annual) specified as a basis for additional share issuances are above that currently attained. In no case would these enter primary EPS; they would, however, enter fully diluted EPS *if dilutive*. Neither of the increased-earnings contingencies is dilutive, and therefore neither enters the computation of fully diluted EPS. (The fact that neither is dilutive is readily seen by reference to the *incremental* factors: the *increment* of $250,000 in earnings will result in an *increment* of 10,000 shares—representing $25 per *incremental* share; *incremental* earnings of $500,000 will result in an *increment* of 30,000 shares—representing $16.67 per *incremental* share.)

IMPLICATIONS FOR ANALYSIS

APB Opinion No. 15 has been criticized, particularly by accountants, because it covers areas outside the realm of accountancy, relies on pro forma presentations which are influenced in large measure by market fluctuations, and because it deals with areas properly belonging to financial analysis.

Whatever the merit of these criticisms, and they do have merit, the financial analyst must welcome this initiative by the accounting profession. It does provide specific and workable guidelines for a meaningful recognition of the dilutive effects, present and prospective, of securities which are the equivalents of common stock. The elements entering the consistent computation of primary EPS and fully diluted EPS are so many and varied and require so many internal data that it is best that the accounting profession has assumed the responsibility for their computation rather than choosing the alternative of disclosing the information and leaving it to outsiders to make their own computations. The financial analyst must, however, have a thorough understanding of the bases on which EPS are computed.

APB Opinion No. 15 has a number of flaws and inconsistencies which the analyst must consider in his interpretations of EPS data:

1.   There is a basic inconsistency in treating certain securities as the equivalent of common stock for purposes of computing EPS while not considering them 'as part of the stockholders equity in the

balance sheet. Consequently the analyst will have difficulty in interrelating reported EPS with the debt-leverage position pertaining to the same earnings.

2. There are a number of arbitrary benchmarks in the Opinion, such as the 20 percent treasury stock repurchase assumption limitation and the 66⅔ percent of prime rate test. The latter is particularly vulnerable to criticism because it does not differentiate among the types of securities issued, their credit standing, or between short-term and long-term interest rates. The prime rate is basically a short-term rate, whereas an interest rate placed on convertibles is mostly a long-term rate.[2] Normally short-term rates are lower than long-term rates. The effect of this is that many low coupon convertibles can be issued which would nevertheless not qualify as CSE under the Opinion.

3. Generally EPS are considered to be a factor influencing stock prices. The Opinion considers options and warrants to be CSE at all times, and whether they are dilutive or not depends on the price of the common stock. Thus, we can get a circular effect in that the reporting of EPS may influence the market price, which, in turn, influences EPS. Also, under these rules earnings may depend on market prices of the stock rather than only on economic factors within the enterprise.

Under these rules the projection of future EPS requires not only the projection of earnings levels but also the projection of future market prices.

4. Since the determination of whether a security is a CSE or not is made only at the time of issuance, it is quite possible that a security which was not originally a CSE is later so recognized in the marketplace. Nevertheless, the status of the security in the computation of EPS cannot be changed to recognize the new reality.

Despite these limitations, primary EPS and fully diluted EPS computed under the provisions of APB *Opinion No. 15* are more valid measurements of EPS than those which were obtained under the rules which were previously in effect.

Statement accounting for changes in earnings per share

When analyzing or projecting EPS the analyst can focus on changes in income on a per share basis. Table 12–1 presents an analysis of the changes in the EPS of a large chemical company for 19X4.

---

[2] When *APB Opinion 15* was issued short- and long-term rates were unusually close to each other. Since then the spread between them has widened thus making comparisons with the prime rate less meaningful.

TABLE 12–1
Analysis of changes in earnings per share

		Earnings per share	
Year 19X3 earnings			$2.77
Additional earnings resulting from:			
Higher sales volume		$1.20	
Manufacturing cost savings		0.37	
Lower raw material prices		0.06	
		$1.63	
Reductions in earnings caused by:			
Lower selling prices	$0.25		
Higher selling, administrative research, development, and other expenses	0.49	0.74	
Increase in operating results			0.89
			$3.66
Nonoperating items:			
Lower income taxes, due primarily to difference in tax rate		$0.12	
Higher investment tax credit on property additions		0.12	
Other income and charges–net		0.03	
Unusual write-offs:			
Obsolescence	$(.06)		
Self-insurance reserve	(.07)		
Other	.03	(.10)	
Effect on earnings of shares issued during the year		(.11)	0.06
Year 19X4 earnings			$3.72
Increase in EPS			$0.95

This published analysis is noteworthy particularly because it contains details such as those pertaining to changes due to sales volume and selling prices, which are normally available only to those with access to internal management records. This information, whenever available, can be of great help to the analyst in the evaluation and prediction of earnings and EPS.

QUESTIONS

1. Why is a thorough understanding of the principles governing the computation of EPS important to the financial analyst?
2. What developments caused the accounting profession to issue an Opinion on the computation of EPS?
3. Discuss uses of EPS and reasons or objectives of the method of reporting EPS under *APB Opinion No. 15*.
4. What is the purpose in presenting fully diluted EPS?

5. How do cumulative dividends on preferred stock affect the computation EPS for a company with a loss?

6. What is the two-class method and when is it used?

7. At the end of the year a company has a simple capital structure consisting only of common stock, as all its preferred stock was converted into common shares during the year. Is a computation of fully diluted EPS required?

8. If a warrant is not exercisable until seven years after the end of the period presented, should it be excluded from the computation of fully diluted EPS?

9. Under *APB Opinion No. 15* how should dividends per share be presented?

10. How does the payment of dividends on preferred stock affect the computation of EPS?

11. When and why would the following securities be considered CSE:
    a. Convertible debentures?
    b. Shares issuable in the future upon satisfaction of certain conditions?

12. EPS can affect market prices. Can market prices affect EPS?

13. Can CSE enter into the determination of EPS in one period and not in another?

14. What is meant by the term *antidilution?* Give an example of this condition.

15. How do we include stock options and warrants as CSE? What is the treasury stock method?

16. Is the treasury stock method always used? Which are the exceptions?

17. What are supplementary EPS? How are they disclosed?

18. *APB Opinion No. 15* has a number of flaws and inconsistencies which the analyst must consider in his interpretation of EPS data. Discuss these.

19. In estimating the value of common stock, the amount of EPS is considered to be a very important element in the determination of such value.
    a. Explain why EPS are important in the valuation of common stock.
    b. Are EPS equally important in valuing a preferred stock? Why or why not? (C.F.A.)

13

STATEMENTS OF CHANGES IN FINANCIAL POSITION—FUNDS AND CASH

SIGNIFICANCE AND PURPOSE

The cash and working capital resources of a business entity represent important indicators of financial health. The ability of an enterprise to meet its obligations as they become due and its ability to expand and grow depend on adequate levels of liquid funds. The statements of changes in financial position provide information regarding the sources and uses of working capital or cash over a period of time as well as information about major financing and investment activities which do not involve sources and uses of working capital or cash.

While fragmentary information on sources and uses of funds can be obtained from comparative balance sheets and from the income statements, a comprehensive picture of this important area of activity can be gained only from a statement of changes in financial position. This fact accounts for the growing importance and use of such statements which can provide information on such questions as:

1. What utilization was made of funds provided by operations?
2. What was the source of funds invested in new plant and equipment?
3. What use was made of funds derived from a new bond issue or the sale of common stock?
4. How was it possible to continue payment of the regular dividend in the face of an operating loss?

5. How was the debt repayment achieved or what was the source of the funds used to redeem the preferred stock?
6. How was the increase in working capital financed?
7. Why, despite record profits, is the working capital position lower than last year?

TWO MAJOR CONCEPTS OF LIQUIDITY

There are a number of recognized indicators of liquidity, but the two most common are working capital and cash (including cash equivalents such as marketable securities). In the present context, the term "funds" is equivalent to "working capital," and these two terms are used interchangeably in practice. The statement of sources and applications of working capital (funds) explains the change in the level of working capital between two dates by listing the factors which contributed to its increase and those which brought about its decrease. Similarly, the statement of sources and applications of cash explains the reasons for increases and decreases of this asset over a given period of time.

STATEMENT OF CHANGES IN FINANCIAL POSITION— A BROADER CONCEPT

Recognizing that the statement of sources and applications of working capital or of cash can omit important financing and investing transactions which do not involve either working capital or cash, *APB Opinion No. 19* called for a broadening of both statements to include such transactions and recommended that it be referred to as a "statement of changes in financial position."

In general, the statement of changes in financial position focuses on changes in working capital or, less frequently, on changes in cash. In addition, either statement includes major financing and investing transactions which do not involve funds or cash such as the following:

1. Issuance of securities to acquire property or other long-term assets.
2. Conversion of long-term debt or preferred stock into common stock.

The intelligent analysis and use of any financial statement requires a thorough understanding of the principles and methods which underlie its preparation. We shall examine below the principles underlying the preparation of the statement of source and application of funds. The principles governing the preparation of the statement of sources and applications of cash will be examined later in this chapter.

Basis of preparation

In order to focus on changes in working capital, let us visualize two highly condensed balance sheets which are divided into sections disclosing (1) current (or working capital) items and (2) all the other (noncurrent) accounts:

	End of Year 1	End of Year 2
Current Items:		
Current assets	$12,000	$16,000
Current liabilities	8,000	10,000
Total Current Items (Net Working Capital)	$ 4,000	$ 6,000
Noncurrent Items:		
Noncurrent assets	$ (6,000)	$ (8,000)
Long-term liabilities	3,000	5,000
Equity (capital) accounts	7,000	9,000
Total Noncurrent Items	$ 4,000	$ 6,000

While the above is certainly not a conventional form of balance sheet presentation, it provides a very useful framework for understanding the interaction between changes in the current (i.e., working capital) section and changes in the noncurrent section. Thus, we can readily observe that the change in working capital from Year-end 1 to Year-end 2 ($2,000) is matched exactly, both in amount and direction, by the change in the net noncurrent items between these two year-ends ($2,000). This is, of course, true because assets always equal liabilities plus capital and, consequently, a change in one sector of the balance sheet must be matched by an equal change in the remaining accounts.

The above-described relationship between the current and noncurrent sectors of the balance sheet provides a useful means for understanding the basis underlying the preparation of the statement of sources and applications of working capital. Visualizing the two sections of the balance sheet as follows,

CURRENT SECTION	Current assets	Current liabilities
NONCURRENT SECTION	Fixed assets Other assets	Long-term liabilities Deferred credits Equity accounts

the following generalizations may be made:

1. Net changes in the current section can be explained in terms of changes in the accounts of the noncurrent section. These are the *only* changes with which the conventional statement of sources and applications of working capital is concerned.
2. Internal changes *within* the current section are not relevant here because the statement indicates the *net* change in working capital without regard to individual changes in the composition of the working capital accounts. Thus, for example, the purchase of inventory for cash or the payment of a current liability, while affecting the composition of the working capital, leaves no effect on its net amount. *APB Opinion No. 19* requires, however, a separate statement explaining the changes in working capital components.
3. Similarly, internal changes *within* the noncurrent section have no effect on working capital. However, changes caused by transactions such as the conversion of debt into equity or the acquisition of fixed assets with long-term debt are significant financial transactions and consequently the statement of changes in financial position would include these.

The best way for us to start the discussion of how the statement of changes in financial position is prepared is to examine a very simple illustration of the principles involved. The following is a pair of simplified and condensed comparative balance sheets as at two consecutive year-ends.

Condensed Balance Sheets
(000 omitted)

| | | December 31 | | Changes during 19X2 | |
		19X1	19X2	Use of funds	Source of funds
1.	Working capital	$320	$ 290		$ 30
2.	Fixed assets	660	874	214	44
3.	Accumulated depreciation	(200)	(244)		
4.	Intangible assets	150	100		50
	Total Assets	$930	$1,020		
5.	Long-term debt	$420	$ 400	20	
6.	Capital stock and paid-in-capital	250	300		50
7.	Retained earnings	260	320		60
	Total Equities	$930	$1,020		
	Total			$234	$234

The extension columns showing the year-end to year-end changes in account balances do not represent a comprehensive statement of sources and applications of funds because they can hide a considerable amount of significant detail. The following analysis of each change will make this clear:

1. The $30,000 change in working capital should be viewed as the difference to be explained because it is the change in funds (i.e., working capital) on which the statement focuses.
2. The $214,000 increase in fixed assets is composed in this case of two elements: purchases of fixed assets of $314,000 and sale of fixed assets with a net book value of $80,000 (cost of $100,000 less accumulated depreciation of $20,000).
3. The net increase in accumulated depreciation of $44,000 is after a charge to that account of $20,000 for accumulated depreciation on the assets sold (see 2 above). Thus the total addition to the accumulated depreciation account (with a contra charge to depreciation expense) was $64,000.
4. In the absence of further data, the decline of $50,000 in the intangible assets can represent a sale of an intangible or the amortization of the intangible by a charge to income. Let us assume here that the latter is true.
5. The net reduction of $20,000 in the long-term debt represents a repayment of $10,000 and the conversion of another $10,000 into common stock which while not affecting working capital is a significant transaction.
6. The increase in the capital stock and paid-in capital accounts is due to the sale of stock of $40,000 and the conversion of debt of $10,000.
7. The change in the retained earnings balance almost always requires further data for proper analysis. The data provided here are as follows:

Balance of retained earnings, 1/1/X2	$260,000
Net income for 19X2	180,000
	$440,000
Less cash dividends paid	120,000
Balance of retained earnings, 12/31/X2	$320,000

From the above it is clear that the cash dividend represented a use of funds of $120,000 and that the net income of $180,000 provides the basis for computing the sources of funds from operations. The reason why the $180,000 cannot be taken to be a source of funds arising from operations is that the income statement includes items of income and expense which do not provide or use funds (working capital items).

The net income figure must be adjusted for such items. Let us now see how this is done.

Arriving at "sources of funds from operations"

Normally, a detailed income statement is provided. In the present example the income statement is as follows:

Sales		$900,000
Cost of Sales:		
Labor	$200,000	
Material	120,000	
Depreciation	64,000	
Other overhead	76,000	460,000
Gross margin		$440,000
Selling, general, and administrative expenses (including $50,000 of intangible amortization)		85,000
Income before taxes		$355,000
Income taxes–current		175,000
Net income		$180,000

An examination of this income statement reveals that the individual items have the following usual (normal) effect on other balance sheet items:

	Items affected	
	Working capital	**Other**
Sales	Cash, accounts receivable	
Labor	Cash, accounts payable	
Material	Cash, accounts payable and inventories	
Depreciation		Fixed assets
Other overhead	Cash, accounts payable and prepaid expenses	
Selling, general, and administrative expenses	Cash, accounts payable and prepaid expenses	
Amortization of intangibles		Intangible assets
Income taxes (current)	Cash, accounts payable	

We see, thus, that in this example depreciation and amortization of intangibles are expenses which, unlike all others, do not require an outlay of current funds. In other words, they "feed" on the noncurrent section of the balance sheet and, since the income statement is included in the Retained Earnings account of the balance sheet, they are internal to the noncurrent section of the balance sheet and are of no concern in the preparation of the statement of sources and applications of funds.

The required adjustment in our case is to start with the net income of $180,000 and add back charges which did not require funds.

Net income		$180,000
Depreciation	$64,000	
Amortizatin of intangibles	50,000	114,000
Funds provided by operations		$294,000

It is obvious that this figure of $294,000 could also have been obtained by reconstructing the income statement so as to include only those items which either provide or require funds (working capital).

The reason the net-income-adjustment method is almost always used in practice to arrive at the "funds provided by operations" figure is that it makes unnecessary the reciting of all the above detail which is to be found in the income statement anyway. Thus, the point to understand here is that the "net income" figure is a convenient starting point for arriving at the adjusted "funds provided by operations" figure. Moreover, doing it this way provides a verifiable and reassuring link to the income statement.

In addition to depreciation and amortization of intangibles the following are further examples of items which may appear in the income statement and which have no effect on funds (working capital).

Income statement item	*Drawn from the following noncurrent balance sheet item*
Amortization of bond premium	Deferred bond premium
Amortization of bond discount	Deferred bond discount
Warranty expenses	Provision for warranty costs
Deferred income tax expense	Deferred taxes
Amortization of leasehold improvements	Leasehold improvements
Subscription income	Deferred subscription income (noncurrent portion)
Equity in earnings of a subsidiary or investee	Investment account

The statement of changes in financial position

Returning to our example, we may now construct a statement of changes in financial position (top of page 361) which is more detailed and more comprehensive than if based solely on the changes which we could have developed from the comparative balance sheets above.

Illustration of "T-account" technique

The simple illustration above indicated some of the more common problems involved in the preparation of the statement of sources and

Sources of funds:
Funds provided by operations:

Net income		$180,000	
Add back–charges not requiring funds in the current period:			
Depreciation	$64,000		
Amortization of intangibles	50,000	114,000	$294,000
Sale of fixed assets			80,000
Capital stock issued in conversion of debt....			10,000
Sale of capital stock			40,000
Decrease in working capital			30,000
Total			$454,000

Use of funds:

Purchases of fixed assets	$314,000
Payment of dividends	120,000
Repayment of long-term debt	10,000
Debt converted into capital stock	10,000
Total	$454,000

applications of funds. These, and others found in more complex examples, are:

1. The analysis of net changes based on further detail provided.
2. The reversal or elimination of transactions internal to the noncurrent accounts.
3. Regrouping and reconstruction of transactions in the noncurrent group which affect, and hence explain, the changes in the working capital sector.

The methods used to implement these adjustments vary from elaborate multicolumn work sheets to highly summarized adjustments which are performed mentally. One of the most direct and most flexible method utilizes the reconstruction of summarized "T-accounts." This method, developed by Professor W. J. Vatter, will be illustrated here.

The basic objective of the T-account method is to reconstruct in summary fashion by means of T-accounts for the noncurrent accounts all the transactions which went through them during the period reported upon. If the reconstructed transaction reveals that it was a source or a use of funds, it is posted to a special Sources and Uses of Funds Summary account. If the transaction has no effect on funds, it is reversed among the applicable noncurrent T-accounts. The following is a summary of the steps involved in this method:

1. A T-account is set up for each noncurrent account appearing in the change column of the comparative balance sheet. The change in each item is posted to the T-account as it appears in the change column, and underlined thus:

Fixed Assets

Change	170	

2. Two additional T-accounts are established.
   a. Operations Summary
   b. Sources and Uses of Funds Summary
3. Based on information supplied and inferences drawn from the changes in the noncurrent account, the balance in the T-account is reconstructed by
   a. Debiting or crediting all income and expense items to the Operations Summary.
   b. Debiting or crediting all other items affecting working capital (funds) to the Sources and Uses of Funds Summary.
4. Finally the Operations Summary is closed out to the Sources and Uses of Funds Summary so that the latter is the only one left after the others have been balanced out.
5. The Sources and Uses of Funds Summary will contain the detail necessary to the preparation of a statement of Sources and Applications of Funds.

ILLUSTRATION 1.   The following are the comparative balance sheets of the Wilson Company, as at December 31, 19X1 and 19X2 and the changes during 19X2.

THE WILSON COMPANY
Comparative Balance Sheet
As of December 31

Assets	19X1	19X2	Increase (decrease)
Current Assets:			
Cash	$ 240,000	$ 120,000	$ (120,000)
Receivables	360,000	450,000	90,000
Inventories	750,000	1,053,000	303,000
Total Current Assets	$ 1,350,000	$ 1,623,000	$ 273,000
Fixed assets	$ 4,500,000	$ 6,438,000	$1,938,000
Accumulated depreciation	(1,500,000)	(1,740,000)	(240,000)
Goodwill	1,950,000	1,980,000	30,000
Total Assets	$ 6,300,000	$ 8,301,000	$2,001,000
Liabilities and Capital			
Accounts payable	$ 360,000	$ 540,000	$ 180,000
Bonds payable	300,000	700,000	400,000
Deferred income taxes	240,000	260,000	20,000
Capital stock	2,400,000	3,200,000	800,000
Paid-in capital	900,000	1,300,000	400,000
Retained earnings	2,100,000	2,301,000	201,000
Total Liabilities and Capital ...	$ 6,300,000	$ 8,301,000	$2,001,000

The following additional information is available:

1. On May 1, 19X2, the company bought the assets of another business—$300,000 worth of equipment and $150,000 worth of inventory and accounts receivable. The amount paid was $510,000, the excess of $60,000 being considered as the cost of goodwill acquired. Of the $510,000 paid, $310,000 was in cash and $200,000 by issuing long-term bonds.
2. Old machinery was sold for $18,000; it originally cost $36,000, and $20,000 of depreciation had been accumulated to date of sale.
3. On February 1, 19X2, The Wilson Company received $1,000,000 in cash for a new issue of capital stock which had a par value of $600,000. $200,000 of convertible bonds were converted into capital stock, par value $200,000. Long-term bonds were also sold for $400,000 (at par).
4. The Wilson Company had a net income of $951,000, after deductions of $260,000 for depreciation, $30,000 for amortization of goodwill, and $20,000 in deferred income taxes. Dividends paid amounted to $750,000.

Based on the above financial statements and the additional data, we are to prepare a statement of sources and applications of funds by means of the T-account method.

The first step is to set up T-accounts for:

1. All noncurrent accounts in order to reconstruct the transactions affecting working capital (funds).
2. The Operations Summary where the sources and uses of funds from operations are summarized.
3. The Sources and Uses of Funds Summary which will equal the change in working capital and which summarizes all sources and uses of funds.

T-Accounts
(in thousand of dollars)

Fixed Assets

Change	1,938		
(c)	1,974	(a)	36

Accumulated Depreciation

		Change	240
(a)	20	(d)	260

Goodwill

Change	30		
(e)	60	(f)	30

Bonds Payable

		Change	400
(h)	200	(b)	200
		(g)	400

Deferred Income Taxes

	Change	20
	(j)	20

Capital Stock

	Change	800
	(i)	200
	(k)	600

Paid-In Capital

	Change	400
	(k)	400

Retained Earnings

		Change	201
(m)	750	(l)	951

Sources and Uses of Funds Summary

Sources		Uses	
Change	93		
(a) Sale of fixed assets	18	(c) Purchase of fixed assets	1,974
(b) Exchange of long-term bonds		(e) Purchase of Goodwill	60
bonds for fixed assets	200	(h) Conversion of bond into	
(g) Sale of bonds	400	capital stock	200
(i) Conversion of bond into		(m) Payment of dividend	750
capital stock	200		2,984
(k) Sale of capital stock	1,000	Increase in working capital	93
	1,818		3,077
Funds provided by operations	1,259		
	3,077		

Operations Summary

(d) Depreciation	260	(a) Gain on sale of fixed assets	2
(f) Goodwill amortization	30	Transfer to sources and uses of	
(j) Deferred income taxes	20	funds summary	1,259
(l) Net income	951		1,261
	1,261		

The following are the entries which record the changes.

Fixed assets

We know that equipment costing $36,000 and having accumulated depreciation of $20,000 was sold for $18,000. Entry (a) reconstructs the transactions in summary fashion.

(a)

Sources and Uses of Funds	18,000	
Accumulated Depreciation	20,000	
Fixed Assets		36,000
Operations Summary		2,000

Since the net change in the Fixed Asset account is $1,938,000, we know, by deduction, that the charges (debits) to the account must have amounted to $1,938,000 plus $36,000 (to offset the credit arising from the sale) or $1,974,000. In the absence of other information, the most logical assumption is that this amount represents purchases of fixed assets (including $300,000 included in the May 1, 19X2 purchase of equipment of a business), and we so treat it. In the purchase of the business $200,000 in long-term bonds were issued in addition to the cash payment. Although this $200,000 issue of bonds is not a use of working capital, it represents a significant financing-investing transaction which should be reflected in a statement of changes in financial position.

(b)

Sources and Uses of Funds	200,000	
Bonds Payable		200,000

(c)

Fixed Assets	1,974,000	
Sources and Uses of Funds		1,974,000

At this point the explained changes in the Fixed Asset T-account (after entries (a), (b), and (c) are made) equal the change we set out to explain and which is entered at the top of the account and underlined, that is, $1,938 thousands.

Accumulated depreciation

The net change of $240,000 and the $20,000 charge for accumulated depreciation on fixed asset sold suggests that $260,000 must have been credited to Accumulated Depreciation for the year, and this is confirmed by the supplementary information given. Since net income was decreased by the amount of depreciation charged, we transfer it to the Operations Summary so as to cancel the charge which did not require funds (working capital).

(d)

Operations Summary	260	
Accumulated Depreciation		260

Goodwill

We know that goodwill in the amount of $60,000 was bought in 19X2. Hence, retracing the original entry, we get:

(e)

Goodwill	60,000	
Sources and Uses of Funds		60,000

The supplementary information tells us that $30,000 of Goodwill was amortized in 19X2. Since this charge to income did not require funds (i.e., it drew a "noncurrent" account), we increase the Operations Summary by this amount, thus:

(f)

Operations Summary	30,000	
Goodwill		30,000

Thus, the net change in the Goodwill account has been accounted for.

Bonds payable

The sale of bonds resulted in a source of funds which is reflected as follows:

(g)

Sources and Uses of Funds	400,000	
Bonds Payable		400,000

The conversion of bonds into capital stock is not a transaction affecting working capital. It is, nevertheless, a significant financing transaction resulting in a change in capital structure and, as such, should be reflected in a statement of changes in financial position. This is done as follows:

(h)

Bonds Payable	200,000	
Sources and Uses of Funds		200,000

(i)

Sources and Uses of Funds	200,000	
Capital Stock		200,000

Deferred income taxes

The charge for deferred income taxes increases a noncurrent deferred credit account and, like that for depreciation and goodwill amortization, does not require current funds, and thus the adjustment is carried to the Operations Summary.

(j)

| Operations Summary | 20,000 | |
| Deferred Income Taxes | | 20,000 |

Capital stock and paid-in capital

The sale of stock is a source of funds and is reconstructed as follows:

(k)

Sources and Uses of Funds	1,000,000	
Capital Stock		600,000
Paid-In Capital		400,000

Retained earnings

Reconstruction of the Retained Earnings account change usually relies on supplementary detail provided. Thus net income amounted to $951,000, and this source of funds (*before* adjustment for nonfund items) is transferred to Operations Summary.

(l)

| Operations Summary | 951,000 | |
| Retained Earnings | | 951,000 |

The cash dividends amounted to $750,000, and this is a use of funds.

(m)

| Retained Earnings | 750,000 | |
| Sources and Uses of Fund | | 750,000 |

We have now accounted for the net changes in all the noncurrent T-accounts differences. The changes internal to the noncurrent group of T-accounts do not affect working capital. However, most of such changes, which represent significant financing and/or investing activities, must be included in the statement of changes of financial position which is more comprehensive than the statement of sources and uses of funds, the information of which it also includes.

The next step is to close out the Operations Summary, which contains the net income and adjustments for nonfund items, to the Sources and Uses of Funds Summary. The gain on sale of fixed assets, which is included in net income, is also removed from it because it was included with the sources of funds from sale of fixed assets. The net amount of $1,259,000 is transferred as a source of funds from operations.

Adding up the "sources" column of the Sources and Uses of Funds Summary, we find that it exceeds the "uses" column by $93,000 which corresponds to the increase in working capital. This is a "use" of funds, and with this addition, the uses and sources of funds are in balance as they always must be. From the Sources and Uses of Funds Summary, we can now proceed to prepare the statement of changes in financial position. The Operations Summary contains the necessary detail needed to reconcile the net income figure with the funds provided by operations figure, as is usually done in the body of the statement of changes in financial position.

The resulting statement of changes in financial position is shown in Exhibit 13–1.

EXHIBIT 13–1

THE WILSON COMPANY
Statement of Changes in Financial Position
For the Year Ended December 31, 19X2

Financial resources were provided by:			
Net income		$ 951,000	
Add: Expenses not requiring outlay of work-			
ing capital in the current period:			
Depreciation of fixed assets	$260,000		
Amortization of goodwill	30,000		
Deferred income taxes	20,000	310,000	
		$1,261,000	
Less: gain on sale of fixed assets (included			
in proceeds from sale)		2,000	
Working capital provided by operations			
for the period			$1,259,000
Sale of fixed assets		$ 18,000	
Net proceeds of sale of bonds		400,000	
Issuance of bonds in exchange of fixed			
assets		200,000	
Conversion of debentures into capital			
stock		200,000	
Sale of capital stock		1,000,000	1,818,000
			$3,077,000
Financial resources were used for:			
Purchase of fixed assets*		$1,974,000	
Purchase of goodwill		60,000	
Retirement of debentures on conversion			
into capital stock		200,000	
Payment of dividends		750,000	$2,984,000
Increase in working capital			93,000
			$3,077,000
Analysis of increase (decrease)			
in working capital:			
Cash		$(120,000)	
Receivables		90,000	
Inventory		303,000	
Net increase in current assets			$ 273,000
Increase of accounts payable			(180,000)
Net increase in working capital			$ 93,000

*Includes $300,000 of fixed assets acquired as part of purchase of business.

Analysis of changes in each element of working capital

It will be noted that the above statement of changes in financial position includes an analysis of increases and decreases in the items comprising working capital. That is in accordance with requirements of *APB Opinion No. 19* which calls for an analysis of this nature even though the reader can prepare one if comparative balance sheets are furnished.

Abbreviated method

Careful examination of The Wilson Company example above will reveal the nature of the flexibility of preparation of the statement of sources and applications of funds which the T-account method affords. Thus, given a little experience in the preparation of the statement by this method, we can omit the step of preparing T-accounts for most of the simple changes and, instead, post the changes directly to the Operations Summary or the Sources and Uses of Funds Summary. T-accounts will then be necessary only for the reconstruction of the accounts containing the most complex entries. These will involve, in most cases, the fixed assets and retained earnings accounts. In this way the time of preparation of the statement of sources and applications of funds statement can be considerably shortened and the process simplified.

STATEMENT OF CHANGES IN FINANCIAL POSITION—CASH FOCUS

Some companies, because of a belief that the changes in the most liquid of resources should be highlighted or because of the nature of their operations, present a statement of changes on financial position focusing on the change in cash rather than in working capital.

The principles of preparation of such a statement are similar to those used in preparing the statement focusing on changes in working capital except that in this case changes in all accounts are used to explain the change in the cash (and cash equivalents) balance.[1]

Conversion of working capital provided by operations to cash flow provided by operations

Analysts are often interested in *Cash Flow* rather than Working Capital from operations. As will be seen in Part III, many useful ratios

---

[1] Attention instructors: The Instructor's Manual contains an illustration of the use of the "T"-account method in preparing a statement of changes in financial position (cash focus).

require a figure of actual cash flow from operations as opposed to the cruder and inaccurate measure of "cash flow" simplistically arrived at by merely adding back depreciation (and possibly other nonfund charges) to net income. To short term credit analysts cash flow from operations is a most important measure of liquidity.

Analytically, the most useful way to compute Net Cash Flow from Operations (NCFO) is to show the elements of revenue that generate cash and the expenses that use cash (the "inflow-outflow" approach) rather than to adjust net income for noncash affecting items (the "net" approach).

The first step is to identify and list all elements of income and expense *that affect* working capital. The second step is to adjust these for changes in *working capital items* (other than cash) which are *assumed* to affect operations. Thus:

Starting with sales

+ Decrease (−increase) in accounts receivable

= Cash collections on sales
+ Other revenues (+ or − adjustments for noncash items)

Total cash collections from operations

Cost of goods sold (excluding depreciation, amortization, etc.).

+ Increase (− decrease) in inventories
+ Decrease (− increase) in trade payables
Operating expenses
Other Expenses (including interest)
+ Increase (− decrease) in prepaid assets
+ Decrease (− increase) in accrued liabilities
Income Tax Expense (excluding deferred taxes—noncurrent).
+ Decrease (− increase) in accrued taxes

Deduct total cash outflows for operations

= Net cash flows from operations (NCFO)

The principle governing the above computation is simple to understand. For example, a net decrease in receivables means that on a net basis not only were all sales collected in cash but that some of the prior year receivables were also collected. Conversely, a net increase in receivables means that on a net basis some sales made this year were not collected, i.e., not all sales brought in cash.

A basic assumption underlying these computations is that all current assets and liabilities are related to operations, i.e., to earning activities. That is, of course, not always true and where the analyst possesses information about nonoperating items included in these accounts (e.g., receivables from sale of equipment) they should be excluded from the NCFO computation. Thus, notes payable to banks relate to financing activities as opposed to earnings activities, while changes in dividends payable relate to the actual amount of cash dividends paid during a period. The analyst must be aware that many other factors may result in the inclusion in current assets and liabilities of non-operating items during a given period. This will result in an inability to arrive at an accurate "cash generated by operations" figure. Examples of such factors are the acquisition of current assets and liabilities of other entities and the exclusion of operating current assets and liabilities of entities disposed of during the period.

ILLUSTRATION 2. Assume that the income statement for the year ending 12/31/19X2 of the Wilson Company (in Illustration 1) is as follows:

		$000
Sales		$20,000
Cost of goods sold (includes $260,000 depreciation)		11,101
Gross Profit		8,899
General, selling and administrative expenses	$ 7,000	
Amortization of goodwill	30	7,030
		1,869
Gain on sale of fixed assets		2
Income before taxes		1,871
Income taxes—Current	900	
Deferred	20	920
Net Income		$ 951

Conversion to cash flow from operation would be as follows:

		$000
Sales		$20,000
Less increase in receivables		90
Cash collections		19,910
Cash outflows		
Cost of goods sold	$11,101	
Less depreciation	260	
	10,841	
Add—Increase in inventories	303	
	11,144	
General, selling and administrative expenses	7,000	
Less—Increase in accounts payable	(180)	17,964
Income taxes—Current		900
Total Outflows		18,864
Net Cash Flow from Operations (NCFO)		$ 1,046

This is to be contrasted with "working capital provided by operations" of $1,259,000 which is referred to by some as "cash flow." This confusion of terms can lead to wrong inferences and wrong decisions since often cash provided by operations can be significantly more or less than working capital so provided.

The "net" basis of converting working capital from operations to cash from operations, while analytically less valuable, is easier to compute. The approach is:

I.   Start with working capital provided by operations.
II. *Add* the amount of change in working capital accounts (other than cash) which experienced a net *credit* change for the period. That is, reductions in current assets (other than cash) or increases in current liabilities, all of which are sources of cash.*
III. *Deduct* the amount of change in working capital accounts (other than cash) which experienced a net *debit* change during the period. That is, increases in current assets (other than cash) and decreases in current liabilities, all of which are uses of cash.*
IV. The result is net cash flow from operations.

The application of the above approach to the Wilson Company figures is as follows:

		$000
Working capital provided by operation		$1,259
Add—Increase in accounts payable (net credit)		180
		1,439
Deduct—Increase in receivables (net debit)	$ 90	
Increase in inventories (net debit)	303	393
		$1,046

It can readily be seen that the above techniques can be used to convert an entire statement of changes in financial position from a working capital focus to a cash focus. In such a conversion, those accounts (other than cash) which do not affect operations (e.g., loans payable, dividends payable) are used to adjust nonoperating sources and uses in order to arrive at their net cash effect.

Additional provisions of *APB Opinion No. 19*

In addition to the already mentioned provisions of *APB Opinion No. 19*, the following requirements are noteworthy:

1. The statement of changes in financial position is now a basic financial statement required to be furnished whenever a profit-oriented

---

* Excluding non-operating items such as changes in marketable securities, bank loans and dividends payable.

business entity issues financial statements that present *both* financial position (balance sheet) *and* results of operations (statement of income and retained earnings).

2. The statement of changes should be based on a broad concept embracing all changes in financial position. Accordingly, transactions such as the following should be included:

    a. Assets acquired in exchange for capital stock or for long-term debt.

    b. Exchanges of property.

    c. Capital donations affecting noncurrent items.

    d. Conversion of debt into equity.

    e. Refinancing of long-term debt.

    f. Issuance, redemption, or purchase of capital stock.

    g. Dividends in kind (except for stock dividends and stock splits).

3. Items such as the following should be shown broad and not netted against each other unless one item is immaterial:

    a. Acquisition and retirement of property, plant, and equipment.

    b. New long-term borrowings and repayment of long-term debt.

4. Effects of extraordinary items should be reported separately.

Implications for analysis

The balance sheet portrays the variety of assets held by an entity at a given moment in time and the manner in which those assets are financed. The income statement portrays the results of operations for a specific fiscal period. Income results in increases of a variety of kinds of assets. Expenses result in the consumption of many kinds of assets (or the incurrence of liabilities)—some current and some noncurrent. Thus, net income cannot be equated with an increment in liquid resources. It is quite conceivable that a very profitable enterprise may find it difficult to meet its current obligations and to lack funds for further expansion. The very fact that a business is successful in expanding sales may bring along with it a worsening of liquidity and the tying up of its funds in assets which cannot be liquidated in time to meet maturing obligations.

The statement of changes in financial position sheds light on the effects of earning activities on liquid resources, and focuses on such matters as what became of net income during the period, and on what assets were acquired and how they were financed. It can highlight clearly the distinction between net income and funds provided by operations. This is very vividly illustrated in a recent funds statement published by City Investing Company where the sources of funds provided by operations are shown as follows:

	Year ended April 30, (in thousands)	
	19Y0	19X9
Source of funds:		
Operations:		
Net income	$68,040	$48,121
Noncash charges and (credits) to income:		
Depreciation and amortization	8,085	6,222
Equity in undisturbed income of unconsolidated subsidiaries	(54,823)	(32,896)
	$21,302	$21,447

Clearly, in the case of this enterprise the actual funds provided by operations are but a fraction of the reported net income. The increasing use of the equity method of accounting in taking up the earnings of investees under *APB Opinion No. 18* (see Chapter 9) will probably serve to increase further the disparity between reported income and funds provided by operations, a disparity to which the analyst must be ever alert.

The statement of changes in financial position is also of great value to the analyst who wants to project operating results on the basis of productive capacity acquired and planned to be acquired, and who wants to assess a company's future capacity to expand, its capital needs, and the sources from which they may be met. The statement is, thus, an essential bridge between the income statement and the balance sheet.

The funds statement probably owes its inception to a desire to learn more about the flow of liquid resources of a business. However, the statement of changes in financial position can provide more than information on the changes in liquid resources and their effect on a company's ability to meet current obligations. To the financial analyst the statement provides clues to important matters such as:

1. Feasibility of financing capital expenditures and possible sources of such financing.
2. Sources of funds to finance an expansion in the volume of business.
3. Future dividend policies.
4. Ability to meet future debt service requirements.
5. An insight into the financial habits of management and resulting indications of future policies.
6. Indications regarding the quality of earnings.

Regarding the last mentioned use the funds statement is useful for identifying faulty or erroneous operating conditions which in the income statement may, for a time, mask true operating results through the use of devices such as premature revenue recognition or unwarranted cost deferrals. A further discussion of earnings quality will be found in Chapter 22.

The statement of changes in financial position as a summary of overall investment and financing activities of an enterprise is, of course, far more reliable and credible evidence of a company's actions and intentions than are the statements and speeches of its management. This is why the statement is so important to the financial analyst and why, in the absence of a formal statement supplied as part of the financial report, many analysts did in the past construct one on an approximate basis using whatever information they could obtain.

The analyst must be careful to examine the form in which the statement of changes in financial position is presented. Thus, some transactions are definitely related such as, for example, the purchase of certain assets and the issurance of debt or the payment of dividends out of specific earnings. The analyst must, however, be careful not to impute relationships among items merely on the basis of their presentation lest he reach misleading conclusions.

The significance of a change in liquidity, whether positive or negative, cannot be judged by means of the statement of sources and applications of funds alone. It must, of course, be related to other variables in a company's financial structure and operating results. Thus, for example, an increase of funds may have been gained by selling off various assets whose earning power will be missed in the future; or the increase may have been financed by means of incurrence of debt which is subject to high costs and/or onerous repayment terms.

The analyst must also be careful to note the scope of coverage of the funds statement he uses. Generally, the most revealing type of statement is the statement of changes in financial position as required by *APB Opinion No. 19*. This funds statement often contains details and information not available elsewhere in the financial report, and the analyst should be alert to the availability of this information.

Cash is the most liquid of assets and is not only the most ready and acceptable means of discharging obligations but is also the ultimate measure of realization of sales transactions. Thus, in certain types of business where liquidity and cash flows are of paramount importance, a statement of sources and applications of cash is often presented. Here the analyst will find the effect of all transactions on the company's cash (or cash plus marketable securities) balance. Although the statement is also referred to as a "statement of cash flow," this term is subject to considerable confusion and requires clarification.

CASH FLOW

The term "cash flow" was probably first coined by financial analysts. Its most common meaning is net income adjusted for charges not involving funds such as, for example, depreciation and depletion. In this sense, the term "cash flow" can be equated with "sources of funds from operations" found in the statement of changes in financial position, except that while the latter term includes adjustments of *all* nonfund items included in net income, the popular concept of "cash flow" is merely one of net income with depreciation expense added back, and hence a much cruder concept. In any event the mixup in terminology only leads to confusion.

The most valid analytical use made of "cash flow" is when security analysts, in an attempt to eliminate distortions which arise from the variety of depreciation methods in use and the loose standards which govern the assumptions of useful lives of assets, try to compare the earnings of companies before depreciation.

The following example points up the distortions in net income comparisons which can occur due to the use of different depreciation methods. The use of different useful-life assumptions for the same kind of fixed assets can, of course, introduce additional distortions.

Assume that two companies (A and B) each invest $50,000 in a machine which generates $45,000 per year from operations before provision for depreciation. Thus, for the five-year assumed useful life of the machine, the results are as follows:

	Five-year period
Funds provided by operations ($45,000 × 5 years)	$225,000
Cost of the machine	50,000
Income from operations of the machine	$175,000
Average yearly net income	$ 35,000

However, the same $175,000 income over five years can be reported quite differently by using straight-line or sum-of-the-years'-digits depreciation. Thus (ignoring taxes), we have:

Year	*Income before depreciation	COMPANY A Straight-line depreciation		COMPANY B Sum-of-the-years'-digits depreciation	
		Depreciation	Net income	Depreciation	Net income
1	$ 45,000	$10,000	$ 35,000	$16,667	$ 28,333
2	45,000	10,000	35,000	13,334	31,666
3	45,000	10,000	35,000	10,000	35,000
4	45,000	10,000	35,000	6,667	38,333
5	45,000	10,000	35,000	3,332	41,668
Total	$225,000	$50,000	$175,000	$50,000	$175,000

* Popularly termed "cash flow."

As the above example shows, while the predepreciation "cash flow" of the two companies is identical, indicating as it should, identical earning power, the after-depreciation income, while identical for the entire five-year period, can be quite different on a year-to-year basis, depending on the depreciation method in use.

The use of "cash flow" or more properly labeled "income before depreciation" is thus a valid analytical tool so long as the user knows specifically what its significance is and what its limitations are.

The limitations of the "cash flow" concept are entirely due to the widespread confusion of the term's meaning and to its misuse.

One source of confusion stems from a lack of definition of what "cash flow" really is. It is, of course, strictly speaking neither "cash" nor "flow" (see earlier description of cash provided by operations). It is not cash because it is used within broader meaning of funds, that is, working capital. It is not "flow" because it represents net change and a very limited aspect of funds flow, that is, funds generated by operations. Moreover the "flow" focuses on an "inflow" and disregards mandatory or necessary outflows. Thus, there are many other flows, even among those identified with operations, which are found in a complete statement of changes in financial position.

The assertion often made that "cash flow" represents a discretionary fund which management can use as it sees fit is also misleading. There are mandatory "outflows" such as debt service, required dividends, preferred stock redemptions, essential capital asset replacements, which cannot be avoided or postponed and which can sharply reduce or even eliminate the discretionary "cash flow" pool generated by operations.

Another and even more serious confusion arises from the assertion of some, and particularly those managements which are dissatisfied by the level of their reported net income, that "cash flow" is a measure of performance superior to or more valid than "net income."[2] This is like saying that depreciation, or other costs not involving the use of current funds, are not genuine expenses. This misconception is also discussed in the chapter dealing with depreciation costs. Only "net income" can be properly regarded as a measure of performance and can be validly related to the equity investment as an indicator of operating success. If we add back depreciation to net income and compute the resulting return on investment, we are, in effect, confusing the return *on* investment with an element of return *of* investment in fixed assets. Moreover, it should also be borne in mind that not only is depreciation a valid cost but that in times of inflation the depreciation funds recov-

---

[2] In ASR 142 (1973) the SEC concluded that certain approaches to "cash flow" reporting may be misleading to investors. Per share data other than that relating to net income, net assets and dividends should be avoided in reporting financial results.

ered from sales may not be sufficient to replace the equipment because the charges are based on the lower historical costs (see also Chapter 14).

Closely linked with the doubts of laymen and even of those who should know better, about the true nature of the depreciation cost is the confusion regarding whether or not depreciation is or is not a source of funds.

DEPRECIATION—A SOURCE OF FUNDS?

One major cause for the belief that depreciation is a source of funds is the manner in which it is presented in some statements of changes in financial position. Thus, the adding back of depreciation to net income is all too often not shown as an *adjustment* of net income in order to arrive at the desired figure of "funds provided by operations" but rather as if it is an independent source of funds similar to that stemming from borrowing of money or the sale of assets.

ILLUSTRATION 3

Misleading presentation			Proper presentation		
Sources of funds:			*Sources of funds:*		
Net income	$ 75,000		Net income	$75,000	
Depreciation	25,000		Add back* depreciation charge	25,000	
Sale of bonds	60,000		Funds provided by operations		$100,000
Sale of machinery	40,000		Sale of bonds		60,000
			Sale of machinery		40,000
Total	$200,000		Total		$200,000

* Expense not requiring current outlay of funds.

It is not hard to understand why the misleading presentation could lead laymen into believing that depreciation is a source of funds. Since it is shown in the same way as all sources of funds, it is a "source" like all others and would seem to suggest that the act of increasing the depreciation expense will increase the total sources of funds. This thinking overlooks, of course, the fact that depreciation acts to reduce net income and thus the act of increasing depreciation can have no effect on funds. On the other hand, the act of increasing permitted depreciation charges for tax return purposes may temporarily conserve funds by reducing the current tax liability.

The thinking regarding depreciation as a source of funds is encouraged by loose discussion in some of our best financial publications. Thus, *Fortune* of June 1970, in an article entitled "An Over Supply of Stocks" which discusses Whittaker Corporation's liquidity difficulties, states that even by utilization of various sources of funds the company would still not be able to cover debt payments due "unless there were a sizable increase in earnings and/or *depreciation* this year" (author's emphasis). To say that an increase in depreciation can supply funds to repay debt is like saying that the higher the costs the better.

The proper presentation brings out the essential fact that the reason depreciation (or similar charges or credits which do not affect current funds) is shown in the statement of sources and applications of funds is in order to show to the reader how the net income figure which is the result of operations is converted to a "funds provided by operations" figure needed in the funds statement.

The essential fact to be understood is that aside from miscellaneous sources of income the *basic* source of funds from operations in any enterprise is sales to customers. It is out of sales that all expenses are recovered and a profit, if any, is earned. If the sales price is sufficient to cover *all* costs, that is, those requiring and those not requiring current funds, then the process of sales will recover the depreciation costs in addition to other costs. If the sales price is not sufficiently high to cover all costs, depreciation will not be recovered or will not be fully recovered. Thus, the importance of revenues as *the* source of funds from operations should never be lost sight of.

The above discussion clearly points out that the financial analyst must approach the funds statements as well as such concepts as "cash flow" and depreciation with understanding and with independence of viewpoint so as to avoid being trapped by the numerous cliches and useless generalizations which are all too often employed even by those who should know better.

QUESTIONS

1. What information can the user of financial statements obtain from the statement of changes in financial position?

2. Which are the two major concepts of liquidity commonly used in the preparation of the statement of changes in financial position?

3. While the "statement of changes in financial position" focuses normally on changes of working capital or cash, it also includes transactions which affect neither. Give three examples of such transactions.

4. In addition to depreciation, what are some other examples of costs and expenses not requiring the outlay of cash or working capital? What are examples of income items not bringing in cash or working capital?

5. Could the form in which revenues are received affect the statement of changes in financial position?

6. The book value of assets sold is often shown as a separate source of working capital or cash. What is the reason for this presentation?

7. *APB Opinion No. 19* states that stock dividends and split-ups are not

required to be disclosed in the statement of changes in financial position. What is the reason for this exception? Would the conversion of preferred stock into common be shown in the statement of changes in financial position?

8. Under the abbreviated "T-account" method of preparing the funds statement which accounts would most likely require reconstruction?

9. What are some of the important clues which an analysis of the statement of changes in financial position can provide for the analyst?

10. What is meant by the term "cash flow"? Why is this term subject to confusion and misrepresentation?

11. *a.* What principles and assumptions underly the conversion of "Working Capital Provided by Operations" to "Cash Provided by Operations"?
    b. Contrast the "inflow-outflow" approach of conversion to the "net" approach.

12. A member of the board of directors of a company which faces shortage of funds in the coming year is told that none of the sources of funds available in the preceding year can be increased. He thereupon suggests increasing the amount shown as "depreciation" in the "sources" section of the funds statement. Comment on his suggestion.

13. A prominent academician wrote some years ago:
    ". . . just as in the first half of this century we saw the income statement displace the balance sheet in importance, so we may now be de-emphasising the income statement in favour of a statement of fund flows or cash flows . . . my own guess is that, so far as the history of accounting is concerned, the next 25 years may subsequently be seen to have been the twilight of income measurement."
    Comment on this prediction.

14

EFFECTS OF PRICE CHANGES
ON FINANCIAL STATEMENTS

The comparability over time of accounting measurements expressed in dollars can be fully valid only if the general purchasing power of the currency remains unchanged. This has only rarely been the case; indeed, the value of the dollar in terms of purchasing power has changed over any length of time. In recent experience, such change has invariably been a decline in purchasing power.

The distortive effect of general price level changes on accounting measurements has long been recognized by leaders of industry and finance as well as by economists and accountants.[1] However, as long as the annual rate of inflation was moderate, accountants, as those best situated to move towards change, elected to rely on education and disclosure rather than on an adjustment of the financial statements as the means of conveying such effects to the general reader.

In times of more severe inflation, there is always clamor for a more formalized and systematic approach designed to adjust for the distortions arising from changes in the price level. There are businessmen who feel that recovery of depreciation based on original cost is not sufficient to provide for replacement of assets used up in production. They are, of course, except under certain imposed circumstances not bound to historical cost depreciation in setting their prices, and thus their arguments are often directed towards the goal of having the tax authorities accept price level adjusted depreciation in computing taxable income. This quest has, so far, not born fruit.

---

[1] We must distinguish between specific price changes and general price level changes affecting the purchasing power of the currency. For example, price changes in goods and services reflecting changes in quality do not affect the general purchasing power of the currency.

Research and professional pronouncements

In the early 1960s the accounting profession recognized that it could no longer ignore the effect of continuing inflation on the financial statements.[2] Accordingly, it commissioned a research study which was published in 1963 as *Accounting Research Study No. 6*, "Reporting the Financial Effects of Price-Level Changes."

Following a period of further significant inflation, the APB issued, in June 1969, its *Statement No. 3* entitled "Financial Statements Restated for General Price-Level Changes." While not carrying the weight of an "Opinion," which requires adherence by all members of the organized accounting profession, the Statement recommendations went further than prior pronouncements and, for the first time, spelled out specific steps to be followed in the preparation of general price level restated financial statements, thus representing a standby framework to be used as the need arose.

After public exposure and discussion, the FASB issued in 1974 an Exposure Draft of a Statement that would have required the inclusion with conventional financial statements, of certain specified financial information stated in terms of units of general purchasing power patterned after the concepts embodied in *APB Statement No. 3*.

In Britain, where the inflation rate has exceeded that of the United States by a significant margin, the professional accounting body issued in 1973 an exposure draft entitled "Accounting for Changes in the Purchasing Power of Money" which essentially recommended an approach similar to that endorsed by the FASB.

Intervention by governmental bodies

As the discussion which will follow indicates, financial statements expressed in terms of units of general purchasing power are subject to significant limitations and this intensified the controversy around the methods chosen as well as the search for better ways to adjust financial statements for the effects of price changes.

In Britain a government appointed committee, known as the Sandilands Committee, was charged "to consider whether, and if so, how company accounts should allow for changes in costs and prices." The Committee's report, issued in 1975, basically rejected accounting in terms of units of general purchasing power in favor of a system of value accounting which is called "Current Cost Accounting."

In the United States, the SEC has in 1976 adopted a new Rule 3-17

---

[2] Further comments on the historical evolution of approaches to the problem of accounting for inflation can be found in the first edition of this work.

of Regulation S-X which requires larger[3] registrants to disclose the current replacement cost of inventories and depreciable and amortiziable assets used in operations at each fiscal year end for which a balance sheet is required, together with the approximate amount of what cost of sales and the provision for depreciation and amortiziation would have been for the most recent fiscal years had they been calculated on the basis of current replacement cost of inventories and productive capacity.

Unlike the British recommendations which envisage a new basis of accountability, the SEC requirements are experimental and extend at present only to supplementary disclosure of the specified data. Disclosure of the effect on net income of applying replacement cost methods is not required. In fact, the Commission cautioned users against a simplistic use of the data presented and warned that they are not designed to be a simple road map to the determination of "true income." At present the basic objective of the Commission is to give investors information about the current economics of business operations rather than the value of business assets.

In mid-1976, the FASB decided to defer further consideration of a Statement of Financial Reporting in Units of General Purchasing Power. The board cited its conclusion that general purchasing power information is not now sufficiently well understood by preparers and users and that the need for it is not now sufficiently well demonstrated to justify imposing the cost of implementation. Other factors influencing the board's decision were the above-mentioned SEC initiative in replacement cost disclosure and the forthcoming review of the entire accounting model as part of the board's project "Conceptual Framework for Financial Accounting and Reporting."

Accounting and reporting alternatives

For hundreds of years accounting has evolved around the concept of historical costs and measurements in terms of money whatever the purchasing power of that money was. In spite of their complexity, accounting presentations enjoyed a degree of acceptance and were understood by informed users. The accelerating erosion of the value of the currency has caused financial statements based on this framework to become less and less relevant to users of financial statements. Now that a departure from the comfort and the familiarity of present conventions is inevitable, the great debate among theorists concerns the best means of measuring the impact of price level changes on financial statements.

---

[3] Exempt initially are companies whose inventories, gross property, plant and equipment total less than $100 million or make up less than 10 percent of total assets.

One school of thought favors the use of general price level adjustments which involve the modification of financial statements expressed in units of money so that relevant information is given in terms of units of general purchasing power (GPL statements). This framework is described and examined in Appendix 14A.

Another school of thought believes that improvements in the utility and relevance of financial statements can be best achieved by reflecting in them the effects of changes in specific prices. Thus, more up-to-date measures of resources employed and results achieved will be provided. A consideration of such an approach, the Replacement Cost Accounting model, follows.

REPLACEMENT COST ACCOUNTING (RCA)

In contrast to the GPL accounting framework (see Appendix 14A) which does not involve a departure from historical cost, Replacement Cost Accounting represents a different response to the need to account for price changes. RCA allows for specific price changes by adjusting assets and liabilities to their current replacement cost.[4] The income statement, in turn, reflects the current replacement cost of goods and services used up in the production of income.

The concept of replacement cost income can be understood best through the following simple illustration:

ILLUSTRATION 1. Assume that A holds for sale 10 widgets which were purchased at a cost of $20 each constituting a starting capital of $200. In a given week three widgets are sold for $30 each and the inventory is replenished at a price of $25 each. As we saw in Chapter 5, conventional accounting can provide three different profit figures for this transaction i.e., $30 under Fifo, $26.50 under average cost and $15 under the Lifo assumption with the latter most closely approximating (but not necessarily equaling, as it does here by coincidence) replacement cost.

RCA goes, however beyond this and departs from both historical cost and the concept of realization. Under the assumption that the units sold had a unit replacement cost equal to those replaced,[5] the operating profit of $15 is arrived at by deducting the replacement cost of sales $75 (3 × $25) from sales $90 (3 × $30) and this profit is represented by cash which can indeed be distributed without affecting the business's ability to carry its normal inventory of 10 widgets i.e.,

---

[4] Most current RCA proposals do not presently envisage the restatement of liabilities.

[5] Just as under historical cost accounting we assume the flow of inventory, under RCA, we conveniently assume that sales occur on inventory purchase dates.

$10 \times \$25 = \$250$. It is in fact, a basic principle of RCA that no profit can be assumed to have been earned until the replacement of inventory (or of productive capacity) has been provided for. In addition, the increment in the value of the original 7 widgets still in inventory $35 ($7 \times \$5$) is recognized as an unrealized holding gain. There is also a cost saving[6] or realized holding gain of $15 by having bought the 3 widgets which were sold at a cost of $20 each instead of the $25 current replacement cost. If we add the $50 total holding gain to operating profit of $15 then RCA gives us a net income of $65 (assuming no other expenses), and this separate classification of results is one of the advantages of RCA. A's RCA Balance Sheet is now as follows:

Cash	$ 15	Owner's equity at beginning		$200
Inventory		Operating profit		15
(10 × $25)	250	Holding gains—Realized	$15	
		Unrealized	35	50
	$265			$265

The income statement could be captioned as follows:

Sales (3 × $30)	$90.00
Cost of sales (3 × $25)	75.00
Sustainable income (1)	$15.00
Realized holding gains	15.00
Realized income (2) (equals conventional net income)	$30.00
Unrealized holding gains	35.00
Net Income	$65.00

    (1) Income which would enable entity to sustain present level of operations were price changes to stop.
    (2) Sustainable income plus Realized holding gains (Income realized in transactions with outsiders).
    These concepts and terms were introduced by S. Davidson and R. L. Weil in "Inflation Accounting," *Financial Analysts Journal*, March–April 1976, pp. 57–66.

Realized holding gains are also referred to as an "inventory profit" particularly by the SEC in *Accounting Series Release 151* which urges their disclosure. It can be argued that unrealized holding gains are also inventory profits, albeit of the unrealized variety.

Two additional things should be noted regarding the above illustration. One is that unlike GPL accounting, RCA in comparison with historical cost changes only the *timing* but not the amount of the total profit recognized. Thus, when the 10 widgets are finally sold the

---

[6] This term appears in Edwards and Bell, *The Theory and Measurement of Business Income* (Berkeley: University of California Press, 1961), a seminal work in this area.

profit under both historical and RCA bases will be identical but the timing will not be, because under RCA we recognize both current replacement costs and holding gains. The other is that some accountants believe that unrealized holding gains do not belong in income and should instead bypass it and be shown directly in stockholder's equity. We are adopting here the position that within the RCA framework it is more useful and informative to show them as part of net income.

ILLUSTRATION 2.   *Extended illustration of replacement cost statements*
     We can now cement our understanding of RCA procedures by restating the historical cost financial statements of the Xtra Corporation appearing in Appendix 14A Exhibits 14A–2B, 14A–4D, 14A–5E and 14A–6F (inclusive of additional data supplied) with the use of the following replacement cost data patterned after the SEC disclosure requirements.

	December 31	
Estimated current replacement costs	*19X1*	*19X2*
Inventories	$ 2,300	$22,000
Equipment	$25,000	$28,000
Less Accumulated Depreciation	2,500	5,600
Net	$22,500	$22,400
For the year ended		
Cost of services (at dates of sale)	$27,000	$51,000
Depreciation of equipment	2,500	2,800

Exhibit 14–1 presents a work sheet which converts the December 31, 19X1 historical cost financial statement of the Xtra Corporation to a replacement cost basis. The following are brief descriptions of the keyed-in adjustments:

1. Holding gains on inventories which have been realized through sales.
2. Incremental replacement cost depreciation realized through sales ($800)[7]
3. Unrealized increase in replacement cost of ending inventory.
4. Total increase in replacement cost of equipment.
4A. Incremental replacement cost depreciation added to accumulated depreciation and reducing the unrealized equipment holding gains.

---

[7] It should be noted that the SEC replacement cost rules call for depreciation provisions based on average replacement cost during the year, in this case 10 percent of ($25,000 + 28,000) ÷ 2 or $2,650 rather than the 10 percent of $28,000 (year end equipment replacement cost) or $2,800 which is the replacement cost depreciation used in year 19X2 in this problem. Many would argue that the additional $150 of depreciation ($2,800 − 2,650) should not be charged to operations.

EXHIBIT 14–1

XTRA CORPORATION
Work Sheet to Prepare Replacement Cost Financial Statements
(dollar amounts in 000s)

	Conventional basis year of 19X1		Adjustments		Replacement cost basis year of 19X1	
			Debit	Credit		
Income Statement:						
Sales		50,000				50,000
Cost of services	25,000		(1) 2,000		27,000	
Depreciation	2,000		(2) 500		2,500	
Other expenses (incl. tax)	13,000				13,000	
Total Expenses		40,000				42,500
Current operating income						7,500
Realized holding gains						
On inventories				(1) 2,000	2,000	
On equipment				(2) 500	500	
Total Realized Holding Gains						2,500
Realized income						10,000
Unrealized holding gains						
On ending inventories				(3) 300	300	
On ending equipment			(4A) 500	(4) 5,000	4,500	
Total Unrealized Holding Gains						4,800
Net Income		10,000				14,800
Balance Sheet:	December 31, 19X1				December 31, 19X1	
Cash		30,000				30,000
Inventories		2,000	(3) 300			2,300
Equipment	20,000		(4) 5,000		25,000	
Less accumulated depreciation	2,000			(4A) 500	(2,500)	
Net		18,000				22,500
Total Assets		50,000				54,800
Capital stock		40,000				40,000
Retained earnings: balance 1/1/X1	—				—	
(Realized) income for year	10,000				10,000	
Balance 12/31/X1		10,000				10,000
Unrealized holding gains balance 1/1/19X1					—	
Unrealized holding gains for 19X1					4,800	
Balance 12/31/19X1						4,800
Total Equity		50,000				54,800
Total Liabilities and Equity		50,000				54,800

EXHIBIT 14–2

XTRA CORPORATION
Work Sheet to Prepare Replacement Cost Financial Statements
(dollar amounts in 000s)

	Conventional basis year of 19X2	Adjustments		Replacement cost basis year of 19X2
		Debit	Credit	
Income Statement:				
Sales	100,000			100,000
Cost of services	50,000	(1) 1,000		51,000
Depreciation	2,000	(2) 800		2,800
Other expenses (incl. taxes)	20,000			20,000
Total Expenses	72,000			73,800
Current operating income				26,200
Realized holding gains				
On inventories			(1) 1,000	1,000
On equipment			(2) 800	800
Total Realized Holding Gains				1,800
Realized Income				28,000
Unrealized holding gains				
On ending inventory		(3A) 300	(3) 2,000	1,700
On equipment		(4A) 5,000	(4) 8,000 ⎫	1,900
		(5A) 1,600	(5) 500 ⎭	
Total Unrealized Holding Gains				3,600
Net Income	28,000			31,600
Balance Sheet:	December 31, 19X2			December 31, 19X2
Cash	45,000			45,000
Accounts receivable	12,000			12,000
Inventories	20,000	(3) 2,000		22,000
Equipment	20,000	(4) 8,000		28,000
Less accumulated depreciation	(4,000)		(5A) 1,600	(5,600)
Net Value of Equipment	16,000			22,400
Total Assets	93,000			101,400
Accounts payable	5,000			5,000
Long-term debt	10,000			10,000
Capital stock	40,000			40,000
Retained earnings 1/1/X2	10,000			10,000
(Realized) income for 19X2	28,000			28,000
Retained earnings 12/31/X2	38,000			38,000
Unrealized holding gains 1/1/X2		(5) 500	(3A, 4A) ⎫ 5,300 ⎭	4,800
Unrealized holding gains for 19X2				3,600
Unrealized holding gains 12/31/X2				8,400
Total Equity	78,000			86,400
Total Liabilities and Equity	93,000			101,400

It should be noted that historical basis "Net Income" equals RCA basis "Realized Income".

Exhibit 14–2 presents a worksheet which converts the December 31, 19X2 historical cost financial statements of the Xtra Corporation to a replacement cost basis. The following explanations of adjustments concern only matters which were not covered in the explanationa of Exhibit 14–1:

(3) and (3A)   The replacement cost of ending inventory is $2,000 in excess of historical cost. However this net figure includes the corresponding excess ($300) of the prior year replacement cost over historical cost of closing inventory. Thus, this year's unrealized holding gain on inventory is $1,700.

(4) and (4A)   The total cumulative excess replacement over historical cost of equipment at 12/31/19X2 was $8,000. Of this $5,000 accrued from the prior year. Thus only $3,000 net of unrealized holding gains on gross equipment accrued in 19X2.

(5) and (5A)   The identical condition with debits and credits reversed is true of accumulated depreciation. The excess of replacement cost accumulated depreciation over the historical counterpart is $1,600 and that reduces the unrealized holding gains originating from gross equipment. However, such an excess of $500 is already attributable to the prior year so that the net reduction in unrealized holding gains on net equipment is $1,100.

It is important to understand the accounting for depreciation expense and accumulated depreciation under RCA. Note that the 19X1 depreciation expense was $2,500 and that of 19X2, $2,800 for a two year total of $5,300. However, the accumulated depreciation properly calculated on the basis of 19X2 year-end replacement cost of the equipment is shown as $5,600. The difference of $300 is known as "catch-up depreciation" and represents the amount of additional depreciation expense that should have been provided (but was not) reflecting the service potential that expired in prior years. This $300 catch-up depreciation instead of affecting operating income is, in effect, reducing the 19X2 "Unrealized Holding Gains" (See adjustment 5A).[8]

---

[8] There are those who maintain that a failure to provide for this catch-up depreciation by a charge to income, results in RCA not really serving to maintain physical plant capacity. In a persuasive article R. F. Vancil and R. L. Weil, "Current Replacement Cost Accounting, Depreciable Assets, and Distributable Income," *Financial Analysts Journal*, July–August 1976) maintain that such arguments ignore the return which the enterprise realizes from the reinvestment of assets retained because of depreciation charges.

The unrealized holding gains for 19X2 on net equipment can be explained as follows:

Replacement cost of net equipment at 12/31/X2	$22,400	
Less—Historical cost net equipment at 12/31/X2	16,000	
Excess of replacement over historical cost		$6,400
Less—Prior year unrealized holding gain		4,500
Unrealized holding gain attributable to 19X2		$1,900*

* This amount can also be shown to represent the year-to-year increase in

Replacement Cost of Gross Equipment ($28,000 − $25,000)		$3,000
Less Excess Replacement Cost over Historical Cost Depreciation	800	
Catch-up Depreciation for prior periods (in this case 19X1)	300	1,100
		$1,900

The unrealized holding gains for 19X2 on inventories can be explained as follows:

Replacement cost of 19X2 ending inventory	$22,000	
Less—Historical cost of 19X2 ending inventory	20,000	
Excess of replacement over historical cost		$2,000
Less—Prior year unrealized holding gain		300
Unrealized holding gain attributable to 19X2		$1,700

EXHIBIT 14–3

XTRA CORPORATION
Income Statement
For Year Ending 12/31-19X2
(based on replacement costs)
(in thousands of dollars)

Sales		$100,000
Cost of services		51,000
Gross Profit..		49,000
Depreciation	$ 2,800	
Other expenses (including taxes)	20,000	22,800
Current operating income		$ 26,200
Realized holding gains:		
Excess of replacement cost over historical cost of services ($51,000 − $50,000)		1,000
Excess of replacement cost over historical cost of depreciation ($2,800 − $2,000)		800
Total realized holding gains		$ 1,800
Realized income		$ 28,000
Unrealized holding gains:		
Excess of replacement cost realized in 19X2 over historical cost of ending inventory		1,700
Excess of replacement cost realizable in 19X2 over historical cost of net equipment		1,900
Total unrealized holding gains		$ 3,600
Net Income		$ 31,600

Exhibit 14–3 presents the replacement cost 19X2 income statement and Exhibit 14–4 the 19X2 balance sheet of the Xtra Corporation.

EXHIBIT 14–4

XTRA CORPORATION
Balance Sheet
As at December 31, 19X2
(based on replacement costs)
(in thousands of dollars)

Assets

Current assets		
Cash		$ 45,000
Accounts receivable		12,000
Inventories		22,000
Total Current Assets		$ 79,000
Equipment	$28,000	
Less: Accumulated depreciation	5,600	
Net cost of equipment		22,400
Total Assets		$101,400

Liabilities and Equity

Accounts payable		$ 5,000
Long-term debt		10,000
Capital stock		40,000
Retained earnings:		
Balance 1/1/19X2	$10,000	
19X2 realized income	28,000	38,000
Unrealized holding gains:		
Balance 1/1/19X2	4,800	
Realized in 19X2	3,600	8,400
Total equity		86,400
Total Liability and Equity		$101,400

Estimating replacement costs

One of the major objections voiced, particularly by accountants, to the adoption of RCA is that this framework involves a great many subjective estimates which are hard to verify and audit. However, the ravages of inflation have undermined the value of historical cost presentations to such an extent that in the words of one critic "it is far better to be approximately right than precisely wrong." What must also be realized in this discussion is that an error in replacement cost estimates will not alter the total profit from the use of an asset over its life time, because over the life of an enterprise profit is still the difference between cash inflows and outflows. An error in replacement cost estimates will, however, affect the year-to-year profit pattern which is something to which those who value securities attach great importance.

In SEC Staff Accounting Bulletin 7 (1976)[9] replacement cost is defined as:

. . . the lowest amount that would have to be paid in the normal course of business to obtain a new asset of equivalent operating or productive capability. In the case of depreciable, depletable, or amoritizable assets, replacement cost (new) and depreciated replacement cost should be distinguished. Replacement cost (new) is the total estimated current cost of replacing total productive capacity at the end of the year while depreciated replacement cost is the replacement cost (new) adjusted for the already expired service potential of such assets.

In the United States where the use of replacement cost data is new, much experimentation will be required before reliable estimation methods are developed. Thus, the SEC will accept a variety of methods of replacement cost determination as well as the presentation of data in ranges rather than single amounts.

The SEC has established a 30 member committee composed of industry members, public accountants, and others to meet with and advise the Commission's chief accountant and his staff on questions concerning implementation of its disclosure rules.

Among the many approaches available to estimate replacement cost are estimation of unit costs of productive capacity, estimation by sampling or otherwise of the cost of a basic unit of output, market quotations, the use of indices whether published or internally developed, and the use of independent appraisals. Expected costs savings to be realized from new equipment may be disclosed but may not be netted against replacement depreciation.

The complexities in the application of such estimation methods are great. For example, in theory the SEC requires that cost of sales be redetermined at the estimated replacement cost of the items sold, at the time they were sold. In practice it is almost impossible to redetermine this cost on a transaction basis. Thus it will be acceptable to estimate it on the basis of *average* cost levels prevailing during the year. This may involve the use of specific price level indices, sampling procedures and information on price volatility and turnover rates.

The question of how to treat the effect of cost savings is similarly complex. The net effect of such savings must take into account not only the effects of replacement cost depreciation but also the financing costs involved in replacing the equipment as well as the impact of the mix of costs (variable versus fixed) on prices.

We must remember that in its rules the SEC focused on specific

---

[9] This and subsequent bulletins, while not bearing the Commission's official approval, represent useful interpretations and contain many further rules concerning replacement cost disclosure requirements.

asset categories exempting many varieties of assets even within them. In a full fledged CRA System the replacement costs of all assets and liabilities would have to be considered.

WHICH FRAMEWORK WILL DO THE JOB?

Exhibits 14–5 and 14–6 present the comparative 19X2 operating results and balance sheets of Xtra Corporation under the two alternates to the conventional accounting model now in use.

The RCA System substitutes current replacement cost for historical costs and thus adjusts financial statements for specific price changes. From the point of view of the analyst, this imparts to the system great relevance and usefulness. Under this concept, as we have seen, only the *timing* but not the ultimate amounts of the elements of the income statements change. The RCA system does not, however, deal with the effects of price level changes, i.e., inflation, on monetary assets and liabilities or with these effects on invested capital. Nor does it resolve the problem of making valid comparisons over time periods when the value of the monetary unit is not stable.

These last mentioned shortcomings of the RCA system are in essence the strengths of GPL accounting. However, as we will see in the

EXHIBIT 14–5

XTRA CORPORATION
Comparative Income Statements
For the Year Ended December 31, 19X2
(in thousands of dollars)

	(1) Conventional	(2) Price-level adjusted	(3) Replacement costs
Sales	$100,000	$104,762	$100,000
Cost of services	50,000	53,438	51,000
Gross profit	$ 50,000	$ 51,324	$ 49,000
Depreciation	2,000	2,640	2,800
Other expenses (including taxes)	20,000	20,952	20,000
	$ 22,000	$ 23,592	$ 22,800
Income before price level loss		27,732	
Current operating income			26,200
Loss: General price-level loss		3,572	
Plus: Realized holding gains			1,800
Realized income			$ 28,000
Plus: Unrealized holding gains			$ 3,600
Net Income	$ 28,000	$ 24,160	$ 31,600

(1) See Exhibit 14A-5 (Appendix 14A).
(2) See Exhibit 14A-7 (Appendix 14A).
(3) See Exhibit 14-4.

EXHIBIT 14–6

XTRA CORPORATION
Comparative Balance Sheets
As at December 31, 19X2
(in thousands of dollars)

	(1) Conventional	(2) Price-level adjusted	(3) Replacement costs
Assets			
Current assets			
Cash	$45,000	$45,000	$ 45,000
Accounts receivable	12,000	12,000	12,000
Inventories	20,000	20,000*	22,000
Total Current Assets	$77,000	$77,000	$ 79,000
Equipment	$20,000	$26,400	$ 28,000
Less: Accumulated depreciation	4,000	5,280	5,600
Net	$16,000	$21,120	$ 22,400
Total Assets	$93,000	$98,120	$101,400
Liabilities and Equity			
Accounts payable	$ 5,000	$ 5,000	$ 5,000
Long-term debt	10,000	10,000	10,000
Capital stock	$40,000	$52,800	$ 40,000
Retained earnings: Balance 1/1/19X2	10,000	6,160	10,000
Net income for 19X2	28,000	24,160	
Realized income for 19X2	n.a.	n.a.	28,000
	$38,000	$30,320	$ 38,000
Unrealized holding gains:			
Balance 1/1/X2			4,800
Additions in 19X2			3,600
			8,400
Total Equity	$78,000	$83,120	$ 86,400
Total Liabilities & Equity	$93,000	$98,120	$101,400

(1) See Exhibit 14A-6 (Appendix 14A).
(2) See Exhibit 14A-10 (Appendix 14A).
(3) See Exhibit 14-5.
* Usually not same as "conventional". See footnote to Exhibit 14A–7 (Appendix 14A).

discussion in Appendix 14A some of its disadvantages are significant indeed. GPL adjusted statements change the amounts, but not the timing, of income statement items by adjusting the historical amounts of items for changes in the purchasing power of money since their acquisition.

The above two systems are not competitive, nor are they incompatible. However, they do involve costs of compilation and presentation and, what is perhaps equally significant, they introduce additional complexity into the reporting process which is in itself a significant cost.

If a choice has to be made then from the point of view of the financial analyst the desirable features of the RCA system far outweigh its disadvantages, certainly to a greater extent than is the case with GPL accounting. However it is possible to incorporate the desirable features of GPL accounting with the RCA system and thus achieve such additional advantages as the measurement of monetary gains and losses and valid comparability of results over a number of years.

One avenue of integration is to recognize that in times of, say, rising price levels not all holding gains arising from the increase in replacement cost of a nonmonetary asset are real. For example, Exhibit 14–1 shows that in 19X1 the replacement cost of equipment of Xtra Corp. rose from $20,000 to $25,000 showing a holding gain of $5,000. But, as shown in Exhibit 14A–4 due to a rise of 20 percent in the general price level the current purchasing power equivalent of the investment in equipment at 12/31/X1 rose to $24,000 from the $20,000 original cost. Thus, of the $5,000 in holding gains only $1,000 were real and the remaining $4,000 were nominal in that they merely made up for the decline in the purchasing power of the capital invested in equipment.

Guided by the above insights, one suggested overall integration of RCA with GPL statements calls for a restatement of the opening (or average) invested capital by the GPL index change for the period with the increment described as "Maintenance of Capital."[10] Only after this amount has been provided for by deduction from net results for the period can the residue be called a real gain for the period.

ILLUSTRATION 3.   The capital investment in Xtra Corp. on 12/31/19X1 was $54,800 and $86,400 at 12/31/19X2 both on a RCA basis (Exhibits 14–1 and 14–2).

The "maintenance of capital" provision may be calculated as follows:

Capital at 1/1/19X2 54,800 × 132/120 (ending index/beginning index) = 60,280 or an increment of	$5,480
Increase in capital during 19X2	
$31,600 ($86,400 − $54,800) × 132/126 (ending index/average index) = $33,105 or an increment of	1,505
"Maintenance of Capital" provision for 19X2	$6,985
Thus a measure of the "real income" for 19X2 is:	
the Net Income (RCA Basis)	$31,600
Less "Capital Maintenance" requirement	6,985
	$24,615

As is the case with monetary gains and losses the "maintenance of capital" charges or credits do not involve funds flows and must be very carefully explained and interpreted.

---

[10] W. D. Hall, "What Will Statements Look Like in Three Years?" *Managerial Planning*, July–August 1976, p. 9–14.

It is interesting to note that in Germany an attempt to recognize the effect of changes in monetary items within a RCA framework takes the form of reducing the increments due to replacement cost factors of cost of sales and depreciation by the proportion of inventories and fixed assets financed by other than equity capital (essentially debt). Under this system, the arbitrary assumption is made that equity capital is used first to finance fixed assets and then inventories.

Certainly in the United States the "jury is still out" on what accounting framework for reflecting price changes will ultimately be adopted. In the meantime, given the information that is now available and will become available the analyst has a framework within which to estimate the effects of price changes on conventionally prepared financial statements.

IMPLICATIONS FOR ANALYSIS

As can be seen from a review of this work so far, the accounting framework is a measurement system of considerable complexity. If we superimpose on this the problem of an unstable measurement unit (money) this complexity is compounded to a mind-boggling degree. And yet, the greater the rate of price level changes, the more critical it becomes for the analyst to comprehend the factors that affect changes in financial statements and the manner in which such changes occur in real terms.

Prices change for many reasons and many such changes are due to changes in technology, product quality, and economies of scale. Thus, even without changes in the purchasing power of money, accounting for historical costs only would not be fully relevant. However, the unquestionably major problem is purchasing power changes, or specifically *inflation*.

Inflation is basically a tax on cash balances. It causes losses on monetary assets, gains on monetary liabilities, and significant changes in the values (expressed in terms of money) of other assets as well as changes in funds flows, the demand for funds, and in the uncertainties and risks affecting with differing impacts business enterprises of various kinds. In the words of Professor John Lintner ". . . higher inflation rates would increase a firm's relative dependence on external funds *even if* there were no phantom inventory profits and depreciation could be charged on replacement costs and there were no added needs due to backups of unsold inventories, increased sales on credit, or delays in collections or credit losses, and so on. Any adverse change in any of these conditions of course merely compounds the adverse effects of increased inflation rates . . ."[11]

---

[11] John Lintner, "Inflation and Security Returns," *The Journal of Finance*, May 1975, pp. 273–74.

We have examined in this chapter two responses to the problems caused by price changes. They also represent two analytical frameworks within which the effects of price changes can be understood and evaluated.

General price level changes

The effect of price level changes on an entity's financial statements depends on both the rate of price level changes and the composition of assets, liabilities, and equities. Empirical studies have shown that even a moderate rate of inflation can, on a cumulative basis, cause very significant changes in reported operating and financial results.[12]

The composition of assets, liabilities, and equities is another important determinant of the effect of price level changes on an entity and on its financial statements.

The following are some useful generalizations regarding such effects in times of significant inflation:

1. The larger the proportion of depreciable assets and the higher their age, the more unrestated income tends to be overstated. Thus the income of capital intensive companies tends to be affected more than that of others by price level restatements.
2. The rate of inventory turnover has a bearing on price level effects. The slower the inventory turnover, the more operating income tends to be overstated.
3. The mix of assets and liabilities as between monetary and nonmonetary is important. A net investment in monetary assets will, in times of rising price levels, lead to purchasing power losses, and purchasing power gains will result from a net monetary liability position.
4. The methods of financing also have an important bearing on results. The larger the amount of debt and the longer its maturities, the better the protection against purchasing power losses or the better the exposure to purchasing power gains.

The analyst must understand that while monetary gains and losses have economic significance they *do not* affect the flow of funds in an enterprise. A GPL statement of changes in financial position would make this abundantly clear.

Specific price changes

RCA overcomes the criticism that businesses experience *specific* price changes rather than general inflation. It divides the total profit

---

[12] Rosenfield, "Accounting for Inflation—A Field Test," *The Journal of Accountancy*, June 1969. Also S. Davidson and R. L. Weil, "Inflation Accounting—What Will General Price Level Adjusted Income Statements Show?," *Financial Analysts Journal*, January and February 1975.

into components which can be meaningfully analyzed and interpreted:

1. Operating profit (or sustainable income), i.e., revenue less the current replacement value of assets consumed or utilized.
2. Holding gains or losses that results from the ownership of assets.

Operating profits result in funds that should be available for distribution to owners. Holding gains plus depreciation recovery on original cost are resources that must be reinvested in order to maintain the enterprise physical capacity.

The market significance of distributable profits as opposed to holding gains which depend on further price increases for recurrence is another matter. Presumably, the market place will value the former at a higher price-earnings ratio than it will the latter.[13]

Many factors will have to be considered before the effect of the SEC mandated replacement cost disclosures on conventionally measured income can be properly evaluated: (1) Ways of incorporating productivity changes of new equipment will have to be devised. (2) The introduction of replacement costs may lead some companies to abandon unrealistically low estimates of the useful lives of equipment which was hitherto a crude means of compensating for a lack of adjustment for inflation. (3) The accounting methods used by various companies will have an effect on the ultimate difference between CVA and conventional accounting figures. Thus companies which kept inventories on the Lifo basis or which used accelerated methods of depreciation for book purposes may not show as dramatically different results under CVA as will companies which have used Fifo inventory accounting and slower depreciation methods.

As we have seen, both systems have analytical significance for the analyst although, if a choice has to be made, RCA seems to have the edge. However, in industries in which most assets and liabilities are monetary in nature, such as banks or other financial institutions, the assessment of the impact of price level changes on those monetary items will be of greatest significance.

APPENDIX 14A

GENERAL PRICE LEVEL RESTATED FINANCIAL STATEMENTS

Preparation and interpretation

The basic purpose of financial statements restated for general price level changes (more briefly referred to as GPL statements) is to pre-

---

[13] See A. Falkenstein and R. L. Weil, "Replacement Cost Accounting," *Financial Analysts Journal,* January–February, 1977.

sent all elements of the financial statements in terms of units of the same purchasing power restated by means of a general price level index. General price level financial statements differ from historical-dollar statements only in the unit of measure used in them. Consequently they do not represent a departure from the historical cost principle. Moreover, they are subject to the same accounting principles as are used in the preparation of historical dollar financial statements with the only exception that gains or losses in the purchasing power of the dollar are recognized in general price level statements.

Different financial statement items are affected differently by restatements. As to effect of price level changes on accounting measurements, it is useful to distinguish between two major categories of items: monetary and nonmonetary.

Monetary items are those which represent a claim to a fixed number of dollars such as cash, accounts and notes receivable, and investments in bonds, or those representing an obligation to pay a fixed number of dollars such as accounts and notes payable, bonds payable, etc.

Since monetary items represent a claim to, or an obligation of, a fixed number of dollars, their value in terms of purchasing power varies with the general price level.

ILLUSTRATION 1A. Assume that A invested $1,000 in a business at the beginning of 19X1 when the price level index stood at 100. The money was kept in a checking account throughout the year, and the balance at 12/31/X1 remained at $1,000 at which time the price index had advanced to 110.

Conventional financial statements would show the financial condition of A at 12/31/X1, unchanged from the beginning of the year, as:

Cash in bank .... $1,000   Capital $1,000

Price level statements, however, would recognize the loss in purchasing power suffered by the cash balance while the price level rose by 10 percent. The first step in such recognition is to restate the balance sheet to the price level prevailing at the end of the year 19X1. Thus:

Cash in bank .... $1,100   Capital $1,100

A glance at the above balance sheet reveals that a further restatement is needed. A failed to preserve his purchasing power because cash as legal tender does not change from its nominal value and hence it can be stated only at its face value of $1,000.

The final presentation of the price level financial statement of A at 12/31/X1 is then as follows:

Cash	$1,000	Capital (as restated)		$1,100
		Less: Loss on monetary		
		items	100	$1,000
	$1,000			$1,000

This financial statement, in effect, tells the reader that in order to preserve the original purchasing power invested, the capital should be $1,100; but owing to the loss in purchasing power of cash of $100, it is only $1,000.

In the same way that the holding of monetary assets during rising price levels results in losses of purchasing power, the owing of money during such periods results in gains of purchasing power because the liability may be satisfied by payment of currency having a lower purchasing power.

ILLUSTRATION 2A.   Assume that in addition to investing $1,000 on 1/1/X1, A also borrowed $1,000 from a friend. At inception his statement of financial condition was as follows:

| Cash in bank .... | $2,000 | Loan payable .... | $1,000 |
| | | Capital .... | 1,000 |

Assuming that A engaged in no further transactions during 19X1, that the price level index rose from 100 on 1/1/X1 to 110 on 12/31/X1 and that interest can be ignored, the conventional financial statements will be unchanged as at 12/31/X1.

Price level financial statements, however, would reflect the changes in purchasing power of money as follows:

Holding of $2,000 cash resulted in a purchasing power *loss* of $2,000 × 10%	$200
Owing $1,000 resulted in a purchasing power *gain* of $1,000 × 10%	100
Net purchasing power loss	$100

The price level financial statement at 12/31/X1 would be as follows:

Cash	$2,000	Loan payable		$1,000
		Capital	$1,100	
		Less: Net purchasing		
		power loss	100	
		Net capital		1,000
	$2,000			$2,000

From the above it can be observed that had the $2,000 kept in the bank been entirely financed by A's capital, he would have incurred a purchasing power loss of $200 (10 percent of $2,000). The fact that he borrowed $1,000 enabled him to pass on to his creditor the purchasing power loss arising from the holding of $1,000 in cash. Moreover, as we shall see below, had A invested the proceeds of the loan in a nonmonetary item, he would have had a purchasing power gain of $100 (10 percent of $1,000).

Nonmonetary items are all items other than the monetary ones. Nonmonetary items are stated in terms of the purchasing power of the dollar at the time they were acquired. Thus, the holding of nonmonetary items does *not* give rise to general price level gains and losses.

ILLUSTRATION 3A. Assume the same facts as in Illustration 1A except that instead of keeping the money in the bank, A invests $1,000 in a plot of land. The conventional financial statements at both the beginning and the end of 19X1 would show:

Land .... $1,000   Capital $1,000

The price level financial statement at 12/31/X1, at which time the price level index had risen from 100 to 110, would be as follows:

Land .... $1,100   Capital $1,100

This gives effect to the assumption that land, a nonmonetary asset, does not lose in purchasing power in times of rising prices, and thus it is restated to $1,100 ($1,000 × 110/100) which is at 12/31/X1 the equivalent in purchasing power that the $1,000 was as at 1/1/X1. This $1,100 for land is historical cost restated in terms of current purchasing power equivalent and has no further significance. Thus it does not represent, except by sheer coincidence, either current market value or replacement cost. However, if its market value is only $900 and it is, for instance, an inventory item rather than a long-term investment, it may have to be written down to this amount under the "lower-of-cost-or-market" principle.

If no write-down is called for the price level statement of A at 12/31/X1, it would remain as shown above indicating, in effect, that the purchasing power of the original $1,000 investment, now stated as $1,100, is assumed to have been maintained.

Two important conclusions arise from the above examples.

1. In times of price level changes the holding of monetary assets and liabilities give rise to general price level gains and losses.
2. Nonmonetary assets and liabilities are restated, by means of the Gross National Product Implicit Price Deflator, to reflect the amount of dollars which represent the purchasing power equivalent to that prevailing at the time of their acquisition. The equity accounts reflect the net result of all changes in the equity including those due to price level changes.

Extended illustration of statement restatement

ILLUSTRATION 4A. We can now solidify our understanding of the process of restatement of GPL statements by means of an extended illustration.

The Xtra Corporation was formed on January 1, 19X1, to perform commercial laundry services. On that date it acquired for $20,000 equipment having an estimated useful life of 10 years. The salvage value at the end of that period is estimated to equal removal costs, and the straight-line method of depreciation is to be used. The opening balance sheet of Xtra Corporation is shown in Exhibit 14A–1.

EXHIBIT 14A–1

XTRA CORPORATION
Balance Sheet, January 1, 19X1
(in 000s)

Assets		*Equity*	
Cash	$20,000	Capital stock	$40,000
Equipment	20,000		
	$40,000		$40,000

During 19X1 the following results were achieved:

Sales.....................................		$50,000
Cost of services	$27,000	
Less—Ending inventory of supplies	2,000	25,000
		$25,000
Depreciation	2,000	
Other expenses (including taxes)	13,000	15,000
Net income..............................		$10,000

The inventory of supplies is accounted for under the Fifo basis. The price level index at the beginning of operations was 100, and by the end of the year it increased to 120. We assume that the increase in the index was spread uniformly throughout the year and that all phases of the company's operations are also spread evenly throughout the period under consideration.

Price level index on January 1, 19X1	100
Price level index on December 31, 19X1	120
Average price level index during 19X1	110

The adjusted income statement shown in Exhibit 14A–2 does not yet include the gain or loss arising from holding monetary items, and we now proceed to determine this effect. The general price level gain or loss computation is best done within the framework of a statement accounting for changes in net monetary assets (in this example assumed to be only cash),

EXHIBIT 14A–2

Restatement of income statement (in thousands of dollars)

	Conventional income statement year ended 12/31/X1		Conversion factor	Price level adjusted income statement in 12/31/X1 dollars	
Sales		$50,000	120/110 (1)		$54,545
Cost of services	$27,000		120/110 (1)	$29,457	
Ending inventory of supplies	2,000	25,000	120/120 (2)	2,000	27,457
		$25,000			$27,088
Depreciation of equipment	2,000		120/100 (3)	2,400	
Other expenses	13,000		120/110 (1)	14,180	
		15,000			16,580
Net income		$10,000			$10,508

(1) Since sales, cost of services, and other expenses are evenly spread over the year they were incurred, on average, at the average price level for 19X1 or at the index level of 110. To convert them to the price level existing at the end of 19X1, when the index stood at 120, we use the conversion factor of 120/110.

(2) Inventory on Fifo basis is assumed to have been acquired during the last quarter when the index stood at 120.

(3) The equipment, which is depreciated, was acquired at the beginning of 19X1 when the price level index was 100. At year-end, the index stood at 120 and the depreciation expense, which is recorded at year-end, is converted by means of a conversion factor of 120/100.

a sort of statement of sources and uses of monetary items as shown in Exhibit 14A–3.

Examination of the computation of price level gain or loss will reveal that it is based on a recognition of the fact that monetary assets lose purchasing power in times of rising price levels (and gain in times of deflation) and that

EXHIBIT 14A–3

General price level gain or loss computation (in thousands of dollars)

	Conventional statement	Conversion	Restated to 12/31/X1 dollars
Monetary items, 1/1/X1	$20,000	120/100 (1)	$24,000
Add: Sales	50,000	(2)	54,545
	$70,000		$78,545
Less: Cost of services and other expenses	40,000	(2)	43,637
Net monetary items at 12/31/X1	$30,000		
Net monetary items—restated (if there were no loss)			$34,908
Net monetary items at 12/31/X1 (as above)			30,000
Price level loss			$ 4,908

(1) In the absence of a change in purchasing power the monetary items (cash in this case) would have been restated to the price level at year-end—hence the 120/100 conversion.

(2) Sales and cost and expenses, with the exception of depreciation, represent inflows or outflows of monetary items. Thus they are converted on the same basis as in the income statement (see Exhibit 14A–2).

the opposite is the case with monetary liabilities. Consequently, the difference between the restated total of monetary items and the nominal amount of these items represents the price level gain or loss. Thus the cash balance of $20,000, had it remained unchanged, should have gone up to $24,000 if the purchasing power residing in the $20,000 balance at the beginning of the year was to have been preserved. However, since cash as legal tender cannot change in face value, a $4,000 price level loss was incurred. Similarly, the proceeds from sales of $50,000 should have become $54,545 by year-end had the purchasing power of these proceeds been preserved. However, since the proceeds were in monetary items (usually cash or accounts receivable), a price level loss of $4,545 has been incurred in this area.

The price level adjusted income of	$10,508
Will now have to be reduced by a price level loss of	4,908
Bring the net income to.....................	$ 5,600

If we assume for the sake of simplicity that the funds from operations merely increased Xtra Corporation's cash balance, we have in Exhibit 14A–4 the conventional and price level adjusted balance sheets at December 31, 19X1.

EXHIBIT 14A–4

(In 000's)

	Conventional balance sheet as at 12/31/X1		Conversion factor	Balance sheet restated in 12/31/X1 dollars	
Cash		$30,000	(1)		$30,000
Inventory		2,000	120/120 (4)		2,000
Total current assets		32,000			32,000
Equipment................	$20,000		120/100	$24,000	
Less: Provision for depreciation	2,000	18,000	120/100	2,400	21,600
		$50,000			$53,600
Capital stock		$40,000	120/100 (2)		$48,000
Retained earnings		10,000	(3)		5,600
		$50,000			$53,600

(1) Monetary items require no restatement because they represent a claim to, or obligation of, a fixed number of dollars.

(2) Capital is a nonmonetary item and thus is converted to the new price level equivalent.

(3) As determined by the restated income statement (see Exhibit 14A-2 and price level adjusted net income computation above).

(4) See footnote (2) of Exhibit 14A-2.

In the second year of its existence, the Xtra Corporation extended its activities somewhat so that it borrowed $10,000 on 7/1/X2, and extended credit to customers. The financial statements at the end of 19X2 were as shown in Exhibits 14A–5 and 14A–6.

EXHIBIT 14A–5

XTRA CORPORATION
Income Statement
For the Year Ending 19X2
(in 000's)

Sales		$100,000
Cost of services:		
Inventory at 1/1/X2	$ 2,000	
Purchases	28,000	
Labor and other costs	40,000	
	$70,000	
Inventory at 12/31/X2	20,000	50,000
		$ 50,000
Depreciation........................	$ 2,000	
Other expenses (including taxes)	20,000	22,000
Net income		$ 28,000

EXHIBIT 14A–6

XTRA CORPORATION
Balance Sheet
As at December 31, 19X2
(in 000's)

Assets

Current Assets:		
Cash......................................		$45,000
Accounts receivable		12,000
Inventories...............................		20,000
Total Current Assets		$77,000
Equipment.................................	$20,000	
Less: Accumulated depreciation	4,000	16,000
Total Assets		$93,000

Liabilities and Capital

Accounts payable		$ 5,000
Long-term debt		10,000
Capital stock..............................	$40,000	
Retained earnings balance		
(1/1/X2)	$10,000	
Net income	28,000	38,000	78,000
Total Liabilities and Capital		$93,000

During 19X2, prices advanced; and by 12/31/X2 the price level index reached the level of 132. The average price level index for 19X2 was 126, and for the last quarter of the year it was 132. On the basis of this information, the restatement process of the Xtra Corporation's 19X2 financial statements, adjusted for price level changes, is shown in Exhibit 14A–7.

EXHIBIT 14A-7

Restatement of income for the year ending 12/31/X2 (in 000's)

	Conventional		Conversion factor	Price level adjusted	
Sales		$100,000	132/126		$104,762
Cost of services inventory					
(1/1/X2)	$ 2,000		132/120	$ 2,200	
Purchases	28,000		132/126	29,333	
Labor and other costs	40,000		132/126	41,905	
	$70,000			$73,438	
Inventory (12/31/X2)	20,000	50,000	132/132 (1)	20,000	53,438
		$ 50,000			$ 51,324
Depreciation	$ 2,000		132/100 (2)	$ 2,640	
Other expenses	20,000	22,000	132/126	20,952	23,592
Net income		$ 28,000			
					$ 27,732

General price level loss (see Exhibit 14A-9) 3,572

Net income (adjusted) .... $ 24,160

(1) Inventory restatement is based on the assumption that under Fifo the ending inventory is the one last purchased. Assuming that the inventory turnover is 4, the entire ending inventory was acquired in the last quarter of 19X2 which had an average price level of 132, that is, identical with that prevailing at year end. Hence the 132/132 conversion factor.

(2) Equipment was acquired when the price level index stood at 100.

EXHIBIT 14A-8

Restatement ("roll forward") of 12/31/X1 price level statements to 12/31/X2 dollars (in 000's)

	Restated in 12/31/X1 dollars		Conversion factor (1)	Restated in 12/31/X2 dollars	
	Balance Sheet				
Cash		$30,000	132/120		$33,000
Inventory		2,000	132/120		2,200
Equipment	$24,000		132/120	$26,400	
Less: Provision for					
depreciation	2,400	21,600	132/120	2,640	23,760
		$53,600			$58,960
Capital stock		$48,000	132/120		$52,800
Retained earnings		5,600	132/120		6,160
		$53,600			$58,960
	Income Statement				
Sales		$54,545	132/120		$60,000
Cost of services	$27,457		132/120	$30,203	
Depreciation	2,400		132/120	2,640	
Other expenses	14,180	44,037	132/120	15,598	48,441
		$10,508			$11,559
General price level loss		4,908	132/120		5,399
Net income		$ 5,600			$ 6,160

(1) Roll forward from 12/31/X1 when index stood at 120 to 12/31/X2 when index reached 132 level.

Next we must roll forward the GPL statements as at 12/31/X1 in order to express them in terms of dollars of 12/31/X2 purchasing power. This must be done in order to:

1. Have prior year financial statements restated in current dollars for comparative purposes.
2. Have the amount of retained earnings at the end of the prior year in current dollars for purposes of current (19X2) year restatement of retained earnings.
3. Utilize figures for purposes such as the computation of general price level gain or loss.

The final comparative price level adjusted financial statements are shown in Exhibits 14A–11 and 14A–12 (p. 410).

What the restated figures mean

The restated financial statements (Exhibits 14A–11 and 14A–12) eliminate the effects of price level changes by stating each item in terms of dollars (in this case 12/31/X2 dollars) of constant purchasing power. As restated, the relationships of these items among themselves as well as over time can be different from those prevailing among the unrestated items. Therein, of course, lies much of their significance as the following examples of selected relationships indicate:

	Conventional ($000s)	Change	Adjusted ($000s)	Change
Sales:				
19X1	$ 50,000		$ 60,000	
19X2	100,000		104,762	
Increase	$ 50,000	+100%	$ 44,762	+ 75%
Net income:				
19X1	$ 10,000		$ 6,160	
19X2	28,000		24,160	
Increase	$ 18,000	+180%	$ 18,000	+292%
Return on investment:				
19X1	22% (1)		11% (3)	
19X2	44% (2)		34% (4)	

(1) Income divided by average capital $= \dfrac{10,000}{(40,000 + 50,000) \div 2}$

(2) Income divided by average capital $= \dfrac{28,000}{(50,000 + 78,000) \div 2}$

(3) Income divided by average capital $= \dfrac{6,160}{(52,800 + 58,960) \div 2}$

(4) Income divided by average capital $= \dfrac{24,160}{(58,960 + 83,120) \div 2}$

The *sales* figure comparison indicates that expressed in unadjusted dollars, sales rose 100 percent from 19X1 to 19X2. On the basis of constant purchasing power dollars (here 12/31/X2 dollars), however, the increase was only 75 percent. Care is needed in interpreting these results. All that the above change means is that in terms of constant purchasing power dollars sales rose 75 percent, and this is a more valid figure of percentage change than the 100 percent change, which compares sales levels expressed in dollars of different purchasing power. However, what cannot be inferred from the adjusted sales figures, for instance, is that the physical volume of sales rose by 75 percent. What the actual change in physical volume was depends on the change in the *specific* sales prices for the company's products or services. If they differ from changes in the *general* price level, no valid inferences regarding changes in physical volume can be drawn. Only if the com-

EXHIBIT 14A–9

General price level restatement—19X2 general price level gain or loss (in 000's)

		12/31/X1	*12/31/X2*
	Conventional	*Restated in 12/31/X2 dollars (1)*	*Conventional restated in 12/31/X2 dollars*
Net monetary items:			
Cash	$ 30,000	$33,000	$ 45,000
Receivables			12,000
Current liabilities			(5,000)
Long-term debt			(10,000)
Net monetary items	$ 30,000	$33,000	$ 42,000

	Conventional	*Conversion factor*	*Restated to 12/31/X2 dollars*
Net monetary items, 12/31/X1	$ 30,000	As above	$ 33,000
Add:			
Sales for 19X2	100,000	(2)	104,762
	$130,000		$137,762
Deduct:			
Purchases	$ 28,000	(2)	$ 29,333
Labor and other costs	40,000	(2)	41,905
Other expenses	20,000	(2)	20,952
	$ 88,000		$ 92,190
Net monetary items (conventional)	$ 42,000		
Net monetary items–restated, 12/31/X2 (if there were no loss)			$ 45,572
Net monetary items (conventional) as above			42,000
General price level loss			$ 3,572

(1) See Exhibit 14A–8.
(2) See income statement conversion (Exhibit 14A–7).

pany's sales price changes coincide exactly with price changes reflected in the general price level index can an adjusted sales change be deemed to reflect changes in the physical volume of sales.

The greater rate of increase in price level adjusted *net income* as compared with the 180 percent increase in net income in the conventional financial statements can be explained as follows:

The general price level loss on monetary items in 19X1 (all in 12/31/X2 dollars) was $5,399 or 47 percent of the $11,559 income before that loss. This depressed considerably the base net income figure in the percentage comparison. By contrast, due in large measure to the monetary liabilities incurred in 19X2, the loss in purchasing power on monetary items in 19X2 was only $3,572 or 13 percent of the $27,732 income before such loss. This accounts for the much stronger year-to-

EXHIBIT 14A–10

Restatement of balance sheet as at December 31, 19X2 (in 000's)

	Conventional		Conversion factor	Price level adjusted 12/31/X2	
Assets					
Current Assets:					
Cash		$45,000	(1)		$45,000
Accounts receivable ..		12,000	(1)		12,000
Inventories		20,000	(2)		20,000
Total Current Assets		$77,000			
Equipment	$20,000		132/100	$26,400	
Less: Provision for depreciation	4,000	16,000	(3)	5,280	21,120
Total Assets		$93,000			$98,120
Liabilities and Capital					
Accounts payable		$ 5,000	(1)		$ 5,000
Long-term debt		10,000	(1)		10,000
Capital stock	$40,000		132/100 (4)	$52,800	
Retained earnings balance (1/1/X2)	$10,000		(5)	$ 6,160	
Net income ...	28,000	38,000	78,000	see Exh. 14A–7	24,160	30,320	83,120
Total Liabilities and Capital		$93,000			$98,120

(1) Monetary items—no restatement needed.
(2) See explanation in income statement conversion schedule (Exhibit 14A–7).
(3) Balance of depreciation provision at 12/31/X1 in 12/31/X1 dollars—2,400 rolled forward to 12/31/X2 dollars (see "roll forward" Exhibit 14A–8) $2,640
Depreciation provided in 19X2 (restated) (Exhibit 14A–7) 2,640

Total depreciation provision $5,280

(4) Capital was invested when price level index stood at 100. To preserve purchasing power, now that the index stands at 132, it must be 132/100 times original amount. This amount can also be taken from Exhibit 14A–8.
(5) From statement showing "roll forward" of restated 12/31/X1 balance sheet to 12/31/X2 dollars (Exhibit 14A–8).

EXHIBIT 14A–11

THE XTRA CORPORATION
Comparative Balance Sheet (price level adjusted)
In 12/31/X2 Dollars (000's)

Assets		12/31/X2		12/31/X1 (1)
Current Assets:				
Cash		$45,000		$33,000
Accounts receivable		12,000		—
Inventories		20,000		2,200
Total Current Assets		$77,000		$35,200
Equipment	$26,400		$26,400	
Less: Provision for depreciation	5,280	21,120	2,640	23,760
Total Assets		$98,120		$58,960
Liabilities and Capital				
Accounts payable		$ 5,000		—
Long-term debt		10,000		—
Capital stock	$52,800			$52,800
Retained earnings balance				
1/1/X2	$ 6,160			
Add: Net income for 19X2				
(Exh. 14A–12)	24,160	30,320	83,120	6,160
Total Liabilities and Capital		$98,120		$58,960

(1) See Exhibit 14A–8.

EXHIBIT 14A–12

THE XTRA CORPORATION
Comparative Statements of Income (price level adjusted)
In 12/31/X2 Dollars (000's)

		Year ended 12/31/X2		Year ended 12/31/X1 (1)
Sales		$104,762		$60,000
Cost of services:				
Inventory, 1/1/X2	$ 2,200			
Purchases	29,333			
Labor and other costs	41,905			
	$73,438		$32,403	
Inventory at year end	20,000	53,438	2,200	30,203
		$ 51,324		$29,797
Depreciation	$ 2,640		$ 2,640	
Other expenses	20,952	23,592	15,598	18,238
Net income...........................		$ 27,732		$11,559
General price level loss		3,572		5,399
Net income...........................		$ 24,160		$ 6,160

(1) See Exhibit 14A–8.

year net profit increase in the restated net income figure as compared with the conventional net income figure.

Finally, the *return on investment* in both years is less on a price level restated basis than on a conventional basis. This is due to the fact that in each year the price level restated net income is less than its conventional counterpart *and* because the capital base, on a restated basis, is larger after giving effect to the increase in the price level than it is in the conventional balance sheet. Thus these twin influences combine to reduce the price level restated return on investment as compared to the conventional figures.

OBJECTIVES OF GENERAL PRICE LEVEL ADJUSTED STATEMENTS

There are a few basic facts about the effect of price level changes on the conventional financial statements which must be thoroughly understood. One is that money, whether expressed in dollars or any other currency, is worth only what it will buy. Thus, if the price level changes, the value of money changes along with it; and hence a dollar received or spent in one period is not comparable with that received or spent in another period, the distortion being in proportion to the cumulative change in the general price level. It is part of the "money illusion" to consider a dollar a dollar and to forget the obvious fact that the 1978 dollar represents a much smaller unit of general purchasing power than did, say, the 1955 dollar. Surely, the known difficulties and complexities of adjusting for the infusion into the financial statements of such disparate bundles of purchasing power, all under the common name of "dollar," and the simplifying assumptions needed in carrying out such restating process do not justify the attempts by many to ignore such effects. In times of changing price levels, the income statement, to single out one of the important measures of corporate performance, is composed of at least two distinct elements: (1) results of business activities expressed in terms of units of equal purchasing power and (2) changes resulting from price level changes. An intelligent assessment and analysis of these results require a separation and an understanding of these two disparate effects. By analogy, if we want to measure the speed of an automobile (business results) by reference to a moving train (price level changes), we must adjust for both the rate of speed and the direction of travel of the train before the true speed of the automobile can be determined.

ILLUSTRATION 4A. A small-loan company whose assets are mostly of a monetary nature must, in times of significant price inflation, charge a rate of interest which will compensate it not only for the use of its capital funds but which will also compensate it for the loss of purchasing power of the funds lent. Thus, the proper interpretation of its income, which by conventional standards may seem unduly large, must include recognition of the offsetting general price level loss on monetary assets incurred by the company.

A major objective of GPL adjusted financial statements is thus to present them in terms of uniform units of purchasing power rather than in terms of units of money which distort interperiod and inter-company comparisons.

LIMITATIONS OF THE RESTATEMENT TECHNIQUE

While facilitating comparisons in terms of a uniform unit of measurement which is, however, not the unit of money in which we conduct day to day transaction, the General Price Level Accounting (GPLA) framework is subject to serious limitations.

General versus specific price changes

One most important shortcoming is the use by this framework of a *general* price level index while in fact price level changes affect businesses in *specific* and dramatically different ways.

ILLUSTRATION 5A
1. Inflation ofen results in a fall in the value of equity securities. The holder of such securities while adjusting them upwards by the change in the general price level index does in actuality experience a decline in the market value of these nonmonetary assets.
2. When dramatic price increases of petroleum products occurred in 1974 the general price level index failed by far to reflect the magnitude of price increases in these specific commodities. Consequently, a restatement of oil inventories by the change in the general price level index was not very meaningful.

Monetary gains and losses

Monetary gains and losses are difficult to understand and to explain. They do not produce parallel cash inflows or outflows and hence they cannot be distributed. What they do show for example, in the case of monetary gains on long term debt, is the reduced economic significance of payments in fixed dollars which the obligations call for in the future. However, the very reporting of such gains, if not understood, may actually mask the significance of a deteriorating liquidity position of a highly leveraged company. This has led some critics to refer to such gains as theoretical or phantom credits.

These limitations as well as the fear that the GPLA framework is not an adequate or fully relevant response to the problem of accounting for price changes has probably resulted in a proposing[1] in Britain of a

---

[1] In mid-1977 British chartered accountants voted down a proposed compulsory system of current cost accounting.

form of current cost accounting and in the United States the SEC replacement disclosure initiatives as earlier described.

QUESTIONS

1. How do changing price levels affect the conventional (unrestated) financial statements of a company operating in an inflationary environment?

2. In what ways have businessmen attempted to meet some of the objectives of price level accounting? Evaluate these attempts briefly.

3. What are the objectives of GPL adjusted statements?

4. In what respect do general price level statements differ from conventional financial statements?

5. Why is the distinction between monetary and nonmonetary items significant in accounting for the effects of price level changes?

6. On the basis of conventional financial statements, the year-to-year sales increase of Company X was 24 percent. Adjusted for price level changes, the increase was only 10 percent. Is it possible to infer from this that the physical volume of sales rose by 10 percent? Explain.

7. Why do general price level adjusted financial statements fail to meet the objectives of those who want to see fair market values or replacement values introduced to accounting?

8. What effect can the composition of the assets and liabilities of an enterprise have on the effect which price level changes can have on it? Elaborate by means of an example or two.

9. In the absence of supplementary financial statements restated for price level changes, how can the financial analyst assess the approximate effects of price level changes on the reported results?

10. *a.* How might it be maintained that a gain or a loss is incurred by holding a constant balance of cash through a period of price level change?

    b. Identify and give a justification for the typical accounting treatment accorded these gains or losses. (AICPA)

11. What is the major objection to the adoption of RCA? What is the major rebuttal voiced against this objection?

12. List some of the approaches available to estimate replacement costs and discuss some of the complexities in the application of such approaches.

13. If a choice has to be made on which framework (conventional, GPL, or RCA) is most desirable from the viewpoint of the financial analyst, which one would you choose and why?

15

THE AUDITOR'S OPINION— MEANING AND SIGNIFICANCE

An entity's financial statements are the representations of its management. Management bears a primary responsibility for the fairness of presentation and the degree of informative disclosure in the financial statements it issues to interested parties, such as present and potential owners, creditors, and others. It has, however, become generally accepted that there is a need for an independent check on management's financial reporting.

The profession that has emerged to serve society's need in this respect by performing the attest function is the public accounting profession. It may be readily observed that the more developed a country's economy and the more diverse, free, and mobile its capital and money markets, the stronger and the more important its public accounting profession is likely to be. Surely, the United States experience supports this conclusion, for the public accounting profession here is perhaps the world's largest and most vital.

Some states recognize and license "Public Accountants" and "Licensed Accountants," and the requirements for practice under these titles vary from strict to feeble. However, there is another title which has the most consistent significance—that of "Certified Public Accountant." It can be acquired only by those who have passed the CPA examination, a rigorous series of tests which are uniform in all states and which are graded centrally under the auspices of the

---

Author's note: Women have been analysts and auditors for years and their numbers are growing. However, in this work masculine pronouns are being used for succinctness and are intended to refer to both males and females.

414

American Institute of Certified Public Accountants (AICPA). While no profession can insure uniformity of quality among its members, the successful completion of these examinations does insure that the candidate has demonstrated acceptable knowledge of accounting and auditing principles and practices.

Since the CPAs represent by far the most important segment of public accounting practice in the United States, our consideration of the auditor's opinion will be confined to that issued by the CPA and governed by the various pronouncements issued by their professional association, the AICPA.

In spite of the many real and imagined shortcomings of the auditor's work, and, as this work illustrates, there are many of both varieties, the auditor's function is of critical importance to the financial analyst. While improvements are needed in many areas of the auditor's work, his attestation to financial statements greatly increases their reliability to the analyst as well as the degree and quality of disclosure provided in them.

As in many areas of endeavor, so in the analysis of financial statements, partial or incomplete knowledge can be more damaging than a complete lack of it. This truth applies to the analyst's understanding and knowledge of the auditor's work and the significance of his opinion.

WHAT THE ANALYST NEEDS TO KNOW

In relying on the auditor's opinion, which covers the financial statements subject to review, the analyst must—

1. Learn as much as he can about the auditor upon whom he is relying.
2. Understand fully what the auditor's opinion means and the message it is designed to convey to the user.
3. Appreciate the limitations to which the opinion is subject, as well as implications which such limitations hold for the analysis of financial statements covered by the opinion.

Knowing the auditor

The possession by the auditor of the CPA certificate does assure the analyst of a reasonable qualification for practice as an auditor. However, as is the case in other professions, differences in ability, competence, and qualifications can be considerable.

The relationship between the auditor and those who rely on his opinion differs markedly from that existing in other professional relationships. While the auditor has both an obligation and a concurrent responsibility to users of his opinion, he is in most cases neither appointed nor compensated by them. He must look mostly to management for both recommendation for his appointment and the determination of his fee. When management's desires with respect to financial reporting are in conflict with the best interests of the outside users of financial statements, the auditor's integrity and independence are put to a stern test. Thus, one criterion of the auditor's reliability is his reputation for integrity and independence in the community at large and among respected members of the financial community. Whatever else the auditor must have, and his qualifications and skill must be considerable, without these attributes nothing else counts for very much. The reputation of an auditor for competence and for knowledge of his work can be established in a variety of ways. The auditor's professional credentials are one element, his membership and standing in state and national accounting associations another, and his participation in professional organizations yet another factor to be assessed by the analyst. An auditing firm's activities and past performance are usually well known in the community in which it operates.

Finally, the analyst, from his own experience is often able to form a judgment about the auditor's reputation for quality work. Since there exists considerable leeway in adherence to audit standards and in the application of accounting principles, an audit firm's "track record" of actual level of performances in these critical areas provides a firsthand guide to its reliability and integrity. The analyst would do well to note instances in which a CPA firm has accepted the least desirable acceptable accounting principle among the available alternatives, has equivocated unnecessarily in its opinion, or was found wanting in its application of auditing procedures.

One of the best sources of information on the capabilities of an audit firm is a local banker.

What the auditor's opinion means

The auditor's opinion is the culmination of a lengthy and complicated process of auditing and investigation. It is here, and only here, that the auditor reports on the nature of his work and on the degree of responsibility he assumes. While his influence may be indirectly felt throughout the financial statements by the presentation, description, and footnote disclosure which he may have suggested or insisted upon, the opinion, and the opinion alone, remains his exclusive domain. Thus, the opinion and the references to the financial statements which it contains should always be carefully read. To ignore the auditor's opinion, or to assume that it does not mean what it says, or that it means more than it says, is foolhardy and unwarranted.

The auditor's responsibility to outsiders whom he does not know and who rely on his representations is considerable, and his exposure to liability arising therefrom is growing. Thus, the obligations which the standards of his profession impose on him, while extensive, are at the same time defined and limited. Consequently, no analyst is justified in assuming that the association of the auditor's name with the financial statements goes beyond what the auditor's opinion says, or is a form of insurance on which the analyst can rely to bail him out of bad decisions.

What exactly does the auditor's opinion say? The best starting point for us is an examination of an auditor's "clean opinion," that is, an opinion which is not qualified in any way. This will give us an idea of the greatest degree of responsibility the auditor is willing to assume. The "clean opinion," which covers two annual examinations, reads as follows:

To the Shareowners and Board of Directors
(Name of Company)

We have examined the balance sheet of (name of company) as of (date), and the related statement of income and retained earnings, and the statement of changes in financial position for the year then ended. Our examination was made in accordance with generally accepted auditing standards, and accordingly included such tests of the accounting records and such other auditing procedures as we considered necessary in the circumstances. We previously examined and reported upon the financial statements of the Company for the year ended (date).

In our opinion, the aforementioned financial statements present fairly the financial position of (name of company) at (date) and (date), and the results of its operations and changes in its financial position for the years then ended, in conformity with generally accepted accounting principles applied on a consistent basis.

(Name of accountants)

(City and date)

THE AUDITOR'S REPORT

The auditor's report is divided into two distinct parts: (1) the scope of the audit and (2) the auditor's opinion.

The scope of the audit

The scope paragraph of the auditor's report sets forth the financial statements examined, the period of time which they cover, and the scope of the audit to which they and the underlying records have been subjected.

The standard terminology refers to an examination made in accordance with "generally accepted auditing standards." This is "shorthand" for a very comprehensive meaning which is elaborated upon in the profession's literature and particularly in *Statement on Auditing Standards No. 1* issued by the Committee on Auditing Procedure of the AICPA in 1972. These auditing standards are broad generalizations classified under three headings: (1) general standards (2) standards of field work, and (3) standards of reporting.

General standards define the personal qualities required of the independent CPA. They are:

a. The examination is to be performed by a person or persons having adequate technical training and proficiency as an auditor.

b. In all matters relating to the assignment an independence in mental attitude is to be maintained by the auditor or auditors.

c. Due professional care is to be exercised in the performance of the examination and the preparation of the report.

Standards of field work embrace the actual execution of the audit and cover the planning of the work, the evaluation of the client's system of internal control, and the quality and sufficiency of the evidence obtained. *Statement on Auditing Standards No. 1* enumerates them as follows:

1. The work is to be adequately planned and assistants, if any, are to be properly supervised.

2. There is to be a proper study and evaluation of the existing internal control as a basis for reliance thereon and for the determination of the resultant extent of the tests to which auditing procedures are to be restricted.

3. Sufficient competent evidential matter is to be obtained through inspection, observation, inquires and confirmations to afford a reasonable basis for an opinion regarding the financial statements under examination.

Reporting standards govern the preparation and presentation of the auditor's report. They are intended to insure that the auditor's position is clearly and unequivocally stated and that the degree of responsibility he assumes is made clear to the reader. These standards are four in number:

1. The report shall state whether the financial statements are presented in accordance with generally accepted principles of accounting.

2. The report shall state whether such principles have been consistently observed in the current period in relation to the preceding period.

3. Informative disclosures in the financial statements are to be regarded as reasonably adequate unless otherwise stated in the report.

4. The report shall either contain an expression of opinion regarding the financial statements, taken as a whole, or an assertion to the effect that an opinion cannot be expressed. When an over-all opinion cannot be expressed, the reasons therefor should be stated. In all cases where an au-

ditor's name is associated with financial statements the report should contain a clear-cut indication of the character of the auditor's examination, if any, and the degree of responsibility he is taking.

Audit standards are the yardsticks by which the quality of audit procedures are measured. The SEC in *Accounting Series Release No. 21* stated:

. . . In referring to generally accepted auditing standards the Commission has in mind, in addition to the employment of generally recognized normal auditing procedures, their application with professional competence by properly trained persons.

Auditing procedures.   The second phrase of the scope section states that the examination "included such tests of the accounting records and such other auditing procedures" as were considered necessary in the circumstances.

This statement encompasses the wide sweep of auditing theory brought to bear on the particular examination, as well as the professional discretion the auditor uses in the performance of his work.

The subject of auditing is, of course, a discipline in itself requiring for successful mastery a period of study and practical application. Thus, while we obviously cannot go with any degree of detail into what constitutes the process of auditing, it behooves all who use its end product to have a basic understanding of the process by which the auditor obtains assurance about the fair presentation of the financial statements as to which he expresses an opinion.

A basic objective of the financial audit is the detection of errors and irregularities, intentional or unintentional, which if undetected would materially affect the fairness of presentation of financial summarizations or their conformity with generally accepted accounting principles.

To be economically feasible and justifiable, auditing can aim only at a reasonable level of assurance in this respect about the data under review. This means that under a testing system, assurance can never be complete, and that the final audit conclusions are subject to this inherent probability of error.

Briefly stated, the auditor's basic approach is as follows: to gain assurance about financial summarizations the auditor must examine the accounting system of which they are a final product. If that system of internal control is well conceived, properly maintained, and implemented, it is assumed that it should result in valid financial records and summarizations.

Thus, the need for and the extent of the testing of the records is dependent on the degree of proper operation of the system of internal control.

The importance of internal control.   The importance of the review of the system of internal control in the total audit framework can be gauged from a reading of the scope paragraph of the original standard opinion (used from about 1939 to 1948) which read in part as follows:

. . . have reviewed the system of internal control and the accounting procedures of the company, and, without making a detailed audit of the transactions, have examined or tested accounting records of the company and other supporting evidence by methods, and to the extent we deemed appropriate.

Even though these specific words have been deleted from the form of the present opinion, the phrase still accurately describes the auditor's work.

After ascertaining, by means of investigation and inquiry, what management's plan and design for a system of internal control is, if any, the auditor proceeds to test the system in order to ascertain whether it is in existence and is, in fact, being implemented as intended. This testing is called procedural testing.

If after application of procedural testing, the system of internal control is found to be well conceived and in proper operation, the amount of testing to which income statement items or individual assets and liabilities will be subjected will be very limited. The latter type of testing, which may be called "validation testing," will have to be increased significantly if procedural testing reveals the system of internal control to be deficient or not operational.

This method of checking out the system and then performing additional sample tests on the basis of its evaluation does, of course, leave room for a great deal of professional discretion, for "corner-cutting," and for a variety of qualities of judgment. Hence, it is subject to the risk of failure. Moreover, the usual audit, according to the accounting profession, is not primarily or specifically designed to disclose fraud, nor can it be relied on to disclose defalcations, although their discovery may result.

From the above discussion it should be clear that reliance on an audit must be based on an understanding of the nature of the audit process and the limitations to which it is subject.

The opinion section

The first paragraph of the auditor's report, which we discussed above, deals with the scope of his examination and the limitations or restrictions, if any, to which it was subject. The second paragraph (in practice the order of these paragraphs may be reversed) sets forth the auditor's opinion on:

1. The fairness of presentation of the financial statements;
2. Their conformity with generally accepted accounting principles; and
3. The consistent application of these principles in the financial statements.

"Fair presentation"

One of the great debates among auditors and between auditors and society in general, particularly the courts, concerns the meaning of the phrase "present fairly" which is found in the auditor's report. Most auditors maintain that financial statements are fairly presented when they conform to generally accepted accounting principles (GAAP) and that "fairness" is meaningful only in this context.

Yet, clearly, in quite a number of cases reaching the courts in recent years financial statements which, according to expert testimony were prepared in accordance with GAAP, were nevertheless found to be misleading in an overall sense. This became particularly apparent in the landmark Continental Vending case where the lack of disclosure of certain highly dubious transactions was defended as not being, at that time, required by GAAP. In refusing to instruct the jury that conformity with GAAP was a complete defense to the charge of fraud, the trial judge maintained that the critical question was whether Continental's financial statements, taken as a whole, "fairly presented" its financial picture. He found that, while conformity with GAAP might be very persuasive evidence of an auditor's good faith, it was not necessarily conclusive evidence of it.

The auditors, in an attempt to respond to a clear divergence between their and society's views of what is meant by "present fairly" issued a statement on the matter in 1975. While still maintaining that "fairness" must be applied within the framework of GAAP, they stated that "fair presentation" also requires that the accounting principles selected and applied must have general acceptance.

The accounting principles must be appropriate in the circumstances.

The financial statements must be "informative of matters that may affect their use, understanding, and interpretation."

The data must be presented and summarized "in a reasonable manner, that is, neither too detailed nor too condensed."

The financial statements must reflect "the underlying events and transactions" in a way that states the results within "a range of acceptable limits that are reasonable and practicable."

As part of the accounting profession's periodic attempts at self-examination and assessment, especially in the face of Congressional and public scrutiny and criticism, an AICPA appointed Commission on Auditor's Responsibilities issued in early 1977 tentative conclusions. These included among others the recommendations that the concept of "fairness" be abandoned, that the "subject to" opinion be dropped in case of uncertainties, that auditors assume greater responsibilities for the detection of fraud and for the search for illegal and questionable acts, and that they report on management's assessment of the corporate internal accounting control systems.

Modification of the opinion

The standard short-form report presented earlier in the chapter contained a "clean opinion," that is, the auditor had no qualifications to record as to any of the three criteria enumerated above. Any modifications of substance in the language of the auditor's opinion paragraph is, technically speaking, considered to be a qualification or a disclaimer. Not all qualifications are, of course, of equal significance to the user. Some deviations in language are explanatory in character reflecting matters which the auditor wishes to emphasize and may not affect the auditor's opinion significantly. References to the work of other auditors is not regarded as a qualification but rather an indication of divided responsibility for the performance of the audit. Other explanatory comments may not carry over to affect the auditor's opinion and, at times, one may wonder why mention of them is necessary. On the other hand, certain qualifications or disclaimers are so significant as to cast doubt on the reliability of the financial statements or their usefulness for decision-making purposes.

Let us then examine the major categories of the auditor's qualifications and disclaimers, the occasions on which they are properly used, and the significance which they hold to the user of financial statements.

CIRCUMSTANCES GIVING RISE TO QUALIFICATIONS, DISCLAIMERS, OR ADVERSE OPINIONS

There are three main categories of conditions which require qualifications, disclaimers, or adverse opinions (collectively referred to as qualified opinions):

1. Limitations in the scope of the auditor's examination affected by (a) conditions which preclude the application of auditing procedures considered necessary in the circumstances or (b) restrictions imposed by the client.

2. The financial statements do not present fairly the financial position and/or results of operations because (a) they fail to conform with generally accepted accounting principles or (b) they do not contain adequate disclosure.
3. There exist uncertainties about the future resolution of material matters, the effect of which cannot presently be estimated or reasonably provided for.

Before a consideration of the variety of conditions which call for qualified opinions, let us consider the major types of qualifications which the auditor may express.

QUALIFICATIONS—"EXCEPT FOR" AND "SUBJECT TO"

These qualifications express an opinion on the financial statements except for repercussions stemming from conditions which must be disclosed. They may arise from limitations in the scope of the audit which, because of circumstances beyond the auditor's control or because of restrictions imposed by the audited company, result in a failure to obtain reasonably objective and verifiable evidence in support of events which have taken place. They may arise from a lack of conformity of the financial statements to generally accepted accounting principles. When they arise because there are uncertainties about future events which cannot be resolved or the effect of which cannot be estimated or reasonably provided for at the time the opinion is rendered the words "subject to" are substituted for "except for". This qualification is meant to be used in instances where the nature of the uncertainties is not so material as to require an adverse opinion.

An uncertainty, such as due to operating losses or serious financial weakness which calls into question the fundamental assumption that an entity can continue to operate as a going concern calls for a "subject to" qualification or, in cases of pervasive uncertainty which cannot be adequately measured, for a disclaimer of opinion.

DISCLAIMER OF OPINION

A disclaimer of opinion is a statement of inability to express an opinion. It must be rendered when, for whatever reason, insufficient competent evidential matter is available to the auditor to enable him to form an opinion on the financial statements. It can arise from limitations in the scope of the audit as well as from the existence of uncertainties the ultimate impact of which cannot be estimated. Material departures from GAAP do not justify a disclaimer of opinion.

ADVERSE OPINIONS

An adverse opinion should be rendered in cases when the financial statements are not prepared in accordance with generally accepted accounting principles, and this has a significant effect on the fair presentation of those statements. An adverse opinion results generally from a situation in which the auditor has been unable to convince his client to amend the financial statements so that they reflect the auditor's estimate about the outcome of future events or so that they otherwise adhere to generally accepted accounting principles. The issuance of an adverse opinion must always be accompanied by a statement of the reasons for such an opinion.

Adverse opinions versus disclaimers of opinion

The difference between adverse opinions and disclaimers of opinion can be best understood in terms of the difference that exists between exceptions that affect the quality of the financial statements on one hand and those which express uncertainties affecting the auditor's opinion on the other. Thus, a situation that may call for an "except for" opinion may at some point result in such a degree of pervasive or material disagreements with management that it will require an adverse opinion. Similarly, pervasive and/or material uncertainties may, at some point, require the conversion of a "subject to" opinion into a disclaimer of opinion.

THE FORM OF THE REPORT

Whenever the auditor expresses a qualified opinion he must disclose in a middle paragraph, or in a footnote which is referred to in that paragraph, the substantive reasons for the qualification. The explanatory paragraph should disclose the principal effects of the subject matter of the qualification on financial position, results of operations and changes in financial position, if reasonably determinable. The paragraph should also make it clear whether the qualification results because of a difference of opinion between the auditor and the client or whether it results because of an uncertainty not subject to present resolution.

All qualifications must be referred to in the opinion paragraph and a qualification due to scope or lack of sufficient evidential matter must be also referred to in the scope paragraph. Thus a mere explanatory statement should not be referred to in either the scope or the opinion paragraphs.

Having covered the various types of opinions an auditor can express, let us now turn to the various conditions which call for qualifications in such opinions.

LIMITATIONS IN THE SCOPE OF THE AUDIT

A limitation in the scope of the auditor's examination, that is, an inability to perform certain audit steps which he considers necessary, will, if material, result in a qualification or disclaimer of his opinion.

Some limitations in the scope of the auditor's examination arise from an inability to perform certain audit steps because of conditions beyond the auditor's and the client's control, for example, an inability to observe the opening inventory where the audit appointment was not made until the close of the year. Other limitations may result from a client-imposed restriction on the auditor's work. Whatever the reason for an incomplete examination, the auditor must report the inadequacy of the examination and the conclusions which flow from such an inadequacy.

The accounting profession has approved "extended procedures" with respect to observation of inventories and the confirmation of accounts receivable. If these steps cannot be reasonably or practically performed, the auditor must, in order to issue an unqualified opinion, satisfy himself about the inventories and accounts receivable by alternative means. He must, however, no longer indicate such an omission of regular procedures in his opinion.

FAILURE OF FINANCIAL STATEMENTS TO CONFORM TO GENERALLY ACCEPTED ACCOUNTING PRINCIPLES

The auditor brings to bear his expertise in the application of auditing techniques and procedures to satisfy himself about the existence, ownership, and validity of presentation of the assets, the liabilities, and net worth as well as the statement of results. As an expert accountant, the auditor judges the fairness of presentation of financial statements and their conformity with generally accepted accounting principles. The latter is one of the most important functions of the auditor's opinion.

Fair presentation is, to an important extent, dependent on the degree of informative disclosure provided. Adherence to generally accepted accounting principles, which is another prerequisite of fairness of presentation, depends on the employment, in the financial statements, of principles having authoritative support. Opinions of the APB and Statements of the FASB enjoy, by definition, authoritative support. If the accountant concurs in a company's use of an accounting principle which differs from that approved by an authoritative body but which he believes enjoys the support of other authoritative sources, he need not qualify his opinion, but he must disclose that the principle used differs from those approved by such authoritative body. This, of course, puts the onus on the auditor in justifying the departure from a principle which enjoys authoritative approval.

If, because of lack of adequate disclosure or the use of accounting principles which do not enjoy authoritative support, the auditor concludes that the financial statements are not fairly presented, he must qualify his opinion or render an adverse opinion. The decision of whether to make his opinion an "except-for" type, which is a qualified opinion, or to render an adverse opinion, which states that the "financial statements do not present fairly . . ." hinges on the materiality of the effect of such a deficiency on the financial statements taken as a whole. The concept of materiality in accounting and auditing is, however, very vague and remains undefined by the accounting profession itself.

It is obvious that a qualification due to a lack of disclosure or a lack of adherence to generally accepted accounting principles is the result of the auditor's inability to persuade his client to modify the financial statements. Thus, an "except for" type of opinion is not proper, and an adverse opinion is called for together with a full description of the shortcomings in the financial statements as well as their total impact thereon.

The following are pertinent excerpts from an opinion qualified because of lack of adherence to generally accepted accounting principles:

As explained in Note A, the 19X3 financial statements include pension expense less than the minimum required by Opinion No. 8 of the Accounting Principles Board.

In our opinion, except that in 19X3 provision had not been made for pension expense as described in the preceding paragraph . . .

FINANCIAL STATEMENTS SUBJECT TO UNRESOLVED KNOWN UNCERTAINTIES

Whenever uncertainties about the future exist which cannot be resolved, or whose effect cannot be estimated or reasonably provided for at the time of the issuance of the auditor's opinion, a qualified opinion or a disclaimer of opinion may be required. Such uncertainties may relate to lawsuits, tax matters, or other contingencies, the outcome of which is dependent upon decisions of parties other than management. Or the uncertainties may relate to the recovery of the investment in certain assets through future operations, or through their disposition.

The practical effect of an uncertainty qualification is to state the auditor's inability to assess the impact of the contingency, or the likelihood of its occurrence, and to pass on to the reader the burden of its evaluation.

One variety of qualification relates to the question of whether the going-concern assumption in accounting (see Chapter 2) is justified. This question arises when a company is incurring continued operating losses, deficits in the stockholder's equity, working capital insufficiencies, or defaults under loan agreements. In such cases the auditor expresses his doubt about the property of applying practices implicit in the going concern concept such as the valuation of fixed assets at cost.

The following are examples of pertinent portions of auditor reports relating to uncertainties:

As discussed in Note 4, because of the uncertainty of mining plans it may be necessary at some indeterminate future date to write off a significant amount of net book investment in the Company's Questa mine and mill.

In our opinion, subject to the realization of the Company's investment in Questa property referred to above . . .

* * * * *

The accompanying financial statements of the Company have been prepared on the basis of a going concern although the ability of the Company to continue as a going concern is dependent upon future earnings. In this connection, it should be noted that in the period from commencement of operations through June 30, 19X8, the Company accumulated a net loss of $150,340.

Except for the appropriateness of the going concern concept and to the ability of the Company to realize its unamortized programming development costs through future profitable operations, in our opinion the accompanying financial statements present fairly . . .

EXCEPTIONS AS TO CONSISTENCY

The second standard of reporting requires that the auditor's report state whether the principles of accounting employed "have been consistently observed in the current period in relation to the preceding period."

The basic objective of the consistency standard is to assure the reader that comparability of financial statements as between periods has not been materially affected by changes in the accounting principles employed or in the method of their application. Thus, if a change has been made affecting the comparability of the financial statements, a statement of the nature of the changes and their effect on the financial statements is required.

There are three types of changes which must be considered here:

1. Changes in accounting principles employed, for example, a change in the method of depreciation.
2. Changes required by altered conditions, for example, a change in the estimated useful life of an asset.
3. Changed conditions unrelated to accounting which nevertheless have an effect on comparability, for example, the acquisition or disposition of a subsidiary.

Changes of type 1 involve the consistency standard and must be dealt with in the auditor's opinion. Changes of type 2 and 3 affect comparability and while not requiring comment in the auditor's report do require footnote disclosure.

SPECIAL REPORTS

There are circumstances where the standard short-form report of the auditor is not appropriate due to special circumstances or the limited scope of the examination which the auditor is requested to undertake. It is particularly important that the analyst read such reports carefully so that he is not misled into believing that the auditor is assuming here his ordinary measure of responsibility. The following are some types of special reports which the reader may encounter:

1. Reports by companies in the development stage where many uncertainties regarding development costs exist.
2. Reports by companies on a cash or incomplete basis of accounting.
3. Reports by nonprofit organizations.
4. Reports prepared for limited purposes. Such reports usually deal with certain aspects of the financial statements (such as computations of royalties, rentals, profit-sharing arrangements, or compliance with provisions of bond indentures, etc.).

In ASR 177 the SEC has called for the auditor's "association" with published interim reports based on performance of a limited review. ASR 190 calls for auditor's association with Replacement Cost data presented in a footnote.

UNAUDITED REPORTS

A certified public accountant may be engaged to prepare, or assist in the preparation of, unaudited financial statements. In such a capacity the auditor performs an accounting service and not an auditing service. Nevertheless, an auditor must disclose deficiencies in financial statements which are known to him, regardless of the capacity in which he is acting.

Unaudited financial statements with which an auditor is associated in any way must be clearly marked as "unaudited" and usually contain the following statement:

The financial statements of Zero Manufacturing Company included in this report have been prepared from the books and records of the Company without audit and we express no opinion on them.

THE SEC'S IMPORTANT ROLE

The Securities and Exchange Commission has in recent years moved particularly forcefully to monitor auditor performance as well as to strengthen the hands of auditors in their dealings with managements.

Disciplinary proceedings against auditors were expanded to include requirements for improvements in internal administration procedures, professional education, and a review of a firm's procedures by outside professionals.

SEC *Accounting Series Release 165* in moving to strengthen the auditor's position requires increased disclosure of the relationship between auditors and their clients, particularly in cases where changes in auditors take place. Disclosure must include details of past disagreements including those resolved to the satisfaction of the replaced auditor as well as footnote disclosure of the effects on the financial statements of methods of accounting advocated by a former auditor but not followed by the client.

In *ASR 194* the commission limits the above disclosure requirements to situations where the successor accountant found acceptable that which the former accountant found unacceptable.

IMPLICATIONS FOR ANALYSIS

Auditing as a function and the auditor's opinion, as an instrument of assurance, are widely misunderstood. The responsibility for this lack of communication cannot be all laid at the auditor's door, for the profession has published a number of pamphlets in which it has endeavored to explain its function. Nor should the readers of financial statements bear the full responsibility for this state of affairs because the accounting profession's message in this area is often couched in technical and cautious language and requires a great deal of effort and background information for a full understanding.

A useful discussion of the implications of the current state of auditing to the user of audited financial statements may be presented in two parts:

1. Implications stemming from the nature of the audit process.
2. Implications arising from the professional standards which govern the auditor's opinion.

Implications inherent in the audit process

Auditing is based on a sampling approach to the data under audit. Statistical sampling is a relatively new concept in auditing, and while lending itself to many applications in theory, it is more limited in actual practice. Thus, most audit tests are based on "judgmental samples" of the data, that is, samples selected by the auditor's intuition, judgment, and evaluation of many factors. Often the size of the sample is necessarily limited by the economics of the accounting practice.[1]

The reader must realize that the auditor does not aim at, nor can he ever achieve, complete certainty. Even a review of every single transaction—a process which would be economically unjustifiable— would not achieve a complete assurance.

Auditing is a developing art. Even its very basic theoretical underpinnings are far from fully understood or resolved. There is, for instance, no clear relationship between the auditor's evaluation of the effectiveness of the system of internal controls, which is a major factor on which the auditor relies, and the extent of audit testing and the nature of audit procedures employed. If we add to that the fact that the qualities of judgment among auditors do vary greatly, we should not be surprised to find that the history of auditing contains many examples of spectacular failure. On the other hand, as is the case with the risk of accidental death in commercial aviation, the percentage of failure to the total number of audits performed is very small indeed. Thus, while the user of audited financial statements can, in general, be reassured about the overall results of the audit function, he must remember that there is substantial risk in reliance on its results in specific cases. Such risks are due to many factors, including the auditor's inability to detect fraud at the highest level and the application of proper audit tests to such an end (McKesson and Robbins case and all the way to the Equity Funding case), the auditor's inability to grasp the extent of a deteriorating situation (the Yale Express case), the auditor's conception of the range of his responsibilities to probe and disclose (the Continental Vending and National Student Marketing cases), and the quality of the audit (Bar Chris Construction, U.S. Financial, Whittaker Corp. and the Mattel cases).

---

[1] This and other "inherent limitations of the auditing process" are emphasized in an SAS issued in 1977 or "The Independent Auditor's Responsibility for the Detection of Errors and Irregularities." The Statement declares that the auditor's examination is subject to the inherent risk that material errors or irregularities, if they exist, will not be detected.

Thus, while the audit function may generally justify the reliance which financial analysts place on audited financial statements, such a reliance cannot be a blind one. The analyst must be aware that the entire audit process is a probabilistic one subject to many risks. Even its flawless application may not necessarily result in complete assurance, and most certainly cannot insure that the auditor has elicited all the facts, especially if there is high-level management collusion to withhold such facts from him. Finally, the heavy dependence of the auditing process on judgment will, of necessity, result in a wide range of quality of performance.

An insight into what can be missed, and why, in the internal and external audit of a large corporation can be obtained from a reading of the *Report of the Special Review Committee of the Board of Direcotrs of Gulf Oil Corporation* (the McCloy report—December 1975). In searching for reasons why Gulf's internal financial controls, its internal auditors, and its external auditors failed to detect or curb the expenditure of large amounts of corporate funds through "off the books" bank accounts for unlawful purposes the review committee concluded that internal control committees choose not to control; that the corporate comptroller did not exercise the control powers vested in him, that the internal auditing department (reporting to the comptroller rather than to an audit committee of the board) lacked in independence and stature and that while it is clear that the external auditors had some knowledge of certain unusual transactions the extent of their knowledge could not be determined.

In relying on audited financial statements, the analyst must be ever aware of the risks of failure inherent in an audit; he must pay attention to the identity of the auditors and to what their record has been; and armed with a knowledge of what auditors do and how they do it, he must himself assess the areas of possible vulnerability in the financial statements.

Implications stemming from the standards which govern the auditor's opinion

In relying on the auditor's opinion the analyst must be aware of the limitations to which the audit process is subject, and this was the subject of the preceding discussion. Moreover, he must understand what the auditor's opinion means and particularly what the auditor himself thinks he conveys to the reader by means of his opinion.

Let us first consider the unqualified opinion or the so-called "clean" opinion. The auditor maintains that he expresses an opinion on *management's* statements. He is very insistent on this point and attaches considerable importance to it. It means that normally he did not pre-

pare the financial statements nor did he choose the accounting principles embodied in them. Instead, he reviews the financial statements
presented to him by management and ascertains that they are in
agreement with the books and records which he audited. He also
determines that generally acceptable principles of accounting have
been employed in the preparation of the financial statements but that
does not mean that they are the *best* principles that could have been
used. It is a well-known fact that management will often rely on the
auditor, as an expert in accounting, to help them pick the principle
which, while still acceptable, will come nearest to meeting their reporting objectives. Finally, the auditor will determine that the
minimum standards of disclosure have been met so that all matters
essential to a fair presentation of the financial statements are included
in them.

One might well ask what difference it makes whether the auditor
prepared the statements or not so long as he expresses an unqualified
opinion on them. The accounting profession has never clearly explained what the implications of this really are to the user of the financial statements. However, a number of such possible implications
should be borne in mind by the analyst:

1. The auditor's knowledge about the financial statements is not as
    strong as that of the preparer who was in more intimate contact
    with all the factors which gave rise to the transactions. He knows
    only what he can see on the basis of a sampling process and may
    not know all that he should know.
2. Since many items in the financial statements are not capable of
    exact measurement, he merely reviews such measurements for
    reasonableness. His are not the original determinations, and un-
    less he can successfully prove otherwise (as for example in the
    case of estimates of useful lives of property), management's de-
    termination will prevail. Thus, the auditor's opinion contains no
    reference to "present exactly" or "present correctly" but rather
    states that the statements "present fairly."
3. While the auditor may be consulted on the use of accounting prin-
    ciples he, as auditor rather than as preparer of such statements,
    does not select the principles to be used. Moreover, he cannot
    insist on the use of the *best* available principle any more than he is
    likely to *insist* on a degree of disclosure above the minimum con-
    sidered as acceptable at the time.
4. The limitations to which the auditor's ability to audit are subject
    have never been spelled out by the accounting profession. Knowl-
    edgeable auditors do, of course, know about them; but there seems
    to be a tacit agreement, of doubtful value to the profession, not to
    discuss them. For example, is the auditor really equipped to audit

the value of complex technical work in progress? Can he competently evaluate the adequacy of insurance reserves? Can he second-guess the client's estimate of the percentage of completion of a large contract? While such questions are rarely raised in public, let alone answered, they cannot be unequivocally answered in the affirmative.

5. While the preparer must, under the rules of double-entry bookkeeping, account for all items, large or small, the auditor is held to less exacting standards of accuracy in his work. Thus the error tolerances are wider. He leans on the doctrine of materiality which in its basic concept simply means that the auditor need not concern himself, in either the auditing or the reporting phases of his work, with trivial or unimportant matters. What is important or significant is, of course, a matter of judgment and so far the profession has neither defined the concept nor set limits or established criteria to govern the application of the concept of mteriality. This has given it an unwarranted degree of reporting latitude.[2]

Of course, auditors even as a profession, in contra-distinction to a business, must pay attention to the economics of their function and to the limits of the responsibilities they should assume. Thus, whether the foregoing limitations on the auditor's function and responsibility are justified or not, the analyst must recognize them as standards applied by auditors and evaluate his reliance on audited financial statements with a full understanding of them.

The auditor's reference to "generally accepted accounting principles" in his opinion should be well understood by the user of the financial statements. Such reference means that the auditor is satisfied that such principles have authoritative support and that they have been applied "in all material respects." Aside from understanding the operation of the concept of materiality, here the analyst must understand that the definition of what constitutes "generally accepted accounting principles" is often vague and subject to significant latitude in interpretation and application. For example, a statement on Auditing Standards issued in 1975 states that "when criteria for selection among alternative accounting principles have not been established to relate accounting methods to circumstances (e.g., as in case of inventory and depreciation methods) the auditor may conclude that more than one accounting principle is appropriate in the circumstances."

Similarly indeterminate are present-day standards relating to disclosure. While minimum standards are increasingly established in

---

[2] See Leopold A. Bernstein, "The Concept of Materiality," *The Accounting Review*, January 1967; and Sam M. Woolsey, "Approach to Solving the Materiality Problem," *The Journal of Accountancy*, March 1973. As of now the FASB has published a Discussion Memorandum on the subject and held public hearings on it.

professional and SEC pronouncements, accountants have not always adhered to them. The degree to which the lack of disclosure impairs the fair presentation of the financial statements remains subject to the auditor's judgment and discretion, and there are no definite standards which indicate at what point lack of disclosure is material enough to impair fairness of presentation and thus require a qualification in the auditor's report.

ILLUSTRATION 1. APB Opinion No. 8 on Pensions requires disclosure re-
garding employee groups covered, a description of pension accounting and funding policies and other salient features of a company's pension plans and the accounting for it. Nevertheless, many companies fail to render a complete disclosure of such details without incurring qualifications in their audit reports.

When the auditor qualifies his opinion, the analyst is faced with an additional problem of interpretation, that is, what is the meaning and intent of the qualification and what effect should such qualifications have on his reliance on the financial statements? The usefulness of the qualification to the analyst depends, of course, on its clarity, its lack of equivocation, and on the degree to which supplementary information and data enable an assessment of its effect.

An additional dimension of confusion and difficulty of interpretation is introduced when the auditor includes explanatory information in his report, merely for emphasis, without a statement of conclusions or of a qualification. The analyst may in such situations be left wondering why the matter was emphasized in this way and whether the auditor is attempting to express an unstated qualification or reservation.

ILLUSTRATION 2. Westinghouse Credit Corporation's auditor report contains the following explanatory middle paragraph:

As described under Interest Expense on page 19, effective January 1, 1974 the terms of the Company's subordinated indebtedness to and credit line support from its parent, Westinghouse Electric Corporation, were changed to eliminate applicable interest and fees.

In light of a full footnote explanation of the matter the analyst is left wondering why the auditors chose to emphasize this particular matter.

Qualification, disclaimers, and adverse opinions

As discussed in an earlier part of this chapter, generally when an auditor is not satisfied with the fairness of presentation of items in the financial statements, he issues an "except-for" type of qualification and when there are uncertainties which he cannot resolve, he issues a "subject to" qualification. At some point the size and importance of items under qualification must result in adverse opinions or disclaim-

ers of opinion respectively. Where is this point? At what stage is a specific qualification no longer meaningful and an overall disclaimer of opinion necessary? Here again, the analyst won't find any guidelines by turning to the auditor's own professional pronounce-ments or literature. The boundaries are left entirely to the realm of judgment without the existence of even the broadest of criteria or guidelines.

ILLUSTRATION 3.   United Park City Mines Company showed on its bal-ance sheet as at December 31, 1972, $10.1 million of Mines and Mining Claims. The auditor's opinion stated in part:

"As set forth in Note 2, mines and mining claims, all of which are leased to Park City Ventures, are not fully developed and consequently the ulti-mate realization of these amounts and of related mining assets depends on circumstances which currently cannot be evaluated.

"In our opinion, based upon our examinations and the report of other independent accountants, subject to the realization of the carrying value of the equipment, mines and mining claims referred to in the preceding paragraph. . . ."

Question: In light of the fact that total assets on the company's balance sheet amounted to $17.6 million and total stockholder's equity to $16.1 million, are the $10.1 million of mining and mining claims not material enough to warrant a disclaimer of opinion rather than a qualification? Of what significance is the use of a qualification rather than a disclaimer of opinion in this case?

Uncertainty qualifications.   When the auditor cannot assess the proper carrying amount of an asset or determine the extent of a possi-ble liability or find other uncertainties or contingencies which cannot be determined or measured, he will issue "subject to" opinion de-scribing such uncertainties. The analyst using financial statements which contain such a qualification is, quite bluntly, faced with a situa-tion where the auditor has passed on to him the uncertainty described and, consequently, the task of evaluating its possible impact. The analyst should recognize the situation for what it really is and not assume that he is dealing with a mere formality designed only for the auditor's self-protection. Moreover, the auditor's efforts to estimate future uncertainties cannot normally be expected to exceed those of management itself. As a Statement on Auditing Standards issued in 1974 put it, "The auditor's function in forming an opinion on financial statements does not include estimating the outcome of future events if management is unable to do so."

In those cases where the "subject to" opinion is given because of uncertainties which cannot be resolved, it is hard to blame the auditor for shifting the burden of evaluation on to the reader. At the same time, it must be remembered that as between the reader and the auditor, the latter, due to his firsthand knowledge of the company's affairs, is far better equipped to evaluate the nature of the contingencies as well as the probabilities of their occurrence. Thus, the analyst is entitled to expect, but will unfortunately not always get, a full explanation of all factors surrounding the uncertainty.

Lest the absence of an uncertainty qualification in the auditor's report lull the analyst into a false sense of security, it must be borne in mind that there are many contingencies and uncertainties which do not call for a qualification but which may nevertheless have very significant impact on the company's financial condition or results of operations. Examples of such contingencies or possibilities are:

1. Obsolescence of a major product line.
2. Loss of a significant customer.
3. Overextension of a business in terms of management capabilities.
4. Difficulty of getting large and complex production units on stream on time.

From the above discussion it should be obvious that the analyst must read with great care the auditor's opinion as well as the supplementary information to which it refers. The analyst can place reliance on the auditor, but regardless of the latter's standing and reputation, the analyst must maintain an independent and open-minded attitude.

Audit risk and its implications

We have in Chapter 2 examined the concept of accounting risk. Audit risk, while related, is of a different dimension and represents, as a study of some of the above mentioned cases will reveal, an equally clear and present danger to lenders and investors who rely on audited financial statements.

It is impossible for the analyst to substitute completely his judgment for that of the auditor. However, armed with an understanding of the audit process and its limitations he can, through identification of special areas of vulnerability, make a better assessment of the degree of audit risk present in a given situation. The following are circumstances which can point to such areas of vulnerability:

Glamour industry and company with need for continuing earnings growth to justify high market price or to facilitate acquisitions.

Company in difficult financial condition requiring credit urgently and frequently.

Company with high market visibility issuing frequent progress reports and earnings estimates.

Managements dominated mostly by one or a few strong-willed individuals or consisting mostly of financial people including CPAs.

Managements which have displayed a propensity for earnings maximization and manipulation by various means.

Problem industry displaying weaknesses, in such areas as receivable collection, inventories, contract cost overruns, dependence on few products, and so forth.

Dealings with insiders or related parties, stockholder lawsuits, frequent turnover of key officers, legal counsel or auditors.[3]

Audit conducted by a firm which has, for whatever reason, experienced a higher than normal incidence of audit failures.

While none of the above situations can be relied on to indicate situations of higher audit risk they have been shown by experience to have appeared in a sufficient number of problem cases to warrant the analyst's close attention.

QUESTIONS

1. In relying on an auditor's opinion what should the financial analyst know about the auditor and his work?
2. What are "generally accepted auditing standards"?
3. What are auditing procedures? What are some of the basic objectives of a financial audit?
4. What does the opinion section of the auditor's report usually cover?
5. The auditors, in an attempt to respond to a clear divergence between their and the society's views of what is meant by "fair presentation," issued a statement on the matter in 1975. What are the major points of that statement?
6. Which are the three major categories of conditions which require the auditor to render qualifications, disclaimers, or adverse opinions?
7. What is an "except-for" type of audit report qualification?
8. What is a (a) disclaimer of opinion and (b) an adverse opinion? When are these properly rendered?
9. What is the practical effect of an uncertainty qualification in an auditor's report?
10. What types of changes may result in a consistency qualification in the auditor's report?
11. What are the major disclosures required by SEC's *Accounting Series Release No. 165* on the relationship between auditors and clients?
12. What are some of the implications to financial analysis which stem from the audit process itself?

---

[3] In *ASR 165* (1974) the SEC required increased disclosure of relationships between registrants and their independent public accountants including disputes, particularly in cases where changes in accountants occur.

13. The auditor does not prepare the financial statements on which he expresses an opinion but instead he samples the data and examines them in order to render a professional opinion on them. List some of the possible implications of this to those who rely on the financial statements.

14. What does the auditor's reference to "generally accepted accounting principles" mean to the analyst of financial statements?

15. Of what significance are "uncertainty qualifications" to the financial analyst? What type of contingencies may not even be considered by the auditor in his report.

16. What are some of the circumstances which can point to areas of higher audit risk?

PART III

FINANCIAL STATEMENT
ANALYSIS—THE MAIN AREAS
OF EMPHASIS

16

ANALYSIS OF SHORT-TERM LIQUIDITY

SIGNIFICANCE OF SHORT-TERM LIQUIDITY

The short-term liquidity of an enterprise is measured by the degree to which it can meet its short-term obligations. Liquidity implies the ready ability to convert assets into cash or to obtain cash. The short term is conventionally viewed as a time span up to a year, although it is sometimes also identified with the normal operating cycle of a business, that is, the time span encompassing the buying-producing-selling and collecting cycle of an enterprise.

The importance of short-term liquidity can best be gauged by examining the repercussions which stem from a lack of ability to meet short-term obligations.

Liquidity is a matter of degree. A lack of liquidity may mean that the enterprise is unable to avail itself of favorable discounts and is unable to take advantage of profitable business opportunities as they arise. At this stage a lack of liquidity implies a lack of freedom of choice as well as constraints on management's freedom of movement.

A more serious lack of liquidity means that the enterprise is unable to pay its current debts and obligations. This can lead to the forced sale of long-term investments and assets and, in its most severe form, to insolvency and bankruptcy.

To the owners of an enterprise a lack of liquidity can mean reduced profitability and opportunity or it may mean loss of control and partial or total loss of the capital investment. In the case of owners with unlimited liability, the loss can extend beyond the original investment.

To creditors of the enterprise a lack of liquidity can mean delay in collection of interest and principal due them or it can mean the partial or total loss of the amounts due them.

Customers as well as suppliers of goods and services to an enterprise can also be affected by its short-term financial condition. Such effects may take the form of inability of the enterprise to perform under contracts and the loss of supplier relationships.

From the above description of the significance of short-term liquidity it can be readily appreciated why the measures of such liquidity have been accorded great importance. For, if an enterprise cannot meet its current obligations as they become due, its continued existence becomes in doubt and that relegates all other measures of performance to secondary importance if not to irrelevance. In terms of the framework of objectives discussed in Chapter 3 the evaluation of short-term liquidity is concerned with the assessment of the unsystematic risk of the enterprise.

While accounting determinations are made, as we have seen in Chapter 2, on the assumption of indefinite continuity of the enterprise, the financial analyst must always submit the validity of such assumption to the test of the enterprise's liquidity and solvency.

One of the most widely used measures of liquidity is working capital. In addition to its importance as a pool of liquid assets which provides a safety cushion to creditors, net working capital is also important because it provides a liquid reserve with which to meet contingencies and the ever present uncertainty regarding an enterprise's ability to balance the outflow of funds with an adequate inflow of funds.

WORKING CAPITAL

The basic concept of working capital is relatively simple. It is the excess of current assets over current liabilities. That excess is sometimes referred to as "net working capital" because some businessmen consider current assets as "working capital." A working capital deficiency exists when current liabilities exceed current assets.

The importance attached by credit grantors, investors, and others to working capital as a measure of liquidity and solvency has caused some enterprises, in the desire to present their current condition in the most favorable light, to stretch to the limit the definition of what constitutes a current asset and a current liability. For this reason the analyst must use his own judgment in evaluating the proper classification of items included in "working capital."

Current assets

Current assets include cash and other assets that are reasonably expected to be realized in cash or sold or consumed during the normal operating cycle of the business or within one year if the operating cycle is shorter than one year. Current liabilities include those expected to be satisfied by either the use of assets classified as current in the same balance sheet or the creation of other current liabilities, or those expected to be satisfied within a relatively short period of time, usually one year. (APB *Statement No. 4,* Par. 198.)

The general rule about the ability to convert current assets into cash within a year is subject to important qualifications. The most important qualification relates to the operating cycle. As more fully described in Chapter 5, the operating cycle comprises the average time span intervening between the acquisition of materials and services entering the production or trading process to the final realization in cash of the proceeds from the sale of the enterprise's products. This time span can be quite extended in industries which require a long inventory holding period (e.g., tobacco, distillery, and lumber) or those which sell on the installment plan. Whenever no clearly defined operating cycle is evident, the arbitrary one-year rule prevails.

The most common categories of current assets are:

1. Cash.
2. Cash equivalents (i.e., temporary investments).
3. Accounts and notes receivable.
4. Inventories.
5. Prepaid expenses.

Cash is, of course, the ultimate measure of a current asset since current liabilities are paid off in cash. However, earmarked cash held for specific purposes, such as plant expansion, should not be considered as current. Compensating balances under bank loan agreements cannot, in most cases, be regarded as "free" cash. SEC *Accounting Series Release* (ASR) 148 requires the disclosure of compensating balance arrangements with the lending banks as well as the segregation of such balances (see also Chapter 5).

Cash equivalents represent temporary investments of cash in excess of current requirements made for the purpose of earning a return on these funds.

The analyst must be alert to the valuation of such investments. Equity investments are now accounted for in accordance with SFAB 12 as detailed in Chapter 5. Debt securities may still be carried above market if management views a decline as merely "temporary" in nature. Similarly, the "cash equivalent" nature of securities investments may sometimes be stretched quite far.

The mere ability to convert an asset to cash is not the sole determinant of its current nature. It is the intention and normal practice that governs. Intention is, however, not always enough. Thus, the cost of fixed assets which are intended for sale should be included in current assets only if the enterprise has a contractual commitment from a buyer to purchase the asset at a given price within the following year or the following operating cycle.

An example where the above principle was not followed is found in the 1970 annual report of International Industries. In this report the company carries as a current asset $37.8 million in "Real estate held for sale." A related footnote explains that "the company intends to sell this real estate during the ensuing operating cycle substantially at cost under sale and leaseback agreements, however, prevailing economic conditions may affect its ability to do so."

This is an obvious attempt to present a current position superior to the one the company can justifiably claim. Without the inclusion of real estate, the company's current ratio would have dropped to 1.1 (with working capital at about $3 million) as against a current ratio, based on reported figures, of 1.8 and a working capital of $40.3 million.

This reinforces the ever-recurring message in this text that the analyst cannot rely on adherence to rules or accepted principles of preparation of financial statements, but instead must exercise eternal vigilance in his use of ratios and all other analytical measures which are based on such statements. If anything, attempts by managements to stretch the rules in order to present a situation as better than it really is should serve as an added warning of potential trouble and risk.

Accounts receivable, net of provisions for uncollectible accounts, are current unless they represent receivables for sales, not in the ordinary course of business, which are due after one year. Installment receivables from customary sales usually fall within the operating cycle of the enterprise.

The analyst must, as the discussion in Chapter 5 indicates, be alert to the valuation as well as validity of receivables particularly in cases such as those where "sales" are made on consignment or subject to the right of return.

Receivables from affiliated companies or from officers and employees can be considered current only if they are collectible in the ordinary course of business within a year or, in the case of installment sales, within the operating cycle.

Inventories are considered current assets except in cases where they are in excess of current requirements. Such excess inventories, which should be shown as noncurrent, must be distinguished from inventories, such as tobacco, which require a long aging cycle. The variations in practice in this area are considerable, as the following illustrations will show, and should be carefully scrutinized by the analyst.

ILLUSTRATION 1.   National Fuel Gas Company (prospectus dated 7/23/69) shows a current as well as a noncurrent portion of gas stored underground and explains this as follows:

"Included in property, plant, and equipment as gas stored underground—noncurrent is $18,825,232 at April 30, 1969, the cost of the volume of gas required to maintain pressure levels for normal operating purposes at the low point of the storage cycle. The portion of gas in underground storage included in current assets does not exceed estimated withdrawals during the succeeding two years."

ILLUSTRATION 2.   Some trucking concerns include the tires on their trucks as current assets presumably on the theory that they will be used up during the normal operating cycle.

The analyst must pay particular attention to inventory valuation. Thus, for example, the inclusion of inventories at Lifo can result in a significant understatement of working capital.

Prepaid expenses are considered current, not because they can be converted into cash but rather because they represent advance payments for services and supplies which would otherwise require the current outlay of cash.

Current liabilities

Current liabilities are obligations which would, generally, require the use of current assets for their discharge or, alternatively, the creation of other current liabilities. The following are current liabilities most commonly found in practice:

1.   Accounts payable.
2.   Notes payable.
3.   Short-term bank and other loans.
4.   Tax and other expense accruals.
5.   Current portion of long-term debt.

The foregoing current liability categories are usually clear and do not require further elaboration. However, as is the case with current assets, the analyst cannot assume that they will always be properly classified for his purposes. Thus, for example, current practice sanctions the presentation as noncurrent of current obligations which are expected to be refunded. The degree of assurance of the subsequent refunding is mostly an open question which in the case of adverse developments may well be resolved negatively as far as the enterprise is concerned.

SEC *ASR 148* has expanded significantly the disclosure requirements regarding short-term bank and commercial paper borrowing. SFAS 6 established criteria for the balance sheet classification of short-term obligations that are expected to be refinanced (see Chapter 7).

The analyst must also be alert to the possibility of presentations designed to present the working capital in a better light than warranted by circumstances.

ILLUSTRATION 3.   Penn Central Company excluded the current maturities of long-term debt from the current liability category and included it in the "long-term debt" section of the balance sheet. In 1969, this treatment resulted in an excess of current assets over current liabilities of $21 million, whereas the inclusion of current debt maturities among current liabilities would have resulted in a working capital *deficit* of $207 million. (The subsequent financial collapse of this enterprise is now a well-known event.)

The analyst must also ascertain whether all obligations, regarding which there is a reasonably good probability that they will have to be met, have been included as current liabilities in computing an effective working capital figure. Two examples of such obligations follow:

1.   The obligation of an enterprise for notes discounted with a bank where the bank has full recourse in the event the note is not paid when due is generally considered a contingent liability. However, the likelihood of the contingency materializing must be considered in the computation of working capital. The same principle applies in case of loan guarantees.

2.   A contract for the construction or acquisition of long-term assets may call for substantial progress payments. Such obligations for payments are, for accounting purposes, considered as commitments rather than liabilities, and hence are not found among the latter. Nevertheless, when computing the excess of liquid assets over short-term obligations such commitments may have to be recognized.

Other problem areas in definition of current assets and liabilities

An area which presented a problem of classification but which has now been settled in favor of consistency is that of deferred tax accounting (see Chapter 11). Thus, if an asset (e.g., installment accounts receivable) is classified as current, the related deferred tax arising from differences in treatment between book and tax return must be similarly classified.

Many concerns which have fixed assets as the main "working assets," such as, for example, trucking concerns and some leasing companies, carry as current prospective receipts from billings out of which their current equipment purchase obligations must be met. Such treatments, or the absence of any distinction between current and noncurrent on the balance sheet, as is the case with real estate companies, is an attempt by such concerns to convey to the reader their "special" financing and operating conditions which make the current versus noncurrent distinction inapplicable and which have no parallel in the regular trading or industrial concern.

Some of these "special" circumstances may indeed be present, but they do not necessarily change the relationship existing between current obligations and the liquid funds available, or reasonably expected to become available, to meet them. It is to this relationship that the analyst, faced with the task of evaluating liquidity, must train his attention.

Working capital as a measure of liquidity

The popularity of working capital as a measure of liquidity and of short-term financial health is so widespread that it hardly needs documentation. Credit grantors compute the relationship between current assets and current liabilities; financial analysts measure the size of the working capital of enterprises they analyze; government agencies compute aggregates of working capital of corporations; and most published balance sheets distinguish between current and noncurrent assets and liabilities. Moreover, loan agreements and bond indentures often contain stipulations regarding the maintenance of minimum working capital levels.

The absolute amount of working capital has significance only when related to other variables such as sales, total assets, and so forth. It is at best of limited value for comparison purposes and for judging the adequacy of working capital. This can be illustrated as follows:

	Company A	Company B
Current assets	$300,000	$1,200,000
Current liabilities	100,000	1,000,000
Working capital	$200,000	$ 200,000

While both companies have an equal amount of working capital, a cursory comparison of the relationship of current assets to current liabilities suggests that Company A's current condition is superior to that of Company B.

CURRENT RATIO

The above conclusion is based on the ratio of current assets to current liabilities. It is 3:1 (300,000/100,000) for Company A and 1.2:1 (1,200,000/1,000,000) for Company B. It is this ratio that is accorded substantial importance in the assessment of an enterprise's current liquidity.

Some of the basic reasons for the widespread use of the current ratio as a measure of liquidity are obvious:

1. It measures the degree to which current assets cover current liabilities. The higher the amount of current assets in relation to current liabilities the more assurance exists that these liabilities can be paid out of such assets.

2. The excess of current assets over current liabilities provides a buffer against losses which may be incurred in the disposition or liquidation of the current assets other than cash. The more substantial such a buffer is, the better for creditors. Thus, the current ratio measures the margin of safety available to cover any possible shrinkage in the value of current assets.

3. It measures the reserve of liquid funds in excess of current obligations which is available as a margin of safety against uncertainty and the random shocks to which the flows of funds in an enterprise are subject. Random shocks, such as strikes, extraordinary losses, and other uncertainties can temporarily and unexpectedly stop or reduce the inflow of funds.

What is not so obvious, however, is the fact that the current ratio, as a measure of liquidity and short-term solvency, is subject to serious theoretical as well as practical shortcomings and limitations. Consequently, before we embark on a discussion of the uses of the current ratio and related measures of liquidity, these limitations must be thoroughly understood.

Limitations of the current ratio

The first step in our examination of the current ratio as a tool of liquidity and short-term solvency analysis is to examine the components which are normally included in the ratio shown in Exhibit 16–1.

EXHIBIT 16–1

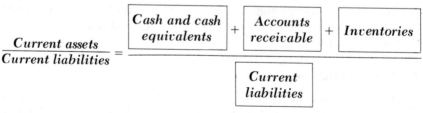

Disregarding, for purposes of this evaluation, prepaid expenses and similar unsubstantial items entering the computation of the current ratio, we are left with the above four major elements which comprise this ratio.

Now, if we define liquidity as the ability to balance required cash outflows with adequate inflows, including an allowance for unexpected interruptions of inflows or increases in outflows, we must ask: Does the relationship of these four elements at a given point in time—

1. Measure and predict the pattern of future fund flows?
2. Measure the adequacy of future fund inflows in relation to outflows.

Unfortunately, the answer to these questions is mostly negative. The current ratio is a static or "stock" concept of what resources are available at a given moment in time to meet the obligations at that moment. The existing reservoir of net funds does not have a logical or causative relationship to the future funds which will flow through it. And yet it is the future flows that are the subject of our greatest interest in the assessment of liquidity. These flows depend importantly on elements *not* included in the ratio itself, such as sales, profits, and changes in business conditions. To elaborate, let us examine more closely the four elements comprising the ratio.

Cash and Cash Equivalents The amount of cash held by a well-managed enterprise is in the nature of a precautionary reserve, intended to take care of short-term imbalances in cash flows. For example, in cases of a business downturn, sales may fall more rapidly than outlays for purchases and expenses. Since cash is a nonearning asset and cash equivalents are usually low-yielding securities, the investment in such assets is kept at a safe minimum. To conceive of this minimum balance as available for payment of current debts would require the dropping of the going-concern assumption underlying accounting statements. While the balance of cash has some relation to the existing level of activity, such a relationship is not very strong nor does it contain predictive implications regarding the future. In fact, some enterprises may use cash substitutes in the form of open lines of credit which, of course, do not enter at all into the computation of the current ratio.

The important link between cash and solvency in the minds of many is due to the well-known fact that a shortage of cash, more than any other factor, is the element which can clinch the insolvency of an enterprise.

Accounts Receivable The major determinant of the level of accounts receivable is sales. The size of accounts receivable in relation to sales is governed by terms of trade and credit policy. Changes in receivables will correspond to changes in sales though not necessarily on a directly proportional basis.

When we look at accounts receivable as a source of cash we must, except in the case of liquidation, recognize the revolving nature of the asset with the collection of one account replaced by the extension of fresh credit. Thus, the level of receivables per se is not an index to future net inflows of cash.

| Inventory | As is the case with accounts receivable, the main determinant of the size of inventories is the level of sales, or expected sales, rather than the level of current liabilities. Given that the level of sales is a measure of the level of demand then, scientific methods of inventory management (economic order quantities, safe stock levels, and reorder points) generally establish that inventory increments vary not in proportion to demand but vary rather with the *square root* of demand.

The relationship of inventories to sales is further accented by the fact that it is sales that is the one essential element which starts the conversion of inventories to cash. Moreover, the determination of future cash inflows through the sale of inventories is dependent on the profit margin which can be realized because inventories are generally stated at the lower of *cost* or market. The current ratio, while including inventories, gives no recognition to the sales level or to profit margin, both of which are important elements entering into the determination of future cash inflows.

Current Liabilities The level of current liabilities, the safety of which the current ratio is intended to measure, is also largely determined by the level of sales.

Current liabilities are a source of funds in the same sense that receivables and inventories tie up funds. Since purchases, which give rise to accounts payable, are a function of the level of activity (i.e., sales), these payables vary with sales. As long as sales remain constant or are rising, the payment of current liabilities is essentially a refunding operation. There again the components of the current ratio give little, if any, recognition to these elements and their effects on the future flow of funds. Nor do the current liabilities which enter into the computation of the current ratio include prospective outlays, such as commitments under construction contracts, loans, leases, or pensions, all of which affect the future outflow of funds.

Implications of the limitations to which the current ratio is subject

There are a number of conclusions which can be reached on the basis of the foregoing discussion:

1. Liquidity depends to some extent on cash or cash equivalents balances and to a much more significant extent on prospective cash flows.
2. There is no direct or established relationship between balances of working capital items and the pattern which future cash flows are likely to assume.
3. Managerial policies directed at optimizing the levels of receivables and inventories are oriented primarily towards efficient and profitable assets utilization and only secondarily at liquidity.[1]

Given these conclusions, which obviously limit the value of the current ratio as an index of liquidity, and given the static nature of this ratio and the fact that it is composed of items which affect liquidity in different ways, we may ask why this ratio enjoys such widespread use and in what way, if any, it can be used intelligently by the analyst.

The most probable reasons for the popularity of the current ratio are evidently the simplicity of its basic concept, the ease with which it can be computed, and the readiness with which data for it can be obtained. It may also derive its popularity from the credit grantor's, and especially the banker's, propensity to view credit situations as conditions of last resort. They may ask themselves: "What if there were a complete cessation of funds inflow? Would the current assets then be adequate to pay off the current liabilities?" The assumption of such extreme conditions is, of course, not always a useful way of measuring liquidity.

To what use can the intelligent analyst put the current ratio?

Let it first be said that the analyst who wishes to measure short-term liquidity and solvency will find cash flow projections and pro forma financial statements to be the most relevant and reliable tools to use. This involves obtaining information which is not readily available in published financial statements and it also involves the need for a great deal of estimation. This area of analysis will be discussed in the next chapter.

The current ratio as a valid tool of analysis

Should the analyst want to use the current ratio as a static measure of the ability of current assets to satisfy the current liabilities, he will be employing a different concept of liquidity from the one discussed above. In this context liquidity means the readiness and speed with which current assets can be converted to cash and the degree to which

---

[1] The nature of the business is also a factor. For example, Fair Lanes, a bowling lanes operator, does obviously not sell on credit and thus has no receivables. It also carries no inventories of any consequences. Consequently it has during most of its 50 year existence operated with a working capital deficiency. With almost all of its current assets in cash it has no problem meeting current obligations.

such conversion will result in shrinkage in the stated value of current assets.

It is not our purpose here to discredit the current ratio as a valid tool of analysis but rather to suggest that its legitimate area of application is far less wide than popularly believed.

Defenders of this, the oldest and best known of financial ratios, may say that they are aware of the multitude of limitations and inconsistencies of concept outlined above but that they will "allow" for them in the evaluation of the ratio. A careful examination of these limitations suggests that such process of "allowing" for such limitations is well nigh impossible.

The better and most valid way to use this ratio is to recognize its limitations and to restrict its use to the analytical job it can do, that is, measuring the ability of *present* current assets to discharge *existing* current liabilities and considering the excess, if any, as a liquid surplus available to meet imbalances in the flow of funds and other contingencies. This should be done with an awareness of the fact that the test envisages a situation of enterprise liquidation[2] whereas in the normal, going-concern situation current assets are of a revolving nature, for example, the collected receivable being replaced with a newly created one, while the current liabilities are essentially of a refunding nature, that is, the repayment of one is followed by the creation of another.

Given the analytical function of the current ratio, as outlined above, there are two basic elements which must be measured before the current ratio can form the basis for valid conclusions:

1. The quality of the current assets and the nature of the current liabilities which enter the determination of the ratio.
2. The rate of turnover of these assets and liabilities that is, the average time span needed to convert receivables and inventories into cash and the amount of time which can be taken for the payment of current liabilities.

To measure the above, a number of ratios and other tools have been devised, and these can enhance the use of the current ratio as an analytic tool.

Measures which supplement the current ratio

The most liquid of current assets is, of course, cash, which is the standard of liquidity itself. A close second to cash is "temporary in-

---

[2] It should be realized that the circumstances leading to bankruptcy or liquidation will have an effect on how much the amounts realized on asset dispositions will shrink. They will, for example, be likely to shrink more severely if the liquidation is caused by overall adverse industry conditions than if caused by specific difficulties such as poor management or inadequate capitalization.

vestments" which are usually highly marketable and relatively safe temporary repositories of cash. These are, in effect, considered as "cash equivalents" and usually earn a modest return.

Cash ratios. The proportion which cash and cash equivalents constitute of the total current assets group is a measure of the degree of liquidity of this group of assets. It is measured by the cash ratio which is computed as follows:

$$\frac{\text{Cash} + \text{Cash Equivalents}}{\text{Total Current Assets}}$$

Evaluation. The higher the ratio the more liquid is the current asset group. This, in turn, means that with respect to this cash and cash equivalents component there is a minimal danger of loss in value in cash of liquidation and that there is practically no waiting period for conversion of these assets into usable cash.

APB *Opinion No. 18* generally requires the carrying of investments, representing an interest of 20 percent or higher, at underlying equity. This is, of course, neither cost nor, necessarily, market value. While such substantial positions in the securities of another company are not usually considered cash equivalents, *should* they nevertheless be so considered, their market value would be the most appropriate figure to use in the computation of liquidity ratios. The equity method of accounting is discussed in Chapters 5 and 9.

As to the availability of cash, the analyst should bear in mind possible restrictions which may exist with respect to the use of cash balances. An example is the so-called "compensating balances" which banks, which extend credit, expect their customers to keep. While such balances can be used, the analyst must nevertheless assess the effect on a company's credit standing and credit availability, as well as on its banking connection, of a breach of the tacit agreement not to draw on the "compensating cash balance."

An additional ratio which measures cash adequacy should be mentioned. The cash to current liabilities ratio is computed as follows:

$$\frac{\text{Cash} + \text{Cash Equivalents}}{\text{Current Liabilities}}$$

It measures how much cash is available to pay current obligations. This is a severe test which ignores the refunding nature of current liabilities. It supplements the cash ratio discussed above in that it measures cash availability from a somewhat different point of view.

To view the cash ratio as a further extension of the acid test ratio (see below) would, except in extreme cases, constitute a test of short-term liquidity too severe to be meaningful. Nevertheless, the importance of cash as the ultimate form of liquidity should never be underestimated. The record of business failures provides many examples of insolvent companies, possessing sizable noncash assets, current and noncurrent, and no cash to pay debts or to operate with.

Measures of accounts receivable liquidity

In most enterprises which sell on credit, accounts and notes receivable are a significant part of working capital. In assessing the quality of working capital and of the current ratio, it is important to get some measure of the quality and the liquidity of the receivables.

Both the quality[3] and liquidity of accounts receivable are affected by their rate of turnover. By quality is meant the likelihood of collection without loss. An indicator of this likelihood is the degree to which receivables are within the terms of payment set by the enterprise. Experience has shown that the longer receivables remain outstanding beyond the date on which they are due, the lower is the probability of their collection in full. Turnover is an indicator of the age of the receivables, particularly when it is compared with an expected turnover rate which is determined by credit terms granted.

The measure of liquidity is concerned with the speed with which accounts receivables will, on average, be converted into cash. Here again turnover is among the best measures to use.

AVERAGE ACCOUNTS RECEIVABLE TURNOVER RATIO

The receivable turnover ratio is computed as follows:

$$\frac{\text{Net Sales on Credit}}{\text{Average Accounts Receivable}}$$

The quickest way for an external analyst to determine the average accounts receivable is to take the beginning receivables of the period, add the ending receivables, and divide the sum by two. The use of monthly or quarterly sales figures can lead to an even more accurate result. The more widely sales fluctuate, the more subject to distortion this ratio is, unless the receivables are properly averaged.

Notes receivable arising from normal sales should be included in the accounts receivable figure in computing the turnover ratio. Discounted notes receivable which are still outstanding should also be included in the accounts receivable total.

The sales figure used in computing the ratio should be that of credit sales only, because cash sales obviously do not generate receivables. Since published financial statements rarely disclose the division be-

---

[3] The validity of the collection claim is also one aspect of quality. Thus, the analyst must be alert to problems which can arise from "sales" on consignment or those with right of return which are further discussed in Chapter 5.

tween cash and credit sales, the external analyst may have to compute the ratio under the assumption that cash sales are relatively insignificant. If they are not insignificant, then a degree of distortion may occur in the ratio. However, if the proportion of cash sales to total sales remains relatively constant, the year-to-year comparison of changes in the receivables turnover ratio may nevertheless be validly based.

The average receivables turnover figure indicates how many *times*, on average, the receivables revolve, that is, are generated and collected during the year.

For example, if sales are $1,200,000 and beginning receivables are $150,000 while year-end receivables are $250,000, then receivable turnover is computed as follows:

$$\frac{1,200,000}{(150,000 + 250,000) \div 2} = \frac{1,200,000}{200,000} = 6 \text{ times}$$

While the turnover figure furnishes a sense of the speed of collections and is valuable for comparison purposes, it is not directly comparable to the terms of trade which the enterprise normally extends. Such comparison is best made by converting the turnover into days of sales tied up in receivables.

Collection period for accounts receivable

This measure, also known as *days sales in accounts receivable* measures the number of days it takes, on average, to collect accounts (and notes) receivable. The number of days can be obtained by dividing the average accounts receivable turnover ratio discussed above into 360, the approximate round number of days in the year. Thus

$$\text{Collection Period} = \frac{360}{\text{Average Accounts Receivable Turnover}}$$

Using the figures of the preceding example, the collection period is:

$$\frac{360}{6} = 60 \text{ days}$$

An alternative computation is to first obtain the average daily sale and then divide the *ending gross* receivable balance by it.

$$\text{Accounts Receivable} \div \frac{\text{Sales}}{360}$$

The result will differ from the foregoing computation because the average accounts receivable turnover figure uses *average* accounts receivable, while this computation uses *ending* accounts receivable only; it thus focuses specifically on the latest accounts receivable balances. Using the figures from our example, the computation is:

$$\text{Average Daily Sales} = \frac{\text{Sales}}{360} = \frac{1,200,000}{360} = \$3,333$$

$$\frac{\text{Accounts Receivable}}{\text{Average Daily Sales}} = \frac{250,000}{3,333} = 75 \text{ days}$$

Note that if the collection period computation would have used ending receivables rather than *average* receivables turnover, the identical collection period, that is, 75 could have been obtained as follows:

$$\frac{\text{Sales}}{\text{Accounts Receivable (ending)}} = \frac{\$1,200,000}{\$250,000} = 4.8 \text{ times}$$

$$\frac{360}{\text{Receivable Turnover}} = \frac{360}{4.8} = 75 \text{ days}$$

The use of 360 days is arbitrary because while receivables are outstanding 360 days (used for computational convenience instead of 365), the sales days of the year usually number less than 300. However, consistent computation of the ratio will make for valid period to period comparisons.

Evaluation

Accounts receivable turnover rates or collection periods can be compared to industry averages (see chapter 4) or to the credit terms granted by the enterprise.

When the collection period is compared with the terms of sale allowed by the enterprise, the degree to which customers are paying on time can be assessed. Thus, if the average terms of sale in the illustration used above are 40 days, then an average collection period of 75 days reflects either some or all of the following conditions:

1. A poor collection job.
2. Difficulty in obtaining prompt payment from customers in spite of diligent collection efforts.
3. Customers in financial difficulty.

The first conclusion calls for remedial managerial action, while the last two reflect particularly on both the quality and the liquidity of the accounts receivable.

An essential analytical first step is to determine whether the accounts receivable are representative of company sales activity. Significant receivables may, for example, be lodged in the captive finance company of the enterprise. In that case the bad debt provision may also relate to receivables not on company books.

It is always possible that an *average* figure is not representative of the receivables population it represents. Thus, it is possible that the 75-day average collection period does not represent an across-the-board payment tardiness on the part of customers but is rather caused by the excessive delinquency of one or two substantial customers.

The best way to investigate further an excessive collection period is to *age* the accounts receivable in such a way that the distribution of each account by the number of days past-due is clearly apparent. An aging schedule in a format such as given below will show whether the problem is widespread or concentrated:

Accounts receivable aging schedule:

	Days past due			
Accounts receivable	*0–30*	*31–60*	*61–90*	*Over 90*

The age distribution of the receivables will, of course, lead to better informed conclusions regarding the quality and the liquidity of the receivables as well as the kind of action which is necessary to remedy the situation. Another dimension of receivables classification is by quality ratings of credit agencies such as Dunn & Bradstreets.

Notes receivable deserve the particular scrutiny of the analyst because while they are normally regarded as more negotiable than open accounts, they may be of poorer quality than regular receivables if they originated as an extension device for an unpaid account rather than at the inception of the original sale.

In assessing the quality of receivables the analyst should remember that a significant conversion of receivables into cash, except for their use as collateral for borrowing, cannot be achieved without a cutback in sales volume. The sales policy aspect of the collection period evaluation must also be kept in mind. An enterprise may be willing to accept slow-paying customers who provide business which is, on an overall basis, profitable, that is, the profit on sale compensates for the extra use by the customer of the enterprise funds. This circumstance may modify the analyst's conclusions regarding the *quality* of the receivables but not those regarding their *liquidity*.

In addition to the consideration of profitability, an enterprise may extend more liberal credit in cases such as (1) the introduction of a new product, (2) a desire to make sales in order to utilize available excess capacity, or (3) special competitive conditions in the industry. Thus, the relationship between the level of receivables and that of sales and profits must always be borne in mind when evaluating the collection period. The trend of the collection period over time is always important in an assessment of the quality and the liquidity of the receivables.

Another trend which may be instructive to watch is that of the relationship between the provision for doubtful accounts and gross accounts receivable. The ratio is computed as follows:

$$\frac{\text{Provision for Doubtful Accounts}}{\text{Gross Accounts Receivable}}$$

An increase in this ratio over time may indicate management's conclusion that the collectibility of receivables has deteriorated. Conversely, a decrease of this ratio over time may lead to the opposite conclusion or may cause the analyst to reevaluate the adequacy of the provision for doubtful accounts.

Measures of accounts receivable turnover are, as we have seen in this section, important in the evaluation of liquidity. They are also important as measures of asset utilization, a subject which will be covered in Chapter 19.

MEASURES OF INVENTORY TURNOVER

Inventories represent in many cases a very substantial proportion of the current asset group. This is so for reasons that have little to do with an enterprise's objective of maintaining adequate levels of liquid funds. Reserves of liquid funds are seldom kept in the form of inventories. Inventories represent investments made for the purpose of obtaining a return. The return is derived from the expected profits which may result from sales. In most businesses a certain level of inventory must be kept in order to generate an adequate level of sales. If the inventory level is inadequate, the sales volume will fall to below the level otherwise attainable. Excessive inventories, on the other hand, expose the enterprise to expenses such as storage costs, insurance and taxes, as well as to risks of loss of value through obsolescence and physical deterioration. Moreover, excessive inventories tie up funds which can be used more profitably elsewhere.

Due to the risk involved in holding inventories as well as the fact that inventories are one step further removed from cash than receivables (they have to be sold before they are converted into receivables), inventories are normally considered the least liquid component of the current assets group. As is the case with most generalizations, this is not always true. Certain staple items, such as commodities, raw materials, standard sizes of structural steel, etc., enjoy broad and ready markets and can usually be sold with little effort, expense, or loss. On the other hand, fashion merchandise, specialized components, or perishable items can lose their value rapidly unless they are sold on a timely basis.

The evaluation of the current ratio, which includes inventories in its computation, must include a thorough evaluation of the quality as well as the liquidity of these assets. Here again, measures of turnover are the best overall tools available for such an evaluation.

Inventory turnover ratio

The inventory turnover ratio measures the average rate of speed with which inventories move through and out of the enterprise.

Computation. The computation of the average inventory turnover is as follows:

$$\frac{\text{Cost of Goods Sold}}{\text{Average Inventory}}$$

Consistency of valuation requires that the cost of goods sold be used because, as is the case with inventories, it is stated principally at *cost*. Sales, on the other hand, normally include a profit. Although the cost of goods sold figure is now disclosed in most published income statements, the external analyst is still occasionally confronted with an unavailability of such a figure. In such a case the sales figure must be substituted. While this results in a theoretically less valid turnover ratio, it can still be used for comparison and trend development purposes, especially if used consistently and when sharp changes in profit margins are not present.

The average inventory figure is most readily obtained as follows:

$$\frac{\text{Opening Inventory} + \text{Closing Inventory}}{2}$$

Further refinement in the averaging process can be achieved, where possible and necessary, by adding up the monthly inventory figures and dividing the total by 12.

Before a turnover ratio is computed the analyst must carefully examine the composition of the inventory figure and make adjustments, such as those from Lifo to Fifo, etc.

Days to sell inventory

Another measure of inventory turnover which is also useful in assessing purchasing policy is the required number of *days to sell inventory*. The computation which follows, i.e.

$$\frac{360 \text{ days}}{\text{Average Inventory Turnover}}$$

measures the number of days it takes to sell the average inventory in a given year and, an alternative computation

$$\frac{\text{Ending Inventory}}{\text{Cost of Average Day's Sales}}$$

measures the number of days which are required to sell off the ending inventory, assuming the given rate of sales where the

$$\text{Cost of an Average Day's Sales} = \frac{\text{Cost of Goods Sold}}{360}$$

Example of computations

Sales	1,800,000
Cost of goods sold	1,200,000
Beginning inventory	200,000
Ending inventory	400,000

$$\text{Inventory Turnover} = \frac{1,200,000}{(200,000 + 400,000) \div 2} = \frac{1,200,000}{300,000} = 4 \text{ times}$$

$$\text{Number of Days to Sell Average Inventory} = \frac{360}{4} = 90 \text{ days}$$

Alternatively the computation based on ending inventory is as follows:

Step 1:

$$\frac{\text{Cost of Goods Sold}}{360} = \frac{1,200,000}{360} = 3,333 \text{ (cost of average day's sales)}$$

Step 2:

$$\frac{\text{Ending Inventory}}{\text{Cost of Average Day's Sales}} = \frac{400,000}{3,333} = 120 \text{ days}$$

Interpretation of inventory turnover ratios. The current ratio computation views its current asset components as sources of funds which can, as a means of last resort, be used to pay off the current liabilities. Viewed this way, the inventory turnover ratios give us a measure of the quality as well as of the liquidity of the inventory component of the current assets.

The quality of inventory is a measure of the enterprise's ability to use it and dispose of it without loss. When this is envisaged under conditions of forced liquidation, then recovery of cost is the objective. In the normal course of business the inventory will, of course, be sold at a profit. Viewed from this point of view, the normal profit margin realized by the enterprise assumes importance because the funds which will be obtained, and which would theoretically be available for payment of current liabilities, will include the profit in addition to the recovery of cost. In both cases costs of sale will reduce the net proceeds.

In practice a going concern cannot use its investment in inventory for the payment of current liabilities because any drastic reduction in normal inventory levels will surely cut into the sales volume.

A rate of turnover which is slower than that experienced historically, or which is below that normal in the industry, would lead to the preliminary conclusion that it includes items which are slow moving because they are obsolete, in weak demand, or otherwise unsaleable. Such conditions do, of course, cast doubt on the feasibility of recovering the cost of such items.

Further investigation may reveal that the slowdown in inventory turnover is due to a buildup of inventory in accordance with a future contractual commitment, in anticipation of a price rise, in anticipation of a strike or shortage, or for any number of other reasons which must be probed into further.

A better evaluation of inventory turnover can be obtained from the computation of separate turnover rates for the major components of inventory such as (1) raw materials, (2) work in process, and (3) finished goods. Departmental or divisional turnover rates can similarly lead to more useful conclusions regarding inventory quality. One should never lose sight of the fact that the total inventory turnover ratio is an aggregate of widely varying turnover rates of individual components.

The biggest problem facing the external analyst who tries to compute inventory turnover ratios by individual components is obtaining the necessary detailed data. This is, at present, rarely provided in published financial statements.

The turnover ratio is, of course, also a gauge of liquidity in that it conveys a measure of the speed with which inventory can be converted into cash. In this connection a useful additional measure is the conversion period of inventories.

Conversion period of inventories. This computation adds the collection period of receivables to the days needed to sell inventories in order to arrive at the time interval needed to convert inventories into cash.

Using figures developed in our examples of the respective ratios above, we get

Days to sell inventory	90
Days to collect receivables	60
Total conversion period of inventories	150 days

It would thus normally take 150 days to sell inventory on credit and to collect the receivable. This is a period identical to the *operating cycle* which we discussed earlier in this chapter.

The effect of alternative methods of inventory management

In evaluating the inventory turnover ratio the analyst must be alert to the influence which alternative accounting principles have on the determination of the ratio's components. The basic discussion on alternative accounting principles of inventory measurement is found in Chapter 5. It is obvious that the use of the Lifo method of inventory valuation may render both the turnover ratios as well as the current ratio practically meaningless. Limited information is usually found in published financial statements which enables the analyst to adjust the unrealistically low Lifo inventory valuation occurring in times of rising price levels so as to render it useful for inclusion in turnover ratio or the current ratio. Even if two companies employ Lifo cost methods for their inventory valuation computation of their ratios, using such inventory figures may nevertheless not be comparable because their respective Lifo inventory pools (bases) may have been acquired in years of significantly different price levels. The inventory figure enters the numerator of the current ratio and also the denominator because the inventory method utilized affects the income tax liability.

The analyst must also bear in mind that companies using the so-called "natural year" may have at their year-end an unrepresentatively low inventory level and that this may increase the turnover ratio to unrealistically high levels.

Prepaid expenses are expenditures made for benefits which are expected to be received in the future. Since most such benefits are recievable within a year or within an enterprise's operating cycle they will conserve the outlay of current funds.

Usually, the amounts included in this category are relatively small compared to the size of the other current assets, and consequently no extensive discussion of their treatment is needed here. However, the analyst must be aware of the tendency of managements of enterprises with weak current positions to include in prepaid expenses deferred charges and other items of dubious liquidity. Such items must consequently be excluded from the computation of working capital and of the current ratio.

CURRENT LIABILITIES

In the computation of working capital and of the current ratio, current liabilities are important for two related reasons:

1. A basic objective of measuring the excess of current assets over current liabilities is to determine whether the latter are covered by current assets and what margin of safety is provided by the excess of such assets over current liabilities.
2. Current liabilities are deducted from current assets in arriving at the net working capital position.

In the computation of the current ratio, the point of view adopted towards current liabilities is *not* one of a continuing enterprise but rather of an enterprise in liquidation. This is so because in the normal course of operations, current liabilities are not paid off but are rather of a refunding nature. As long as the sales volume remains stable, purchases will also remain at a stable level, and that in turn will cause current liabilities to remain level. Increasing sales, in turn, will generally result in an increasing level of current liabilities. Thus, it can be generally stated that the trend and direction of sales is a good indication of the future level of current liabilities.

In assessing the quality of the current ratio, the nature of the current liabilities must be carefully examined.

Differences in the "nature" of current liabilities

Not all liabilities represent equally urgent and forceful calls for payment. At one extreme we find liabilities for taxes of all kinds which must be paid promptly regardless of current financial difficulties. The powers of collection of federal and local government authorities are as well known as they are powerful.

On the other hand, current liabilities to suppliers with whom the enterprise has a long standing relationship and who depend on, and value, the enterprise's business are of a very different degree of urgency. Postponement and renegotiation of such debts in times of financial stringency are both possible and are commonly found.

The "nature" of current liabilities in terms of our present discussion must be judged in the light of the degree of urgency of payment which attaches to them. It should be understood that if fund inflows from current revenues are viewed as sources of funds available for the payment of current liabilities, then labor costs and other current fund-requiring costs and expenses have a first call on sales revenues and that trade bills and other liabilities can be paid only after such recurring outlays have been met. This dynamic aspect of funds flow will be examined more closely in the chapter which follows.

The analyst must also be aware of unrecorded liabilities which may have a claim to current funds. Examples of these are purchase commitments and obligations under pensions and leases. Moreover, under long-term loan acceleration clauses, a failure to meet current installments of long-term debt may render the entire debt due and payable, that is, cause it to become current.

Days purchases in accounts payable ratio

A measure of the degree to which accounts payable represent current rather than overdue obligations can be obtained by calculating the *days purchases in accounts payable ratio*. This ratio is computed as follows:

$$\text{Accounts Payable} \div \frac{\text{Purchases}}{360}$$

The difficulty which the external analyst will encounter here is that normally purchases are not separately disclosed in published financial statements. A very rough approximation of the amount of purchases can be obtained by adjusting the cost of goods sold figure for depreciation and other nonfund requiring charges as well as for changes in inventories. However, the cost of goods sold figure may contain significant cash charges, and this may reduce the validity of a computation which contains such an approximation of purchases.

The capacity to borrow

An important aspect of an enterprise's liquidity which can be determined only after careful analysis and interpretation of its financial statements is its capacity to borrow. It can be a very significant off-balance sheet liquidity resource.

The capacity to borrow depends on numerous factors and is subject to rapid change. It depends on profitability, stability, relative size, industry position, asset composition and capital structure. It will depend, moreover, as such external factors as credit market conditions and trends.

The capacity to borrow is important as a source of funds in time of need for funds and is also important when an enterprise must roll over its short-term debt.

INTERPRETATION OF THE CURRENT RATIO

In the foregoing sections we have examined the means by which the quality and the liquidity of the individual components of the current ratio is measured. This evaluation is, of course, essential to an overall interpretation of the current ratio as an indicator of short-term liquidity and financial strength.

The analyst must, however, exercise great care if he wants to carry the interpretation of the current ratio beyond the conclusion that it represents an excess of current resources over current obligations as of a given point in time.

Examination of trend

An examination of the trend of the current ratio over time can be very instructive. Two tools of analysis which were discussed in Chapter 4 are useful here. One is *trend analysis*, where the components of working capital as well as the current ratio would be converted into an index to be compared over time. The other is *common-size analysis*, by means of which the *composition* of the current asset group is examined over time. A historical trend and common-size comparison over time, as well as an intra-industry comparison of such trends can also be instructive.

Interpretation of changes over time

Changes in the current ratio over time must, however, be interpreted with great care. They do not automatically imply changes in liquidity or operating results. Thus, for example, in a prosperous year an increased liability for taxes may result in a lowering of the current ratio. Conversely, during a business contraction, current liabilities may be paid off while there may be a concurrent involuntary accumulation of inventories and uncollected receivables causing the ratio to rise.

In times of business expansion, which may reflect operating successes, the enterprise may suffer from an expansion in working capital requirements, otherwise known as a "prosperity squeeze" with a resulting contraction of the current ratio. This can be seen in the following example:

	Year 1	Year 2
Current assets	$300,000	$600,000
Current liabilities	100,000	400,000
Working capital	$200,000	$200,000
Current ratio	3:1	1.5:1

As can be seen from the above example, a doubling of current assets, accompanied by a quadrupling of current liabilities and an unchanged amount of working capital will lead to a halving of the current ratio. This is the effect of business expansion unaccompanied by an added capital investment. Inflation can have a similar effect on a business enterprise in that it will lead to a substantial increase in all current items categories.

Possibilities of manipulation

The analyst must be aware of the possibilities of year-end manipulation of the current ratio, otherwise known as "window dressing."

For example, towards the close of the fiscal year the collection of receivables may be pressed more vigorously, advances to officers may be called in for temporary repayment, and inventory may be reduced to below normal levels. Proceeds from these steps can then be used to pay off current liabilities. The effect on the current ratio of the reduction of current liabilities through the use of current assets can be seen in the following example:

	Payoff of $50,000 in liabilities	
	Before	*After*
Current asets	$200,000	$150,000
Current liabilities	100,000	50,000
Current ratio	2:1	3:1

The accounting profession, sensing the propensity of managements to offset liabilities against assets, has strengthened its prohibitions against offsets by restricting them strictly to situations where the legal right to offset exists.

To the extent possible, the analyst should go beyond year-end measures and should try to obtain as many interim readings of the current ratio as possible, not only in order to guard against the practice of "window dressing" described above but also in order to gauge the seasonal changes to which the ratio is exposed. The effect of a strong current ratio in December on an assessment of current financial condition may be considerably tempered if it is discovered that at its seasonal peak in July the enterprise is dangerously close to a serious credit squeeze.

The use of "rules of thumb" standards

A popular belief that has gained considerable currency is that the current ratio can be evaluated by means of "rules of thumb." Thus, it is believed that if the current ratio is 2:1 (or 200 percent), it is sound and anything below that norm is bad while the higher above that figure the current ratio is, the better.

This rule of thumb may reflect the lender's, and particularly the banker's, conservatism. The fact that it is down from the norm of 2.5:1 prevailing at the turn of the century may mean that improved financial reporting has reduced this size of the "cushion" which the banker and other creditors would consider as the minimum protection they need.

What the 2:1 standard means is that there are $2 of current assets available for each dollar of current liabilities or that the value of current assets can, on liquidation, shrink by 50 percent before it will be inadequate to cover the current liabilities. Of course, a current ratio much higher than 2:1, while implying a superior coverage of current liabilities, may also mean a wasteful accumulation of liquid resources which do not "carry their weight" by earning an appropriate return for the enterprise.

It should be evident by now that the evaluation of the current ratio in terms of rules of thumb is a technique of dubious validity. This is so for two major reasons:

1. As we have learned in the preceding sections, the quality of the
    current assets, as well as the composition of the current liabilities
    which make up this ratio, are the most important determinants in
    an evaluation of the quality of the current ratio. Thus, two com-
    panies which have identical current ratios may nevertheless be in
    quite different current financial condition due to variations in the
    quality of the working capital components.
2. The need of an enterprise for working capital varies with industry
    conditions as well as with the length of its own particular *net trade
    cycle*.

The net trade cycle

An enterprise's need for working capital depends importantly on
the relative size of its required inventory investment as well as on the
relationship between the credit terms it receives from its suppliers as
against those it must extend to its customers.

ILLUSTRATION 4.   Assume a company shows the following data at the end
of 19X1:

Sales for 19X1	$360,000
Receivables	40,000
Inventories	50,000
Accounts payable	20,000

The following tabulation measures the company's cash cycle in terms
of days:

$$\text{Sales per day } \frac{\$360,000}{360} = \quad \$1,000$$

Number of days sales in:	
Accounts receivable	40 days
Inventories	50
Total trade cycle	90 days
Less: Accounts payable	20
Net trade cycle	70 days

From the above we can see that the company is keeping 50 days of sales
in inventory and that it receives only 20 sales days of trade credit while it
must extend 40 sales days of credit to its customers. Obviously the higher
the *net trade cycle* a company has the larger its investment in working
capital is likely to be. Thus, in our above example, if the company could
lower its investment in inventories by 10 sales days, it could lower its
investment in working capital by $10,000. A similar result can be achieved
by increasing the number of days sales in accounts payable by 10.

It should be noted that for the sake of simplicity and uniformity the net trade cycle computation uses number of *days sales* as a common factor. This does introduce, however, a degree of distortion because, while receivables can be related directly to sales, inventories are more logically related to cost of goods sold and accounts payable to purchases. This distortion will, however, not normally be large enough to invalidate the tool for analytical and comparison purposes and the degree of distortion will depend on factors such as the profit margin.

The working capital requirements of a supermarket with its high inventory turnover and low outstanding receivables are obviously lower than those of a tobacco company with its slow inventory turnover.

Valid working capital standards

Comparison with industry current ratios as well as analyses of working capital requirements such as the net trade cycle analysis described above can lead to far more valid conclusions regarding the adequacy of an enterprise's working capital than can a mechanical comparison of its current ratio to the 2 : 1 "rule of thumb" standard.

The importance of sales

In an assessment of the overall liquidity of current assets, the trend of sales is an important factor. Since it takes sales to convert inventory into receivables or cash, an uptrend in sales indicates that the conversion of inventories into more liquid assets will be easier to achieve than when sales remain constant. Declining sales, on the other hand, will retard the conversion of inventories into cash.

Common-size analysis of current assets composition

The composition of the current asset group, which can be analyzed by means of common-size statements, is another good indicator of relative working capital liquidity.

Consider, for example, the following comparative working capital composition:

	Year 1		Year 2	
	$	%	$	%
Current Assets:				
Cash	30,000	30	20,000	20
Accounts receivable	40,000	40	30,000	30
Inventories	30,000	30	50,000	50
Total Current Assets	100,000	100	100,000	100

From the simple illustration above it can be seen, even without the computation of common-size percentages, that the liquidity of the current asset group has deteriorated in year 2 by comparison with year 1. However, the use of common-size percentage comparisons will greatly facilitate the evaluation of comparative liquidity, regardless of the size of the dollar amounts involved.

The liquidity index

The measurement of the comparative liquidity of current assets can be further refined through the use of a *liquidity index*. The construction of this index (first suggested by A. H. Finney) can be illustrated as follows:

Using the working capital figures from the common-size computation above, and assuming that the conversion of inventories into accounts receivable takes 50 days on average and that the conversion of receivables into cash takes an average of 40 days, the index is computed as follows:

Year 1

	Amount ×	Days removed from cash	= Product dollar-days
Cash	30,000	—	—
Accounts receivable	40,000	40	1,600,000
Inventories	30,000	90	2,700,000
Total	100,000 (a)		4,300,000 (b)

$$\text{Liquidity index} = \frac{b}{a} = \frac{4{,}300{,}000}{100{,}000} = \underline{\underline{43}}$$

Year 2

	Amount ×	Days removed from cash	= Product dollar-days
Cash	20,000	—	—
Accounts receivable	30,000	40	1,200,000
Inventories	50,000	90	4,500,000
Total	100,000		5,700,000

$$\text{Liquidity index} \frac{5{,}700{,}000}{100{,}000} = \underline{\underline{57}}$$

The computation of the respective liquidity indices for the years 1 and 2 tells what we already knew instinctively in the case of this simple example, that is, that the liquidity has deteriorated in year 2 as compared to year 1.

The liquidity index must be interpreted with care. The index is in itself a figure without significance. It gains its significance only from a comparison between one index number and another as a gauge of the period to period change in liquidity or as a company to company comparison of relative liquidity. Increases in the index signify a deterioration in liquidity while decreases signify changes in the direction of improved liquidity. The index which is expressed in days is a weighing mechanism and its validity depends on the validity of the assumptions implicit in the weighing process.

An additional popular technique of current ratio interpretation is to submit it to a somewhat sterner test.

ACID-TEST RATIO

This test is the acid-test ratio, also known as the "quick ratio" because it is assumed to include the assets most quickly convertible into cash.

The acid-test ratio is computed as shown in Exhibit 16–2.

The omission of inventories from the acid-test ratio is based on the belief that they are the least liquid component of the current asset group. While this is generally so, we have seen in an earlier discussion in this chapter that this is not always true and that certain types of inventory can be more liquid than are slow-paying receivables. Another reason for the exclusion of inventories is the belief, quite often warranted, that the valuation of inventories normally requires a greater degree of judgment than is required for the valuation of the other current assets.

EXHIBIT 16–2

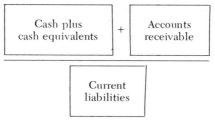

Since prepaid expenses are usually insignificant in relation to the other current assets, the acid test ratio is sometimes computed simply by omitting the inventories from the current asset figure.

The interpretation of the acid-test ratio is subject to most of the same considerations which were discussed regarding the interpretation of the current ratio. Moreover, the acid-test ratio represents an even sterner test of an enterprise's liquidity than does the current ratio, and the analyst must judge by himself what significance to his conclusions the total omission of inventories, as a source of current funds, is.

OTHER MEASURES OF SHORT-TERM LIQUIDITY

The static nature of the current ratio which measures the relationship of current assets to current liabilities, at a given moment in time, as well as the fact that this measure of liquidity fails to accord recognition to the great importance which funds or cash flows play in an enterprise's ability to meet its maturing obligations has lead to a search for more dynamic measures of liquidity.

Funds flow ratios

Funds flow ratios relate obligations to funds (working capital) generated by operations which are available to meet them. These resources do consequently not include funds from nonoperating sources such as borrowing or the sale of fixed assets.

One such ratio relates current liabilities to the funds from operations for the year:

$$\frac{\text{Funds Provided by Operations}}{\text{Current Liabilities}}$$

This is a measure of how many times current liabilities are covered by the funds flow of the year just elapsed. It is, of course, backward looking while current liabilities as of a certain date must be paid out of *future*, rather than past, funds flow. Nevertheless, in the absence of drastic changes in conditions, the latest yearly funds flow represents at least a good basis for an estimate of the next period's funds flow.

Importance of nonfund items in net income. Since the conversion of income into funds flow depends on the size of the net *nonfund* items included in it, a useful comparison measure is the relationship between the net nonfund items in income and net income. The computation of this ratio is as follows:

$$\frac{\text{Net Nonfund Items in Income}}{\text{Net Income}}$$

The higher the relationship of net nonfund requiring items to net income the greater the funds flow is in relation to reported net income and, thus, the higher the funds flow will be in relation to a given net income figure. An example of the computation of the *net nonfund items* follows:

Depreciation	$3,500,000
Depletion	1,200,000
Patent amortization	400,000
Deferred income taxes	2,800,000
Total nonfund charges	$7,900,000
Less: Unremitted earnings of foreign subsidiaries	2,100,000
Net nonfund requiring items	$5,800,000

If net income is $58,000,000, the net nonfund items ratio is as follows:

$$\frac{5,800,000}{58,000,000} = .1 \text{ or } 10 \text{ percent}$$

This means that funds flow will normally be expected to approximate 110 percent of net income.

Cash flow related measures

A ratio, which focuses on cash expenses of the year, and measures how many days of expenses the most liquid current assets could finance, assuming that all other cash inflows were to suddenly dry up, can be computed as follows:

$$\frac{\text{Cash} + \text{Cash Equivalents} + \text{Receivables}}{\text{Year's Cash Expense}}$$

Like the acid test ratio, the sternness of this test is such that its usefulness must be carefully weighed by the analyst.

A variation in the measurement of the relationship of current liabilities to funds which are expected to become available to meet them is to relate them to expected actual cash flows from operations:

$$\frac{\text{Current liabilities}}{\text{Sources of Cash from Operations}}$$

The computation of cash generated by operations is discussed in Chapter 13.

Projecting changes in conditions or policies

It is possible and often very useful to trace through the effects of changes in conditions and/or policies on the funds or cash resources of an enterprise.

ILLUSTRATION 5.   Assume that the Foresight Company has the following account balances at December 31, 19X1:

	Debit	Credit
Cash	$ 70,000	
Accounts receivable	150,000	
Inventory	65,000	
Accounts payable		$130,000
Notes payable		35,000
Accrued taxes		18,000
Fixed assets	200,000	
Accumulated depreciation		43,000
Capital stock		200,000

The following additional information is available for 19X1:

Sales	$750,000
Cost of sales	520,000
Purchases	350,000
Depreciation	25,000
Net income	20,000

The company anticipates a growth of 10 percent in sales for the coming year. All corresponding revenue and expense items will also increase by 10 percent, except for depreciation which will remain the same. All expenses are paid in cash as they are incurred during the year. 19X2 ending inventory will be $150,000. By the end of 19X2 the company expects to have a notes payable balance of $50,000 and no balance in the accrued taxes account. The company maintains a minimum cash balance of $50,000 as a managerial policy.

I. Assume that the company is considering a change in credit policy so that the ending accounts receivable balance will represent 90 days of sales. What impact will this change have on the company's cash balance. Will it have to borrow?

This can be computed as follows:

Cash 1/1/X2		$ 70,000
Accounts Receivable 1/1/X2	$150,000	
Sales	825,000	
	$975,000	
Less: Accounting Receivable 12/31/X2 (a)	206,250	768,750
Total Cash available		$838,750
Cash Disbursements		
Accounts Payable 1/1/X2	$130,000	
Purchases (b)	657,000	
	787,000	
Accounts Payable 12/31/X2 (c)	244,000	543,000
Notes Payable 1/1/X2	35,000	
Notes Payable 12/31/X2	50,000	(15,000)
Accrued Taxes	18,000	
Cash Expenses (d)	203,500	749,500
		$ 89,250
Cash Balance Desired		50,000
Cash Excess		$ 39,250

Explanation

(a) $\$825,000 \times \dfrac{90}{360} = \$206,250$

(b) 19X2 cost of sales: $\$520,000 \times 1.1 = \$572,000$

    Ending inventory   150,000

    Goods available for sale $722,000
    Beginning inventory   65,000

    Purchases $657,000

(c) $\text{Purchases} \times \dfrac{\text{Old Accounts Payable}}{\text{Old Purchases}} = \$657,000 \times \dfrac{\$130,000}{\$350,000}$

                             $= \$244,000$

(d) Gross profit ($\$825,000 - \$572,000$) $253,000
    Less: Net income $24,500*
            Depreciation   25,000   49,500

    Other cash expenses $203,500

    * 110 percent of $20,000 (19X1 N.I.) + 10 percent of $25,000 (19X1 Depreciation).

II. What would the effect be if the change, instead of as in I, is to an *average* accounts receivable turnover of 4?

We compute this as follows:

Excess cash balance as computed
  above $39,250
Change from an *ending* to an *average* ac-
  counts receivable turnover will increase
  year-end accounts receivable balance to:

$\dfrac{825,000}{4} = 206,250 \times 2 =$

              $412,500 - 150,000 =$ $262,500$ (e)
  Less: Accounts receivable balance
    as above (I)   206,250   56,250 (cash decrease)

Cash Required to Borrow $17,000

(e) $\dfrac{\text{Sales}}{\text{Average A/R Turnover}} = \text{Average A/R};$ Ending A/R $= [(\text{Average A/R}) \times 2] -$

                                            Beginning A/R

III. Assuming that, in addition to the conditions prevailing in II above, suppliers require the company to pay within 60 days—What would be the effect on the cash balance?

The computation is as follows:

Cash required to borrow (from II above) .... $ 17,000
Ending accounts payable (I above) $244,000
Ending accounts payable under 60-day payment =

  Purchases $\times \dfrac{60}{360} = \$657,000 \times \dfrac{60}{360} =$ $109,500

Additional disbursements required.................... $134,500

Cash to be borrowed.................................. $151,500

QUESTIONS

1. Why is short-term liquidity so significant? Explain from the viewpoint of various parties concerned.

2. The concept of working capital is simple, that is, the excess of current assets over current liabilities. What are some of the factors that make this simple computation complicated in practice?

3. What are "cash equivalents"? How should an analyst value them in his analysis?

4. Can fixed assets be included in current assets? If so, explain the situation under which the inclusion may be allowed.

5. Some installment receivables are not collectible within one year. Why are they included in current assets?

6. Are all inventories included in current assets? Why or why not?

7. What is the theoretical justification for including prepaid expenses in current assets?

8. The company under analysis has a very small amount of current liabilities but the long-term liabilities section shows a significant balance. In the footnote to the audited statements, it is disclosed that the company has a "revolving loan agreement" with a local bank. Does this disclosure have any significance to you?

9. Some industries are subject to peculiar financing and operating conditions which call for special consideration in drawing the distinction between what is "current" and what is "noncurrent." How should the analyst recognize this in his evaluation of working capital?

10. Your careful computation of the working capitals of Companies A and B reveals that both have the same amount of working capital. Are you ready to conclude that the liquidity position of both is the same?

11. What is the current ratio? What does it measure? What are the reasons for its widespread use?

12. The holding of cash generally does not yield a return. Why does an enterprise hold cash at all?

13. Is there a relationship between the level of inventories and that of sales? Are inventories a function of sales? If there is a functional relationship between the two, is it proportional?

14. What are the major objectives of management in determining the size of inventory and receivables investment?

15. What are the theoretical limitations of the current ratio as a measure of liquidity?

16. If there are significant limitations attached to the current ratio as a measure of liquidity, what is the proper use of this tool?

17. What are cash ratios? What do they measure?

18. How do we measure the "quality" of various current assets?

19. What does the average accounts receivable turnover measure?

20. What is the collection period for accounts receivable? What does it measure?

21. A company's collection period is 60 days this year as compared to 40 days of last year. Give three or more possible reasons for this change.

22. What is an accounts receivable aging schedule? What is its use in the analysis of financial statements?

23. What are the repercussions to an enterprise of (a) overinvestment or (b) underinvestment in inventories?

24. What problems would you expect to encounter in an analysis of a company using the Lifo inventory method in an inflationary economy? What effects do the price changes have (a) on the inventory turnover ratio and (b) on the current ratio?

25. Why does the "nature" of the current liabilities have to be analyzed in assessing the quality of the current ratio?

26. Why is a firm's capacity to borrow significant? What factors does it depend on?

27. An apparently successful company shows a poor current ratio. Explain the possible reasons for this.

28. What is "window dressing"? Is there any way to find out whether the financial statements are "window dressed" or not?

29. What is the "rule of thumb" governing the expected size of the current ratio? What dangers are there in using this rule of thumb mechanically?

30. Describe the importance which the sales level plays in the overall current financial condition and liquidity of the current assets of an enterprise.

31. What is the liquidity index? What significance do the liquidity index numbers have?

32. What do cash flow ratios attempt to measure?

33. What is the importance of projecting the effects of changes in conditions or policies on the cash resources of an enterprise?

17

FUNDS FLOW ANALYSIS AND FINANCIAL FORECASTS

The preceding chapter examined the various measures which are derived from past financial statement data and which are useful in the assessment of short-term liquidity. The chapter which follows will focus on the use of similar data in an evaluation of longer term solvency. The limitations to which these approaches are subject are due mainly to their static nature, that is, to their reliance on status reports, as of a given moment, of claims against an enterprise and the resources available to meet these claims.

An important and, in many cases, superior alternative to such static measures of conditions prevailing at a given point in time is the analysis and projection of more dynamic models of cash and funds flow. Such models use the present only as a starting point, and while building on reliable patterns of past experience, utilize the best available estimates of future plans and conditions in order to forecast the future availability and disposition of cash or working capital.

OVERVIEW OF CASH FLOW AND FUNDS FLOW PATTERNS

Before we examine the methods by means of which funds flow projections are made, it would be useful to get a thorough understanding of the nature of funds flow. Exhibit 17–1 presents a diagram of the flow of funds through an enterprise. This diagram parallels the accounting cycle diagram presented in Chapter 1 (Exhibit 1–1).

The flow of funds diagram focuses on two concepts of funds: cash and working capital (also known as "funds").

EXHIBIT 17–1
Flow of funds through an enterprise

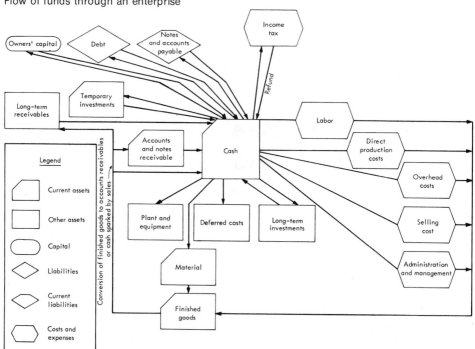

Cash (including cash equivalents) is the ultimate liquid asset. Almost all decisions to invest in assets or to incur costs require the immediate or eventual use of cash. This is why managements focus, from an operational point of view, on *cash* rather than on working capital. The focus on the latter represents mainly the point of view of creditors who consider as part of the liquid assets pool other assets, such as receivables and inventories, which are normally converted into cash within a relatively short time span.

Careful examination of the flows depicted in Exhibit 17–1 should contribute greatly to the reader's understanding of the importance of liquid funds in an enterprise as well as the factors which cause them to be converted into assets and costs. The following factors and relationship are worthy of particular note:

Since the diagram focuses on cash and funds flows only, assets, liabilities, and other items which are not directly involved, such as prepayments and accruals, as well as the income account are not included in it. Some flows are presented in simplified fashion for an easier understanding of relationships. For example, accounts payable are presented as direct sources of cash, whereas in reality they represent a temporary postponement of cash payment for the acquisition of goods and services.

It is recognized that the holding of cash provides no return or a very low return and that in times of rising price levels, cash as a monetary asset is exposed to purchasing power loss. However, these considerations aside, the holding of this most liquid of assets represents, in a business sense, the lowest exposure to risk. Management must make the decision to invest cash in assets or costs, and such a conversion increases risk because the certainty of ultimate reconversion into cash is less than 100 percent. There are, of course, a variety of risks. Thus, the risk involved in a conversion of cash into temporary investments is lower than the risk involved in committing cash to long-term, long-payout assets such as plant, machinery, or research costs. Similarly, the investment of cash in a variety of assets and costs for the creation and marketing of a new product involves serious risk regarding the recovery in cash of amounts so committed. The short-term liquidity as well as the long-term solvency of an enterprise depends on the recovery and realizability of such outlays.

The inflow and outflow of cash (or funds) are highly interrelated. A failure of any part of the system to circulate can affect the entire system. A cessation of sales affects the vital conversion of finished goods into receivables or cash and leads, in turn, to a drop in the cash reservoir. Inability to replenish this reservoir from sources such as owners' capital, debt, or accounts payable (upper left-hand corner of diagram) can lead to a cessation of production activities which will result in a loss of future sales. Conversely, the cutting off of expenses, such as for advertising and marketing, will slow down the conversion of finished goods into receivables and cash. Longer term blockages in the flows may lead to insolvency.

The diagram clarifies the interrelationship between profitability, income, and cash flow. The only real source of funds from operations is sales. When finished goods, which for the sake of simplicity represent the accumulation of *all* costs and expenses in the diagram, are sold, the profit margin will enhance the inflow of liquid funds in the form of receivables and cash. The higher the profit margin the greater the accretion of these funds.

Income, which is the difference between the cash and credit sales and the cost of goods sold, can have a wide variety of effects on cash flow. For example, the costs which flow from the utilization of plant and equipment or from deferred charges generally do not involve the use of current funds. Similarly, as in the case of land sales on long-term installment terms, the creation of long-term´ receivables through sales reduces the impact of net income on cash flow. It can be readily seen that adding back depreciation to net income creates a very crude measure of cash flow.

The limitation of the cash flow concept can be more clearly seen. As cash flows into its reservoir management has a *degree* of discretion as to where to direct it. This discretion depends on the amount of cash already committed to such outlays as dividends, inventory accumulation, capital expenditures, or debt repayment. The total cash inflow also depends on management's ability to tap sources such as equity capital and debt. With respect to noncommitted cash, management has, at the point of return of the cash to the reservoir, the discretion of directing it to any purpose it deems most important. It is this noncommitted cash flow segment that is of particular interest and importance to financial analysts.

Under present accounting conventions certain cash outlays, such as those for training or sales promotion, are considered as business (period) costs and are not shown as assets. These costs can, nevertheless, be of significant future value in either the increasing of sales or in the reduction of costs.

SHORT-TERM CASH FORECASTS

In the measurement of short-term liquidity the short-term cash forecast is one of the most thorough and reliable tools available to the analyst.

Short-term liquidity analysis is of particular interest to management in the financial operations of an enterprise and to short-term credit grantors who are interested in an enterprise's ability to repay short-term loans. The security analyst will pay particular attention to the short-term cash forecast when an enterprise's ability to meet its current obligations is subject to substantial doubt.

Realistic cash forecasts can be made only for relatively short time spans. This is so because the factors influencing the inflows and outflows of cash are many and complex and cannot be reliably estimated beyond the short term.

Importance of sales estimates

The reliability of any cash forecast depends very importantly on the forecast of sales. In fact, a cash forecast can never reach a higher degree of reliability than the sales forecast on which it is based. Except for transactions involving the raising of money from external sources or the investment of money in long-term assets, almost all cash flows relate to and depend on sales.

The sales forecast involves considerations such as:

1. The past direction and trend of sales volume.
2. Enterprise share of the market.
3. Industry and general economic conditions.
4. Productive and financial capacity.
5. Competitive factors.

These factors must generally be assessed in terms of individual product lines which may be influenced by forces peculiar to their own markets.

Pro forma financial statements as an aid to forecasting

The reasonableness and feasibility of short-term cash forecasts can be checked by means of pro forma financial statements. This is done by utilizing the assumptions underlying the cash forecast and constructing, on this basis, a pro forma statement of income covering the period of the forecast and a pro forma balance sheet as at the end of that period. The ratios and other relationships derived from the pro forma financial statements should then be checked for feasibility against historical relationships which have prevailed in the past. Such relationships must be adjusted for factors which it is estimated will affect them during the period of the cash forecast.

Techniques of short-term cash forecasting

ILLUSTRATION 1. The Prudent Corporation has recently introduced an improved product which has enjoyed excellent market acceptance. As a result, management has budgeted sales for the six months ending June 30, 19X1 as follows:

	Estimated sales
January	$100,000
February	125,000
March	150,000
April	175,000
May	200,000
June	250,000

The cash balance at January 1, 19X1 is $15,000, and the treasurer foresees a need for additional funds necessary to finance the sales expansion. He has obtained a commitment from an insurance company for the sale to them of long-term bonds as follows:

April .... $50,000 (less $2,500 debt costs)
May   60,000

He also expects to sell real estate at cost: $8,000 in May and $50,000 in June. In addition, equipment with an original cost of $25,000 and a book value of zero was to be sold for $25,000 cash in June.

The treasurer considers that in the light of the expanded sales volume the following minimum cash balances will be desirable:

January $20,000
February   25,000
March   27,000
April, May, and June   30,000

He knows that during the next six months he will not be able to meet his cash requirements without resort to short-term financing. Consequently he approaches his bank and finds it ready to consider his company's needs. The loan officer suggests that in order to determine the cash needs and the sources of funds for loan repayment, the treasurer prepare a cash forecast for the six months ending June 30, 19X1 and pro forma financial statements for that period.

The treasurer, recognizing the importance of such a forecast, proceeded to assemble the data necessary to prepare it.

The pattern of receivables collections based on experience was as follows:

Collections	Percent of total receivable
In month of sale	40
In the second month	30
In the third month	20
In the fourth month	5
Write-off of bad debts	5
	100

On the basis of this pattern and the expected sales the treasurer constructed Schedule A shown in Exhibit 17–2.

An analysis of past cost patterns resulted in the estimates of cost and expense relationships for the purpose of the cash forecast (Schedule B) shown in Exhibit 17–3.

It was estimated that all costs in Schedule B (exclusive of the $1,000 monthly depreciation charge) will be paid for in cash in the month incurred, except for material purchases which are to be paid 50 percent in the month of purchase and 50 percent in the following month. Since the product is manufactured to specific order, no finished goods inventories are expected to accumulate.

Schedule C (Exhibit 17–4) shows the pattern of payments of accounts payable (for materials).

EXHIBIT 17-2

SCHEDULE A
Estimates of Cash Collections
For the Months January–June, 19X1

	January	February	March	April	May	June
Sales...............	$100,000	$125,000	$150,000	$175,000	$200,000	$250,000
Collections:						
1st month—40%.....	$ 40,000	$ 50,000	$ 60,000	$ 70,000	$ 80,000	$100,000
2nd month—30%....		30,000	37,500	45,000	52,500	60,000
3rd month—20%			20,000	25,000	30,000	35,000
4th month—5%				5,000	6,250	7,500
Total cash collections........	$ 40,000	$ 80,000	$117,500	$145,000	$168,750	$202,500
Write-offs—5%				$5,000	$6,250	$7,500

EXHIBIT 17-3

SCHEDULE B
Cost and Expense Estimates for Six Months
Ending June 30, 19X1

Materials	30% of sales
Labor	25% of sales
Manufacturing overhead:	
Variable	10% of sales
Fixed	$48,000 for six months (including $1,000 of depreciation per month)
Selling expenses	10% of sales
General and administrative expenses:	
Variable	8% of sales
Fixed	$7,000 per month

EXHIBIT 17-4

SCHEDULE C
Pro Forma Schedule of Cash Payments for Materials Purchases
For the Months January–June 19X1

	January	February	March	April	May	June
Materials purchased during month	$40,000	$38,000	$43,000	$56,000	$58,000	$79,000
Payments:						
1st month—50%	$20,000	$19,000	$21,500	$28,000	$29,000	$39,500
2nd month—50%		20,000	19,000	21,500	28,000	29,000
Total payments	$20,000	$39,000	$40,500	$49,500	$57,000	$68,500

EXHIBIT 17–5

THE PRUDENT CORPORATION
Cash Forecast
For the Months January–June 19X1

	January	February	March
Cash balance—beginning	$15,000	$20,000	$ 25,750
Add: Cash receipts:			
Collections of accounts receivable (Schedule A)	40,000	80,000	117,500
Proceeds from sale of real estate			
Proceeds from additional long-term debt			
Proceeds from sale of equipment			
Total cash available	$ 55,000	$100,000	$143,250
Less: Disbursements:			
Payments for:			
Materials purchases (Schedule C)	$20,000	$39,000	$ 40,500
Labor	25,000	31,250	37,500
Fixed factory overhead	7,000	7,000	7,000
Variable factory overhead.........	10,000	12,500	15,000
Selling expenses	10,000	12,500	15,000
General and administrative	15,000	17,000	19,000
Taxes			
Purchase of fixed assets		1,000	1,000
Total disbursements	87,000	120,250	135,000
Tentative cash balance (negative)	$(32,000)	$ (20,250)	$ 8,250
Minimum cash balance required	20,000	25,000	27,000
Additional borrowing required	$ 52,000	$ 46,000	$ 19,000
Repayment of bank loan			
Interest paid on balance outstanding at rate of ½ per month*			
Ending cash balance	$ 20,000	$ 25,750	$ 27,250
Loan balance	$ 52,000	$ 98,000	$117,000

* Interest is computed at the rate of ½% per month and paid on date of repayment which occurs at month end. Loan is taken out at beginning of month.

Equipment costing $20,000 will be bought in February for notes payable which will be paid off, starting that month, at the rate of $1,000 per month. The new equipment will not be fully installed until sometime in August 19X1.

Exhibit 17–5 presents the cash forecast for the six months ending June 30, 19X1 based on the data given above. Exhibit 17–6 presents the pro forma income statement for the six months ending June 30, 19X1. Exhibit 17–7 presents the actual balance sheet of The Prudent Corporation as at January 1, 19X1 and the pro forma balance sheet as at June 30, 19X1.

The financial analyst should examine the pro forma statements critically and submit to feasibility tests the estimates on which the fore-

April		May		June		Six-month totals	
$ 27,250		$ 30,580		$ 30,895		$ 15,000	
145,000		168,750		202,500		753,750	
		8,000		50,000		58,000	
47,500		60,000				107,500	
				25,000		25,000	
	$219,750		$267,330		$308,395		$959,250
$ 49,500		$ 57,000		$ 68,500		$274,500	
43,750		50,000		62,500		250,000	
7,000		7,000		7,000		42,000	
17,500		20,000		25,000		100,000	
17,500		20,000		25,000		100,000	
21,000		23,000		27,000		122,000	
				19,000		19,000	
1,000		1,000		1,000		5,000	
	157,250		178,000		235,000		912,500
	$ 62,500		$ 89,330		$ 73,395		$ 46,750
	30,000		30,000		30,000		
	—		—		—		$117,000
	$ 30,000		$ 58,000		$ 29,000		(117,000)
	1,920		435		145		2,500
	$ 30,580		$ 30,895		$ 44,250		$ 44,250
	$ 87,000		$ 29,000		—		—

casts are based. The ratios and relationships revealed by the pro forma financial statements should be analyzed and compared to similar ratios of the past in order to determine whether they are reasonable and feasible of attainment. For example, the current ratio of The Prudent Corporation increased from 2.6 on 1/1/X1 to 3.2 in the pro forma balance sheet as of 6/30/X1. During the six months ended 6/30/X1 a pro forma return on average equity of almost 16 percent was projected. Many other significant measures of turnover, common-size statements, and trends can be computed. The reasonableness of these comparisons and results must be assessed. They can help reveal serious errors and inconsistencies in the assumptions which underly the projections and thus help strengthen confidence in their reliability.

EXHIBIT 17–6

THE PRUDENT CORPORATION
Pro Forma Income Statement
For the Six Months Ending June 30, 19X1

Source of estimate

Sales	$1,000,000	Based on sales budget (page 481)
Cost of sales:		
Materials	$ 300,000	Schedule B
Labor	250,000	Schedule B
Overhead	148,000	Schedule B
	$ 698,000	
Gross profit	$ 302,000	
Selling expense	$ 100,000	Schedule B
Bad debts expense	18,750	Schedule A
General and administrative expense	122,000	Schedule B
Total	$ 240,750	
Operating income	$ 61,250	
Gain on sale of equipment	25,000	
Interest expense	(2,500)	Exhibit 17–5, footnote
Income before taxes	83,750	
Income taxes	38,050	30% of first $25,000; 52% of balance. Pay ½ in June and accrue balance
Net income	$ 45,700	

Differences between short-term and long-term forecasts

The short-term cash forecast is, as we have seen, a very useful and reliable aid in projecting the state of short-term liquidity. Such a detailed approach is, however, only feasible for the short term, that is, up to about 12 months. Beyond this time horizon the uncertainties become so great as to preclude detailed and accurate cash forecasts. Instead of focusing on collections of receivables and on payments for labor and materials, the longer term estimates focus on projections of net income and on other sources and uses of funds. Over the longer term the emphasis on cash becomes less important, and the estimation process centers on funds, that is, working capital. Over the short term the difference between cash and other working capital assets is significant. Over the longer term, however, the distinction between cash, receivables, and inventories becomes less significant because the conversion period of these assets to cash is not significant relative to the period encompassed by the longer term. In other words, if the trade cycle is 90 days long, such a period is not as significant in a 3-year forecast as it is in relation to a 6 or 12 months span. The further we peer

EXHIBIT 17–7

THE PRUDENT CORPORATION
Balance Sheets

	Actual January 1, 19X1		Pro forma June 30, 19X1	
Assets				
Current Assets:				
Cash	$ 15,000		$ 44,250	
Accounts receivable (net)	6,500		234,000	
Inventories–raw materials	57,000		71,000	
Total Current Assets		$ 78,500		$349,250
Real estate	$ 58,000		—	
Fixed assets	206,400		$201,400	
Accumulated depreciation	(36,400)		(17,400)	
Net Fixed Assets		228,000		184,000
Other assets		3,000		3,000
Deferred debt expenses				2,500
Total Assets		$309,500		$538,750
Liabilities and Equity				
Current Liabilities:				
Accounts payable	$ 2,000		$41,500	
Notes payable	28,500		43,500	
Accrued taxes	—		19,050	
Total Current Liabilities		$ 30,500		$104,050
Long-term debt	$ 15,000		$125,000	
Common stock	168,000		168,000	
Retained earnings	96,000		141,700	
		279,000		434,700
Total Liabilities and Equity		$309,500		$538,750

into the future, the broader are the financial statement categories which we must estimate and the less detailed can the data behind the estimates be.

The projection of future statements of changes in financial position is best begun with an analysis of prior year funds statements. To this data can then be added all available information and estimates about the future needs for funds and the most likely sources of funds needed to cover such requirements.

ANALYSIS OF STATEMENTS OF CHANGES IN FINANCIAL POSITION

In Chapter 13 we examined the principles underlying the preparation of the statement of changes in financial position (funds statement) as well as the uses to which the statement may be put by the analyst.

We shall now focus on the analysis of the statement of changes in financial position paying particular attention to the value of such an analysis to a projection of future funds flows.

In any analysis of financial statements the most recent years are the most important because they represent the most recent experience. Since there is an inherent continuity in business events, it is this latest experience that is likely to have the greatest relevance to the projection of future results. So it is with the statement of changes in financial position.

It is important that the analyst obtain statements of changes in financial position for as many years as possible. This is particularly important in the case of an analysis of this statement since the planning and execution of plant expansions, of modernization schemes, of working capital increases as well as the financing of such activities by means of short-term and long-term debt and by means of equity funds is an activity which is likely to encompass many years. Thus, in order for the analyst to be able to assess management's plans and their execution, statements of changes in financial position covering a number of years must be analyzed. In this way a more comprehensive picture of management's financial habits can be obtained and an assessment of them made.

First illustration of statement of changes in financial position analysis

Exhibits 17–8 and 17–9 present the statement of changes in financial position of the Migdal Corporation and the same data expressed in common-size percentages. The common-size statement of changes in financial position is a useful tool of analysis in that it enables the analyst to compare readily the changes which occurred over time in the relative contributions of various categories of sources and uses of funds.

The statements in Exhibit 17–8 and 17–9 reveal that net income has been steadily growing since 19X1 and contributed increasingly, on an absolute basis, to funds from operations. As a percentage of total funds generated, funds from operations fluctuated from a low of 33.5 percent in 19X1 to a high of 97.4 percent in 19X4. This is due to substantial inflows from borrowings in 19X1 and an absence of external financing in 19X4. To finance its significant additions to equipment and to working capital, the company resorted mostly to substantial equity financing in 19X3 and in 19X6. More modest additions to debt occurred in 19X1 to 19X3. The relationship of depreciation to income has exhibited sufficient stability over the years to facilitate the projection of this element.

EXHIBIT 17–8

MIGDAL CORPORATION
Statement of Changes in Financial Position
For the Years Ended 19X1–19X6

	19X6	19X5	19X4	19X3	19X2	19X1
Funds were provided from:						
Current operations:						
Net income	$1,641,889	$1,385,021	$1,140,113	$ 822,362	$ 532,872	$ 422,065
Depreciation	596,207	436,102	335,019	275,331	193,827	114,096
Amortization of preoperating expenses	152,525	135,156	184,726	73,394	52,885	36,036
Deferred taxes	38,000	(80,000)	43,500	(7,053)	(22,447)	18,881
Funds from operations	$2,428,621	$1,876,279	$1,703,358	$1,164,034	$ 757,137	$ 591,078
Net proceeds from sale of stock	2,526,871			1,340,375		424,982
Exercise of stock options	94,458	7,445	44,663	2,922		
Transfer of deferred taxes to current assets		86,000				
Long-term borrowing				500,000	300,000	750,000
Total	$5,049,950	$1,969,724	$1,748,021	$3,007,331	$1,057,137	$1,766,060
Funds were used for:						
Additions to equipment	$2,256,821	$1,326,761	$ 678,101	$ 535,708	$1,000,593	$ 610,406
Additions to other assets	331,397	188,205	170,063	147,291	127,250	89,017
Reduction in long-term debt	175,000	175,000	100,000	25,000	69,174	32,863
Other		18,975	3,721			30,349
Total	$2,763,218	$1,708,941	$ 951,885	$ 707,999	$1,197,017	$ 762,635
Increase (decrease) in working capital	$2,286,732	$ 260,783	$ 796,136	$2,299,332	$ (139,880)	$1,003,425
Increases (decreases) to working capital:						
Cash and U.S. Treasuries	$ 103,288	$ (60,252)	$ 340,304	$2,124,704	$ (97,370)	$ 263,161
Receivables	279,010	(72,138)	122,950	(79,788)	77,086	30,741
Inventories	2,244,180	1,848,771	737,350	1,184,078	1,416,723	645,078
Prepaid expenses	253,689	149,772	28,075	(4,739)	98,623	62,461
Current portion of long-term debt	(75,000)	(75,000)	(75,000)	500,000	(453,642)	164,515
Accounts payable	(458,504)	(1,394,811)	(87,807)	(809,927)	(897,663)	(681)
Income taxes payable	302,593	217,493	(143,122)	(389,473)	(128,063)	(41,195)
Other payables	(437,524)	(353,052)	(126,614)	(225,523)	(155,574)	(120,655)
Total	$2,286,732	$ 260,783	$ 796,136	$2,299,332	$ (139,880)	$1,003,425

EXHIBIT 17–9

MIGDAL CORPORATION
Statement of Changes in Financial Position
Common Size
For the Years Ended 19X1–19X6

	19X6	19X5	19X4	19X3	19X2	19X1
Funds were provided from:						
Current operations:						
Net income	32.5%	70.3%	65.2%	27.3%	50.4%	23.9%
Depreciation	11.8	22.1	19.1	9.2	18.3	6.5
Amortization of preoperating expenses	3.0	6.9	10.6	2.4	5.0	2.0
Deferred taxes	0.8	(4.1)	2.5	(0.2)	(2.1)	1.1
Funds from operations	48.1%	95.2%	97.4%	38.7%	71.6%	33.5%
Net proceeds from sale of stock	50.0			44.6		24.0
Exercise of stock options	1.9	0.4	2.6	0.1		
Transfer of deferred taxes to current assets		4.4				
Long-term borrowing				16.6	28.4	42.5
Total	100.0%	100.0%	100.0%	100.0%	100.0%	100.0%
Funds were used for:						
Additions to equipment	44.7%	67.4%	38.8%	17.8%	94.7%	34.6%
Additions to other assets	6.6	9.5	9.7	4.9	12.0	5.0
Reduction in long-term debt	3.5	8.9	5.7	0.8	6.5	1.9
Other		1.0	0.2			1.7
Total	54.8%	86.8%	54.4%	23.5%	113.2%	43.2%
Increase (decrease) in working capital	45.2%	13.2%	45.6%	76.5%	(13.2)%	56.8%
Increases (decreases) in working capital:						
Cash and U.S. Treasuries	4.5%	(23.1)%	42.7%	92.4%	(69.6)%	26.2%
Receivables	12.2	(27.7)	15.4	(3.5)	55.1	3.1
Inventories	98.1	708.9	92.6	51.5	1012.8	64.3
Prepaid expenses	11.1	57.4	3.5	(0.2)	70.5	6.2
Current portion of long-term debt		(28.7)	(9.4)	21.7	(324.3)	16.4
Accounts payable	(20.1)	(534.8)	(11.0)	(35.2)	(641.7)	(0.1)
Income taxes payable	13.2	83.4	(18.0)	(16.9)	(91.6)	(4.1)
Other payables	(19.1)	(135.4)	(15.8)	(9.8)	(111.2)	(12.0)
Total	100.0%	100.0%	100.0%	100.0%	100.0%	100.0%

Deferred taxes have, on the other hand, exhibited a more erratic pattern. The constantly increasing additions to equipment have not resulted in commensurate increases in the provision for deferred taxes indicating that the company has, in general, probably not elected faster depreciation methods for tax purposes relative to the amounts booked. However, the swing in the provision from 19X5 to 19X6 may indicate some new book–tax differentials.

During the entire period under review, fixed asset additions have significantly exceeded the provision for depreciation. Thus, even allowing for the effects of inflation on replacement costs it is clear that Migdal is going through a period of significant capital investment. The constantly increasing net income is testimony to the productivity of these investments. In all years, except 19X2, funds provided by operations have exceeded additions to equipment. Net borrowing during the period was only about $1 million. New capital from the sale of stock was more significant approaching $4 million. In all years but one working capital increased, probably as a result of increasing sales, and the total increase was substantial. Particularly heavy were investments in inventory, again to support higher sales. The rate of increase in accounts payable, while substantial, did not equal the growth in the investment in receivables further explaining the substantial working capital expansion.

A forecast of future statements of changes in financial position would have to take into consideration all above discussed trends which the enterprise has exhibited, such as those relating to income, the elements that convert it to sources of funds from operations, fixed assets additions, the relationship of sales to growth in working capital and possibly to sources of funds provided by operations as well. The size of nonfund adjustments, such as depreciation, depends on future depreciation policies and equipment acquisitions. The latter as well as write-off methods to be used for tax purposes will in turn determine the size of the deferred tax adjustments. The more we know about factors such as these the more reliable the forecast will be.

Second illustration of statement of changes in financial position analysis

The Exeter Chemical Company presents the five-year statement of changes in financial position shown in Exhibit 17–10. This statement has a column for totals encompassing the period covered by the statement. This is a useful feature since it affords a view of the cumulative totals of sources and uses of funds over the longer term. Since cash and cash equivalents are the most liquid portions of the current assets group, the changes in working capital are separated to indicate

EXHIBIT 17-10

EXETER CHEMICAL COMPANY
Statement of Changes in Financial Position
(in thousands)

	Total	19X4	19X3	19X2	19X1	19X0
Source of funds:						
Net income:	$ 412,712	$114,891	$ 82,990	$ 78,368	$ 68,656	$ 67,807
Provision for:						
Depreciation, depletion, etc.	498,427	120,268	114,606	97,639	86,876	79,038
Deferred income taxes	35,804	11,980	12,373	11,451		
Insurance reserve	2,000	2,000				
Outside financing:						
5¾% promissory notes	99,593			99,593		
Other	4,945	3,276	1,669			
Common shares issued under options	40,245	12,108	14,532	2,639	9,926	1,040
Other—net	(13,622)	(429)	(5,368)	2,366	(7,918)	(2,273)
	$1,080,104	$264,094	$220,802	$292,056	$157,540	$145,612
Disposition of funds:						
Dividends on common shares	$ 155,029	$ 37,606	$ 34,978	$ 29,470	$ 27,316	$ 25,659
Plant additions and replacements	776,511	218,105	114,502	168,833	153,818	121,253
Investment in affiliated companies	60,913	13,340	18,443	9,597	9,810	9,723
Retirement of debt	73,590	10,418	13,452	17,877	21,928	9,915
Increase in working capital*	95,001	29,845	18,042	14,614	5,021	27,479
Increase–(decrease) in cash and securities	(80,940)	(45,220)	21,385	51,665	(60,353)	(48,417)
	$1,080,104	$264,094	$220,802	$292,056	$157,540	$145,612

* Exclusive of cash and securities.

changes in working capital exclusive of these liquid items and changes in the cash items.

An analysis of the statement in Exhibit 17–10 reveals that the sources of funds from operations over the five-year period were as follows:

		Millions
Net income		$413
Nonfund requiring charges:		
Depreciation, depletion, etc.	$498	
Deferred income taxes	36	
Insurance reserves	2	536
Total		$949

From funds provided by operations of $949 million we must deduct essential capital equipment replacement requirements before we can arrive at the balance of discretionary funds available to management for dividend payments (here $155 million), plant expansion and so forth. Here we know only that both replacement and possibly expansion of plant added up to $776 million, an amount which is exceeded by sources of funds from operations less dividends. Thus, investments in affiliated companies, the retirement of debt, and the increase in net working capital over the period were financed by means of promissory notes and the issuance of common stock under options. It is also interesting to note that while working capital increased by $95 million over the five years ending 19X4, cash and marketable securities decreased by almost $81 million. Undoubtedly the substantial increase in activity, as evidenced by a near doubling of net income over the five-year period, necessitated an expansion of funds invested in receivables and inventories.

EVALUATION OF THE STATEMENT OF CHANGES IN FINANCIAL POSITION

The foregoing examples of analyses of the statement of changes in financial position illustrate the variety of information and insights which can be derived from them. Of course, the analysis of statements of changes in financial position is to be performed within the framework of an analysis of all the financial statements, and thus the conclusion reached from an analysis of one statement may be strengthened and corroborated by an analysis of the other financial statements.

There are some useful generalizations that can be made regarding the value of the analysis of the statement of changes in financial position to the financial analyst.

This statement enables the analyst to appraise the quality of management decisions over time, as well as their impact on the results of operations and financial condition of the enterprise. When the analysis encompasses a longer period of time, the analyst can evaluate management's response to the changing economic conditions as well as to the opportunities and the adversities which invariably present themselves.

Evaluation of the statement of changes in financial position analysis will indicate the purposes to which management chose to commit funds, where it reduced investment, the source from which it derived additional funds, and to what extent it reduced claims against the enterprise. Such an analysis will also show the disposition of earnings over the years, as well as how management has reinvested the internal fund inflow over which it had discretion. The analysis will also reveal the size and composition of sources of funds from operations, as well as their pattern and degree of stability.

As depicted in Exhibit 17–1 earlier in this chapter, the circulation of funds in an enterprise involves a constant flow of funds and their periodic reinvestment. Thus, funds are invested in labor, material, and overhead costs as well as in long-term assets, such as inventories and plant and equipment, which join the product-cost stream at a slower rate. Eventually, by the process of sales, these costs are converted back into accounts receivable and into cash. If operations are profitable the funds recovered will exceed the amounts invested, thus augmenting the funds inflow or cash flow. Losses have, of course, the opposite effect.

What constitutes funds inflow, or cash flow, as it is often more crudely referred to, is the subject of considerable confusion. Generally the funds provided by operations, that is, net income adjusted for nonfund requiring or supplying items, is an index of management's ability to redirect funds away from areas of unfavorable profit opportunity into areas of greater profit potential. However, not all the funds provided by operations may be so available because of existing commitments for debt retirement, stock redemption, equipment replacement, and dividend payments. Nor are funds provided by operations the only potential cash inflows, since management can avail itself of external sources of capital in order to bolster its funds inflow. The components of the "sources of funds from operations" figure hold important clues to the stability of that source of funds. Thus, for example, depreciation is a more stable element in the total than net income itself in that it represents a recovery by the enterprise of the investment in fixed assets out of selling prices even before a profit is earned.

In evaluating the statement of changes in financial position, the analyst will judge a company's quality of earnings by the impact which changes in economic and industry conditions have on its flow of funds. The statement will also reveal nonfunds generating income which may have a bearing on the evaluation of earnings quality.

If in his estimates of future earnings potential the analyst foresees a need for additional capital, his analysis of the funds statement will be directed towards a projection of the source from which these funds will be obtained, and what dilution of earnings per share, if any, this will involve.

The analysis and evaluation of the statement of changes in financial position is, as the foregoing discussion suggests, an important early step in the projection of future statements of changes in financial position.

PROJECTION OF STATEMENTS OF CHANGES IN FINANCIAL POSITION

No thorough model of an enterprise's future results is complete without a concurrent forecast of the size of funds needed for the realization of the projections in the model as well as an assessment of the possible sources from which such funds can be derived.

If a future expansion of sales and profits is forecast, the analyst must know whether the enterprise has the "financial horsepower" to see such an expansion through by means of internally generated funds and, if not, where the required future funds are going to come from.

The projection of the statement of changes in financial position will start with a careful estimate of the expected changes in each individual category of assets and the funds which will be derived from or required by such changes. Some of the more important factors to be taken into consideration follow:

1. The net income expected to be generated by future results will be adjusted for nonfund items, such as depreciation, depletion, deferred income taxes, and nonremitted earnings of subsidiaries and investees, in order to arrive at estimates of funds provided by operations.
2. Sources of funds from disposals of assets, sale of investments, and the sale of stocks and bonds will be estimated.
3. The needs for working capital will be arrived at by estimating the required level of the individual working capital items such as cash, receivables, and inventories and reducing this by the expected levels of payables. There is usually a relationship between incremental sales and the corresponding increment in required working capital amounts.
4. Expected capital expenditures will be based on the present level of operations as compared with productive capacity, as well as on

an estimate of the future level of activity implied by the profit projections.

5. Mandatory debt retirement and desirable minimum levels of dividend payments will also be estimated.

The impact of adversity

The projected statement of changes in financial position is useful not only in estimating the funds implications of future expansion and opportunity but also in assessing the impact on the enterprise of sudden adversity.

A sudden adversity, from the point of view of its impact on the flow of funds, will usually manifest itself in a serious interruption in the inflow of funds. This can be brought about by such events as recessions, strikes, or the loss of a major customer or market. In this context a projection of the statement of changes in financial position would be a first step in the assessment of the defensive posture of an enterprise. The basic question to which such an analysis is directed is this: what can the enterprise do; and what resources, both internal and external, can it marshal to cope with a sudden and serious reduction in the inflow of funds?

The strategies and alternatives available to an enterprise faced with such adversities are ably examined and discussed in a work by Professor Donaldson. Dr. Donaldson defines financial mobility as the capacity to redirect the use of financial resources in response to new information about the company and its environment.[1]

The projected "sources and uses of funds" statement is an important tool in the assessment of the resources available to meet such "new information" as well as in planning the changes in financial strategy which this may require.

To the prospective credit grantor such an approach represents an excellent tool in the assessment of risk. In estimating the effects of, for example, a recession, on the future flow of funds he can trace through not only the potential shrinkage in cash inflows from operations but also the effects of such shrinkage on the uses of funds and on the sources from which they can be derived.

The funds flow adequacy ratio

The purpose of this ratio is to determine the degree to which an enterprise generated sufficient funds from operations to cover capital

---

[1] Gordon Donaldson, *Strategy for Financial Mobility* (Boston: Graduate School of Business Administration, Harvard University, 1969).

expenditures, net investment in inventories, and cash dividends. To remove cyclical and other erratic influences a five-year total is used in the computation of the ratio, thus:

$$\frac{\text{Five year sum of sources of funds from operations}}{\begin{array}{c}\text{Five year sum of capital expenditures, inventory}\\\text{additions, and cash dividends}\end{array}}$$

The investment in the other important working capital item, receivables, is omitted on the theory that it can be financed primarily by short term credit, i.e., growth in payables, and so forth.

A ratio of 1 indicates that an enterprise has covered its needs based on attained levels of growth without the need for external financing. To the degree that the ratio falls below 1 internally generated funds may be inadequate to maintain dividends and current operating growth levels. This ratio may also reflect the effect of inflation on the fund requirements of an enterprise. The reading of this, like any other ratio, can provide no definitive answers and is only a pointer to further analysis and investigation. The ratio for Migdal Corporation (see Exhibit 17–8 above) for the five years ending 19X6 is

$$\frac{7,929}{13,230} = 0.60.$$

Funds reinvestment ratio

This ratio is useful in measuring the percentage of the investment in assets, which is being retained and reinvested in the enterprise for the replacement of assets and for growth in operations. The formula is:

$$\frac{\text{Funds provided by operations} - \text{Dividends}}{\text{Gross plant} + \text{Investment} + \text{Other assets} + \text{Working capital}}$$

A reinvestment rate of 8 to 10 percent is considered generally to be at a satisfactory level. The ratio for Beta Company (Appendix 4B pp. 89–103) for 19X6 is

$$\frac{509.4 - 91.4}{4,750.5} \text{ or } 8.8\%.$$

CONCLUSION

In the assessment of future liquidity, the use of cash forecasts for the short term and of projected statements of changes in financial position for the longer term represent some of the most useful tools available to the financial analyst. In contrast to ratio measures of liquidity, these tools involve a detailed examination of sources and uses of cash or funds. Such examination and estimation processes can be subjected to feasibility tests by means of pro forma statements and to the discipline inherent in the double-entry accounting system.

QUESTIONS

1. What is the primary difference between funds flow analysis and ratio analysis? Which is superior and why?

2. "From an operational point of view, management focuses on cash rather than working capital." Do you agree with the statement? Why or why not?

3. What is the relationship between inflows and outflows of cash?

4. Why is the short-term cash forecast important to the financial analyst?

5. What is the first step to be taken in preparing a cash forecast, and what considerations are required in such a step?

6. What are pro forma financial statements? How are they utilized in conjunction with funds flow projections?

7. What are the limitations of short-term cash forecasts?

8. If the usefulness of a short-term cash forecast is limited, what analytical approach is available to the financial analyst who wants to analyze future flows of working capital?

9. What useful information do you, as a financial analyst, expect to get from the analysis of past statements of changes in financial position (funds statement)?

10. What would a forecast of future statements of changes in financial position have to take into consideration?

11. What are the differences between short-term and long-term financial forecasts?

12. What analytical function does the common-size statement of changes in financial position serve?

13. Why is a projected statement of changes in financial position necessary when you have historical data which are based on actual performance?

14. If actual operations are seriously affected by unforeseen adversities, would a projected statement of changes in financial position still be useful?

15. "Cash flow per share" is sometimes used in common stock analysis in the same fashion as *earnings per share*. In financial analysis, shouldn't the former be used more often than the latter? Explain. (C.F.A.)

18

ANALYSIS OF CAPITAL STRUCTURE AND LONG-TERM SOLVENCY

The financial strength and stability of a business entity, the probability surrounding its ability to weather random shocks, and to maintain its solvency in the face of adversity are important measures of risk associated with it. This evaluation of risk is critical because, as discussed in Chapter 3, the equity investor as well as the lender require returns which are commensurate with the levels of risk which they assume. This and the preceding two chapters deal with the evaluation of the financial strength and viability of enterprises within different time frames.

KEY ELEMENTS IN THE EVALUATION OF LONG-TERM SOLVENCY

The process of evaluation of long-term solvency of an enterprise differs markedly from that of the assessment of short-term liquidity. In the latter the time horizon is short and it is often possible to make a reasonable projection of funds flows. It is not possible to do this for the longer term, and thus the measures used in the evaluation of longer term solvency are less specific but more all-encompassing.

There are a number of key elements involved in the evaluation of the long-term solvency of an enterprise. The analysis of capital structure is concerned with the types of capital funds used to finance the enterprise, ranging from "patient" and permanent equity capital to short-term funds which are a temporary, and consequently, a much more risky source. There are different degrees of risk associated with the holding of different types of assets. Moreover, assets represent secondary[1] sources of security for lenders ranging from loans secured by specific assets to assets available as general security to unsecured creditors.

On a long-term basis earnings and earning power (which implies the recurring ability to generate cash in the future) are some of the most important and reliable indications of financial strength available. Earnings are the most desirable and reliable sources of funds for the longer term payment of interest and repayment of principal. As a surrogate for funds generated by operations, earnings are the yardstick against which the coverage of interest and other fixed charges is measured. Moreover, a reliable and stable trend of earnings is one of the best assurances of an enterprise's ability to borrow in times of funds shortage and its consequent ability to extricate itself from the very conditions which lead to insolvency.

In addition to general measures of financial strength and long-term solvency lenders rely on the protection afforded by loan covenants or the pledges of specific assets as security. Some loan covenants define default and the legal remedies available when it occurs. Others are designed to insure against deterioration in such key measures of financial health as the current ratio and the debt equity ratio, against the issuance of further debt, or against the disbursement of resources through the payments of dividends above specified levels or through acquisitions. Of course, there can be no prohibition against operating losses, a core problem attending most cases of deterioration in financial condition. Thus, the existence of protective provisions cannot substitute for alertness and a continuous monitoring of the financial condition of an enterprise in which long-term funds are at risk.[2]

The vast amount of public and private debt outstanding has led to standardized approaches to its analysis and evaluation. By far the most important is the rating of debt securities by rating agencies which is discussed in Appendix 18–A to this chapter. Appendix 18–B examines the use of ratios as predictors of failure.

In this chapter we shall examine in further detail the tools and the measures available for the analysis of long-term solvency.

---

[1] When lending to going concerns lenders should regard the liquidation of assets for the purpose of recovery of principal and interest as a measure of last resort and as an undesirable source of funds to rely on at the time credit is granted.

[2] Lenders have learned that senior positions in the debt hierarchy do not afford in practice the security they seem to afford in theory. Thus, subordinated debt is not akin to capital stock because subordinated creditors have a voice in determining whether a debtor should be rescued or be thrown into bankruptcy. This interdependence between junior and senior lenders has led some to the belief that one might as well buy the highest yielding obligation of an enterprise since any situation serious enough to affect the value of the junior security is likely to affect the senior security as well.

IMPORTANCE OF CAPITAL STRUCTURE

The capital structure of an enterprise consists basically of equity funds and debt. It is measured in terms of the relative magnitude of the various sources of funds of the enterprise. The inherent financial stability of an enterprise and the risk of insolvency to which it is exposed are importantly dependent on the sources of its funds as well as on the type of assets it holds and the relative magnitude of such asset categories. Exhibit 18–1 presents an example of the distribution of assets of an enterprise and the sources of funds used to finance their acquisition. It is evident from the diagram in Exhibit 18–1 that within the framework of equality prevailing between assets and liabilities plus capital, a large variety of combinations of assets and sources of funds used to finance them is possible.

ACCOUNTING PRINCIPLES

The amounts at which liabilities and equity accounts are shown on the financial statements are governed by the application of generally

EXHIBIT 18–1
Asset distribution and capital structure of an enterprise

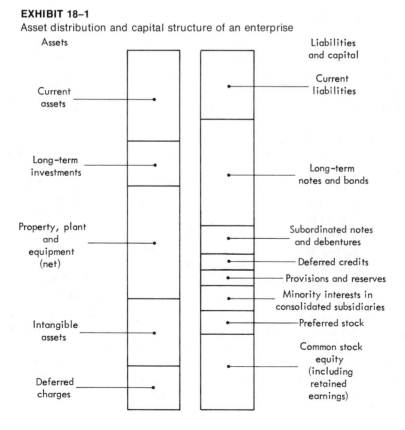

accepted accounting principles. The principles governing the measurement of liabilities are discussed in Chapter 7, and those governing the accounting for equities are covered in Chapter 8. The analyst must keep these principles in mind when analyzing the capital structure and its effect on long-term solvency. While it can be stated, as a broad generalization, that the accounting principles governing the measurement of liabilities and equities do not affect the analysis of financial statements as importantly as do those governing the measurement of assets, a study of the above-mentioned chapters will reveal aspects of real importance to the analyst.

There are liabilities which are not fully reflected in the balance sheet and there are accounts whose accounting classification as debt or equity should not be automatically accepted by the analyst. The proper decision of how to classify or deal with these depends on a thorough understanding of their nature and/or the particular conditions of issue to which they are subject. The discussion which follows supplements the important analytical considerations covered in Chapters 7 and 8:

Deferred credits

Most deferred credits, such as premiums on bonds, represent allocation accounts designed primarily to aid in the measurements of income. They do not present an important problem of analysis because they are relatively insignificant in size. Deferred income items, such as subscription income received in advance, represent an obligation for future service and are, as such, clearly liabilities.

One type of deferred credit which is much more sizable, and consequently much more important, is *deferred income taxes*. As already pointed out in Chapter 11, this account is not a liability in the usual sense because the government does not have a definite short-term or even longer term claim against the enterprise. Nevertheless, this account does represent the aggregate exhaustion in tax deductibility of assets and other items, over and above that recorded for book purposes, and this means that at some time in the future the deferred tax account will be used to reduce the higher income tax expense which corresponds to *increased* tax liabilities. Even if the likelihood of the deferred tax account "reversing" in the foreseeable future is quite good, there still remains the question of whether the time-adjusted present value of such future "reversals" should not be used instead of the nominal face value amount of the deferred credit.

To the analyst the important question here is whether to treat the deferred tax account as a liability, as an equity item, or as part debt and part equity. The decision depends on the nature of the deferral, the past experience with the account (e.g., has it been constantly grow-ing?), and the likelihood of future "reversal." To the extent that such future "reversal" is only a remote possibility, the deferred credit can be viewed as a source of funds of such long-term nature as to be classifiable as equity. On the other hand, if the possibility of a "draw-ing down" of the deferred tax account in the foreseeable future is quite strong, then the account is more in the nature of a long-term liability.[3] In classifying the deferred tax account as between debt and equity, the analyst must be guided by considerations such as the ones discussed above.

Long-term leases

SFAS 13 has, beginning in 1977, restricted further the capital (fi-nancing) leases which companies can avoid showing as recorded liabilities. However, until 1980 older financing leases which are exempt from the SEC's immediate disclosure requirements may still not be reflected on balance sheets and the analyst will have to make adjustments on the basis of supplementary data which must be provided in footnotes.

Liabilities for pensions

The excess of vested benefits of employees over pension fund assets represents one kind of unrecorded liability under presently accepted accounting practices. Contingent liabilities which may exist on the liquidation of an enterprise or the termination of a pension plan are other factors which must be taken into consideration by analysts asses-sing the total obligations to which an enterprise may be subject. Un-recorded pension obligations are particularly substantial in some in-dustries, such as tire and steel.

Unconsolidated subsidiaries

Information on unconsolidated subsidiaries is important because bondholders of such subsidiaries may look only to the latter's assets as security for their bonds. Moreover, bondholders of the parent company (particularly holding companies) may derive a significant portion of their fixed charge coverage from the dividends of the unconsolidated subsidiaries. Yet, in the event of the subsidiary's bankruptcy the par-ent bondholders may be in a junior position to the bondholders of the subsidiary.

---

[3] H. C. Herring and F. A. Jacobs in "The Expected Behavior of Deferred Tax Credits," *Journal of Accountancy*, August 1976, argue that statistically the probability of the deferred tax accounting reversing is quite good.

Provisions, reserves and contingent liabilities

Provisions such as for guarantees and warranties represent obligations to offer future service and should be classified as such. Generally speaking, reserves created by charges to income may also be considered as liabilities. However, general contingency reserves or reserves for very indeterminate purposes (most of which are now prohibited by SFAS 5) should not be considered as genuine liabilities.

The analyst must make a judgment regarding the probability of commitments or contingencies becoming actual liabilities and should then treat these items accordingly.

Minority interests

Minority interests in consolidated financial statements represent an obligation of the consolidated group to minority shareholders of the subsidiaries included therein. The analyst should recognize, however, that these are not liabilities similar in nature to debt because they have neither mandatory dividend payment nor principal repayment requirements. Capital structure measurements concentrate on the mandatory payments aspects of liabilities. From this point of view, minority interests are more in the nature of outsider's claim to a portion of the equity or an offset representing their proportionate ownership of assets.

Convertible debt

Convertible debt is generally classified among liabilities. However, if the conversion terms are such that the only reasonable assumption that can be made is that the debt will be converted into common stock, then it may be classified as equity for purposes of capital structure analysis.

Preferred stock

Most preferred stock entails no absolute obligation for payment of dividends or repayment of principal, possessing thus the characteristics of true equity. However, as was discussed in Chapter 7, preferred stock with a fixed maturity or subject to sinking fund requirements should, from an analytical point of view, be considered as debt.

Effect of intangible assets

Intangible assets and deferred items of dubious value which are included on the asset side of the balance sheet have an effect on the computation of the total equity of an enterprise. To the extent that the analyst cannot evaluate or form an opinion on the present value or future utility of such assets, he may exclude them from consideration and thus reduce the amount of equity capital by the amounts at which such assets are carried. However, the arbitrary exclusion of all intangible assets from the capital base is an unjustified exercise in overconservatism.

The foregoing discussion related to the classification of balance sheet items as between debt and equity. Let us now turn to an examination of the significance of capital structure in financial analysis.

The significance of capital structure

The significance of capital structure is derived, first and foremost, from the essential difference between debt and equity.

The equity is the basic risk capital of an enterprise. Every enterprise must have some equity capital which bears the risk to which it is inevitably exposed. The outstanding characteristic of equity capital is that it has no guaranteed or mandatory return which must be paid out in any event and no definite timetable for repayment of the capital investment. Thus, capital which can be withdrawn at the contributor's option is not really equity capital and has, instead, the characteristics of debt.[4] From the point of view of an enterprise's stability and exposure to the risk of insolvency, the outstanding characteristic of equity capital is that it is permanent, can be counted on to remain invested in times of adversity, and has no mandatory requirement for dividends. It is such funds that an enterprise can most confidently invest in long-term assets and expose to the greatest risks. Their loss, for whatever reason, will not necessarily jeopardize the firm's ability to pay the fixed claims against it.

Both short-term and long-term debt, in contrast to equity capital, must be repaid. The longer the term of the debt and the less onerous its repayment provisions, the easier it will be for the enterprise to service it. Nevertheless, it must be repaid at certain specified times regardless of the enterprise's financial condition; and so must interest be paid in the case of most debt instruments. Generally, the failure to pay principal or interest will result in proceedings under which the common stockholders may lose control of the enterprise as well as part or all of their investment. Should the entire equity capital of the enterprise be wiped out by losses, the creditors may also stand to lose part or all of their principal and interest due.

---

[4] For example, during the financial crisis which befell many brokerage houses in the late 1960s it was discovered that much "equity" capital which was thought to lend strength to the enterprise and additional security to customers and creditors was in effect subject to withdrawal by owners. At the sign of real trouble these owners withdrew their capital thus compounding the financial problems even more.

It can be readily appreciated that the larger the proportion of debt in the total capital structure of an enterprise, the higher the resulting fixed charges and repayment commitments and the greater the probability of a chain of events leading to an inability to pay interest and principal when due.

To the investor in the common stock of an enterprise, the existence of debt represents a risk of loss of his investment, and this is balanced by the potential of high profits arising from financial leverage. Excessive debt may also mean that management's initiative and flexibility for profitable action will be stifled and inhibited.

The creditor prefers as large a capital base as possible as a cushion which will shield him against losses which can result from adversity. The smaller the relative capital base, or conversely, the larger the proportionate contribution of funds by creditors, the smaller is the creditors' cushion against loss and consequently the greater their risk of loss.

While there has been a considerable debate, particularly in academic circles, over whether the *cost of capital* of an enterprise varies with different capital structures, that is, with various mixes of debt and equity, the issue seems significantly clearer from the point of view of outsiders to the enterprise, such as creditors or investors, who must make decisions on the basis of conditions as they are. In the case of otherwise identical entities the creditor exposes himself to greater risk if he lends to the company with 60 percent of its funds provided by debt (and 40 percent by equity capital) than if he lends to a similar company which derives, say, only 20 percent of its funds from debt.

Under the Modigliani-Miller thesis the cost of capital of an enterprise in a perfect market is, except for the tax deductibility of interest, not affected by the debt-equity relationship.[5] This is so, they assert, because each individual stockholder can inject, by use of personally created leverage, his own blend of risk into the total investment position. Thus, under this theory, the advantage of debt will be offset by a markdown in a company's price-earnings ratio.

The degree of risk in an enterprise, as judged by the outside prospective investor is, however, a given; and our point of view, as well as our task here, is to measure the degree of risk residing in the capital structure of an enterprise.

REASONS FOR EMPLOYMENT OF DEBT

In addition to serving as an inflation hedge, a primary reason for the employment of debt by an enterprise is that up to a certain point,

---

[5] F. Modigliani and M. Miller, "The Cost of Capital, Corporation Finance and the Theory of Investment," *American Economic Review*, June 1958, pp. 261–97.

debt is, from the point of view of the ownership, a less expensive source of funds than equity capital. This is so for two main reasons:

1. The interest cost of debt is fixed, and thus, as long as it is lower than the return which can be earned on the funds supplied by creditors, this excess return accrues to the benefit of the equity.
2. Unlike dividends, which are considered a distribution of profits, interest is considered an expense and is, consequently, tax deductible.

A further discussion of these two main reasons follows.

The concept of financial leverage

Financial leverage means the use in the capital structure of an enterprise of debt which pays a fixed return. Since no creditor or lender would be willing to put up loan funds without the cushion and safety provided by the owners' equity capital, this borrowing process is also referred to as "trading on the equity," that is, utilizing the existence of a given amount of equity capital as a borrowing base.

In Exhibit 18–2, a comparison is made of the returns achieved by two companies having identical assets and earnings before interest expense. Company X derives 40 percent of its funds from debt while Company Y has no debt. In Year 1, when the average return on total assets is 7.5 percent, the return on the stockholders' equity of Company X is 10.3 percent. This higher return is due to the fact that the stockholders benefited from the excess return on total assets over the cost of debt. For Company Y the return on equity always equals the return on total assets. In Year 2 the return on total assets of Company X was equal to the interest cost of debt and, consequently, the effects of leverage were neutralized. The results of Year 3 show that leverage is a double-edged sword. Thus, when the return on total assets falls below the cost of debt, Company X's return on the equity is lower than that of debt-free Company Y.

The effect of tax deductibility of interest

The second reason given for the advantageous position of debt is the tax deductibility of interest as opposed to the distribution of dividends. This can be illustrated as follows:

Assume the facts given in Exhibit 18–2 for Year 2, and that the operating earnings of Co. X and Co. Y, $60,000 for each, are both of equal quality.[6] The results of the two companies can be summarized as follows:

---

[6] The concept of the quality of earnings is discussed in Chapter 22.

EXHIBIT 18-2

Trading on the equity—results under different earning assumptions (in thousands of dollars)

	Assets	Debt payable	Stock-holders' equity	Income before interest and taxes	6% debt interest	Taxes (1)	Net income	Net income + (Interest) (1 – tax rate)	Return on Total assets (2)	Return on Stock-holders' equity (3)
Year 1										
Co. X	$1,000,000	$400,000	$ 600,000	$150,000	$24,000	$63,000	$63,000	$75,000	7.5%	10.5%
Co. Y	1,000,000	—	1,000,000	150,000	—	75,000	75,000	75,000	7.5	7.5
Year 2										
Co. X	1,000,000	400,000	600,000	60,000	24,000	18,000	18,000	30,000	3.0	3.0
Co. Y	1,000,000	—	1,000,000	60,000	—	30,000	30,000	30,000	3.0	3.0
Year 3										
Co. X	1,000,000	400,000	600,000	25,000	24,000	500	500	12,500	1.25	.08
Co. Y	1,000,000	—	1,000,000	25,000	—	12,500	12,500	12,500	1.25	1.25

(1) Assuming a 50% effective tax rate.

(2) $\dfrac{\text{Net Income} + \text{Interest } (1 - .50)}{\text{Total Assets}}$

(3) $\dfrac{\text{Net Income}}{\text{Stockholders' Equity}}$

	Company X	Company Y
Operating earnings	$60,000	$60,000
Interest (6% of $400,000)	24,000	
Income before taxes	$36,000	$60,000
Taxes	18,000	30,000
Net income	$18,000	$30,000
Add back interest paid to bondholder	24,000	
Total return to security holders	$42,000	$30,000

Disregarding leverage effects which are neutral in the above example, even if the return on assets is equal to the interest rate, the total amount available for distribution to the bondholders and stockholders of Company X is $12,000 higher than the amount available for the stockholders of Company Y. This is due to the lower total tax liability to which the security holders of Company X are subject.

It should be borne in mind that the value of the tax deductibility of interest is dependent on the existence of sufficient earnings. However, unrecovered interest charges can be carried back and carried forward as part of tax loss carry-overs permitted by law.

Other advantages of leverage

In addition to the advantages accruing to equity stockholders from the successful employment of financial leverage and the tax deductibility of interest expenses, a sound longer term debt position can result in other advantages to the equity owner. A rapidly growing company can avoid earnings dilution through the issuance of debt. Moreover, if interest rates are headed higher, all other things being equal, a leveraged company will be more profitable than its nonleveraged competitor. Finally, there is a financial benefit from advantageously placed debt because debt capital is not always available to an enterprise and the capacity to borrow may disappear should adverse operating results occur.

Measuring the effect of financial leverage

The effect of leverage on operating results is positive when the return on the equity capital exceeds the return on total assets. This difference in return isolates the effect which the return on borrowed money has on the return on the owner's capital. As was seen in the example in Exhibit 18–2, leverage is positive when the return on assets is higher than the cost of debt. It is negative when the opposite conditions prevail. The terms "positive" and "negative" are not used here in the strict algebraic sense.

The effect of financial leverage can be measured by the following formula:

$$\text{Financial Leverage Index} = \frac{\text{Return on Equity Capital}^7}{\text{Return on Total Assets}}$$

Using the data in Exhibit 18–2 we compute the financial leverage indices of Company X for Years 1, 2, and 3 as follows:

Financial leverage index

$$\text{Year 1:} \quad \frac{10.5}{7.5} = 1.4$$

$$\text{Year 2:} \quad \frac{3.0}{3.0} = 1$$

$$\text{Year 3:} \quad \frac{.08}{1.25} = .07$$

In Year 1 when the return on equity exceeded that on total assets, the index at 1.4 was positive. In Year 2 when the return on equity equaled that on total assets, the index stood at 1 reflecting a neutralization of financial leverage. In Year 3 the index, at .07, was way below 1.0, thus indicating the very negative effect of financial leverage in that year. The subject of return on investment is discussed in Chapter 19.

Measuring the effect of capital structure on long-term solvency

From the foregoing discussion it is clear that the basic risk involved in a leveraged capital structure is the risk of running out of cash under conditions of adversity.

Debt involves a commitment to pay fixed charges in the form of interest and principal repayments. While certain fixed charges can be postponed in times of cash shortage, those associated with debt cannot be postponed without adverse repercussion to the ownership and also to the creditor groups.

Another important repercussion of excessive debt is a loss of financing flexibility i.e., the ability to raise funds particularly in adverse capital markets.

Long-term projections—usefulness and limitations

If a shortage of cash required to service the debt is the most adverse possibility envisaged, then the most direct and most relevant measure

---

[7] This can include or exclude preferred stock depending on how the effect of leverage is to be measured.

of risk inherent in the leveraged capital structure of an enterprise would be a projection of future cash resources and flows which would be available to meet these cash requirements. These projections must assume the worst set of economic conditions which are likely to occur, since this is the most realistic and useful test of safety from the creditor's point of view. If only prosperous and normal times are to be assumed, then the creditor would not need his preferred position and would be better off with an equity position where the potential rewards are higher.

In Chapter 17 we concluded that detailed cash flow projections can be reliably made only for the short term. Consequently they are useful only in the measurement of short-term liquidity.

The statement of changes in financial position can be projected over a relatively longer term because such a projection is far less detailed than a projection of cash flows. However, as we saw in the discussion of such projections in the proceding chapter, this lack of detail as well as the longer time horizon reduces the reliability of such projections.

The short term is understood to encompass, generally, a period of up to one year. The longer term, however, is a much wider ranging period. Thus, it may include a solvency analysis with respect to a three-year term loan, or it may encompass the evaluation of risk associated with a 30-year bond issue. Meaningful projections covering the period over which the interest and principal of the term loan will be paid can still reasonably be made. However, a 30-year projection of funds flow covering the bond issue would be an unrealistic exercise. For this reason longer term debt instruments often contain sinking fund provisions which act to reduce the uncertain time horizon, and stipulations of additional security in the form of specific assets pledged as collateral. Moreover, they contain provisions such as for the maintenance of minimum working capital levels or restrictions on the payment of dividends, all of which are designed to insure against a deterioration in the financial ratios prevailing at the time the bonds are issued.

Desirable as funds flow projections may be, their use for the extended longer term is severely limited. For this reason, a number of measures of long-term solvency have evolved which are more static in nature and are based on asset and earnings coverage tests. These measures will be considered below.

CAPITAL STRUCTURE ANALYSIS—COMMON-SIZE STATEMENTS

A simple measure of financial risk in an enterprise is the composition of its capital structure. This can be done best by constructing a common-size statement of the liabilities and equity section of the balance sheet as shown in Exhibit 18–3.

EXHIBIT 18–3

Liabilities and equity section—with common-size percents

Current liabilities	$ 428,000	19.0%
Long-term debt.........................	$ 500,000	22.2%
Equity capital:		
Preferred stock	$ 400,000	17.8%
Common stock	800,000	35.6
Paid-in capital	20,000	.9
Retained earnings	102,000	4.5
Total Equity	$1,322,000	58.8%
Total Liabilities and Equity	$2,250,000	100.0%

An alternative way of analyzing capital structure with common-size percentages would be to focus only on the longer term capital funds by excluding the current liabilities from total funds.

The advantage of a common-size analysis of capital structure is that it presents clearly the relative magnitude of the sources of funds of the enterprise, a presentation which lends itself readily to a comparison with similar data of other enterprises.

A variation of the approach of analyzing capital structure by means of common-size percentages is to analyze it by means of ratios.

CAPITAL STRUCTURE RATIOS

The basic ratio measurements of capital structure relate the various components of the capital structure to each other or to their total. Some of these ratios in common use are explained below.

Equity capital/total liabilities

This ratio measures the relationship of the equity capital, inclusive of preferred stock, to total liabilities, that is, both current and long-term liabilities. A ratio in excess of 1 to 1 indicates that the owners of the enterprise have a greater financial stake in it than do the creditors. Additionally, assuming that the assets are presented at close to realizable values, a ratio of 1 to 1 would mean that creditors have $2 in assets as security for each $1 of credit they extended to the enterprise. This generalization would have to be modified, of course, if some creditors have a prior claim on specific assets or all assets. To the extent that senior creditors have prior claims, the relative security of junior debt is diminished.

A reciprocal measure is total liabilities as a percentage of stockholder's equity.

Equity capital/long-term debt

This ratio measures the relative contributions of equity capital and of long-term debt to the total capitalization of an enterprise.[8] A ratio in excess of 1 : 1 indicates a higher equity capital participation as compared to long-term debt. The complement of this ratio is the familiar debt/equity ratio which is computed as follows:

$$\frac{\text{Long-Term Debt}}{\text{Equity Capital}}$$

Ratios measuring the proportion which equity capital represents of the total funds invested in the enterprise are a variation the common-size analysis approach. The following are among the ratios which accomplish this purpose.

$$\frac{\text{Equity Capital}}{\text{Equity Capital plus all Liabilities (total capitalization)}}$$

is a ratio which expresses the relationship between equity capital and the total funds available to the entity.

$$\frac{\text{Long-Term Debt}}{\text{Equity Capital plus all Liabilities (total capitalization)}}$$

measures the relative contribution of long-term debt to the total funds available to the enterprise.

Short-term debt

The ratio of debt which matures over the short term (five years) to total debt is an important indicator of the short-run fund and financing needs of an enterprise. Short-term debt, as opposed to maturing long-term debt or sinking fund requirements, is an indicator of enterprise reliance on bank financing.

Equity capital at market value

Accounting principles in current use place primary emphasis on historical costs rather than on current values. Since the shareholder's capital is the residual of assets minus liabilities, this accounting can result in equity capital book value figures which are far removed from realistic market values.

One method of correcting this flaw in the stated equity capital amounts, particularly when they enter importantly into the computation of many of the ratios which we have considered above, is to restate

---

[8] The term "long-term debt" usually includes *all* liabilities which are not current.

them by converting the assets from historical cost to current market values.

Although SEC disclosure requirements affecting certain companies will provide analysts with some replacement cost data (see Chapter 14) we are still far from having complete market values available.

One way of overcoming the problem of giving recognition to market values is to compute the equity capital at current (or some kind of average) market value of the stock issues which comprise it. On the assumption that the valuation placed by the market on the equity capital recognizes the current values of assets and their earning power, this amount can then be used in the computation of the various debt-equity ratios.

A serious objection to this method is that stock prices fluctuate widely and may, particularly in times of overspeculation, not be representative of "true" values at a given moment. However, this argument can be countered with considerable evidence that the judgment of the marketplace is most of the time superior to that of other judgmental processes and that use of average market prices would solve the problem of temporary aberrations. Thus, the use of equity capital figures computed at current, or at average, market values has much to commend it. Being more realistic they can improve the ratio measurements in which they are used and can provide a more realistic measure of the asset cushion which bondholders can count on.[9]

One important advantage of earnings-coverage ratios, as will be seen in the subsequent discussion of this subject, is that they are based on the earning power of assets rather than on the amount at which they are carried in the financial statements. Market values do, of course, give recognition to such earning power of an entity's assets. Thus, ratio measures, such as debt-equity ratios, which use equity capital amounts at market value, are more consistent with earnings-coverage ratios than are ratios using historical book values.

Interpretation of capital structure measures

The common-size and ratio analyses of capital structure, which have been examined above, are all measures of risk inherent in the capital structure of an enterprise. The higher the proportion of debt, the larger the fixed charges of interest and debt repayment, and the

---

[9] B. Graham, D. L. Dodd, and S. Cottle in their *Security Analysis*, 4th ed., (New York: McGraw-Hill Book Co., Inc., 1962), p. 361 suggest that the ratio of

$$\frac{\text{Market Value of Junior Equity}}{\text{Par Value of Bonds}}$$

should not be less than .5 and can be used to corroborate earnings coverage measures. It would not be prudent to have to assume, they maintain, that the junior equity is undervalued by the market.

greater the likelihood of insolvency during protracted periods of earnings decline or other adversities.

One obvious value of these measures is that they serve as screening devices. Thus, when the ratio of debt to equity capital is relatively small, say 10 percent or less, there is normally no need to be concerned with this aspect of an enterprise's financial condition; and the analyst may well conclude that he can spend his time better by directing his attention to the more critical areas revealed by his analysis.

Should an examination of the debt-equity ratios reveal that debt is indeed a significant factor in the total capitalization, then further analysis is necessary.

Such an analysis will encompass many aspects of an enterprise's financial condition, results of operations, and future prospects.

An analysis of short-term liquidity is always important because before the analyst starts to assess long-term solvency he has to be satisfied about the short-term financial survival of the enterprise. Chapter 16 examines the analysis of short-term liquidity, and the analyst will use the tools discussed there to assess the situation and also to relate the size of working capital to the size of long-term debt. Loan and bond indenture covenants requiring the maintenance of minimum working capital ratios attest to the importance attached to current liquidity in insuring the long-term solvency of an enterprise.

Additional analytical steps of importance will include an examination of debt maturities (as to size and spacing over time), interest costs, and other factors which have a bearing on the risk. Among those, the earnings stability of the enterprise and its industry as well as the kind of assets its resources are invested in are important factors.

MEASURES OF ASSETS DISTRIBUTION

The type of assets an enterprise employs in its operations should determine to some extent the sources of funds used to finance them. Thus, for example, it is customarily held that fixed and other long-term assets should not be financed by means of short-term loans. In fact, the most appropriate source of funds for investment in such assets is equity capital, although debt also has a place in such financing. On the other hand, working capital, and particularly seasonal working capital needs, can be appropriately financed by means of short-term credit. The ratio of working capital to long-term debt should not fall below 1 and in most industries which are affected by the business cycle a ratio below 1.5 to 2 may indicate weakness and vulnerability.

In judging the risk exposure of a given capital structure, the asset composition is one of the important factors to consider. This asset composition is best measured by means of common-size statements of the asset side of the balance sheet. For example, Exhibit 18–4 shows the common-size asset section of the balance sheet whose liabilities and equity section was presented in Exhibit 18–3.

EXHIBIT 18–4
Assets section—with common-size percents

Current Assets:		
Cash	$ 376,000	16.7%
Accounts receivable (net)	425,000	18.9
Merchandise inventory	574,000	25.5
Total Current Assets	$1,375,000	61.1%
Investments	$ 268,000	11.9%
Land, property, and equipment (net)	368,000	16.4
Intangibles	239,000	10.6
Total Assets	$2,250,000	100.0%

Judging *only* by the distribution of assets and the related capital structure, it would appear that since a relatively high proportion of assets is current (61 percent), a 41 percent debt and current liabilities position (see Exhibit 18–3) is not excessive. Other considerations and measurements may, however, change this conclusion.

Asset coverage is an important element in the evaluation of long-term solvency. Assets of value provide protection to holders of debt obligations both because of their earning power and because of their liquidation value. Additionally, they represent the bases on which an enterprise can obtain the financing which may be required to tie it over a period of financial stringency.

The relationship between asset groups and selected items of capital structure can also be expressed in terms of ratios.

Fixed assets/equity capital is a ratio which measures the relationship between long-term assets and equity capital. A ratio in excess of 1 : 1 means that some of the fixed assets are financed by means of debt.

Net tangible assets as a percentage of long-term debt is a measure of asset coverage of long-term obligations. It excludes assets of doubtful realizability or value and represents a measure of safety of debt based on liquidation of assets.

If the financial structure ratios are such that they require further analysis, one of the best means for further investigation are tests which measure an enterprise's ability to service its debt requirements out of earnings. This is the area we shall turn to next.

MEASURES OF EARNINGS COVERAGE

One conclusion of our discussion of debt-equity ratios was that a major usefulness of these measurements lies in their function as a screening device, that is, a means of deciding whether the apparent risk inherent in the capital structure of an enterprise requires further investigation and analysis. An important limitation of the measurements of debt-equity relationships is that they do not focus on the availability of funds, or cash, flows which are necessary to service the enterprise's debt. In fact, as a debt obligation is repaid the debt-equity ratio tends to improve whereas the yearly amount of cash needed to pay interest and sinking fund requirements may remain the same or may even increase, as for example, in the case of level payment debt or loans with "balloon" repayment provisions.

Earnings-coverage ratios measure directly the relationship between debt related fixed charges and the earnings available to meet these charges.[10] While the concept behind this measurement is simple and straightforward, its practical implementation is complicated by the problem of defining what should be included in "earnings" and in "fixed charges."

EARNINGS AVAILABLE TO MEET FIXED CHARGES

As was seen in Chapter 13, net income determined under the principles of accrual accounting is not the same thing as sources of funds provided by operations. Specifically, certain items of income, such as undistributed earnings of subsidiaries and controlled companies or sales on extended credit terms, do not create funds, that is, working capital. Similarly, certain expenses such as depreciation, amortization, depletion, and deferred income tax charges do not require the outlay of current funds. On the other hand, it should be borne in mind that a parent company can determine the dividend policy of a controlled subsidiary.

Fixed-debt charges are paid out of current funds rather than out of net income. Thus, the analyst must realize that an unadjusted net income figure may not be a correct measure of funds available to meet fixed charges.

Since fixed charges are paid off with cash, a clarification is needed as to why we accept here working capital as a surrogate for cash. The reason is that over the longer term the conversion period of current assets into cash becomes relatively insignificant. Thus, even if the conversion period of inventories into receivables, and ultimately into cash, is 120 days this period is not significant compared with the longer term period over which the fixed charges of debt must be paid.

The use of net income as an approximation of funds provided by

---

[10] Fixed charge coverage ratios represent important inputs in bond rating decisions. Bond indentures often specify that minimum levels of this ratio must be maintained before additional debt can be issued.

operations may, in some instance, be warranted while in others it may significantly overstate or understate the amount actually available for the servicing of debt. Thus, the soundest approach to this problem lies not in generalizations but rather in a careful analysis of the nonfund generating items included in income as well as the nonfund requiring expenses charged to that income. Thus, for example in considering depreciation as a nonfund requiring expense, the analyst must realize that over the long run an enterprise must replace its plant and equipment.

The problem of determining the amount of income to be included in fixed-charge-coverage ratios requires consideration of a number of additional factors:

1. *The treatment of extraordinary gains and losses.* As pointed out in the more comprehensive discussion of this subject in Chapters 11 and 22, extraordinary gains and losses enter into the determination of longer term average earnings power. As such they must be recognized as a factor which may, over the longer term, contribute to or reduce the funds available to pay fixed charges. Any computation of earnings-coverage ratios utilizing average earnings figures must recognize the existence of extraordinary gains and losses over the years. This is particularly true of earnings-coverage ratios where what we measure is the risk of loss of sources of funds for payment of fixed charges.

2. *Preferred dividends* need not be deducted from net income because the payment of such dividends is not mandatory. However, in consolidated financial statements, preferred dividends of a subsidiary whose income is consolidated must be deducted because they represent a charge which has priority over the distribution of earnings to the parent.

3. Earnings which are attributed to *minority interests* are usually deducted from net income available for fixed charges even though minority shareholders can rarely enforce a cash claim under normal operating conditions. An exception arises where preferred stock dividend requirements of a consolidated subsidiary are considered fixed charges and where they also represent a significant portion of the total minority interest. In such instances, the coverage ratio should be computed on the basis of earnings before deducting minority interests.

If a subsidiary with a minority interest has a loss, the credit in the income statement which results from the minority's share in the loss should be excluded from consolidated earnings for purposes of the coverage ratio computation. The parent would, in most cases, meet fixed-charge obligations of its subsidiary to protect its own credit standing, whether or not legally obligated to do so.

4. *The impact of income taxes* on the computation of earnings-coverage ratios should always be carefully assessed. Since interest is a tax-deductible expense, it is met out of pretax income. Thus, the income out of which interest payments are met is pretax income. On the other hand, preferred dividends or sinking fund payments are not tax deductible and must be paid out of after-tax earnings.

5. The *level of income* used in the computation of earnings-coverage ratios deserves serious consideration. The most important consideration here is: what level of income will be most representative of the amount that will actually be available in the *future* for the payment of debt-related fixed charges. An average earnings figure encompassing the entire range of the business cycle, and adjusted for any known factors which may change it in the future, is most likely to be the best approximation of the average source of funds from future operations which can be expected to become available for the payment of fixed charges. Moreover, if the objective of the earnings-coverage ratio is to measure the creditor's maximum exposure to risk, then the proper earnings figure to use is that achieved at the low point of the enterprise's business cycle.

FIXED CHARGES TO BE INCLUDED

Having considered the amount of earnings which should be included in the earnings coverage, we shall now turn to an examination of the types of fixed charges properly includable in the computation of this ratio.

1. Interest on long-term debt

Interest on long-term debt is the most direct and most obvious fixed charge which arises from the incurrence of long-term debt. Interest expense includes the amortization of deferred bond discount and premium. The bond discount and issue expenses represent the amount by which the par value of the bond indebtedness exceeded the proceeds from the bond issue. As such, the discount amortization represents an addition to the stated interest expense. The amortization of bond issue premium represents the reverse situation, and thus results in a reduction of interest expense over the period of amortization.[11]

If low coupon bonds have only a short period to run before maturity and it is likely that they will have to be refinanced with higher coupon bonds, it may be appropriate to incorporate in fixed charges the expected higher interest costs.

---

[11] Bond discount or premium amortization, which are usually relatively insignificant in amount, do not, strictly speaking, require a current outlay of funds. They represent cost or income item allocations over the term of the loan.

Interest on income bonds must, at best, be paid only as earned. Consequently, it is not a fixed charge from the point of view of the holder of fixed interest securities. It must, however, be regarded as a fixed charge from the point of view of the income bond issuer.

In public utilities, interest on funds tied up in construction projects which earn, as yet, no return, are usually excluded from interest costs and capitalized as costs of construction. For purposes of earnings-coverage calculations the exclusion of this interest factor from fixed charges results in a failure to measure the total burden of servicing long-term debt. Consequently, a more realistic measure of coverage can be arrived at by adding the "interest during construction" credit back to interest expense. At the same time the total interest amount, without benefit of a credit for interest charged during construction, is used in the coverage computation.

The SEC has been paying increasing attention to the computation of the ratio of earnings to fixed charges in prospectuses and has clarified the point that the amount of interest added back to income must not necessarily equal the interest amount included in the "fixed charges" part of the ratio computation.

In determining the earnings side of the ratio of earnings to fixed charges, interest is to be added back to pretax net earnings. The amount of interest to be added back should include the amount shown as interest expense plus the amount of interest which has found its way into other captions of the income statement such as, for example, capitalized interest expense now being written off to cost of sales as a part of the cost of land, construction, or other items sold. The add-back should not include the amounts of interest expense capitalized which are still carried in the balance sheet as, for instance, inventory, since such interest charges have already been removed from the income statement. The reason for this is to remove from the amount considered to be earnings of the enterprise, all amounts which have been paid out or accrued as interest and which have not been otherwise excluded from the income statement.

For the purpose of determining fixed charges, however, interest expense should include all interest applicable to the period which has been paid or accrued by the company on its total debt structure which existed during the period, including the amounts capitalized, even though some of the capitalized amount will remain in inventory or other balance sheet accounts.

Exhibit 18-5 presents an example of the computation of the ratio of earnings to fixed charges illustrating the principles discussed above: [12]

---

[12] The basic objective of pro forma earnings coverage computations is to incorporate in them fixed charges associated with contemplated issuances of debt while recognizing at the same time the income statement benefits to be derived from the proceeds of such debt issues.

EXHIBIT 18–5
Computation of actual and pro forma ratio of earnings to fixed charges

	19X1	19X2
Earnings:		
Income before provision for income taxes	$225,700	$370,200
Interest and debt expense included in cost of sales	279,400	523,100
Interest charged direct to income	1,800	9,600
Interest component of noncapitalized leases	1,700	5,100
Total	$508,600	$908,000
Fixed charges:		
Interest and debt expenses capitalized in real estate	$583,700	$727,300
Interest charged direct to income	1,800	9,600
Interest component of noncapitalized leases	1,700	5,100
Total	$587,200	$742,000
Interest on debentures to be issued at assumed rate of 7½%		187,500
Interest on debt to be retired		(5,400)
Pro forma fixed charges		$924,100
Ratio of earnings to fixed charges:		
Historical	.87	1.22
Pro forma		0.98

2. Interest implicit in lease obligations

Chapter 7 on the analysis of liabilities discussed the present status of accounting recognition of leases as financing devices. SFAS 13 now requires the capitalization of most financing leases.

When a lease is capitalized (see Chapter 7), the interest portion of the lease payment is designated as such on the income statement while most of the balance is usually considered as repayment of the principal obligation. A problem arises, however, when the analyst feels that certain leases which should have been capitalized are not so treated in the financial statements. The issue here actually goes beyond the pure accounting question of whether capitalization is, or is not, appropriate. It stems rather from the fact that a long-term lease represents a fixed obligation which must be given recognition in the computation of the earnings coverage ratio. Thus, even long-term leases which, from an accounting theory point of view, need not be capitalized may be considered as including fixed charges which have to be included in the coverage ratio computation.

The problem of extracting the interest portion of long-term lease payments is not a simple one. The external analysts can possibly obtain the implicit interest rate of financing leasing from an examination of the more extensive disclosure now available on the subject. Otherwise a rough rule of thumb, such as that interest represents one third of rentals, originally suggested by Graham and Dodd, may have to be used.[13] The SEC, which had used this rule, no longer accepts it automatically and insists on a more reliable estimate of the portion of rentals which represent interest.[14] "Delay rentals" in the extractive industries represent payment for the privilege of deferring the development of properties and, being in the nature of not regularly recurring compensation to owners, are not considered as rentals includable in the earnings-coverage ratio.

As with the offsetting of interest income against interest expense, the general rule is that rental income should not be offset against rental expense when determining fixed charges. An exception is made, however, where the rental income represents a direct reduction in rental expense.

3. Capitalized interest

The interest cost reflected in the income statement (wherever found, e.g., as financial cost or as part of cost of sales) is not the only one to be considered in arriving at the amount of interest to be included in fixed charges. Thus, interest that is not currently expensed but which is capitalized during the period (e.g., in inventory) must also be considered as a fixed charge. Capitalization occurs, for example, in the case of real estate development companies where interest costs are added to the cost of land held for sale and expensed as part of the cost of land only when it is sold.

4. Other elements to be included in fixed charges

The foregoing discussions concerned the determination of fixed financing charges, that is, interest and the interest portion of lease rentals. These are the most widely used measures of "fixed charges" included in earnings-coverage ratios. However, if the purpose of this ratio is to measure an enterprise's ability to meet fixed commitments which if unpaid could result in repercussions ranging all the way from financial embarrassment to insolvency, there are other fixed charges to be considered. Thus, when consolidated financial statements are presented, preferred stock dividend requirements of consolidated subsidiaries must be included as part of fixed charges. The most important category to be considered here, however, are principal repayment obligations such as sinking fund requirements, serial repayment provisions, and the principal repayment component of lease rentals.

---

[13] Graham, Dodd, and Cottle. *Security Analysis*, p. 344. (This rule was developed in a previous edition of this work.)

[14] SEC *Accounting Series Release 155.*

5. Principal repayment requirements

Principal repayment obligations are, from a cash-drain point of view, just as onerous as obligations to pay interest. In the case of rentals, the obligations to pay principal and interest must be met simultaneously.

A number of reasons have been advanced to indicate why the requirements for principal repayments are not given recognition in earnings-coverage ratio calculations:

1. It is claimed that sinking fund payment requirements do not have the same degree of urgency as do interest payments and that, consequently, they should be excluded. This is based on the assumption that creditors would be willing to agree to a temporary suspension of such payments even though this generally constitutes an act of bankruptcy. This is an assumption of doubtful validity. Moreover, if the coverage ratio is designed to measure safety, then a situation where an enterprise must renegotiate or forego adhering to debt repayment provisions is in itself symptomatic of a rather unsafe condition.

2. Another objection to the inclusion of sinking fund or other periodic principal repayment provisions in the calculation of the earnings-coverage ratio is that this may result in double counting, that is, the funds recovered by depreciation already provide for debt repayment. Thus, if earnings reflect a deduction for depreciation, then fixed charges should not include provisions for principal repayments.

   There is some merit in this argument if the debt was used to acquire depreciable fixed assets and if there is some correspondence between the pattern of depreciation charges and that of principal repayments. It must, moreover, be borne in mind that depreciation funds are recovered generally only out of profitable, or at least break-even, operations, and consequently this argument is valid only under an assumption of such operations.

   Our discussion of the definition of "earnings" to be included in the coverage-ratio calculations emphasized the importance of funds provided by operations as the measure of resources available to meet fixed charges. The use of this concept would, of course, eliminate the double counting problem since nonfund-requiring charges such as depreciation would be added back to net income for the purpose of the coverage computations.

A more serious problem regarding the inclusion of debt repayment provisions among "fixed charges" arises from the fact that not all debt agreements provide for sinking fund payments or similar repayment obligations. Any arbitrary allocation of indebtedness over time would be an unrealistic theoretical exercise and would ignore the fact that to the extent that such payments are not required in earlier years, the immediate pressure on the cash resources of the enterprise is reduced. In the longer run, however, larger maturities as well as "balloon" payments will have to be met.

The most useful solution to this problem lies in a careful analysis and assessment of the yearly debt repayment requirements which will serve as the basis on which to judge the effect of these obligations on the long-term solvency of the enterprise. The assumption that debt can always be refinanced, rolled over, or otherwise paid off from current operations is not the most useful approach to the problem of risk evaluation. On the contrary, the existence of debt repayment obligations as well as the timing of their maturity must be recognized and included in an overall assessment of the long-term ability of the enterprise to meet its fixed obligations. The inclusion of sinking fund or other early repayment requirements in fixed charges is one way of recognizing the impact of such requirements on fund adequacy. Another method would, as a minimum, call for scheduling total debt repayment requirements over a period of 5–10 years into the future and relating these to after tax funds expected to be available from operations.

6. Other fixed charges

While interest payments and debt repayment requirements are the fixed charges most directly related to the incurrence of debt, there is no logical justification to restrict the evaluation of long-term solvency only to these charges and commitments. Thus, a complete analysis of fixed charges which an enterprise is obliged to meet must include all long-term rental payment obligations[15] (not only the interest portion thereof) and particularly those rentals which must be met under any and all circumstances, under noncancellable leases, otherwise known as "hell-and-high-water" leases.

The reason why short-term leases can be excluded from consideration as fixed charges is that they represent an obligation of limited duration, usually less than three years, and can consequently be discontinued in a period of severe financial stringency. Here, the analyst must, however, evaluate how essential the rented items are to the continuation of the enterprise as a going concern.

---

[15] Capitalized long-term leases affect income by the interest charge implicit in them as well as by the amortization of the property right. Thus, to consider the "principal" component of such leases as fixed charges (after income was reduced by amortization of the property right) would amount to double counting.

Other charges which are not directly related to debt, but which must nevertheless be considered as long-term commitments of a fixed nature, are long-term purchase contracts not subject to cancellation and other similar obligations.

7. Guarantees to pay fixed charges

Guarantees to pay fixed charges of unconsolidated subsidiaries should result in additions to fixed charges if the requirement to honor the guarantee appears imminent.

ILLUSTRATION OF EARNINGS-COVERAGE RATIO CALCULATIONS

Having discussed the various considerations which enter into the decision of what factors to include in the earnings-coverage ratio computation, we will address ourselves now to the simpler question of how the ratio is computed. The computation of the various coverage ratios will be based on the illustration in Exhibit 18-6.

EXHIBIT 18-6

THE LEVERED CORPORATION
Abbreviated Income Statement

Net sales		$13,400,000
Equity in earnings of unconsolidated affiliates		600,000
		$14,000,000
Cost of goods sold	$7,400,000	
Selling, general, and administrative expenses	1,900,000	
Depreciation (excluded from above costs)	800,000	
Interest expense (inclusive of interest portion of rents) (1)	700,000	
Rental expense (3)	800,000	
Share of minority interests in consolidated income	200,000	11,800,000
Income before taxes		$ 2,200,000
Income taxes:		
Current	$ 800,000	
Deferred	300,000	1,100,000
Income before extraordinary items		$ 1,100,000
Gain on sale of investment in land (net of $67,000 tax)		200,000
Net income		$ 1,300,000
Dividends:		
On common stock	$ 400,000	
On preferred stock	200,000	600,000
Earnings retained for the year		$ 700,000

Selected notes to the financial statements

1. The interest expense is composed of the following charges:

   a. Interest on $6 million 6% senior notes due 19X0 .... $360,000
   b. Interest on $4 million 7% subordinated convertible debentures ...   280,000
   c. Interest portion of $160,000 in rents which have been capitalized .   50,000
   d. Other interest costs   10,000

   $700,000

   Sinking fund requirements on the 6 percent senior notes are $500,000 annually.
2. The company has a 10-year noncancellable raw material purchase commitment amounting to $100,000 annually.
3. Interest implicit in noncapitalized leases amounts to $300,000.

TIMES-INTEREST-EARNED RATIO

This is the simplest and one of the most widely used coverage ratios. The ratio is computed as follows:

$$\frac{\text{Income before Taxes} + \text{Interest Expense}}{\text{Interest Expense}}$$

Using the data in Exhibit 18–6 the computation of the times-interest-earned ratio is as follows:

$$\frac{2,200,000 + 700,000}{700,000} = 4.1 \text{ times}$$

As was pointed out in our discussion earlier in this chapter, since interest is a tax-deductible expense it is met out of pretax income. Interest is added back to pretax income because it was deducted in arriving at such income.

Ratio of earnings to fixed charges

The simplistic computation of the times-interest-earned ratio often omits the interest portion of long-term uncapitalized lease rentals. Under SFAS 13, there should be significantly fewer of these in the future. The ratio of earnings to fixed charges must, as a minimum, include all interest charges including those implicit in noncaptialized lease rentals.

Coverage ratios of senior bonds

If payment of senior bond interest takes precedence over the subordinated or junior bond interest, the fact remains that default in the payment of any contractual obligation may set in motion a chain of events which could prove detrimental to, and perhaps even result in loss, to senior bondholders.

If we compute the coverage ratio for a senior bond only, we omit from fixed charges the interest due to holders of junior issues but include the interest component of rentals on the assumption that the rentals are essential to the conduct of operations. Based on the data in Exhibit 18–6, we compute the fixed-charge coverage ratio for the 6 percent senior notes as follows:

$$\frac{\text{Income before Taxes} + \text{Interest Expense} + \text{Interest in Rentals}}{\text{Interest on Senior Issue} + \text{Interest in Rentals}}$$

$$\frac{2,200,000 + 700,000 + 300,000}{360,000 + 300,000} = 4.8 \text{ times}$$

The analyst should be careful to avoid the error, now rarely made, of computing the fixed-charge coverage ratio on a junior bond issue by omitting the senior bond interest from it. The junior issue can, of course, not be better covered than the senior one.

Fixed-charges-coverage ratio—the SEC standard

According to the SEC's definition, fixed charges include, in addition to (A) interest costs (inclusive of amortization of debt discount, expense and premium), (B) the interest portion implicit in rentals. Earnings in our example would exclude undistributed income of un-consolidated[16] persons (C). Again, using data in Exhibit 18–6:

$$\frac{\text{Income before Taxes} - (C) + (A) + (B)}{(A) + (B)}$$

$$= \frac{2,200,000 - 600,000 + 700,000 + 300,000}{700,000 + 300,000} = 2.6 \text{ times}$$

Fixed-charges-coverage ratios—expanded concept of fixed charges

If we adopt the point of view that failure to meet any fixed obligations can lead to trouble or to a chain of events leading to insolvency, then we want to establish how well such fixed obligations are covered by earnings. Thus, in addition to the fixed charges included in the computation in the preceding example, the following must now be considered for inclusion:

Annual sinking fund requirements on 6 percent senior note ($500,000). This represents an obligation which if not met may result

---

[16] It is assumed that the enterprise can direct consolidated subsidiaries to transfer funds in the form of dividends or otherwise.

in financial embarrassment or even insolvency. This fixed charge differs from the others considered so far in that it is not tax deductible. In order to bring it to a basis comparable to that of the tax-deductible fixed charges, we must convert it into the pretax amount which is needed to yield an after-tax outlay equal to the fixed charge. This is done by multiplying the fixed charge by a step-up factor computed as follows:

$$\frac{1}{1 - \text{Tax Rate}}$$

Assuming a tax rate of 50 percent in this case we get:

$$\$500,000 \times \left(\frac{1}{1 - 0.50}\right) = \$1,000,000$$

The converted sinking fund fixed charge of $1,000,000 will be used in the computation of the coverage ratio.

Long-term rental ($800,000). The earnings coverage computation, defined by the SEC, included as fixed charges only that portion of uncapitalized rentals which is attributable to the interest factor. This approach views as fixed charges only those fixed obligations which are in the nature of interest. Under the expanded concept of fixed charges, any obligation to pay fixed amounts over the longer term is considered a fixed charge because a failure to make such payments can set in motion a chain of events whose end result may be similar to that flowing out of a failure to pay interest.

The data in Exhibit 18–6 indicate that the uncapitalized leases represent long-term obligations. In the case of these lease rentals the interest portion is, from a contractual point of view, indistinguishable from the principal repayment portion ($500,000). Consequently, under the expanded concept of fixed charges the entire amount of rentals ($800,000), rather than only the interest portion, is viewed as a fixed charge whose degree of coverage by earnings it is important to establish.

Noninterest portion of capitalized rents ($110,000)

The principal or noninterest portion of capitalized rentals represents as urgent a call on the liquid resources of the enterprise as does the interest portion. It should, however, be borne in mind that since income is already charged with depreciation of the property rights stemming from the capitalized leases, inclusion in fixed charges of the noninterest portion of capitalized rentals would amount to a double counting.

Noncancellable raw material purchase commitments

According to Exhibit 18-6 the annual noncancellable long-term purchase commitment amounts to $100,000. The reason why this payment may be considered a fixed charge under the "expanded" concept is that it represents a noncancellable obligation to pay out a fixed annual sum of money over a 10-year period.

From the point of view of the income tax impact, this item is akin to interest or rental payments in that it is a tax-deductible charge because it enters ultimately into the cost of goods sold.

Recognition of benefits stemming from fixed charges

Consideration must be given to the question whether the benefits derived by an enterprise from the incurrence of fixed charges are given recognition in the earnings included in the coverage ratio. In the case of interest the benefits stem from the use of the funds derived from the loan. Similarly, rental payments benefit revenues through the productive use of the items leased. The benefits derived from the raw material commitments are reflected in sales revenues. Since outlays for raw materials represent a variable cost, they would ordinarily not be included in fixed charges because they represent an expense that can be varied in accordance with the volume of business transacted. In our example the fixed nature of the charge for raw materials stems from a noncancellable commitment to buy. This reduces discretion and variability. If, in the judgment of the analyst, such commitments represent rock-bottom requirements which will exist even under the most pessimistic estimates of product demand, then he may decide not to consider the purchase commitment as a fixed charge. This will be the assumption in our computational example.

Computation of coverage ratio—expanded concept of fixed charges

In accordance with the preceding discussion the earnings-coverage ratio would, based on the data in Exhibit 18–6, be computed as follows:

$$\frac{\text{Income before Taxes} + \text{Interest} + \text{Rental Expense}}{\text{Interest} + \text{Rental Expense} + \text{Sinking Fund}\left(\frac{1}{1-0.50}\right)}$$

$$= \frac{2,200,000 + 700,000 + 800,000}{700,000 + 800,000 + 1,000,000} = 1.48 \text{ Times}$$

Pro forma computations of coverage ratios

In cases where fixed charges yet to be incurred are to be recognized in the computation of the coverage ratio, for example, interest costs under a prospective incurrence of debt, it is quite proper to estimate the benefits which will ensue from such future inflows of funds and to include these estimated benefits in the pro forma income. Benefits to be derived from a propsective loan can be measured in terms of interest savings obtainable from a planned refunding operation, income from short-term investments[17] in which the proceeds may be invested, or similarly reasonable estimates of future benefits.

The SEC will usually insist on the presentation of pro forma computation of the ratio of earnings to fixed charges which reflects changes to be effected under prospective financing plans. Exhibit 18–5 presented an example of such a computation.

Funds flow coverage of fixed charges

The discussion earlier in this chapter pointed out that net income is generally not a reliable measure of funds provided by operations which are available to meet fixed charges. The reason is, of course, that fixed charges are paid with cash or, from the longer term point of view, with funds (working capital) while net income includes items of revenue which do not generate funds as well as expense items which do not require the current use of funds. Thus, a better measure of fixed charges coverage may be obtained by using as numerator funds obtained by operations rather than net income. This figure can be obtained from the statement of changes in financial condition.

Under this concept the coverage ratio would be computed as follows:

$$\frac{\text{Funds provided by Operations} + \text{Fixed Charges}}{\text{Fixed Charges}}$$

Using the data in Exhibit 18–6 and the broadest definition of "fixed charges," we compute the coverage ratio as follows:

Funds provided by operations (pretax)

Income before extraordinary items*	$1,100,000
Add back—income taxes	1,100,000
Pretax income	$2,200,000
Less: Nonfund generating income:	
Equity in earnings of unconsolidated affiliates	600,000
	$1,600,000

---

[17] *Accounting Series Release 119* of the SEC prohibits such offset of investment income.

Add: Expenses not requiring funds:

Depreciation	$800,000	
Share of minority interests in consolidated income	200,000	
Deferred income taxes (already added above)		1,000,000
Funds provided by operations (before taxes)		$2,600,000

* Assuming that a one-year calculation can properly omit extraordinary items.

Using the fixed charges we discussed under the "expanded concept" in the previous example, that is,

Interest	$ 700,000
Rental expense	800,000
Sinking fund requirement $\left(\dfrac{1}{1-0.50}\right)$	1,000,000
Total	$2,500,000

We compute the times fixed charges covered by funds provided by operations as follows:

$$\frac{\$2,600,000 + 700,000 + 800,000}{2,500,000} = 1.64 \text{ times}$$

It is interesting to note that the SEC definition of "income to be included in the coverage calculation" recognizes only one type of non fund generating revenue, that is, undistributed earnings of unconsolidated persons. It seems rather arbitrary to insist on only one type of "nonfund" adjustment to the exclusion of others. Perhaps it is a measure of conservatism that the SEC coverage-ratio formula ignores nonfund-requiring charges such as depreciation while requiring deduction of nonfund generating credits. However, it must be recognized that over the long run, and coverage ratios are concerned with the longer term, asset replacement needs may well equal, if not exceed, the amounts charged as depreciation. Thus, while such needs cannot be exactly anticipated and scheduled by external analysts, they must be taken into account, and one way of doing this is to omit depreciation from consideration as a charge not requiring the outlay of funds.

If depreciation is added back to net income, then there is little justification for not including principal repayment requirements, such as sinking fund requirements, among the fixed charges. In this case, the "double counting" problem discussed earlier is clearly eliminated.

A case, similar to the involved in the consideration of depreciation, can be made, under certain circumstances, against considering deferred income taxes as a non fund requiring charge in the computation of the coverage ratio of a long-term bond. Here we must recognize that over the long term, the higher charges of expenses for tax purposes which may have given rise to the tax deferral will result in lower future expense charges for tax purposes, thus causing the tax deferral to "reverse" and requiring higher taxes in the future. The treatment of deferred taxes in the coverage ratio computation will then depend on the analyst's judgment as to the expected future behavior of the deferred tax account, that is, whether it is likely to grow, stabilize, or decline. Also, the fact that deferred tax computations ignore present value concepts may also have to be considered.

Should the analyst wish to base the computation on "cash flow" or, more accurately, cash provided by operations the "funds from operations" figure must be appropriately adjusted for changes in such current items as accounts receivable, inventories, prepayments, accounts payable and accruals (see Chapter 13).

Other useful tests of funds flow relationships

Net funds (or cash) flows as a percentage of capital expenditures relates funds provided by operations *after* dividends to needed capital plant and equipment replacements and additions. This is a measure of fund committments to outlays which do not enter the fixed charges total but which may nevertheless be vital or important to the continuing operation of an enterprise.

Cash or funds flow as a percentage of long-term debt is an additional measure of safety which relates fund availability to total long term indebtedness.

Stability of "flow of funds from operations"

Since the relationship between the "flow of funds from operations" to the fixed charges of an enterprise is so important to an evaluation of long-term solvency, it is important to assess the stability of that flow. This is done by a careful evaluation of the elements which comprise the sources of funds from operations. For example, the depreciation add-back to net income is a more stable element than is net income itself because the recovery of the depreciation cost from selling prices precedes the earning of any net income, and has thus a higher degree of probability of happening. Even in very competitive industries selling prices must, in the long run, reflect the cost of plant and equipment used up in production.

EARNINGS COVERAGE OF PREFERRED DIVIDENDS

In the evaluation of preferred stock issues, it is often instructive to calculate the earnings coverage of preferred dividends, much in the same way the interest or fixed charges coverage of debt issues is computed.

In our discussion of coverage ratios for individual bond issues, earlier in this chapter, we pointed out the misleading results which can result from a class by class coverage computation where junior and senior bonds are outstanding. Thus, we concluded that the computation of a coverage ratio on an overall basis is a more meaningful approach. The same principle applies to the computation of the coverage of preferred dividends, that is, the computation must include as charges to be covered by earnings all fixed charges which take precedence over the payment of preferred dividends.[18]

As in the case of the interest or fixed-charge coverage computations, the final ratio depends on a definition of "fixed charges."

Since preferred dividends are not tax deductible, after-tax income must be used to cover them. Consequently the basic formula for computing preferred dividend coverage is:

$$\frac{\text{Income before Tax} + \text{Fixed Charges*}}{\text{Fixed Charges*} + \text{Preferred Dividends}\left(\dfrac{1}{1 - \text{Tax Rate}}\right)}$$

* Which *are* tax deductible.

If, for example, we adopt the SEC definition of fixed charges and assume a tax rate of 50 percent, then, based on the data in Exhibit 18–6, we compute the preferred dividend coverage ratio as follows:

Fixed charges:
Interest costs .... $ 700,000
Interest portion implicit in rentals 300,000
Total $1,000,000

$$\frac{2,200,000 - 600,000 + 1,000,000}{1,000,000 + 200,000 \left(\dfrac{1}{1 - 0.50}\right)} = 1.9 \text{ times}$$

If there are two or more preferred issues outstanding, a by-class coverage computation can be made by omitting from it the dividend requirements of the junior issue but always including all prior fixed charges and preferred dividends.

A refinement of the above computation (now required by the SEC) is achieved by substituting for the assumed tax rate the actual composite average tax rate incurred by the entity for the period. This actual tax rate is computed by relating the actual tax provision for the period

---

[18] This is also the position of the SEC as now formalized in *ASR 155* (1974). Care must be exercised in comparing these coverage ratios because some analysts and financial services include only the preferred dividend requirements in the computation.

to income before such taxes. It can, however, be argued that the tax incidence with respect to any one item is measured by the marginal (incremental) rather than the *average* tax rate.

EVALUATION OF EARNINGS-COVERAGE RATIOS

The earnings-coverage ratio test is a test of the ability of an enterprise to meet its fixed charges out of current earnings.[19] The orientation towards earnings is a logical one because the bondholder or other long-term creditor is not as much interested in asset coverage or what he can salvage in times of trouble, as he is interested in the ability of the enterprise to stay out of trouble by meeting its obligations currently and as a going concern. Given the limited returns obtainable from debt instruments, an increase in the interest rate cannot compensate the creditor for a serious risk of loss of principal. Thus, if the probability of the enterprise meeting its obligations as a going concern is not strong, then a creditor relationship can hardly be advantageous.

The coverage ratio is influenced by the level of earnings and by the level of fixed charges which in turn depends importantly on the debt-equity within the capitalization.

Importance of earnings variability

One very important factor in the evaluation of the coverage ratio is the pattern of behavior of cash flows over time, or the behavior of its surrogate—earnings. The more stable the earnings pattern of an enterprise or industry the lower the relative earnings coverage ratio that will be acceptable. Thus, a utility, which in times of economic downturn is likely to experience only a mild falloff in demand, can justify a lower earnings coverage ratio than can a cyclical company such as a machinery manufacturer which may experience a sharp drop in sales in times of recession. Variability of earnings is, then, an important factor in the determination of the coverage standard. In addition, the durability and the trend of earnings are important factors which must be considered apart from their variability.[20]

---

[19] W. B. Hickman, *Corporate Bond Quality and Investor Experience* (Princeton, N.J.: Princeton University Press, 1958), p. 11, found, for example, that bonds with poor earnings coverage had a probability of default 17 times greater than those with good coverage.

[20] Most factors which will affect an entity's equity securities will also affect its bonds. For example, when Consolidated Edison Co. passed its dividend in 1974 its bonds plunged along with its common stock which was the security directly affected. The market, aside from taking its cue from this action, may also have concluded that the company's ability to sell equity securities as well as its overall financing flexibility have been impaired.

Importance of method of computation and of underlying assumptions

The coverage standard will also depend on the method of computation of the coverage ratio. As we saw above, varying methods of computing the coverage ratio assume different definitions of "income" and of "fixed charges." It is reasonable to expect lower standards of coverage for the ratios which employ the most demanding and stringent definitions of these terms. For example, based on data in Exhibit 18–6, the earnings-coverage ratio of interest was 4.1 times, while the coverage ratio under an expanded concept of fixed charges worked out to only 1.46 times.

The standards will also vary with the kind of earnings which are utilized in the coverage computation, that is, average earnings, the earnings of the poorest year, etc. Moreover, the quality of earnings is an important consideration (see Chapter 22).

It is not advisable to compute earnings-coverage ratios under methods which are not theoretically sound and whose only merit is that they are conservative. Thus, using after-tax income in the computation of the coverage ratio of fixed charges which are properly deductible for tax purposes is not logical and introduces conservatism in the wrong place. Any standard of coverage adequacy must, in the final analysis, be related to the willingness and ability of the lender to incur risk.

Example of minimum standard of coverage

A standard suggested by a well-known work on security analysis[21] lists the following minimum coverage ratios of fixed charges:

1. *By 7 to 10 year average earnings:*

	Coverage	
	Before taxes	*After taxes*
Public utilities	4x	2.4x
Railroads	5x	2.9x
Industrials	7x	3.8x

2. *By earnings of the poorest year:*

Public utilities	3x	1.9x
Railroads	4x	2.4x
Industrials	5x	2.9x

Over the years an ever growing debt load, undertaken undoubtedly in many cases as protection against the effects of inflation, has resulted

---

[21] Graham, Dodd, and Cottle, *Security Analysis* p. 348.

in lower coverage ratios for most U.S. companies. This lowering in fixed-charge coverage ratios has been accompanied by an apparent erosion of the coverage standards against which they are judged. More recent standards of coverage will be found in Appendix 18A.

APPENDIX 18A

THE RATING OF DEBT OBLIGATIONS

Since the turn of the century, there has become established in the United States a comprehensive and sophisticated system for rating debt securities. Most ratings are performed by two highly regarded investment research firms, Moody's and Standard & Poor's (S&P).

A bond credit rating is a composite expression of judgment about the credit worthiness of the bond issuer as well as the quality of the specific security being rated. A rating measures credit risk, that is the probability of occurence of developments adverse to the interests of the creditor.

This judgment of credit worthiness is expressed in a series of symbols which express degrees of credit risk. Thus, the top four rating grades of Standard & Poor's are:

AAA Bonds rated AAA are highest grade obligations. They possess the ultimate degree of protection as to principal and interest. Marketwise they move with interest rates, and hence provide the maximum safety on all counts.

AA Bonds rated AA also qualify as high grade obligations, and in the majority of instances differ from AAA issues only in small degree. Here, too, prices move with the long-term money market.

A Bonds rated A are regarded as upper medium grade. They have considerable investment strength but are not entirely free from adverse effects of changes in economic and trade conditions. Interest and principal are regarded as safe. They predominantly reflect money rates in their market behavior, but to some extent, also economic conditions.

BBB The BBB, or medium grade category is borderline between definitely sound obligations and those where the speculative element begins to predominate. These bonds have adequate asset coverage and normally are protected by satisfactory earnings. Their susceptibility to changing conditions, particularly to depressions, necessitates constant watching. Marketwise, the bonds are more responsive to business and trade conditions than to interest rates. This group is the lowest which qualifies for commercial bank investment.

The major reason why debt securities are widely rated while equity securities are not lies in the fact that there is a far greater uniformity of approach and homogeneity of analytical measures used in the evaluation of credit worthiness than there can be in the evaluation of the future market performance of equity securities. Thus, the wide agreement on what is being measured in credit risk analysis has resulted in a widespread acceptance of and reliance on published credit ratings.

The criteria which enter into the determination of a rating have never been precisely defined and they involve both quantitative measures (e.g., ratio analysis) as well as qualitative factors such as market position and management quality. The major rating agencies refuse to be pinned down on what precise mix of factors enter into their rating process (which is a committee decision) because it is both art and science and also because to do so would cause endless arguments about the validity of the many judgmental factors which enter into a rating decision.

We can then see that in arriving at ratings these agencies must undertake analyses along the lines discussed throughout this work, the differences being mainly in the vast number of debt issues covered and the standardization of approaches which this entails. The following description of factors entering the rating process is based on published sources as well as on discussions with officials of the rating agencies.

The rating of corporate bonds

In rating an industrial bond issue the rating agency will focus on the issuing company's asset protection, financial resources, earning power, management, and the specific provisions of the debt security.

Also of great importance are size of firm, market share, industry position, susceptibility to cyclical influences[1] and other broad economic factors.

Asset protection is concerned with measuring the degree to which a company's debt is covered by the value of its assets. One measure is net tangible assets to long-term debt. At S&P an industrial needs a ratio of 5 to 1 to get an AAA rating; a ratio of over 4 to 1 to qualify for an AA rating; 3 to 3.5 to 1 for an A; and about 2.5 to 1 for a BBB rating.

Understated assets, such as those of companies in the natural resource or real estate fields, are generally accorded recognition in the rating process.

The long term debt as a percentage of total capitalization calls for a ratio of under 25 percent for an AAA, around 30 percent for a AA, 35 percent for an A and about 40 percent for a BBB rating.

---

[1] There are, for example, no AAA rated companies in the steel or paper industries.

Other factors entering the consideration of asset protection include the determination of book value, the makeup of working capital, the quality and age of property, plant, and equipment as well as questions of off balance sheet financing and unrecorded liabilities.

Financial resources encompass, in particular, such liquid resources as cash and other working capital items. Quality measures here include the collection period of receivables and inventory turnover. These are judged by means of industry standards. The use of debt, both short term and long term as well as the mix between the two is also investigated.

Future earning power and the resulting cash generating ability is a factor of great importance in the rating of debt securities because the level and the quality of future earnings determine importantly an enterprise's ability to meet its obligations. Earning power is generally a more reliable source of security than is asset protection.

A prime measure of the degree of protection afforded by earning power is the fixed-charge coverage ratio. To qualify for consideration for an AAA rating an industrial company's earnings should cover its interest and rental charges after taxes above seven to eight times, for an AA rating above six times, for an A rating over four times and a BBB over three times.

Another measure of debt service paying ability is cash flow (crudely-net income plus depreciation) to total funded debt. It should be 65 percent or more for an AAA; 45 to 60 percent for an AA; 35 to 45 percent for an A; and 25 to 30 percent for a BBB rating.

Management abilities, philosophy, depth, and experience always loom importantly in any final rating judgment. Through interviews, field trips, and other analyses the raters probe into the depth and breadth of management, as well as into its goals, the planning process and strategies in such areas as research and development, product promotion, new product planning, and acquisitions.

The specific provisions of the debt security are usually spelled out in the bond indenture. What is analyzed here are the specific provisions in the indenture which are designed to protect the interests of bondholders under a variety of future conditions. Included in consideration here are, among others, conditions for issuance of future debt issues, specific security provisions such as mortgaging, sinking fund and redemption provisions, and restrictive covenants.

As can be seen, debt rating is a complex process involving quantitative as well as qualitative factors all of which culminate in the issuance of a single quality rating. The weights which may be assigned to each factor will vary among analysts but the final conclusion will generally represent the composite judgment of several experienced raters.

THE RATING OF MUNICIPAL SECURITIES

Buyers of Municipal Bonds depend for their security of principal and interest on factors which are quite different from those which determine the quality of corporate debt. Hence, the processes of analysis differ.

Municipal securities, those issued by state and local governmental authorities, comprise a number of varieties. Many are general obligation bonds backed by the full faith and credit of the governmental unit which issues them. Others are special tax bonds that are limited in security to a particular tax that will be used to service and retire them. Then there are revenue bonds secured only by revenues of municipal enterprises. Other categories comprise housing authority bonds, tax anticipation notes, and so forth. Although the amount of information provided to buyers of municipal bonds is of very uneven quality moves are afoot to correct this, primarily by way of legislation.

Raters require a great variety of information from issuers of municipal debt. In case of general obligation bonds, the basic security rests on the issuer's ability and willingness to repay the debt from general revenues under a variety of economic conditions.[2] The fundamental revenue source is the taxing power of the local municipality. Thus, the information they require includes: current population and the trend and composition of population, the largest ten tax payers, the current market value of taxable properties, the gross indebtedness, and the net indebtedness (i.e., after deducting self-sustaining obligations, sinking fund, etc.) recent annual reports, budgets, and estimates of capital improvement and future borrowing programs, as well as an overall description of the area's economy.

While rating techniques have the same objectives as in the case of corporate bonds the ratios used are adapted to the specific conditions which exist with respect to municipal debt obligations. Thus, debt as a percentage of market value of real estate is an important indicator: 10 percent is considered high while 3–5 percent is on the low side. Annual debt service of 10 percent of total revenue is considered comfortable while percentages in the high teens are considered as presenting a warning sign. Per capita debt of $400 or less is considered low while debt in the $900 to $1,000 area is considered excessive and, hence, a

---

[2] The decision of New York State's highest court to overturn the New York City Moratorium on its notes strengthens the meaning of the concept of "full faith and credit." Said Chief Justice C. J. Breitel: "A pledge of the city's faith and credit is both a commitment to pay and a commitment of the city's revenue generating powers to produce the funds to pay . . . that is the way both words "faith" and "credit" are used and they are not tautological."

negative factor. Tax delinquencies should generally not exceed 3–4 percent.

Other factors of interest include unfunded pension liabilities as well as the trend of indebtedness. A steady increase in indebtedness is usually a danger sign. As in all cases of debt rating, the factor of management, though largely intangible and subject to measurement only through ultimate results, is of critical importance.

LIMITATIONS OF THE RATING PROCESS

As valuable and essential as the rating process is to buyers of the thousands upon thousands of bond issues of every description, the limitations of this standardized procedure must also be understood. As is true in any phase of security analysis the analyst who can, through superior analysis, improve on what is conventionally accepted stands to benefit accordingly. As was seen in Chapter 3 this is even more true in the case of debt securities than in the case of equity securities.

Bond ratings are very wide and they consequently present opportunities for those who can identify these differences within a rating classification. Moreover, rating changes generally lag the market and this presents additional opportunities to the analyst who with superior skill and alertness can identify important changes before they become generally recognized.

References

"The Rating Game," The Twentieth Century Fund, New York, 1974.

"Higher Stakes in the Bond-Rating Game," *Fortune*, April 1976.

H. C. Sherwood, *How Corporate and Municipal Debt is Rated: An Inside Look at Standard & Poor's Rating System.* New York: John Wiley & Sons, Inc., 1976.

APPENDIX 18B

RATIOS AS PREDICTORS OF BUSINESS FAILURE

The most common use to which financial statement ratios are put is to use them as pointers in the direction of further investigation and analysis. Some investigation and experimentation has been undertaken to determine to what extent ratios can be used as predictors of failure. As such they could provide valuable additional tools in the analysis of long-term solvency.

The basic idea behind bankruptcy prediction models is that through observation of the trend and behavior of certain ratios of various firms before failure, those characteristics in ratios which predominate in failing firms can be identified and used for prediction purposes. The expectation is that signs of deterioration observed in ratio behavior can be detected early enough and clearly enough so that timely action can be taken to avoid substantial risk of default and failure.

Empirical studies

Among the earliest studies to focus on the behavior of ratios prior to the failure of firms were those of Winakor and Smith who studied a sample of 183 firms which experienced financial difficulties for as long as 10 years prior to 1931, the year when they failed.[1] Analyzing the 10-year trend of 21 ratios they concluded that the ratio of net working capital to total assets was among the most accurate and reliable indicator of failure.

Fitzpatrick analyzed the three- to five-year trends of 13 ratios of 20 firms that had failed in the 1920–29 period.[2] By comparing them to the experience of a control group of 19 successful firms, he concluded that all of his ratios predicted failure to some extent. However, the best predictors were found to be the return on net worth and the net worth to total debt ratio.

Merwin studied the experience of a sample of 939 firms during the 1926–36 period.[3] Analyzing an unspecified number of ratios he found that three ratios were most sensitive in predicting "discontinuance" of a firm as early as four to five years before such discontinuance. The three ratios were the current ratio, net working capital to total assets, and net worth to total debt. They all exhibited declining trends before "discontinuance" and were at all times below estimated normal ratios.

Focusing on the experience of companies which experienced defaults on debt and bank credit difficulties, Hickman studied the experience of corporate bond issues during 1900–1943 and reached the conclusion that the times-interest-earned ratio and the net-profit-to-sales ratio were useful predictors of bond issue defaults.[4]

In a study using more powerful statistical techniques than used in its predecessors, Beaver found that financial ratios proved useful in the

---

[1] Arthur Winakor and Raymond F. Smith, *Changes in Financial Structure of Unsuccessful Firms,* Bureau of Business Research (Urbana, Ill.: University of Illinois Press, 1935).

[2] Paul J. Fitzpatrick, *Symptoms of Industrial Failures* (Washington: Catholic University of America Press, 1931); and Paul J. Fitzpatrick, *A Comparison of the Ratios of Successful Industrial Enterprises with Those of Failed Companies* (Washington: The Accountants Publishing Co., 1932).

[3] Charles L. Merwin, *Financing Small Corporations: In Five Manufacturing Industries, 1926–36* (New York: National Bureau of Economic Research, 1942).

[4] W. Braddock Hickman, *Corporate Bond Quality and Investor Experience* (Princeton, N.J.: Princeton University Press, 1958), pp. 395–431.

prediction of bankruptcy and bond default at least five years prior to such failure. He determined that ratios could be used to distinguish correctly between failed and nonfailed firms to a much greater extent than would be possible by random prediction.[5]

Among his conclusions were that both in the short-term and the long-term cash-flow-to-total-debt ratios were the best predictors, capital structure ratios ranked second, liquidity ratios third, while turnover ratios were the worst predictors.

In an investigation of the ability of ratios to predict bond rating changes and bond ratings of new issues, Horrigan found that the rating changes could be correctly predicted to a much greater extent by the use of ratios than would be possible through random prediction.[6]

Altman extended Beaver's univariate analysis to allow for multiple predictors of failure.[7] Altman used multiple discriminant analysis (MDA) which attempts to develop a linear function of a number of explanatory variables to classify or predict the value of a qualitative dependent variable; e.g., bankrupt or nonbankrupt. Twenty-two financial ratios, based on data one period before bankruptcy, were examined and Altman selected five of these to be included in his final discriminant function: Working capital/Total assets (liquidity), Retained earnings/Total assets (age of firm and cumulative profitability), Earnings before interest and taxes/Total assets (profitability), Market value of equity/Book value of debt (financial structure), Sales/Total assets (capital turnover rate).

Altman was not able to use a cash flow variable, which Beaver found to be the most discriminating in his study since apart from other elements, Altman did not have depreciation figures.

Conclusions

The above research efforts, while pointing out the significant potential which ratios have as predictors of failure, nevertheless indicate that these tools and concepts are in an early stage of development.

The studies focused on experience with failed firms *after the fact*. While they presented evidence that firms which did not fail enjoyed stronger ratios than those which ultimately failed, the ability of ratios alone to predict failure has not been conclusively proved. Another important question yet to be resolved is whether the observation of

[5] William H. Beaver, "Financial Ratios as Predictors of Failure," *Empirical Research in Accounting, Selected Studies, 1966*, Supplement to vol. 4, *Journal of Accounting Research*, pp. 71–127.

[6] James O. Horrigan, "The Determination of Long-term Credit Standing with Financial Ratios," *Empirical Research in Accounting, Selected Studies, 1966*, Supplement to Vol. 4, *Journal of Accounting Research*, pp. 44–62.

[7] Edward Altman, "Financial Ratios, Discriminant Analysis, and the Prediction of Corporate Bankruptcy," *Journal of Finance* 22 (September 1968) 589–609.

certain types of behavior by certain ratios can be accepted as a better means of the analysis of long-term solvency than is the integrated use of the various tools described throughout this work. Further research may show that the use of ratios as predictors of failure will best complement and precede, rather than supplement, the rigorous financial analysis approaches suggested in this work. However, as screening, monitoring, and attention-directing devices they hold considerable promise.

QUESTIONS

1. Generally speaking, what are the key elements in the evaluation of long-term solvency?
2. Why is the analysis of capital structure important?
3. How should deferred income taxes be treated in the analysis of capital structure?
4. In the analysis of capital structure how should lease obligations which have not been capitalized be treated? Under what conditions should they be considered the equivalent of debt?
5. What are liabilities for pensions? What factors should analysts assessing total pension obligations of the firm take into consideration?
6. How would you classify (i.e., equity or liability) the following items. State your assumptions and reasons:
    a. Minority interest in consolidated financial statement.
    b. General contingency reserve for indefinite purpose.
    c. Reserve for self-insurance.
    d. Guarantee for product performance on sale.
    e. Convertible debt.
    f. Preferred stock.
7. What is meant by "financial leverage," and in what case(s) is such leverage most advantageous?
8. In the evaluation of long-term solvency why are long-term projections necessary in addition to a short-term analysis? What are some of the limitations of long-term projections?
9. What is the difference between common-size analysis and capital structure ratio analysis? Why is the latter useful?
10. The amount of equity capital shown on the balance sheets, which is based on historical cost, at times differs considerably from realizable market value. How should a financial analyst allow for this in the analysis of capital structure?
11. Why is the analysis of assets distribution necessary?
12. What does the earnings coverage ratio measure and in what respects is it more useful than other tools of analysis?
13. Your analysis of additional information leads you to conclude that the rental payment under a long-term lease should have been capitalized. If

it was not capitalized on the financial statement, what approaches would you take?

14. For the purpose of earnings-coverage ratio computation, what are your criteria for inclusion of an item in "fixed charges"?

15. The company under analysis has a purchase commitment of raw materials under a noncancellable contract which is substantial in amount. Under what conditions would you include the purchase commitment in the computation of fixed charges?

16. Is net income generally a reliable measure of funds available to meet fixed charges? Why or why not?

17. What are some of the useful tests of funds flow relationships?

18. Company B is a wholly owned subsidiary of Company A. The latter is also Company B's principal customer. As potential lender to Company B, what particular facets of this relationship would concern you most? What safeguards, if any, would you require?

19. Comment on the statement: "debt is a supplement to, not a substitute for, equity capital."

20. A company in need of additional equity capital decides to sell convertible debt thus postponing equity dilution and ultimately selling its shares at an effectively higher price. What are the advantages and disadvantages of such a course of action?

21. *a.* What is the basic function of restrictive covenants in long-term debt indentures (agreements)?
    b. What is the function of provisions regarding:
    (1) Maintenance of minimum working capital (or current ratio).
    (2) Maintenance of minimum net worth.
    (3) Restrictions on the payment of dividends.
    (4) Ability of creditors to elect a majority of the board of directors of the debtor company in the event of default under the terms of the loan agreement.

22. What is your opinion on the use of ratios as predictors of failure? Your answer should recognize the empirical research which has been recently done in this area.

23. Dogwood Manufacturing, Inc., a successful and rapidly growing company, has always had a favorable difference between the rate of return on its assets and the interest rate paid on borrowed funds. Explain why the company should *not* increase its debt to the 90% level of total capitalization and thereby minimize any need for equity financing. (C.F.A.)

24. Why are debt securities widely rated while equity securities are not?

25. On what aspects do the rating agencies focus in rating an industrial bond? Elaborate.

26. *a.* Municipal securities compromise a number of varieties. Discuss.
    b. What factors are considered in the rating of municipal securities?

27. Can the analyst improve on a rating judgment? Discuss.

19

ANALYSIS OF RETURN ON
INVESTMENT AND OF ASSET
UTILIZATION

DIVERSE VIEWS OF PERFORMANCE

In this age of increasing social consciousness there exist many views of what the basic objectives of business enterprises are or should be. There are those who will argue that the main objective of a business enterprise should be to make the maximum contribution to the welfare of society of which it is capable. That includes, aside from the profitable production of goods and services, consideration of such immeasurables as absence of environmental pollution and a contribution to the solution of social problems. Others, who adhere to the more traditional *laissez faire* school, maintain that the major objective of a business enterprise organized for profit is to increase the wealth of its owners and that this is possible only by delivering to society (consumers) that which it wants. Thus, the good of society will be served.

An extended discussion of these differing points of view on performance is beyond the purpose of this text. Since the analysis of financial statements is concerned with the application of analytical tools to that which can be measured, we shall concentrate here on those measures of performance which meet the objectives of financial analysis as outlined in Chapter 3. In that context performance is the source of the rewards required to compensate investors and lenders for the risks which they are assuming.

CRITERIA OF PERFORMANCE EVALUATION

There are many criteria by which performance can be measured. Changes in sales, in profits, or in various measures of output are among the criteria frequently utilized.

No one of these measurements, standing by itself, is useful as a comprehensive measure of enterprise performance. The reasons for this are easy to grasp. Increases in sales are desirable only if they result in increased profits. The same is true of increases in volume of production. Increases in profits, on the other hand, must be related to the capital that is invested in order to attain these profits.

IMPORTANCE OF RETURN ON INVESTMENT (ROI)

The relationship between net income and the capital invested in the generation of that income is one of the most valid and most widely recognized measures of enterprise performance. In relating income to invested capital the ROI measure allows the analyst to compare it to alternative uses of capital as well as to the return realized by enterprises subject to similar degrees of risk. The investment of capital can always yield some return. If capital is invested in government bonds, the return will be relatively low because of the small risk involved. Riskier investments require higher returns in order to make them worthwhile.[1] The ROI measure relates income (reward) to the size of the capital that was needed to generate it.

MAJOR OBJECTIVES IN THE USE OF ROI

Economic performance is the first and foremost purpose of business enterprise. It is, indeed, the reason for its existence. The effectiveness of operating performance determines the ability of the enterprise to survive financially, to attract suppliers of funds, and to reward them adequately. ROI is the prime measure of economic performance. The analyst uses it as a tool in two areas of great importance:

1. An indicator of managerial effectiveness.
2. A method of projecting earnings.

An indicator of managerial effectiveness

The earning of an adequate or superior return on funds invested in an enterprise depends first and foremost on the resourcefulness, skill, ingenuity, and motivation of management. Thus, the longer term ROI is of great interest and importance to the financial analyst because it

---

[1] See Chapter 3 for an examination of the importance of the evaluation of risk and return in investing and lending decisions.

offers a prime means of evaluating this indispensible criterion of business success: the quality of management.

A method of projecting earnings

A second important function served by the ROI measure is that of a means of earnings projection. The advantage of this method of earnings projection is that it links the amount of earnings which it is estimated an enterprise will earn to the total invested capital. This adds discipline and realism to the projection process, which applies to the present and expected capital investment the return which is expected to be realized on it. The latter will usually be based on the historical and incremental rates of return actually earned by the enterprise, and adjusted by projected changes, as well as on expected returns on new projects.

The rate of ROI method of earning projection can be used by the analyst as either the primary method of earnings projection or as a supplementary check on estimates derived from other projection methods.

Internal decision and control tool

While our focus here is on the work of the external financial analyst, mention should be made of the very important role which ROI measures play in the individual investment decisions of an enterprise as well as in the planning, budgeting, coordination, evaluation, and control of business operations and results.

It is obvious that the final return achieved in any one period on the total investment of an enterprise is composed of the returns (and losses) realized by the various segments and divisions of which it is composed. In turn, these returns are made up of the results achieved by individual product lines, projects, and so forth.

The well-managed enterprise exercises rigorous control over the returns achieved by each of its "profit centers" and rewards its managers on the basis of such results. Moreover, in evaluating the advisability of new investments of funds in assets or projects, management will compute the estimated returns it expects to achieve from them and use these estimates as a basis for its decision.

BASIC ELEMENTS OF ROI

The basic concept of ROI is relatively simple to understand. However, care must be used in determining the elements entering its computation because there exist a variety of views, which reflect different objectives, of how these elements should be defined.

The basic formula for computing ROI is as follows:

$$\frac{\text{Income}}{\text{Investment}}$$

We shall now examine the various definitions of "investment" and of the related "income."

Defining the investment base

There is no one generally accepted measure of capital investment on which the rate of return is computed. The different concepts of investment reflect different objectives. Since the term "return on investment (ROI)" covers a multitude of concepts of investment base and income, there is need for more specific terms to describe the actual investment base used.

Total assets.   Return on total assets is perhaps the best measure of the *operating efficiency* of an enterprise. It measures the return obtained on *all* the assets entrusted to management. By removing from this computation the effect of the method used in financing the assets, the analyst can concentrate on the evaluation or projection of operating performance.

Modified asset bases.   For a variety of reasons some ROI computations are based not on total assets but rather on an adjusted amount.

One important category of adjustments relates to "unproductive" assets. In this category assets omitted from the investment base include idle plant, facilities under construction, surplus plant, surplus inventories and surplus cash, intangible assets, and deferred charges. The basic idea behind these exclusions is not to hold management responsible for earning a return on assets which apparently do not earn a return. While this theory may have validity in the use of ROI as an internal management and control tool, it lacks merit when applied as a tool designed to evaluate management effectiveness on an overall basis. Management is entrusted funds by owners and creditors, and it has discretion as to where it wants to invest them. There is no reason for management to hold on to assets which bring no return. If there are reasons for keeping funds invested in such assets, then there is no reason to exclude them from the investment base. If the long-run profitability of an enterprise is benefited by keeping funds invested in assets which have no return or a low return in the interim, then the longer term ROI should reflect such benefits. In conclusion, it can be said that from the point of view of an enterprise evaluation by the external analyst there is rarely any justification to omit assets from the investment base merely because they are not productively employed or do not earn a current return.

The exclusion of intangible assets from the investment base is often due to skepticism regarding their value or their contribution to the earning power of the enterprise. Under generally accepted accounting principles intangibles are carried at cost. However, if the cost exceeds their future utility, they must be written down or else the analyst will at least find an uncertainty exception regarding their carrying value included in the auditor's opinion. Accounting for intangible assets is discussed in Chapter 6. The exclusion of intangible assets from the asset (investment) base must be justified on more substantial evidence than a mere lack of understanding of what these assets represent or an unsupported suspicion regarding their value.

Depreciable assets in the investment base.   An important difference of opinion prevails with respect to the question of whether depreciable assets should be included in the investment base at original cost or at an amount net of the accumulated allowances for depreciation.

One of the most prominent advocates of the inclusion of fixed assets at gross amount in the investment base, for purposes of computing the return on investment, is the management of E. I. duPont de Nemours and Company which pioneered the use of ROI as an internal management tool.

In a pamphlet describing the company's use of the ROI method in the appraisal of operating performance, this point of view is expressed as follows:

Calculation of return on investment. Return on investment as presented in the chart series is based upon *gross* operating investment and earnings *net* of depreciation.

Gross operating investment represents all the plant, tools, equipment and working capital made available to operating management for its use; no deduction is made for current or other liabilities or for the reserve for depreciation. Since plant facilities are maintained in virtually top productive order during their working life, the depreciation reserve being considered primarily to provide for obsolescence, it would be inappropriate to consider that operating management was responsible for earning a return on only the net operating investment. Furthermore, if depreciable assets were stated at net depreciated values, earnings in each succeeding period would be related to an ever-decreasing investment; even with stable earnings, Return on Investment would continually rise, so that comparative Return on Investment ratios would fail to reveal the extent of trend of management performance. Relating earnings to investment that is stable and uniformly compiled provides a sound basis for comparing the "profitability of assets employed" as between years and between investments.

In the case of any commitment of capital—e.g., an investment in a security—it is the expectation that in addition to producing earnings while committed, the principal will eventually be recovered. Likewise, in the case of funds invested in a project, it is expected that in addition to the return earned while invested, the working capital will be recovered through liquidation at the end of the project's useful life and the plant investment will be recovered through depreciation accruals. Since earnings must allow for this recovery of plant investment, they are stated net of depreciation.[2]

It is not difficult to take issue with the above reasoning. It must, however, be borne in mind that the duPont system is designed for use in the internal control of separate productive units as well as for the control of operating management. Our point of view here is, however, that of evaluating the operating performance of an enterprise taken as a whole. While the recovery of capital out of sales and revenues (via depreciation), by an enterprise operating at a profit, can be disregarded in the evaluation of a *single* division or segment, it cannot be disregarded for an enterprise taken as a whole because such recovery is reinvested somewhere within that enterprise even if it is not reinvested in the particular segment which gave rise to the depreciation and which is evaluated for internal purposes. Thus, for an enterprise taken as a whole, the "net of depreciation" asset base is a more valid measure of investment on which a return is computed. This is so for the reasons given above and also because the income which is usually related to the investment base is net of the depreciation expense.

The tendency of the rate of return to rise as assets are depreciated (see also Chapter 10) is offset by the retention of capital recovered by means of depreciation, on which capital a return must also be earned. Moreover, maintenance and repair costs rise as equipment gets older, thus tending to offset the reduction, if any, in the asset base.

Among other reasons advanced in support of the use of fixed assets at their gross amount is the argument that the higher amounts are designed to compensate for the effects of inflation on assets expressed in terms of historical cost. In the discussion of the price level problem in Chapter 14 it was pointed out that price level adjustments can validly be made only within the framework of a complete restatement of all elements of the financial statements. Crude "adjustments," such as using the gross asset amount, are apt to be misleading and are generally worse than no adjustments at all.

Long-term liabilities plus equity capital. The use of long-term liabilities plus equity capital as the investment base differs from the "total assets" base only in that current liabilities are excluded as suppliers of funds on which the return is computed. The focus here is on the two major suppliers of longer term funds, that is, long-term creditors and equity shareholders.

---

[2] American Management Association, *Executive Committee Control Charts*, AMA Management Bulletin No. 6, 1960, p. 22.

Shareholders' equity.   The computation of return on shareholders' equity measures the return accruing to the owners' capital. As was seen in the discussion of financial leverage in Chapter 18, this return reflects the effect of the employment of debt capital on the owners' return. Since preferred stock, while in the equity category, is usually nevertheless entitled only to a fixed return, it is also omitted from the calculation of the final return on equity computation.

BOOK VERSUS MARKET VALUES IN THE INVESTMENT BASE

Return on asset calculations are most commonly based on book values appearing in the financial statements rather than on market or fair values which are, in most cases, analytically more significant and relevant. Also, quite often, a return is earned by enterprises on assets which either do not appear in the financial statements or are significantly understated therein. Examples of such assets are intangibles such as patents, trademarks, expensed research and development costs, advertising and training costs, and so forth. Other excluded assets may include leaseholds and the value of natural resources discovered.

As was discussed in Chapter 14, there exists a trend towards fair value accounting and information on the replacement cost of assets of large corporations is already available. In the interim one alternative to the use of such sketchy data is to rely on the valuation which the market places the equity securities of the enterprise in order to approximate fair values. Thus we can substitute the market value of equity securities and debt for the book value of total assets in computing a proper investment base.

Difference between investor's cost and enterprise investment base

For purposes of computing the ROI, a distinction must be drawn between the investment base of an enterprise and that of an investor. The investor's investment base is, of course, the price he paid for his equity securities. Except for those cases in which he acquired such securities at book value, his investment base is going to differ from that of the company in which he has invested. In general, the focus in ROI computations is on the return realized by the enterprise rather than the return realized on the investment cost of any one shareholder.

Averaging the investment base

Regardless of the method used in arriving at the investment base, the return achieved over a period of time is always associated with the investment base that was, on average, actually available to the enterprise over that period of time. Thus, unless the investment base did not change significantly during the period, it will be necessary to average it. The most common method of averaging for the external analyst is that of adding the investment base at the beginning of the year to that at the end of the year and dividing their total by two. A more accurate method of averaging, where the data is available, is to average by month-end balances, that is, adding the month-end investment bases and dividing the total by 12.

Relating income to the investment base

In the computation of ROI, the definition of return (income) is dependent on the definition of the investment base.

If the investment base is defined as comprising total assets, then income *before* interest expense is used. The exclusion of interest from income deductions is due to its being regarded as a payment for the use of money to the suppliers of debt capital in the same way that dividends are regarded as a reward to suppliers of equity capital. Income, before deductions for interest or dividends, is used when it is related to total assets or to long-term debt plus equity capital.

When the return on the equity capital is computed, net income after deductions for interest and preferred dividends is used. If the preferred dividends are cumulative, they are deducted in arriving at the balance of earnings accruing to the common stock, whether these dividends were declared or not.

The final ROI must always reflect all applicable costs and expenses and that includes income taxes. Some computations of ROI nevertheless omit deductions of income taxes. One reason for this practice is the desire to isolate the effects of tax management from those of operating performance. Another reason is that changes in tax rates affect comparability over the years. Moreover, companies which have tax loss carry-forwards find that the deduction of taxes from income adds confusion and complications to the ROI computations.

It must, however, be borne in mind that income taxes reduce the final return and that they must be taken into consideration particularly when the return on shareholders' equity is computed.

Illustration of ROI computations

The computation of ROI under the various concepts of "investment base" discussed above will now be illustrated by means of the data contained in Exhibits 19–1 and 19–2. The computations are for the year 19X9 and based on figures rounded to the nearest million dollars.

EXHIBIT 19–1

AMERICAN COMPANY
Statement of Income
For Years Ended December 31, 19X8 and 19X9
(in thousands of dollars)

	19X8	19X9
Net sales	$1,636,298	$1,723,729
Costs and expenses	1,473,293	1,579,401
Operating income	$ 163,005	$ 144,328
Other income net.........................	2,971	1,784
	$ 165,976	$ 146,112
Interest expense*	16,310	20,382
Provision for federal and other taxes on income	71,770	61,161
Net income	$ 77,896	$ 64,569
Less dividends:		
Preferred stock	2,908	2,908
Common stock	39,209	38,898
	$ 42,117	$ 41,806
Net income reinvested in the business	$ 35,779	$ 22,763

* All assumed to be on long-term debt.

Return on total assets

$$\frac{\text{Net Income} + \text{Interest}}{\text{Total Assets}}$$

$$\frac{65 + 20}{1,372} = 6.2\%$$

Two refinements are possible in this computation and become necessary if their use would make a significant difference in the result.

One refinement recognizes that the year-end total asset figure may be different from the average amount of assets employed during the year. This calls for adding the total assets at the beginning and end of the year and dividing by two.

The second refinement recognizes that interest is a tax-deductible expense and that if the interest cost is excluded the related tax benefit must also be excluded from income. If we assume the average tax rate[3] to be 50 percent that means that we add back only *half* the interest cost.

Reflecting these two refinements the formula becomes:

$$\frac{\text{Net Income} + \text{Interest Expense} \times (1 - \text{Tax Rate})}{(\text{Beginning Total Assets} + \text{Ending Total Assets}) \div 2}$$

---

[3] As was already argued in Chapter 18, the incremental (marginal) tax rate, rather than the average effective tax rate of the enterprise may be the appropriate rate to use.

EXHIBIT 19–2

AMERICAN COMPANY
Statements of Financial Position
As at December 31, 19X8 and 19X9
(in thousands of dollars)

	19X8	19X9
Assets		
Current Assets:		
Cash	$ 25,425	$ 25,580
Eurodollar time deposits and temporary cash investments	38,008	28,910
Accounts and notes receivable—net	163,870	176,911
Inventories	264,882	277,795
Total Current Assets	$ 492,185	$ 509,196
Investments in and receivables from nonconsolidated subsidiaries	33,728	41,652
Miscellaneous investments and receivables	5,931	6,997
Funds held by trustee for construction	6,110	
Land, buildings, equipment, and timberlands—net	773,361	790,774
Deferred charges to future operations	16,117	16,452
Goodwill and other intangible assets	6,550	6,550
Total Assets	$1,333,982	$1,371,621
Liabilities		
Current Liabilities:		
Notes payable to banks—principally Eurodollar	$ 7,850	$ 13,734
Accounts payable and accrued expenses	128,258	144,999
Dividends payable	10,404	10,483
Federal and other taxes on income	24,370	13,256
Long-term indebtedness payable within one year	9,853	11,606
Total Current Liabilities	$ 180,735	$ 194,078
Long-term indebtedness	350,565	335,945
Deferred taxes on income	86,781	101,143
Total Liabilities	$ 618,081	$ 631,166
Capital		
Preferred, 7% cumulative and noncallable, par value $25 per share; authorized 1,760,000 shares	$ 41,538	$ 41,538
Common, par value $12.50 per share; authorized 30,000,000 shares	222,245	222,796
Capital in excess of par value	19,208	20,448
Earnings reinvested in the business	436,752	459,515
Less: Common treasury stock	(3,842)	(3,842)
Total Capital	$ 715,901	$ 740,455
Total Liabilities and Capital	$1,333,982	$1,371,621

Using the data in Exhibits 19–1 and 19–2,

$$\frac{65 + 20(1 - 0.5)}{(1,334 + 1,372) \div 2} = 5.5\%$$

Since the return on total assets shown by the refined method differs significantly from the uncorrected method, the use of the refined method, which is the theoretically correct one, is indicated.

Return on modified asset bases. Since our discussion earlier in the chapter came to the conclusion that in normal circumstances most of the modifications in the amount of total assets are not logically warranted, no illustrations of such computation will be given.

Return on long-term liabilities plus equity capital

$$\frac{\text{Net Income} + \text{Interest Expense*} \times (1 - \text{Tax Rate})}{\text{Average Long-Term Liabilities plus Equity Capital}}$$

Using the data in Exhibits 19–1 and 19–2:

$$\frac{65 + (20 \times 0.5)}{(437 + 716 + 437 + 740) \div 2} = 6.4\%$$

* On long-term debt.

It should be noted that deferred taxes on income are included among the long-term liabilities. In the computation of return on long-term liabilities and equity capital, the question of how to classify deferred taxes does not really present a problem because after careful consideration of the circumstances giving rise to the deferrals, the analyst will decide whether they are to be considered as either debt or equity. In this computation both debt and equity are aggregated anyway. The problem of classification becomes more real in computing the return on shareholders' equity. In the examples which follow we assume circumstances where deferred taxes are considered to be more in the nature of a long-term liability than of an equity nature.

Return on stockholders' equity. The basic computation of return on the equity excludes from the investment base all but the common stockholders' equity.

$$\frac{\text{Net Income} - \text{Preferred Dividends}}{\text{Average Common Stockholders' Equity}}$$

Using data in Exhibits 19–1 and 19–2:

$$\frac{65 - 3}{(674 + 699) \div 2} = 9 \text{ percent}$$

The higher return on shareholders' equity as compared to the return on total assets reflects the positive workings of financial leverage.

Should it be desired, for whatever reason, to compute the return on total stockholders' equity, the investment base would include the preferred shareholders' equity, while net income would not reflect a deduction for preferred dividends. The formula[4] would then be:

$$\frac{\text{Net Income}}{\text{Average Total Shareholders' Equity (common and preferred)}}$$

Where convertible debt sells at a substantial premium above par and is clearly held by investors for its conversion feature, there is justification for treating it as the equivalent of equity capital. This is particularly true when the company can choose at any time to force conversion of the debt by calling it.

Analysis and interpretation of ROI

Earlier in the chapter we mentioned that ROI analysis is particularly useful to the analyst in the areas of evaluation of managerial effectiveness, enterprise profitability, and as an important tool of earnings projection.

Both the evaluation of management and the projection of earnings by means of ROI analysis are complex processes requiring thorough analysis. The reason for this is that the ROI computation usually includes components of considerable complexity.

Components of the ROI ratio. If we focus first on return on total assets we know that the primary formula for computing this return is:

$$\frac{\text{Net Income} + \text{Interest} \, (1 - \text{Tax Rate})}{\text{Average Total Assets}}$$

For purposes of our discussion and analysis let us look at this computation in a simplified form:

$$\frac{\text{Net Income}}{\text{Total Assets}}$$

Since sales are a most important yardstick in relation to which profitability is measured and are, as well, a major index of activity, we can recast the above formula as follows:

$$\frac{\text{Net Income}}{\text{Sales}} \times \frac{\text{Sales}}{\text{Total Assets}}$$

The relationship of net income to sales measures operating performance and profitability. The relationship of sales to total assets is a

---

[4] The return on common stockholders equity may also be computed thus:

$$\frac{\text{Earnings per Share}}{\text{Book Value per Share}}$$

but the results will often not be identical because the earnings per share computation includes adjustments for common stock equivalents, etc. (see Chapter 12) measure of asset utilization or turnover, a means of determining how effectively (in terms of sales generation) the assets are utilized. It can be readily seen that both factors, profitability as well as asset utilization, determine the return realized on a given investment in assets.

Profitability and asset utilization are, in turn, complex ratios which normally require thorough and detailed analysis before they can be used to reach conclusions regarding the reasons for changes in the return on total assets.

Exhibit 19–3 presents the major factors which influence the final return on total assets. In the next section we shall be concerned with the interaction of profitability (net income/sales) and of asset utilization or turnover (sales/total assets) which, in Exhibit 19–3 is regarded as the first level of analysis of the return on total assets. As can be seen from Exhibit 19–3, the many important and complex factors which, in turn, determine profitability and asset utilization represent a second level of analysis of the return on total assets. Chapters 20 and 21 will take up the analysis of results of operations, and Chapter 22 will deal with the evaluation and projection of earnings. The analysis of asset utilization will be discussed in subsequent sections of this chapter.

EXHIBIT 19–3

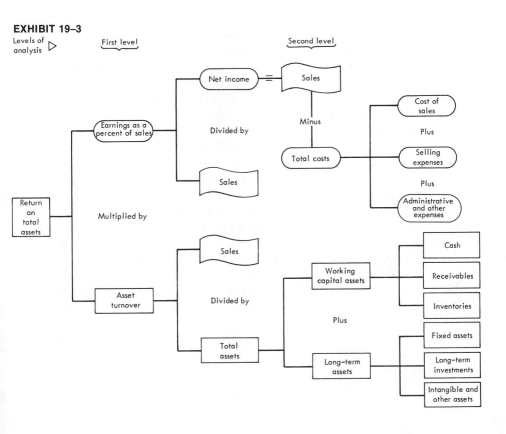

Relationship between profitability and asset turnover. The relationship between return on total assets, profitability, and capital turnover (utilization) is illustrated in Exhibit 19–4, which indicates that when we multiply profitability (expressed as a percentage) by asset utilization (expressed as a turnover) we obtain the return on total assets (expressed as a percentage relationship).

EXHIBIT 19–4
Analysis of return on total assets

	Company X	Company Y	Company Z
1. Sales	$5,000,000	$10,000,000	$10,000,000
2. Net income	500,000	500,000	100,000
3. Total assets	5,000,000	5,000,000	1,000,000
4. Profit as % of sales $\left(\frac{2}{1}\right)$	10%	5%	1%
5. Asset turnover $\left(\frac{1}{3}\right)$	1	2	10
Return on total assets (4 × 5)	10%	10%	10%

Company X realizes its 10 percent return on total assets by means of a relatively high profit margin and a low turnover of assets. The opposite is true of Company Z, while Company Y achieves its 10 percent return by means of a profit margin half that of Company X and an asset turnover rate twice that of Company X. It is obvious from Exhibit 19–4 that there are many combinations of profit margins and turnover rates which can yield a return on assets of 10 percent.

In fact, as can be seen from Exhibit 19–5, there exist an infinite variety of combinations of profit margin and asset turnover rates which yield a 10 percent return on assets. The chart in the exhibit graphically relates asset turnover (vertical axis) to profitability (horizontal axis).

The curve, sloping from the upper left area of low profit margins and high asset turnover rates, traces out the endless combinations of profitability and asset turnover rates which yield a 10 percent return on total assets. The data of Companies X and Y (from Exhibit 19–4) are represented by dots on the graph, while the data of Company Z cannot be fitted on it since the full curve has not been shown. The other lettered dots represent the profit-turnover combination of other companies within a particular industry. This clustering of the results of various companies around the 10 percent return on assets slope is a useful way of comparing the returns of many enterprises within an industry and the major two elements which comprise them.

The chart in Exhibit 19–5 is also useful in assessing the relative

EXHIBIT 19–5

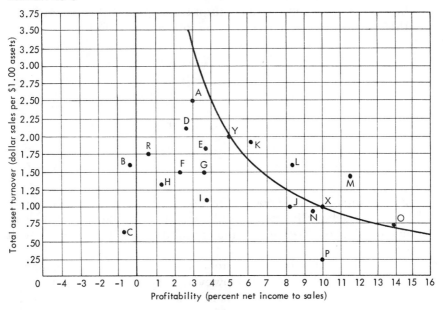

courses of action open to different enterprises which want to improve their respective returns on investments.

Companies B and C must, of course, restore profitability before the turnover rate becomes a factor of importance. Assuming that all the companies represented in Exhibit 19–5 belong to the same industry and that there is an average representative level of profitability and turnover in it, Company P will be best advised to pay first and particular attention to improvement in its turnover ratio, while Company R should pay foremost attention to the improvement of its profit margin. Other companies, such as Company I, would best concentrate on both the turnover and the profit margin aspects of ROI improvement.

While the above analysis treats profitability and turnover as two independent variables, they are, in fact, interdependent. As will be seen from the discussion of break-even analysis in Chapter 21, a higher level of activity (turnover), when fixed expenses are substantial, will tend to increase the profit margin because, within a certain range of activity, costs increase proportionally less than sales. In comparing two companies within an industry the analyst, in evaluating the one having the lower asset turnover, will make allowance for the potential increase in profitability that can be associated with a projected increase in turnover that is based primarily on an expansion of sales.

Analysis of return on total assets can reveal the weaknesses as well as the potential strengths of an enterprise. Assume that two companies in the same industry have returns on total assets as follows:

		Company A	Company B
1.	Sales	$ 1,000,000	$20,000,000
2.	Net income	100,000	100,000
3.	Total assets	10,000,000	10,000,000
4.	Profitability $\left(\frac{2}{1}\right)$	10%	0.5%
5.	Turnover of assets $\left(\frac{1}{3}\right)$	0.1 times	2 times
	Return on investment (4×5)	1%	1%

Both companies have poor returns on total assets. However, remedial action for them lies in different areas and the analyst will concentrate on the evaluation of the feasibility of success of such improvement.

Company A has a 10 percent profit on sales which, let us assume, is about average for the industry. However, each dollar invested in assets supports only 10 cents in sales whereas Company B gets $2 of sales for each dollar invested in its assets. The analyst's attention will naturally be focused on Company A's investment in assets. Why is its turnover so low? Are there excess assets which yield little or no return or are there idle assets which should be disposed of? Or, as often is the case, are the assets inefficiently or uneconomically utilized? Quite obviously, Company A can achieve more immediate and significant improvements by concentrating on improving turnover (by increasing sales, reducing investment, or both) than by striving to increase the profit margin beyond the industry average.

The opposite situation prevails with respect to Company B where attention should first be focused on the reasons for the low profit margin and to the improvement of it as the most likely avenue of success in increasing ROI. The reasons for low profitability can be many, including inefficient equipment and production methods, unprofitable product lines, excess capacity with attendant high fixed costs, excessive selling or administrative costs, etc.

The company with the low profitability may discover that changes in tastes and in technology have resulted in an increased investment in assets being needed to finance a dollar of sales. This means that in order to maintain its return on assets the company must increase its profit margin or else production of the product is no longer worthwhile.

There is a tendency to regard a high profit margin as a sign of high earnings quality. This view was rebutted by W. M. Bennett who pointed out the importance of return on capital as the ultimate test of profitability.[5] He presented the following table comparing during a given year the similar profit margins of five companies with their respective returns on capital:

	Profit margin as % of sales	Profit as % of capital
Whirlpool	5.3%	17.1%
Corn Products	5.9	12.0
Goodyear	5.5	9.6
U.S. Plywood	5.5	8.0
Distillers Seagram	5.0	6.7

It is evident that in the case of these five companies, which have similar profit margins, the rate of capital turnover made the difference in the return on capital performance, and this must be taken into account by the analyst. Thus, a supermarket chain will be content with a net profit margin of 1 percent or less because it has a high rate of turnover due to a relatively low investment in assets and a high proportion of leased assets (such as stores and fixtures). Similarly, a discount store will accept a low profit margin in order to obtain a high rate of asset turnover (primarily of inventories). On the other hand, capital intensive industries such as steels, chemicals, and autos, which have heavy investments in assets and resulting low asset turnover rates, must achieve high net profit margins in order to offer investors a reasonable return on capital.

ANALYSIS OF ASSET UTILIZATION

As is graphically illustrated in Exhibit 19–3, the return on total assets depends on (1) getting the largest profit out of each dollar of sales and (2) obtaining the highest possible amount of sales per dollar of invested capital (net assets).

The intensity with which assets are utilized is measured by means of asset turnover ratios. That utilization has as its ultimate measure the amount of sales generated since sales are in most enterprises the first and essential step to profits. In certain special cases, such as with enterprises in developmental stages, the meaning of turnover may have to be modified in recognition of the fact that most assets are committed to the development of future potential. Similarly, abnormal supply problems and strikes are conditions which will affect the state of capital utilization and, as such, will require separate evaluation and interpretation.

[5] William M. Bennett, "Capital Turnover vs. Profit Margins," *Financial Analysts Journal*, March–April 1966, pp. 88–95.

Evaluation of individual turnover ratios

Changes in the basic turnover ratio which enters the determination of the ROI calculation, that is,

$$\frac{\text{Sales}}{\text{Total Assets}}$$

can be evaluated meaningfully only by an analysis of changes in the turnover rates of individual asset categories and groups which comprise the total assets.

Sales to cash.   As was seen in the discussion in Chapter 16, cash and cash equivalents are held primarily for purposes of meeting the needs of day-to-day transactions as well as a liquidity reserve designed to prevent the shortages which may arise from an imbalance in cash inflows and outflows. In any type of business there is a certain logical relationship between sales and the cash level that must be maintained to support it.

Too high a rate of turnover of cash may be due to a cash shortage which can ultimately result in a liquidity crisis if the enterprise has no other ready sources of funds available to it.

Too low a rate of turnover may be due to the holding of idle and unnecessary cash balances. Cash accumulated for specific purposes or known contingencies may result in temporary decreases in the rate of turnover.

The basic trade-off here is between liquidity and the tying up of funds which yield no return or a very modest return.

Sales to receivables.   Any organization which sells on credit will find that the level of its receivables is a function of sales. A relatively low rate of turnover here is, among other reasons, likely to be due to an overextension of credit, to an inability of customers to pay, or to a poor collection job.

A relatively high rate of turnover may indicate a strict credit extension policy or a reluctance or inability to extend credit. Determining the rate of turnover here is the trade-off between sales and the tying up of funds in receivables.

Sales to inventories.   The maintenance of a given level of sales generally requires a given level of inventories. This relationship will vary from industry to industry depending on the variety of types, models, colors, sizes, and other classes of varieties of items which must be kept in order to attract and keep customers. The length of the production cycle as well as the type of item (e.g., luxury versus necessity; perishable versus durable) has a bearing on the rate of turnover.

A slow rate of turnover indicates the existence of problems such as overstocking, slow-moving or obsolete inventories, overestimating of sales or a lack of balance in the inventory. Temporary problems such as strikes at important customers may also be responsible for this.

A higher than normal rate of turnover may mean an underinvestment in inventory which can result in lack of proper customer service and in loss of sales.

In this case the trade-off is between tying up funds in inventory, on one hand, and sacrificing customer service and sales on the other.

Sales to fixed assets. While the relationship between property, plant, and equipment and sales is a logical one on a long-term basis, there are many short-term and temporary factors which may upset this relationship. Among these factors are conditions of excess capacity, inefficient or obsolete equipment, multishift operations, temporary changes in demand, and interruptions in the supply of raw materials and parts.

It must also be remembered that increases in plant capacity are not gradual but occur, instead, in lumps. This too can create temporary and medium-term changes in the turnover rates. Often, leased facilities and equipment, which do not appear on the balance sheet, will distort the relationship between sales and fixed assets (see, however, Chapter 7).

The trade-off here is between investment in fixed assets with a correspondingly higher break-even point on one hand, and efficiency, productive capacity, and sales potential on the other.

Sales to other assets. In this category we find, among others, such assets as patents and deferred research and development costs. While the direct relationship between these individual categories of assets and current sales levels may not be evident, no assets are held or should be held by an enterprise unless they contribute to sales or to the generation of income. In the case of deferred research and development costs, the investment may represent the potential of future sales. The analyst, must, in his evaluation of rates of asset utilization, allow for such factors.

Sales to short-term liabilities. The relationship between sales and short-term trade liabilities is a predictable one. The amount of short-term credit which an enterprise is able to obtain from suppliers depends on its needs for goods and services, that is, on the level of activity (e.g., sales). Thus, the degree to which it can obtain short-term credit depends also importantly on the level of sales. This short-term credit is relatively cost-free and, in turn, reduces the investment of enterprise funds in working capital.

Use of averages

Whenever the level of a given asset category changes significantly during the period for which the turnover is computed, it is necessary to use averages of asset levels in the computation. The computation then becomes

$$\frac{\text{Sales}}{(\text{Asset at beginning of period} + \text{Asset at end of period}) \div 2}$$

To the extent that data is available and the variation in asset levels during the period warrants it, the average can be computed on a monthly or quarterly basis.

Other factors to be considered in return on asset evaluation

The evaluation of the return on assets involves many factors of great complexity. As will be seen from the discussion in Chapter 22, the inclusion of extraordinary gains and losses in single period and average net income must be evaluated. Chapter 14 has examined the effects of price level changes on ROI calculations, and these, too, must be taken into account by the analyst.

In analyzing the trend of return on assets over the years, the effect of acquisitions accounted for as poolings of interest (see Chapter 9) must be isolated and their chance of recurrence evaluated.

The external analyst will not usually be able to obtain data on ROI by segments, product lines, or divisions of an enterprise. However, where his bargaining power or position allows him to obtain such data, they can make a significant contribution to the accuracy and reliability of his analysis.

A consistently high return on assets is the earmark of an effective management and can distinguish a growth company from one experiencing merely a cyclical or seasonal pickup in business.

An examination of the factors which comprise the return on assets will usually reveal the limitations to which their expansion is subject. Neither the profit margin nor the asset turnover rate can expand indefinitely. Thus, an expanding asset base via external financing and/or internal earnings retention will be necessary for further earnings growth.

Equity growth rate

The equity growth rate by means of earnings retention can be calculated as follows:

$$\frac{\text{Net Income} - \text{Dividend Payout}}{\text{Common Shareholders' Equity}} = \text{Percent Increase in Common Equity}$$

This is the growth rate due to the retention of earnings. It indicates the possibilities of earnings growth without resort to external financing. These increased funds, in turn, will earn the rate of return which the enterprise can obtain on its assets and thus contribute to growth in earnings.

Return on shareholders' equity

Up to now we have examined the factors affecting the return on total assets. However, of great interest to the owner group of an enterprise is the return on the stockholders' equity. The rate of return on total assets and that on the stockholders' equity differs because a portion of the capital with which the assets are financed is usually supplied by creditors who receive a fixed return on their capital or, in some cases, no return at all. Similarly, the preferred stock usually receives a fixed dividend. These fixed returns differ from the rate earned on the assets (funds) which they provide, and this accounts for the difference in returns on assets and those of stockholders' equity. This is the concept of financial leverage which was already discussed at length in Chapter 18.

Equity turnover

The computation of the return on shareholders' equity is composed of the following two major elements:

$$\frac{\text{Net Income}}{\text{Sales}} \times \frac{\text{Sales}}{\text{Average Shareholders' Equity}}$$

The equity turnover (sales/average shareholder's equity) can be further analyzed by breaking it down into two elements:

$$\frac{\text{Sales}}{\text{Net Operating Assets}} \times \frac{\text{Net Operating Assets}}{\text{Average Shareholders' Equity}}$$

The first factor measures asset utilization which we have discussed earlier in the chapter. The second factor is a measure of the use of financial leverage by the enterprise. The more an enterprise uses borrowed funds to finance its assets the higher this ratio will be.

Measuring the financial leverage index

The financial leverage index, as we already saw in Chapter 18, can be measured as follows:

$$\frac{\text{Return on Equity}}{\text{Return on Total Assets}} = \frac{\text{Assets}}{\text{Equity}}$$

$$\times \frac{\text{Net Income}}{\text{Net Income} + \text{Interest}\,(1 - \text{Tax Rate})}$$

The formula for return on total assets

$$\frac{\text{Net Income} + \text{Interest}\,(1 - \text{Tax Rate})}{\text{Total Assets}}$$

can be converted to a return on stockholders' equity formula by multiplying it by the financial leverage index.

$$\frac{\text{Net Income} + \text{Interest}\,(1 - \text{Tax Rate})}{\text{Total Assets}} \times (\text{Financial leverage index})$$

In the discussion that follows, the leverage index for American Company, based on the data of Exhibits 19–1 and 19–2 in this chapter, is as follows:

$$\frac{\text{Return on Stockholders' Equity}}{\text{Return on Total Assets}} = \frac{8.8\%}{5.47\%} = 1.61$$

A financial leverage index greater than 1 is positive, that is, it indicates that the use of borrowed and other noncommon equity funds increases the common stockholders' return. A leverage index below 1 has the opposite effect.

Analysis of financial leverage effects

The effect which each noncommon equity capital source has on the return on the common equity can be analysed in detail. Using the data of American Company which was included in Exhibits 19–1 and 19–2, earlier in this chapter we can undertake such an analysis as follows:

An analysis of the American Company balance sheet as at 12/31/X9 discloses the following major sources of funds (in thousands):

Current liabilities (exclusive of current portion of long-term debt)		$ 182,472
Long-term debt	$335,945	
Current portion	11,606	347,551
Deferred taxes		101,143
Preferred stock		41,538
Common stockholders' equity		698,917
Total Investment or Total Assets		$1,371,621

The income statement for 19X9 includes (in thousands):

Income before taxes	$ 125,730
Income (and other) taxes	61,161*
Net income	$ 64,569
Preferred dividends	2,908
Income accruing to common shareholders	$ 61,661
Total Interest Expense	$ 20,382
Assumed interest on short-term notes (5%)	687
Balance of interest on long-term debt	$ 19,695

* Average tax rate of 49%.

The return on total assets is computed as follows:

$$\frac{\text{Net Income} + \text{Interest} (1 - \text{Tax Rate})}{\text{Total Assets}}$$

$$= \frac{64,569 + 20,382 \, (1 - 0.49)}{1,371,621} = 5.47\%$$

The 5.47 percent return represents the average return on all assets employed by the company. To the extent that suppliers of capital other than the common stockholders get a lower reward than an average of 5.47 percent the common equity benefits by the difference. The opposite is true when the suppliers of capital receive more than a 5.47 percent reward in 19X9.

Exhibit 19–6 presents an analysis showing the relative contribution and reward of each of the major suppliers of funds and their effect on the returns earned by the common stockholders.

EXHIBIT 19–6

Analysis of composition of return on shareholders' equity (slide rule accuracy computations in thousands of dollars)

Category of fund supplier	Fund supplied	Earnings on fund supplied at rate of 5.47%	Payment to suppliers of funds	Accruing to (detracting from) return on common stock
Current liabilities	182,472	9,981	350 (1)	9,631
Long-term debt	347,551	19,011	10,044 (2)	8,967
Deferred taxes	101,143	5,533	None	5,533
Preferred stock	41,538	2,272	2,908 (3)	(636)
Earnings in excess of compensation to suppliers of funds				23,495
Add: Common stockholder's equity	698,917	38,231	—	38,231
Totals	1,371,621	75,028 (4)	13,302	
Total income (return) on stockholders' equity				61,726 (4)

(1) Interest cost of $687 less 49% tax.
(2) Interest cost of $19,695 less 49% tax.
(3) Preferred dividends—not tax deductible.
(4) Slight differences with statement figures are due to rounding.

As can be seen from Exhibit 19–6 the $9,631,000 accruing to the common equity from use of current liabilities is largely due to its being free of interest costs. The advantage of $8,967,000 accruing from the use of long-term debt is substantially due to the tax deductability of interest. Since the preferred dividends are not tax deductible, the unimpressive return on total assets of 5.45 percent resulted in a disadvantage to the common equity of $636,000. The value of tax deferrals can be clearly seen in this case where the use of cost-free funds amounted to an annual advantage of $5,533,000.

We can now carry this analysis further (all dollar amounts in thousands):

The return on the common stockholder equity is as follows:

$$\frac{\text{Net Income less Preferred Dividends}}{\text{Common Stockholders' Equity}} = \frac{61,661^6}{698,917} = 8.8\%$$

The net advantage which the common equity reaped from the working of financial leverage (Exhibit 19–6) is $23,495.

As a percentage of the common stockholders' equity, this advantage is computed as follows:

$$\frac{\begin{array}{c}\text{Earnings in excess of compensation}\\ \text{to outside suppliers of funds}\end{array}}{\text{Common Stockholders' Equity}} = \frac{\$23,495}{\$698,917} = 3.36\%$$

The return on common stockholders' equity can now be viewed as being composed as follows:

Return on assets 5.47%
Leverage advantage accruing to common equity 3.36
Return on common equity 8.8%

QUESTIONS

1. Why is "return on investment (ROI)" one of the most valid measures of enterprise performance? How is this measure used by the financial analyst?

2. How is ROI used as an internal management tool?

3. Discuss the validity of excluding "nonproductive" assets from the asset base used in the computation of ROI. Under what circumstances is the exclusion of intangible assets from the asset base warranted?

4. Why is interest added back to net income when the ROI is computed on total assets?

5. Under what circumstances may it be proper to consider convertible debt as equity capital in the computation of ROI?

---

[6] Ties in (except for rounding difference) with total income accruing to common stockholders in Exhibit 19–6.

6. Why must the net income figure used in the computation of ROI be adjusted to reflect the asset base (denominator) used in the computation?

7. What is the relationship between ROI and sales?

8. Company A acquired Company B because the latter had a record of profitability (net income to sales ratio) exceeding that of its industry. After the acquisition took place a major stockholder complained that the acquisition resulted in a low return on investment. Discuss the possible reasons for his complaint.

9. Company X's profitability is 2 percent of sales. Company Y has a turnover of assets of 12. Both companies have ROIs of 6 percent which is considered unsatisfactory by industry standards. What is the asset turnover of Company X and what is the profitability ratio of Company Y? What action would you advise to the managements of the respective companies?

10. What is the purpose of measuring the asset utilization of different asset categories?

11. What factors enter into the evaluation of the ROI measures?

12. How is the equity growth rate computed? What does it signify?

13. How is the "financial leverage index" computed? What is the significance of a financial leverage index reading of 1?

14. *a.* What is "equity turnover" and how is it related to the rate of return on equity?

   b. "Growth in per share earnings generated from an increase in equity turnover probably cannot be expected to continue indefinitely." Do you agree or disagree? Explain briefly, bringing out in your answer the alternative causes of an increase in equity turnover. (C.F.A.)

20

ANALYSIS OF RESULTS OF OPERATIONS—I

THE SIGNIFICANCE OF INCOME STATEMENT ANALYSIS

The income statement presents in summarized fashion the results of operations of an enterprise. These results, in turn, represent the major reason for the existence of a profit-seeking entity, and they are important determinants of its value and solvency.

As was brought out in the discussion of objectives of financial analysis in Chapter 3, some of the most important decisions in security analysis and credit evaluation are based on an evaluation of the income statements. To the security analyst income is often the single most important determinant of security values, and hence the measurement and the projection of income are among his most important analytical objectives. Similarly, to the credit grantor income and funds or cash provided by operations are the most natural as well as the most desirable source of interest and principal repayment. In almost all other aspects of financial analysis the evaluation and projection of operating results assume great importance.

THE MAJOR OBJECTIVES OF INCOME ANALYSIS

In the evaluation of the income of an enterprise the analyst is particularly interested in an answer to the following questions:

1. What is the relevant net income of the enterprise and what is its quality?
2. What elements in the income statement can be used and relied upon for purposes of earnings forecasting?

3. How stable are the major elements of income and expense and what is their trend?
4. What is the "earning power" of the enterprise?

What is the relevant net income of the enterprise?

Based on the simple proposition that net income is the excess of revenues over costs and expenses during an accounting period, many people, including astute professional analysts, are exasperated at the difficulties they encounter in their search for the "true earnings" or the "real earnings" of an enterprise.

Why, they ask, should it be possible for so many different "acceptable" figures of "net income" to flow out of one set of circumstances? Given the economic events which the enterprise experienced during a given period, is there not only *one* "true" result, and is it not the function of accountancy to identify and measure such result?

Those who have studied Part II of this text will know why the answer to the last question must be "no". In this chapter, dealing with the analysis of income, it is appropriate to summarize *why* this is so.

"Net income" is not a specific quantity. Net income is not a specific flow awaiting the perfection of a flawless meter with which it can be precisely measured. There are a number of reasons for this:

1. The determination of income is dependent on estimates regarding the outcome of future events. This peering into the future is basically a matter of judgment involving the assessment of probabilities based on facts and estimates.

While the judgment of skilled and experienced professionals, working on the basis of identical data and information, can be expected to fall within a narrow range, it will nevertheless *vary* within such a range. The estimates involve the allocation of revenues and costs as between the present and the future. Put another way, they involve the determination of the future utility and usefulness of many categories of unexpired costs and of assets as well as the estimation of future liabilities and obligations.

2. The accounting principles governing the determination and measurement of income at any given time are the result of the cumulative experience of the accounting profession, of regulatory agencies, of businessmen, and others. They reflect a momentary equilibrium which is based partly on knowledge and experience and partly on the compromise of widely differing views on methods of measurement. Chapter 10 indicates the great variety of these views. While the accounting profession has moved to narrow the range of acceptable alternative measurement principles, alternatives nevertheless remain; and their complete elimination in the near future is unlikely.

3. Beyond the problem of honest differences in estimation and other judgments, as well as of the variety of alternative acceptable principles, is also the problem arising from the diverse ways in which the judgments and principles are applied.

Theoretically, the independent professional accountant should be concerned first and foremost with the fair presentation of the financial statements. He should make accounting a "neutral" science which gives expression and effect to economic events but does not itself affect the results presented. To this end he should choose from among alternative principles those most applicable to the circumstances and should disclose all facts, favorable and adverse, which may affect the user's decision.

In fact, the accounting profession as a whole has not yet reached such a level of independence and detachment of judgment. It is subject to the powerful pressures on the part of managements who have, or at least feel that they have, a vital interest in the way in which results of operations are presented. The auditors are most vulnerable to pressures in those areas of accounting where widely differing alternatives are equally acceptable and where accounting theory is still unsettled. Thus, they may choose the lowest level of acceptable practice rather than that which is most appropriate and fair in the circumstances. Although relatively less frequent, cases of malpractice and collusion in outright deception by independent accountants nevertheless still surface from time to time.

The analyst cannot ignore these possibilities, must be aware of them and be ever alert to them. It calls for constant vigilance in the analysis of audited data, particularly when there is reason to suspect a lack of independence and objectivity in the application of accounting principles.

In addition to the above reasons which are inherent in the accounting process, there exists another reason why there cannot be such a thing as an absolute measure of "real earnings." It is that financial statements are general-purpose presentations designed to serve the diverse needs of many users. Consequently, a single figure of "net income" cannot be relevant to all users, and that means that the analyst must use this figure and the additional information disclosed in the financial statements and elsewhere as a starting point and adjust it so as to arrive at a "net income" figure which meets his particular interests and objectives.

ILLUSTRATION 1.   To the buyer of an income-producing property, the depreciation expense figure which is based on the seller's cost is not relevant. In order to estimate the net income he can derive from such property, depreciation based on the expected purchase price of the property must be substituted.

ILLUSTRATION 2.   To the analyst who exercises independent judgment and uses knowledge of the company he is analyzing and the industry of which it is a part, the reported "net income" marks the start of his analysis. He adjusts the "net income" figure for changes in income and expense items which he judges to be warranted. These may include, for example, estimates of bad debts, of depreciation, and of research costs as well as the treatment of gains and losses which are labeled "extraordinary." Comparisons with other companies may call for similar adjustments so that the data can be rendered comparable.

From the above discussion it should be clear that the determination of *a* figure of "net income" is from the point of view of the analyst secondary to the objective of being able to find in the income statement all the disclosures needed in order to arrive at an income figure which is relevant for the purpose at hand.

The questions regarding the quality of earnings, of what elements in the income statement can be relied on for forecasting purposes, of what the stability and the trend of the earning elements are, and finally, of what the "earning power" of the enterprise is, will all be considered in Chapter 22.

We shall now proceed to examine the specific tools which are useful in the analysis of the various components of the income statement.

ANALYSIS OF COMPONENTS OF THE INCOME STATEMENT

The analysis of the income statements of an enterprise can be conceived as being undertaken at two levels: (1) obtaining an understanding of the accounting principles used and of their implication and (2) using the appropriate tools of income statement analysis.

Accounting principles used and their implication

The analyst must have a thorough understanding of the principles of income, cost, and expense accounting and measurement employed by the enterprise. Moreover, since most assets, with the exception of cash and receivables actually collectible, represent costs deferred to the future, the analyst must have a good understanding of the principles of asset and liability measurements employed by the enterprise so that he can relate them to the income accounting of the enterprise as a means of checking the validity of that accounting. Finally, he must understand and assess the implications which the use of one accounting principle, as opposed to another, has on the measurement of the income of an enterprise and its comparison to that of other enterprises.

Most chapters in Part II of this work deal with this important phase of financial statement analysis.

Tools of income statement analysis

The second level of analysis consists of applying the appropriate tools of analysis to the components of the income statement and the interpretation of the results shown by these analytical measures. The application of these tools is aimed at achieving the objectives of the analysis of results of operations mentioned earlier, such as the projection of income, the assessment of its stability and quality, and the estimation of earning power.

The remainder of this chapter will be devoted to an examination of these tools and to the interpretation of the results achieved through their use.

THE ANALYSIS OF SALES AND REVENUES

The analysis of sales and revenues is centered on answers to these basic questions:

1. What are the major sources of revenue?
2. How stable are these sources and what is their trend?
3. How is the earning of revenue determined and how is it measured?

Major sources of revenue

Knowledge of major sources of revenues (sales) is important in the analysis of the income statement particularly if the analysis is that of a

EXHIBIT 20–1

Analysis of sales by product line over time

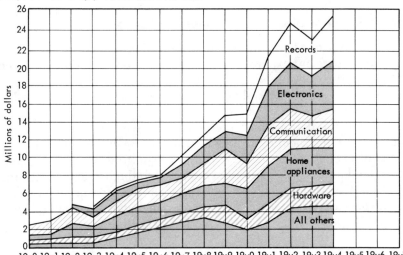

EXHIBIT 20–2

	Year ended				
	Sept. 25, 19X0	Sept. 24, 19X1	Sept. 29, 19X2	Sept. 28, 19X3	Sept. 27, 19X4
Net sales	(dollar amounts in thousands)				
Mining systems equipment	$133,927	$149,673	$157,096	$145,889	$191,345
Industrial and general products	76,971	72,699	67,964	84,806	97,634
Air pollution control equipment	28,391	40,610	62,679	58,702	55,811
Ore processing and petroleum equipment	34,113	37,868	36,062	38,784	51,652
Total	$273,402	$300,850	$323,801	$328,181	$396,442
*Income before income taxes and extraordinary items**					
Mining systems equipment	$ 15,869	$ 20,434	$ 19,622	$ 13,301	$ 20,038
Industrial and general products	5,524	2,647	2,304	8,216	9,120
Air pollution control equipment	2,560	3,636	(1,852)	(2,747)	663
Ore processing and petroleum equipment	3,907	4,507	3,610	2,839	5,823
Total	$ 27,860	$ 31,224	$ 23,684	$ 21,609	$ 35,644

* Generally, corporate costs and expenses have been allocated to each of the lines of business on the basis of sales or investment employed depending on the nature of the item.

multimarket enterprise. Each major market or product line may have its own separate and distinct growth pattern, profitability, and future potential.

The best way to analyze the composition of revenues is by means of a common-size statement which shows the percentage of each major class of revenue to the total. This information can also be portrayed graphically on an absolute dollar basis as shown in Exhibit 20–1. With inclusion of an increasing amount of product line information in published financial statements the external analyst will be able to obtain more readily the data necessary for this analysis. Exhibit 20–2 presents an example of disclosure in a prospectus.

FINANCIAL REPORTING BY DIVERSIFIED ENTERPRISES

The user of the financial statements of diversified enterprises faces, in addition to the usual problems and pitfalls of financial analysis, the problem of sorting out and understanding the impact which the different individual segments of the business have on the sum total of reported results of operations and financial condition. The author of an important study in the reporting by diversified companies has defined a conglomerate company as follows:

. . . one which is so managerially decentralized, so lacks operational integration, or has such diversified markets that it may experience rates of profitability, degrees of risk, and opportunities for growth which vary within the company to such an extent that an investor requires information about these variations in order to make informed decisions.[1]

Reasons for the need for data by significant enterprise segments

The above definition suggests some of the most significant reasons why financial analysts require as much information and detailed data as possible about the various segments of an enterprise. The analysis, evaluation, projection, and valuation of earnings requires that these be broken down into categories which share similar characteristics of variability, growth potential, and risk. Similarly, the asset structure and the financing requirements of various segments of an enterprise can vary significantly and thus require separate analysis and evaluation. Thus, the credit grantor may be interested in knowing which segments of an enterprise provide funds and which are net users of funds.

TABLE 20–1
Earnings contribution and growth rates by industry segments

Industry	Earnings contributions (in $000)	Growth rate of earnings contribution over the past 3 years (in %)
Leisure time:		
1. Camp equipment	100	11
2. Fishing equipment	50	2
3. Boats	72	15
4. Sporting goods	12	3
	234	
Agribusiness:		
1. Milk processing	85	2
2. Canning	72	8
3. Chicken farming	12	15
	169	
Education:		
1. Text publishing	40	3
2. Papers and supplies	17	6
	57	
Total	460	

---

[1] R. K. Mautz, "Identification of the Conglomerate Company," *Financial Executive,* July 1967, p. 26.

TABLE 20–2
Segmented earnings contribution matrix

	Growth rate (in %)			
Industry	0–5	5–10	10–15	Total
Leisure time	$ 62	$ 0	$172	$234
Agribusiness	85	72	12	169
Education	40	17	0	57
Total	$187	$89	$184	$460

The composition of an enterprise, the relative size and profitability of its various segments, the ability of management to make profitable acquisitions, and the overall performance of management represents additional important information which the analyst seeks from its segmented data.[2] As will be seen from the discussion in Chapter 22, among the best ways to construct an earnings forecast is to build the projections, to the extent possible, segment by segment.

The evaluation of the growth potential of earnings requires that as much information as possible be obtained about the different product lines or segments which make up the aggregate earnings. Rappaport and Lerner have illustrated the use of a segmented earnings contribution matrix which may prove useful in an assessment of earnings quality and growth potential, as well as in the valuation of aggregate earnings.[3] These are shown in Tables 20–1 and 20–2.

Disclosure of "line of business" data

The degree of informative disclosure about the results of operations and the asset base of segments of a business can vary widely. Full disclosure would call for providing detailed income statements, statements of financial position, and statements of changes in financial position for each significant segment. This is rarely found in practice because of the difficulty of obtaining such breakdowns internally, and also because of management's reluctance to divulge information which could harm the enterprise's competitive position. Short of the disclosure of complete financial statements by business segment, a great variety of partial detail has been suggested.

[2] D. W. Collins in a study of 150 multisegment firms found that "SEC product-line revenue and profit disclosures together with industry sales projections published in various government sources provide significantly more accurate estimates of future total-entity sales and earnings than do those procedures that rely totally on consolidated data." *Journal of Accounting Research,* Spring 1976, pp. 163–77.

[3] A. Rappaport and E. M. Lerner, *A Framework for Financial Reporting by Diversified Companies* (New York: National Association of Accountants, 1969), pp. 18–19.

Income statement data

Revenues only. In most enterprises this should not present great difficulties.

Gross profit. This involves complex problems of interdivisional transfer pricing as well as allocation of indirect overhead costs.

Contribution margin. Contribution margin reporting (see also Chapter 21) is based on assigning to each segment the revenues, costs, and expenses for which that segment is solely responsible. It is a very useful concept in management accounting, but for purposes of public reporting of segment data it presents problems because there are no generally accepted methods of cost allocation and, consequently, they can vary significantly from company to company and even within one enterprise. Disclosure of allocation methods, while helpful, will not remove all the problems facing the user of such data.

Net income (after full cost allocation). The further down the income statement we report by segment, the more pervasive and the more complex the allocation procedures become. Reporting segment net income would require allocating all joint expenses to each specific business activity on some rational basis, even though they may not be directly related to any particular one.

Balance sheet data

A breakdown by segments of assets employed would be needed in an assessment of the efficiency of operations by segment, in the evaluation of segmental management, as well as in the computation of divisional return on investment.

In most companies only certain assets, such as, for example, plant and equipment, inventories, and certain intangibles, are identified directly with a specific segment. An allocation of all assets would have to be arbitrary since in many enterprises cash, temporary investments, and even receivables are centralized at the group or corporate headquarters level.

Research studies

Interest in the subject of reporting by diversified companies has sparked research efforts into the types of disclosures which are necessary and feasible and the problems related thereto.[4] The most exten-

---

[4] See Morton Backer and Walter B. McFarland, *External Reporting for Segments of a Business* (New York: National Association of Accountants, 1968). Also see Robert T. Sprouse, "Diversified Views about Diversified Companies," *Journal of Accounting Research*, Vol. 7, No. 1 (Spring 1969), pp. 137–59; and A. Rappaport and E. H. Lerner, *A Framework for Financial Reporting by Diversified Companies* (New York: National Association of Accountants, 1969).

sive research effort was that undertaken by Professor R. K. Mautz[5] and in 1974 the FASB published an extensive Discussion Memorandum on the subject.

Statement of Financial Accounting Standards 14

In late 1976, the FASB issued *Statement of Financial Accounting Standards No. 14,* "Financial Reporting for Segments of a Business Enterprise." This *Statement,* which is effective for fiscal years beginning on or after 12/16/76, establishes requirements for disclosures to be made in company financial statements concerning information about operations in different industries, foreign operations, export sales, and major customers.

The *Statement* recognizes that evaluation of risk and return is the central element of investment and lending decisions. Since an enterprise operating in various industry segments or geographic areas may have different rates of profitability, degrees and types of risk and opportunities for growth, disaggregated information will assist analysts in analyzing the uncertainties surrounding the timing and amount of expected cash flows—and hence the risks—related to an investment in or a loan to an enterprise that operates in different industries or areas of the world.

The *Statement* requires companies to report in their financial statements the revenues, operating profit (revenue less operating expenses), and identifiable assets of each significant industry segment of their operations. Certain other related disclosures are required. The *Statement* does not prescribe methods of accounting for transfer pricing or cost allocation. However, it does require that the methods in use be disclosed.

A segment is regarded as significant, therefore reportable, under the *Statement* if its sales, operating profit, or identifiable assets are 10 percent or more of the related combined amounts for all of a company's industry segments.[6] To ensure that the industry segments for which a company reports information represent a substantial portion of the company's overall operations, the *Statement* requires that the

---

[5] R. K. Mautz, *Financial Reporting by Diversified Companies* (New York: Financial Executives Research Foundation, 1968).

[6] Specifically, an industry segment is significant if in the latest period for which statements are presented:

1. Its revenue is 10 percent or more of the *combined* revenue of all industry segments; or
2. Its operating profit (loss) is 10 percent or more of the greater of: (*a*) the combined operating profit of all segments that did not incur a loss, or (*b*) the combined operating loss of all segments that did incur a loss; or
3. Its identifiable assets are 10 percent or more of the combined identifiable assets of all industry segments.

combined sales of all segments for which information is reported shall be at least 75 percent of the company's total sales. The Statement also suggests ten as a practical limit to the number of industry segments for which a company reports information. If that limit is exceeded, it may be appropriate to combine certain segments into broader ones to meet the 75 percent test with a practical number of segments.

Under SFAS 14, if a company derives 10 percent or more of its revenue from sales to any single customer, that fact and the amount of revenue from each such customer also must be disclosed.

The Statement provides guidelines for determining a company's foreign operations and export sales and for grouping operations by geographic areas. Information similar to that required for industry segments also is required for a company's operations in different geographic areas of the world.

SEC reporting requirements

In 1969 the SEC amended its registration forms S-1 and S-7 under the 1933 Act, and Form 10 under the 1934 Act. The effect of the amendment was to include a requirement for comprehensive lines of business information to be disclosed by registrants who, with their subsidiaries, are engaged in more than one line of business.

In 1970 the Commission revised its annual report form (Form 10-K) to include a requirement of annual reporting of line of business information identical with the requirements referred to above.

These provisions are intended to elicit information with respect to those lines of business that contributed, during either of the last two fiscal years, a certain proportion of (1) the total of sales and revenues, or (2) income before income taxes and extraordinary items and without deduction of loss resulting from operations of any line of business. For companies with total sales and revenues of more than $50 million, the proportion is 10 percent; for smaller companies, 15 percent. Similar disclosure is also required with respect to any line of business which resulted in a loss of 10 percent or more (15 percent or more for smaller companies) of income before income taxes, extraordinary items, and loss operations. The period to be covered by the information is each of a maximum of the last five fiscal years.

In 1974 these reporting requirements were extended to annual reports to security holders of companies filing with the SEC. It is likely that, following issuance of SFAS 14, the SEC will conform its requirements to those of that statement.

Implications for analysis

The increasing complexity of diversified business entities and the loss of identity which acquired companies suffer in the published financial statements of conglomerates have created serious problems for the financial analyst.

The disclosure requirements of SFAS 14 and those of the SEC which preceded them will increase the amount of segmental information available for analysis. However the analyst will have to be very careful in his assessment of the reliability of the data on which he bases his conclusions.

The more specific and detailed the information provided is the more likely it is to be based on extensive allocations of costs and expenses. Allocation of common costs, as practiced for internal accounting purposes, are often based on such concepts as "equity," "reasonableness," and "acceptability to managers." These concepts have often little relevance to the objective of financial analysis.

Bases of allocating joint expenses are largely arbitrary and subject to differences of opinions as to their validity and precision. Some specific types of joint expenses which fall into this category are general and administrative expenses of central headquarters, research and development costs, certain selling costs, advertising, interest, pension costs, and federal and state income taxes.

There are, at present, no generally accepted principles of cost and expense allocation or any general agreement on the methods by which the costs of one segment should be transferred to another segment in the same enterprise. Moreover, the process of formulating such principles or of reaching such agreement has barely begun. The analyst who uses segmented data must bear these limitations firmly in mind.

In SFAS 14 the board has, in effect, recognized the above described limitations and realities. Consequently the disclosure of profit contribution (revenue less only those operating expenses that are directly traceable to a segment), which was proposed in the exposure draft issued for public comment was not required in the final Statement. Similarly, the board concluded that revenue from intersegment sales or transfers shall be accounted for on whatever basis is used by the enterprise to price intersegment sales or transfers. No single basis was prescribed or proscribed.

Moreover, the board concluded that certain items of revenue and expense either do not relate to segments or cannot always be allocated to segments on the basis of objective evidence and consequently there is no requirement in SFAS 14 that net income be disclosed for reportable segments. The board also noted in the Statement that "determination of an enterprise's industry segments must depend to a considerable extent on the judgment of the management of the enterprise."

The implication for analysts of this lack of firmer guidelines and definitions is that segmental disclosures are and must be treated as "soft" information which is subject to manipulation and pre-interpretation by managements. Consequently, such data must be treated with a healthy degree of skepticism and conclusions can be derived from them only through the exercise of great care as well as analytical skill.

Stability and trend of revenues

The relative trend of sales of various product lines or revenues from services can best be measured by means of trend percentages as illustrated in Table 20-3.

TABLE 20-3
Trend percentage of sales by product line (19X1 = 100)

	19X1	19X2	19X3	19X4	19X5
Product A	100	110	114	107	121
Product B	100	120	135	160	174
Product C	100	98	94	86	74
Service A	100	101	92	98	105

Sales indices of various products lines can be correlated and compared to composite industry figures or to product sales trends of specific competitors.

Important considerations bearing on the quality and stability of the sales and revenues trend include:

1. The sensitivity of demand for the various products to general business conditions.
2. The ability of the enterprise to anticipate trends in demand by the introduction of new products and services as a means of furthering sales growth and as replacement of products for which demand is falling.
3. Degree of customer concentration (now required to be disclosed by SFAS 14), dependence on major customers, as well as demand stability of major customer groups.[7]
4. Degree of product concentration and dependence on a single industry.
5. Degree of dependence on relatively few star salesmen.
6. Degree of geographical diversification of markets.

---

[7] Statement on Auditing Standards 6 (AICPA) requires disclosure of the economic dependency of a company on one or more parties with which it transacts a significant volume of business, such as a sole or major customer, supplier, franchisor, franchisee, distributor, borrower or lender.

MANAGEMENT'S DISCUSSION AND ANALYSIS OF THE SUMMARY OF EARNINGS

A significant new concept of disclosure from the analyst's point of view was instituted in 1974 with the promulgation by the SEC of *ASR 159.*

The release is concerned with additional disclosures of an interpretative or explanatory nature which are necessary to enable investors to understand and evaluate significant period-to-period changes in the various items included in the summary of earnings (or summary of operations). A separate section to be captioned "Management's Discussion and Analysis of the Summary of Earnings" must contain an explanation of such changes as well as changes in accounting principles or practices or in the method of their application that have a material effect on reported net income. An explanation is also required when due to the presence of "material facts" historical operations or earnings as reported are not indicative of future operations or earnings.

To help determine whether a change should be discussed or elaborated upon, the release offers the following guide as to materiality:

A change in an item of revenue or expense is generally required to be discussed when it increased or decreased by more than 10 percent compared to its level in a prior period presented *and* it also increased or decreased by more than 2 percent of the average net income or loss for the most recent three years presented. In the calculation of the three year average, loss years are excluded; if losses were incurred in each of the most recent years, the average net loss shall be used for purposes of this test of materiality.

If a change is immaterial under the foregoing test, it should still be discussed or explained if that is necessary for a full understanding of the earnings summary. Conversely, if management finds that a change exceeds the percentage criteria but need not be explained, it must furnish to the SEC a written *supplemental* statement explaining why, in its opinion, such explanation is not necessary.

While it is recognized that the release cannot cover all situations which may arise it cites the following as examples of the types of subjects which should be covered:

1. Material changes in product mix or in the relative profitability of lines of business.
2. Material changes in advertising, research, development, product introduction or other discretionary costs.
3. The acquisition or disposition of a material asset other than in the ordinary course of business.
4. Material and unusual charges or gains, including credits or charges associated with discontinuation of operations.

5. Material changes in assumptions underlying deferred costs and the plan for amortization of such costs.
6. Material changes in assumed investment return and in actuarial assumptions used to calculate contributions to pension funds.
7. The closing of a material facility or material interruption of business or completion of a material contract.

Disclosure of the dollar amount of each item or change covered and its effect on reported results as well as a discussion of causes of material changes in each item are also required.

The discussion of "material facts" is not intended to be retrospective only. Such discussion must also cover material factors known to management which are likely to influence, favorably or unfavorably *future* trends and results. However, a discussion of such factors may be in broad terms only; no specific quantitative estimates or projections are required.

Implications for analysis

In the explanatory portion of the release the commission staff sets forth the following objectives of the required narrative disclosure:

a. They should enable investors to appraise the "quality of earnings".
b. They should facilitate an understanding of the extent to which changes in accounting as well as changes in business activity affect the comparability of year-to-year data.
c. They should facilitate an assessment of the source as well as the probability of recurrence of net income (or loss).

While *ASR 159* leaves to the discretion of management the determination of how to communicate most effectively to the reader the significant elements which are necessary for a clear understanding of the company's financial results, it is emphasized that a mechanistic approach which uses "boiler plate or compliance jargon" should be avoided. Thus, the aim is meaningful disclosure in narrative form by those in charge of operations who are really in a position to know and who can supply significant additional details not usually found in the financial statements.

Since the issuance of *ASR 159*, experience has shown that the quality and the depth of the disclosures is uneven. The analyst, without having to take them at face value, can nevertheless use them as valuable analytical supplements for both the information that they provide and the insights into the thinking and the attitude of managements which they afford.

Methods of revenue recognition and measurement

Chapter 10 contains a discussion of the variety of methods of revenue recognition and measurement which coexist in various industries. Some of these methods are more conservative than others. The analyst must understand the income recognition methods used by the enterprise and their implications as well as the methods used by companies with which the results of the enterprise under analysis are being compared. A foremost consideration is whether the revenue recognition method in use accurately reflects an entity's economic performance and earnings activities.

QUESTIONS

1. What are the major objectives of income analysis?
2. Why can "net income" not be a single specific quantity?
3. Two levels can be identified in the analysis of the income statement. Name them.
4. Why is knowledge of major sources of revenue (sales) of an enterprise important in the analysis of the income statement?
5. Why are information and detailed data about the segments of diversified enterprises important to financial analysts?
6. What are the major provisions of SFAS 14?
7. Disclosure of various types of information by "line of business" has been proposed. Comment on the value of such information and the feasibility of providing it in published financial statements.
8. To what limitations of public segmental data must the analyst be alert?
9. Which important considerations have a bearing on the quality and the stability of a sales and revenue trend?
10. *a.* What is the test, offered by *ASR 159*, of the materiality of a change that should be discussed by management in its discussion and analysis of the summary of earnings?
    b. If a change is immaterial under the above test, should it still be discussed?
11. Cite some of the examples of the types of subjects which should be covered in the management's discussion and analysis of the summary of earnings.
12. What are the objectives of discussions required by *ASR 159*?

21

ANALYSIS OF RESULTS OF OPERATIONS—II

This chapter continues and concludes the discussion of the analysis of results of operations begun in the preceding chapter.

ANALYSIS OF COST OF SALES

In most enterprises[1] the cost of goods or services sold is, as a percentage of sales, the single most significant cost category. As the discussion in Chapter 10 shows, the methods of determining cost of sales encompass a wide variety of alternatives. Moreover, there is, particularly in unregulated industries, no agreed-to uniform cost classification method which would result in a clear and generally accepted distinction among such basic cost and expense categories as cost of sales, administrative, general, sales, and financial expenses. This is particularly true in the classification of general and administrative expenses. Thus, in undertaking cost comparisons the analyst must be ever alert to methods of classification and the effect they can have on the validity of comparisons within an enterprise or among enterprises.

GROSS PROFIT

The excess of sales over the cost of sales is the gross profit or gross margin. It is commonly expressed as a percentage:

---

[1] Exceptions can be found, for example, in some land sales companies where selling and other costs may actually exceed the cost of land sold.

Sales	$10,000,000	100%
Cost of sales	7,200,000	72
Gross profit	$ 2,800,000	28%

The gross profit percentage is a very important operating ratio. In the above example the gross profit is $2,800,000 or 28 percent of sales. From this amount all other costs and expenses must be recovered and any net income that is earned is the balance remaining after all expenses. Unless an enterprise has an adequate gross profit, it can be neither profitable nor does it have an adequate margin with which to finance such essential future-directed discretionary expenditures as research and development and advertising. Gross profit margins vary from industry to industry depending on such factors as competition, capital investment, the level of costs other than direct costs of sales which must be covered by the gross profit, and so forth.

Factors in the analysis of gross profit

In the analysis of gross profit the analyst will pay particular attention to—

1. The factors which account for the variation in sales and costs of sales.
2. The relationship between sales and costs of sales and management's ability to control this relationship.

ANALYSIS OF CHANGES IN GROSS MARGIN[2]

A detailed analysis of changes in gross margin can usually be performed only by an internal analyst because it requires access to data such as the number of physical units sold, unit sales prices, as well as unit costs. Such data are usually not provided in published financial statements. Moreover, unless the enterprise sells a single product, this analysis requires detailed data by product line. The external analyst, unless he has special influence on the company analyzed, will usually not have access to the data required for the analysis of gross margin.

Despite the above limitations to which gross margin analysis is subject, it is instructive to examine its process so that the elements accounting for variations in gross margin can be more fully understood.

---

[2] In this discussion the terms "gross profit" and "gross margin" are used interchangeably. Some writers reserve the term "gross margin" for situations where the cost of goods sold excludes overhead costs, that is, direct costing. This is not the intention here.

EXAMPLE OF ANALYSIS OF CHANGE IN GROSS MARGIN

Company A shows the following data for two years:

| | Unit of measure | Year ended December 31, | | In-crease | De-crease |
		19X1	19X2		
1. Net sales	Thousands of dollars	657.6	687.5	29.9	
2. Cost of sales	Thousands of dollars	237.3	245.3	8.0	
3. Gross margin	Thousands of dollars	420.3	442.2	21.9	
4. Units of product sold	Thousands	215.6	231.5	15.9	
5. Selling price per unit (1 ÷ 4)	Dollars	3.05	2.97		.08
6. Cost per unit (2 ÷ 4)	Dollars	1.10	1.06		.04

Based on the above data, Exhibit 21–1 presents an analysis of the change in gross margin of $21,900 from 19X1 to 19X2. This analysis is

EXHIBIT 21–1

COMPANY A
Statement Accounting for Variation in Gross Margin
Between Years 19X1 and 19X2

Thousands of dollars

I. Analysis of variation in sales
    (1) Variation due to change in volume of products sold
        Change in volume (15.9) × 19X1 unit selling price (3.05) $48.5
    (2) Variation due to change in selling price
        Change in selling price (−$0.08) × 19X1 sales
          volume (215.6) ....   −17.2

                                                    $31.3
    (3) Variation due to combined change in sales volume
        (15.9) and unit sales price (−$0.08) .... − 1.3

    Increase in net sales $30.0*

II. *Analysis of variation in cost of sales*
    (1) Variation due to change in volume of products sold:
        Change in volume (15.9) × 19X1 cost per unit ($1.10) $17.5
    (2) Variation due to change in cost per unit sold: change in
        cost per unit (−$0.04) × 19X1 sales volume (215.6) .... − 8.6

                                                    $ 8.9
    (3) Variation due to combined change in volume (15.9)
        and cost per unit (−$0.04) .... − .6

    Increase in cost of sales .... $ 8.3*

        Net variation in gross margin $21.7*

* Differences are due to rounding.

based on the principle of focusing on one element of change at a time. Thus, in Exhibit 21–1 the analysis of variation in sales involves the following steps:

Step 1:   We focus on the year-to-year change in volume while *assuming* that the unit selling price remained unchanged at the former, 19X1, level. Since both the volume change (15.9) and the unit selling price ($3.05) are positive, the resulting product ($48.5) is positive.

Step 2:   We focus now on the change in selling price which represents a year-to-year decrease (−$0.08) and *assume* the volume (215.6) to be unchanged from the prior year level so as to single out the change due to price change. Algebraically here the multiplication of a negative (price change) by a positive (volume) results in a negative product (−$17.2).

Step 3:   We must now recognize that the *assumptions* used in steps 1 and 2 above, that is, that the volume remained unchanged while the unit price changed and vice versa, are temporary expedients used to single out major causes for change. To complete the computation we must recognize that by making these assumptions we left out the *combined* change in volume and unit price. The change in volume of 15.9 represents an *increase* and, consequently, is *positive*. The unit selling price change represents a *decrease* (−$0.08) and hence is *negative*. As a result the product is negative (−$1.3).

Step 4:   Adding up the—

Variation due to volume change $48.5
Variation due to price change .... −17.2
Combined change of volume and unit price .... − 1.3

We account for the causes behind the sales increase $30.0

The analysis of variation in the cost of sales follows the same principles.

Interpretation of changes in gross margin

The analysis of variation in gross margin is useful in identifying major causes of change in the gross margin. These changes can consist of one or a combination of the following factors:

1.   Increase in sales volume.
2.   Decrease in sales volume.
3.   Increase in unit sales price.
4.   Decrease in unit sales price.
5.   Increase in cost per unit.
6.   Decrease in cost per unit.

The presence of the "combined change of volume and unit sales price" and the "combined volume and unit cost" in the analysis presents no problem in interpretation since their amount is always minor in relation to the main causative factors of change.

The interpretation of the results of the analysis of gross margin involves the identification of the major factors responsible for change in the gross margin and an evaluation of the reasons for change in the factors. Such an analysis can also focus on the most feasible areas of improvement (i.e., volume, price, or cost) and the likelihood of realizing such improvements. For example, if it is determined that the major reason for a decline in gross margin is a decline in unit sales prices and that it reflects a situation of overcapacity in the enterprise's industry with attendant price cutting, then the situation is a serious one because of the limited control management has on such a development. If, on the other hand, the deterioration in the gross margin is found to be due to increases in unit costs, then this may be a situation over which management can exercise a larger measure of control and, given its ability to do so, an improvement is a more likely possibility.

BREAK-EVEN ANALYSIS

The second level of cost analysis is importantly concerned with the relationship between sales and the cost of sales but goes beyond that segment of the income statement. This level encompasses break-even analysis and is concerned with the relationship of sales to most costs, including, but not limited to, the cost of sales.

Concepts underlying break-even analysis

The basic principle underlying break-even analysis is the behavior of costs. Some costs vary directly with sales while others remain essentially constant over a considerable range of sales. The first category of costs is classified as *variable* while the latter are known as *fixed* costs.

The distinction among costs according to their behavior can be best understood within the framework of an example. In order to focus first on the basic data involved and on the technique of break-even analysis, we shall examine it by means of a simple illustration:

An enterprising graduate student saw an opportunity to sell pocket calculators at a financial analysts convention due to take place in his hometown. Upon inquiry he learned that he would have to get a vendor's license from the convention organizing committee at a cost of $10 and that the rental of a room in which to sell would amount to $140. The cost of calculators was to be $3 each with the right to return any that were not sold. The student decided that $8 was the proper sales price per calculator and wondered whether the undertaking will be

worthwhile. As a first step he decided to compute the number of calculators he will have to sell in order to break even.

Equation approach

We start from the elementary proposition that

Sales = Variable Cost + Fixed Costs + Profit (or − Loss)

Since at break even there is neither gain nor loss the equation is

Sales = Variable Cost + Fixed Costs

If we designate the number of calculators which must be sold to
break even as X, we have

$$8X = 3X + 150$$

where

Sales = Unit sales Price (8) × X
Variable Costs = Variable cost per unit (3) × X
Fixed Costs = License fee ($10) + Rental ($140)

These costs are fixed because they will be incurred regardless of the
number of calculators sold.
Solving the equation we get

$$5X = 150$$
$$X = 30 \quad \text{units or calculators}$$
to be sold to break even

In this example the number of calculators to be sold is important
information because the student needs to assess the likelihood of
obtaining the size of demand which will make his venture profitable.
This approach is, however, limited to a single product enterprise.

If, as is common in business, an enterprise sells a mix of goods, the
unit sales break-even computation becomes impracticable and the
focus is on dollar sales. This would be the situation if our student sold
stationery and books in addition to calculators.

This more prevalent break-even computation can be illustrated
with the data already given.

If we designate the dollar sales at break even as Y, we get:

$$Y = \text{Variable cost percentage } Y + \text{Fixed costs}$$
$$= 0.375Y + 150$$
$$0.625Y = 150$$
$$Y = \$240 \text{ (sales at break even)}$$

In this computation the variable cost percentage is the ratio of variable costs ($3) to sales price ($8). This means that each dollar of sales

entails an incurrence of $.375 for variable costs or 37.5 percent of the sales price.

Graphic presentation

Exhibit 21–2 portrays the results attained above in graphic form. A graph drawn to scale will yield a solution approximating in accuracy that obtained by the formula method. Moreover it portrays under one set of assumptions not only the break-even point but also a whole range of profitable operations above that point as well as the losses below it.

EXHIBIT 21–2
Calculator illustration—break-even chart

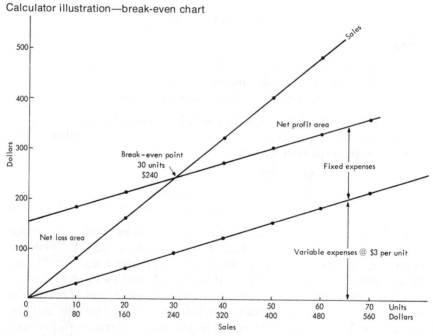

Contribution margin approach

Another technique of break-even analysis which can produce additional insights into the relationship of sales, costs, and profits is the contribution margin approach. It will be illustrated here by means of the foregoing pocket calculator example.

The contribution margin is what is left of the net sales price after deduction of the variable costs. It is from this margin that fixed costs must first be met and after that a profit earned.

Sales price per calculator	$8.00
Variable costs per calculator	3.00
Unit contribution margin	$5.00

Since each unit (calculator) sold contributes $5 to overhead and for profit, the break-even point in units is

$$\frac{\text{Fixed Costs}}{\text{Unit Contribution Margin}} = \frac{\$150}{\$5} = 30 \text{ units}$$

Thus, after 30 units are sold the fixed costs are covered and each additional unit sale yields a profit equal to the unit contribution margin, that is, $5.

If, as is more usual, the break-even point is to be expressed in dollars of sales, the formula involves use of the contribution margin ratio rather than the unit contribution margin. The contribution margin ratio is a percentage relationship computed as follows:

$$\frac{\text{Unit Contribution Margin}}{\text{Unit Sales Price}} = \frac{5}{8} = 0.625 \text{ or } 62.5 \text{ percent}$$

The calculator problem dollar break-even point can now be calculated as follows:

$$\frac{\text{Fixed Costs}}{\text{Contribution Margin Ratio}} = \frac{150}{0.625} = \$240$$

The contribution margin is an important tool in break-even analysis, and its significance will be the subject of further discussion later in this section.

Pocket calculator problem—additional considerations

The break-even technique illustrated above lends itself to a variety of assumptions and requirements. The following are additional illustrations, all using the original data of our example, unless changed assumptions are introduced:

ILLUSTRATION 1: Assume that our student decided that in order to make the venture worthwhile he requires a net profit of $400. How many calculators must be sold to achieve this objective?

$$\text{Sales} = (\text{Variable cost \%})(\text{sales}) + \text{Fixed costs} + \text{Profit}$$
$$S = 0.375S + \$150 + \$400$$
$$0.625S = 550$$
$$S = \$880$$
$$\frac{880}{8} = 110 \text{ units}$$

ILLUSTRATION 2: Assume that the financial analysts convention committee offered to provide the student with a room free of charge if he agreed to imprint on the calculators the Financial Analysts Society's seal. However, this would increase the cost of calculators from $3 to $4 per unit. Under the original assumptions the break-even point was 30 calculators. What should it be if the student accepts the committee's proposal?

Here we have a reduction of fixed costs by $140 and an increase in variable costs of $1 per unit.

If X be the number of calculators sold at break-even point, then:

$$\text{Sales} = \text{Variable costs} + \text{Fixed costs}$$
$$8X = 4X + \$10$$
$$4X = 10$$
$$X = 2.5 \text{ calculators (rounded to 3)}$$

This proposal obviously involves a much lower break-even point and hence reduced risk. However, the lower contribution margin will at higher sales levels reduce total profitability. We can determine at what level of unit sales the original assumption of a $3 per unit variable cost and $150 fixed cost will equal the results of the $4 per unit variable cost and $10 fixed costs.

Let X be the number of units (calculators) sold, then:

$$4X + \$10 = 3X + \$150$$
$$1X = 140$$
$$X = 140 \text{ calculators}$$

Thus, if more than 140 calculators are sold, the alternative which includes the $3 variable cost will be more profitable.

Having examined the break-even analysis technique and some types of decisions for which it is useful, we will now turn to a discussion of the practical difficulties and the theoretical limitations to which this approach is subject.

Break-even technique—problem areas and limitations

The intelligent use of the break-even technique and the drawing of reasonably valid conclusions therefrom depends on a resolution of practical difficulties and on an understanding of the limitations to which the techniques are subject.

Fixed, variable, and semivariable costs. In the foregoing simple examples of break-even analysis, costs were clearly either fixed or variable. In the more complex reality found in practice, many costs are not so clearly separable into fixed and variable categories. That is, they do not either stay constant over a considerable change in sales volume or respond in exact proportion to changes in sales.

We can illustrate this problem by reference to the costs of a food supermarket. As was discussed above, some costs will remain fixed within a certain range of sales. Rent, depreciation, certain forms of maintenance, utilities, and supervisory labor are examples of such fixed costs. The level of fixed costs can, of course, be increased by simple management decision unrelated to the level of sales, for example, the plant superintendent's salary may be increased.

Other costs, such as the cost of merchandise, trading stamps, supplies, and certain labor will vary closely with sales. These costs are truly variable. Certain other costs may, however, contain both fixed and variable elements in them. Examples of such "semivariable" costs are repairs, some materials, indirect labor, fuel, utilities, payroll taxes, and rents which contain a minimum payment provision and are also related to the level of sales. Break-even analysis requires that the variable component of such expenses be separated from the fixed component. This is often a difficult task for the management accountant and an almost impossible task for the outside analyst to perform without the availability of considerable internal data.

Simplifying assumptions in break-even analysis. The estimation of a variety of possible results by means of break-even calculations or charts requires the use of simplifying assumptions. In most cases these simplifying assumptions do not destroy the validity of the conclusions reached. Nevertheless, in reaching such conclusions the analyst must be fully aware of these assumptions and of their possible effect.

The following are some of the more important assumptions implicit in break-even computations:

1. The factors comprising the model, implicit in any given break-even situation, actually behave as assumed, that is,

    a. That the costs have been reasonably subdivided into their fixed and variable components;

    b. That variable costs fluctuate proportionally with volume;

    c. That fixed costs remain fixed over the range relevant to the situation examined; and

    d. That unit selling prices will remain unchanged over the range encompassed by the analysis.

2. In addition, there are certain operating and environmental assumptions which emphasize the static nature of any one break-even computation. It is assumed:

    a. That the mix of sales will remain unchanged,

    b. That efficiency of operations will remain constant,

    c. That prices of costs factors will not change,

    d. That the only factor affecting costs is volume,

    e. That beginning and end of period inventory levels will remain substantially unchanged, and

    f. That there is no substantial change in the general price level during the period.

The formidable array of assumptions enumerated above points out the susceptibility of break-even computations to significant error. Not all the assumptions are, however, equally important, or, if not justified, will have an equal impact on the validity of conclusions. For example, the assumption that the selling price will not change with volume is contrary to economic theory and often is contrary to reality. Thus, the sales line is a curved rather than a linear function. However, the degree of error will depend on the actual degree of deviation from a strict linear relationship. Another basic assumption is that volume is *the* major, if not the only, factor affecting costs. We know, however, that strikes, political developments, legislation, and competition, to name a few other important factors, have a decided influence on costs. The analyst must, consequently, keep these simplifying assumptions firmly in mind and be aware of the dynamic factors which may require modifications in his conclusions.

Break-even analysis—uses and their implications

The break-even approach can be a useful tool of analysis if its limitations are recognized and its applications are kept in proper perspective.

The emphasis on the break-even, that is, zero profit, point is an unfortunate distortion of the objective of this type of analysis. Instead, the break-even situation represents but one point in a flexible set of projections of revenues and of the costs which will be associated with them under a given set of future conditions.

The managerial applications of break-even analysis are many. It is useful, among others, in price determination, expense control, and in the projection of profits. Along with standard cost systems it gives management a basis for pricing decisions under differing levels of activity. In conjunction with flexible budgets it represents a powerful tool of expense control. The break-even chart is also a useful device with which to measure the impact of specific managerial decisions, such as plant expansion and new product introduction or of external influences, on the profitability of operations over various levels of activity.

To financial analysts the function of profit projections is one of vital importance. Moreover, the ability to estimate the impact of profitability of various economic conditions or managerial courses of action is also an extremely important one. Both of these are importantly aided by break-even analysis. The intelligent use of this technique and a thorough understanding of its operation are the factors which account for its importance to the external financial analyst.

Illustration of break-even technique application. Exhibit 21–3 presents the break-even chart of the Multi-Products Company at a

EXHIBIT 21–3
Multi-Products Company
Break-even chart—all operations

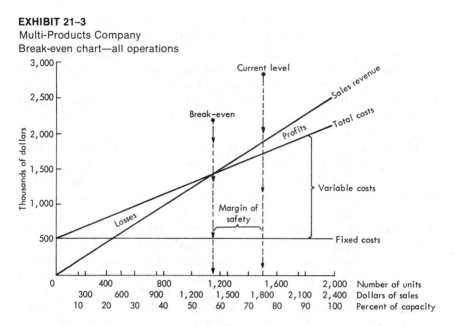

given point in time. It is subject to the various assumptions which were discussed above including that relating to the ability to separate costs into their fixed and variable components.

At break even a very condensed income statement of Multi-Products Company will be as follows:

Sales		$1,387,000
Costs:		
Variable	$887,000	
Fixed	500,000	1,387,000
Net income		0

The variable cost percentage is 887/1387 or about 64 percent. The contribution margin ratio is 36 percent (100 − Variable cost percentage of 64). The variable cost percentage means that on average, out of every dollar of sales 64 cents go to meet variable costs, that is, costs which would not be incurred if the sale did not occur. The contribution margin ratio is basically the complement of the variable cost percentage.

Break-even point:	
Sales	$1,387,000
Units	1,156,000
Average selling price per unit	$1.20

It indicates that each dollar of sales generates a contribution of 36 cents towards meeting fixed expenses and the earning of a profit beyond the break-even point. The contribution margin earned on sales of $1,387,000 is just sufficient to cover the $500,000 in fixed costs. Quite obviously, the lower the fixed costs, the less sales it would take to cover them and the lower the resulting break-even point. In the most unlikely event that the Multi-Products Company would have no fixed costs, that is, all costs varied directly with sales, the company would have no break-even point, that is, it would start making a profit on the very first dollar of sales.

The break-even chart reflects the sale of a given mix of products. Since each product has different cost patterns and profit margins, any significant change in the product mix will result in a change in the break-even point and consequently in a change in the relationship between revenues, costs, and results. Although Exhibit 21–3 shows the number of units on the sales (volume) axis, this figure and the average selling price per unit are of limited significance because they represent averages prevailing as a result of a given mix of products.

The importance of a relatively stable sales mix to the successful application of break-even analysis suggests that this technique cannot be usefully employed in cases where the product mix varies greatly over the short term. Nor, for that matter, can break-even analysis be usefully applied in cases where there are sharp and frequent fluctuations in sales prices or in costs of production, such as raw materials.

Exhibit 21–3 indicates that given the existing mix of products, the present level of fixed costs of $500,000 can be expected to prevail up to a sales level of approximately $2,400,000. This is the point at which 100 percent of theoretical capacity will be reached. The break-even point is at 60 percent of capacity while the current level of sales is at about 75 percent of capacity. This means that when the 100 percent capacity level is reached, the fixed costs may have to undergo an upward revision. If Multi-Products is reluctant to expand its capacity and thus increase its fixed costs and break-even point, assuming that variable costs do not decrease, it may have to consider other alternatives such as:

1. Forgoing an increase in sales.
2. Increasing the number of shifts, which could increase variable costs significantly.
3. Subcontracting some of its work to outsiders, thus forgoing some of the profit of increased activity.

Exhibit 21–3 also presents to the analyst at a glance the company's present position relative to the break-even point. The current level of sales of $1,800,000 is about $413,000 above the break-even point. This is also known as the "safety margin," that is, the margin that separates the company from a no-profit condition. This concept can be expanded to indicate on the chart at what point the company will earn a desired return on investment, at what point the common dividend may be in jeopardy, and at what point the preferred dividend may no longer be covered by current earnings.

It is obvious that the data revealed by a reliably constructed break-even chart or by the application of break-even computations is valuable in profit projection, in the assessment of operating risk, as well as in an evaluation of profit levels under various assumptions regarding future conditions and managerial policies.

Analytical implications of break-even analysis

From the above discussion of a specific situation, such as that illustrated in Exhibit 21–3, we will now turn to a more general review of conclusions which can be derived from break-even analysis.

The concept of operating leverage. Leverage and fixed costs go together. As we have seen in Chapter 18, financial leverage is based on fixed costs of funds for a portion of the resources used by the enterprise. Thus, earnings above that fixed cost magnify the return on the residual funds and vice versa.

The fixed costs of a business enterprise, in the sense in which we have discussed them so far in this chapter, form the basis of the concept of operating leverage. Until an enterprise develops a volume of sales which is sufficient to cover its fixed costs, it will incur a loss. Once it has covered the fixed costs, further increments in volume will result in more than proportionate increases in profitability. The following will illustrate the nature of operating leverage:

Illustration of the working of operating leverage. In a given enterprise the cost structure is as follows:

$$\text{Fixed costs} = \$100,000$$
$$\text{Variable cost percentage} = 60 \text{ percent}$$

The following tabulation presents the profit or loss at successively higher levels of sales and a comparison of relative percentage changes in sales volume and in profitability:

Sales	Variable costs	Fixed costs	Profit (loss)	Percentage increase over preceding step	
				Sales	Profit
$100,000	$ 60,000	$100,000	$(60,000)	—	—
200,000	120,000	100,000	(20,000)	100%	—
250,000	150,000	100,000	—	25	—
300,000	180,000	100,000	20,000	20	Infinite
360,000	216,000	100,000	44,000	20	120%
432,000	259,200	100,000	72,800	20	65%

The working of operating leverage is evident in the above tabulation. Starting at break even, the first 20 percent sales increase resulted in an infinite increase in profits because they started from a zero base. The next 20 percent increase in sales resulted in a 120 percent profit increase over the preceding level while the sales increase that followed resulted in a 65 percent profit increase over the preceding level. The effects of leverage diminish as the sales increase above the break-even level because the bases to which increases in profits are compared get progressively larger.

Leverage, of course, works both ways. It will be noted that a drop in sales from $200,000 to $100,000, representing 50 percent decrease, resulted in a tripling of the loss.

One important conclusion from this to the analyst is that enterprises operating near their break-even point will have relatively larger percentage changes of profits or losses for a given change in volume. On the upside the volatility will, of course, be desirable. On the downside, however, it can result in adverse results which are significantly worse than those indicated by changes in sales volume alone.

Another aspect is operating *potential,* sometimes erroneously referred to as leverage, which derives from a high level of sales accompanied by very low profit margins. The potential here, of course, is the room for improvements in profit margins. Even relatively slight improvements in profit margins, applied on a large sales level, can result in dramatic changes in profits. Thus, the popular reference to a semblance of leverage for what is really a potential for improvement.

Another aspect of the same *potential* occurs when the sales volume *per share* is large. Obviously an improvement in profitability will be translated into larger earnings per share improvements.

The significance of the variable cost percentage

The volatility of profits is also dependent on the variable cost percentage. The low variable cost enterprise will achieve higher profits for a given increment in volume once break-even operations are reached than will the high variable-cost enterprise.

ILLUSTRATION 3.   Company A has fixed costs of $700,000 and a variable cost equal to 30 percent of sales. Company B has fixed costs of $300,000 and variable costs equal to 70 percent of the sales. Assume that both companies have now reached sales of $1,000,000 and are, consequently, at break even. A $100,000 increment in sales will result in a profit of $70,000 for Company A and only in a profit of $30,000 for Company B. Company A has not only greater operating leverage but can, as a result, afford to incur greater risks in going after the extra $100,000 in sales than can Company B.

From the above example it is evident that the *level* of the break-even point is not the only criterion of risk assessment but that the analyst must also pay attention to the variable cost ratio.

The significance of the fixed-cost level

Given a certain variable cost percentage, the higher the fixed costs, the higher the break-even point of an enterprise. In the absence of change in other factors, a given percentage change in fixed costs will result in an equal percentage change in the break-even point. This can be illustrated as follows:

First break-even situation

Sales		$100,000
Variable expenses	$60,000	
Fixed costs	40,000	100,000
Profit		–0–

Second break-even situation—20% increase in fixed costs

Sales (increase of 20%)		$120,000
Variable expenses (60%)	$72,000	
Fixed cost (40,000 + 20%)	48,000	120,000
		–0–

Thus a fixed cost increase of 20 percent, with the variable cost ratio remaining unchanged, resulted in a 20 percent increase in the break-even point.

An increase in the break-even point of an enterprise generally increases operational risk. It means that the enterprise is dependent on a higher volume of sales in order to break even. Looked at another way, it means that the enterprise is more vulnerable to economic downturns as compared to its situation with a lower break-even point. The substantial acquisition of the large capacity Boeing 747 aircraft by the airlines provides an example of the effects of high break-even points. While these large aircraft lowered the variable cost per passenger, they relied also on a projected increase in the number of passengers. When this failed to materialize, the airlines' profit margins deteriorated swiftly with many of them going into the red. There are other repercussions to high levels of fixed costs. Thus, for example, a higher break-even point may mean that the enterprise has less freedom of action in fields such as labor relations. A high level of fixed costs makes strikes more expensive and subjects the enterprise to added pressure to submit to higher wage demands.

Often, added fixed costs in the form of automatic machinery are incurred in order to save variable costs, such as labor, and to improve efficiency. That can be very profitable in times of reasonably good demand. In times of low demand, however, the higher level of fixed costs sets in motion the process of reverse operational leverage discussed above, with attendant rapidly shrinking profits or even growing losses. High fixed costs reduce an enterprise's ability to protect its profits in the face of shrinking sales volume.

Investments in fixed assets, particularly in sophisticated machinery, can bring about increases in fixed costs far beyond the cost of maintaining and replacing the equipment. The skills required to operate such equipment are quite specialized and require skilled personnel which the enterprise may be reluctant to dismiss for fear of not being able to replace them when business turns up again. This converts what should be variable costs into de facto fixed costs.

While fixed costs are incurred in order to increase capacity or to decrease variable costs, it is often advisable to cut fixed costs in order to reduce the risks associated with a high break-even point. Thus, a company may reduce fixed costs by switching from a salaried sales force to one compensated by commissions based on sales. It can avoid added fixed costs by adding work shifts, buying ready-made parts, subcontracting work, or discontinuing the least profitable product lines.

In evaluating profit performance, past and future, of an enterprise, the analyst must always keep in mind the effect that the level of fixed costs can have on operating results under a variety of business conditions. Moreover, in projecting future results the analyst must bear in mind that any given level of fixed costs is valid only up to the limits of practical capacity within a range of product mixes. Beyond such a point a profit projection must take into consideration not only the increased levels of fixed costs required but also the financial resources which an expansion will require as well as the cost and sources of the funds which will be needed.

The importance of the contribution margin

The analyst must be alert to the absolute size of an enterprise's contribution margin because operating leverage is importantly dependent on it. He must, moreover, be aware of the factors which can change this margin, that is, changes in variable costs as well as changes in selling prices.

While we have focused on the individual factors which affect costs, revenues, and profitability, in practice changes result from a combination of factors. Projected increases in sales volume will increase profits only if costs, both fixed and variable, are controlled and kept within projected limits. Break-even analysis assumes that efficiency remains constant. However, experience teaches us that cost controls are more lax in times of prosperity than they are in times of recession. Thus, the analyst cannot assume constant efficiency any more than he can assume a constant product mix. The latter is also an important variable which must be watched by the analyst. Questions of why an enterprise realized lower profits on a higher volume of sales can often be explained, at least in part, by reference to changes in sales mix.

In spite of its important limitations, the break-even approach is an important tool of analysis to the financial analyst.

Its ability to aid the external analyst in performance evaluation and in profit projection makes its use worthwhile to him in spite of the laborious work which it often entails and the fragmentary and scarce amounts of information on which, of necessity, it must be based.

ADDITIONAL CONSIDERATIONS IN THE ANALYSIS OF COST OF SALES

Gross margin analysis focuses on changes in costs, prices, and volume. Break-even analysis, in turn, focuses on the behavior of costs in relation to sales volume and on management's ability to control costs in the face of rising and falling revenues. The effectiveness of these and other methods of cost analysis depends on the degree of data availability as well as on an understanding of the accounting principles which have been applied.

The ability of the analyst to make the rough approximations which are necessary to separate costs into fixed and variable components depends on the amount of detail available. Disclosure of major cost components such as materials, labor, and various overhead cost categories can be helpful. The more detailed the breakdowns of expense categories the more likely is the analyst to be able to construct meaningful break-even estimates.

In the evaluation of the cost of sales and the gross margin, and particularly in its comparison with those of other enterprises, the analyst must pay close attention to distortions which may arise from the utilization of a variety of accounting principles. While this is true of all items of cost, attention must be directed particularly to inventories and to depreciation accounting. These two areas, considered in detail in Chapters 6 and 10, merit special attention not only because they represent costs which are usually substantial in amount but also because of the proliferation of alternative principles which may be employed in accounting for them.

DEPRECIATION

Depreciation is an important cost element particularly in manufacturing and service enterprises. It is mostly fixed in nature because it is computed on the basis of elapsed time. However, if its computation is based on production activity the result is a variable cost.

Because depreciation is computed in most cases on the basis of time elapsed, the ratio of depreciation expense to income is not a particularly meaningful or instructive relationship. In the evaluation of depreciation expense the ratio of depreciation to gross plant and equipment is more meaningful. The ratio is computed as follows:

$$\frac{\text{Depreciation Expense}}{\text{Assets subject to Depreciation}}$$

This ratio can, of course, be computed by major categories of assets. The basic purpose is to enable the analyst to detect changes in the composite rate of depreciation used by an enterprise as a means of evaluating its adequacy and of detecting attempts at income smoothing.

AMORTIZATION OF SPECIAL TOOLS AND SIMILAR COSTS

The importance of the cost of special tools, dies, jigs, patterns, and molds costs varies from industry to industry. It is of considerable importance, for example, in the auto industry where special tool costs are associated with frequent style and design changes. The rate of amortization of such costs can have an important effect on reported income and is important to the analyst in an assessment of that income as well as in its comparison with that of other entities within an industry. The ratios that can be used to analyze changes in the deferral and amortization policies of such costs are varied and focus on their relationship to sales and other classes of assets.

The yearly expenditure for special tools can be related to and expressed as a percentage of (1) sales and (2) net property and equipment.

The yearly amortization of special tools can be related to (1) sales, (2) unamortized special tools, and (3) net property and equipment.

A comparison of the yearly trend in these relationships can be very helpful in an analysis of the consistency of income reporting of a single enterprise. The comparison can be extended further to an evaluation of the earnings of two or more enterprises within the same industry. This approach is indicative of the type of analysis which various elements of costs lend themselves to.

MAINTENANCE AND REPAIRS COSTS

Maintenance and repairs costs vary in significance with the amount invested in plant and equipment as well as with the level of productive activity. They have an effect on the cost of goods sold as well as on other elements of cost. Since maintenance and repairs contain elements of both fixed and variable costs, they cannot vary directly with sales. Thus, the ratio of repairs and maintenance costs to sales, while instructive to compare from year to year or among enterprises, must be interpreted with care. To the extent that the analyst can determine the fixed and the variable portions of maintenance and repairs costs, his interpretation of their relationship to periodic sales will be more valid.

Repairs and maintenance are, to a significant extent, discretionary costs. That is, the level of expense can, within limits, be regulated by management for a variety of reasons including those aimed at the improvement of reported income or at the preservation of liquid resources. Certain types of repairs cannot, of course, be postponed without resulting breakdowns in productive equipment. But many types of preventive repairs and particularly maintenance can be postponed or skimped on with results whose effects lie mainly in the future. Thus, the level of repair and maintenance costs both in relation to sales and to plant and equipment is of interest to the analyst. It has, of course, a bearing on the quality of income, a subject which we shall consider in the next chapter.

The level of repair and maintenance costs is also important in the evaluation of depreciation expense. Useful lives of assets are estimated by the use of many assumptions including those relating to the upkeep and maintenance of the assets. If, for instance, there is a deterioration in the usual or assumed level of repairs and maintenance, the useful life of the asset will, in all probability, be shortened. That may, in turn, require an upward revision in the depreciation expense or else income will be overstated.

OTHER COSTS AND EXPENSES—GENERAL

Most, although not all, cost and expense items found in the income statement have some identifiable or measurable relationship to sales. This is so because sales are the major measure of activity in an enterprise except in instances when production and sales are significantly out of phase.

Two analytical tools whose usefulness is based, in part, on the relationship that exists between sales and most costs and expenses should be noted here:

1. The *common-size income statement* expresses each cost and expense item in terms of its percentage relationship to net sales. This relationship of costs and expenses to sales can then be traced over a number of periods or compared with the experience of other enterprises in the same industry. Appendix 4B of Chapter 4 contains an illustration of a common-size income statement covering a number of years.

2. The *index number analysis of the income statement* expresses each item in the income statement in terms of an index number related to a base year. In this manner relative changes of income statement items over time can be traced and their significance assessed. Expense item changes can thus be compared to changes in sales and to changes in related expense items. Moreover, by use of common-size balance sheets, percentage changes in income statement items can be related to changes in assets and liabilities. For example, a given change in sales would normally justify a commensurate change in inventories and in accounts receivable. Appendix 4B of Chapter 4 contains an illustration of an index number analysis.

Selling expenses

The analysis of selling costs has two main objectives:

1. The evaluation over time of the relationship between sales and the costs needed to bring them about.
2. An evaluation of the trend and the productivity of future-directed selling costs.

The importance of selling costs in relation to sales varies from industry to industry and from enterprise to enterprise. In some enterprises selling costs take the form of commissions and are, consequently, highly variable in nature, while in others they contain important elements of fixed costs.

After allowing for the fixed and variable components of the selling expenses, the best way to analyze them is to relate them to sales. The more detailed the breakdown of the selling expense components is—the more meaningful and penetrating can such analysis be. Exhibit 21–4 presents an example of such an analysis.

Analysis of Exhibit 21–4 indicates that for the entire period selling costs have been rising faster than sales and that in 19X3 they took 5.6 percent more of the sales dollar than they did in 19X0. In this period salesmen's salaries increased by 1.0 percent of sales, advertising by 3.6 percent of sales, and branch expenses by 2.2 percent of sales. The drop in delivery expense may possibly be accounted for by the offsetting increase in freight costs.

EXHIBIT 21–4

TRYON CORPORATION
Comparative Statement of Selling Expenses
(dollar amounts in thousands)

	19X3		19X2		19X1		19X0	
	$	%	$	%	$	%	$	%
Sales	1,269		935		833		791	
Trend percentage		160		118		105		100
Selling expenses (% are of sales):								
Advertising	84	6.6	34	3.6	28	3.4	24	3.0
District branch expenses*	80	6.3	41	4.4	38	4.6	32	4.1
Delivery expense (own trucks)	20	1.6	15	1.6	19	2.3	22	2.8
Freight-out	21	1.7	9	1.0	11	1.3	8	1.0
Salesmen's salary expense	111	8.7	76	8.1	68	8.1	61	7.7
Salesmen's travel expense	35	2.8	20	2.1	18	2.2	26	3.3
Miscellaneous selling expense	9	.7	9	1.0	8	.9	7	.9
Total	360	28.4	204	21.8	190	22.8	180	22.8

* Includes rent, regional advertising, etc.

A careful analysis should be made of advertising costs in order to determine to what extent the increase is due to the promotion of new products or the development of new territories which will benefit the future.

When selling expenses as a percentage of sales show an increase, it is instructive to focus on the selling expense increase which accompanies a given increase in sales. It can be expected that beyond a certain level greater sales resistance is encountered in effecting additional sales. That sales resistance or the development of more remote territories may involve additional cost. Thus, it is important to know what the percentage of selling expense to sales is or to new sales as opposed to old ones. This may have, of course, implications on the projection of future profitability. If an enterprise can make additional sales only by spending increasing amounts of selling expenses, its profitability may suffer. Offsetting factors, such as those related to break-even operations or to economies of scale must also be considered.

Future directed marketing costs

Certain categories of sales promotion costs, particularly advertising, result in benefits which extend beyond the period in which they were incurred. The measurement of such benefits is difficult if not impossible, but it is a reasonable assumption that there is a relationship between the level of expenditures for advertising and promotion and the sales level, present and future.

Since expenditures for advertising and other forms of promotion are discretionary in nature, the analyst must carefully follow the year to year trend in these expenditures. Not only does the level of such expenditures have a bearing on future sales estimates, but it also indicates whether management is attempting to "manage" reported earnings. The effect of discretionary costs on the "quality" of earnings reported will be the subject of further discussion in the chapter that follows.

GENERAL, ADMINISTRATION, FINANCIAL, AND OTHER EXPENSES

Most costs in this category tend to be fixed in nature. This is largely true of administrative costs because such costs include significant amounts of salaries and occupancy expenditures. However, there may be some "creep" or tendency for increases in this category, and this is particularly true in prosperous times. Thus, in analyzing this category of expense the analyst should pay attention to both the trend of administrative costs as well as to the percentage of total sales which they consume.

Financial costs

Financial costs are, except for interest on short-term indebtedness, fixed in nature. Moreover, unless replaced by equity capital, most borrowed funds are usually refinanced. This is because of the long-term nature of most interest-bearing obligations. Included in these costs are the amortization of bond premium and discount as well as of debt issue expenses. A good check on an enterprise's cost of borrowed money as well as credit standing is the calculation of the average effective interest rate paid. This rate is computed as follows:

$$\frac{\text{Total Interest Cost}}{\text{Total Indebtedness subject to Interest}}$$

The average effective interest rate paid can be compared over the years or compared to that of other enterprises. It is also significant in that it sheds light on the credit standing of the enterprise.

A measure of sensitivity to interest changes is obtained by determining the portion of debt which is tied to the prime rate. In periods of rising interest rates a significant amount of debt tied to the prime rate exposes an enterprise to sharply escalating interest costs. Conversely, falling interest rates are a beneficial factor to such an enterprise.

"Other" expenses

"Other" expenses are, of course, a nondescript category. The total amount in this category should normally be rather immaterial in relation to other costs. Otherwise, it can obscure substantial costs which, if revealed, may provide significant information about the enterprise's current and future operations. Nonrecurring elements may also be included in the "other expense" category, and this may add to the significance of this category to the analyst.

The analyst must also be alert to the tendency to offset "other" expenses against "other" income. Here too the major problem is one of concealment of important information and data. Here it is important that details of the major items comprising the offset amount be given.

OTHER INCOME

Miscellaneous income items which are small in amount are usually of no significance to the analyst. However, since "other income" may include returns from various investments, it may contain information about new ventures and data regarding investments which is not available elsewhere. Such investments may, of course, have future implications, positive or negative, which exceed in significance the amounts of current income which are involved.

INCOME TAXES

Income taxes represent basically a sharing of profits between an enterprise and the governmental authority by which they are imposed. Since most enterprises with which this text is concerned are organized in corporate form, we shall focus primarily on corporate income taxes.

Income taxes are almost always significant in amount and normally can take about half of a corporation's income before taxes. For this reason the analyst must pay careful attention to the impact which income taxes have on net income.

Except for a lower rate on a first modest amount of income, corporate income is normally taxed at the rate of about 50 percent. Differences in the timing of recognition of income or expense items as between taxable income and book income should not influence the effective tax rate because of the practice of interperiod income tax allocation which aims to match the tax expense with the book income regardless of when the tax is paid. Income tax allocation is discussed in Chapter 11.

The relationship between the tax accrual and the pretax income, otherwise known as the effective tax rate or tax ratio, will, however, be influenced by permanent tax differences. These are differences which arise from provisions in the tax law which:

1. Do not tax certain revenues (e.g., interest on municipal obligations and proceeds from life insurance).
2. Do not allow certain expenses as deductions in arriving at taxable income (e.g., goodwill amortization, fines, premiums on officers' life insurance).
3. Tax certain income at reduced rates (e.g., dividend income, capital gains).
4. Allow certain costs beyond the amount taken for book purposes (e.g., excess of statutory depletion over book depletion).

The effective tax rate or tax ratio is computed as follows:

$$\frac{\text{Income Tax Expense for Period}}{\text{Income before Income Taxes}}$$

This ratio may also deviate from the normal or expected rate because, among others, of the following additional reasons:

1. The basis of carrying property for accounting purposes may differ from that for tax purposes as a result of reorganizations, business combinations, etc.
2. Nonqualified as well as qualified stock-option plans may result in book-tax differences.
3. Certain industries, such as savings and loan associations, shipping lines, and insurance companies enjoy special tax privileges.
4. Credits, such as the Investment Tax Credit.

The important thing is that both for income evaluation as well as for net income projection the analyst must know the reasons why the tax ratio deviates from the normal or the expected. Income taxes are such an important element of cost that even relatively small changes in the effective tax rate can explain important changes in net income. Moreover, without an understanding of the factors which cause changes in the effective tax rate of a company, the analyst is missing an important ingredient necessary in the forecasting of future net income.

In *ASR 149* (1973) the SEC issued rules which expanded significantly the analytical disclosures concerning regular and deferred income taxes. Chapter 11 includes a description of these as well as a discussion of their significance to the analyst.

While the focus on net income and on earnings per share requires a thorough analysis of changes in the effective tax rate, it must be borne in mind that many analysts attach relatively greater importance

to pretax earnings. This is due to the greater importance which is assigned to pretax operating results, which require management skills
of a high order, as compared with changes due to variations in the
effective tax rate over which, it is assumed, management has comparatively more limited control.

THE OPERATING RATIO

The operating ratio is yet another intermediate measure in the
analysis of the income statement. It measures the relationship between all operating costs and net sales and is computed as follows:

$$\frac{\text{Cost of Goods Sold} + \text{Other Operating Expenses}}{\text{Net Sales}}$$

The ratio is designed to enable a comparison within an enterprise or
with enterprises of the proportion of the sales dollar absorbed by all
operating costs. Only other income and expense items as well as income taxes are excluded from the computation of this ratio.

In effect this ratio represents but an intermediate step in the com-
monsize analysis of the income statement. It is, in and of itself, not of
great analytical significance because it is a composite of many factors
which require separate analysis. These factors comprise the analysis of
gross margin and of other major expense categories discussed earlier.
Thus, the operating ratio cannot be properly interpreted without a
thorough analysis of the reasons accounting for variations in gross margin and for changes in selling, general, administrative, and other costs.

NET INCOME RATIO

The net income ratio is the relationship between net income and
total revenues and is computed as follows:

$$\frac{\text{Net Income}}{\text{Total Revenues}}$$

It represents the percentage of total revenue brought down to net
income. In addition to its usefulness as an index of profitability, the
net profit ratio represents, as was seen in Chapter 19, a main component of the computation of the return on investment.

Statement accounting for variation in net income

In the analysis of year-to-year changes in net income it is useful to
separate the elements which contributed to an increase in net income
from those which contributed to a decrease. A statement which does

that and which also indicates the percentage increase or decrease in these factors is the "statement accounting for the variations in net income."

Exhibit 21–5 presents comparative statements of income of the Alliance Company. Based on the data in these income statements, Exhibit 21–6 presents a "statement accounting for variations in net income." This statement is simple to prepare and allows the analyst to single out for further analysis those elements of income and expense which had the greatest impact on the change in net income from one period to another.

EXHIBIT 21–5

ALLIANCE COMPANY
Income Statements
For Years Ended March 31, 19X1, 19X2
(amounts in thousands)

	19X1	19X2	Dollar increase (decrease) 19X2	Percentage increase (decrease) 19X2
Net sales	$94,313	$102,888	$8,575	9%
Cost of sales	71,516	77,922	6,406	9
Gross profit	$22,797	$ 24,966	$2,169	10
Selling, general, and administrative and other expenses:				
Selling expenses	$ 3,300	$ 4,298	$ 998	30
General and administrative expenses	2,610	3,191	581	22
Financing expenses	4,627	4,916	289	6
Total Operating Expenses	$10,537	$ 12,405	$1,868	18
Operating profit	$12,260	$ 12,561	$ 301	2
Other income and expenses (Net)	1,447	1,752	305	21
Profit before taxes on income	$13,707	$ 14,313	$ 606	4
Taxes on income	4,500	4,604	104	2
Net income	$ 9,207	$ 9,709	$ 502	5

EXHIBIT 21-6

ALLIANCE COMPANY
Statement Accounting for Variation in Net Income
For the Year Ended December 31, 19X2
(amounts in thousands)

			Percentage increase
Items tending to increase net income:			
Increase in gross margin on sales:			
Increase in net sales:			
Net sales, 19X2 ..../.........	$102,888		
Net sales, 19X1	94,313	$8,575	9
Deduct: Increase in cost of goods sold:			
Cost of goods sold, 19X2	77,922		
Cost of goods sold, 19X1	71,516	6,406	9
Net increase in gross margin:			
Gross margin, 19X2	24,966		
Gross margin, 19X1	22,797	2,169	10
Increase in other revenue and expense (net)			
Net 19X2	1,752		
Net 19X1	1,447	305	21
Total of items tending to increase net income		$2,474	
Items tending to decrease in income:			
Increase in selling expenses:			
Selling expenses, 19X2	4,298		
Selling expenses, 19X1	3,300	998	30
Increase in general and administrative expenses:			
General and administrative expenses, 19X2	3,191		
General and administrative expenses, 19X1	2,610	581	22
Increase in financing expenses:			
Financing expenses, 19X2	4,916		
Financing expenses, 19X1	4,627	289	6
Increase in estimated federal income taxes:			
Estimated federal income taxes, 19X2.....	4,604		
Estimated federal income taxes, 19X1.....	4,500	104	2
Total of items tending to decrease net income		1,972	
Net increase in net income:			
Net income, 19X2	9,709		
Net income, 19X1	9,207	$ 502	5

QUESTIONS

1. What are the most important elements in the analysis of gross profit?

2. What is the basic principle underlying break-even analysis? What are fixed costs? Variable costs? Semivariable costs?

3. Certain assumptions which underlie break-even computations are often referred to as simplifying assumptions. Name as many of these as you can.

4. In break-even computation what is the "variable cost percentage"? What is its relationship to "contribution margin ratio"?

5. What alternatives to an increase in fixed costs can an enterprise when it approaches 100 percent of theoretical capacity?

6. What is operating leverage? Why do leverage and fixed costs go together? What are the analytical implications of operating leverage?

7. Of what analytical significance are (a) the break-even point and (b) the variable cost ratio?

8. What is a useful measure of the adequacy of current provisions for depreciation?

9. To what factors can maintenance and repair costs be meaningfully related?

10. What are the main objectives of an analysis of selling expenses?

11. List some of the reasons why the effective tax rate of one enterprise may vary from that of another enterprise?

22

THE EVALUATION AND
PROJECTION OF EARNINGS

OBJECTIVES OF EARNINGS EVALUATION

In the preceding chapters we examined the steps which have to be taken and the understanding which must be brought to bear on the analysis of the operating performance of an enterprise. This chapter will examine the additional considerations involved in the achievement of the major objectives of income statement analysis:

The evaluation of the earnings level and its quality.

Evaluation of the stability and the trend of earnings.

The forecasting of earnings.

The estimation of "earning power."

Monitoring performance and results.

EVALUATION OF EARNINGS LEVEL AND ITS QUALITY

The discussions through Part II of this work have pointed out that much of the accounting process of income determination involves a high degree of estimation. Chapters 10 and 11 on the analysis of the income statement have explained that the income of an enterprise, as measured by the accounting process, is not a specific amount but can vary depending on the assumptions used and the various principles applied. Complicating these measurements still further is the fact that numerous accounting periods can receive benefits from a single cash outlay and that it may take a number of periods before a transaction results in the collection of all amounts due. For that reason, creditors, in particular, are greatly interested in the cash equivalent of reported earnings (see also Chapter 13).

This distinction between accrual income and the related cash flows has led some of those uninitiated in the income determination process to doubt the validity of all accounting measurements. This, however, is an extreme and unwarranted position because, as any student of accounting should know, the concept of income is the result of a series of complex assumptions and conventions, and exists only as the creation and the approximation of this system of measurement. This system is always subject to reexamination and is, despite its shortcomings, still the most widely accepted method of income determination.

In examining the level of reported income of an enterprise, the analyst must determine the effect of the various assumptions and accounting principles used on that reported income. Beyond that he must be aware of the "accounting risk" as well as the "audit risk" to which these determinations are subject.

Over the years, and especially since the enactment of the Securities Acts of 1933 and 1934, and with improvement in the audit function in this country, the incidence of outright fraud and deliberate misrepresentation in financial statements has diminished markedly. But they have not been completely eliminated and probably never will. Nor can the analyst ever rule out the possibility of spectacular failures in the audit function. While each major audit failure tends to contribute to the improvement of regulation and of auditing, they have not prevented the recurrence of such failures as the security holders of McKesson & Robbins, of Seabord Commercial Corporation, of H. L. Green, of Miami Window, of Yale Express, of BarChris Construction Company, of Continental Vending Company, of Mill Factors Corporation, and Equity Funding Company, well know.

The analyst must always assess the vulnerability to failure and to irregularities of the company under analysis and the character and the propensities of its management, as a means of establishing the degree of risk that it will prove to be the relatively rare exception to the general rule. (The audit process is discussed in Chapter 15.)

The evaluation of the earnings level and of the earnings trend is intimately tied in with the evaluation of management. The evaluation of the management group cannot be separated from the results which they have actually achieved. Whatever other factors may have to be considered, results over a period of time are the acid test of management's ability, and that ability is perhaps the most important intangible (i.e., unquantifiable) factor in the prediction of future results. The analyst must be alert to changes in the management group and must assess its depth, stability, and possible dependence on the talents of one or a few individuals.

The analyst must also realize that not only is it impossible to arrive at a single figure of "net income" but that identical earnings figures may possess different degrees of "quality."

THE CONCEPT OF EARNINGS QUALITY

The concept of earnings quality arose out of a need to provide a basis of comparison among the earnings of different entities as well as from the need to recognize such differences in "quality" for valuation purposes. There is almost no general agreement on definitions of or on assumptions underlying this concept. The elements which comprise the "quality of earnings" can be classified as follows:

a. One type of factor that affects the quality of earnings is the accounting and computational discretion of management and that of the attesting accountants in choosing from among accepted alternative accounting principles. These choices can be liberal, that is, they can assume the most optimistic view of the future, or they can be conservative. Generally, the quality of conservatively determined earnings is higher because they are less likely to prove overstated in the light of future developments than those determined in a "liberal" fashion. They also minimize the possibility of earnings overstatement and avoid retrospective changes. On the other hand, unwarranted or excessive conservatism, while contributing to the temporary "quality" of earnings, actually results in a lack of reporting integrity over the long run and cannot be considered as a desirable factor. Quite apart from the impact which these accounting choices have on the financial statements they also hold important clues to management's propensities and attitudes.

b. The second type of factor affecting the quality of earnings is related to the degree to which adequate provision has been made for the maintenance of assets and for the maintenance and enhancement of present and future earning power. In most enterprises there exists considerable managerial discretion over the size of income streams and particularly over the reported amounts of costs and expenses. Discretionary types of expenses, such as repairs and maintenance, advertising, and research and development costs can be varied for the sole purpose of managing the level of reported net income (or loss) rather than for legitimate operating or business reasons. Here, too, the analyst's task is to identify the results of management practices and to judge its motivations.

c. The third major factor affecting the quality of earnings is not primarily a result of discretionary actions of managements, although skillful management can modify its effects. It is the effect of cyclical and other economic forces on earnings, on the stability of their sources, and particularly on their variability. Variability of earnings is generally an undesirable characteristic and, consequently, the higher the variability the lower the quality of these earnings.

The fairly broad tolerances within which generally accepted accounting principles can be applied have been discussed throughout this work. There follows a consideration of other aspects which affect earnings quality.

Evaluation of discretionary and future-directed costs

Discretionary costs are outlays which managements can vary to some extent from period to period in order to conserve resources and/or to influence reported income. For this reason they deserve the special attention of analysts who are particularly interested in knowing whether the level of expenses is in keeping with past trends and with present and future requirements.

Maintenance and repairs

As was already discussed in the preceding chapter, management has considerable leeway in performing maintenance work and some discretion with respect to repairs. The analyst can relate these costs to the level of activity because they do logically vary with it. Two ratios are particularly useful in comparing the repair and maintenance levels from year to year:

$$\frac{\text{Repairs and Maintenance}}{\text{Sales}}$$

This ratio relates the costs of repairs and maintenance to this most available measure of activity. In the absence of sharp inventory changes, sales are a good indicator of activity. If year-to-year inventory levels change appreciably, an adjustment may be needed whereby ending inventories at approximate selling prices are added to sales and beginning inventories, similarly adjusted, are deducted from them.

The other ratio is:

$$\frac{\text{Repairs and Maintenance}}{\substack{\text{Property, Plant, and Equipment (exclusive of land)} \\ \text{Net of Accumulated Depreciation}}}$$

It measures repair and maintenance costs in relation to the assets for which these costs are incurred. Depending on the amount of information available to the analyst, the ratio of repair and maintenance costs to specific categories of assets can be developed. It should be noted that substandard repairs and maintenance on assets may require revisions in the assumptions of useful lives for depreciation purposes.

The absolute trend in repair and maintenance costs from year to year can be expressed in terms of index numbers and compared to those of related accounts. The basic purpose of all these measurements is to determine whether the repair and maintenance programs of the enterprise have been kept at normal and necessary levels or whether they have been changed in a way that affects the quality of income and its projection into the future.

Advertising

Since a significant portion of advertising outlays has effects beyond the period in which it is incurred, the relationship between advertising outlays and short-term results is a tenuous one. This also means that managements can, in certain cases, cut advertising costs with no commensurate immediate effects on sales, although it can be assumed that over the longer term sales will suffer. Here again, year-to-year variations in the level of advertising expenses must be examined by the analyst with the objective of assessing their impact on future sales and consequently on the quality of reported earnings.

There are a number of ways of assessing the trend in advertising outlays. One is to convert them into trend percentages using a "normal" year as a base. These trend percentages can then be compared to the trend of sales and of gross and net profits. An alternative measure would be the ratio of

$$\frac{\text{Advertising Expenses}}{\text{Sales}}$$

which, when compared over the years, would also indicate shifts in management policy. The ratio of

$$\frac{\text{Advertising}}{\text{Total Selling Costs}}$$

must also be examined so as to detect shifts to and from advertising to other methods of sales promotion.

An analysis of advertising to sales ratios over several years will reveal the degree of dependence of an enterprise on this promotional strategy. Comparison of this ratio with that of other companies in the industry will reveal the degree of market acceptance of products and the relative promotional efforts needed to secure it.

Research and development costs

The significance and the potential value of research and development costs are among the most difficult elements of the financial statements to analyze and interpret. Yet they are important, not only because of their relative size, but even more so because of their significance for the projection of future results.

Research and development costs have gained an aura of glowing potential in security analysis far beyond that warranted by actual experience. Mentioned most frequently are some of the undeniably spectacular and successful commercial applications of industrial research in the post-World War II era in such fields as chemistry, electronics, and photography. Not mentioned are the vast sums spent for endeavors labeled "research" which are expensed or written off while benefits from these fall far short of the original costs.

The analyst must pay careful attention to research and development costs and to the absence of such costs. In many enterprises they represent substantial costs, much of them fixed in nature, and they can represent the key to future success or failure. We must first draw a careful distinction between what can be quantified in this area and, consequently, analyzed in the sense in which we consider analysis in this work, and what cannot be quantified and must consequently be evaluated in qualitative terms.

In the area of research and development costs the qualitative element looms large and important. The definition of what constitutes "research" is subject to wide-ranging interpretations as well as to outright distortion. The label "research" is placed on activities ranging from those of a first-class scientific organization engaged in sophisticated pure and applied research down to superficial and routine product and market testing activities.

Among the many factors to be considered in the evaluation of the quality of the research effort are the caliber of the research staff and organization, the eminence of its leadership, as well as the commercial results of their research efforts. This qualitative evaluation must accompany any other kinds of analysis. Finally, a distinction must be drawn between government or outsider sponsored research and company directed research which is most closely identified with its own objectives. From the foregoing discussion it is clear that research cannot be evaluated on the basis of the amounts spent alone. Research outlays represent an expense or an investment depending on how they are applied. Far from guaranteeing results, they represent highly speculative ventures which depend on the application of extraordinary scientific as well as managerial skills for their success. Thus, spending on research cannot guarantee results and should not be equated with them.

Having considered the all-important qualitative factors on which an evaluation of research and development outlays depends, the analyst should attempt to determine as best he can how much of the current research and development outlays which have been expensed have future utility and potential.

The "future potential" of research and development costs is, from the point of view of the analyst, a most important consideration. Research cost productivity can be measured by relating research and development outlays to:

1. Sales growth
2. New product introductions
3. Acquisition of plant and equipment (to exploit the results of research)
4. Profitability

It must be recognized, however, that often the analyst will not have the adequate information which is necessary for him to check on the judgment of management and their independent accountants in their treatment of research and development outlays.

Another important aspect of research and development outlays is their discretionary nature. It is true that those enterprises which have established research and development departments impart a fixed nature to a segment of these costs. Nevertheless they can be increased or curtailed at the discretion of managements, often with no immediate adverse effects on sales. Thus, from the point of view of assessing the quality of reported income, the analyst must evaluate year-to-year changes in research and development outlays. This he can do by means of trend percentage analysis as well as by years of analysis of ratios such as the ratio of

$$\frac{\text{Research and Development Outlays}}{\text{Sales}}$$

A careful comparison of outlays for research and development over the years will indicate to the analyst whether the effort is a sustained one or one which varies with the ups and downs of operating results. Moreover, "one shot" research efforts lack the predictability or quality of a sustained, well organized longer term research program.

Other future-directed costs

In addition to advertising and research and development, there are other types of future-directed outlays. An example of such outlays are the costs of training operating, sales, and managerial talent. Although these outlays for the development of human resources are usually expensed in the year in which they are incurred, they may have future utility, and the analyst may want to recognize this in his evaluation of current earnings and of future prospects.

BALANCE SHEET ANALYSIS AS A CHECK ON THE VALIDITY AND QUALITY OF REPORTED EARNINGS

The amounts at which the assets and liabilities of an enterprise are stated hold important clues to an assessment of both the validity as well as the quality of its earnings. Thus, the analysis of the balance sheet is an important complement to the other approaches of income analysis discussed in this chapter, and elsewhere in this work.

Importance of carrying amounts of assets

The importance which we attach to the amounts at which assets are carried on the balance sheet is due to the fact that, with few exceptions such as cash, some investments, and land, the cost of most assets enters ultimately the cost stream of the income statement. Thus, we can state the following as a general proposition: Whenever assets are overstated the cumulative income[1] is overstated because it has been relieved of charges needed to bring such assets down to realizable values.

It would appear that the converse of this proposition should also hold true, that is, that to the extent to which assets are understated, cumulative income is also understated. Two accounting conventions qualify this statement importantly. One is the convention of conservatism, already discussed in Chapter 2, which calls for the recognition of gains only as they are actually realized. Although there has been some movement away from a strict interpretation of this convention, in general most assets are carried at original cost even though their current market or realizable value is far in excess of that cost.

The other qualifying convention is that governing the accounting for business combinations. As was seen in the discussions in Chapter 9, the "pooling of interests" concept allows an acquiring company to carry foward the old book values of the assets of the acquired company even though such values may be far less than current market values or the consideration given for them. Thus, the analyst must be aware of the fact that such an accounting will allow the recording of profits, when the values of such understated assets are realized, which represents nothing more than the surfacing of such hitherto understated assets. Since such profits have, in effect, previously been bought and

---

[1] The effect on any one period cannot be generalized on.

paid for, they cannot be considered as representing either the earning power of the enterprise or an index of the operating performance of its management.

Importance of provisions and liabilities

Continuing our analysis of the effect of balance sheet amounts on the measurement of income, we can enunciate the further proposition that an understatement of provisions and liabilities will result in an overstatement of cumulative income because the latter is relieved of charges required to bring the provision or the liabilities up to their proper amounts. Thus, for example, an understatement of the provision for taxes, for product warranties, or for pensions means that cumulative income is overstated.

Conversely, an overprovision for present and future liabilities or losses results in the understatement of income or in the overstatement of losses. As was seen in the discussion in Chapter 11, provisions for future costs and losses which are excessive in amount represent attempts to shift the burden of costs and expenses from future income statements to that of the present.

Bearing in mind the general propositions regarding the effect on income of the amounts at which assets and liabilities are carried in the balance sheet, the critical analysis and evaluation of such amounts represents an important check on the validity of reported income.

Balance sheet analysis and the quality of earnings

There is, however, a further dimension to this kind of analysis in that it also has a bearing on an evaluation of the quality of earnings. This approach is based on the fact that various degrees of risk attach to the probability of the future realization of different types of assets.

Thus, for example, the future realization of accounts receivable has generally a higher degree of probability than has the realization of, say, inventory or unrecovered tools and dies costs. Moreover, the future realization of inventory costs can, generally, be predicted with greater certainty than can the future realization of goodwill or of deferred start-up costs. The analysis of the assets carried in the balance sheet by risk class or risk category holds clues to and is an important measure of the quality of reported income. Stated another way, if the income determination process results in the deferral of outlays and costs which carry a high degree of risk that they may not prove realizable in the future, then that income is of a lower quality than income which does not involve the recording of such high-risk assets.

Effect of valuation of specific assets on the validity and quality of reported income

In order to illustrate the importance of balance sheet analysis to an evaluation of reported income, let us now examine the effect of the valuation of specific assets on the validity and quality of that income.

Accounts receivable.   The validity of the sales figure depends on the proper valuation of the accounts receivable which result from it. This valuation must recognize the risk of default in payment as well as the time value of money. On the later score, *APB Opinion No. 21* provides that if the receivable does not arise from transactions with customers or suppliers in the normal course of business under terms not exceeding a year, then, except for some other stated exceptions, it must be valued using the interest rate applicable to similar debt instruments. Thus, if the receivable bears an interest rate of 5 percent while similar receivables would, at the time, be expected to bear an interest rate of 7 percent, both the receivable and the sale from which it arose would be restated at the lower discounted amount.

Inventories.   Overstated inventories lead to overstated profits. Overstatements can occur due to errors in quantities, errors in costing and pricing, or errors in the valuation of work in process. The more technical the product and the more dependent the valuation is on internally developed cost records, the more vulnerable are the cost estimates to error and misstatement. The basic problem here arises when costs which should have been written off to expense are retained in the inventory accounts.

An understatement of inventories results from a charge-off to income of costs which possess future utility and which should be inventoried. Such an understatement of inventories results in the understatement of current income and the overstatement of future income.

Deferred charges.   Deferred charges such as deferred tooling or start-up and preoperating costs must be scrutinized carefully because their value depends, perhaps more than that of other assets, on estimates of future probabilities and developments. Experience has shown that often such estimates have proven overoptimistic or that they did not contain sufficient provisions for future contingencies. Thus, the risk of failure to attain expectations is relatively higher here than in the case of other assets.

The effect of external factors on the quality of earnings

The concept of earnings quality is so broad that it encompasses many additional factors which, in the eyes of analysts, can make earnings more reliable or more desirable.

The effect of changing price levels on the measurement of earnings was examined in Chapter 14. In times of rising price levels the inclusion of "inventory profits" or the understatement of expenses such as depreciation lowers in effect the reliability of earnings and hence their quality.

The quality of foreign earnings is affected by factors such as difficulties and uncertainties regarding the repatriation of funds, currency fluctuations, the political and social climate as well as local customs and regulation. With regard to the latter, the inability to dismiss personnel in some countries in effect converts labor costs into fixed costs.

Regulation provides another example of external factors which can affect earnings quality. The "regulatory environment" of a public utility affects the "quality" of its earnings. Thus an unsympathetic or even hostile regulatory environment which causes serious lags in the obtaining of rate relief will detract from earnings quality because of uncertainty about the adequacy of future revenues.

The stability and reliability of earnings sources affect earnings quality. Defense related revenues can be regarded as nonrecurring in time of war and affected by political uncertainties in peace time.

Finally, some analysts regard complexity of operations and difficulties in their analysis (e.g., of conglomerates) as negative factors.

EVALUATION OF EARNINGS STABILITY AND TREND

The analyst will concentrate on identifying those elements in the income and cost streams which show stability, proven relationships, and predictability, and will separate them from those elements which are random, erratic, or nonrecurring and which, consequently, do not possess the elements of stability required for a reasonably reliable forecast or for inclusion in an "earning power" computation. To the intelligent analyst the most desirable income statement is the one containing a maximum of meaningful disclosure which will allow him to do this, rather than one containing built-in interpretations which channel him to specific conclusions.

The analyst must be on his guard against the well-known tendency of managements to practice income smoothing, thus trying to give to the income and expense streams a semblance of stability which in reality they do not possess. This is usually done in the name of "removing distortions" from the results of operations, whereas what is really achieved is the masking of the natural and cyclical irregularities which are part of the reality of the enterprise's experience and with which reality it is the analyst's primary task to come to grips.[2]

---

[2] The dissatisfaction of many managements with SFAS 8 (see Chapter 9) stems in large part from the instability which the current recognition of foreign exchange gains and losses introduces into the income statement. And yet, for the analyst the real question is whether these are not, in fact, a portrayal of underlying realities and risks.

Need to identify erratic elements. In the analysis of the income statement the analyst will strive to identify erratic and unstable factors which will be separated from what may be called the enterprise's stable or basic "earning power." These factors include temporary demand (as was the case with the temporary shortage of color-TV tubes which in the 1960s temporarily increased the fortunes of National Video Company), unusual costs, such as those due to strikes, and items which are genuinely unusual or extraordinary. This analysis will separate results of discontinued operations, restate for accounting changes and assign unusual or extraordinary items to (say, five year) average earnings rather than to the earnings of a single year.

An example of an analytical format which can be used to modify a conventional income statement in order to segregate and highlight special or unusual items bearing on comparability or on income evaluation follows:

	Millions of dollars		
	19X3	*19X2*	*19X1*
Net sales	291	283	197
Other income (a)	12	6	7
Total	303	289	204
Cost of sales (b)	198	154	145
Selling, general & adm. (c)	21	16	18
Advertising (c)	12	6	9
Repair & maintenance (b)	5	7	4
Research & development	4	3	1
Interest	5	3	2
	245	189	179
	58	100	25
Income taxes (before items shown below) (d)	26	48	10
Income from continuing operations	32	52	15
Loss form discontinued operations*		(8)	(2)
Equity in associated companies (a)	12	8	6
Investment tax credit (d)	6	7	—
Tax exempt earnings of subsid. (d)		4	
Loss on disposal of oil oper.* (b)			(7)
Gain on patent suit*		12	
Flood loss*			(16)
Net income (loss)	50	75	(4)

* Net of tax.

The keying-letters above (e.g. (a), (b), . . .) indicate where rearranged or highlighted items have been segregated from by the analyst. The analyst will have to decide how to treat these items and whether to include them in a specific year or in the average earnings of a number of years.

The tax information comes from the tax disclosure footnote (see Chapter 11). Discretionary cost information comes from disclosure required by the SEC. While this example covers three years, a more valid trend analysis will usually involve a larger number of years.

Determining the trend of income over the years

Having determined the size of a company's basic earnings as well as the factors which require adjustment before those earnings can be used as a basis for forecasts, the analyst will next determine the variability of these earnings, that is, changes in their size over the business cycle and over the longer term.

Evaluation of earnings variability. Earnings which fluctuate up and down with the business cycle are less desirable than earnings which display a larger degree of stability over such a cycle. The basic reason for this is that fluctuating earnings cause fluctuations in market prices. Earnings which display a steady growth trend are of the most desirable type. In his evaluation of earnings, the intelligent analyst realizes the limitations to which the earnings figure of any one year is subject. Therefore, depending on his specific purposes, he will consider the following earnings figures as improvements over the single year figure:

1. *Average earnings* over periods, such as 5 to 10 years, smooth out erratic and even extraordinary factors as well as cyclical influences, thus presenting a better and more reliable measure of "earning power" of an enterprise.
2. *Minimum earnings* are useful in decisions, such as those bearing on credit extension, which are particularly sensitive to risk factors. They indicate the worst that could happen based on recent experience.

The importance of earnings trends. In addition to the use of single, average, or minimum earnings figures, the analyst must be alert to earnings trends. These are best evaluated by means of trend statements such as those presented in Exhibit 7 of Chapter 4. The earnings trend contains important clues to the nature of the enterprise (i.e., cyclical, growth, defensive) and the quality of its management.

Distortions of trends. Analysts must be alert to accounting distortions which affect trends. Among the most important are changes in accounting principles and the effect of business combinations, particularly purchases. These must be adjusted for.

Some of the most common and most pervasive manipulative practices in accounting are designed to affect the presentation of earnings trends. These manipulations are based on the assumptions, generally true, that the trend of income is more important than its absolute size; that retroactive revisions of income already reported in prior periods have little, if any, market effect on security prices[3], and that once a company has incurred a loss, the size of the loss is not as significant as the fact that the loss has been incurred.

These assumptions and the propensities of some managements to use accounting as a means of improving the appearance of the earnings trend has led to techniques which can be broadly described as income smoothing.

Income smoothing.   A number of requirements must be met by the income-smoothing process so as to distinguish it from outright falsehoods and distortions.

The income-smoothing process is a rather sophisticated and insidious device. It does not rely on outright or patent falsehoods and distortions but rather uses the wide leeway existing in accounting principles and their interpretation in order to achieve its ends. Thus, income smoothing is performed within the framework of "generally accepted accounting principles." It is a matter of form rather than one of substance. Consequently, it does not involve a real transaction (e.g., postponing an actual sale to another accounting period in order to shift revenue) but only a redistribution of credits or charges among periods. The general objective is to moderate income variability over the years by shifting income from good years to bad years, by shifting future income to the present (in most cases presently reported earnings are more valuable than those reported at some future date), or vice versa. Similarly, income variability can be moderated or modified by the shifting of costs, expenses, or losses from one period to another.

Income smoothing may take many forms. Hereunder are listed some forms of smoothing to which the analyst should be particularly alert:

1.   The retroactive revision of results already reported, generally with the objective of relieving future income of charges which would have otherwise been made against it. The accounting profession has moved to limit the abuses in this area. (See discussion in Chapters 7 and 11.)
2.   Misstatements, by various methods, of inventories as a means of redistributing income among the years. The Londontown Manufacturing Company case provides a classic example of such practices.[4]
3.   The offsetting of extraordinary credits by identical or nearly identical extraordinary charges as a means of removing an unusual or

---

[3] This was recognized by *APB Opinion No. 20* which, with but three exceptions, forbids the retroactive restatement of prior year financial statements. For a discussion of this *Opinion* see Chapter 11.

[4] Details can be found in an SEC decision issued October 31, 1963 (41 SEC 676–688).

sudden injection of income which may interfere with the display of a growing earnings trend. (For examples and further discussion see Chapter 11.)

4. The provision of reserves for future costs and losses as a means of increasing the adverse results of what is already a poor year and utilizing such reserves to relieve future years of charges against income which would otherwise be properly chargeable against it. (Abuses in this area have been curtailed by SFAS 5.)

5. The substantial write-downs of operating assets (such as plant and equipment) or of intangibles (such as goodwill) in times of economic slowdown when operating results are already poor. The reason usually given for such write-downs is that carrying the properties at book value cannot be economically justified. (For example, Cudahy Packing Company has effected such a write-down of plant but had to reverse it in a subsequent year.) Particularly unwarranted is the practice of writing down operating assets to the point at which a target return on investment (which management thinks it *should* earn) is realized.

6. Timing the inclusion of revenues and costs in periodic income in such a way as to influence the overall trend of income (or loss) over the years. (Examples are the timing of sales or other disposition of property, incurring and expensing of discretionary costs such as research and development, advertising, maintenance, etc.) This category, unlike most others, entails more than accounting choice in that it may involve the timing of actual business transactions.

EXTRAORDINARY GAINS AND LOSSES

Both the evaluation of current earnings levels and the projection of future earnings rely importantly on the separation of the stable elements of income and expense from those which are random, nonrecurring, and erratic in nature.

Stability and regularity are important characteristics affecting the quality of earnings. Moreover, in making earnings projections the forecaster relies, in addition, on repetitiveness of occurrence. Thus, in order to separate the relatively stable elements of income and expense of an enterprise from those which are random or erratic in nature, it is important, as a first step, to identify those gains and losses which are nonrecurring and unusual as well as those which are truly extraordinary.

This separation is a first step which is mostly preparatory in nature. Following it is a process of judgment and analysis which aims at determining how such nonrecurring, unusual, or truly extraordinary items should be treated in the evaluation of present income, and of management performance as well as in the projection of future results.

Significance of accounting treatment and presentation

The validity of any accounting treatment and presentation is largely dependent on its usefulness to those who make decisions on the basis of financial statements. Unfortunately, particularly in the area of the accounting for, and the presentation of, extraordinary gains and losses, the usefulness of this accounting has been impaired because of the great importance attached to it by those who report the results of operations and who are judged by them.

The accounting for, and the presentation of, extraordinary gains and losses has always been subject to controversy. Whatever the merits of the theoretical debate surrounding this issue, the fact remains that one of the basic reasons for the controversial nature of this topic is reporting management's great interest in it. Managements are almost always concerned with the amount of net results of the enterprise as well as with the manner in which these periodic results are reported. This concern is reinforced by a widespread belief that most investors and traders accept the reported net income figures, as well as the modifying explanations which accompany them, as true indices of performance. Thus, extraordinary gains and losses often become the means by which managements attempt to modify the reported operating results and the means by which they try to explain these results. Quite often these explanations are subjective and are slanted in a way designed to achieve the impact and impression desired by management.

The accounting profession has tacitly, if not openly, recognized the role which the foregoing considerations play in the actual practice of reporting extraordinary gains and losses. Its latest pronouncements on this subject, which has been discussed in Chapter 11, have at least insured a fuller measure of disclosure of extraordinary gains and losses and their inclusion in the income statement. This represents an improvement over prior pronouncements which, in an attempt to arrive at a "true" index of operating performance, sanctioned the exclusion of certain extraordinary gains and losses from the income statement.

Analysis and evaluation

The basic objectives in the identification and evaluation of extraordinary items by the analyst are:

1. To determine whether a particular item is to be considered "extraordinary" for purposes of analysis, that is, whether it is so unusual, nonoperating, and nonrecurring in nature that it requires special adjustment in the evaluation of current earnings levels and of future earning possibilities.
2. To decide what form the adjustment for items which are considered as "extraordinary" in nature should take.

Determining whether an item of gain or loss is extraordinary. The infirmities and shortcomings of present practice as well as the considerations which motivate it lead to the inescapable conclusion that the analyst must arrive at his own evaluation of whether a gain or loss should be considered as extraordinary and, if so, how to adjust for it.

In arriving at this decision it is useful to subdivide items, commonly classified as unusual or extraordinary, into three basic categories:

a. Nonrecurring operating gains or losses. By "operating" we usually identify items connected with the normal and usual operations of the business. The concept of normal operations is more widely used than understood and is far from clear and well defined. Thus, in a company operating a machine shop, operating expenses would be considered as those associated with the work of the machine shop. The proceeds from a sale above cost of marketable securities held by the company as an investment of excess cash would be considered a nonoperating gain. So would the gain (or loss) on the sale of a lathe, even if it were disposed of in order to make room for one that would increase the productivity of the shop.

The concept of recurrence is one of frequency. There are no predetermined generally accepted boundaries dividing the recurring event from the nonrecurring. An event (which in this context embraces a gain or loss) occurring once a year can be definitely classified as "recurring." An event, the occurrence of which is unpredictable and which in the past has either not occurred or occurred very infrequently, may be classified as nonrecurring. On the other hand, an event that occurs infrequently but whose occurrence is predictable raises some question as to its designation. An example of the latter would be the relining of blast furnaces. They last for many years; while their replacement is infrequent, the need for it is predictable. Some companies provide for their replacement by means of a reserve. Casualties do not, however, accrue in similar fashion.

Nonrecurring operating gains or losses are, then, gains or losses connected with or related to operations that recur infrequently and/or unpredictably.

In considering how to treat nonrecurring, operating gains and losses, the analyst would do best to recognize the fact of inherent abnormality and the lack of a recurring annual pattern in business and treat them as belonging to the results of the period in which they are reported.

We must also address ourselves to the question of what should be considered as "normal operations." Thus, it is a bakery's purpose to bake bread, rolls, and cakes, but it is presumably outside its normal purpose to buy and sell marketable securities for gain or loss, or even to sell baking machinery that is to be replaced for the purpose of more efficient baking.

This narrow interpretation of the objectives of a business has undergone considerable revision in modern financial theory. Thus, rather than the "baking bread" or any other specific objective, the main objective and task of management is viewed as that of increasing the capital of the owners, or expressed differently, the enhancing of the value of the common stock. This, according to modern financial theory, can be accomplished by means of the judicious combination of an optimal financing plan and any mix of operations opportunities that may be available to achieve the desired purpose.

The analyst should not be bound by the accountant's concept of "normal operations," and thus he can usefully treat a much wider range of gains and losses as being derived from "operations." This approach reinforces our conclusion that most nonrecurring, *operating* gains and losses should, from the point of view of analysis, be considered part of the operating results of the year in which they occur.

This approach is offered as a general guideline rather than as a mechanical rule. The analyst may, after examination of all attendant circumstance, conclude that some such items require separation from the results of a single year. The relative size of an item could conceivably be a factor requiring such treatment. In this case the best approach is to emphasize *average earnings* experience over, say, five years rather than the result of a single year. This approach of emphasizing average earnings becomes almost imperative in the case of enterprises which have widely fluctuating amounts of nonrecurring and other extraordinary items included in their results. After all, a single year is too short and too arbitrary a period on the basis of which to evaluate the earnings power of an enterprise or the prospects for future results. Moreover, we are all familiar with enterprises which defer expenses and postpone losses and come up periodically with a loss year which cancels out much of the income reported in preceding years.

b. Recurring, nonoperating gains or losses. This category includes items of a nonoperating nature that recur with some frequency. An example would be the recurring amortization of a "bargain purchase credit." Other possible examples are interest income and the rental received from employees who rent company-owned houses.

While items in this category may be classified as "extraordinary" in published financial statements, the narrow definition of "nonoperating" which they involve as well as their recurrent nature are good reasons why they should not be excluded from current results by the analyst. They are, after all, mostly the result of the conscious employment of capital by the enterprise, and their recurrence requires inclusion of these gains or losses in estimates designed to project future results.

c. Nonrecurring, nonoperating gains or losses. Of the three categories, this one possesses the greatest degree of "abnormality." Not only are the events here nonrepetitive and unpredictable, but they do not fall within the sphere of normal operations. In most cases these events are extraneous, unintended, and unplanned. However, they can rarely be said to be totally unexpected. Business is ever subject to the risk of sudden adverse events and to random shocks, be they natural or man-made. In the same manner, business transactions are also subject to unexpected windfalls. One good example in this category is the loss from damage done by the crash of an aircraft on a plant not located in the vicinity of an airport. Other, but less clear-cut, examples in this category may also include:

1. Substantial uninsured casualty losses which are not within the categories of risk to which the enterprise can reasonably be deemed to be subject.
2. The expropriation by a foreign government of an entire operation owned by the enterprise.
3. The seizure or destruction of property as a result of an act of war, insurrection, or civil disorders, in areas where this is totally unexpected.

It can be seen readily that while the above occurrences are, in most cases, of a nonrecurring nature, their relation to the operations of a business varies. All are occurrences in the regular course of business. Even the assets destroyed by acts of God were acquired for operating purposes and thus were subject to all possible risks.

Of the three categories this one comes closest to meeting the criterion of being "extraordinary." Nevertheless, truly unique events are very rare. What looks at the time as unique may, in the light of experience turn out to be the symptom of new sets of circumstances which affect and may continue to affect the earning power as well as the degree of risk to which an enterprise is subject.

The analyst must bear in mind such possibilities, but barring evidence to the contrary, items in this category can be regarded as extraordinary in nature and thus can be omitted from the results of operations of a *single* year. They are, nevertheless, part of the longer term record of results of the enterprise. Thus, they enter the computation of *average earnings,* and the propensity of the enterprise to incur such gains or losses must be considered in the projection of future average earnings.

The foregoing discussion has tried to point out that the intelligent classification of extraordinary items provides a workable solution to their treatment by the analyst. There are, however, other aspects of the evaluation of extraordinary items which must be considered here. One is the effect of extraordinary items on the resources of an enterprise; the other is their effect on the evaluation of management performance.

Effect of extraordinary items on enterprise resources. Every extraordinary gain or loss has a dual aspect. In addition to recording a gain (whether extraordinary or not) a business records an increase in resources. Similarly, a loss results in a reduction of resources. Since return on investment measures the relationship of net income to resources, the incurrence of extraordinary gains and losses will affect this important measure of profitability. The more material the extraordinary item, the more significant that influence will be. In other words if earnings and events are to be used to make estimates about the future, then extraordinary items convey something more than past performance. Thus, if an extraordinary loss results in the destruction of capital on which a certain return is expected, that return may be lost to the future. Conversely, an extraordinary gain will result in an addition of resources on which a future return can be expected.

This means that in projecting profitability and return on investment, the analyst must take into account the effect of recorded "extraordinary" items as well as the likelihood of the occurrence of future events which may cause extraordinary items.

Effect on evaluation of management. One implication frequently associated with the reporting of extraordinary gains and losses is that they have not resulted from a "normal" or "planned" activity of management and that, consequently, they should not be used in the evaluation of management performance. The analyst should seriously question such a conclusion.

What is "normal activity" in relation to management's deliberate actions? Whether we talk about the purchase or sale of securities, of other assets not used in operations, or of divisions and subsidiaries that definitely relate to operations, we talk about actions deliberately taken by management with specific purposes in mind. Such actions require, if anything, more consideration or deliberation than do ordinary everyday operating decisions because they are most often unusual in nature and involve substantial amounts of money. They are true tests of management ability. The results of such activities always qualify or enhance the results of "normal" operations, thus yielding the final net results.

Similarly, management must be aware of the risk of natural or manmade disasters or impediments in the course of business. The decision to engage in foreign operations is made with the knowledge of the special risks which this involves and the decision to insure or not is a normal operating decision. Nothing can really be termed completely unexpected or unforeseeable. Management does not engage, or is at least not supposed to engage, in any activity unconsciously;

hence, whatever it does is clearly within the expected activity of a business. Every type of enterprise is subject to specific risks which are inherent in it, and managements do not enter such ventures blindly.

When it comes to the assesment of results that count and results that build or destroy value, the distinction of what is normal and what is not fades almost into insignificance. Management's beliefs about the quality of its decisions are nearly always related to the normalcy, or lack thereof, of surrounding circumstances. This can be clearly seen in the management report section of many annual reports. Of course, management has to take more time to explain failure or shortcomings than to explain success. Success hardly needs an explanation, unless it involves circumstances not likely to be repeated. Failure often evokes long explanations, and more often than not, unusual or unforeseeable circumstances are blamed for it. If only normal conditions had prevailed, everything would have been much better. But in a competitive economy, normal conditions hardly ever prevail for any length of time. Management is paid to anticipate and expect the unusual. No alibis are permitted. Explanations are never a substitute for performance.

EARNINGS FORECASTING

A major objective of income analysis is the projection of income. The evaluation of the level of earnings is, from an analytical point of view, closely related to their projection. This is so because a valid projection of earnings involves an analysis of each major component of income and a considered estimate of its probable future size. Thus, some of the factors discussed in the preceding section are also applicable to earnings projection.

Projection must be differentiated from extrapolation. The latter is based on an assumption of the continuation of an existing trend and involves, more or less, a mechanical extension of that trend into the uncharted territory of the future.

Projection, on the other hand, is based on a careful analysis of as many individual components of income and expense as is possible and a considered estimate of their future size taking into consideration interrelationships among the components as well as probable future conditions. Thus, forecasting requires as much detail as is possible to obtain. In addition the "stability" of the individual components must be assessed in terms of the likelihood of their future recurrence. This lends particular importance to the analysis of nonrecurring factors and of extraordinary items. Some of the mechanics of earnings forecasting were considered in Chapter 17 as part of the process of projecting short-term fund flows.

Projection requires the use of an earnings record covering a number of periods. Repeated or recurring performance can be projected with a better degree of confidence than can random events.

Projection also requires use of enterprise data by product line or segment wherever different segments of an enterprise are subject to different degrees of risk, possess different degrees of profitability, or have differing growth potentials.

For example, the following tabulation of divisional earnings results indicates the degree to which the results of a component of an enterprise can be masked by the aggregate results:

	Earnings in million dollars			
	19X1	19X2	19X3	19X4
Segment A	1,800	1,700	1,500	1,200
Segment B	600	800	1,100	1,400
Total net income	2,400	2,500	2,600	2,600

Judgment on the earnings potential of the enterprise depends, of course, importantly on the relative importance of, as well as the future prospects of, segment B. The subject of product line reporting is discussed in Chapter 20.

SEC disclosure requirements—aid to forecasting

The "Management's discussion and analysis of the summary of earnings" disclosure requirements of the SEC (see Chapter 20) contain a wealth of information on management's views and attitudes as well as on factors which can influence enterprise operating performance. Consequently, the analyst may find much information in these analyses to aid him in the forecasting process.

Another important SEC disclosure requirement which can identify factors which the analyst should consider in forecasts is found in *ASR 166* (1974) entitled "Disclosure of Unusual Risks and Uncertainties in Financial Reporting." In this release the Commission indicates considerable concern over the number of situations it has noted in which significant and increasing business uncertainties have not been fully reflected in the financial reporting of registrants. It recognizes that investors and others are aware of the large number of estimates required in the preparation of financial statements, but points out that when unusual circumstances arise or there are significant changes in the degree of business uncertainty, a registrant has the responsibility of including comprehensive and specific disclosure of such risks and uncertainties in its financial reports.

The release contains specific examples of unusual risks and uncertainties such as *loans of financial institutions, marketable securities, deferred fuel costs* of public utilities, *crude oil purchase prices* subject to negotiation with foreign governments, and *single major projects* which will significantly affect the *success or failure* of a company. However, the importance of the release to the analyst lies in the principle of disclosure promulgated here. Thus, while these disclosures are not requirements under the Commission's rules, adherence to their spirit and intent by management should provide valuable information to the analyst.

Elements in earnings forecasts

Granted that the decision maker is interested primarily in future prospects, his approach to assessing them must be based primarily on the present as well as on the past. While expected future changes in conditions must be given recognition, the experience of the present and the past form the base to which such adjustments are applied. In doing this the analyst relies on the degree of continuity and perseverance of momentum which is the common experience of the enterprise and the industry of which it is part. Random shocks and sudden changes are always possible, but they can rarely be foreseen with any degree of accuracy.

The importance to the analyst of the underlying continuity of business affairs should not be overemphasized. One should not confuse the basis for the projection of future results, which the past record represents, with the forecast which is the end product. As a final objective the analyst is interested in a projection of net income. Net income is the result of the offset of two big streams: (1) total revenues and (2) total costs.

Considering that net income represents most frequently but a relatively small portion of either stream, one can see how a relatively minor change in either of these large streams can cause a very significant change in net income.

A significant check on the reasonableness of an earnings projection is to test it against the return on invested capital which is implicit in the forecast. If the result is at variance with returns realized in the past the underlying assumptions must be thoroughly examined so that the reasons for such deviations can be pinpointed.

In terms of the framework examined in Chapter 19 the return on investment depends on earnings which are a product of *management* and of *assets* which require funds for their acquisition.

1. Management. That it takes resourceful management to "breathe life" into assets by employing them profitably and causing their optimum utilization is well known. The assumption of stability of relationships and trends implies that there has been no major change in the skill, the depth, and the continuity of the management group or a radical change in the type of business in which their skill has been proven by a record of successful performance.

2. *Assets.* The second essential ingredient to profitable operations is funds or resources with which the assets essential to the successful conduct of business are acquired. No management, no matter how ingenious, can expand operations and have an enterprise grow without an adequate asset base. Thus, continuity of success and the extrapolation of growth must be based on an investigation of the sources of additional funds which the enterprise will need and the effect of the method of financing on net income and earnings per share.

The financial condition of the enterprise, as was seen in Chapters 16 and 18, can have a bearing on the results of operations. A lack of liquidity may inhibit an otherwise skillful management, and a precarious or too risky capital structure may lead to limitations by others on its freedom of action.

The above factors, as well as other economic, industry, and competitive factors, must be taken into account by the analyst when projecting the earnings of an enterprise. Ideally, in projecting earnings, the analyst should add a lot of knowledge about the future to some knowledge of the past. Realistically the analyst must settle for a lot of knowledge about the past and present and only a limited knowledge of the future.

In evaluating earnings trends the analyst relies also on such indicators of future conditions as capital expenditures, order backlogs, as well as demand trends in individual product lines.

It is important to realize that no degree of sophistication in the techniques used in earnings projections can eliminate the inevitable uncertainty to which all forecasts are subject. Even the best and most soundly based projections retain a significant probability of proving widely off the mark because of events and circumstances which cannot be foreseen.

The most effective means by which the analyst and decision maker can counter this irreducible uncertainty is to keep close and constant watch over how closely actual results conform to his projections. This requires a constant monitoring of results and the adjustment and updating of projections in the light of such results. The monitoring of earnings is considered later in this chapter.

Publication of financial forecasts

Recent years have witnessed intensified interest in publication by companies of forecasts of earnings and other financial data. The publication of forecasts in Britain in certain specialized situations as well as a belief that forecasts would be useful to investors were major factors behind this interest. This type of forecasting by insiders (i.e., management) is to be distinguished from forecasts made by financial analysts which are based on all the information which they can obtain.

In early 1977 an advisory committee to the SEC recommended that the agency design procedures to encourage companies to make forecasts of their economic performance.

So far, the commission has not formally encouraged or discouraged forecasting, but in 1975 it put forward rules governing those that do so. These were considered so restrictive, however, that businessmen warned that they would be forced to sharply reduce communications about their companies and the SEC withdrew them.

The SEC did, however, delete in its regulations a reference to predictions of "earnings" as possibly misleading in certain situations. Thus the commission will no longer object to disclosure in filings with it of projections which are made in good faith and have a reasonable basis provided that they are presented in appropriate form and are accompanied by information adequate for investors to make their own judgments.

The issue of forecasts is being considered again in connection with a major study of the agency's disclosure policy. The advisory committee said a so-called safe harbor rule should be adopted to clarify the potential liability of those making voluntary projections. It also said filings should include a cautionary statement about the inherent uncertainty of such data.

The interest in financial forecasts has resulted in a formal consideration of some of the issues by the AICPA which in 1975 issued two statements on the subject.[5]

These statements recommend, among others, that financial forecasts should be presented in a historical financial statement format and that they include regularly a comparison of the forecast with attained results.

Both statements recognize the primary importance which assumptions play in the reliability and creditability of a financial forecast. Consequently, those assumptions which management thinks most crucial or significant to the forecast—or are key factors upon which the financial results of the enterprise depends—should be disclosed to provide the greatest benefit to users of forecasts. There ordinarily should be some indication of the basis or rationale for these assumptions.

Speagle, Clark, and Elgers have categorized assumptions underly-

---

[5] "Guidelines for Systems for the Preparation of Financial Forecasts" and "Presentation and Disclosure of Financial Forecasts," AICPA 1975. (Auditing implication are also being considered.)

ing forecasted financial statements as: (1) "On going assumptions relating to the forecast methodology, company operating characteristics and so on; (2) Standard assumptions bearing upon the continuity in accounting policy, company management, supply sources, etc.; and (3) Transitory assumptions covering events in a particular year such as recapitalizations, labor settlements, new product introductions, facilities expansion, etc.[6]

The validity of any forecasted financial data depends to a high degree on the assumptions, both implicit and explicit, upon which the forecasting technique is based. The financial analyst who uses a management forecast as input to his own projections should pay first and primary attention to the assumptions on which it is based.

Estimating earning power

A culmination of the foregoing analytical and evaluative processes are often the estimation of the earning power of an enterprise. Earning power is a concept of financial analysis, not of accounting. It focuses on stable, and recurring elements and thus aims to arrive at the best possible estimate of repeatable *average* earnings over a span of future years. Accounting, as we have seen, can supply much of the essential information for the computation of earning power. However, the process is one involving knowledge, judgment, experience, a time horizon as well as a specialized investing or lending point of view, such as those described in Chapter 3.

Investors and lenders look ultimately to future cash flows as sources of rewards and safety. Accrual accounting, which underlies income determination, aims to relate sacrifices and benefits to the periods in which they occur. In spite of its known shortcomings, this framework represents the most reliable and relevant indicator of future probabilities of cash inflows and outflows presently known.

In our discussion of the analysis and the prediction of earnings, we recognized that a year represents too short and too arbitrary a time period for purposes of income measurement and evaluation. Because of the length of time required to assess the ultimate workout and the results of many investments and outlays and because of the presence of numerous nonrecurring and extraordinary factors, the determination of the normal earnings level or earning power of an enterprise is best measured by means of average earnings realized over a number of years.

The period of time over which an earnings average should be calculated will vary with the industry of which the enterprise is part

---

[6] R. E. Speagle, J. J. Clark, and P. Elgers, *Publishing Financial Forecasts: Benefits, Alternatives, Risk* (Laventhol Krekstein Horwath & Horwath, 1974).

and with other special circumstances. However, in general, a from 5-
to 10-year earnings average will smooth out many of the distortions
and the irregularities which impair the significance of a single year's
results.

Monitoring performance and results

The judgments of what the proper financial forecast of an enterprise
is or what its earning power is, are based on estimates which hinge on
future developments which can never be fully forseen. Consequently,
the best course of action is to monitor performance closely and frequently and to compare it with earlier estimates and assumptions. In
this way one can constantly revise one's estimates and judgments and
incorporate the unfolding reality into earlier judgments and conclusions. One of the best ways of monitoring performance is to follow
interim reports closely.

INTERIM FINANCIAL STATEMENTS

The need to follow closely the results achieved by an enterprise
requires frequent updatings of such results. Interim financial statements, most frequently issued on a quarterly basis, are designed to fill
this need. They are used by decision makers as means of updating
current results as well as in the prediction of future results.

If, as we have seen, a year is a relatively short period of time in
which to account for results of operations, then trying to confine the
measurement of results to a three-month period involves all the more
problems and imperfections. For this and other reasons the reporting
of interim earnings is subject to serious limitations and distortions. The
intelligent use of reported interim results requires that we have a full
understanding of these possible problem areas and limitations. The
following is a review of some of the basic reasons for these problems
and limitations, as well as their effect on the determination of reported
interim results.

Year-end adjustments

The determination of the results of operations for a year requires a
great many estimates, as well as procedures, such as accruals and the
determination of inventory quantities and carrying values. These procedures can be complex, time-consuming, and costly. Examples of
procedures requiring a great deal of data collection and estimation
include estimation of the percentage of completion of contracts, determination of cost of work in process, the allocation of under- or over-

absorbed overhead for the period, and the estimation of year-end inventory levels under the Lifo method. The complex, time-consuming, and expensive nature of these procedures can mean that they are performed much more crudely during interim periods and are often based on records which are less complete than are their year-end counterparts. The result inevitably is a less accurate process of income determination which, in turn, may require year-end adjustments which can modify substantially the interim results already reported.

Seasonality

Many enterprises experience at least some degree of seasonality in their activities. Sales may be unevenly distributed over the year, and so it may be with production and other activities. This tends to distort comparisons among the quarterly results of a single year. It also presents problems in the allocation of many budgeted costs, such as advertising, research and development, and repairs and maintenance. If expenses vary with sales, they should be accrued on the basis of expected sales for the full year. Obviously, the preparer of yearly financial statements has the benefit of hindsight which the preparer of interim statements does not. There are also problems with the allocation of fixed costs among quarters.

ILLUSTRATION 1.　A study of the affairs of Mattel, Inc. reveals how company executives came up with targeted earnings quarter by quarter in fiscal years ending January 31, 1971 and 1972 using misleading or blatantly false methods to increase recorded sales or to decrease recorded expenses to reach targets. Mattel used an accounting practice known as "annualization" to match incurred expenses against sales on a year to date basis and these were juggled to achieve preselected results.

ILLUSTRATION 2.　The tenuous nature of quarterly gross profit estimates is exemplified by this note by Bristol Products, Inc.: "Results of Fourth Quarter, 1974—As indicated in Note 1, the Company's interim financial statements for 1974 reflected results of operations using estimated gross profit percentages for its wholesale divisions. Physical inventories of these divisions at December 31, 1974 disclosed that the interim gross profit estimates and resultant net income were understated. If fourth quarter, 1974 results were computed using the annual gross profit percentages determined for the wholesale divisions, fourth quarter net income would have amounted to approximately $114,000 or $.10 per share. This compares with fourth quarter net income of $228,645 or $.24 per share computed by substracting interim results reported for the first three quarters of 1974 from results for the year."

ILLUSTRATION 3.　The following is an example of adjustments which can result from seasonal variations: "Because of a seasonal production cycle, and in accordance with practices followed by the Company in reporting interim financial statements prior to 19X4, $435,000 of unabsorbed factory overhead has been deferred at July 4, 19X5. Due to uncertainties as to production and sales in 19X4, $487,000 of such unabsorbed overhead was expensed during the first 6 months of 19X4."

APB Opinion No. 28

In its *Opinion No. 28* the APB concluded that interim reports should be prepared in accordance with generally accepted accounting principles used in the preparation of the latest financial statements. Adopting mostly the point of view that a quarterly report is an integral part of a full year rather than a discrete period, it calls for the accrual of revenues and for the spreading of certain costs among the quarters of a year. For example, it sanctions the accrual of such year-end adjustments as inventory shrinkages, quantity discounts, and uncollectible accounts; but it prohibits the accrual of advertising costs on the ground that benefits of such costs cannot be anticipated. Losses cannot, generally, be deferred beyond the interim period in which they occur. Lifo inventory liquidations should be considered on an annual basis. Only permanent declines in inventory values are to be recorded on an interim basis. Moreover, the Opinion calls for the inclusion of extraordinary items in the interim period in which they occur.[7] Income taxes should be accrued on the basis of the effective tax rate expected to apply to the full year.

SEC interim reporting requirements

The SEC took a relatively early and strong interest in interim reporting and as a result brought about very significant improvements in reporting and disclosure in this area. In 1972 it required quarterly reports (on Form 10-Q) and reports on current developments (Form 8-K), disclosure of separate fourth quarter results and details of year-end adjustments.

In 1975 the SEC issued requirements (principally in *ASR 177*) which served to expand substantially the content and the utility of interim reports filed with the Commission. The principal requirements include:

Comparative quarterly and year-to-date abbreviated income statement data—this information may be labelled "unaudited" and

---

[7] SFAS 3 specifies that "If a cumulative effect type accounting change is made in other than the first interim period of an enterprise's fiscal year, no cumulative effect of the change shall be included in net income of the period of change. Instead, financial information for the pre-change interim periods of the fiscal year in which the change is made shall be restated by applying the newly adopted accounting principle to those pre-change interim periods."

must also be included in annual reports to shareholders. (Small companies are exempted).

Year-to-date statements of changes in financial position.

Comparative balance sheets.

Increased pro forma information on business combinations accounted for as purchases.

Conformity with the principles of accounting measurement as set forth in professional pronouncements on interim financial reports.

Increased disclosure of accounting changes with a letter from the registrant's independent public accountant stating whether or not he judges the changes to be preferable.

Management's narrative analysis of the results of operations, explaining the reasons for material changes in the amount of revenue and expense items from one quarter to the next. (See discussion in Chapter 20).

Indications as to whether a Form 8-K was filed during the quarter—reporting either unusual charges or credits to income or a change of auditors.

Signature of the registrant's chief financial officer or chief accounting officer.

In promulgating these expanded disclosure requirements the Commission indicated that it believed that these disclosures will assist investors in understanding the pattern of corporate activities throughout a fiscal period. It maintained that presentation of such quarterly data will supply information about the trend of business operations over segments of time which are sufficiently short to reflect business turning points.

Implications for analysis

While there have been some notable recent improvements in the reporting of interim results, the analyst must remain constantly aware that accuracy of estimation and the objectivity of determinations are and remain problem areas which are inherent in the measurement of results of very short periods. Moreover, the limited association of auditors with interim data, while lending as yet some unspecified degree of assurance, cannot be equated to the degree of assurance which is associated with fully audited financial statements. SEC insistence that the professional pronouncements on interim statements (such as *APB Opinion 28*) be adhered to should offer analysts some additional comfort. However, not all principles promulgated by the APB on the subject of interim financial statements result in presentations useful to the analyst. For example, the inclusion of extraordinary items in the results of the quarter in which they occur will require careful adjustment to render them meaningful for purposes of analysis.

While the normalization of expenses is a reasonable intraperiod accounting procedure, the analyst must be aware of the fact that there are no rigorous standards or rules governing its implementation and that it is, consequently, subject to possible abuse. The shifting of costs between periods is generally easier than the shifting of sales; and, therefore, a close analysis of sales may yield a more realistic clue to a company's true state of affairs for an interim period.

Since the price of the common stock influences the computation of earnings per share (see Chapter 12) the analyst should in his evaluation of per share results be alert to the separation of these market effects from those related to the operating fundamentals of an enterprise.

Some problems of seasonality in interim results of operations can be overcome by considering in the analysis not merely the results of a single quarter, but also the year-to-date cumulative results which incorporate the results of the latest available quarter. This is the most effective way of monitoring the results of an enterprise and bringing to bear on its analysis the latest data on operations that are available.

QUESTIONS

1. Distinguish between income and cash flow. Why is there a distinction between the two?
2. a. What is meant by "quality of earnings"? Why do analysts assess it?
   b. On what major elements does the quality of earnings depend?
3. a. What are discretionary costs?
   b. Of what significance are discretionary costs to an analysis of the quality of earnings?
4. a. Why is the evaluation of research and development costs important to the analysis and projection of income?
   b. What are some of the precautions required in analyzing research and development expenses?
5. a. What is the relationship between the carrying amounts of various assets and earnings reported?
   b. What is the relationship between the amounts at which liabilities, including provisions, are carried and earnings reported?
6. Explain briefly the relationship between the quality of earnings and the following balance sheet items:
   a. Accounts receivable.
   b. Inventories.
   c. Deferred charges.
7. In what way is balance sheet analysis a check on the validity as well as the quality of earnings?

8. Comment on the effect which the "risk category" of an asset has on the quality of reported earnings.

9. What is the effect of external factors on the quality of earnings?

10. What is income smoothing? How can it be distinguished from outright falsehoods?

11. Name three forms of income smoothing.

12. Why are managements so greatly interested in the reporting of extraordinary gains and losses?

13. What are the basic objectives of the analyst in the identification and the evaluation of extraordinary items?

14. *a.* Into what categories can items which are described as unusual or extraordinary in the financial statements be usefully subdivided into for purposes of analysis?
    b. Give examples of each such category.
    c. How should the analyst treat items in each category? Is such a treatment indicated under all circumstances? Explain.

15. What are the effects of extraordinary items on—
    a. Enterprise resources?
    b. The evaluation of managements?

16. Comment on the following statement:
    "Extraordinary gains or losses have not resulted from a 'normal' or 'planned' activity of management and, consequently, they should not be used in the evaluation of managerial performance."
    Do you agree?

17. What is the difference between projection and extrapolation of earnings?

18. Cite some of the examples of unusual risks and uncertainties that should be disclosed according to SEC's *ASR No. 166* and their importance to the financial analyst.

19. What are the categories of assumptions underlying forecasted financial statements? Give examples of each category. What is the importance of these assumptions to the financial analyst?

20. *a.* What are interim financial statements used for?
    b. What accounting problems which are peculiar to iterim statements must the analyst be aware of?

21. Why are interim earnings reports particularly useful in the monitoring of earnings trends?

22. Interim financial reporting can be subject to serious limitations and distortions. Discuss some of the reasons for this.

23. What factors (*a*) within the company, and (*b*) within the economy, have and are likely to affect the degree of variability in the earnings per share, dividends per share, and market price per share, of common stock? (C.F.A.)

24. What are the major disclosure requirements by the SEC with regard to interim reports? What are the objectives behind them?

25. What implications do interim reports hold for the financial analyst?

23

COMPREHENSIVE ANALYSIS OF FINANCIAL STATEMENTS

THE METHODOLOGY OF FINANCIAL STATEMENT ANALYSIS

The marshalling, arrangement, and presentation of data for purposes of financial statement analysis can be standardized to some extent in the interest of consistency and organizational efficiency. However, the actual process of analysis must be left to the judgment of the analyst so that he may allow for the great diversity of situations and circumstances which he is likely to encounter in practice, and thus give full reign to his own initiative, originality, and ingenuity. Nevertheless, there are some useful generalizations and guidelines which may be stated as to a general approach to the task of financial statement analysis.

To begin with, financial statement analysis is oriented towards the achievement of definite objectives. In order that the analysis best accomplish these objectives, the first step is to define them carefully. The thinking and clarification leading up to such a definition of objectives is a very important part of the analytical process, for it insures a clear understanding of objectives, that is, of what is pertinent and relevant and what is not, and thus also leads to avoidance of unnecessary work. This clarification of objectives is indispensable to an *effective* as well as to an *efficient* analysis: *effective,* in that, given the specifications, it focuses on the most important and most relevant elements of the financial statements; *efficient,* in that it leads to an analysis with maximum economy of time and effort.

ILLUSTRATION 1. The bank's loan officer, dealing with a request for a short-term loan to finance inventory, may define his objective as assessing the intention and the ability of the borrower to repay the loan on time. Thus, the analyst can concentrate on what is needed to achieve this objective and need not, for instance, address himself to industry conditions which can affect the borrowing entity only over the longer term.

Once the objective of the analysis has been defined, the next step is the formulation of specific questions the answers to which are needed in the achievement of such objectives.

ILLUSTRATION 2.   The loan officer in Illustration 1 now needs to define the critical criteria which will affect his decision. For instance, the question of the borrower's *willingness* to repay the short-term loan bears on his character; and financial statement analysis can reveal only the history of past loans granted it. Thus, tools other than financial statement analysis will have to be employed to get complete information on the borrower's character.

Among the other questions on which the loan officer will need information are the following:

1.   What is the enterprise's short-term liquidity?
2.   What will its sources and uses of cash be during the duration of the loan agreement?

Financial statement analysis can go far towards providing answers to such questions.

Having defined the objective and having translated it into specific questions and criteria which must be resolved, the analyst is ready for the third step in the analysis process. This is to decide which tools and techniques of analysis are the most appropriate, effective, and efficient ones to use in working on the particular decision problem at hand.

ILLUSTRATION 3.   Following the sequence developed in Illustrations 1 and 2, the loan officer will now decide which financial statement analysis tools are most appropriate to use in this case. He may choose one or more of the following:

1.   Short-term liquidity ratios.
2.   Inventory turnover measures.
3.   Cash flow projections.
4.   Analyses of changes in financial position.

These analyses will have to include estimates and projections of future conditions toward which most, if not all, financial analysis is oriented.

The fourth and final step in analysis is the interpretation of the data and measures assembled as a basis for decision and action. This is the most critical and difficult of the steps, and the one requiring the application of a great deal of judgment, skill, and effort. Interpretation is a process of investigation and evaluation, and of envisaging the reality which lies behind the figures examined. There is, of course, no mechanical substitute for this process of judgment. However, the proper definition of the problem and of the critical questions which must be answered, as well as the skillful selection of the most appropriate tools of analysis available in the circumstances, will go a long way towards a meaningful interpretation of the results of analysis.

ILLUSTRATION 4. Following the sequence of the first three examples above, the collection, by the loan officer, of the data described in Illustration 3 is, of course, not the end result of his analysis. These data must be integrated, evaluated, and interpreted for the purposes of reaching the basic decision of whether to make the loan and, if so, in what amount.

By way of analogy, the weather forecasting function provides an example of the difference between the availability of analytical data and its successful interpretation. Thus, the average listener to weather information does not know how to interpret barometric pressure, relative humidity, or wind velocity. What one needs to know is the weather forecast which results from an interpretation of these data.

The intelligent analyst and interpreter of financial statement data must always bear in mind that a financial statement is at best an abstraction of an underlying reality. Further mathematical manipulation of financial data can result in second, third, and even further levels of abstractions; and the analyst must always keep in mind the business reality behind the figures. No map of the Rocky Mountains can fully convey the grandeur of the terrain. One has to see them in order to appreciate them because maps, like financial statements, are, at best abstractions. That is why security analysts must, at some point, leave the financial statements and visit the companies which they analyze in order to get a full understanding of the phenomena revealed by their analysis. This is particularly true because the static reality portrayed by the abstractions found in the financial statements cannot remain static for very long. Reality is ever changing.

A recognition of the inherent limitations of financial data is needed for intelligent analysis. This does not detract from their importance because financial statements and data are the only means by which the financial realities of an enterprise can be reduced to a common denominator which is quantified and which can be mathematically manipulated and projected in a rational and disciplined way.

SIGNIFICANCE OF THE "BUILDING BLOCK" APPROACH TO FINANCIAL ANALYSIS

The six major "building blocks" of financial analysis which we have examined in this text are:

1. Short-term liquidity.
2. Funds flow.

3. Capital structure and long-term solvency.
4. Return on investment.
5. Asset utilization.
6. Operating performance.

The "building block" approach to financial statement analysis involves:

1. The determination of the major objectives which a particular financial analysis is to achieve.
2. Arriving at a judgment about which of the six major areas of analysis (i.e., our "building blocks") must be evaluated with what degree of emphasis and in what order of priority.

For example, the security analyst, in the evaluation of the investment merit of a particular issue of equity securities, may attach primary importance to the earning capacity and potential of the enterprise. Thus, the first "building block" of the analysis will be the evaluation of "operating performance" and the next, perhaps, "return on investment." A thorough analysis will, of course, require that attention be paid to the other four major areas of analysis, although with perhaps lesser degrees of emphasis, that is, depth. This attention to the other major areas of analysis is necessary in order to detect possible problem areas, that is, areas of potential risk. Thus, further analysis may reveal a liquidity problem arising from a "thin" working capital condition, or it may reveal a situation of inadequate capital funds which may stifle growth and flexibility. It is conceivable that these problem areas may reveal themselves to be so important as to overshadow the question of earning power, thus leading to a change in the relative emphasis which the analyst will accord to the main areas of his particular analysis.

While the subdivision of the analysis into six distinct aspects of a company's financial condition and performance is a useful approach, it must be borne in mind that these areas of analysis are highly interrelated. For example, the operating performance of an enterprise can be affected by the lack of adequate capital funds or by problems of short-term liquidity. Similarly, a credit evaluation cannot stop at the point where a satisfactory short-term liquidity position has been determined because existing or incipient problems in the "operating performance" area may result in serious drains of funds due to losses. Such drains can quickly reverse the satisfactory liquidity position which may prevail at a given point in time.

At the start of his analysis the analyst will tentatively determine the relative importance of the areas which he will examine and the order in which they will be examined. This order of emphasis and priority may subsequently change in the light of his findings and as the analysis progresses.

THE EARMARKS OF GOOD FINANCIAL ANALYSIS

As we have noted, the foundation of any good analysis is a thorough understanding of the objectives to be achieved and the uses to which it is going to be put. Such understanding leads to economy of effort as well as to a useful and most relevant focus on the points that need to be clarified and the estimates and projections that are required.

In practice, rarely can all the facts surrounding a particular analysis be obtained, so that most analyses are undertaken on the basis of incomplete and inadequate facts and data. The process of financial analysis is basically one of reducing the areas of uncertainty—which can, however, never be completely eliminated.

A written analysis and report is not only a significant medium of communication to the reader but it also serves importantly to organize the thinking of the analyst as well as to allow him or her to check the flow and the logic of the presentation. The process of writing reinforces our thinking and vice versa. As we revise our words, we also refine our thoughts—and improvements in style lead, in turn, to the sharpening and improvement in the thinking process itself.

A good analysis separates clearly for the reader the interpretations and conclusions of the analysis from the facts and data upon which they are based. This not only separates fact from opinion and estimate, but also enables the reader to follow the rationale of the analyst's conclusions and allows him to modify them as his judgment dictates. To this end the analysis should contain distinct sections devoted to:

1. General background material on the enterprise analyzed, the industry of which it is a part, and the economic environment in which it operates.
2. Financial and other data used in the analysis as well as ratios, trends, and other analytical measures which have been developed from them.
3. Assumptions as to the general economic environment and as to other conditions on which estimates and projections are based.
4. A listing of positive and negative factors, quantitative and qualitative, by important areas of analysis.
5. Projections, estimates, interpretations, and conclusions based on the aforementioned data.(Some analyses list only the positive and negative factors developed by the analysis and leave further interpretations to the reader.)

A good analysis should start with a brief "Summary and Conclusion" section as well as a table of contents to help the busy reader decide how much of the report he wants to read and on which parts of it to concentrate.

The writer of an analytical report must guard against the all-too-common tendency to include irrelevant matter. For example, the reader need not know the century-old details of the humble beginnings of the enterprise under analysis nor should he be taken on a "journey" along all the fruitless byways and missteps which the analyst inevitably encountered in his process of ferreting out and separating the important from the insignificant. Irrelevant bulk or "roughage" can only serve to confuse and distract the reader of a report.

Ambiguities and equivocations which are employed to avoid responsibility or to hedge conclusions do not belong in a good analytical report. Finally, the writers of such reports must recognize that we are all judged on the basis of small details. Consequently, the presence of mistakes in grammar or of obvious errors of fact in a report can plant doubt in the reader's mind as to the competence of the author and the validity of the analysis.

SPECIAL INDUSTRY OR ENVIRONMENTAL CHARACTERISTICS

In this text, the analysis of the various segments of financial statements was treated from the point of view of the regular commercial or industrial enterprise. The financial analyst must, however, recognize that there are industries with distinct accounting treatments which arise either from their specialized nature or from the special conditions, such as governmental regulation, to which they are subject. The analysis of the financial statements of such enterprise requires a thorough understanding of the accounting peculiarities to which they are subject, and the analyst must, accordingly, prepare himself for his task by the study and the understanding of the specialized areas of accounting which affect his particular analysis.

Thus, for example, the analysis of a company in the Oil and Gas Industry requires a thorough knowledge of such accounting concepts peculiar to that industry such as the determination of "cost centers," prediscovery costs, discovery costs, and the disposition of capitalized costs. There are particular problems in the treatment of exploratory, development, and other expenditures as well as in amortization and depletion practices.

Life insurance accounting, to cite another example, also requires specialized knowledge which arises from the peculiarities of this industry and from the regulation to which it is subject. There are special problems in the area of recognition of premium revenues, the accounting for acquisition costs of new business, and the determination of policy reserves.

Public utility regulation has resulted in specialized accounting concepts and problems of which every utility analyst must be aware. There are tax allocation problems resulting in differences among companies which "normalize" taxes versus those which "flow" them through. Then there are problems related to the adequacy of provisions for depreciation, and problems concerning the utility's "rate base" and the method by which it is computed.

As in any field of endeavor specialized areas of inquiry require that specialized knowledge be brought to bear upon them. Financial analysis is, of course, no exception.

ILLUSTRATION OF A COMPREHENSIVE ANALYSIS OF FINANCIAL STATEMENTS—MARINE SUPPLY CORPORATION

The following analysis of the financial statements and other data of the Marine Supply Corporation will serve as an illustration of this process.

Introduction

The Marine Supply Corporation, a leader in the outboard motor industry, was incorporated some 40 years ago. While outboard motor engines and related marine products still account for the bulk of the company's sales, other products are gaining in importance and growing at a rate much faster than the primary products (see Exhibit 23–1, sales breakdown).

Snow vehicle production was launched in fiscal year 19X4. Its growth rate looks dramatic because it starts from an extremely low

EXHIBIT 23–1

MARINE SUPPLY CORPORATION
Sales Breakdown
(in millions of dollars)

	19X5		19Y0		Sales increase 19X5– 19Y0	Annual growth rates*
Product	Sales	%	Sales	%	%	%
Marine products	135.0	74.5	217.3	71.0	+ 61	10
Lawn care equipment	16.2	9.0	30.5	10.0	+ 88	13
Vehicles	14.1	7.8	19.6	6.4	+ 39	7
Chain saws	9.4	5.2	9.5	3.1	+ 1	0
Snow vehicles	5.1	2.8	23.4	7.7	+359	36
Miscellaneous............	.9	.7	4.2	1.8	+367	36
Total	180.7	100.0	304.5	100.0	+ 69	11.2

* Five-year period, compounded annually.

base. Outboard motors can be regarded as the primary base of the company's growth, and outboard engines contribute an even larger portion of corporate profits.

While most of Marine Supply Corporation's products have some commercial applications, they are sold primarily for recreation or leisure-time purposes. Being generally big-ticket items, the company's sales are greatly subject to swings in consumer buying cycles.

The use of outboard motors and the majority of the company's other products is largely confined to the warmer months of late spring, summer, and early fall. This means peak retail demand for these items is seasonal; dealer buying tends to be concentrated in this period as well. As a result, the first quarter of the company's fiscal year (ending December) frequently produces a nominal deficit while the June quarter generates 40 percent or more of annual profits.

Marine Supply is one of the world's largest manufacturers of outboard motors; its twin lines command something more than one half the U.S.-Canadian market (by far the most important), and the company estimates a similar proportion overseas. Competition in the industry is keen but is generally centered on performance (racing) results rather than price. Marine Supply's principal advantages are:

1. A highly efficient sales-distribution-repair network (currently about 8,000 dealers) in North America.
2. Exceptional brand loyalty.
3. Almost total domination of the lower horsepower ranges where the vast majority of engines are still sold.

Marine Supply's position in golf carts is also dominant, but its degree of domination is less pronounced. While an important factor in snow vehicles, lawn care, and chain saws, these are highly fragmented markets with many competitors. Still, the company's marketing strategy is the same as in outboards: build a quality product with a strong dealer organization, use intensive advertising, and maintain a premium price structure. This approach has been successful in lawn mowers where Lawn King is a strong competitor despite tremendous product similarity among all brands. In snow vehicles—a comparatively new product to which Marine Supply was a comparative late comer—the company has not yet been totally successful in building its market share.

Financial statements

The financial statements of Marine Supply Corporation are presented in Exhibits 23–2, 23–3, and 23–4 below.

The auditor's opinion on the financial statements has been unqualified for the past six years.

Additional information

Marine Supply has a good, if very cyclical, historic operating performance record. In 19W4, for example, sales were only $73 million as against $304.5 million in 19Y0, more than 300 percent increase. Over the same span net income grew from $5.5 million to $13.4 million, an increase of 144 percent. The slower gain in net income, reflecting sharply reduced operating margins due largely to Federal Trade Commission action in the mid 19W0s, has meant erosion of the company's return on investment from an exceptional 25 percent (on net worth) in the 19W4–W6 period to just over 11 percent for the last three years.

EXHIBIT 23–2

MARINE SUPPLY CORPORATION
Balance Sheets
As of September 30 for Years 19X5–Y0
(in millions of dollars)

	19X5	19X6	19X7	19X8	19X9	19Y0
Assets						
Current Assets:						
Cash and equivalents	15.00	24.30	12.10	17.40	19.50	17.48
Receivables	22.50	24.50	31.40	35.40	46.50	53.70
Inventories	49.50	57.60	64.70	78.90	100.80	97.32
Other current assets	—	.00	.0	.10	.0	.00
Total Current Assets	87.00	106.40	108.20	131.80	166.80	168.50
Gross plant	85.20	88.60	98.70	114.70	129.70	137.90
Accumulated depreciation	(45.20)	(48.70)	(52.50)	(56.10)	(60.80)	(65.88)
Net plant	40.00	39.90	46.20	58.60	68.90	72.02
Intangibles and other assets	7.00	6.40	10.70	11.90	12.70	15.45
Total Assets	134.00	152.70	165.10	202.30	248.40	255.97
Liabilities and Capital						
Current Liabilities:						
Accounts payable	1.10	1.10	7.00	15.20	24.60	24.53
Other current liabilities	15.80	24.90	23.50	26.90	35.00	36.75
Total Current Liabilities	16.90	26.00	30.50	42.10	59.60	61.28
Long-term debt	14.50	13.50	12.40	28.70	45.70	46.04
Deferred taxes and investment credits	1.94	2.19	2.57	4.58	5.38	7.14
Other liabilities	2.39	2.57	2.03	1.52	2.57	1.05
Total Liabilities	35.73	44.26	47.50	76.90	113.25	115.51
Net worth	98.27	108.44	117.60	125.40	135.15	140.46
Total Liabilities and Capital	134.00	152.70	165.10	202.30	248.40	255.97

EXHIBIT 23–3

MARINE SUPPLY CORPORATION
Income Statements
For Years Ending September 30
(in millions of dollars)

	19X5	19X6	19X7	19X8	19X9	19Y0
Net sales	180.70	212.50	233.40	280.20	327.10	304.48
Other income	—	—	—	—	—	.19
Total revenue	180.70	212.50	233.40	280.20	327.10	304.67
Cost of goods sold*						
(excluding depreciation)	113.35	130.95	145.03	180.16	209.52	190.58
Depreciation	4.28	4.26	4.40	4.75	5.59	6.25
Gross profit	63.07	77.29	83.97	95.29	111.99	107.84
Selling, general, and administrative						
expenses	41.98	47.04	54.04	61.99	71.44	72.99
Operating income	21.09	30.25	29.93	33.30	40.55	34.85
Fixed interest charges	.70	1.05	1.23	2.10	4.73	6.60
Other expenses	.62	.54	.62	1.05	1.54	—
Net income before tax	19.77	28.66	28.08	30.15	34.28	28.25
Income taxes:						
Deferred	.47	.26	.38	.37	.80	1.75
Current	8.66	12.73	12.47	14.12	16.40	13.11
Net income	10.64	15.67	15.23	15.66	17.08	13.39
Common dividends	5.13	6.35	6.37	7.98	8.06	8.08
Retained earnings	5.51	9.32	8.86	7.68	9.02	5.31
* Includes:						
Research and development costs	11.8	11.2	13.4	12.1	12.4	12.8
Maintenance and repairs	10.3	10.4	11.6	12.4	12.7	11.5

Exhibit 23–5, fifteen-year growth rates—annually compounded, compares various growth rates, first using single years, then a three-year span.

Note that with the exception of sales per share, the growth rates are still higher for the single year comparisons. This is attributable to the very low 19W4 base and the tremendous gains from 19W4 through 19W6—a three-year span in which sales, net income, dividends, and book value each increased from 75 percent to 133 percent.

Exhibit 23–6, five-year growth rates—annually compounded, indicates the most recent five-year performance, first on a single-year basis, then using three-year "smoothed" base. On either basis, the company's record looks better in recent years than over the long pull.

Two noteworthy points should be made about this record:

1. The gains represent almost solely internal growth. Acquisitions have been few, their relative size quite small, and their profit contributions have often been negative.

EXHIBIT 23–4

MARINE SUPPLY CORPORATION
Statement of Changes in Financial Position
For Years Ending September 30
(in thousands of dollars)

	19X5	19X6	19X7	19X8	19X9	19Y0	Total %	Total Amount
Source:								
From operations:								
Net earnings	10,642	15,666	15,375	15,662	17,078	13,390	46.5	87,813
Depreciation	4,284	4,264	4,448	4,747	5,587	6,254	15.7	29,584
Amortization of tooling	—	3,360	2,755	4,595	6,484	6,637	12.6	23,831
Other—principally provision for deferred income taxes	755	527	493	372	800	1,753	2.5	4,700
Total from operations	15,681	23,817	23,071	25,376	29,949	28,034	77.3	145,928
Proceeds from sale of:								
Long-term borrowings	—	—	—	17,030	18,202	1,391	19.4	36,623
Plant and equipment (net)	174	662	326	146	347	112	.9	1,767
Common stock	52	859	294	317	732	—	1.2	2,254
Other items, net	—	—	45	1,808	413	—	1.2	2,266
Total sources	15,907	25,338	23,736	44,677	49,643	29,537	100.0	188,838
Application:								
Additions to plant and equipment	2,964	4,739	11,177	16,639	16,109	9,461	32.3	61,089
Tooling expenditures	—	2,565	7,635	6,430	6,825	7,398	16.3	30,853
Long-term debt maturing currently	1,136	1,073	1,126	1,035	1,142	1,073	3.6	6,585
Dividends paid	5,128	6,351	6,369	7,981	8,060	8,080	22.2	41,969
Other items, net	408	355	—	1,199	—	3,526	2.9	5,488
Total applications	9,636	15,083	26,307	33,284	32,136	29,538	77.3	145,984
Working capital increase (decrease)	6,271	10,255	(2,571)	11,393	17,507	(1)	22.7	42,854

2. No adjustments need be made for dilution. The company has no convertible securities outstanding; stock options are also insignificant.

Exhibits 23–7 through 23–10 are based on the financial statements of Marine Supply Corporation.

EXHIBIT 23–5

MARINE SUPPLY CORPORATION
Fifteen-Year Growth Rates
(annually compounded)

Per share	19W4–Y0	19W4–W6 to 19X8–Y0
Sales	8.0%	8.0%
Net income	4.6	3.3
Dividends	10.0	7.4
Book value	11.0	7.4

EXHIBIT 23–6

MARINE SUPPLY CORPORATION
Five-Year Growth Rates
(annually compounded)

Per share	19X5–Y0	19X4–X6 to 19X8–Y0
Sales	10.5%	9.7%
Net income	4.2	5.7
Dividends	9.0	9.6
Book value	7.0	5.7

EXHIBIT 23–7

MARINE SUPPLY CORPORATION
Common-Size Balance Sheets

	19X5	19X6	19X7	19X8	19X9	19Y0
Assets						
Current Assets:						
Cash and equivalents	11%	16%	7%	9%	8%	7%
Receivables	17	16	19	17	18	21
Inventories	37	38	39	39	41	38
Total current assets	65	70	65	65	67	66
Land, plant, and equipment, net	30	26	28	29	28	28
Intangibles and other assets	5	4	7	6	5	6
Total Assets	100	100	100	100	100	100
Liabilities and Equity						
Current liabilities	13	17	18	21	24	24
Long-term debt	11	9	8	14	18	18
Deferred taxes and investment credits	1	1	2	2	2	3
Other liabilities	2	2	1	1	1	—
Total Liabilities	27	29	29	38	45	45
Net worth	73	71	71	62	55	55
Total Liabilities and Equity	100	100	100	100	100	100

EXHIBIT 23–8

MARINE SUPPLY CORPORATION
Common-Size Income Statements

Item	19X5	19X6	19X7	19X8	19X9	19Y0	Industry composite 19Y0
Net sales	100.0%	100.0%	100.0%	100.0%	100.0%	100.0%	100.0%
Cost of goods sold* (excluding depreciation)	62.7	61.6	62.1	64.3	64.1	62.6	64.6
Depreciation	2.4	2.0	1.9	1.7	1.7	2.0	2.8
Gross profit	34.9	36.4	36.0	·34.0	34.2	35.4	32.6
Selling, general, and administrative expenses	23.2	22.2	23.2	22.1	21.8	24.0	21.0
Operating income	11.7	14.2	12.8	11.9	12.4	11.4	11.6
Interest expense	.4	.5	.5	.8	1.4	2.2	0.8
Other income (expense)	(.3)	(.2)	(.3)	(.4)	(.5)	.1	0.2
Net income before tax	11.0	13.5	12.0	10.7	10.5	9.3	11.0
Deferred taxes	.3	.1	.2	.1	.3	.6	.3
Income taxes	4.8	6.0	5.3	5.0	5.0	4.3	4.9
Net income	5.9	7.4	6.5	5.6	5.2	4.4	5.8
* Including:							
Research and development	6.5	5.2	5.7	4.3	3.8	4.2	5.4
Maintenance and repairs	5.7	4.9	5.0	4.4	3.9	3.8	6.2

EXHIBIT 23–9

MARINE SUPPLY CORPORATION
Trend Index of Selected Accounts
(19X5 = 100)

Account	19X6	19X7	19X8	19X9	19Y0
Cash	162	81	116	130	117
Accounts receivable	109	140	157	207	239
Inventory	116	131	159	204	197
Total current assets	122	124	151	192	194
Total current liabilities	154	180	249	353	363
Working capital	115	111	128	153	153
Fixed assets	100	116	147	172	180
Other assets	94	157	175	187	227
Long-term debt	93	86	198	315	318
Total liabilities	124	133	215	317	323
Equity capital	110	120	128	138	143
Net sales	118	129	155	181	169
Cost of goods sold	116	128	159	185	168
Gross profit	123	133	151	178	171
Selling, general, and administrative expenses	112	132	148	170	174
Interest expense	150	176	300	676	945
Total expenses	114	128	155	182	172
Operating income	143	142	158	192	165
Profit before taxes	145	142	153	173	143
Net income	147	143	147	161	126

EXHIBIT 23–10

MARINE SUPPLY CORPORATION
Selected per Share Results

Item	19X5	19X6	19X7	19X8	19X9	19Y0
Sales	$22.90	$26.71	$29.28	$34.85	$40.48	$37.68
Net income	1.35	1.97	1.91	1.95	2.11	1.66
Dividends	.65	.80	.80	1.00	1.00	1.00
Book value	12.43	13.63	14.76	15.60	16.73	17.38

While the economy in general was slow in 19Y0, 19X8 and 19X9 were good years for boat sales; and responses at boat shows across the country were strong in those years. Compared to automobiles, revolutionary model changes are rare in the boating industry.

The company's contract with the union expired at the end of 19Y0, and the company was not sure during 19Y0 whether it could avoid a strike.

After careful analysis, we conclude that about one half of deferred taxes and investment credits account balances will be reversed in the future; however, the possibility of reversal in the foreseeable future for the remaining one half is very remote. "Other liabilities" represent various debts having the characteristic of long-term debt. "Other current liabilities" represent amounts owing to various banks under revolving credit agreement.

The company is nearing its production capacity limits, necessitating new construction. For example, in 19X8 and 19X9, the company was forced to utilize some aging facilities on a multishift basis.

The period 19X5–Y0 has been by far the most prosperous in Marine Supply's history. Sales and earnings have each reached peak levels, although the last six years have not been as profitable as mid 19W0s.

Based on the foregoing data and information we are to analyze the financial statements of Marine Supply Corporation with the following alternative points of view (objectives) in mind:

1. That of a bank to extend to the company a short-term loan of $15 million.
2. That of an insurance company to whom the company wants to sell privately $30 million of 25-year bonds.
3. That of an investor considering a substantial investment in the company.

These diverse and broad points of view require that we analyze all major aspects of the company's financial condition and results of operations, that is:

1. Short-term liquidity.
2. Funds flow.

3. Capital structure and long-term solvency.
4. Return on investment.
5. Asset utilization.
6. Operating performance.

The following assumptions will be used in the projection of operating results and of fund flows for 19Y1:

It is expected that the annual growth rate by product line will continue except that snow vehicles and miscellaneous are expected to grow at a rate of 29 percent and 30 percent respectively. Improvements in production facilities will lower the cost of goods (exclusive of depreciation) to 60 percent of sales. The composite depreciation rate (depreciation expense as a percent of ending net plant) is expected to be 10 percent. Amortization of tooling costs included in cost of goods sold will be 10 percent higher than in 19Y0. Selling expenses, which amount to one fourth of the selling, general, and administrative group of expenses are expected to go up by 10 percent in 19Y1. The other three fourths of this category will remain unchanged. Taxes will average 53 percent of income before taxes, and the amount of deferred taxes will amount to the same proportion of the total tax accrual as in 19Y0. Dividend payout is expected to amount to 50 percent of net income.

In order to retire $15 million in revolving credit notes (shown under current liabilities) and to finance a major plant expansion and modernization program just starting, the company expects to sell at par, early in 19Y1, $30 million in 30-year 7 percent sinking fund bonds. That will leave $20 million in revolving credit notes outstanding. Interest expenses in 19Y1 are estimated at $5,810,000. The maturities and sinking fund requirements of long-term debt are as follows:

	Million $
19Y1	1.0
19Y2	2.3
19Y3	4.4
19Y4	8.6
19Y5	12.2

Research and development outlays are expected to amount to $3 million in 19Y1, and outlays for tooling are planned at $13 million.

The company plans to spend $30 million in 19Y1 on plant and equipment. Sales of equipment are expected to bring in $200,000 after tax. The chain-saw division which has a book value of $5 million is expected to be disposed of for $2 million, net of tax.

The problem of obtaining a meaningful and valid standard of external comparison for this analysis has been a difficult one. Two major sources of such data are industry statistics, such as those compiled by

Robert Morris Associates, Standard & Poor's, or Dun & Bradstreet, or comparative data derived from companies of similar size and in similar lines of business. In this case comparative data was developed from the published reports of companies in lines of business similar to those of Marine Supply Company.

Analysis of short-term liquidity

Exhibit 23–11 presents some important liquidity measures of Marine Supply Corporation over the last six years. Both the current ratio and the acid test ratio have been declining over this period. However, they are still at sound levels in 19Y0 on an absolute basis and also when compared to industry averages. The downward trend in these measures must be interpreted in the light of management's possible policy and intent. It is quite conceivable, particularly in view of the lower levels of the comparable industry ratios, that the current position in earlier years was unnecessarily strong and represented a wasteful tying up of resources which did not earn an acceptable return for the company. A glance at the common-size analysis in Exhibit 23–7 reveals the changes which have occurred in the composition of working capital elements over the past six years; the proportion of cash and cash equivalents among the current assets has dropped by almost half even though the absolute amount of cash and equivalents has not diminished on average. There has been a significant increase in current liabilities; they now represent almost a quarter of the funds invested in the enterprise whereas in 19X5 they represented 13 percent of the total. This is confirmed in the trend index analysis (Exhibit 23–9) which shows that since 19X5 current liabilities have increased 3.63 times while cash increased 1.17 times, receivables 2.39 times, and inventories only 1.97 times. That the increase in current liabilities was out of proportion to that of sales is seen by the fact that during the same period sales increased only 1.69 times. That means that Marine Supply Corporation was somehow able to secure short-term credit from suppliers and banks at a rate twice as fast as that warranted by growth in sales. This, in turn, is importantly responsible for the steady decline in the current and the acid-test ratios.

A more serious problem area is the quality of the two important elements of current assets: accounts receivable and inventories. The accounts receivable turnover has undergone constant decline over the past six years, reaching a low point of 5.67 in 19Y0. In that year it compared unfavorably as to 8.2 turnover in the industry. The alternative measure of "days' sales in accounts receivable" presents a similar picture with an increasing number of "days' sales" tied up in receivables. The 19Y0 figure of 63.5 days compares to an industry experi-

EXHIBIT 23–11

MARINE SUPPLY CORPORATION
Short-Term Liquidity Analysis

	Units	19X5	19X6	19X7	19X8	19X9	19Y0	Industry composite 19Y0
Current ratio	Ratio	5.15	4.09	3.55	3.13	2.80	2.75	2.40
Acid-test ratio	Ratio	2.22	1.88	1.43	1.26	1.11	1.16	.90
Accounts receivable turnover	Times	8.03	8.67	7.43	7.92	7.03	5.67	8.20
Inventory turnover	Times	2.29	2.27	2.24	2.28	2.08	1.96	2.30
Days sales in receivables	Days	44.8	41.5	48.5	45.5	51.2	63.5	43.9
Days to sell inventory	Days	157.2	158.6	160.7	157.9	173.1	183.7	156.5
Conversion period	Days	202.0	200.1	209.2	203.4	224.3	247.2	200.4
Cash to current assets	%	17.24	22.84	11.18	13.20	11.69	10.37	9.80
Cash to current liabilities	%	88.76	93.46	39.67	41.33	32.72	28.52	29.60
Working capital	$(MM)	70.10	80.40	77.70	89.70	107.20	107.22	—
Liquidity index	#	127	118	139	134	150	163	—

ence of 44.0 days. It also compares unfavorably to the company's most common terms of sales of net 30 days. Thus, it is possible that the collectibility and the liquidity of accounts receivable have deteriorated.

Inventory turnover has also decreased over the past six years, although the deterioration has not been as marked as has been the case with receivables. A number of factors could account for this, including a larger number and variety of outboard motors, lawn mowers, and snow vehicles models which must be stocked, the larger variety of spare parts that these require, as well as a possible accumulation of raw materials in anticipation of a strike at suppliers. It is also possible that Marine Supply Corporation overestimated sales for 19Y0, while sales dropped 7 percent from the 19X9 level, inventories dropped by only 3 percent, thus contributing to the turnover slowdown. The 19Y0 turnover of Marine Supply Corporation of 1.96 compares unfavorably with the 2.3 industry average. In 19Y0 it took 183.7 days to sell the average inventory compared to an industry average of 156.2 days. The comparable figure for the company in 19X5 was 157.2 days.

The deterioration in the liquidity of the principal operating assets of the current asset group, accounts receivable, and inventories is also seen in the period of days it takes to convert inventories into cash. It grew from 202 days in 19X5 to 247.2 days in 19Y0 and compares to an industry average of only 200.2 days in the latter year.

The liquidity index at 163 in 19Y0 up from 127 in 19X5, also corroborates the deterioration in the liquidity of the current assets which we have already determined in the analysis of individual components of working capita.

It is conceivable that further analysis and inquiry from management will reveal that the slowdown in the turnover of accounts receivable and inventories does not affect their ultimate realization even if that would take a longer time. In that case the repercussions of such a slowdown lie in the area of liquidity and funds flow as well as in the area of asset utilization which will be examined later in this analysis.

Analysis of funds flow

This analysis has two main objectives:

1. To supplement the static measures used to assess short-term liquidity by means of a short-term funds flow forecast.
2. To analyze the statement of changes in financial position in order to assess its implications on the longer term flow of funds (i.e., long-term solvency).

Our first step will be to build a funds flow forecast for Marine Supply Corporation in 19Y1. Since sources of funds from operations are an important element of funds and a projection of earnings will be necessary anyway, we start with such a projection for 19Y1, using the data and the supplementary information provided (see Exhibit 23–12).

EXHIBIT 23–12

MARINE SUPPLY CORPORATION
Projected Income Statement for 19Y1
(millions of dollars)

	19Y0 sales level	Incre- ment factor	19Y1 esti- mated amount	Total	%
Net sales:					
Marine products	217.3 ×	1.10	239.03		
Lawn care equipment	30.5 ×	1.13	34.47		
Vehicles	19.6 ×	1.07	20.97		
Snow vehicles	23.4 ×	1.29	30.19		
Miscellaneous	4.2 ×	1.30	5.46	330.12	100.0
Cost of goods sold (exclusive of depreciation)			198.07		60.0
Depreciation (1)			8.70		2.6
				206.77	62.6
Gross profit				123.35	37.4
Selling, general, and administrative expenses:					
General and administrative (2)			54.74		
Selling (3)			20.08		
Amortization of deferred startup costs			1.00	75.82	23.0
				47.53	14.4
Interest expenses				5.81	1.8
Income before taxes				41.72	12.6
Income taxes:					
Current			19.24		
Deferred (4)			2.88	22.12	6.7
				19.60	5.9
Loss on disposal of chain-saw division (net of tax)				3.00	0.9
Net income				16.60	5.0

(1) Beginning net plant plus half of 19Y1 additions times 10%: (72.2 + 15.0) × 10%. It is assumed that the plant additions were in use, on average, half of the year.
(2) Three fourths of 72.99 (last year selling, general, and administrative).
(3) Selling expenses at 10% above the 19Y0 level (72.99 − 54.74) × 1.10.
(4) Deferred taxes at 13% of the total provision for the year which amounts to 53% of pretax income.

Having established the estimated net income for 19Y1 we can now proceed, using the data and the additional information we now have, to construct an estimated statements of sources and uses of working capital (funds) for 19Y1.

Exhibit 23–13 projects an increase in working capital of about $16 million. If this forecast proves reasonably accurate, the current ratio should improve to about 3:1. As is true of all forecasts, their reliability depends on the validity of the assumptions on which they are based.

EXHIBIT 23–13

MARINE SUPPLY CORPORATION
Projected Statement of Sources and Uses of Funds for 19Y1
(in millions of dollars)

Sources of funds:
  From operations:

Net income	16.60	
Add: Items not requiring current funds:		
Depreciation	8.70	
Amortization of tooling costs	7.30	
Deferred income taxes	2.88	
Amortization of startup costs	1.00	
Loss on sale of chain-saw division	3.00	
Total from operations		39.48
Proceeds from sale of 7% sinking fund bonds		30.00
Sale of chain-saw division		2.00
Sale of equipment		0.20
Total sources		71.68
Uses of funds:		
Additions to plant and equipment	30.00	
Outlays for tooling	13.00	
Outlays for research and development	3.00	
Long-term debt maturities	1.00	
Dividends declared	8.30	
Total uses		55.30
Increase in working capital		16.38

The assumption that Marine Supply Corporation can sell $30 million in 7 percent sinking fund bonds appears reasonable in the light of the company's present capital structure. Its failure to do so would require either the abandonment or deferral of expansion and modernization plans or it will result in a deterioration of the current ratio to about 2.5

The projected net income of $16.6 million for 19Y1 appears reasonable because it is based on the assumption of a continuation of present sales trends and a reduction in the growth rate of two product line categories. However, it is more vulnerable on the expense side. The increase in the gross margin is predicated on increases in productivity which are envisaged but which are yet to be realized. Moreover, any program of expansion and modernization is subject to the risk of delays, misjudgments, and short falls which may delay, postpone, or completely undermine the realization of improvements and economies.

On the other hand, the increases in fixed costs which such a program entails are a reality with which the enterprise must live for a long time.

Any degree of failure to realize savings and improvements will also affect the short-term flow of funds. Thus, for example, continuing the assumption that 50 percent of the net income will be distributed as dividends, a 5 percent increase in cost of goods sold (exclusive of depreciation) will lower the inflow of funds as follows:

	Millions of dollars (approximately)
Increase in cost of goods sold (exclusive of depreciation)—5% of $198 million	9.90
Less tax effect at 53%	5.25
	4.65
Less: Dividend reduction (50%)	2.32
	2.33
Less: Deferred taxes (13% of 5.25)	0.68
Reduction in funds available from operations	1.65

A similar computation can, of course, be made for any other change in assumptions. The likelihood of any of the above assumptions materializing and the probability attached to them is, ultimately, a matter of judgment.

The longer range funds flow picture is subject to a great many uncertainties. Examination of the company's historical pattern of fund flows over the 19X5 to 19Y0 period (see Exhibit 23–4) is revealing. Funds from operations provided 77 percent of all funds inflows while long-term borrowing provided most of the rest. Such borrowing occurred mostly in 19X8 and 19X9. Equity financing was negligible.

Additions to plant and equipment used about 32 percent of all funds available. These outlays were, however, twice as high as the provision for depreciation. With the company bumping against the ceiling of its practical capacity in many lines this trend is likely to continue. Already in 19Y1 capital expenditures are planned at three times the 19Y0 level and long-term debt will be incurred to finance this as well as the working capital needs of an expanding business. As will be discussed further under "capital structure" there is, of course, a limit to the company's debt capacity, and equity financing will be required. This may explain the company's relatively generous dividend policy over the recent years.

In spite of relatively heavy long-term borrowing in 19X8 and 19X9 long-term debt maturities and sinking fund requirements are low. These will, however, increase sharply from $1 million in 19Y1 to $12 million in 19Y5. The proposed $30 million bond issue in 19Y1 will undoubtedly add to these maturities.

The longer term fund flow outlook of Marine Supply Corporation is one of increasing demand for funds due to accelerating outlays for plant equipment and tooling as well as sharply rising debt service outlays. While funds from operations have been significant and are growing, they will have to continue to do so to meet increasing demands. Since funds from operations represented 77 percent of all sources of funds in the past six years, the company's fund flow is particularly vulnerable to any reduction in net income. Working capital needs will also increase along with the expected increase in sales volume.

It should be borne in mind that focusing on *net* working capital does not tell the whole story of Marine Supply Corporation's borrowing. Included in current liabilities are $35 million in revolving credit notes. The company may well want to convert this short-term interest sensitive debt into a longer term type of obligation. A beginning towards this goal is expected to be made in 19Y1. That too will require using up some of the company's shrinking capacity to finance by means of long-term debt.

Analysis of capital structure and long-term solvency

Having just examined the funds aspect of Marine Supply Corporation's long-term solvency we now turn to an examination of its capital structure and the risk inherent in it. The change in the company's capital structure can be gauged by means of a number of measurements and comparisons.

Looking at Exhibit 23–7 we see that the contribution of equity capital to the total funds invested in the enterprise has shrunk from 73 percent in 19X5 to 55 percent in 19Y0. With the expected issuance of $30 million on additional bonds, this proportion can be expected to dip below 50 percent. The long-term debt portion of the total funds invested in the enterprise increased from 11 percent in 19X5 to 18 percent in 19Y0 and is headed considerably higher in 19Y1.

In Exhibit 23–9 we can see the relative change in debt, equity, and other related elements in the financial statements. On a basis of 19X5 = 100 long-term debt rose to 318 while equity capital increased only to 143. In the same period net sales rose only to 169, net income to 126, while interest costs soared to 945. Quite clearly the company decided to finance its needs by means of debt, both short and long term. Reasons for this could be an unwillingness to dilute the equity or a desire to incur monetary liabilities in times of inflation. Whatever the reason, the leverage and hence the risk in the capital structure increased substantially. This is particularly true because Marine Supply Corporation is in a relatively cyclical industry and relies on a share of the consumer's discretionary dollar.

The capital structure and long-term solvency ratios in Exhibit 23–14 bear out these conclusions. Equity to total debt stands at 1.29 in 19Y0 compared to 2.86 in 19X5, and compares to an industry composite of 1.4. Similarly, equity to long-term debt stands at 2.84 in 19Y0 compared to an industry composite of 3.1. The times interest earned ratio plummeted from 29.24 in 19X5 to 5.28 in 19Y0 and compares with an industry composite of 8.6. The income projections as well as the borrowing plans for 19Y1 would result in an improved interest coverage ratio of 8.2 as a consequence of the refinancing of high-interest short-term debt and also because the 7 percent bonds will be outstanding for only part of the year. This improvement in the coverage ratio may, however, prove to be only temporary in nature.

EXHIBIT 23–14

MARINE SUPPLY CORPORATION
Capital Structure and Long-Term Solvency Ratios

	19X5	19X6	19X7	19X8	19X9	19Y0	19Y0 industry composite
Equity to total debt	99.24*	109.54	118.89	127.69	137.84	144.03	
	34.76	43.16	46.21	74.61	110.56	111.94	
	= 2.86	= 2.54	= 2.57	= 1.71	= 1.25	= 1.29	1.4
Equity to long-term debt	99.24	109.54	118.89	127.69	137.84	144.03	
	17.86*	17.16	15.71	32.51	50.96	50.66	
	= 5.56	= 6.38	= 7.57	= 3.93	= 2.70	= 2.84	3.1
Equity to net fixed assets	2.48	2.75	2.57	2.18	2.00	2.00	2.2
Times interest earned	29.24	28.30	23.83	15.36	8.25	5.28	8.6

* Computed as following:

One half of deferred income taxes	0.97
Net worth shown	98.27
Adjusted net worth	99.24
Total liabilities shown	35.73
Less: One half of deferred income taxes	0.97
Adjusted total liabilities	34.76
Less: Total current liabilities	16.90
Adjusted long-term debt	17.86

As we saw from the longer term funds flow analysis, the company is now entering a period of increasing capital investment needs and of increasingly heavy debt service schedules. It does this at a time when its debt is high in relation to its equity capital and when shrinking interest coverage ratios exert downward pressure on its credit rating. Moreover, the increasing fixed charges which stem from recent substantial additions to plant and equipment make operating results more vulnerable to cyclical downturn with the result that sources of funds from operations are similarly vulnerable.

Analysis of return on investment

The return which the company realizes on total assets, Exhibit 23–15, has been on the decline in recent years, having declined from 10.6 percent in 19X6 (which was the best year in this respect) to 6.4 percent in 19Y0. Even if we regard 19X6 as an unusually good year, the decline from the prior year return levels is quite significant. In comparison with an industry return on total assets in 19Y0 of 9.3 percent, the company's 6.4 percent return is also significantly worse. This negative trend over the past six years is reason for concern and requires further investigation. The two major elements which make up the return on total assets, that is, net profit margin and asset turnover, will be examined later in this analysis.

EXHIBIT 23–15

MARINE SUPPLY CORPORATION
Return on Investment Ratios

	19X5	19X6	19X7	19X8	19X9	19Y0	19Y0 industry composite
Return on total assets	8.2% (1)	10.6%	9.6%	8.3%	7.8%	6.4%	9.3%
Return on equity capital	10.8% (2)	14.5%	13.0%	12.5%	12.6%	9.5%	12.8%
Return on long-term liabilities and equity	9.4% (3)	12.8%	11.8%	10.5%	10.3%	8.5%	10.6%
Financial leverage index	1.32 (4)	1.37	1.23	1.27	1.32	1.33	1.38
Equity growth rate	5.6 (5)	8.6	7.5	6.1	6.7	3.88	—

Notes:

$$(1)\quad \frac{\text{Net income} + \text{Interest expense } (1 - \text{Tax rate})}{\text{Total assets}} = \frac{10.64 + .7(1 - .46)}{134}$$

$$(2)\quad \frac{\text{Net income}}{\text{Net worth}} = \frac{10.64}{98.27}$$

$$(3)\quad \frac{\text{Net income} + \text{Interest expense } (1 - \text{Tax rate})}{\text{Long-term liabilities} + \text{Equity}} = \frac{11.018}{134.0 - 16.90}$$

$$(4)\quad \frac{\text{Return on equity capital}}{\text{Return on total assets}} = \frac{10.8}{8.2}$$

$$(5)\quad \frac{\text{Net income} - \text{Payout}}{\text{Common shareholders' equity}} = \frac{\text{Amount retained}}{\text{Common shareholders' equity}} = \frac{5.51}{98.27}$$

In comparison with the return on total assets, the decline in the return on equity has not been quite as significant. This is mainly due to the relatively advantageous use of short-term and long-term credit. The financial leverage index (Exhibit 23–15) which in 19Y0 stands at 1.33 is practically unchanged from its 19X5 level. It must be noted, however, that the company cannot expand its debt much more from the present level since over the past six years debt has expanded very significantly. Thus, in the immediate future an adequate return on equity will be dependent primarily on improvements in profitability and in asset utilization. As can be seen from Exhibit 23–15, the equity growth rate from earnings retention has shrunk in 19Y0 to 3.8 percent from over 6 percent in the two years before that and from 8.6 percent in 19X6. This is largely due to the maintenance of a generous dividend policy in the face of shrinking earnings. This shrinkage in the internal equity growth rate comes at a time when the company is increasingly in need of additional equity capital. Conceivably, however, a liberal dividend record can facilitate in the future the raising of equity capital.

Analysis of asset utilization

Exhibit 23–16 indicates that in most categories the asset utilization ratios have been declining over the past six years. The sales to total assets ratio is down to 1.2 in 19Y0 from the 1.4 level in 19X8 and compares to an industry average 1.5 times. The impact of this change can be assessed as follows:

EXHIBIT 23–16

MARINE SUPPLY CORPORATION
Asset Utilization Ratios

	19X5	19X6	19X7	19X8	19X9	19Y0	19Y0 industry composite
Sales to cash and equivalents	12.0	8.7	19.3	16.1	16.8	17.4	9.1
Sales to receivables	8.0	8.7	7.4	7.9	7.0	5.7	10.6
Sales to inventories	3.7	3.7	3.6	3.6	3.2	3.1	4.1
Sales to working capital	2.6	2.6	3.0	3.1	3.1	2.8	4.0
Sales to fixed assets	4.5	5.3	5.1	4.8	4.7	4.2	6.4
Sales to other assets	25.8	33.2	21.8	23.4	25.8	19.7	22.3
Sales to total assets	1.3	1.4	1.4	1.4	1.3	1.2	1.5
Sales to short-term liabilities	10.7	8.2	7.7	6.7	5.5	5.0	—

Given the company's net income to sales ratio in 19Y0 of 4.4 percent and a net of tax interest expense of about 1.1 percent (Exhibit 23–8) a total asset turnover of 1.4 (the 19X8 rate) would have yielded a return on total assets of 7.7 percent $[(4.4 + 1.1) \times 1.4]$ rather than the 6.4 percent return actually realized in 19Y0. At a rate of turnover of 1.5 (industry average) the present profit rate would yield a return on investment of about 8.2 percent $[(4.4 + 1.1) \times 1.5]$.

The asset categories where the turnover rate has dropped most sharply over the six years are "other assets" and "receivables." Only cash showed an increase in turnover (utilization). Judging by the fact that there were significant fixed asset additions in 19X8 and 19X9 (see Exhibit 23–9), the drop in the fixed asset turnover rate was moderate. It must be borne in mind that it takes time before fixed asset additions become sufficiently productive to generate an expected volume of sales. In addition, certain types of fixed asset outlays represent improvements in production facilities which lead to efficiencies and savings rather than to expansion of productive capacity. Such outlays, consequently, do not lead to greater sales but rather to savings in variable costs and result in improvements in profit margins. Exhibit 23–8 indicates that while profit margins are below the 19X6–X7 levels, they have been in an improving trend in the last three years. The drop over the six-year span in the turnover of the "other assets" group reflects growth in deferred charges, particularly tooling.

Analysis of operating performance

Exhibit 23–8 presents common-size income statements of the company for the six years, 19X5–Y0.

The gross profit of Marine Supply Corporation has held within a relatively narrow range over the last six years. In 19Y0 at 35.3 percent the gross profit margin is higher than in the preceding two years but is below the levels reached in 19X6 and 19X7. It does compare favorably to the industry gross margin of 32.6 percent. However, the research and development costs as well as the repair and maintenance costs included in the cost of goods sold figure are lower, as a percentage of sales than the industry composite. This aspect of the quality of earnings will be further discussed below.

In 19Y0 the percentage relationship between depreciation expense and sales was 2.1 percent up from 1.7 percent the year before. The disparity between this percentage and the industry composite of 2.8 percent is noteworthy because it may affect the quality of Marine Supply Corporation's earnings. It would appear that an inadequate amount of depreciation is recorded by Marine Supply Corporation. Before a definite judgment can be made, additional information would be required. The company is now approaching the limit of practical capacity in many of its product lines. Competitors may have more reserve capacity available and that may express itself in a relatively higher composite depreciation rate. It is also possible that Marine Supply Corporation's equipment is, on average, of an older vintage, and hence lower cost, than its competitors'. On the other hand, a lower composite depreciation rate than necessary is a factor which lowers the quality of the company's earnings.

We have two more measures available to judge the size of the yearly depreciation charge:

	19X5	19X6	19X7	19X8	19X9	19Y0
Accumulated depreciation as a percentage of gross plant	53	55	53	49	47	48
Annual depreciation expense as a percentage of gross plant	5.0	4.8	4.4	4.2	4.3	4.5

The decline in the percentage of accumulated depreciation in relation to gross plant most likely reflects the substantial additions of new equipment in recent years. The decline of depreciation expense as a percentage of gross plant is, however, indicative of a less conservative depreciation policy in the more recent years.

Selling, general, and administrative expenses as a percentage of sales have, generally, been on the rise. In 19Y0 they stood at 24 percent which compares to an industry composite figure of only 21 percent. Thus, by the time we reach operating income, the advantage which the company held over the industry because of larger gross margin has now been neutralized. Operating income for Marine Supply Corporation represents 11.4 percent of sales, and that compares with 11.6 percent for the industry. Further inquiries should be made to determine whether the selling expense component or the general and administrative part are responsible for the increase in this category.

Interest expenses have shown by far the steepest increase over the past six years. On the basis of 19X5 = 100 they have grown to 945 (almost tenfold) by 19Y0 (Exhibit 23–9). This is due, of course, primarily to the sharp expansion of debt. Moreover, the short-term revolving debt is interest sensitive and thus introduces a measure of uncertainty in the forecasting of future interest charges.

Two other aspects of the quality of Marine Supply Corporation's earnings should be noted.

Research and development costs as a percentage of sales have been in a declining trend having reached 4.2 percent in 19Y0 down from 6.5 percent in 19X5 (Exhibit 23–3). This raises a question about the effect on future sales and profits of the decline in the research and development cost outlays in relation to sales. Similarly, the percentage of sales devoted to reparis and maintenance has declined from 5.7 percent in 19X5 to 3.8 percent in 19Y0, a matter of concern particularly in the light of the fact that Marine Supply Corporation's facilities are, on average, older now than in 19X5. In the latter year the percentage of repair and maintenance expense in relation to gross plant was 12.1 percent. In 19Y0 that relationship dropped to 8.3 percent. This *prima facie* evidence of a deterioration in the quality of Marine Supply Corporation's earnings merits further investigation.

The total effective tax rate of Marine Supply Corporation in 19Y0 is
52 percent which compare to industry composite effective rate of 47
percent. The net income to sales of Marine Supply Corporation is 4.4
percent for 19Y0 significantly below the industry composite of 5.8
percent for that year. However, since 19Y0 was a year of labor trouble
and recession for the company, the percentages of net income to sales
prevailing in the prior years, which are closer to the industry average,
may be taken as more representative of the company's earning power.

Exhibit 23–17 analyzes the change occurring in net income between the 19X5–X7 period and the 19X8–Y0 period. Sales increased
by 46 percent, but due largely to greater increases in the cost of good
sold (49 percent) and interest expenses (353 percent) the increase in
net income was held to only 11 percent.

EXHIBIT 23–17

MARINE SUPPLY CORPORATION
Statement Accounting for Variations in Net Income
Three-Year Period 19X5–X7 (average) Compared to
Three-Year Period 19X8–Y0 (average)
(in millions of dollars)

Items tending to increase net income:				
Increase in net sales:				
Net sales, 19X8–Y0	303.93			
Net sales, 19X5–X7	208.87	95.06		46%
Deduct increase in cost of goods sold:				
Cost of goods sold, 19X8–Y0	193.42			
Cost of goods sold, 19X5–X7	129.78	63.64		49
Net increase in gross margin			31.42	
Items tending to decrease in net income:				
Increase in depreciation:				
Depreciation, 19X8–Y0	5.53			
Depreciation, 19X5–X7	4.31	1.22		28
Increase in selling, general, and				
administrative expenses:				
S.G.A., 19X8–Y0	68.81			
S.G.A., 19X5–X7	47.69	21.12		44
Increase in interest expense:				
Interest expense, 19X8–Y0	4.48			
Interest expense, 19X5–X7	.99	3.49		353
Increase in other income and expense:				
Other income and expense, 19X8–Y0	.80			
Other income and expense, 19X5–X7	.59	.21		36
Net increase in expenses			26.04	
Net increase in profit before taxes			5.38	21
Increase in income taxes:				
Income taxes, 19X8–Y0	15.52			
Income taxes, 19X5–X7	11.66		3.86	33
Net increase in net income			1.52	11

Summary and conclusions

This analysis has examined all facets of Marine Supply Corporation's record of results of operations and financial position and has estimated the projected results and fund flows for one year. An analysis such as this is an indispensable step in arriving at a decision on the three questions posed. Nevertheless, essential as the data and information developed by this analysis is, it is not sufficient in most cases to arrive at a final conclusion. This is so because qualitative and other factors can have an important bearing on the final conclusion. Only when all the factors, those developed by the analysis as well as the others, have been assembled can a decision be reached by the application of judgment.

For example, the *bank* which is asked to extend short-term credit must take into consideration the character of the management, past loan experience, as well as the ongoing relationship with the loan applicant.

In addition to the foregoing intangibles, the long-term lender will focus on such matters as security arrangements and provisions which safeguard the solvency of the recipient of the loan.

The *equity investor* is, of course, interested in earning power and in earnings per share, but many considerations and judgments must be joined with these data before an investment decision is made. Thus, for instance, what earnings are, and what they are likely to be, is the product of financial analysis. At what price-earnings ratio they should be capitalized is a question for investment judgment. Similarly, the risk inherent in an enterprise, the volatility of its earnings, and the breadth and quality of the market for its securities are factors which must also be considered. They determine whether an investment fits into the investor's portfolio and whether it is compatible with his investment objectives.

Since the ultimate conclusions regarding problems, such as the lending and investing decision which we consider in this case, is based on more than the data and facts brought out by financial analysis alone, it follows that the most useful way to present the results of financial analysis is to summarize them by listing the most relevant and salient points which were developed by the analysis and which the decision maker should consider. This we shall do in this case.

The following are the main points which have been developed by our analysis of Marine Supply Corporation.

Short-term liquidity. The current ratio is in a downtrend but still stands at a relatively sound level. The downtrend may, in part, represent a correction of former excessive levels in the ratio.

The current assets are, as a whole, less liquid than in former years.

The slower turnover in accounts receivable indicates a possible deterioration in collectibility. The decline in inventory turnover may be due to diversity of product line rather than to unsaleable or obsolete items in stock.

Current liabilities have risen sharply in recent years, and they now represent one fourth of all funds available to the enterprise.

The decline in liquidity is evidenced by a rise in the liquidity index.

Fund projections for 19Y1 indicate a projected increase in working capital of $16 million by the end of that year. This assumes, however, the successful sale of $30 million in bonds and that expense projections which incorporate benefits of efficiencies will be realized. There is a moderate amount of risk that these projections may not be realized.

Capital structure and long-term solvency. In 19Y0 equity capital represented 55 percent of total funds invested in the enterprise down from 73 percent in 19X5. In recent years (see Exhibit 23–9) long-term debt increased drastically (3.18 times), out of proportion to such measures as growth in sales (1.69 times) or in equity (1.43 times).

The reduction of equity capital relative to debt and all funds invested in the company is not a favorable development in view of the fact that Marine Supply Corporation is in a cyclical industry. The company may be nearing the limit of its debt capacity.

Times interest earned is down to 5.28 in 19Y0 (from 29.24 to 19X5). If a portion of rentals would be included as fixed charges, the coverage ratio would drop lower still. Next year, assuming the $30 million in long-term bonds are sold, this ratio is slated to improve to 8.2 times.

Over the last six years 77 percent of all funds inflows were funds generated by operations. Thus, a very substantial source of funds is vulnerable to changes in operating results. Over the longer term, demand for funds is expected to increase significantly. Long-term debt maturities are slated to increase sharply even excluding those from the $30 million bond issue which is expected to be sold in 19Y1. There will be a growing need of funds for plant and equipment. Provisions for depreciation were consistently below fixed-asset additions in recent years.

Return on investment and asset utilization. The return on investment is in a declining trend. In 19Y0 the return on total assets was 6.4 percent compared with an industry composite of 9.3 percent in 19Y0 where the disparity with the industry composite of 12.8 percent is less marked.

The decline in return on total assets is due to the twin effects of declining asset utilization rates as well as a decline in profitability per dollar of sales.

Operating performance. The company's gross profit percentage has held relatively steady over the past six years. Other costs have neutralized Marine Supply Corporation's higher gross margin compared to the industry. Interest expenses have risen sharply over recent years. Both research and development expenses and repair and maintenance outlays have declined as a percentage of sales in recent years.

The significant decline in net income as a percentage of sales to 4.4 percent in 19Y0 (industry composite 5.8 percent) is due to the particularly adverse labor and economic conditions of that year. In prior years the company's net as a percentage of sales, compared more favorably to industry experience.

Projected income for 19Y1, based on the assumptions stated in the analysis, is $16.6 million after a loss of $3 million on disposal of the chain-saw division. On a per share basis the net income per share is expected to be $2.06 per share compared to earnings per share in 19Y0 of $1.66 and in 19X9 of $2.11. In 19Y0 income per share before the loss on the chain-saw division is projected at $2.43.

USES OF FINANCIAL STATEMENT ANALYSIS

The foregoing analysis of the financial statements of Marine Supply Corporation consists of two major parts: (1) the detailed analysis and (2) the summary and conclusions. As was mentioned earlier, in a formal analytical report the summary and conclusions section may precede the detailed analysis so that the reader is presented with material in the order of its importance to him.

The *bank* loan officer who has to decide on the short-term loan application by the company will normally give primary attention to short-term liquidity analysis and to the funds flow projection and secondarily to capital structure and operating results.

The investment committee of the *insurance company* may, in taking a longer term point of view, pay attention first to capital structure and long-term solvency and then to operating performance, return on investment, asset utilization, and short-term liquidity, and in that order of emphasis.

The *potential investor* in Marine Supply Corporation's shares will, of course, be interested in all the aspects of our analysis. His emphasis may, however, be different again and take the following order of priority: results of operations, return on investment, capital structure, and long-term solvency and short-term liquidity.

An adequate financial statement analysis will, as the Marine Supply Corporation analysis illustrates, contain in addition to the analysis of the data, enough information and detail so as to allow the decision maker to follow the rationale behind the analyst's conclusions as well as allow him to expand it into areas not covered by the analysis.

QUESTIONS

1. What kind of processes should normally precede an analysis of financial statements?
2. What are the analytical implications of the fact that financial statements are, at best, an abstraction of underlying reality?
3. Name the six major "building blocks" of financial analysis. What does the "building block" approach involve?
4. What are some of the earmarks of a good analysis? Into what distinct sections should a well-organized analysis be divided?
5. What additional knowledge and analytical skills must an analyst bring to bear upon the analysis of enterprises in specialized or regulated industries?

PROBLEMS*

CHAPTER 2

2-1. Russell J. Morrison wrote in the *Financial Analysts Journal:*

"Strictly speaking, the objectives of financial reporting are the objectives of society and not of accountants and auditors, as such. Similarly, society has objectives for law and medicine—namely, justice and health for the people—which are not necessarily the objectives of lawyers and doctors, as such, in the conduct of their respective 'businesses.'

"In a variety of ways, society exerts pressure on a profession to act more nearly *as if* it actively shared the objectives of society. Society's pressure is to be measured by the degree of accommodation on the part of the profession under pressure, and by the degree of counter-pressure applied by the profession. For example, doctors accommodate society by getting better educations than otherwise and reducing incompetence in their ranks. They apply counter-pressure and gain protection by forming medical associations."

Required:

a. In what way has society brought pressure on accountants to serve it better?

---

* In addition to the odd-numbered problems presented in this section, a series of even-numbered supplementary problems can be found in the Instructor's Manual.

b. How has the accounting profession responded to these pressures? Are there better responses?

2–3. A leading banker stated:

Today we are faced with a widening gap in the communications between the accounting fraternity and its audience of bankers, managers, investors, and the general public. The intellectual accounting exercises which are now starting to move from drawing room dialogues to the marketplace appear to be entirely self-propelled in the sense that virtually no one outside of a relatively small group of accounting theorists is demanding such sweeping changes. There just is no demand for a whole new accounting system from people who must use the product. Investors are already being confused by the current overrecording of short-term swings, which tends to obscure the basic long-term trends of the business in which they have invested. In a world of floating exchange rates, to wash each jiggle in the international currency markets through current earnings merely distorts a company's results without taking note of the relationship between currencies over a longer time frame. Bankers and other lenders make no demands for current-value accounting for the simple reason that one of the first rules of credit analysis is to study comparable data over time. There is no real demand from industry generally for sweeping changes in accounting concepts, since rule changes are justified only when they improve information and yield better decisions. Most businessmen and bankers believe that accounting conventions should not drive business decisions, but rather should reflect them in a meaningful manner."

Required:

a. Why is the banker concerned with developments in accounting?
b. What processes are designed to assure that users of financial statements are heard before accounting standards are changed?

2–5. "Despite its intrinsic intellectual appeal, complete uniform accounting seems unworkable in a complex industrial society that relies, at least in part, on economic market forces."

Required:

a. Discuss briefly at least three disadvantages of national or international accounting uniformity.
b. Does uniformity in accounting necessarily mean comparability? Explain.

(C.F.A.)*

2–7. A professor of finance wrote:

"An accountant's job is to conceal, not to reveal. An accountant is not asked to give outsiders an accurate picture of what's going on in a company. He is asked to transform the figures on a company's operations in such a way that it will be impossible to recreate the original figures.

An income statement for a toy company doesn't tell how many toys of various kinds the company sold, or who the company's best customers are. The balance sheet doesn't tell how many of each kind of toy the company has in

---

* Material from the C.F.A. Candidate Examinations published by The Institute of Chartered Financial Analysts. Reprinted by permission of the publisher.

inventory, or how much is owed by each customer who is late in paying his bills.

"In general, anything that a manager uses to do his job will be of interest to some stockholders, customers, creditors or government agencies. Managerial accounting differs from financial accounting only because the accountant has to hide some of the facts and figures managers find useful. The accountant simply has to throw out most of the facts and some of the figures that the managers use when he creates the financial statements for outsiders."

The rules of accounting reflect this tension. Even if the accountant thought of himself as working only for the good of society, he would conceal certain facts in the reports he helps write. Since the accountant is actually working for the company, or even for the management of the company, he conceals many facts that outsiders would like to have revealed.

Required:

a. Comment on the professor's view of the accountant's job.
b. What type of omitted information is the writer referring to?

2–9. A leader of the accounting profession has stated: "Most users of financial statements believe that they understand the objectives of those statements. They accept the attestation of the auditor to a fair presentation of 'financial position' and 'results of operations' as if these objectives were precisely formulated, and a standard methodology available to achieve them. Few investors realize how much disagreement exists not only on the methodology but on the objectives themselves. Even fewer, perhaps, grasp the implications of this disagreement for the value of the document on which they are relying."

Required:

What are the implications to the financial statement analyst of the disagreement on objectives and methodology in accounting?

CHAPTER 4

4–1. The following question is based on the financial statements of Beta Company (pages 89–103).
Following is additional information about 19X4:

1. Composition of current assets:

	($ millions)
Cash	34.0
Temporary investments	296.9
Accounts receivable	333.8
Inventories	324.4
Deferred income tax	28.0
	1017.1

2. Total equity 1367.2

3. Total assets 2729.9

Required:

To the list of ratios already computed for Beta Company for 19X6 (on page 000) add comparable ratios for 19X5. Comment on the year to year changes in these measurements.

4–3. Complete the following comparative operating statement of XYZ Corporation:

XYZ CORPORATION
Operating Statement
Years Ending on December 31
(in thousands of dollars)

	19X4	*19X3*	*19X2*	*Cumulative amount*	*Annual average amount*
Net sales		2,280	1,998		
Cost of goods sold	2,000				1,920
Gross profit		300			327
Total operating expenses					280
Income before taxes	96	25	20		
Net income	76	13	10		

4–5. Compute the increases (decreases) from the preceding year in percentage and fill in the blanks in the following table:

	19X9		*19X8*		*19X7*
	Index No.	*Change in in %*	*Index No.*	*Change in in %*	*Index No.*
Net sales		50	100		80
Cost of goods sold	165		100		90
Gross profit	127		100		85
Total operating expenses		30	100		70
Income before tax		25	100		60
Net Income	130		100		65

4–7.   Comparative financial position and operating statements are commonly used tools of analysis and interpretation.

Required:

a.   Discuss the inherent limitations of single-year statements for purposes of analysis and interpretation. Include in your discussion the extent to which these limitations are overcome by the use of comparative statements.
b.   Comparative balance sheets and comparative income statements that show a firm's financial history for each of the last 10 year's may be misleading. Discuss the factors or conditions that might contribute to misinterpretations. Include a discussion of the additional information and supplementary data that might be included in or provided with the statements to prevent misinterpretations.

(AICPA adapted)*

4–9.   While you were analyzing a balance sheet of a newly acquired company your assistant spilled coffee over the paper obliterating most of the figures. All that remained was the following:

XYZ Corporation
Balance Sheet
As of December 31, 1974

Assets
Cash ....
Accounts receivable ....
Inventory ....
Building ....
Land ....   _____

     Total Assets ....   ════════

Liabilities and equity
Accounts payable   50,000
Bonds payable ....
Common stock ....
Retained earnings   100,000

     Total Liabilities and Equity ....   ════════

On a separate sheet you had made the following notations:

Net assets $400,000
Debt to equity ratio 1:4
Current ratio 3:1
Sales $450,000
Average age of accounts receivable—60 days
Gross profit %—10%
Inventory turnover—8.1 times
Depreciation on 20 year life will be $12,500

Required:

From the information you will reconstruct the balance sheet.

* Material from the Uniform CPA Examinations and Unofficial Answers, copyright © by the American Institute of Certified Public Accountants, Inc., is reprinted (or adapted) with permission.

4–11. Given the information below, complete the following balance sheet (these are the only items in the balance sheet.)

Cash	
Accounts receivable	
Inventory	66
Prepaid expenses........................	
Land	
Building	
Furniture and fixtures	
Machinery and equipment	
Accounts payable	
Bonds payable—due within 1 year	
Bonds payable	200
Capital stock	
Retained earnings	220

Current ratio = 3 : 1

Cash: Current liabilities ratio = 0.6 : 1

* Credit terms of suppliers are 2/10, net 30. Purchases, which are spread out evenly during the year, were 360, and were paid on the last date the discount was available.

* Number of days sales in accounts receivable = 54

Gross profit is 34% of sales

* Number of days to sell inventory = 72

Bonds payable are serial bonds, payable evenly over the next 5 years

Net worth to long term debt = 1.5 : 1

Net income to sales = 5%

Common size analysis of fixed assets:

Land	10%
Building	40
Furniture and fixtures	15
Machinery and equipment	35
	100%

4–13. The Tutco Corporation has maintained the following relationships among the data on its financial statements in recent years as well as in the 19X6 year.

1.	Gross profit as a percentage of net sales	40%
2.	Net profit rate on net sales	10%
3.	Rate of selling expenses to net sales	12%
4.	Accounts Receivable turnover	12 per year
5.	Ratio of accumulated depreciation to cost of fixed assets	.375 to 1
6.	Current Ratio	2 to 1
7.	Accounts Receivable to Cash	2.5 to 1
8.	Inventory to Accounts Receivable	1.8 to 1
9.	Asset Turnover	1.5 per year

* Turnover ratios are explained in chapter 16.

10. Ratio of total Assets to intangible
    Assets .... 10 to 1
11. Ratio of Notes Payable–Short term
    to Accounts Payable .... 1 to 1.5
12. Total Equity to Total Liabilities
    ratio .... 1.5 to 1
13. Times Interest Earned 16

The corporation had a net income of $150,000 for 19X6 which resulted in EPS of $15. Additional information includes the following:

1. Capital stock consists of only common shares of par value $10 per share The market price at time of issue was $30. All shares issued and outstanding.
2. Balance of retained earnings on January 1, 19X6 was $150,000.
3. The notes payable–short term had an interest rate of 10% per year and were outstanding for only 6 months.
4. Bonds payable had an interest rate of 8% per year.
5. All Purchases and Sales were "on account".
6. Income Tax Rate is 50%.

Required:

Prepare in good form the income statement for the year ended December 31, 19X6 and the balance sheet as at that date. Supporting computations should be in good form. The balance sheet includes only the items referred to in the problem.

CHAPTER 5

5–1. The following question(s) are based on the financial statements of Beta Company (pages 89–103).

Required:

a. Beta Corporation uses the Lifo cost-flow assumption in determining its cost of goods sold and beginning and ending inventory amounts for most of its inventory items. Determine the actual gross profit of Beta Corporation for 19X6 if Fifo had been used for all items of inventory.
b. How would the financial statements have differed if Beta Corporation accounted for temporary investments (all equity securities) in accordance with SFAS 12 and the aggregate market value of these investments had been $280 million at the end of 19X6? Ignore income taxes.

5–3. Don Paul Machinery Company sold used machinery to Carlos & Sons in exchange for a note, issued on December 31, 19X0, to mature on December 31, 19X9. The note stipulates that the price of the used machine is $10,000 and an annual interest of 2 percent is to be accrued and compounded annually until maturity of the note. Upon maturity, the principal plus interest accrued will be paid. The prevailing market rate of interest is 8 percent. The following is a partial table of present value and amount of $1:

Years	Amount of $1 at 2%	Present value of $1 at 8%
0	1.0000	1.000
1	1.0200	.926
2	1.0404	.857
3	1.0612	.794
4	1.0824	.735
5	1.1041	.681
6	1.1262	.630
7	1.1487	.583
8	1.1717	.540
9	1.1951	.500

Required:

a. Compute note receivable on December 31, 19X0–X9 and interest income for the nine years under "traditional" method and the present-value method. Use the following format:

	"Traditional" method		Present-value method			Difference in Int. Inc.
Years	Note Rec.	Int. Inc.	Note Rec.	Int. Inc.	Unamortized discount	

b. What effect does the use of present-value method have on the balance sheet and income statement of Don Paul Machinery Company?

5–5. 1. Given the following data:

Beginning inventory   30 desks $900 (at cost)

Purchases			Sold	
June 1	30 desks @30	$900	June 5	20 desks
10	40 desks @32	1,280	15	30 desks
20	30 desks @31	930	25	40 desks

Required:

a. Compute the cost of goods sold under the Fifo, Lifo and Moving-Average cost inventory accounting for Company A.

b. Compute the cost of goods sold under the three methods of inventory for Company B which has exactly same beginning inventory, purchases and sales as Company A above, except that it sold 20 more desks on June 30. Thus, on June 30, Company B has an ending inventory of 20 desks.

2. Because of a fire, all the inventory and records of the Climax Co. were burned. For insurance claim purposes, you are asked to estimate the inventory of desks burned. There was no inventory at the beginning of the period and purchases during the period amounted to $3,000. The company usually makes 15% gross profit and the sales during the period were $3,200.

Required:

What was the inventory burned by the fire?

5–7. XYZ Corporation uses Fifo method for inventory valuation. The company maintains 3,000 units in inventory at all times.

It buys and sells 4,000 units every year or about 1,000 units every quarter.

Following are the actual purchases cost and selling prices per unit for 19X2 and the 1st two quarters of 19X3.

	Purchase cost per unit	*Sale price per unit*	*Economic condition*
1st quarter, 19X2	$10	13	
2nd quarter, 19X2	11	14	inflation
3rd quarter, 19X2	12	15	inflation
4th quarter, 19X2	13	16	inflation
1st quarter, 19X3	13	16	level price
2nd quarter, 19X3	12	15	price decline

The company determines its sale price by applying a constant $3 markup on cost per unit.

Required:

a. Determine the effect of the Fifo method on reported gross profit during inflation and when prices level off and then when they decline. Also show cost of inventory on hand at the beginning of each quarter.

b. Answer (a) above assuming the company was using Lifo method. Compare the results with (a).

5–9. The Falcon Store purchases its merchandise, a standard item, at the current market price and resells the same product at a price 20 cents higher. The purchase price remains the same throughout the year. Data on number of units in inventory at the beginning of year, unit purchases, and unit sales are shown as follows:

No. units in inventory—
 beginning of year ($1 cost) 1,000
No. units purchased in year @ $1.50 1,000
No. units sold in year @ $1.70 1,000

Required:

a. Calculate the after-tax profit for the Falcon Store under the (1) Fifo and (2) Lifo methods of inventory valuation if the company has no expenses other than cost of goods sold but pays income taxes at the rate of 50 percent. Taxes are accrued currently and paid the following year.

The beginning-of-year balance sheet for Falcon Store is as follows:

Inventory	*Net worth*
(1,000 units @ $1) = $1,000	$1,000

b. If all sales and purchases are for cash, construct the balance sheets as of the end of the year using both methods of inventory valuation.
c. What is the significance of each of these methods of inventory valuation upon profit determination and financial position in a period of increasing prices?
d. What problem does the Lifo method pose in constructing interim financial statements?

(C.F.A.)

5–11. The controller of the Investor Corporation, a retail company, made three different schedules of gross margin for the first quarter ended September 30, 1974. These schedules appear below.

	Sales ($10 per unit)	Cost of goods sold	Gross margin
Schedule A	$280,000	$118,550	$161,450
Schedule B	280,000	116,900	163,100
Schedule C	280,000	115,750	164,250

The computation of cost of goods sold in each schedule is based on the following data:

	Units	Cost per unit	Total cost
Beginning inventory, July 1	10,000	$4.00	$40,000
Purchase, July 25	8,000	4.20	33,600
Purchase, August 15	5,000	4.13	20,650
Purchase, September 5	7,000	4.30	30,100
Purchase, September 25	12,000	4.25	51,000

The president of the corporation cannot understand how three different gross margins can be computed from the same set of data. As controller, you have explained to him that the three schedules are based on three different assumptions concerning the flow of inventory costs; i.e., first-in, first-out; last-in, first-out; and weighted average. Schedules A, B, and C were not necessarily prepared in this sequence of cost-flow assumptions.

Required:

Prepare three separate schedules computing cost of goods sold and supporting schedules showing the composition of the ending inventory under each of the three cost-flow assumptions.

(AICPA)

CHAPTER 6

6–1. The following question is based on the financial statements of Beta Company (pages 89–103).

Required:

Explain all changes during 19X6 in the plant and properties accounts.

6-3.   The following is a recent news item:

"GENOA, Italy"—The twin luxury liners Michelangelo and Raffaello, once the proud representatives of Italy's passenger fleet, have been sold to Iran, it was announced by officials of the state-controlled shipping line.

"The price wasn't disclosed but reports put the figure at $35 million, compared with the 1963 construction cost of $145 million.

"The announcement said the two vessels will be transferred to Iran after being refurbished as floating hotels."

It was followed by another news item which stated:

"The greatest nonevent in the annals of the sea occurred last Thursday in Japan, when the world's biggest oil tanker, the 484,377-ton Nissei Maru, was completed—and went straight into lay-up. Between the time the keel of the monster vessel was laid and its delivery, its hypothetical market value plunged 90%. Moreover, it will cost a small fortune to maintain it in lay-up. Then there is the delicate problem of accepting a ship without putting it through its sea trials. What will be the validity of the shipyard's guarantees if it is put through its paces for the first time two or three years hence?"

Required:

a.   What determines the value of assets?
b.   Do present day accounting principles give prompt recognition to changes in economic values? Discuss.

6-5.   A prospectus of the Connecticut Light and Power Company contained a footnote which read in part: "Commencing in 1968, the Company and its affiliated companies established a uniform practice of determining the amount of overhead expenses allocable to the cost of construction of utility plant. Such capitalized overhead expenses include portions of engineering and supervision expenses and *administrative and general expenses.* As a result, the earnings for the year 1968 are approximately $1,025,000 higher than they would have been if the change in practice had not been made."

Required:

a.   On the basis of what information would the utility decide on the allocation of overhead expenses to plant and equipment?
b.   What additional information, if any, would the analyst be interested in this regard?

6-7.   The *Wall Street Journal* carried the following news-item on June 25, 1970:

"KIN-ARK TO WRITE OFF APARTMENT PROPERTIES LOSING $40,000 MONTHLY.
"Setting Value Lower on Buildings in Tulsa Will Allow Boost in Operating Net in '70, Firm Says.

"Tulsa—Kin-Ark Corp. said it will write-off its equity in two high-rise apartment properties here that have been losing about $40,000 a month.

"The apartments, in which Kin-Ark had invested about $10 million, will be valued on its books at about $8.5 million (the amount of the outstanding mortgage debt) effective June 30, the company said. The difference of about $1,230,000 will be treated as a nonrecurring operating loss for 1970, the company said.

"Howard K. Edwards, president, said this will allow the company 'to achieve a significant increase in earnings from operations in the balance of 1970 and in future years.'

"The company also said that unless 'satisfactory arrangements' can be made with the mortgage holder or the Federal Housing Authority 'to continue operation of the property without further cash expenditures, the properties may be turned back to the FHA.' "

Required:

a. What will Kin-Ark Corporation achieve by the write-off of its equity in the apartment properties?
b. Is it usual for companies to write-off properties which are money-losers?
c. What particular circumstance will enable the company to cut itself loose from the losses which the apartments cause?

6–9. On June 30, 1970, your client, The Vandiver Corporation, was granted two patents covering plastic cartons that it has been producing and marketing profitably for the past three years. One patent covers the manufacturing process and the other covers the related products.

Vandiver executives tell you that these patents represent the most significant breakthrough in the industry in the past 30 years. The products have been marketed under the registered trademarks Safetainer, Duratainer, and Sealrite. Licenses under the patents have already been granted by your client to other manufacturers in the United States and abroad and are producing substantial royalties.

On July 1, Vandiver commenced patent infringement actions against several companies whose names you recognize as those of substantial and prominent competitors. Vandiver's management is optimistic that these suits will result in a permanent injunction against the manufacture and sale of the infringing products and collection of damages for loss of profits caused by the alleged infringement.

The financial vice president has suggested that the patents be recorded at the discounted value of expected net royalty receipts.

Required:

a. What is an intangible asset? Explain.
b. (1) What is the meaning of "discounted value of expected net receipts"? Explain.
   (2) How would such a value be calculated for net royalty receipts?
c. What basis of valuation for Vandiver's patents would be generally accepted in accounting? Give supporting reasons for this basis.
d. (1) Assuming no practical problems of implementation and ignoring

generally accepted accounting principles, what is the preferable basis of evaluation for patents? Explain.

(2) What would be the preferable theoretical basis of amortization? Explain.

e. What recognition, if any, should be made of the infringement litigation in the financial statements for the year ending September 30, 1970? Discuss.

(AICPA)

CHAPTER 7

7-1. The following question is based on the financial statements of Beta Company (pages 89–103).

Required:

How much long-term debt was paid during 19X6?

7-3. The equityholders of a business entity usually are considered to include both creditors and owners. These two classes of equityholders have some characteristics in common, and sometimes it is difficult to make a clear-cut distinction between them. Examples of this problem include (1) convertible debt and (2) debt issued with stock purchase warrants. While both examples represent debts of a corporation, there is a question as to whether there is an ownership interest in each case which requires accounting recognition.

Required:

a. Identify:
   (1) Convertible debt.
   (2) Debt issued with stock purchase warrants.
b. With respect to convertible debt and debt issued with stock purchase warrants, discuss:
   (1) The similarities.
   (2) The differences.
c. (1) What are the alternative accounting treatments for the proceeds from convertible debt? Explain.
   (2) Which treatment is preferable? Explain.
d. (1) What are the alternative accounting treatments for the proceeds from debt issued with stock purchase warrants? Explain.
   (2) Which treatment is preferable? Explain.

(AICPA)

7-5. The Hawk Company (the lessor) leased a machine to the Dove Corporation (the lessee) for 5 years, the life of the machine, at an annual rental, paid in advance, of $120,000. The machine cost Hawk $480,000, and it determined the rental based on a 10% rate of return. Dove uses the same rate. The present value of the lease payments amounts to $480,000. The machine has no salvage value and is depreciated under the straight-line method.

Required:

Please prepare all journal entries for the first and second years for both the lessor and lessee.

7-7. On 1/1/19X5 the Myer Corporation leased a machine from the Hawkins Corporation at an annual rental of $20,000. Hawkins' cost of the leased machine and its fair value on 1/1/19X5 is $152,120. The machine had a useful life of 15 years. The lessor's rate of interest implicit in the lease is not known. It is estimated that the residual value of the machine at the end of its useful life will be about $1,000 but it is not guaranteed by the lessee.

The term of the lease is for 15 years. The incremental borrowing rate of Myer Corporation is 10 percent.

The tables of the present value of $1 received annually at the end of each period for N periods indicate that the present value of $1 received annually for 15 periods (at 10 percent rate) is $7.606. The tables of present value of $1 received at the end of a period indicates that the present value of $1 received at the end of 15 years (at 10 percent) is $.239.

Required:

a. Assuming the lease is capitalized, show the entries required in the Myer Corporation's books for 19X5 and 19X7.
b. Show the effect on the income statement for the years ended 12/31/X5 and 12/31/X6 and on the balance sheet at 12/31/19X5 and 12/31/19X7.

7-9. The following are condensed financial statements of F. W. Woolworth Co. and Consolidated Subsidiaries for the fiscal year (FY) ended January 31, 1975:

Income Account	Millions	Balance Sheet	Millions
Net sales	$4,177.1	Current assets	$1,203.6
Cost of sales	2,947.9	Investments, principally in	
Gross Profit	1,229.2	English subsidiary	197.2
		Net properties, at cost	649.1
Selling, general and		Intangible assets	14.7
administration expense	1,007.4	Deferred charges	12.9
Depreciation and			
amortization	63.0	Total Assets	$2,077.5
Total Operating		Current liabilities	$ 643.3
Expense	1,070.4	Long-term debt	413.1
		Other liabilities & reserves	24.6
Net profit from		Deferred income taxes	50.5
operations	158.8	Preferred stock	8.2
Other income	12.8	Common shareholders'	
Income before interest		equity (29.4 million	
and taxes	171.6	shares)	937.8
Interest expense	70.3	Total Liabilities	
Consolidated income		and Share-	
before income tax	$ 101.3	holders' Equity	$2,077.5
Provision for income taxes	48.1		
Consolidated income	53.2		
Equity in net income of			
english subsidiary			
after taxes	11.6		
Net Income	$ 64.8		

Footnote 9 to the financial statements states in part as follows (dollar amounts in millions):

The aggregate present value of minimum rental commitments of SEC-defined financing leases at January 31, 1975 was $978.9 (January 31, 1974–$961.0). Present values were determined by discounting minimum commitments under the lease commitments at interest rates in effect at the time the leases became effective. Such interest rates range from 1.0% to 14.0% and their weighted average is 6.7% (FY 1974–6.21%). The present value of rentals, to be received under more than 1,100 non-cancellable subleases of property and included above, amounted to $10.6 at January 31, 1975 (January 31, 1974– $11.3). On the assumption that SEC-defined financing leases had been capitalized, and the related property rights amortized on a straight-line basis and interest expense computed on the basis of the present value of the declining outstanding balance of the lease commitments, *net income* would have been decreased by $3.1 in FY 1975 and $3.1 in FY 1974. Under such assumptions amortization of property rights would have amounted to $66.1 (FY 1974–$59.2) and the additional interest expense would have amounted to $62.4 (FY 1974–$53.7).

Required:

a. Explain the $3.1 million reduction in net income (after taxes) if financial leases had been capitalized. Show calculations to support your answer. (Assume a 48% income tax rate.)

b. Certain important financial relationships are affected by the method used to account for leases on financial statements. Calculate the values of the following financial relationships based on (1) reported statements *and* (2) reported statements adjusted for capitalized leases. Show calculations.
   (1) Times interest earned.
   (2) Total debt to net worth including reserves.
   (3) Earnings per share.

c. Explain the usefulness to the analyst of information on lease capitalization.

(C.F.A.)

CHAPTER 8

8–1. The following questions are based on the financial statements of Beta Company (pages 89–103).

Required:

a. Give the journal entry that explains the change in the treasury stock account during 19X6 (see Note 9) assuming that there were no other transactions affecting stockholders' equity beside issuance of common stock.

b. What caused the $325 million increase in stockholders' equity during 19X9?

c. Compute the book value per share of both the common and preferred stock rounded to nearest to dollar. (1) For 19X6 and for (2) 19X5 (there were 53,995 shares of $4 preferred stock outstanding on 12/31/19X5).

d. (1) What is the stated value of the cumulative $4 preferred stock?
(2) How does the company present the preferred treasury stock in the balance sheet?

8–3. On a given day, the stock of the Golden Chemical Corp. sold on the N.Y. Stock Exchange for $1,492, while Silver Chemical Corp. was selling for $64.

Required:

a. How can you account for the fact that Golden Chemical was selling for a much greater price? What can you conclude about the relative profitability of the two companies?
b. On the previous day, Golden Chemical stock had sold for $1,471, while Silver Chemical sold for $62. Which stock had the greater price rise?
c. If you had purchased Silver Chemical at $62 and sold it the next day for $64, what effect would this have on the accounting records of the company?

8–5. The ownership interest in a corporation is customarily reported in the balance sheet as stockholders' equity.

Required:

a. List the principal transactions or items that reduce the amount of retained earnings. (Do not include appropriations of retained earnings.)
b. In the stockholders' equity section of the balance sheet a distinction is made between contributed capital and earned capital. Why is this distinction made? Discuss.
c. There is frequently a difference between the purchase price and sale price of treasury stock, but accounting authorities agree that the purchase or sale of its own stock by a corporation cannot result in a profit or loss to the corporation. Why isn't the difference recognized as a profit or loss to the corporation? Discuss.

(AICPA)

8–7. The A.B.C. Corporation has paid its preferred dividends over the past two years. The preferred stock is of the nonparticipating variety. No dividends were paid on the common stock in 19X5.

A.B.C. CORPORATION

	19X5	19X4
Stockholders' Equity:		
Preferred stock—7% noncumulative—par value $25 per share:		
Authorized—93,200 shares		
Issued—93,200 shares—including shares in treasury 19X5, 38,548 shares and 19X4, 21,508 shares	$ 2,330,000	$ 2,330,000
Common stock—no par value:		
Authorized—2,400,000 shares		
Issued—1,831,400 shares—including shares in treasury 19X5, 34,380 shares and 19X4, 62,900 shares	14,943,700	14,943,700
Retained earnings	18,649,861	17,146,574
	$35,923,561	$34,420,274
Less: Cost of shares in treasury	2,616,583	2,707,499
Total Stockholders' Equity	$33,306,978	$31,712,775
	$47,216,729	$40,694,371

Required:

Compute the book value per share of both the common and preferred stock for 19X4 and 19X5.

CHAPTER 9

9–1. The following questions are based on the financial statements of Beta Company (pages 89–103).

Required:

a. For the asset "investment in affiliates—at equity":
  (1) Explain all changes during 19X6.
  (2) Identify all effects in the working capital statement which relate to this investment.
  (3) How much cash dividends were received by Beta Corporation from these affiliated companies?
b. What was the effect of foreign currency translation on earnings in 19X5 and 19X6? How can you tell?
c. Was the acquisition of General Crude Oil Company in 19X5 accounted for as a purchase or as a pooling of interests? How can you tell? Assume that Beta Corporation did not acquire any business prior to 19X5.
d. Assume that the stock in affiliated companies was acquired at book value at the time of acquisition, what were the total dividends distributed by these affiliates during 19X6? How can you tell?
e. What proportions of total sales, working capital and assets are derived from operations outside the United States for 19X6?

9–3. A current accounting controversy concerns the widespread use of pooling in mergers. Opponents of the use of pooling believe that the surviving company often uses pooling (rather than purchase) to hide the "true" effects of the merger.

Required:

What may be "hidden" and how is the analysis of a company's securities affected by pooling practices?

(C.F.A.)

9–5. The following are condensed balance sheets of Purchase Company and Sale Company as of December 31, 19X0.

Balance Sheets
As of December 31, 19X0

	Purchase Co.	Sale Co.
Assets		
Cash and receivables	$200,000	$ 50,000
Other assets	400,000	150,000
Total Assets	$600,000	$200,000
Liabilities and Equity		
Liabilities	$100,000	$ 60,000
Capital stock, $100 par value	300,000	100,000
Paid-in capital	50,000	—
Retained earnings	150,000	40,000
Total Liabilities and Equity	$600,000	$200,000

Purchase Company acquired an 80 percent interest in Sale Company on January 1, 19X1 for $120,000, by paying $60,000 in cash and the balance in notes payable to Sale Company's shareholders.

Required:

Prepare a consolidated financial statement.

9–7. Axel Company acquired 100% of the stock of Wheal Company on December 31, 19X4. The following information pertains to Wheal Co. on that date:

	Book value	Fair value
Cash	$ 40,000	$ 40,000
Accounts receivable	60,000	55,000
Inventory	50,000	75,000
Property, plant, and equipment (net)	100,000	200,000
Secret formula		30,000
	$250,000	$400,000
Accounts payable	30,000	30,000
Accrued employee pensions	20,000	22,000
Long-term debt	40,000	38,000
Capital stock	100,000	—
Other contributed capital	25,000	—
Retained earnings	35,000	—
	$250,000	$ 90,000

Axel Company issued $110,000 par value (Market value on December 31, 19X4 − $350,000) of its own stock to the stockholders of Wheal to consummate the transaction, and Wheal became a wholly-owned, consolidated subsidiary of Axel Company.

Required:

a. Entries to record the acquisition of Wheal Co. Stock,
b. Entries to eliminate the Investment in Wheal Company Stock in working papers for a consolidated balance sheet at December 31, 19X4,
c. A calculation of consolidated retained earnings at December 31, 19X4— Axel's retained earnings at that date are $150,000—if:
   1. Axel uses the pooling of interest method for the business combination.
   2. Axel uses the purchase method for acquisition of Wheal.

9–9. Data on two companies planning a combination are as follows:

	ABC Company	XYZ Company
Book value of common stock	$200 million	$30 million
Common shares outstanding........	4 million	1 million
Net earnings for common	$ 20 million	$ 3 million
Market price of common	$ 75 per share	$30 per share

Assume this is all the information available. Assume a 50 percent tax rate. APB *Opinions Nos. 16* and *17* on "Business Combinations and Intangible Assets" apply.

Required:

a. In the combination .5 shares of ABC Company are to be exchanged for each XYZ Company share.
   (1) Is this (i) A pooling, (ii) A purchase, (iii) Part pooling, part purchase, (iv) Either, depending on intent?
   (2) What are the total dollar earnings of the new entity?
   (3) How much goodwill is created in the consolidation?
   (4) Calculate earnings per share of the new entity—show calculations.
b. In the combination .2 shares of ABC Company plus $25 worth of 6 percent debt is to be exchanged for each share of XYZ Company.
   (1) Is this (i) A pooling, (ii) A purchase, (iii) Part pooling, part purchase, (iv) Either, depending on intent?
   (2) How much goodwill is created in the consolidation?
   (3) What is the yearly write-off of goodwill assuming the maximum life allowed for goodwill?
   (4) On a pro forma basis, assuming the combination had taken place a year ago, calculate the net earnings and per share earnings of the new entity. Show calculations.

(C.F.A.)

9–11. Following are the financial statements of AMEX of Italia, a subsidiary of AMEX of America.

Income Statement
For the Year Ended 12/31/19X5
(in thousands of Italian liras)

Sales		150,000
Beginning inventory	12,000	
Purchases	120,000	
	132,000	
Less: Ending inventory	22,000	
Cost of sales		110,000
Gross profit		40,000
Selling and administrative expenses	20,000	
Depreciation	10,000	30,000
Pre-Tax income		10,000
Taxes @ 40%		4,000
Net Income		6,000

Balance Sheet
As at 12/31/19X5
(in thousands of Italian liras)

Assets		Liabilities & Equities		
Cash	5,000	Accounts payable		8,000
Accounts receivable	10,000	Income taxes payable .		2,000
Inventory	22,000	Total Current		
Total Current Assets	37,000	liabilities		10,000
Plant and equipment	50,000	Long-term debt		15,000
Less: Accumulated		Capital stock	40,000	
depreciation	20,000	Retained earnings	15,000	
Net plant & equipment	30,000	Stockholders'		
Land	13,000	equity		55,000
Total fixed assets	43,000	Total Liabilities		
		and Equities		80,000
Total Assets	80,000			

You were given the following additional information:
1. Plant and equipment was originally purchased on 1/1/19X4 when the foreign exchange rate was $1 = 600 Liras.
2. AMEX of Italia was established on 1/1/19X3 at which time the land was the only fixed asset and the exchange rate was $1 = 580 Liras.
3. The foreign exchange rates during 19X5 were as follows:

1/1/19X5	$1 = 620
Average for 19X5	$1 = 630
12/31/19X5	$1 = 640

4. Balance of retained earnings on 1/1/19X5 was equal to $14.75 thousands.
5. Ending inventory was purchased when the exchange rate was $1=640 Liras.

Required:

Translate the financial statements of AMEX of Italia into dollars in accordance with the principles of SFAS8.

CHAPTER 10

10–1. After the presentation of your report on the examination of the financial statements to the board of directors of the Savage Publishing Company, one of the new directors says he is surprised the income statement assumes that an equal proportion of the revenue is earned with the publication of every issue of the company's magazine. He feels that the "crucial event" in the process of earning revenue in the magazine business is the cash sale of the subscription. He says that he does not understand why—other than for the smoothing of income—most of the revenue cannot be "realized" in the period of the sale.

Required:

a. List the various accepted methods for recognizing revenue in the accounts and explain when the methods are appropriate. Do not limit your listing to the methods for the recognition of revenue in magazine publishing.
b. Discuss the propriety of timing the recognition of revenue in the Savage Publishing Company's accounts with—
   (1) The cash sale of the magazine subscription.
   (2) The publication of the magazine every month.
   (3) Both events, by recognizing a portion of the revenue with cash sale of the magazine subscription and a portion of the revenue with the publication of the magazine every month.

(AICPA)

10–3. The Cosmo Construction Company commenced doing business in January 19X5. Construction activities for the year 19X5 are summarized below:

Project	Total contract price	Contract expenditures to Dec. 31, 19X5	Estimated additional costs to complete contracts	Cash collections to Dec. 31, 19X5	Billings to Dec. 31, 19X5
A	$ 310,000	$187,500	$ 12,500	$155,000	$155,000
B	500,000	200,000	350,000	250,000	300,000
C	400,000	340,000	—	300,000	400,000
D	300,000	16,500	183,500	—	4,000
	$1,510,000	$744,000	$546,000	$705,000	$859,000

The company is your client. The president has asked you to compute the amounts of revenue for the year ended December 31, 19X5 that would be reported under the completed-contract method and the percentage-of-completion method of accounting for long-term contracts.

The following information is available:
1. All contracts are with different customers.
2. Any work remaining to be done on the contracts is expected to be completed in 19X6.
3. The company's accounts have been maintained on the completed-contract method.

Required:

a. Prepare a schedule computing the amount of revenue by project for the year ended December 31, 19X5 that would be reported under—
   (1) The completed-contract method.
   (2) The percentage-of-completion method.
b. Prepare a schedule under the completed-contract method computing the amounts that would appear in the company's balance sheet at December 31, 19X5 for (1) costs in excess of billings and (2) billings in excess of costs.
c. Prepare a schedule under the percentage-of-completion method that would appear in the company's balance sheet at December 31, 19X5 for (1) costs and estimated earnings in excess of billings and (2) billings in excess of costs and estimated earnings.

(AICPA adapted)

10–5. Trinket Company started with $3,000 cash in a business to produce trinkets using a simple assembly process. During the first month of business, the Company signed sales contracts for 1,300 units (sales price of $9 per unit), produced 1,200 units (production cost of $7 per unit), shipped 1,100 units and collected in full for 900 units.

Production costs are paid at the time of production. The Company has only two other costs: (a) sales commissions of 10% of sales price are paid at the same time that the Company collects from the customer and (b) shipping costs of $.20 per unit are paid at time of shipment.

The sales price and all costs have been constant per unit and are likely to remain the same.

Required:

Prepare comparative (side-by-side) balance sheets and income statements for the first month of Trinket Company for *each* of the following *three* alternatives:
a. Profit is recognized at the time of shipment.
b. Profit is recognized at the time of collection.
c. Profit is recognized at the time of production.

Note: Net income for each of the three alternatives should be (a) $990; (b) $810; (c) $1080.

10–7. An accountant must be familiar with the concepts involved in determining earnings of a business entity. The amount of earnings reported for a business entity is dependent on the proper recognition, in general, of revenue and expense for a given time period. In some situations, costs are recognized as expenses at the time of product sale; in other situations, guidelines have been developed for recognizing costs as expenses or losses by other criteria.

Required:

a. Explain the rationale for recognizing costs as expenses at the time of product sale.

b. What is the rationale underlying the appropriateness of treating costs as expenses of a period instead of assigning the costs to an asset? Explain.

c. In what general circumstances would it be appropriate to treat a cost as an asset instead of as an expense? Explain.

d. Some expenses are assigned to specific accounting periods on the basis of systematic and rational allocation of asset cost. Explain the underlying rationale for recognizing expenses on the basis of systematic and rational allocation of asset cost.

e. Identify the necessary conditions in which it would be appropriate to treat a cost as a loss.

(AICPA)

10–9. The Smith Company, just starting business, builds a new plant costing $2,000,000. The plant will be fully depreciated over a 10-year period. The company has 100,000 shares of common stock outstanding and no debt. Operating earnings are $500,000 each year before depreciation and income taxes. The tax rate is 50 percent.

Required:

a. Calculate the provision for depreciation on the new plant in Year 1 and Year 10 using:
  (1) Straight-line method.
  (2) Sum-of-the-years'-digits method.

b. Construct condensed income statements, as reported to stockholders, for Year 1 and Year 10 if:
  (1) Straight-line depreciation method used for both tax and reporting purposes.
  (2) Sum-of-the-years'-digits depreciation method used for both tax and reporting purposes.
  (3) Sum-of-the-years'-digits depreciation method used for tax purposes and the report to stockholders presented on a "normalized" basis.

c. Show the earnings per share for each of the situations, in (b) above, for Year 1 and Year 10. Explain briefly how you account for the different earnings per share figures.

(figures may be rounded to thousands)

(C.F.A. adapted)

10–11. Company S, a profitable organization, has built and equipped a $2,000,000 plant which was brought into operation early in 19X1. Earnings of the company before depreciation on the new plant and before income taxes have been projected as follows:

19X1	$1,500,000
19X2	2,000,000
19X3	2,500,000
19X4	3,000,000
19X5	3,500,000

The company may use the straight-line, double-declining balance, or sum-of-the-years'-digits methods of depreciation for the new plant.

Required:

Calculate the effect that each of these methods of depreciation would have on—
a. Federal income taxes.
b. Net income.
c. Cash flow.

Assume income tax rate of 50 percent, and that the useful life of the plant is 10 years. (No salvage value)

(C.F.A. adapted)

CHAPTER 11

11–1. The following questions are based on the financial statements of Beta Company (pages 89–103).

Required:

a. Estimate the amount of depreciation expense shown on Beta 19X6 tax return. Use a tax rate of 48% and assume that the entire depreciation expense is as shown in the income statement.
b. Identify the amounts for 19X6 of the following (combine federal, foreign and state taxes) and show your source.
   (1) Earnings before income taxes.
   (2) Expected income tax at 48%.
   (3) Total income tax expense.
   (4) Total income tax due to governments.
   (5) Total income tax due and not yet paid at December 31, 19X6 (ignore deferred taxes).
c. (1) Why does the effective tax rate for 19X6 differ from 48% of income before tax? (Note 3)
   (2) Is it likely that the effective tax rate will continue to be low in the future?
d. Was the company's effective tax rate in 19X6 different from that in 19X5? And if it was, what were the main reason(s)?
e. Reconstruct all entries related to income taxes for 19X6 and show the amount of income tax paid.
f. What effect did the investment tax credit have on the 19X6 and 19X5 financial statements?

11–3. The following paragraph is part of the notes to the financial statements of International Harvester Company for the year ended October 31, 1970:

". . . Total pension expense for the years 1970 and 1969 was $43,535,000 and $56,609,000, respectively. Pension costs are computed on the basis of accepted actuarial methods and include amortization of prior service cost, generally over a 30-year period. It is the Company's policy to fund accrued pension costs."

During the 1970 fiscal year, the Company changed certain actuarial assumptions; the principal change was in the assumed interest rate which reduced annual pension costs by $9,275,000.

The actuarially computed value of vested benefits for all plans as of December 31, 1969, exceeded the total of the pension funds by approximately $166,000,000.

The following additional data is supplied:

Income available to common—year ended 10/31/70	$52,432,000
Number of common shares	27,267,000
Dividend rate per common share	$ 1.80
Assume that the tax rate on incremental corporate income is 50 percent.	

Required:

From the viewpoint of the common stockholder, discuss the significance of the changes in actuarial assumptions underlying pension fund expenses for the year 1970.

(C.F.A.)

11–5. HI HAT Corp. was formed in 19X4 to take over the operations of a small business. This business proved to be very stable for HI HAT as can be seen (000 omitted):

	19X4	19X5	19X6
Sales	$10,000	$10,000	$10,000
Expenses (except income tax)	9,000	9,000	9,000
Income before taxes	$ 1,000	$ 1,000	$ 1,000

In addition, HI HAT expended $1,400,000 on preoperating costs for a new product during 19X4. These costs were deferred for financial reporting purposes but were deducted in calculating 19X4 taxable income. During 19X5 the new product line was delayed and in 19X6 HI HAT abandoned the new product and charged the deferred cost of $1,400,000 to the 19X6 income statement.

Required:

a.   Prepare comparative income statements in good form for the three years. Be certain to identify all tax amounts as either "current" or "deferred".

b.   List each tax item on the balance sheets at the end of each year (assume all tax payments and refunds occur in the year following the reporting year and that the tax rate is 50% in each year).

11–7. The 19X7 earnings of the ABC Corporation are summarized below. The company did not use accelerated depreciation for tax purposes.

Operating earnings	$1,000,000
Depreciation	100,000
Pretax net	900,000
Federal income tax	450,000
Net income	450,000

Required:

a. At the year-end, the company added $300,000 new equipment, with an estimated life of five years. Assume no change in operating earnings and tax rate for 19X8. Based on the use of straight-line depreciation in the annual report, show the summarized earnings as reported to stockholders, using:

(1) Straight-line depreciation for tax purposes.

(2) Double-declining balance depreciation for tax purposes, "normalized."

(3) Double-declining balance depreciation for tax purposes with "flow-through."

b. What would be the 19X8 depreciation, for tax purposes, on the new facilities using the sum-of-the-years' digits?

c. Under what conditions might the "flow-through" concept be justified?

(C.F.A.)

11–9. SEC *Accounting Series Release 163* states:

"The conventional accounting model applicable to companies other than public utilities has not traditionally treated the cost of capital as part of the cost of an asset and, except for two specific industries, no authoritative statement on this subject presently exists. Interest cost on debt is generally treated as a period expense of the period during which debt capital is used, while the cost of equity capital is reflected neither in asset cost nor in the income statement."

Required:

Discuss the reasons for the adoption of this approach to the accounting for interest costs.

11–11. The Century Company, a diversified manufacturing company, had four separate operating divisions engaged in the manufacture of products in each of the following areas: food products, health aids, textiles, and office equipment.

Financial data for the two years ended December 31, 1975, and 1974 are presented below:

	Net sales		Cost of sales		Operating expenses	
	1975	1974	1975	1974	1975	1974
Food products .	$3,500,000	$3,000,000	$2,400,000	$1,800,000	$ 550,000	$ 275,000
Health aids	2,000,000	1,270,000	1,100,000	700,000	300,000	125,000
Textiles	1,580,000	1,400,000	500,000	900,000	200,000	150,000
Office equipment	920,000	1,330,000	800,000	1,000,000	650,000	750,000
	$8,000,000	$7,000,000	$4,800,000	$4,400,000	$1,700,000	$1,300,000

On January 1, 1975, Century adopted a plan to sell the assets and product line of the office equipment division and expected to realize a gain on this disposal. On September 1, 1975, the division's assets and product line were sold for $2,100,000 cash resulting in a gain of $640,000 (exclusive of operations during the phase-out period).

The company's textiles division had six manufacturing plants which produced a variety of textile products. In April 1975, the company sold one of these plants and realized a gain of $130,000. After the sale, the operations at the plant that was sold were transferred to the remaining five textile plants which the company continued to operate.

In August 1975, the main warehouse of the food products division, located on the banks of the Bayer River, was flooded when the river overflowed. The resulting damage of $420,000 is not included in the financial data given above. Historical records indicate that the Bayer River normally overflows every four to five years causing flood damage to adjacent property.

For the two years ended December 31, 1975, and 1974, the company had interest revenue earned on investments of $70,000 and $40,000 respectively.

For the two years ended December 31, 1975, and 1974, the company's net income was $960,000 and $670,000 respectively.

The provision for income tax expense for each of the two years should be computed at a rate of 50%.

Required:

Prepare in proper form a comparative statement of income of the Century Company for the two years ended December 31, 1975, and December 31, 1974. Footnotes are **not** required.

(AICPA)

11–13. The following quotation from an article written by Leopold Bernstein highlights the issue concerning the use of reserves to recognize future costs and losses—are they valid or merely a means of further clouding reports?

"The growing use of reserves for future costs and losses impairs the significance of periodically reported income and should be viewed with skepticism by the analyst of financial statements. That is especially true when the reserves are established in years of heavy losses, when they are established in an arbitrary amount designed to offset an extraordinary gain, or when they otherwise appear to have as their main purpose the relieving of future income of expenses properly chargeable to it.

"The basic justification in accounting for the recognition of future losses stems from the doctrine of conservatism which, according to one popular application, means that one should anticipate no gains, but take all the losses one can clearly see as already incurred."

Required:

a. Discuss the merits of Bernstein's arguments and apprehensions.
b. Explain how such information may be factored into your review of past trends, the estimates of future earnings, and valuation of the common stock.

(C.F.A.)

CHAPTER 12

12–1. Earnings per share (EPS) is the most featured single financial statistic about modern corporations. Daily published quotations of stock prices have recently been expanded to include a "times earnings" figure for many securities which is based on EPS. Often the focus of analysts' discussions will be on the EPS of the corporations receiving their attention.

Required:

a. Explain how dividends or dividend requirements on any class of preferred stock that may be outstanding affect the computation of EPS.
b. One of the technical procedures applicable in EPS computations is the "treasury-stock method."
   (1) Briefly describe the circumstances under which it might be appropriate to apply the treasury-stock method.
   (2) There is a limit to the extent to which the treasury-stock method is applicable. Indicate what this limit is and give a succinct indication of the procedures that should be followed beyond the treasury-stock limits.
c. Under some circumstances convertible debentures would be considered "common stock equivalents" while under other circumstances they would not.
   (1) When is it proper to treat convertible debentures as common stock equivalents? What is the effect on computation of EPS in such cases?
   (2) In case convertible debentures are not considered as common stock equivalents, explain how they are handled for purposes of EPS computations.

(AICPA)

12–3. On 10/1/X5 the management of the Morning Corporation decided to merge with the Afternoon and Evening Corporations. Following is some additional information: (assume pooling accounting)

	Afternoon Corporation	Evening Corporation	Morning Corporation
Net income from 1/1 to 9/30/X5	$200,000	$300,000	$100,000
Common shares outstanding on 10/1/X5	100,000	80,000	300,000
Shares issued on 7/1/X5	50,000		
Shares issued on 9/1/X5		20,000	
Net income from 10/1 to 12/31/X5			$400,000
Number of shares issued for acquisition of:			
Afternoon Corp. (2 for 1)			200,000
Evening Corp. (5 for 1)			400,000

Required:

Compute earnings per share for the Consolidated Company on 12/31/X5.

12–5. The Smith Company, in its annual reports for the years ending December 31, reported per share earnings as shown below:

19X0	$3.00
19X1	2.00
19X2	1.50
19X3	3.00
19X4	1.80
19X5	2.50
19X6	2.50

The following changes in capitalization took place in December of each of the years shown:

19X1 .... 50% stock dividend paid
19X2 .... 400,000 shares of common stock issued for cash
19X3 .... 2-for-1 split effective
19X5 .... 300,000 shares issued on conversion of an outstanding debenture issue
19X6 .... 80% stock dividend paid

Required:

The head of the research department has asked you to make the necessary adjustments to the reported figures so that a better comparison of changes in earnings on the common stock can be made.

(C.F.A. adapted)

12–7. Company A has a net income for the year of $4 million and the number of common shares outstanding is 3 million (there was no change during the year). The Company also has options and warrants outstanding to purchase 1 million common shares at $15 per share.

Required:

a. If the average market value of the common share was $20, the year-end price was $25, interest rate on borrowings is 6 percent and the tax rate is 50 percent. Compute the primary and the fully diluted EPS.
b. Do the same requirement as in (a) above, assuming that net income for the year was only $3 million and average market value per common share was $18 and year-end price was $20 per share.

12–9. The officers of Environmental Protection, Inc. had considered themselves fortunate when the company had been able to sell a $9,000,000 subordinated convertible debenture issue on June 30, 19X0 with only a 6 percent coupon. They had had the alternative of refunding and enlarging the outstanding term loan, but the interest cost would have been one half a point above the prime rate. The latter had been as high as 8½ percent until March 29, 19X0 when it was lowered to 8 percent, the rate that prevailed until September 21, 19X0 when it was lowered again to 7½ percent.

Environmental Protection, Inc. had the following capital structure at December 31, 19X0:

7% term loan*	$3,000,000
6% convertible subordinated debentures 19Y5†	9,000,000
Common stock, $1 par, authorized 2,000,000 shares, issued and outstanding 900,000	900,000
Warrants, expiring July 1, 19X5 900,000‡	
Capital surplus	1,800,000
Retained earnings	4,500,000

  * The term loan (originally $5,000,000) is repayable in semiannual installments of $500,000.

  † The convertible subordinated debentures, sold June 30, 19X0 are convertible at any time at $18 until maturity. Sinking fund of $300,000 per year to start in 19X5.

  ‡ Warrants entitle holder to purchase one share for $10 to expiration on July 1, 19X5.

Additional data for year 19X0:

Interest expense	$ 500,000
Net income....................................	1,500,000
Dividends paid	135,000
Earnings retained..............................	900,000
Market prices December 31, 19X0 (which are also the averages for 19X0)	
Convertible debentures 6% 75.................	107
Common	13.00
Warrants	4.50
Treasury bills interest rate at 12/31/19X0	6%

Required:

a. Calculate (show your computations) the earnings per share figures for the common stock as they would be required to be shown in the 19X0 annual report.

b. What would be the times interest earned before tax on the 6 percent convertible subordinated debentures (assume a 50 percent federal income tax rate for the company) for the year 19X1 assuming net earnings before interest and taxes were the same as in 19X0.

(C.F.A. adapted)

CHAPTER 13

13–1. The following questions are based on the financial statements of Beta Company (pages 89–103).

Required:

a. Prove that the changes in the company's balance sheets (19X5 to 19X6) are explained in the 19X6 statement of changes in financial position. Draw T-accounts for the balance sheet items showing the beginning and ending balances and one T-account for *all* working capital accounts. Post the items shown in the 19X6 statement of changes in financial position to these T-accounts. "Key" each figure to an explanation.

b. How much cash was collected from customers (accounts and notes receivable) during 19X6?

c. Investments in timberlands for 19X6 are shown as $37.5 million in the statement of changes in financial position. Independently calculate this figure from other information available in the financial statements.

d. Determine the Net Cash Flow from operations for 19X6 (NCFO) using:
   (1) The "Inflow-Outflow" approach.
   (2) The "Net" approach.

e. How much was the gain on sale of capital assets for 19X6? Where did the company report this gain? Did the company use the proper presentation of this gain on the statement of changes in financial position? How can you tell?

f. How much was *paid* in cash dividends on common stock during 19X6?

g. Was any portion of the $133 million notes payable and current maturities of long-term debt due at the end of 19X5 paid during 19X6?

h. How much was the cost of finished goods produced during 19X6? (Consider total cost of all inventory items, labor and overhead).

i. How much was the deferred tax provision for 19X6? What effect did it have on current liabilities?

j. What effect did the 19X6 depreciation expense have on working capital (i.e., on current assets and/or current liabilities)?

k. Can you identify the items in the 19X6 income statement which were sources and uses of working capital and explain the *net* working capital from operations during 19X6 of $509.4 million per the statement of changes in financial position? (*Hint:* Consider only items which affect current assets or current liabilities).

l. What was the main cause of the increase in "funds provided from operations" ($509.4 million vs. $459.6 million)?

13–3. Part A. There have been considerable discussion and research in recent years concerning the reporting of changes in financial position (sources and applications of funds). *Accounting Principles Board Opinion No. 19* concluded

" . . . That the statement summarizing changes in financial position should be based on a broad concept embracing all changes in financial position and that the title of the statement should reflect this broad concept. The Board therefore recommends that the title be Statement of Changes in Financial Position."

Required:

a. What are the two common meanings of "funds" as used when preparing the statement of changes in financial position? Explain.

b. What is meant by " . . . a broad concept embracing all changes in financial position . . ." as used by the Accounting Principles Board in its *Opinion No. 19?* Explain.

Part B. Chen Engineering Company is a young and growing producer of electronic measuring instruments and technical equipment. You have been retained by Chen to advise it in the preparation of a statement of changes in financial position. For the fiscal year ended October 31, 1975, you have obtained the following information concerning certain events and transactions of Chen.

1. The amount of reported earnings for the fiscal year was $800,000, which included a deduction for an extraordinary loss of $93,000 (See item 5 below).
2. Depreciation expense of $240,000 was included in the earnings statement.
3. Uncollectible accounts receivable of $30,000 were written off against the allowance for uncollectible accounts. Also, $37,000 of bad debts expense was included in determining earnings for the fiscal year, and the same amount was added to the allowance for uncollectible accounts.
4. A gain of $4,700 was realized on the sale of a machine; it originally cost $75,000 of which $25,000 was undepreciated on the date of sale.
5. On April 1, 1975, a freak lightning storm caused an uninsured inventory loss of $93,000 ($180,000 loss, less reduction in income taxes of $87,000). This extraordinary loss was included in determining earnings as indicated in 1. above.
6. On July 3, 1975, building and land were purchased for $600,000; Chen gave in payment $100,000 cash, $200,000 market value of its unissued common stock, and a $300,000 purchase-money mortgage.
7. On August 3, 1975, $700,000 face value of Chen's 6% convertible debentures were converted into $140,000 par value of its common stock. The bonds were originally issued at face value.
8. The board of directors declared a $320,000 cash dividend on October 20, 1975, payable on November 15, 1975, to stockholders of record on November 5, 1975.

Required:

For each of the eight (8) numbered items above, explain whether each item is a source or use of working capital and explain how it should be disclosed in Chen's statement of changes in financial position for the fiscal year ended October 31, 1975. If any item is neither a source nor a use of working capital, explain why it is **not** and indicate the disclosure, if any, that should be made of the item in Chen's statement of changes in financial position for the fiscal year ended October 31, 1975.

(AICPA)

13–5. The following data were taken from the accounting records of Sprouse Corporation and subsidiaries for 19X1:

	Thousands
Income before extraordinary items	$5,000
Extraordinary items (net of tax)	1,200
Depreciation, depletion, and amortization	8,300
Major disposals of property, plant, and equipment (book value)	1,000
Deferred income taxes for 19X1	200
Undistributed earnings of unconsolidated subsidiary and affiliates	100
Amortization of discount on bonds payable	20
Amortization of deferred "investment tax credit"	30
Decrease in noncurrent assets	1,300
Proceeds from exercise of stock options	200

Required:

Determine the amount of working capital provided by operations in 19X1.

13–7.   Exhibit 13–A gives the balance sheet of XYZ Corporation.

EXHIBIT 13–A

XYZ CORPORATION
Balance Sheets
As of December 31, 19X1 and 19X2

	19X2	19X1
Cash	$300,000	$100,000
Accounts receivable	200,000	150,000
Inventories	320,500	300,000
Property, plant, and equipment	550,000	400,000
Patents, net of $500 amortization	4,500	—
Accounts payable	(50,000)	(175,000)
Accumulated depreciation	(350,000)	(250,000)
Convertible debt	—	(80,000)
Common stock, $1 par	(280,000)	(100,000)
Additional paid-in capital	(400,000)	(200,000)
Retained earnings	(295,000)	(145,000)
	—0—	—0—

In addition, the following information is available:

1. Net income for the year was $300,000.
2. Cash dividends paid during the year were $150,000.
3. During the year the convertible debt was converted to 80,000 shares of common stock.
4. During the year the company sold 100,000 shares of common stock at $3 per share.
5. Depreciation charged to income during the year was $100,000.
6. During the year the company purchased patents for $5,000. Amortization of patents during the year amounted to $500.

Required:

a. Prepare a statement of changes in financial position.
b. Determine net cash flow from operations (NCFO) based on the net approach.

13–9.   Exhibits 13–B and 13–C are financial statements for Mason Company for years 19X5 and 19X6.

EXHIBIT 13–B

MASON COMPANY
Balance Sheets
As of December 31, 19X5 and 19X6
(in thousands of dollars)

	19X5	*19X6*	*Change*
Assets			
Current Assets:			
Cash	2,600	3,000	400
Marketable securities	500	800	300
Accounts receivable	8,000	10,000	2,000
Notes receivable	115	50	(65)
Inventories	16,308	15,302	(1,006)
Total Current Assets	27,523	29,152	1,629
Plant and equipment	61,712	63,008	1,296
Less: Accumulated depreciation	23,400	25,605	(2,205)
Total Fixed Assets	38,312	37,403	(909)
Other assets	35	20	(15)
Total Assets	65,870	66,575	705
Total Liabilities and Capital			
Current Liabilities:			
Accounts payable	4,100	5,000	900
Notes payable	1,602	1,333	(269)
Accrued expenses	58	24	(34)
Accrued federal income tax	3,000	3,900	900
Current portion of long-term debt	4,000	4,000	—
Total Current Liabilities	12,760	14,257	1,497
Long-term debt	12,221	8,799	(3,422)
Preferred stock	13,110	15,640	2,530
Common stock	22,379	22,379	—
Retained earnings	5,400	5,500	100
Total Liabilities and Capital	65,870	66,575	705

EXHIBIT 13–C

MASON COMPANY
Income Statement
For the Year Ended December 31, 19X6
(in thousands of dollars)

Sales (net)	88,432
Cost of goods sold	53,976
Gross margin	34,456
Selling and administrative expense	22,394
Operating profit	12,062
Interest expense	650
Other income	(312)
Profit before taxes	11,724
Provision for federal income tax	6,176
Net income after tax	5,548
Dividends paid	5,448
Addition to retained earnings	100

The following is additional information:

1. Long-term debt was converted into preferred stock, dollar for dollar. The excess of the long-term debt over the amount converted was retired by a payment in cash.
2. Plant and equipment retired during the year was fully depreciated and did not have any salvage value.
3. Other income represents gains resulting from marketable security transactions.
4. Depreciation of $4,625 is included in costs of goods sold.
5. Both notes receivable and notes payable relate to operations.

Required:

a. Prepare a statement of changes in financial position for year 19X6 (working capital concept).
b. Prepare a statement of changes in financial position for year 19X6 (cash concept).
c. Determine net cash flow from operations based on "inflow-outflow" approach.

13–11. On 1/1 year 1, Company Z desired to expand by investing in new production facilities to support expected larger sales. The management decided to borrow $200 million and service the debt by the proceeds from its operations within 5 years (the expected useful life of new facilities is 10 years). The lender (a big insurance company) required projected income statements for the following five years to be able to evaluate the debt paying ability of Z Company. Exhibit 1 shows these projected income statements:

EXHIBIT 1

COMPANY Z
Projected Income Statements
(in $ millions)

	Year 1	Year 2	Year 3	Year 4	Year 5
Sales	$525	$550	$575	$600	$625
Cost of sales	480	495	510	525	540
Gross profit	45	55	65	75	85
Depreciation (1)	30	30	30	30	30
Other expenses (2)	15	15	15	15	15
	45	45	45	45	45
Net Income	0	10	20	30	40

(1) Includes $20 million depreciation of new facilities
(2) Include interest and taxes

Based on the projected income statements the lender provided a $200 million loan to Z Company based on determination of net cash flow from operations (net income + depreciation). The lender did not ask for projected balance sheets. Z Company paid the first installment of $20 million on 1/1 year 2 but when the installment of $30 million of 1/1 year 3 became due, Z Company did not have more than $27 million in cash. The insurance company called upon you as a financial analyst to see what went wrong. You asked for the balance sheet as at Dec. 31, Year 1 which appears in Exhibit 2, and expected changes in the level of accounts receivable, inventory and accounts payable.

EXHIBIT 2

COMPANY Z
As at 12/31 (in million $)

	Year 1
Cash	30
Accounts receivable	105
Inventory	65
Total current assets	200
Fixed assets	300
Less: Acc dep.	80
Total fixed assets	220
Total Assets	420
Accounts payable	80
Long-term debt	200
Total Liability	280
Equity: Capital	140
R/E	—
Total equity	140
Total Liabilities and Equity	420

You learned that starting in Year 2 accounts receivable will increase by $5 million each year, inventory by $10 million each year and accounts payable by $2 million each year. There was no change during Year 1. Z Company maintains a $10 million minimum cash balance at all times.

Required:

a. Prepare a table showing net cash flows from operations based on net income plus depreciation.
b. Prepare a table showing net cash inflows from operations based on the tabulation presented in this chapter.
c. Explain to the insurance company what went wrong by comparing the results in (a) and (b) above.

13–13.   A popular analytical tool employed by financial analysts and other readers of financial statements is the computation of the amount of cash flow. To provide more meaningful cash flow information that cannot readily be obtained from the balance sheet and the statement of income and retained earnings, it has been suggested that a funds statement be provided along with the other financial statements. The title of the funds statement should be descriptive, such as "statement of source and application of funds" or "summary of changes in financial position."

Required:

a. Define the term cash flow from an accounting standpoint.
b. Discuss each of the following statements:
   (1) Cash flow provides a more significant indication of the results of a company's operations than does net income.
   (2) A large cash flow permits steady expansion and the regular payment of cash dividends.
c. Discuss the uses to which funds statements may be put by the readers of the statements.

(AICPA)

CHAPTER 14

14–1.   The following question(s) are based on the financial statements of Beta Company (pages 89–103).

Beta Company has included in form 10-K, information on replacement costs as follows:

Replacement cost information (unaudited).   In accordance with the Securities and Exchange Commission's *Accounting Series Release No. 190* issued in March 1976, the Company has estimated the replacement costs of its inventories, productive capacity, and timberlands at December 31, 19X6, together with estimates of the cost of products sold, depreciation, and cost of timber harvested for the year then ended on the basis of such replacement costs.

The following table summarizes the quantitative disclosures required by the SEC.

	In millions December 31, 19X6	
	Estimated replacement cost	Comparable historical amounts
Inventories	$ 456	$ 348
Plants and properties	$7,684	$3,573
Less: Accumulated depreciation	4,017	1,625
Total Plants and Properties	$3,667	$1,948
Cost of products sold..................	$2,514	$2,514
Depreciation & Depletion	$ 346	$ 180
Cost of timber harvested	33	33

In accordance with *ASR No. 190,* the amounts shown above include land and certain assets at historical cost which, in management's present opinion, will not be replaced at the end of their economic lives, in addition to oil and gas properties also at historical cost, since the methodology for mineral resource replacement cost calculations has not yet been established by the SEC.

Required:

a. Based on this information, restate by format of a work sheet, the Company's balance sheet and income statement on a replacement cost basis.
b. What general conclusions can we draw from the restated financial statements?
c. Of which limitations must the analyst be aware in using and interpreting such restated statements?

14–3. Part A. Valuation of assets is an important topic in accounting theory. Suggested valuation methods include the following:
1. Historical cost (past purchase prices).
2. Historical cost adjusted to reflect general price-level changes.
3. Discounted cash flow (future exchange prices).
4. Market price (current selling prices).
5. Replacement cost (current purchase prices).

Required:

a. Why is the valuation of assets a significant issue?
b. Explain the basic theory underlying **each** of the valuation methods cited above. **Do not discuss advantages and disadvantages of each method.**

Part B. Valuation to reflect general price-level adjustments, as opposed to replacement cost, would yield differing amounts on a firm's financial statements.

Several transactions concerning one asset of a calendar-year company are summarized as follows:

1974   Purchased land for $40,000 cash on December 31.
        Replacement cost at year end was $40,000.
1975   Held this land all year.
        Replacement cost at year end was $52,000.
1976   October 31—sold this land for $68,000.
General price-level index:
    December 31, 1974 100
    December 31, 1975 110
    October 31, 1976 120

Required:

On your answer sheet, duplicate the following schedules and complete the information required based upon the transactions described above.

Valuation of land on statement of financial position	General price-level	Replacement cost
December 31, 1974	$	$
December 31, 1975		

Gain on earnings statement	General price-level	Replacement cost
1974	$	$
1975		
1976		
Total	$	$

(AICPA)

14–5. Financial policies which are advantageous in an extended inflationary period can lead to liquidity problems for a corporation in a business slowdown.

Required:

a. Illustrate this point by discussing appropriate balance sheet items.
b. How can inflation result in overstating net income?
c. How can inflation result in overstating a company's return on net worth?

(C.F.A.)

14–7. You have deposited $20,000 in a savings account at a local bank on January 2, 19X1. The balance on December 31, 19X1, is $21,200. You made no withdrawals during the year. The general price level index on January 1, 19X1, was 110 but it increased to 121 by December 31, 19X1. Inflation progressed evenly throughout the year.

Required:

a. Compute the interest rate and amount of interest earned.
b. Compute the loss due to inflation on principal, if any.
c. Compute the net increase or decrease in your wealth caused by the savings account, inclusive of interest earned.

14–9. Sweeny Corporation was founded on January 1, 19X1. The price level index was at 100 on that day. The price index increased by 10 percent in each of the following two years. It is assumed that these increases and all phases of the business occur uniformly throughout the year.

Below are the balance sheets and income statements for the periods under consideration:

	1/1/X1	12/31/X1	12/31/X2
Cash	$ 20,000	$ 40,000	$ 64,000
Land	80,000	80,000	80,000
Total	$100,000	$120,000	$144,000
Capital	$100,000	$100,000	$100,000
Retained earnings		20,000	44,000
Total	$100,000	$120,000	$144,000

	12/31/X1	12/31/X2
Sales	$ 50,000	$ 70,000
Cost of sales	(25,000)	(36,000)
Other expenses	(5,000)	(10,000)
Net Income	$ 20,000	$ 24,000

Required:

a. Restate the above statements and show the effect of price level changes. All amounts are to be brought up to the current (12/31/X2) level.
b. Assume that the following replacement cost estimates for certain of the company's assets have been provided by management. Develop a work-sheet to prepare the financial statements for 19X1 and 19X2 based on replacement costs:

	Estimated replacement costs	
	19X1	19X2
At December 31		
Land	$85,000	$91,000
For year ended December 31		
Cost of sales	$29,000	$39,000

14–11. Revsine Company was organized on 1/1/19X5. Following are its financial statements for 19X5.

REVSINE COMPANY
Balance Sheet (conventional basis)
(in millions of dollars)

	At 1/1/19X5	At 12/31/19X5
Cash	20	10
Accounts receivable	—	30
Inventory	—	50
Equipment	100	100
Less: Accumulated depreciation	—	10
Net Cost	100	90
Total Assets	120	180
Accounts payable	—	40
Capital stock	120	120
Retained earnings	—	20
Total Liabilities and Equity	120	180

REVSINE COMPANY
Income Statement for 19X5
(historical basis)
(in millions of dollars)

Sales		200
Cost of sales	100	
Depreciation	10	
Other expenses (including taxes)	70	180
Net Income		20

The management has provided the following estimates of replacement costs:

	Estimated replacement costs (in millions of dollars)
1. For year ending December 31, 19X5	
Cost of goods sold at date(s) of sale	110
Depreciation	12
2. At December 31, 19X5	
Inventory	55
Equipment	120

Required:

Develop a worksheet to prepare replacement cost financial statements for 19X5.

14–13. Following are the conventional financial statements of Edwards & Bell Corporation for 19X8.

EDWARDS & BELL CORPORATION
Income Statement
For the Year Ended December 31, 19X8
(in thousands of dollars)

Sales		$100,000
Beginning inventory	$ 10,000	
Purchases	60,000	
	70,000	
Less: Ending inventory	15,000	
Cost of sales		55,000
Gross profit		45,000
Depreciation........................	5,000	
Other expenses (including taxes)	20,000	
		25,000
Net Income		$ 20,000

Balance Sheet
As at December 31

	19X7	19X8
Assets		
Cash	$ 5,000	$ 7,000
Accounts receivable	15,000	18,000
Marketable securities	12,000	20,000
Inventory	10,000	15,000
Total Current Assets	42,000	60,000
Land	40,000	40,000
Equipment	50,000	50,000
Less: Accumulated depreciation	—	(5,000)
Total Assets	$132,000	$145,000
Liabilities and Equity		
Accounts payable	12,000	15,000
Long-term notes payable	30,000	10,000
Capital stock	50,000	60,000
Retained earnings	40,000	60,000
Total Equity	90,000	120,000
Total Liabilities and Equity	$132,000	$145,000

The following are the replacement costs estimates that were provided by management for certain of the company's assets:

	19X7	19X8
At December 31		
Inventory	12,000	19,000
Land	42,000	45,000
Equipment	50,000	60,000
Marketable securities	13,000	22,000
For Year Ended December 31		
Depreciation		6,000
Cost of goods sold		60,000

Required:

Develop a worksheet to prepare replacement cost financial statements for Edwards & Bell Corporation for 19X8.

CHAPTER 16

16–1. The following questions are based on the financial statements of Beta Company (pages 89–103).

Management projects for 19X7 a 15 percent growth in sales, purchases, and expenses except depreciation which is to increase by only 10 percent. Other income will increase by 5 percent. Depletion and cost of timber harvested will remain the same. The average inventory turnover for 19X7 will be 6. To achieve these operating goals, management will lengthen the receivable collection period to 90 days, based on year-end accounts receivable. Ending accounts payable turnover of 6 will remain the same. Notes payable of $15 million will be due in 19X7. Management desires to maintain a minimum cash balance of $40 million. Effective income tax rate for 19X7 will be 40 percent, of which 10 percent will be deferred. Dividends on preferred stock will be the same as in 19X6 and on common stock will be $95 million.

Required:

a. Will the company have to borrow in 19X7?
b. If Beta Company is planning to request a 9-month loan from the bank for $150 million in 19X7, how can you, as the bank's senior financial analyst, assess Beta's liquidity to determine whether the loan should be approved?

16–3. The management of Fire Corp. wants to improve the appearance of their current position, i.e., current and quick ratios, on their financial statements.

Required:

a. List and briefly describe 4 ways in which they might accomplish this goal.
b. For each, state the procedures, if any, which an analyst can use to detect these window dressing devices.

16–5. The "Z" Company had the following unrelated transactions during 19X0:

1. Determined that $3,000 of accounts receivable were uncollectible.
2. The bank notified the company that a customer's check for $225 had been returned marked "insufficient funds." The customer went bankrupt.
3. The owners of the company made an additional cash investment of $12,000.
4. Inventory which had cost $300 was considered obsolete when the physical inventory was taken.
5. Declared a $4,700 cash dividend to be paid during the first week of the next accounting period.
6. The company purchased a long-term investment of cash, $6,000.
7. Accounts payable of $9,500 were paid in cash.

8. The company borrowed $1,875 from the bank and gave a 90-day, 6 percent promissory note.
9. Sold a vacant lot that had been used in the business for cash, $24,600.
10. Purchased a three-year insurance policy for $2,100.

Assume that prior to any of the above transactions the company's current ratio was 2 : 1.

Required:

Considering the above transactions separately, how would each affect the company's:
a. Current ratio?
b. Quick ratio (acid-test ratio)?
c. Net working capital?

16–7.   Benston Corporation has the following operating results in 19X5

Income Statement
For Year Ending December 31, 19X5

Sales		800,000
Cost of goods sold		480,000
Gross profit		320,000
Depreciation	25,000	
Other expenses (including taxes)	160,000	185,000
Net Income		135,000

Purchases in 19X5 were $500,000

Balance Sheet Data
As at December 31, 19X5

Cash	$ 60,000
Accounts receivable	200,000
Merchandise inventory	70,000
Accounts payable	100,000
Notes payable	300,000

In 19X6 management expects a 20% growth in sales and expenses other than depreciation. To keep control over inventory costs and to avoid stockouts, management will keep the average inventory turnover ratio at 6. To achieve these operating goals, there will be a lengthening of the receivable collection period, based on the year-end accounts receivable, to 120 days. No other policy changes are contemplated. Notes payable of $100,000 become due in 19X6.

Required:

Will Benston Corporation have to borrow in 19X6? Assume that management wants to maintain a minimum cash balance of $50,000.

16–9.   Below are some of the accounts of RST Corporation as of March 31, 19X5.

	Debit	Credit
Cash	50,000	
Accounts receivable	200,000	
Inventory	100,000	
Accounts payable		150,000
Notes payable		75,000
Income taxes payable		25,000
Capital stock		250,000
Sales		800,000
Purchases	400,000	
Depreciation	35,000	
Net Income		40,000

Cost of goods sold for the year ended March 31, 19X5 was $600,000, including depreciation above and the company desires to maintain a minimum cash balance of $75,000. In all situations below notes payable and income taxes payable remain constant.

Required:

a.   The company has decided to change the ending inventory turnover rate to 5 times the cost of goods sold, effective as of the coming year. Sales as well as the other revenue and expense items are expected to increase by 10 percent over 19X5 with the exception of depreciation which is expected to increase by only 5 percent. Calculate the effect of the change in the inventory turnover rate on the funds available to the company if it also intends to change its collection policy so that receivables equal on the average 120 days of sales. Will this change cause a need for more funds or an excess of funds and by how much?

b.   Assume the same information as in (a), except that the company decided to change to a policy of extending credit to an average of 60 days of sales. Will this result in a need for or an excess of funds?

c.   Evaluate separately from (a) and (b) above what the effect would be if the company changes its accounts payable policy as follows. The terms for purchases are a 2 percent discount if paid on receipt, net/60 days. The company has determined that it would take the discount for one-fourth the amount of the purchases and use the credit arrangement for the other three-quarters. Assume that all revenue and expense items will remain constant and that no discounts were taken in 19X5. The average income tax rate is 50 percent. What would be the effect of such policy on the company's availability of funds?

16–11.   In the problems cited below, indicate whether X is equal to, greater than, or less than Y and give the reasons for your answer.

1.   The following data concerning Company A and Company B were compiled from their records. Compare Company A's inventory turnover (X) with that of Company B (Y).

	Co. A	Co. B
Sales	$200,000	$550,000
Gross profit percentage:		
Based on cost of goods sold	25%	
Based on selling price		30%
Initial inventory	$ 30,000	$102,500
Ending inventory	34,000	90,000

2. The following data concerning the sales and collections of Company C and Company D were compiled from their records. Compare the average collection period of Company C's accounts receivable (X) with that of Company D (Y).

	Co. C	Co. D
Sales	$220,500	$90,000
Accounts receivable, 1/1	21,000	4,000
Accounts receivable, 12/31	· 15,700	8,000

3. "Cost or market, whichever is lower," may be applied to the inventory as a whole (procedure "a") or to categories of inventory items (procedure "b"). Compare the reported value of inventory which would generally obtain when procedure "a" is used (X) with the reported value of inventory when procedure "b" is used (Y).

4. Prices have been rising steadily, and the inventory turnover ratio was four in the last year. Compare the ending inventory computed by the Lifo method (X) with the same ending inventory computed by the moving-average method (Y).

5. The authorized capital stock of the Alpha Corporation consisted of one million shares of $5 par value common, of which 800,000 shares were issued and outstanding. The balance in the Retained Earnings account was $1,260,000. A 10 percent stock dividend was declared and issued when the market value of the stock was $7.50 per share. Compare the total net worth before issuance of the stock dividend (X) with the total net worth after the issuance of the stock dividend (Y).

6. The cash sale of a fixed asset has resulted in a loss. Compare the current ratio before the sale (X) with the ratio after the sale (Y).

7. The Omega Corporation has written off an uncollectible account receivable against the allowance account. Compare the current ratio before the write-off (X) with the ratio after the write-off (Y).

8. The current ratio of the Segma Corporation is 2 to 1. If cash is used to pay a current liability, compare the ratio before payment (X) with the ratio after payment of the current liability (Y).

16–13. Part A. Arthur, CPA, is auditing the RCT Manufacturing Company as of February 28, 1975. As with all engagements, one of Arthur's initial procedures is to make overall checks of the client's financial data by reviewing significant ratios and trends so that he has a better understanding of the business and can determine where to concentrate his audit efforts.

The financial statements prepared by the client with audited 1974 figures and preliminary 1975 figures are presented below in condensed form.

RCT MANUFACTURING COMPANY
Condensed Balance Sheets
February 28, 1975 and 1974

Assets	1975	1974
Cash	$ 12,000	$ 15,000
Accounts receivable, net	93,000	50,000
Inventory	72,000	67,000
Other current assets	5,000	6,000
Plant and equipment, net of depreciation	60,000	80,000
	$242,000	$218,000

Equities		
Accounts payable	$ 38,000	$ 41,000
Federal income tax payable	30,000	14,400
Long-term liabilities	20,000	40,000
Common stock	70,000	70,000
Retained earnings	84,000	52,600
	$242,000	$218,000

RCT MANUFACTURING COMPANY
Condensed Income Statements
Years Ended February 28, 1975 and 1974

	1975	1974
Net sales	$1,684,000	$1,250,000
Cost of goods sold	927,000	710,000
Gross margin on sales	757,000	540,000
Selling and administrative expenses	682,000	504,000
Income before federal income taxes	75,000	36,000
Income tax expense	30,000	14,400
Net income	$ 45,000	$ 21,600

Additional information:
1. The company has only an insignificant amount of cash sales.
2. The end of year figures are comparable to the average for each respective year.

Required:

For each year compute the current ratio and a turnover ratio for accounts receivable. Based on these ratios, identify and discuss audit procedures that should be included in Arthur's audit of (1) accounts receivable and (2) accounts payable.

Part B. In connection with the annual examination of Johnson Corp., a manufacturer of janitorial supplies, you have been assigned to audit the fixed assets. The company maintains a detailed property ledger for all fixed assets. You prepared an audit program for the balances of property, plant, and equipment but have yet to prepare one for accumulated depreciation and depreciation expense.

Required:

Prepare a separate comprehensive audit program for the accumulated depreciation and depreciation accounts.

(AICPA)

CHAPTER 17

17–1. The following questions are based on the financial statements of Beta Company (pages 89–103).

Following are projections of some items of the statement of changes in financial positions for 19X7 and 19X8:

	19X8	19X7
Sources of Funds	*(in $ millions)*	
Issuance of common stock	5.0	—
Reduction of long-term investments	10.0	30.0
Sales of properties	6.0	4.0
Other sources—net.....................	3.5	8.4
Applications of Funds		
Cash Dividends	98.0	95.0
Investments in plant and properties	450.0	400.0
Investments in timber lands	50	100
Purchase of treasury stock	0.2	0.5
Environmental construction fund held		
by trustees	1.0	3.0
Other Projections		
Sales.................................	4,680	4,070

You are to estimate the remaining sources and uses of funds based on the following assumptions:
1. Net income in 19X7 and 19X8 will represent the average percentage of sales as prevailed in the five-year period ended December 31, 19X6.
2. Depletion of oil and gas properties is estimated at $50 million each year, and cost of timber harvested will be $35 million in 19X7 and $38 million in 19X8.
3. Depreciation in 19X7 and 19X8 will bear the same relationship to net income as has average depreciation over the five year period 19X2–19X6 borne to average net income over the same period.
4. Deferred income taxes—noncurrent will be in 19X7 at a level reflecting the relationship of total 5-year deferred tax (noncurrent) to total 5-year net income. They will change in 19X8 by the percentage change which 19X8 net income bears to 19X7 net income.
5. Net borrowing change in 19X7 and 19X8 will be at the level needed to meet the year-end working capital relationship to sales reflecting the level which prevailed in 19X6.

Required:

a. (1) Analyze the statement of changes in financial position of Beta Company for the 5-year period 19X2–19X6.
   (2) Prepare projected statements of changes in financial position for 19X7 and 19X8 based on the above projections and assumptions.
b. Did the $67.5 million increase in working capital during 19X6 improve Beta's liquidity? Discuss briefly.

c. Compute the following ratios:
(1) Funds flow adequacy ratio for 19X2–19X6 period
(2) Funds reinvestment ratio for: (*a*) 19X6 and (*b*) 19X5.

17–3. Prepare a cash projection for Max Manufacturing Company indicating receipts and disbursements for May, June and July. The firm wishes to maintain at all times a minimum cash balance of $20,000. Determine whether or not borrowing will be necessary during the period, and, if it is, when and how much. As of April 30, the firm had a cash balance of $20,000.

	Actual sales		Estimated sales
January	50,000	May	70,000
February	50,000	June	80,000
March	60,000	July	100,000
April	60,000	August	100,000

Additional Information
1. 50 percent of total sales are for cash and the remaining 50 percent will be collected equally during the following two months (the firm incurs a negligible bad-debt loss).
2. Cost of goods manufactured and sold is 70 percent of sales. Ninety percent of this cost is paid during the first month after incurrence, the remaining 10 percent is paid the following month.
3. Sales and administrative expenses amount to $10,000 per month plus 10 percent of sales. All of these expenses are paid during the month of incurrence.
4. A semi-annual interest payment on $300,000 of bonds outstanding, (6 percent coupon) will be paid during July. An annual $50,000 sinking fund payment is also to be made during July.
5. Capital expenditures of $40,000 will be invested in plant and equipment in June.
6. Income tax payment of $1,000 will be made in July.
7. A $10,000 dividend is expected to be declared and paid in July.

17–5.

INSELROCK CORPORATION
Balance Sheet
Oct. 31, 19X6

Assets		*Liabilities and equity*	
Current Assets:		Current Liabilities:	
Cash	$ 35,000	Accounts payable	$ 33,000
Accts receivable	60,000	Notes payable	5,000
Inventory	45,000	Total Current Liabilities	38,000
Total Current Assets	140,000	Capital stock	100,000
Fixed assets	120,000	Retained earnings	82,000
Accumulated depreciation	(40,000)		
Total Assets	$220,000	Total Liabilities and Equity	$220,000

The following supplementary information is available:
1. Sales for the three (3) months October to December are estimated as follows:
    October $50,000, November $55,000, and December $65,000.
    Present collection policy calls for monthly collections equal to 60 percent of current months sales and 40 percent of the preceding months sales.
2. The firm anticipates the following purchases, the terms of which are n/30:
    October $40,000, November 51,000 and December $62,000
3. Wages and salaries are $3,000 per month.
4. Operating expenses are ten percent (10%) of sales.
5. Rent is $2,000 monthly.
6. A $5,000 note is payable November 15
7. Depreciation is $1,200 monthly; income tax is estimated at 50 percent (50%); cost of sales amounts to 50 percent (50%) of sales.
8. The minimum cash balance the company desires to keep is $30,000.

Required:

a. Prepare a cash forecast for the two months, November, 19X6 and December, 19X6.
b. Prepare a pro forma income statement for the two months and a balance sheet as at December 31, 19X6.

17–7. Following are the consolidated statements of changes in financial position of Moon Company and its subsidiaries for the five years ending December 31, 19X5 as well as some projections for 19X6 and 19X7.

Required:

a. Analyze and evaluate the statement for the 5-year period presented.
b. Prepare projected statements of changes in financial position of Moon Company for 19X6 and 19X7 based on the following assumptions as well as on some of the projections provided:
    1. Net income in 19X6 and 19X7 will be at a level representing average percentage of net income to sales as prevailed in 19X1–19X5.
    2. Depreciation in 19X6 and 19X7 will bear the same relationship to net income as has average depreciation over the 5-year period 19X1–19X5 borne to average net income over the same period.
    3. The best estimate of deferred income taxes is that they will be in 19X6 at a level reflecting the relationship of total 5-year net income. In 19X7, they will change by the percentage change of 19X7 net income relative to 19X6 net income.
    4. Net borrowing change in 19X6 and 19X7 will be at the level needed to meet the year end working capital relationship to sales reflecting the level which prevailed in 19X5.

17–9. David Construction, builds heavy construction equipment for commercial and government purposes. Because of two new contracts and the anticipated purchase of new equipment, the management needs certain projections for the next three years. You have been requested to prepare these projections.

You have acquired the following information from the company's records and personnel.

1. David Construction uses the completed-contract method of accounting whereby construction costs are capitalized until the contract is completed. Since all general and administrative expenses can be identified with a particular contract, they also are capitalized until the contract is completed.

2. David's December 31, 1973, balance sheet follows:

Assets

Cash		$ 72,000
Due on contracts		—
Costs of uncompleted contracts in excess of billings		—
Plant and equipment	$2,800,000	
Less accumulated depreciation	129,600	2,670,400
Total		$2,742,400

Liabilities and Stockholders' Equity

Loans payable..	$ —
Accrued construction costs	612,400
Accrued income tax payable	65,000
Common stock ($10 par value)........................	500,000
Paid in capital......................................	100,000
Retained earnings	1,465,000
Total..	$2,742,400

3. Two contracts will be started in 1974—Contract A and Contract B. Contract A and Contract B are expected to be completed in December 1975 and December 1976, respectively. No other contracts will be started until after Contracts A and B are completed. All other outstanding contracts had been completed in 1973.

4. Total estimated revenue for Contract A is $2,000,000 and for Contract B is $1,500,000. The estimated cash collections per year follow:

	1974	1975	1976
Contract A	$ 800,000	$1,200,000	$ —
Contract B	300,000	450,000	750,000
	$1,100,000	$1,650,000	$750,000

5. Estimated construction costs to be incurred per contract, per year follow:

	Contract A	Contract B
1974	$ 720,000	$ 250,000
1975	1,000,000	400,000
1976	—	650,000
	$1,720,000	$1,300,000

MOON COMPANY, INC. AND CONSOLIDATED SUBSIDIARIES
Consolidated Statement of Changes in Financial Position

	Year Ended December 31					Projected	
	19X1	19X2	19X3	19X4	19X5	19X6	19X7
	(thousands of dollars)						
Sources of working capital							
Operations:							
Net income	$ 151,616	$ 154,709	$ 229,731	$ 377,727	$ 220,054		
Charges to income not involving working capital:							
Recovery of capital (Depreciation, cost depletion, amortization and retirements)	146,106	156,146	181,079	219,423	283,552		
Deferred Income Taxes	33,636	22,096	43,698	4,994	81,087		
Other	7,093	10,714	8,874	7,304	8,867	$ 8,700	$ 8,900
Working capital provided from operations	338,451	343,665	463,382	609,448	593,560		
Net Decrease in long-term receivables and investments	—	—	—	—	—		
Contribution of common stock to stock purchase and savings plans	19,239	—	10,242	7,428	6,142	6,000	—
Borrowings		105,611	90,429	92,033	71,026		
Disposition of properties, plants and equipment	21,602	26,844	31,025	36,220	118,470	89,000	45,000
Contribution of common stock to pension fund	15,385	—	—	—	—		
Increase in deferred credits	—	—	—	50,604	27,062	—	—
Other sources	—	—	6,009	—	9,808	10,000	9,000
Total Sources of Working Capital	394,677	476,120	601,087	795,733	826,068		

Uses of working capital

Capital expenditures	323,916	269,756	283,926	776,495	537,285	500,000	600,000
Cash dividend payments	70,539	69,604	70,524	73,651	77,669	100,000	105,000
Prepayment of pension costs	18,765	—	9,109	—	—	—	—
Purchase of company's own stock	50,262	40,999	4,387	2,012	5,132	15,000	10,000
Decrease in long-term debt	35,943	30,144	32,009	40,482	92,672	40,000	45,000
Net increase in long-term receivables and investments	15,093	20,229	45,407	3,780	16,369	—	—
Portion of other deferred credits transferred to current	—	—	—	—	—	—	—
Other uses	1,652	7,685	—	10,700	—	—	—
Total Uses of Working Capital	516,170	438,417	445,362	907,120	729,127		
Increase (Decrease) in Working Capital	$ (121,493)	$ 37,703	$ 155,725	$ (111,387)	$ 96,941		
Additional information							
Working capital at Dec. 31	725,870	763,573	919,298	807,911	904,852		
Sales	1,520,610	1,550,875	2,307,200	3,607,879	2,905,550	3,200,000	3,500,000

6. Depreciation expense is included in these estimated construction costs. For 1974, 10% of the estimated construction costs represents depreciation expense. For 1975 and 1976, 15% of the estimated construction costs represents depreciation expense. The cash portion of these estimated construction costs is paid as follows: 70% in the year incurred and 30% in the following year.

7. Total general and administrative expenses (not included in construction costs) consist of a fixed portion each year for each contract, and a variable portion which is a function of cash collected each year. For the two prior years, cash collected and total general and administrative expenses (based on one contract each year) were as follows:

	Cash collected	Total general and administrative expenses
1973	$1,350,000	$27,250
1972	1,180,000	24,700

These general and administrative expenses all represent cash expenses and are paid in the year incurred.

8. Dividends are expected to be distributed as follows:

> 1974 Stock—10% of common shares outstanding (estimated fair market value is $15 per share).
> 1975 Stock split—2 for 1 (par value to be reduced to $5 per share).
> 1976 Cash—$1.00 per share.

9. David will acquire a new asset in 1975 for $700,000 and plans to pay for it that year.

10. When the cash balance falls below $70,000, David obtains short-term loans in multiples of $10,000. For purposes of this problem, ignore interest on short-term loans and ignore any repayments on these loans.

11. Assume income taxes are paid in full the following year.

Required:

a. Prepare projected income statements for each of the calendar years 1975 and 1976 (when contracts are to be completed). The income tax rate is 40%, and the company uses the same methods for accounting and tax purposes.

b. Prepare cash budgets for each of the calendar years 1974, 1975, and 1976. The budgets should follow this format:

Cash (beginning of year) .... $
Plus: collections
Less: disbursements (enumerated)
Plus: borrowing (if any) _____
Cash (end of year) .... $ ____

CHAPTER 18

18-1.   The following questions are based on the financial statements of
Beta Company (pages 89–103).

Required:

a. Compute the following for 19X6:
    (1) Times interest earned ratio.
    (2) Fixed charges coverage ratio
       (a) Per SEC standard
       (b) Per expanded concept
    Assume that selling and administrative expenses include $30 million in
    rentals of which $12 million represent implicit interest and that the com-
    pany has a sinking fund requirement of $20 million annually. (For pur-
    poses of this question the above data supercede the information found in
    footnote 16)
    (3) Funds flow coverage of fixed charges as per expanded concept.
b. What is Beta's debt/equity ratio at 12/31/X6 if we consider as debt (1) the
    excess of actuarially computed value of vested pension benefits over the
    value of pension fund assets, (2) reserves and deferred liabilities, (3) 75
    percent of deferred income taxes as well as (4) total long-term debt.

18-3.   The following information is available for Companies A, B, and C.

	A	B	C
Total assets	$1,000,000	$2,000,000	$3,000,000
Total liabilities	300,000	—	1,500,000
Interest rate on total liabilities	10%	—	5%
Operating income	80,000	200,000	270,000
Percentage of operating income to			
total assets	8%	10%	9%

Required:

Compute the financial leverage indexes for Companies A, B, and C. Assume a tax rate of 48 percent. What do the respective levels of the leverage
indexes for these companies mean?

18-5.   Susan Corporation needs additional funds for plant expansion. The
board of directors is considering obtaining the funds by issuing additional
short-term notes, long-term bonds, preferred stock, or common stock.

Required:

a. What primary factors should the board of directors consider in selecting
    the best method of financing plant expansion?
b. One member of the board of directors suggests that the corporation should
    maximize trading on equity, that is, using stockholders' equity as a basis
    for borrowing additional funds at a lower rate of interest than the expected
    earnings from the use of the borrowed funds.

(1) Explain how trading on equity affects earnings per share of common stock.
(2) Explain how a change in income tax rates affects trading on equity.
(3) Under what circumstances should a corporation seek to trade on equity to a substantial degree?

c. Two specific proposals under consideration by the board of directors are the issue of 7 percent subordinated income bonds or 7 percent cumulative, nonparticipating, nonvoting preferred stock, callable at par. In discussing the impact of the two alternatives on the debt to stockholders' equity ratio, one member of the board of directors stated that he felt the resulting debt-equity ratio would be the same under either alternative because the income bonds and preferred stock should be reported in the same balance sheet classification. What are the arguments (1) for and (2) against using the same balance sheet classification in reporting the income bonds and preferred stock?

(AICPA)

18–7. Following is the income statement of Duke Corporation for the year ended 12/31/19X1.

DUKE CORPORATION
Income Statement
For Year Ending 12/31/19X1
(in thousands)

Sales		$13,400
Add: Equity in earnings of uncon-		
solidate subsidiary		600
		14,000
Less: Cost of goods sold		7,000
Gross profit		7,000
Selling and administrative expenses	$1,800	
Depreciation	600	
Rental charges (1)	700	
Share of minority interests in consoli-		
dated income	300	
Interest expense (2)	600	4,000
Pre-tax income		3,000
Income taxes—Current	$1,000	
Deferred	500	1,500
Net Income		1,500
Dividends—Preferred Stock	$ 200	
On common stock	500	700
Earnings retained for the year		$ 800

(1) Include implicit interest of $200,000
(2) Includes interest portion of $100,000 in rents which have been capitalized.

Additional information
1. The company has a 5-year noncancellable purchase commitment of $50,000 annually.
2. The company has a sinking fund requirement of $100,000 annually.

Required

Compute the following coverage ratios:
a. Times interest earned.
b. Fixed charges coverage ratio:
   (1) Per SEC standard.
   (2) Per expanded concept.
c. Funds flow coverage of fixed charges.
d. Earnings coverage of preferred dividends.

18–9.   Following is the income statement for OPQ Co. for the year ending December 31, 19X8.

Revenues		
Net sales		$51,075,000
Undistributed earnings of subsidiaries		363,000
		51,438,000
Cost and expenses		
Costs of products sold (1)		41,191,000
Selling, general and administrative		
expenses (2)		2,396,000
Provision for depreciation		605,000
		44,192,000
Income before provision for income taxes		7,246,000
Provision for income taxes—Current	$2,200,000	
Deferred	1,562,000	3,762,000
Net income		$3,484,000

(1) Includes Rentals of $800,000 of which $340,000 is the implicit interest component.

(2) Includes Interest Expense of	$650,000
Amortization of Bond Discount	50,000
Interest of Capitalized Lease	70,000
	$770,000

There is an annual sinking fund obligation of $300,000. The average tax rate is 45 percent.

Required

a. Compute times-interest-earned ratio.
b. Compute the fixed charges coverage ratio:
   (1) Per SEC standard.
   (2) Per expanded concept of fixed charges.
c. Compute the funds flow coverage of fixed charges, under expanded concept.

18–11.   Late in December 1975, Mr. Paul Lawrence, senior analyst for the Taconite Life Insurance Company, was asked to decide which of two steel company bonds should be sold to make room for forthcoming private placements of steel companies which would bear significantly higher yields. In the opinion of the financial vice president of the company such placements, together with present holdings of steel industry bonds, would represent a disproportionate investment in steel industry securities, even though Taconite was one of the larger life insurance companies.

Price data on the two securities as of December 19, 1975, are as follows:

Issuer	Description	Maturity	Current call price	Closing price 12/19/75	Yield to maturity	Bond quality rating
Armco Steel	Deb. 8.70s	10/1/95	106.96	94	9.36%	A
Republic Steel	Deb. 8.90s	11/15/95	107.12	96	9.44%	A

Armco Steel Corporation is the nation's fifth largest steel company with raw steel output of 8.9 million tons in 1974. Major markets included: construction (22% of steel sales), distributors (18%), automotive (21%), industrial machinery (10%), appliances (12%), oil and gas (5%). The company has over 40-year reserves of iron ore, coal and limestone. Nonsteel Armco Enterprises group included: Hitco (nonmetallic composite materials), Equipment Leasing Division, Insurance Division, National Supply (oil industry equipment).

Republic Steel Corporation is the nation's third largest steel producer. It is also an important producer of specialty steels. The automotive industry is the largest customer (22% of shipments), followed by distributors (18%), machinery (14%), and construction (10%). Steel output in 1974 was 10.6 million tons. Republic Steel is 66% self-sufficient in iron ore (owns 50% of Reserve Mining with Armco owning the other 50%), and is 54% self-sufficient in coal.

As part of his analysis of the two companies, Mr. Lawrence had his assistant prepare the analyses shown in Table 1. Ratios 2 through 5 assume that the debt service burden anticipated as of December 1975 had been serviced in each of the years 1965–74. Such anticipated burden included a full year's interest on the $100 million Armco debenture 9.20s issued on July 15, 1975, and also assumed that Republic Steel would issue $100 million debentures at an assumed cost of 10% in view of its forthcoming $350 million capacity expansion program. Also, sinking fund requirements of $5 million per year to begin in 1977 for both companies are included in prospective debt service.

Required:

a. In reviewing the data prepared by Mr. Lawrence's assistant in Table 1, identify and explain which of the ratios have shown greater significance in appraising the debt-service ability of the two companies.

b. Based solely on the data in Table 1, select the company which appears to have better prospects for servicing its indebtedness. Explain.

c. Select one of the two bonds for Mr. Lawrence to sell. (Assume that the marketability of each of the two issues is similar.) Explain your choice.

d. Based on this comparative analysis and debt-service capacity for the two debentures, explain the significance of their bond quality ratings.

(C.F.A.)

TABLE 1

ARMCO STEEL CORPORATION vs. REPUBLIC STEEL CORPORATION
Comparative Analysis of Debt Service Capacity

Ratio number	Description of ratio	5-year average 1970–74	10-year average 1965–74	Poorest year 1965–74	1974	9 mos. 1975
1.	Times actual interest earned (before income taxes)					
	Armco Steel	5.91x	9.79x	3.31x(1971)	11.28x	5.95x
	Republic Steel	5.62x	8.04x	0.31x(1971)	15.66x	6.36x
2.	Times anticipated interest earned (before income taxes)					
	Armco Steel	5.85x	4.42x	2.67x(1970)	9.84x	5.95x
	Republic Steel	5.22x	4.49x	0.28x(1971)	10.87x	4.78x
3.	Times anticipated interest and sinking fund earned (before income taxes)					
	Armco Steel	2.58x	2.33x	1.44x(1967)	4.93x	4.27x
	Republic Steel	1.98x	2.05x	0.17x(1971)	4.95x	2.17x
4.	Earnings before depreciation, interest and income taxes (EBDIT) divided by interest, lease payments and sinking fund*					
	Armco Steel	5.60x	4.86x	3.39x(1970)	9.43x	4.27x
	Republic Steel	4.23x	4.20x	1.76x(1971)	8.35x	4.70x
5.	Excess EBDIT over anticipated interest, lease payments, and sinking fund as a percent of net sales*					
	Armco Steel	10.2%	11.2%	7.4%(1970)	13.7%	12.3%
	Republic Steel	7.5%	9.3%	2.6%(1971)	12.9%	7.2%
6.	Capital structure—Armco					
	Long-term debt	32.4%	29.5%	34.9%(1970)	26.8%	N/A
	Net worth	67.6%	70.5%	65.1%(1970)	73.2%	N/A
	Capital structure—Republic					
	Long-term debt	24.0%	23.9%	27.4%(1970)	17.7%	N/A
	Net worth	76.0%	76.1%	72.6%(1970)	82.3%	N/A
7.	Net tangible assets per 1,000 bond					
	Armco Steel	$3,020	$3,555	$2,008(1971)	$3,515	N/A
	Republic Steel	$4,292	$4,195	$3,637(1970)	$5,648	N/A
8.	Net working capital per $1,000 bond					
	Armco Steel	$ 728	$1,016	$ 614(1971)	$1,008	N/A
	Republic Steel	$ 826	$ 806	$ 547(1969)	$1,322	N/A
9.	Average market price as a percent of book value common stock					
	Armco Steel	67.2%	82.7%	57.1%(1974)	57.1%	69.3%
	Republic Steel	41.2%	57.7%	32.7%(1974)	32.7%	37.7%

* For all years depreciation expense was substantially in excess of sinking fund requirements.

CHAPTER 19

19–1. The following questions are based on the financial statements of Beta Company (pages 89–103).

Required:

a. Compute return on investment for 19X6 under the following investment bases:
  (1) Total assets.
  (2) Gross productive assets, assuming that property includes gross idle facilities of $50 million in 19X6 and $40 million in 19X5 and that 20 percent of total other assets are not productive.
  (3) Year-end market value of common stock assuming that the market value at year end was equal to the average price for the last quarter of 19X6.
  (4) Long-term debt plus stockholders' equity. Assume that average interest rate on other long-term debt and on the current maturities is 7%. (Note: Consider Reserves and Deferred Liabilities as well as 75 percent of Deferred Income Taxes as long-term debt).

b. (1) Compute the financial leverage index.
  (2) From (1) above, discuss how well the company is utilizing its leverage.
  (3) Present a tabulation showing the composition of the return on common equity.
  (4) From (3) above what can be concluded about the relative "cost" of different sources of funds?

19–3. The following data relate to the Simplex Company for 19X0:

Sales revenue	$400,000
Average total assets	180,000
Average stockholders' equity	120,000
Net income after tax	18,000

Required:

a. Compute the rate of return on average stockholders' equity.
b. Calculate the rate of return on average total assets.
c. Determine the percentage of net income to revenue.
d. Calculate the number of times the assets were turned over in 19X0.
e. Compute the following for 19X1, assuming no change in any factor other than that described:
  (1) *Net income* if the net income as a percentage of total revenue is 18 percent.
  (2) *Average total assets* if the number of asset turnovers is three.
  (3) *Sales revenue* if the number of asset turnovers is four.
  (4) *Rate of return on stockholders' equity* if the percentage of net income to revenue is 3 percent.
  (5) *Sales revenue* if average total assets increase by $30,000 and the number of turnovers during 19X1 doubles over 19X0.

(6) *Rate of return on stockholders' equity* if owners' equity increases by $12,000.

f. For each of the changes in part (e) indicate whether or not the expected results are favorable from the stockholders' viewpoint.

19–5. The ABC Corporation's total capital structure consists of 40 percent bonds and 60 percent common equity. The total capital structure amounts to $50,000,000. The bonds have a 6 percent coupon. The tax rate is 50 percent. Retained earnings amount to 7,500,000. The operating margin (before deduction of interest and taxes) is 10 percent.

Required:

a. What operating margin has to be attained in order to earn 10 percent on stockholders' equity?
b. If the corporation's operating margin was $3,000,000 for the year, was financial leverage (trading on equity) beneficial, detrimental, or niether? Show all computations.

19–7. The Benston Corp. supplied you with the following operating results for 19X5

Sales	$200,000
Earnings before interest and taxes	16,000
Tax rate	50%
Bond payable—at 6% interest	$ 40,000
Stockholders' equity (1)	50,000
Current liabilities	10,000
Total Assets	$100,000

(1) Includes $10,000, 6 percent cumulative preferred stock.

Required:

a. Compute the return on total assets, asset turnover, and rate of return on sales.
b. Discuss the meaning of the relationships in (a) above.
c. Compute return on common equity and the financial leverage index.

19–9. The LMO Corporation's total capital structure consists of 30 percent bonds and 70 percent common equity. The total capital structure amounts to $20,000,000. The bonds have a 5 percent coupon. The tax rate is 50 percent. Retained earnings amount to $4,000,000. The operating margin (before deduction of interest and taxes) is 15 percent.

Required:

a. What level of net operating income has to be attained in order to earn 15 percent on stockholders' equity?
b. If the corporation had net operating income of $1,000,000 for the year, was financial leverage (trading on equity) beneficial, detrimental, or neither? Prove it.
    Show all computations.

(C.F.A. adapted)

19–11. You have made a very preliminary analysis of three common stocks with the information as set forth below. All three stocks have the same investment grade or quality. Assume that the same important numerical financial ratios and relationships which currently exist (such as price-earnings ratio, payout ratio, dividend yield, etc.) will extend into the future, with small cyclical variations, for as far as you can see. For the investments being considered, you require a rate of return of 10 percent a year.

Required:

Based solely on the information given in this problem:
a. Which, if any, of the stocks meet your requirements? Show your calculations.
b. Which one of the three stocks is most attractive for purchase?

		Stock	
Data description	A	B	C
Return on total assets	10%	9%	12%
Return on stockholders' equity	14%	12%	15%
Estimated earnings per share in the current year	$ 2.00	$ 1.67	$ 1.43
Estimated dividends per share in the current year	$ 1.00	$ 1.00	$ 1.00
Current market price	$27.00	$24.00	$23.00

(C.F.A. adapted)

CHAPTER 20

20–1. The most recently published statement of consolidated income of Standard Industries, Inc. appears as follows:

STANDARD INDUSTRIES, INC.
Statement of Consolidated Income
For the Year Ended March 31, 19X8

Net sales....................................	$38,040,000
Other revenue	408,600
Total revenue	$38,448,600
Cost of products sold	$27,173,300
Selling and administrative expenses	8,687,500
Interest expense	296,900
Total cost and expenses	$36,157,700
Income before income taxes	$ 2,290,900
Provision for income taxes..................	1,005,000
Net income	$ 1,285,900

Charles Norton, a representative of a firm of security analysts, visited the central headquarters of Standard Industries for the purpose of obtaining more information about the company's operations.

In the annual report Standard's president stated that Standard was engaged in the pharmaceutical, food processing, toy manufacturing, and metal-working industries. Mr. Norton complained that the published income statement was of limited utility in his analysis of the firm's operations. He said Standard should have disclosed separately the profit earned in each of its component industries. Further he maintained that several items appearing on the statement of consolidated retained earnings should have been included on the income statement, namely a gain of $633,400 on the sale of the furniture division in early March of the current year and an assessment of additional income taxes of $164,900 resulting from an examination of the returns covering the years ended March 31, 19X5 and 19X6.

Required:

a. Explain what is meant by the term "conglomerate" company.
b. (1) Discuss the accounting problems involved in measuring net profit by industry segments within a company.
   (2) With reference to Standard Industries' statement of consolidated income identify the specific items where difficulty might be encountered in measuring profit by each of its industry segments and explain the nature of the difficulty.
c. (1) What criteria should be applied in determining whether a gain or loss should be excluded from the determination of net income?
   (2) What criteria should be applied in determining whether a gain or loss that is properly includable in the determination of net income should be included in the results of ordinary operations or shown separately as an extraordinary item after all other items of revenue and expense?
   (3) How should the gain on the sale of the furniture division and the assessment of additional taxes each be presented in Standard's financial statements?

(AICPA adapted)

20–3. The following is a statement of Sales and Results by Operating Group Builder Corporation and Consolidated Subsidiaries for the two years ended August 31, 19X4 and 19X3:

	For the year ended August 31,	
	19X4	19X3
	(in thousands)	
Net sales and revenues:		
Mineral and fiber products group	$ 444,071	$ 366,275
Coal, iron and chemicals group	86,054	60,519
Pipe products group	201,348	174,936
Homebuilding group	114,954	94,246
Metal and wood products group	257,933	219,366
Stone and concrete products group	37,975	36,761
Paper group	82,856	68,491
Sugar operations	51,593	31,143
Oil and gas operations	4,821	4,165
Other	12,432	12,734
Consolidated Net Sales and Revenues	$1,294,037	$1,068,636
Contribution to operating income:		
Mineral and fiber products group	$ 47,036	$ 43,542
Coal, iron and chemicals group	30,674	10,480
Pipe products group	14,278	16,275
Homebuilding group	16,831	19,879
Metal and wood products group	15,134	12,827
Stone and concrete products group	4,591	4,736
Paper group	4,142	1,629
Sugar operations	8,433	746
Oil and gas operations	2,478	1,270
Other	432	1,337
Savings and loan operations*	1,963	3,211
	145,992	115,932
Less: Unallocated corporate interest and other expense	(34,467)	(20,465)
Income taxes	(48,195)	(41,370)
Consolidated Net Income	$ 63,330	$ 54,097

* Unconsolidated subsidiary.

Required:

a. Prepare common-size statements which show the percentage of each group sales to total sales for the two years. Include a column for percent increase or decrease of 19X4 amounts from 19X3. Round to the nearest tenth of one percent.

b. Prepare a common-size statement showing the percentage of each group contribution to operating income to the total contribution by all groups for the two years. Again include a column showing the percent change in 19X4 from 19X3 rounded to the nearest tenth of one percent.

c. Prepare a statement showing the percentage of each group's contribution to each group's sales. Also show a column for percent change in 19X4 from 19X3 for these contributions.

d. Are favorable trends indicated by the comparative computations? In what areas do these measurements display weaknesses? What are they likely to be?

20–5. Within the last three or four years, several requirements for fuller disclosure in the footnotes to corporate financial statements have been imposed by the Accounting Principles Board, the Financial Accounting Standards Board, and the Securities and Exchange Commission.

Required:

a. List at least five of these requirements, indicating their nature.
b. For each of the requirements that you have listed, discuss how the additional information aids financial analysis.

(C.F.A.)

CHAPTER 21

21–1. The following question is based on the financial statements of Beta Company (pages 89–103).

Required:

Prepare a statement to account for variations in net income for the three-year period 19X1–X3 (average) compared to the three-year period 19X4–X6 (average) in millions of dollars.
You may combine some items, for example, cost of goods sold would equal cost of products sold plus distribution expenses.

21–3. The following is a comparative income statement of Day & Sons, Inc:

DAY & SONS, INC.
Comparative Income Statement
For Years Ending December 31, 19Y1 and 19Y2

	19Y2	19Y1
Net sales	$162,000	$160,600
Cost of goods sold	102,000	104,500
Gross profit	$ 60,000	$ 56,100
Selling expenses	$ 15,630	$ 16,802
General and administrative		
expenses	7,215	7,560
Other expenses	1,205	1,095
Total expenses	$ 24,050	$ 25,457
Income before income taxes	$ 35,950	$ 30,643
Income taxes	18,089	14,472
Net income	$ 17,861	$ 16,171
Units of merchandise sold	10,000	11,000

Required:

a. Prepare an analysis of the variation in gross margin.
b. Prepare an analysis of the variation in net income.

21–5. While your sales dropped by 20,000 units in 19X2 as compared to 19X1, you were delighted to find that your gross profit increased substantially. You have sold 100,000 units in 19X2 at $7 per unit with a gross margin of 35 percent. In 19X1 you sold the same item at $5 with a cost of $4.

Required:

a. What is the difference in gross profit?
b. Prepare an analysis of the variation in gross margin.

21–7. The following statistics are available for the Disco Company for 19X1 and 19X2:

	19X2	19X1
Gross profit percentage	40%	35%
Ending accounts receivable	$150,000	$90,000
Number of days sales in A/C rec.	60	45
Income tax rate	50%	40%
Net income as a percentage of sales	6%	9%

Required:

a. Prepare income statements in comparative form for the two years.
b. Comment on the trend in sales volume, gross profit percentage, and net income percentage.

21–9. ABC Company has recently leased manufacturing facilities for production of a new product. Based on studies made, the following data have been generated:

Estimated annual sales .... 24,000 Units

	Total amount	Amount per unit
Estimated costs:		
Material	$ 96,000	$4.00
Direct labor	14,400	0.60
Overhead	24,000	1.00
Administrative expense	28,800	1.20
	$163,200	$6.80

Selling expenses are expected to be 15 percent of sales and profit is to amount to $1.02 per unit. Ignore income taxes.

Required (showing all computations in good form):

a. Compute the selling price per unit.
b. Project a statement of income for the year.

c. Compute a break-even point expressed in dollars and in units assuming that overhead and administrative expenses are fixed but all other costs are fully variable. (Round to the nearest whole dollar.)

21–11. Cost-volume-earnings analysis (break-even analysis) is used to determine and express the interrelationships of different volumes of activity (sales), costs, sales prices, and sales mix to earnings. More specifically, the analysis is concerned with what will be the effect on earnings of changes in sales volume, sales prices, sales mix, and costs.

Required:

a. Certain terms are fundamental to cost-volume-earnings analysis. Explain the meaning of each of the following terms:
   (1) Fixed costs.
   (2) Variable costs.
   (3) Relevant range.
   (4) Break-even point.
   (5) Margin of safety.
   (6) Sales mix.
b. Several assumptions are implicit in cost-volume-earnings analysis. What are these assumptions?
c. In a recent period Zero Company had the following experience:

Sales (10,000 units @ $200)			$2,000,000
	Fixed	*Variable*	
Costs:			
Direct material	$ —	$ 200,000	
Direct labor	—	400,000	
Factory overhead	160,000	600,000	
Administrative			
expenses	180,000	80,000	
Other expenses	200,000	120,000	
Total costs	$540,000	$1,400,000	1,940,000
Net income			$ 60,000

Each item below is independent.
   (1) Calculate the break-even point for Zero in terms of units and sales dollars. Show your calculations.
   (2) What sales volume would be required to generate a net income of $96,000? Show your calculations.
   (3) What is the break-even point if management makes a decision which increases fixed costs by $18,000? Show your calculations.

(AICPA)

21–13. The following information pertains to the Deck Corporation:

Fixed cost	$170,000	
Variable cost per unit of product	$ 5.00	
Selling price per unit of product	$ 10.00	

Required:

a. What is the break-even point?
b. Determine the effect on net income of a 7 percent increase in volume if the present sales volume is:
  (1) 50,000 units.
  (2) 120,000 units.
c. Do identical percentage increases in volume always have the same effect on net income?
d. Determine separately the effect on net income under the assumptions given in Problems (b) (1) and (b) (2) if in addition:
  (1) The selling price drops by 40 cents per unit.
  (2) The variable costs drop by 10 percent.
  (3) The fixed costs increase by $50,000.
  (4) Changes in (1), (2), and (3) occur simultaneously.
    You are to recompute volume break-even points and percentage changes in profits resulting from the volume increases. Comment on the results.

21–15.   The Credit manager of L. Green, Inc. feels that the credit policy of the firm needs to be tightened. In support of his argument to the president, the credit manager contrasts the 90-day terms of L. Green with the 30-day terms of the industry. L. Green is selling $1.6 million a year, its variable costs are 85 percent and its fixed costs are $100,000. On the basis of a survey of Green's customers the credit manager expects the following relationship between terms and sales.

Policy	Terms	Annual sales
A	90	1,600,000
B	75	1,575,000
C	60	1,550,000
D	45	1,500,000
E	30	1,425,000
F	15	1,300,000

Required:

a. Determine the break-even point in units and dollars for each policy. (Assume sale price of $10 per unit.)
b. If the company can earn 15 percent interest on the money market, which policy should be adopted? (Assume that the average collection period corresponds to the terms extended.)
c. Discuss the qualitative factors which should be considered before making a final decision.

CHAPTER 22

22–1.   The following questions are based on the financial statements of Beta Company (pages 89–103). (See Note 14.)

Required:

a. Construct an index of seasonal variability (between quarters) of sales and net income for 19X6.

b. Compute the percentage of net earnings to sales for each quarter and comment on the changes.

22–3. XYZ is a small company of $500,000 sales a year. The company was in need of a short term loan of $100,000 to finance its working capital requirements. Two banks were ready to give the required loan to the company but each bank required certain conditions to be satisfied. Bank A expects at least a 25 percent gross margin on sales and Bank B requires a 2 : 1 current ratio.

The following information is available:

1. Sales returns and allowances—10 percent of sales
2. Purchases returns and allowances—2 percent of purchases
3. Sales discount—2 percent of sales
4. Purchase discount—1 percent of purchases
5. Ending inventory—$138,000
6. Cash is 10 percent of accounts receivable.
7. Credit terms that the company gives to its customers are 45 days, while credit that company gets from its suppliers is 90 days.
8. Purchases for the year were $400,000.
9. The percentage increase in inventory at end over beginning inventory was 38 percent.
10. Accounts payable is the only item of current liabilities.

Required:

From which, if any, bank can the company get a loan?

22–5. Companies A and B each had operating income of $250,000 in 19X2. The following additional information is available:

Company A

1. First year additional depreciation of $60,000 was taken.
2. Auditor's opinion reads: "The company became liable for damages of $20,000 as a result of a lawsuit in January 19X3 but no provision had been made in the financial statement presented above."
3. The company adopted in 19X2 a policy to capitalize all research and development costs and to amortize them one third annually. The amortization this year amounted to $12,000.
4. The company adopted in 19X2 a policy to capitalize executive training expenses and plans to amortize them over 10 years (19X2, $2,000).
5. The company takes an annual depletion allowance of $10,000 on assets which have been fully amortized.

Company B

1. Company capitalized marketing expenses of $60,000 incurred in 19X2 and plans to amortize them over three years in equal amounts.
2. Due to the new company policy of "tighten your belts," necessary repairs and maintenance expenses were cut by one half to $10,000.

3. To take advantage of a lower tax liability, the company continued to take depreciation on assets retired in 19X1. Depreciation applicable to such assets amounted to $9,000.
4. In order to lessen the burden on future income, inventories were written down by $15,000 below the current appropriate carrying costs.
5. The company provided a "reserve for future losses" of $100,000 three years ago and has been absorbing it one tenth annually by credits to income.
6. The company expenses all research and development costs which amounted to $50,000 in 19X2.

Required:

Adjust the operating incomes of the two companies so as to state them on a comparable basis. If there are any irregular accounting practices, indicate the adjustments you would make.

22–7. Following are the financial statements of Morning Star Corporation for 19X4 and 19X5:

Income Statements

	19X4		19X5	
Sales		2,000,000		2,700,000
Beginning inventory	500,000		300,000	
Purchases	1,300,000		2,000,000	
	1,800,000		2,300,000	
Less: Ending inventory	300,000		600,000	
Cost of Goods Sold		1,500,000		1,700,000
Gross Profit.....................		500,000		1,000,000
Repairs and maintenance	60,000		70,000	
Training programs for operating, sales, executive and managerial talents	50,000		50,000	
Other general and administrative expenses	150,000		300,000	
Advertising and promotion	40,000		45,000	
Other selling expenses	80,000		300,000	
		380,000		765,000
Net Income		120,000		235,000

	Balance Sheets		
	19X4		19X5
Current Assets		$1,000,000	$1,500,000
Fixed Assets:			
Land	500,000		500,000
Property, plant and equipment	1,500,000		2,000,000
	2,000,000		2,500,000
Less: Accumulated depreciation, property, plant and equipment	700,000		900,000
Total Fixed Assets		1,300,000	1,600,000
Total Assets		$2,300,000	$3,100,000
Liabilities		800,000	1,000,000
Shareholders Equity		1,500,000	2,100,000
Total Liabilities and Capital		$2,300,000	$3,100,000

Required:

a. What are, in your opinion, the significant changes in Morning Star's managerial policies with regard to operational expenses in 19X5 (Limit your analysis to discretionary and future-directed expenses)

b. Do you think the changes may have an effect on future earnings?

22–9. A prominent financial analyst recently stated:

"For my part I think we should drop the word extraordinary and leave it to each reader to decide whether a strike will recur next year or not, to decide whether a lease abandonment will recur or not. In other words, an all-inclusive statement, with no category of 'extraordinary.' Let the reader use that statement for predictive purposes by eliminating those items which will not recur next year. But let the record show all the events which had an impact, with no 'below the line' items, no adjustments which 'really don't count.'

"The 'current operating performance' philosophy really has no point, I am arguing. Everything is to be included; it is all part of the collapse or success this year. By omitting items from 'current operating performance' we are relegating them to a lesser role. I do not believe that is conceptually correct. Thus, (1) we include everything in order to judge the performance of management and (2) we are also trying to guess at next year's results.

"For this purpose the reader may well decide that there will not be a big inventory write-off, and that no plant will be sold or abandoned. Both items deserve to adversely affect income because they are measuring management performance. Both items may be excluded by the reader in predicting the next year.

"Finally, the existing system has resulted in abuses. An earthquake is part of the picture. A defalcation in Basel is part of banking. A lease abandonment recurs in the oil industry. No man is wise enough to cut the Gordian knot on this issue by picking and choosing what is extraordinary, recurring, typical, different from typical or customary."

Required:

Evaluate this statement and present clearly and concisely your views of—
a. How "extraordinary items" should be presented.
b. How the analyst should evaluate such items.

22–11. Your client, Ocean Company, manufactures and sells three different products—Ex, Why, and Zee. Projected income statements by product line for the year ended December 31, 1976, are presented below:

	Ex	Why	Zee	Total
Unit sales	10,000	500,000	125,000	635,000
Revenues	$925,000	$1,000,000	$575,000	$2,500,000
Variable cost of units sold	285,000	350,000	150,000	785,000
Fixed cost of units sold	304,200	289,000	166,800	760,000
Gross margin	335,800	361,000	258,200	955,000
Variable general and administrative (G&A) expenses	270,000	200,000	80,000	550,000
Fixed G&A expenses	125,800	136,000	78,200	340,000
Income (loss) before tax	$ (60,000)	$ 25,000	$100,000	$ 65,000

Production costs are similar for all three products. The fixed G&A expenses are allocated to products in proportion to revenues. The fixed cost of units sold is allocated to products by various allocation bases, such as square feet for factory rent and machine hours for repairs, etc.

Ocean management is concerned about the loss for product Ex and is considering two alternative courses of corrective action.

Alternative A. Ocean would purchase some new machinery for the production of product Ex. This new machinery would involve an immediate cash outlay of $650,000. Management expects that the new machinery would reduce variable production costs so that total variable costs (cost of units sold and G&A expenses) for product Ex would be 52 percent of product Ex revenues. The new machinery would increase total fixed costs allocated to product Ex to $480,000 per year. No additional fixed costs would be allocated to products Why or Zee.

Alternative B. Ocean would discontinue the manufacture of product Ex. Selling prices of products Why and Zee would remain constant. Management expects that product Zee production and revenues would increase by 50 percent. Some of the present machinery devoted to product Ex could be sold at scrap value which equals its removal costs. The removal of this machinery would reduce fixed costs allocated to product Ex by $30,000 per year. The remaining fixed costs allocated to product Ex include $155,000 of rent expense per year. The space previously used for product Ex can be rented to an outside organization for $157,000 per year.

Required:

Prepare a schedule analyzing the effect of Alternative A and Alternative B on projected total company income before tax.

22–13. The following is a summary of earnings information reported by Gulf and Western Industries, Inc. to stockholders for the three months ended October 31, 1970 and 1969:

	Three months ended October 31	
	1970	1969 (Note A)
Net earnings per share (Notes B and C)	$0.73	$0.71
Net sales and other operating revenue	$390,764,000	$387,249,000
Net earnings—after income taxes of $4,000,000 for 1970 and $7,950,000 for 1969	$ 15,206,000	$ 15,863,000

Note A—Amounts shown for 1969 have been restated to reclassify the operations of businesses subsequently disposed of or not presently consolidated.

Note B—Net earnings for the three months ended October 31, 1969 includes $134,000 or $0.01 per share from gains on sales of securities. There were no gains or losses from sales of securities for the 1970 period.

Note C—Earnings per share amounts are based on average common and common-equivalent shares outstanding during the respective periods. Average shares outstanding were 19,022,000 for 1970 and 20,247,000 for 1969. The reduction of average shares outstanding is the result of the company purchasing its shares from time to time.

Required:

a. How useful are the reported earnings per share for 1969 and 1970 as measures of earning power and growth? Give reasons for your answer based on the *above data only*.

b. Identify and explain briefly the problems involved in interpreting quarterly earnings figures.

c. What is meant by the term "common-equivalent shares"?

(C.F.A.)

22–15. What factors (a) within the company, and (b) within the economy, have and are likely to affect the degree of variability in the earnings per share, dividends per share, and market price per share, of common stock?

(C.F.A.)

CHAPTER 23

23–1. The following questions are based on the financial statements of Beta Company (pages 89–103).

Required:

Evaluate Beta Company for the six-year period ending December 31, 19X6. Your evaluation should be supported by extensive analysis of the following aspects:

1. Short-term liquidity
2. Capital structure and long term solvency
3. Return on Investment
4. Asset utilization
5. Operating performance

You were given the following additional information:

Composition of current assets for 19X0–19X4 (*in millions of dollars*)

	19X0	19X1	19X2	19X3	19X4
Current Assets:					
Cash		25.7	58.6	15.0	34.0
Temporary investments		1.0	101.7	206.7	296.9
Accounts receivable	278.8	256.5	267.4	275.1	333.8
Inventories	291.1	278.3	230.6	227.9	324.4
Deferred income tax		7.7	16.1	13.3	28.0
Total Current Assets		569.2	674.4	738.0	1,017.1
Total Assets		2,031.6	2,076.2	2,917.1	2,729.9
Total Equity		1,081.3	1,117.8	1,179.8	1,367.2

Total Debt includes: current liabilities, long-term liabilities, deferred income taxes and reserves and deferred liabilities, i.e., difference between total assets and total equity.

23–3. Select a company from a nonregulated industry for which you can obtain adequately informative financial statements for at least six years.

Required:

Based on the financial statements, background information on the company and its industry, as well as financial measures of other companies in the industry, prepare a *comprehensive analysis and report* covering the following specific points:

a. General (brief) description of the company and its industry.

b. An evaluation of the following areas:
  (1) Short-term liquidity (current debt paying ability)
  (2) Capital structure and long term solvency
  (3) Return on investment
  (4) Operating performance
  (5) Capital utilization

c. Comment on the degree of informative disclosure, useful to the analyst, which was found in the financial statements examined.

d. In what way did alternative principles of accounting used in the financial statements affect the analytical measures used in this report?

You are expected to use a broad variety of financial analysis tools in your analysis and evaluation leading to a conclusion regarding the five areas detailed above.

23–5. Discuss the factors which would determine the relative price-earnings ratios to be applied to each of these two makers of industrial machinery for which the following financial data are available:

	A	B
Capital structure:		
5% 20-year notes	$10,000,000	$ None
Common and surplus	20,000,000	30,000,000
Number of common shares	500,000	750,000
Earnings per share:		
1966	$ 4.25	$ 3.00
1965	3.50	2.50
1964	2.25	1.67
1963	2.75	2.00
1962	1.70	1.95
Sales (1966)	30,000,000	30,000,000
Net income	2,125,000	2,250,000
Balance sheet data at 12/31/66:		
Cash	3,000,000	5,850,000
Receivables....................	5,000,000	3,750,000
Inventories	12,000,000	10,000,000
Total Current Assets	$20,000,000	$19,600,000
Accounts payable	4,000,000	3,500,000
Accruals	2,000,000	2,000,000
Taxes	1,000,000	1,100,000
Total Current Liabilities	$ 7,000,000	$ 6,600,000
Net plant	13,000,000	15,900,000
Patents, etc....................	4,000,000	100,000

(C.F.A.)

23–7.   As the CPA responsible for an "opinion" audit engagement, you are requested by the client to organize the work to provide him at the earliest possible date with some key ratios based on the final figures appearing on the comparative financial statements. This information is to be used to convince creditors that the client business is solvent and to support the use of going-concern valuation procedures in the financial statements. The client wishes to save time by concentrating on only these key data.

The data requested and the computations taken from the financial statements follow:

	Last year	This year
Current ratio	2.0:1	2.5:1
Quick (acid-test) ratio	1.2:1	.7:1
Property, plant, and equipment		
to owners' equity	2.3:1	2.6:1
Sales to owners' equity	2.8:1	2.5:1
Net income.........................	Down 10%	Up 30%
Earnings per common share	$2.40	$3.12
Book value per common share	Up 8%	Up 5%

Required:

a.   The client asks that you prepare a list of brief comments stating how each of these items supports the solvency and going-concern potential of his business. He wishes to use these comments to support his presentation of data to his creditors. You are to prepare the comments as requested, giving the implications and the limitations of each item separately and then the collective inference one may draw from them about the client's solvency and going-concern potential.

b. Having done as the client requested in part (a), prepare a brief listing of additional ratio-analysis-type data for this client which you think his creditors are going to ask for to supplement the data provided in part (a). Explain why you think the additional data will be helpful to these creditors in evaluating this client's solvency.

c. What warnings should you offer these creditors about the limitations of ratio analysis for the purpose stated here?

(AICPA)

23–9.   Aluminum Company of America (Alcoa) is the world's largest aluminum producer. Exports account for 4.4 percent of sales. In 1972 its tonnage breakdown was:

Fabricated products . . . .   76.5 percent
Primary aluminum . . . .   23.5 percent

The company's captive electrical generators supply about 50 percent of its requirements. Power purchases in the Pacific Northwest are almost all under "firm contract." In the long term, all of the company's existing aluminum reduction plants will be converted to a new proprietary process which will reduce electricity consumption by 40 percent per pound of product. At the end of 1973 Alcoa announced that it may have to allocate output to its customers due to heavy demand, especially from capital goods firms.

Kaiser Aluminum and Chemical Corporation is the third largest U.S. aluminum producer. Chemicals, other metals and real estate development are other major business areas for the firm. Eighteen percent (18%) of the firm's sales are to foreign customers. Kaiser's sales mix is as follows:

Aluminum products:
Fabricated products 60%
Primary aluminum 12%
Chemicals 14%
Refractory produces 7%
Other 7%

About 40 percent of Kaiser's power requirements for aluminum is generated by Pacific Northwest hydroelectric facilities. Although power shortages have idled approximately 9 percent of the company's aluminum capacity in the Pacific Northwest, this capacity is expected to be back in use shortly. Power for Kaiser's Ravenswood, West Virginia facility is supplied by Ohio Power Company under a firm contract extending to 1993. This contract is renewable under specified conditions. Electric power for its Chalmette,

Louisiana facility is supplied by a company-owned, gas-fueled plant. Natural gas is supplied to this plant under a long-term, intrastate contract which is not currently subject to direct Federal regulation.

Table 1 compares production of primary aluminum in the United States to the Federal Reserve Board Index of Industrial Production, and shows statistics on aluminum production of Alcoa and Kaiser.

TABLE 1

Aluminum production and prices in the United States compared to industrial production and wholesale commodity prices (years 1960–1972)

		Primary aluminum production in U.S.			*Price indexes*	
Year	*FRB index of ind. prod. (1967 = 100)*	*Total (mil. tons)*	*Alcoa (thous. tons)*	*Kaiser (thous. tons)*	*Wholesale commodities (1967 = 100)*	*Aluminum products*
1972	115.2	4.1	1392	773	119.1	110.2
1971	106.8	3.9	1434	737	113.9	109.5
1970	106.7	3.9	1450	n.a.	110.4	109.8
1969	110.7	3.8	1370	819	106.5	106.3
1968	105.7	3.4	1192	780	102.5	101.3
1967	100.0	3.1	1140	724	100.0	100.0
1966	97.9	3.0	1060	667	99.8	98.5
1965	89.2	2.8	965	627	96.6	99.4
1964	81.7	2.6	878	599	94.7	101.4
1963	76.5	2.4	777	579	94.5	102.9
1962	72.2	2.2	682	560	94.8	108.7
1961	66.7	2.0	662	461	94.5	111.3
1960	66.2	1.9	727	488	94.9	110.8

Source: *Federal Reserve Bulletin*, November 1973, p. A62; *Moody's Manual of Investments: Industrials*, Company data in various issues, 1962 to 1973.

Required:

a. Based solely on the data presented in Table 1 draw conclusions regarding the growth and stability of aluminum production and the competitive position of Alcoa and Kaiser. Support your conclusions with statistical analyses for 1961, 1966 and 1972.

Table 2 summarizes financial statement ratios dealing with the determinants of earning power and financial position.

b. Compare the trends in those ratios of the two companies which show return on equity and its components. Identify factors which account for any differences you may note.

TABLE 2
Statistical analysis of earning power and financial position—Aluminum Company of America and Kaiser Aluminum and Chemical Corporation

Period	After-tax return on common shareholders' equity A (%)	K (%)	Operating profit margin A (%)	K (%)	Ratio of other expenses to net sales[1] A (%)	K (%)	Ratio of income taxes to pre-tax income[2] A (%)	K (%)
10 yr. average (63–72)	8.5	9.5	11.8	10.2	0.8	2.9	38.2	33.2
5 yr. average (63–67)	8.5	11.4	12.1	12.0	1.2	3.5	38.7	31.8
5 yr. average (68–72)	8.4	7.6	11.4	8.5	0.3	3.5	37.6	34.7
3 yr. average (70–72)	7.4	4.9	9.7	6.9	0.0	2.6	33.3	33.8
1972	8.3	2.6	8.4	5.2	0.0	3.3	29.3	34.9

Period	Operating asset turnover A (x)	K (x)	Ratio of operating assets to common equity A (x)	K (x)	Payout ratio A (%)	K (%)	Total liabilities and preferred stock divided by common equity A (x)	K (x)	Acid test ratio A (x)	K (x)
10 yr. average (63–72)	0.72	0.69	1.9	2.8	42.4	49.8	1.1	2.2	1.4	1.0
5 yr. average (63–67)	0.75	0.66	1.8	3.1	41.1	47.8	1.0	2.5	1.4	1.2
5 yr. average (68–72)	0.70	0.71	1.9	2.4	43.6	51.9	1.2	2.0	1.4	0.8
3 yr. average (70–72)	0.68	0.70	1.9	2.4	49.2	63.7	1.2	2.0	1.4	0.7
1972	0.74	0.74	2.0	2.4	39.2	80.6	1.2	2.0	1.5	0.7

[1] Preferred stock dividends are included as other expenses since these companies receive depletion allowances and other tax deductions which bring their effective income tax rates substantially below statutory rates for corporations.

[2] Pre-tax income figures consist of reported pre-tax income minus preferred stock dividends.

TABLE 3
Compound annual growth rates of sales, earnings and dividends per share (1963–1973*)

Years	Sales per share common		Earnings per share common		Dividends per share common	
	A	K	A	K	A	K
1963–73	6.2%	5.4%	4.9%	−4.0%	4.7%	−4.8%
1963–68	7.6	11.4	17.4	19.2	9.6	5.6
1969–73	7.0	6.0	−3.4	−25.1	1.2	−18.8
1971–73	19.4	17.3	43.2	17.4	3.0	−24.6

* 1973 figures estimated by Value Line.

c. Compare the ratios of the two companies which reflect the strength of their financial position. Identify important differences and explain their implications.

Table 3 shows growth rates of sales, earnings and dividends per share for each company.

d. Compare and contrast the data for the two companies with regard to growth and stability. Based on data in Tables 2 and 3, estimate the rate of earnings growth that each company can sustain. Show calculations.

The future outlook of the aluminum industry is summarized in U.S. Industrial Outlook: 1974 (p. 80) as follows:

"The aluminum industry has a promising long-range growth outlook. By 1980 shipments should range between 20 billion and 24 billion pounds, reflecting an annual growth rate from 1973 averaging 5.6 percent to 8.4 percent. Value of shipments should show an annual average growth of 7.1 to 10 percent."

In December, 1973, price ceilings on aluminum ingot and fabricated products were removed and effective prices were raised 16 percent. Labor costs of both companies are expected to increase at least 7 percent a year beginning July 1, 1974.

The following additional information is supplied:

	Price/Earnings ratio				Dividend yields			
	Alcoa		Kaiser[1]		Alcoa		Kaiser[1]	
	High (x)	Low (x)	High (x)	Low (x)	High (%)	Low (%)	High (%)	Low (%)
1963–73 average	20.6	14.3	21.4	13.5	3.0	2.0	3.4	2.1
1969–73 average	17.3	10.7	19.7	10.5	3.8	2.3	4.0	2.2
1971–73 average	19.1	10.9	24.5	11.0	4.5	2.7	4.4	2.0
1963–73 range	31.0	8.5	34.2	8.4	5.0	1.4	5.0	1.7

[1] Excludes 1972 because earnings and dividends per share were abnormally low.

	Alcoa[2]	Kaiser
Current market price 1/4/74	72	21
Range of market price-year 1973	81–48	29–21
Est. E.P.S. 1974 (Value Line)	$5.00	$1.55
Est. D.P.S. 1974 (Value Line)	$1.91	$0.50

[2] Prior to a stock split on February 1, 1974.

e. You are a security analyst in the trust investment department of the Fourth National Bank and Trust Company with the responsibility of following the stocks of non-ferrous metal companies. The bank has been shifting its purchases from established growth stocks to companies likely to benefit from an expected surge in capital expenditures. Early in January, 1974, the bank received the regular quarterly payment on a pension fund account. The client company expected the bank to pursue an aggressive investment policy. It was desired to add one of these stocks to the portfolio based on its relative long-range attractiveness. Select one of these two stocks and explain your reasons.

INDEX